A Historical Theology of the Hebrew Bible

A HISTORICAL THEOLOGY
OF THE HEBREW BIBLE

Konrad Schmid

Translated by Peter Altmann

WILLIAM B. EERDMANS PUBLISHING COMPANY
GRAND RAPIDS, MICHIGAN

Wm. B. Eerdmans Publishing Co.
4035 Park East Court SE, Grand Rapids, Michigan 49546
www.eerdmans.com

Originally published in German as *Theologie des Alten Testaments*
2018 © Mohr Siebeck in Tübingen, Germany
English translation © 2019 William B. Eerdmans Publishing Co.
Published 2019
Printed in the United States of America

28 27 26 25 24 23 22 21 20 19   1 2 3 4 5 6 7 8 9 10

ISBN 978-0-8028-7693-5

Library of Congress Cataloging-in-Publication Data

A catalog record for this book is available from the Library of Congress

Contents

Contents

Preface

Whoever is of the opinion that a theology of the Hebrew Bible could only be written by a representative of the field within the framework of a retrospective life's work is probably correct. The complexity of the subject as well as the question demand both a broad overview and deep insight into the related content and problems. At least in the German-speaking academic context, a theology of the Hebrew Bible is traditionally a later work in the life of a scholar. The trend in the past 85 years has increased virtually linearly. At the appearance (where applicable of the first volume) of their theologies, Walther Eichrodt was 43 (1933), Ludwig Köhler 56 (1936), Gerhard von Rad also 56 (1957), Georg Fohrer 58 (1972), Walther Zimmerli 65 (1972), Claus Westermann 69 (1978), Horst Dietrich Preuß 63 (1990), Otto Kaiser 69 (1993), Rolf Rendtorff 74 (1999), and Jörg Jeremias 76 years old (2015).[1]

Whoever would counter that the end of an academic career is actually too late for a theology, for such a late work no longer entirely emerges from the active discussion community of the university, need not be wrong. Whoever approaches the question of a theology of the Hebrew Bible can, therefore, hardly win. It is always an untimely undertaking. However, the alternative option—that is, to let the matter rest—is no better. To do so is

---

1. One would not be mistaken in assuming that the increasing curve after 1960 is at least in part causally connected to von Rad's monumental work, which set the standard extremely high for all successors. Cf. also Jesper Høgenhaven, *Problems and Prospects of Old Testament Theology*, BibSem 6 (Sheffield: JSOT Press, 1987), 25: "The publication of von Rad's *Theologie* was followed by almost ten years' pause in the stream of OT theologies. For obvious reasons it cannot be determined whether this pause was in fact due to the impact of von Rad's work, but undoubtedly his 985 pages may well have caused ambitious successors to lose their nerve." Cf. also Edmond Jacob, *Grundfragen alttestamentlicher Theologie* (Stuttgart: Kohlhammer, 1970); James Barr, "Trends and Prospects in Biblical Theology," *JTS*, n.s., 25 (1974): 265–82.

to neglect treatment of an important field of Hebrew Bible studies. The consequences of this omission also have negative effects on the other subdisciplines of Hebrew Bible studies. The loss of the theological question has led—at least in German-speaking exegesis—to a mechanization of biblical studies, which is not really appropriate to its subject.

The present work understands itself primarily as an outline that attempts to bring the theological dimension of Hebrew Bible studies into accord with the changing literary-historical and historical state of the discussion. The often cited statement by Henry Wheeler Robinson that a theology of the Hebrew Bible should be written afresh in every generation speaks to this book as well,[2] even if it cannot and does not claim to be the theology of the Hebrew Bible of its generation. It is temporally contingent—however, not primarily for the reasons articulated by Robinson—because there is no *theologia perennis* (everlasting theology), but also because historical reconstructions as such cannot be made from a trans-historical point of view.

It goes without saying that the present book is open to revision and critique with respect to both the details and the whole. At the same time, it takes itself to be a stimulus for integrating theology into the current scholarly discussion of the Hebrew Bible. In any case—speaking again for German-language scholarship—it is surprising what enormous upheavals have taken place in the Hebrew Bible subdisciplines of introductory studies,[3] the history of Israel,[4] and the history of Israelite religion[5] in the

2. Henry Wheeler Robinson, *Inspiration and Revelation in the Old Testament* (Oxford: Clarendon, 1946), 232. Cf. Rolf Rendtorff, "Theologie des Alten Testaments: Überlegungen zu einem Neuansatz," in *Kanon und Theologie: Vorarbeiten zu einer Theologie des Alten Testaments* (Neukirchen-Vluyn: Neukirchener Verlag, 1991), 1; George A. F. Knight, *A Christian Theology of the Old Testament* (London: Paternoster, 1959), 7: "This is *a* Theology of the Old Testament. *The* Theology of the Old Testament will never be written."

3. See, for example, Jan C. Gertz, ed., *Grundinformation Altes Testament*, 5th ed., Uni-Taschenbücher 2745 (Göttingen: Vandenhoeck & Ruprecht, 2016); Walter Dietrich et al., *Die Entstehung des Alten Testaments* (Stuttgart: Kohlhammer, 2016).

4. See Ernst Axel Knauf and Philippe Guillaume, *A History of Biblical Israel: The Fate of the Tribes and Kingdoms from Merenptah to Bar Kochba* (Sheffield: Equinox, 2015); Christian Frevel, *Geschichte Israels* (Stuttgart: Kohlhammer, 2016); Wolfgang Oswald and Michael Tilly, *Geschichte Israels: Von den Anfängen bis zum 3. Jahrhundert n. Chr.* (Darmstadt: Wissenschaftliche Buchgesellschaft, 2016). Cf. Thomas Krüger, "Recent Developments in the History of Ancient Israel and Their Consequences for a Theology of the Hebrew Bible," *BN* 144 (2010): 5–13.

5. See, e.g., Othmar Keel and Christoph Uehlinger, *Gods, Goddesses, and the Images of God in Ancient Israel* (Edinburgh: T&T Clark, 2008); Ziony Zevit, *The Religions of Ancient*

past forty years, while contributions in the sphere of the theology of the Hebrew Bible—not in their own right, but in light of the possible over-all directions—have remained comparatively diffuse. Whether one could currently speak of a "certain blossoming of the discipline" (while simultaneously of the often observed "contestation of its legitimacy")[6] seems questionable. Important drafts have again been published in recent years, after the 1980s in particular were marked by new editions of the classic books on the topic. However, unlike the close interaction between new conclusions and approaches in the non-theological subdisciplines of Hebrew Bible studies, the theology of the Hebrew Bible maintains an almost extra-territorial existence; it is not really integrated into the communal discourse of Hebrew Bible studies. A "blossoming" would also entail, to stay with the image, a rootedness in the topsoil of Hebrew Bible studies, which is not entirely recognizable in the current discussion.

Where should one seek reasons for the eccentric existence of the theology of the Hebrew Bible within the context of Hebrew Bible studies? First, there is a certain lack of orientation holding sway over the meaning of "theology" in relation to the Hebrew Bible.[7] While the famous opening statement of Ludwig Köhler's theology that "[o]ne can designate a book as theology of the Old Testament if it offers the opinions, thoughts, and concepts of the OT brought into the correct contextual configuration, justified by its content, which is or could be theologically significant"[8] is still charming, it is in reality little more than a tautology. A theology of the Hebrew Bible should, in the first place, establish what a "theological" statement is. Surprisingly, the tendency to speak of inner-Hebrew Bible theologies has increased almost in correlation to the degree that the question of a

---

Israel: A Synthesis of Parallactic Approaches (London: Continuum, 2001); Friedhelm Hartenstein, "Religionsgeschichte Israels: Ein Überblick über die Forschung seit 1990," *VF* 48 (2003): 2–28; Michael Tilly and Wolfgang Zwickel, *Religionsgeschichte Israels: Von der Vorzeit bis zu den Anfängen des Christentums* (Darmstadt: Wissenschaftliche Buchgesellschaft, 2011).

6. Hermann Spieckermann, "Die Liebeserklärung Gottes: Entwurf einer Theologie des Alten Testaments," in *Gottes Liebe zu Israel: Studien zur Theologie des Alten Testaments*, FAT 33 (Tübingen: Mohr Siebeck, 2001), 197. Cf. also Friedhelm Hartenstein, *Die bleibende Bedeutung des Alten Testaments: Studien zur Relevanz des ersten Kanonteils für Theologie und Kirche*, Biblisch-theologische Studien 165 (Göttingen: Vandenhoeck & Ruprecht, 2016).

7. On the question of theological exegesis, cf. Konrad Schmid, "Sind die Historisch-Kritischen kritischer geworden? Überlegungen zu Stellung und Potential der Bibelwissenschaften," *Jahrbuch für Biblische Theologie* 25 (2011): 63–78.

8. Ludwig Köhler, *Theologie des Alten Testaments*, 4th ed., NTG (Tübingen: Mohr Siebeck, 1966), v.

theology brought in from the outside has receded into the background.[9] This plural and almost inflationary use of the term *theology* has virtually supplanted the classical conception, along with the project of a theology of the Hebrew Bible in many places.

Furthermore, a rising consciousness of the problem concerning the textual object, the Hebrew Bible, should also be pointed out. There is no such thing as *the* Hebrew Bible/Old Testament. We have the Hebrew Bible of Judaism and different Old Testaments in numerous editions in Christianity, each of which strictly speaking requires its own theology.

The project of a "theology of the Hebrew Bible" is, then, in need of clarification both from the side of theology as well as from the side of the Hebrew Bible/Old Testament. Accordingly, the present sketch initially devotes two sections (B and C) to the discussion of these questions: What can the term "theology" reasonably mean in application to the Hebrew Bible? And how can the conception of "Hebrew Bible/Old Testament" attain a nuanced understanding?

According to the conclusions of these clarifications—this much can be anticipated—"theology of the Hebrew Bible" should essentially be carried out as a reconstructive (and not a constructive) undertaking. So, the aspirations of this book are less hybrid than its comprehensive title might seem. "Theology" is understood in a limited sense: Where does the Hebrew Bible/Old Testament (in its various orders and inventories) allow for the recognition of reflexive and synthesizing efforts that could be described at least rudimentarily as theology?

Theology is thereby perceived essentially as a descriptive project, and therefore I have entitled this book: *A Historical Theology of the Hebrew Bible*.[10] It will not be difficult to find scholarly voices that consider such a

---

9. See Erhard Gerstenberger, *Theologies of the Old Testament*, trans. John Bowden (Minneapolis: Fortress, 2002); Georg Fischer, *Theologien im Alten Testament* (Stuttgart: Katholisches Bibelwerk, 2014); cf. for discussion Konrad Schmid, *Is There Theology in the Hebrew Bible?*, trans. Peter Altmann, Critical Studies in the Hebrew Bible 4 (Winona Lake, IN: Eisenbrauns, 2015). See also Rolf Knierim, *The Task of Old Testament Theology: Substance, Method, and Cases* (Grand Rapids: Eerdmans, 1995), 1: "The Old Testament contains a plurality of theologies."

10. Albert de Pury and Ernst Axel Knauf, eds., "La théologie de l'Ancien Testament, kérygmatique ou descriptive?" *ETR* 70 (1995): 323–34; cf. already Carl Steuernagel, "Alttestamentliche Theologie und alttestamentliche Religionsgeschichte," in *Vom Alten Testament: Karl Marti zum siebzigsten Geburtstage gewidmet von Freunden, Fachgenossen, und Schülern*, ed. Karl Budde, BZAW 41 (Gießen: Töpelmann, 1925), 266–73; and recently Dalit Rom-Shiloni, "Hebrew Bible Theology: A Jewish Descriptive Approach," *JR* 96 (2016): 165–84.

conclusion deficient with regard to a project of theology, for the question of theology concerns not only the genesis of the Hebrew Bible but also its application.[11] Far be it from me to dispute this categorically. Under certain presuppositions and by means of certain definitions it is quite possible to pursue "theology" of the Hebrew Bible/Old Testament as a "normative" undertaking. However, this path will not be taken; instead it will be presented as an alternative that cannot claim exclusivity, but nevertheless is reckoned as theology in a very precise sense.

A historical theology of the Hebrew Bible, as understood and developed in the pages that follow, is based on an inquiry oriented toward the Hebrew Bible itself, which elevates the textually-indicated theological profile of the canon as a whole, divisions of canon, books, texts, and themes of the Hebrew Bible and presents their inner-biblical interconnectedness. In this respect it is neither a Christian nor a Jewish, but rather a Hebrew Bible undertaking. It is not a project immediately related to present-day application; it instead has an initially historical focus. Correspondingly, it is not accorded any immediate kerygmatic or normative functions. This is not a deficiency within the framework of a collaborative theology.[12] Especially from a Protestant perspective, the thought should not be absurd that the authority of Scripture does not come in the form of imperatives, but that imperatives come through the mediation of encultured propositions of thought that have proven increasingly normative on the basis of the weight of their content.

The German original of this book lacks the qualifier "historical," because "Theologie" is a less loaded term in German than "theology" in English and may very well denote a historical approach without a kerygmatic perspective.

11. Bernd Janowski, "Theologie des Alten Testaments: Zwischenbilanz und Zukunftsperspektiven," in *Theologie und Exegese des Alten Testaments / der Hebräischen Bibel: Zwischenbilanz und Zukunftsperspektiven*, ed. Bernd Janowski, SBS 200 (Stuttgart: Katholisches Bibelwerk, 2005), 112.

12. Cf. similarly Jörg Frey: "A New Testament theology does not have the task of contemporary proclamation. It is indeed related through its conclusions to other disciplines and can count on the fact that the reality addressed in the New Testament texts is also relevant for the present and in principle accessible to contemporary recipients, but it remains fundamentally bound to the historical context of the New Testament texts also in its presentation of New Testament themes and does not claim to distill out a 'pure' theology by stripping away time-bound elements or the ability to present some kind of Christian 'normative dogmatics.'" "Zum Problem der Aufgabe und Durchführung einer Theologie des Neuen Testaments," in *Aufgabe und Durchführung einer Theologie des Neuen Testaments*, ed. Cilliers Breytenbach and Jörg Frey, WUNT 205 (Tübingen: Mohr Siebeck, 2007), 44–45.

On the basis of the canonically, historically, as well as thematically focused order of the subsequent chapters, some overlap necessarily occurs. Certain sections of text and topics are addressed several times and in different places. This overlap also allows the reader to review the book in individual parts and not only as an entire study.

The present book is the English translation of my *Theologie des Alten Testaments*, published by Mohr Siebeck in Tübingen. It is supported by preliminary works that are adopted here in a partial and summary manner. Part B goes back to a detailed preliminary study on the question *Is There Theology in the Hebrew Bible?*, some sections of which are reproduced here.[13] The literary-historical judgments in the following rest on my presentation of *The Old Testament: A Literary History*.[14] Individual case studies or examples—such as on the Torah as an overarching complex in §18 or the interpretation of history in §32—adopt examples treated in more detail in my volume of collected essays *Schriftgelehrte Traditionsliteratur*.[15] The considerations on the theology of creation in Part H §31 are oriented toward my contributions to the volume *Schöpfung*.[16]

My thanks go to my colleagues Friedhelm Hartenstein, Thomas Krüger, Manfred Oeming, and Markus Witte for their willingness to read and provide critical comments on earlier forms of the present book as well as especially to Peter Altmann for the preparation of the translation. I am also grateful to Andrew Knapp and his team at Eerdmans for the careful, smooth, and swift publication process.

KONRAD SCHMID
Zurich, August 2018

---

13. Konrad Schmid, *Is There Theology in the Hebrew Bible?*, trans. Peter Altmann, Critical Studies in the Hebrew Bible 4 (Winona Lake, IN: Eisenbrauns, 2015).

14. Konrad Schmid, *The Old Testament: A Literary History,* trans. Linda M. Maloney (Minneapolis: Fortress, 2012).

15. Konrad Schmid, *Schriftgelehrte Traditionsliteratur: Fallstudien zur innerbiblischen Schriftauslegung im Alten Testament*, FAT 77 (Tübingen: Mohr Siebeck, 2011).

16. Konrad Schmid, *Schöpfung*, TdT 4, Uni-Taschenbücher 3514 (Tübingen: Mohr Siebeck, 2012).

A. Introduction

§1 Is There a Theology of the Hebrew Bible?

David M. Carr, *Writing on the Tablet of the Heart: Origins of Scripture and Literature* (Oxford: Oxford University Press, 2005) ◆ Herbert Donner, "'Wilde Exegese': Ein Argument zum Problem der Scheinmodernität des Alten Testaments," *Wege zum Menschen* 23 (1971): 417–24 ◆ Stephen A. Geller, *Sacred Enigmas: Literary Religion in the Hebrew Bible* (London: Routledge, 1996) ◆ Paul Hanson et al., eds., *Biblische Theologie: Beiträge des Symposiums "Das Alte Testament und die Kultur der Moderne" anlässlich des 100. Geburtstags Gerhard von Rads (1901–1971) Heidelberg, 18.–21. Oktober 2001*, Altes Testament und Moderne 14 (Münster: LIT, 2005) ◆ Friedhelm Hartenstein, "JHWHs Wesen im Wandel: Vorüberlegungen zu einer Theologie des Alten Testaments," *TLZ* 137 (2012): 3–20 ◆ Friedhelm Hartenstein, *Die bleibende Bedeutung des Alten Testaments: Studien zur Relevanz des ersten Kanonteils für Theologie und Kirche*, Biblisch-theologische Studien 165 (Göttingen: Vandenhoeck & Ruprecht, 2016) ◆ Jörg Jeremias, *Theologie des Alten Testaments*, GAT 6 (Göttingen: Vandenhoeck & Ruprecht, 2015) ◆ Hans-Jürgen Hermisson, *Alttestamentliche Theologie und Religionsgeschichte Israels*, Forum Theologische Literaturzeitung 3 (Leipzig: Evangelische Verlaganstalt, 2000) ◆ Bernd Janowski, "Theologie des Alten Testaments: Plädoyer für eine integrative Perspektive," in *Congress Volume Basel 2001*, ed. André Lemaire, VTSup 92 (Leiden: Brill, 2002), 241–76 ◆ Bernd Janowski and Norbert Lohfink, eds., *Religionsgeschichte Israels oder Theologie des Alten Testaments?* Jahrbuch für biblische Theologie 10 (Neukirchen-Vluyn: Neukirchener Verlag, 1995) ◆ Melanie Köhlmoos, "Evangelische Theologie und das Alte Testament," in *Evangelische Theologie: Eine Selbstverständigung in enzyklopädischer Absicht*, ed. Heiko Schulz (Leipzig: Evangelische Verlagsanstalt, 2016), 31–53 ◆ Reinhard G. Kratz, "Noch einmal: Theologie im Alten Testament," in *Vergegenwärtigung des Alten Testaments: Beiträge zur biblischen Hermeneutik: Festschrift für Rudolf Smend zum 70. Ge-*

burtstag, ed. Christoph Bultmann et al. (Göttingen: Vandenhoeck & Ruprecht, 2002), 310–26 ◆ Manfred Oeming, "Ermitteln und Vermitteln: Grundentscheidungen bei der Konzeption einer Theologie des Alten Testaments," in *Verstehen und Glauben: Exegetische Bausteine zu einer Theologie des Alten Testaments*, BBB 142 (Berlin: Philo, 2003), 9–48 ◆ Matthew R. Schlimm, *This Strange and Sacred Scripture: Wrestling with the Old Testament and Its Oddities* (Grand Rapids: Baker Academic, 2015) ◆ William M. Schniedewind, *How the Bible Became a Book: The Textualization of Ancient Israel* (Cambridge: Cambridge University Press, 2004) ◆ Konrad Schmid, "Sind die Historisch-Kritischen kritischer geworden? Überlegungen zu Stellung und Potential der Bibelwissenschaften," *Jahrbuch für Biblische Theologie* 25 (2011): 63–78 ◆ Konrad Schmid, *Is There Theology in the Hebrew Bible?*, Critical Studies in the Hebrew Bible 4 (Winona Lake, IN: Eisenbrauns, 2015) ◆ Rudolf Smend, "Theologie im Alten Testament," in *Die Mitte des Alten Testaments*, BEvT 99 (Munich: Kaiser, 1986), 104–17 ◆ Brent A. Strawn, *The Old Testament Is Dying: A Diagnosis and Recommended Treatment* (Grand Rapids: Baker Academic, 2017) ◆ Andrew Teeter, "The Hebrew Bible and/as Second Temple Literature: Methodological Reflections," *DSD* 20 (2013): 349–77 ◆ Karel van der Toorn, *Scribal Culture and the Making of the Hebrew Bible* (Cambridge MA: Harvard University Press, 2007)

THE ISSUES SURROUNDING A THEOLOGY OF THE OLD TESTAMENT The theology of the Old Testament has been an established part of Christian theology since the late eighteenth century.[1] However, ever since then it has participated in the changes and developments both of Hebrew Bible studies and of theology as a whole. As a result, the problematic of the theology of the Hebrew Bible requires an outline that engages with these historical developments. Such engagement brings with it the acknowledgment of a variety of possible approaches to the project of a theology of the Hebrew Bible.

The traditional endeavor of a theology of the Old Testament arose in the wake of the separation and then further distancing that took place between systematic theology and exegetical studies. As such, it arose as compensation for the loss of the unity between Scripture and Christian doctrine.[2] Today, such an approach has become impossible and inadvis-

---

1. For the reluctant reception within Jewish biblical scholarship see below §6.

2. Cf. the more trenchant statement by Erich Zenger, "Ist das Projekt 'Theologie der Hebräischen Bibel/des Alten Testaments' überhaupt bibelgemäß? Response auf den Vortrag von Shimon Gesundheit," *Biblische Theologie: Beiträge des Symposiums "Das Alte Testament*

able. The texts of the Hebrew Bible do not allow for a particular "biblical" synthesis with regard to doctrine; they are too divergent both historically and conceptually. In addition, theology as a whole does not require such a synthesis from a theology of the Hebrew Bible with regard to its—in classical terms—*Lehrbegriffe* ("leading principles"). In itself this would represent nothing more than a provisional systematic theology, which New Testament theology and systematic theology would supplement, correct, and ultimately supersede.

Nevertheless, the premature calls that have arisen in different formulations and with varying amounts of intensity over the past century for both the dismissal of the discipline of "Old Testament theology" as well as the suggestion to replace it with the "religious history of ancient Israel" prove inadequate. At least two fundamental observations demonstrate the useful and even necessary presence of a theology of the Hebrew Bible—as a historical and conceptually differentiated concept—within Hebrew Bible studies, if one is to understand the Hebrew Bible as completely as possible. The first observation points out that the Old Testament and the Hebrew Bible—in the divergent forms that have come down to us—comprise different systemizations and organizations of material, which partially overlap and partially compete with one another. These organizations and systemizations put the theological designs of the biblical authors and redactors on display. Second, the literary nature of the Hebrew Bible, in many ways reconstructable as updating (*Fortschreibung*) literature—the texts and the books of the Hebrew Bible only reached their current forms over a period of time through inner-biblical commentary and expansion—constitutes a unique body of literature that genuinely and prominently includes elements of theological reflection. Biblical texts themselves actually formulate the fact that it is updating literature (see, e.g., Jer 36:32) as well as theologically reflective literature (see, e.g., Deut 1:5), even if this theology often remains to a large degree implicit rather than explicit.

THE ACADEMIC CHARACTER OF A THEOLOGY OF THE HEBREW BIBLE A theology of the Hebrew Bible is as important and necessary as is an account of Plato's philosophy. Plato's work also displays diversity because it was written at different times and addresses various topics. However, while con-

und die Kultur der Moderne" anlässlich des 100. Geburtstags Gerhard von Rads (1901-1971) Heidelberg, 18.–21. Oktober 2001, ed. Paul Hansen et al., Altes Testament und Moderne 14 (Münster: LIT, 2005), 65–66.

tinuing to respect its internal diversity, one can investigate the trajectories, developments, and types of logic involved in Plato's philosophy without subsuming his thought into the study of the entire subsequent history of Platonic philosophy, however much the later historical dimension may necessarily be present in the study. In the same way, one can also investigate the diverse (but not endlessly diverse) theology of the Hebrew Bible, which does not merge completely with its later history of reception, without ignoring or denying this history. The fact that one can investigate the Hebrew Bible with regard to its *theology*—instead of, for example, its philosophy (which is also in principle a possibility, cf. below, §5)—arises unproblematically and easily from the fact that its texts speak in manifold ways of God, even when this only takes place implicitly. One may also view the Hebrew Bible, in similar fashion to Plato's works, in terms of a unity from the perspective of its reception history. Unlike Plato, however, the Hebrew Bible even demonstrates overarching structural elements in its literary presentation, which indicate a certain degree of textual unity (cf. below, Part E).

THEOLOGY AND THEOLOGIES OF THE HEBREW BIBLE To a certain extent, one can describe the theology of the Hebrew Bible as a conglomeration of its theologies (cf. below, Parts F and H), so this book could in principle bear the title *Theologies of the Hebrew Bible*. However, this choice would provide a different emphasis. The unifying literary elements would then receive less value than the various individual positions. The Hebrew Bible is in fact marked by both—the plurality of positions as well as their literary mediation. Therefore, the use of "theology" both in singular and plural forms is defensible with regard to the Hebrew Bible.

METHODOLOGICAL DECISIONS The approach to the theology of the Hebrew Bible and its structure are topics of a contentious debate with widely divergent positions in current scholarship. Should it represent the perspective of a specific confession? Should it be laid out in terms of comparative religious history? Should it treat ethical questions? Should the various parts of the canon receive equal weight? Should it be descriptive or normative? Should it also treat perspectives that crisscross the Christian Bible (OT and NT) as a whole? Should its contents be ordered historically or systematically? And finally, should it make note of individual scholarly discussions?[3] There are no

---

3. These are the significant points of view mentioned by Manfred Oeming, "Ermitteln und Vermitteln," 17, 47–48.

clear answers to these questions. One can only articulate the various options, which serve different kinds of interests.

ORIGIN AND APPLICATION Especially the English-speaking tradition of biblical studies, but also certain strands of German-speaking scholarship, often perceives "Hebrew Bible/Old Testament theology" as an investigation that seeks the meaning and normativity of texts of the Hebrew Bible for the contexts of its present-day interpreters. Unlike introductions to the Hebrew Bible, which investigate the origins of biblical literature, theology of the Hebrew Bible focuses on its application (cf. also below, §15). This perspective is possible, justified, and profitable, although it is helpful to distinguish between the aspects of contemporary meaning and normativity. However, in this approach the historical development of theology and the theologies of the Hebrew Bible will instead be the focus. Four remarks are necessary for clarification.

HISTORICAL AND THEOLOGICAL EXEGESIS? First, within current Hebrew Bible studies, "historical" and "theological" interpretative approaches of the Hebrew Bible exist strangely separate from one another. They are appreciated by different groups, who in turn view one another with a certain amount of skepticism. Whoever works more historically with the texts of the Hebrew Bible tends to hold theological approaches in low regard, viewing them as subjective, confessionally determined, and unscholarly. On the flip side, theologically interested interpreters often show little concern for the results of historical exegesis, which are viewed as arbitrary, artificial, and irrelevant. However, such a separation remains unconvincing. The charges of arbitrariness raised by both sides have some basis in reality, and they can only be resolved through reciprocal clarification. Historical-critical exegesis renders itself *historically* implausible when it devalues the theological dimension of the biblical texts; theological interpretation of biblical texts deteriorates into Docetism when it prioritizes the theological "y-coefficient" before the historical "x-coefficient" of textual interpretation. Historical exegesis only holds true as *historical* if one carries it out with a concurrent theological sensibility. On the other hand, theological exegesis—if it intends to remain true to the text and content—cannot radically diverge in its approach from textually oriented historical exegesis. As soon as theological exegesis threatens to remove itself from the foundation of historical biblical scholarship, suspicion of Gnosticizing or even Docetic tendencies of biblical interpretation become warranted.

Theology of the Hebrew Bible as Normative Discipline? Second, in terms of the history of scholarship, the notion of "Old Testament theology" as an explicitly normative discipline is comparatively new. Its roots lie in the Enlightenment, and it first gained significant ground in modern Hebrew Bible studies under the influence of neo-orthodox theology at the beginning of the twentieth century, as Part B will demonstrate in more detail. Premature demands for normativity with regard to the interpretation of the Bible should, however, be met with healthy skepticism, especially in Protestant theology. Protestantism reads the Bible as gospel and not as demand. Reading the Bible as gospel means—to put it bluntly—letting its content and declarations address the audience and, when appropriate, win them over, even if this may not be accorded canonical authority. As a result of the texts of the Bible functioning in this persuasive manner over many centuries, the Bible has become canonical, though it would be theologically (and also historically) incorrect to base its ability to persuade on its canonicity, rather than on the nature of its content.

Canonicity as a Result of Liturgical Use Third, it should be remembered that the canonicity of the biblical books originates in their liturgical use. The prestige of the canonical books refers to their recognition as writings worthy of liturgical use and not as specific content that is now declared normative. The validity of the biblical canon is a phenomenon of the Bible's reception history, not of its texts in and of themselves. This historical growth of the authority of the biblical writings cannot simply be retrojected onto themselves. The nature of the content should be investigated for what led to these books, rather than others, becoming those that now belong among the recognized books of the Bible. However, under the auspices of a historical-critical approach to the theology of the Hebrew Bible, one should maintain distance from the postulation of the inherent authority of these writings in mythical fashion. The reception history of the Bible is rife with such mythical retrojections. The most prominent among them in this regard are the theories of inspiration that have appeared since the first century CE, which themselves are quite interesting historical objects of study. However, within the framework of a theology of the Hebrew Bible, the inquiry remains focused on the objective weight of the texts and their content.

Theology as a Descriptive Historical Term Fourth, applying the concept of theology solely to its normative and currently relevant decla-

6

rations would overly reduce the notion of theology. Especially in English-speaking scholarship, the term *theology* is often understood as complementary to historical or philological inquiries, but this limited application of the concept is only a few decades old. Theological statements can be meaningful for the present and normative, but they do not necessarily have to serve that purpose. Theology is also an inner-biblical phenomenon, and new directions in scholarship have opened a wide field of inquiry that points to the connections between the processes of inner-biblical interpretation and theological processes in the Hebrew Bible. Here as well, further clarification comes from the history of scholarship and the divergent emphases that appear in the conceptions of theology in various formulations of theology throughout scholarship (Part B).

THE DIFFERENCES AND PROXIMITY OF THE THEOLOGY OF THE HEBREW BIBLE TO A CHRISTIAN OR A JEWISH THEOLOGY The theology of the Hebrew Bible and, at the same time, the promotion of the theology of the Hebrew Bible as historical description means that the results of such a project can neither be a Christian theology of the Old Testament, nor—with qualifications—a Jewish theology of the Hebrew Bible. The Hebrew Bible is older than Christianity, and this is also the case for the relationship of the Hebrew Bible to Judaism with regard to the preexilic texts. There is, therefore, some difference in content between what a historically descriptive approach to the theology of the Hebrew Bible will reconstruct from its subject matter and what is to be expected in Christian and Jewish tradition. However, it will not be completely alien, as these traditions have developed from, among other sources, the Hebrew Bible. The nature of the difference and also the proximity will be considered at the end of this book in Part I.

THE STRUCTURE AND APPROACH The following section briefly outlines the approach chosen for this book, which begins with the elaboration of the concept of theology (Part B) and what exactly should be understood by Hebrew Bible and Old Testament (Part C). Part D then will investigate related questions in more detail. The material in Parts E–H begins with an investigation of the natures of the various parts of the current Hebrew Bible (Part E). What follows is discussion of the sections of the canon and their constituent parts (Part F), a sketch of their theological history with regard to the composition of the literature of the Hebrew Bible (Part G), and then inquiry of the thematic focal points in light of their historical differentiations (Part H). The concluding Part I addresses the differences in theological conceptions of the Hebrew Bible with regard to their reception within Judaism and Christianity.

Such an open course of action connected to methodological questions is necessary because Hebrew Bible studies has lost a clear notion of what exactly should constitute a theology of the Hebrew Bible and what it should accomplish. This loss was necessary; the upheavals in Hebrew Bible studies in the last four decades have brought about a number of new insights and a new, more differentiated understanding of the literature of the Hebrew Bible. These changes require fresh orientation for the sub-disciplines within Hebrew Bible studies. This is not only the case for the theology of the Hebrew Bible, but also for approaches to questions of historical introductions, the history of Israel, the literary history of the Hebrew Bible, and the religious history of ancient Israel.

1. *The Subject of the Theology of the Hebrew Bible as the Literarily Formed, Historically Complex, and Factually Connected Thought World of the Hebrew Bible*

If one attempts to approach the question of the theology of the Hebrew Bible—which remains an essential element of Hebrew Bible studies on the basis of the two observations above among others—while eschewing an ahistorical approach, then the subject of such an investigation becomes the literary collection of the Hebrew Bible, including its literary forms, conceptual developments, historical differentiations, and textual as well as redactional connections. The task of the theology of the Hebrew Bible that follows should be understood as the reconstruction and presentation of the thought world of the literature of the Hebrew Bible. This thought world can be considered theological to the degree that its worldview is essentially constituted by, or primarily influenced by, its referential connection to God. The degree to which the use of the term *theological* is appropriate or not requires further explanation, which appears in the discussion found in Part B.

It is also integral to the task of a theology of the Hebrew Bible to combine the various points of view that arise in its literary presentations, conceptual emphases, and historical differentiations. The theological relevance of the Hebrew Bible appears not only in the various positions taken by different texts, arising from the disparate situations of their historical origins. Also significant are the interpretive dynamics that combine the texts with one another into a larger whole. For almost none of the theological positions surveyed and mentioned in the Hebrew Bible were drafted in complete isolation. As a rule they developed as reactions, further developments, critique, etc., of previously given texts.

OUTSIDER AND INSIDER PERSPECTIVES It is also evident that this approach to the theology of the Hebrew Bible must be accessible to those outside the discipline. Theology of the Hebrew Bible must satisfy the usual scholarly standards, such that its questions, implementation, and results both make sense and are plausible for those (whether they accept or reject the results) who, for example, locate themselves outside Judaism or Christianity. Those affiliated with Judaism or Christianity might have a certain advantage or head start in understanding the Hebrew Bible or Old Testament because of their prior acquaintance with its texts, but knowledge of or historical proximity to a subject does not represent a prerequisite for possible understanding. Both non-Jews and non-Christians can study, interpret, and understand the Hebrew Bible. Sometimes the distance from a subject can even allow for increased awareness; outsider perspectives can supplement insider perspectives in important aspects.

In the same way that was true for Julius Wellhausen (1844–1918), who apparently planned a critique of Old Testament theology in light of the approaches that were available to him, which he evidently found unconvincing. As with his "attempt [to work out and publish] a critique of the so-called Old Testament theology as a scholarly discipline,"[4] the saying remains applicable: *abuse does not preclude [proper] use*. Hebrew Bible studies will not be justified with regard to its subject as long as it forgoes the subdiscipline of theology of the Hebrew Bible. Neither will it be justified if this subdiscipline is approached in an ahistorical or uncritical manner.

4. Cf. Rudolf Smend, "Der Greifswalder Julius Wellhausen und die Biblische Theologie," in *Beyond Biblical Theologies*, ed. Heinrich Assel et al., WUNT 295 (Tübingen: Mohr Siebeck, 2012), 3–18.

2. *The Historical and Socio-Literary Character of the Literature of the Hebrew Bible as Elite Literature*

THE SCRIBAL CULTURE OF ANCIENT ISRAEL What exactly do we have before us in the Hebrew Bible? Is it divine revelations that have become words, religious texts from daily life, or the theological writings of experts? Who wrote these texts and for whom? These questions are difficult to answer because the answers diverge depending on the part of the Hebrew Bible under discussion. In addition, too little material exists for solid historical judgments about the sources. However, it is likely that the texts of the Hebrew Bible were produced and read within the comparably small circle of individuals who were able to read and write quite proficiently within a widely illiterate society. Comparative evidence from Greece and Egypt points in a similar direction. While the ability to read and write was limited to a small part of the population, the existence of professional scribes does not mean that the rest of the population was completely illiterate. The situation was much more complex. There is no exact line between literacy and illiteracy. Then as now, the ability to read and write was acquired through a gradual process. A short notice of delivery for goods, such as those found in the Samaria Ostraca from the eighth century BCE, could undoubtedly be comprehended by a larger circle than the Siloam Inscription from Hezekiah's Tunnel in Jerusalem, not to mention a book of prophecy.

Contrary to the self-presentation of the Hebrew Bible, which ascribes small sections of the Pentateuch to Moses (cf. Exod 17:14; 24:4; 34:28; Num 33:2), it appears that only in the ninth century BCE in Israel and in Judah only in the eighth century BCE did writing and scribal culture first become pronounced to such a degree that one would expect the production of more extensive literary works.[5] In addition to general evidence on the cultural-historical development of the southern Levant that is important for understanding scribal culture, this conclusion is supported by the historical distribution of ancient Hebrew inscriptions. This contention is not based on the statistical evidence, but it is apparently still tied to rise

---

5. Israel Finkelstein and Benjamin Sass, "Epigraphic Evidence from Jerusalem and Its Environs at the Dawn of Biblical History: Facts First," in *New Studies in the Archaeology of Jerusalem and Its Region: Collected Essays.* Volume XI, ed. Yuval Gadot et al. (Jerusalem: Israel Antiquities Authority, 2017), 21*–26*, conclude that "Alphabetic writing developed slowly between the 13th century and the early 9th, with a first peak occurring only in the late Iron IIA, the 9th century BCE" (25*).

of literacy. The number of ancient Hebrew inscriptions increases dramatically from the ninth to the eighth century. The opposite argument made by some American and Israeli scholars, namely that due to the absence of *Hebrew* inscriptions from the Persian period one should primarily place the formation of the Hebrew Bible in the preexilic period, goes against historical probability. Persian period inscriptions were written in the *lingua franca* of the time, Aramaic. Furthermore, their number is significantly larger than the number of Hebrew inscriptions. In principle, the number of Persian period inscriptions, if anything, confirms the importance of the Persian period for the formation of the literature of the Hebrew Bible rather than constituting an argument against it.

One should, however, interpret the statistical evidence with caution because most of the writing in this time took place on materials that did not survive (especially papyrus), so the preserved inscriptions, such as the ostraca, only reflect the culture of writing in a fragmentary manner. In any case, the overall impression remains significant, particularly because it is supported by two further observations. The first observation is that written prophecy in Israel and Judah appears at the very point in time when one can reckon with a certain level of literary culture—the eighth century BCE. The second is the temporal convergence with the fact that from this point onward Israel and Judah—though somewhat later for Judah—are perceived as states in ancient Near Eastern sources, which allows for the corresponding conclusion of a certain level of state development, which itself is related to the writing culture.

There is, however, contrary evidence that should be noted. The most wide-ranging inscriptions from the Southern Levant, the Mesha Stela[6] and the Balaam Inscription from Tell Deir 'Alla,[7] are, on the one hand, early (ninth century BCE and eighth–seventh century BCE respectively) and, on the other, from the periphery in terms of geography.[8] They discourage an overly narrow and mechanical connection between the advancement of a state apparatus and the advancement of its writing culture. By themselves, however, they provide insufficient evidence for an alternative set of parameters.

6. "The Inscription of King Mesha," trans. K. A. D. Smelik (*COS* 2.23:137–38).

7. "The Deir 'Alla Plaster Inscriptions," trans. Baruch A. Levine (*COS* 2.27:140–45).

8. Cf. Erhard Blum, "Die altaramäischen Wandinschriften aus Tell Deir 'Alla und ihr institutioneller Kontext," in *Metatexte: Erzählungen von schrifttragenden Artefakten in der alttestamentlichen und mittelalterlichen Literatur*, ed. Friedrich-Emanuel Focken and Michael Ott, Materiale Textkulturen 15 (Berlin: de Gruyter, 2016), 21–52.

THE DISSEMINATION OF HEBREW BIBLE LITERATURE For understanding
the literary production of the Hebrew Bible, it is also important to note
that the books of the Hebrew Bible were likely originally written as single
copies. This hypothesis is supported by their character as agglutinative
(growing by supplementation) interpretive literature. It is hardly imaginable that the process of literary updating, consisting of multiple steps for
the biblical books (which the evidence of the Bible's transmission shows
beyond dispute), could have taken place if numerous copies of the books
were in circulation. This hypothesis is supported further by information
within the Hebrew Bible itself. Typical, for example, is the statement of
Deut 17:18:

> When [the king] sits on the throne of his kingdom, he shall have *the*
> copy of this law (את־משנה התורה הזאת, *'t-mšnh htwrh hz't*) writ-
> ten for him in a book in accord with what is found with the Levitical
> priests.

This text does not call for the king to make *a* copy of the Deuteronomic
law. It instead assumes that the duplicate produced for the king remains the
sole additional copy besides the original. The texts of 2 Chr 17:7–9; Neh
8:1–2; and 2 Macc 2:13–15 can be similarly understood as pointing to the
very limited distribution of the books of the Hebrew Bible from the Iron
Age through the Hellenistic period. In fact, 2 Macc 2:15 shows that not
even the Jewish community of Alexandria possessed a complete Bible in
the second century BCE. The narrow circulation of biblical writings hardly
comes as a surprise when one considers the cumbersome and therefore
expensive nature of the production of scrolls. The copying of an Isaiah
scroll in the rabbinic period equaled about six months' income for a scribe.

It appears that the Jerusalem temple played a special role in literary
production. One can reckon with a model exemplar being stored there,
which would then serve as the basis for a newly augmented (by literary
updating) copy.

2 Macc 2:13–15 speaks of a library founded by Nehemiah in Jerusalem,
whose inventory of books ("the books about the kings and prophets, and
the writings of David, and letters of kings about votive offerings") could
apparently—as the conspicuous absence of the Torah might indicate—
only be described as eclectic, or rather characterized as an ensemble consisting of the Enneateuch (the Torah would then be the prophecy of Moses) and the Latter Prophets as well as the Psalms. This description would

have fit for the library of the Jerusalem temple. The narrative of the book discovery in the temple by Hilkiah the priest in 2 Kgs 22, as well as 1 Sam 10:25, indicate that the Hebrew Bible itself imagines a collection of books in the temple. Most libraries in the ancient Near East were selective, containing a limited collection of texts. These libraries were not public; they were reserved for temple and educational activities, reflecting the fact there was not a strict separation between libraries and archives in the ancient Near East. In addition were the apparently much rarer depository libraries, which aimed to collect every possible text available. Examples of this type of library are the Library of Ashurbanipal, the Library of Alexandria, and probably the one from Qumran. The extent of the Jerusalem library is difficult to determine. The text of 2 Macc 2:13–15 indicates that it likely contained more than merely the literature that eventually became the Hebrew Bible. Further support for this conclusion comes from the Qumran scrolls. It is hard to believe that the library at Qumran, which includes far more than the Hebrew Bible, was larger than the Jerusalem temple's library.

One should not reckon with the homogeneous makeup of Jerusalem's scribal community. Though the group responsible for the formation of the books of the Hebrew Bible was likely quite manageable and geographically limited to Jerusalem, at least from the Persian period onward, they appear to have represented a rather broad spectrum of theological views. Viewpoints that are at times almost diametrical now appear next to each other in the biblical books, which in any case points to such a conclusion.

SCHOOLS IN ANCIENT ISRAEL Historical knowledge about scribes and scribal schools in ancient Israel is very limited. Both evidence from the Bible and extant seals (and seal impressions)[9] from the preexilic period sufficiently testify to the existence of professional scribes (cf., e.g., 2 Sam 8:17; 1 Kgs 4:3; Jer 32; 36; 43; 45 ["Baruch the scribe"]; Ezra 7:6, 11–26 ["Ezra the scribe of the law of the God of heaven"]; Neh 13:12–13; Sir 38–39; Mark 11:27–33; Matt 23). Their function shifted throughout history in the direction of scribal scholarship, which was not merely responsible for the recording of texts (though this remained necessary due to the limited durability of the textual media), but also for the expansionistic interpretation of the texts they transmitted (cf. Jer 36:32).

9. Cf. Matthieu Richelle, "Elusive Scrolls: Could Any Hebrew Literature Have Been Written Prior to the Eighth Century BCE?," *VT* 66 (2016): 556–94.

In light of similar cultural-historical analogies, one can reckon with scribes trained at schools located in the temple or the palace. The Bible hardly mentions these schools (only Sir 51:23; Acts 19:9), so they must instead be deduced from analogous situations, which does not necessarily speak against this hypothesis. Neither was there a strict separation between the temple and palace schools. The temple was not an autonomous institution; it instead depended on the royal court.

The Talmudic tradition is aware of four hundred and eighty schools in Jerusalem (y. Meg. 73b), which may, however, be exaggerated. In any case, there were likely a significant number of schools in operation, especially in Jerusalem, beginning in the Hellenistic period. One need not necessarily imagine a freestanding building for such schools. What was central was the teacher-student relationship (1 Chr 25:8; Prov 5:12–14; Ps 119:99). The instruction of students could have taken place in the rooms of the temple or in the teachers' private dwellings. It should be expected that there were private libraries among priestly families, which played a role in the transmission of scribal knowledge within the family.

Scholars sometimes find the absence of the attestation of schools in ancient Israel significant, tracing back scribal education instead to the transmission of knowledge more likely taking place within scribal "families." One should probably combine both hypotheses, rather than viewing them as mutually exclusive. This conclusion is suggested by the close proximity of the Jerusalem scribal family of the Shaphanids to both the royal court and the temple (cf. 2 Kgs 22:3; Jer 36).

THE HEBREW BIBLE AS A WITNESS TO A LITERARY RELIGION The Hebrew Bible does not provide an unmediated window into the lived experience of folk religion, as many scholars supposed in the heyday of form-critical studies. The Hebrew Bible—as Stephen Geller poignantly states[10]—bears witness to a literary religion, which, as such, was never lived, but instead gave rise to an extraordinarily strong reception history.

10. Stephen A. Geller, *Sacred Enigmas: Literary Religion in the Hebrew Bible* (London: Routledge, 1996).

B. The Use of the Concept of Theology in Relation to the Bible

There is a lack of clarity on the nature of the project of theology of the Hebrew Bible in current scholarship. This issue calls for an explanation from the history of the scholarship of the origins and development of the discipline. Such a historical study can also render the prominent concept of "theology" comprehensible in light of the contexts and intellectual frameworks from which these various approaches to it have emerged.

Clarification from the history of scholarship does not mean an exhaustive discussion of every position to date, but rather the attempt to trace the inner logic and the changes in the external context of the discussion that has led to the current convoluted situation.

There are primarily two forces that have driven the discussion that should be taken into account. First, the existence of the subdiscipline "theology of the Old Testament" can be described as the outgrowth of a development in scholarship attested since the eighteenth century that essentially consists of a double movement of differentiation. First, the rise of historical-critical biblical scholarship expedited the rupture between systematics and biblical studies as well as the unity of biblical studies itself. Because the Old Testament/Hebrew Bible contains a different theology than the New Testament, it should in principle be described separately. However, the accent on the plurality of content in the Bible is only one of the driving forces that formed the present situation.

The second concerns the concept of theology itself. Within the university contexts arising during the High and Late Middle Ages (eleventh–twelfth centuries), the concept of theology was influenced by Scholasticism. Theology came to denote the systematic and logical portrait of the Christian doctrinal edifice. For Luther, however, theology was applied to the soteriological function of Christian faith.

Protestant orthodoxy then returned more or less to the Scholastic uses of the term.[1]

§2 The Premodern Conception of Theology: From Mythology to Systematic Doctrine

Gerhard Ebeling, "Theologie I: Begriffsgeschichtlich," *RGG*, 3rd ed., 6:754–69 ◆ John H. Hayes and Frederick C. Prussner, *Old Testament Theology: Its History and Development* (London: SCM, 1985) ◆ Friedrich Kattenbusch, "Die Entstehung einer christlichen Theologie," *ZTK* 38 (1930): 161–205 ◆ Horst Dietrich Preuss, *JHWHs erwählendes und verpflichtendes Handeln*, vol. 1 of *Theologie des Alten Testaments* (Stuttgart: Kohlhammer, 1991), 2–23

1. "Theology" in Plato, Aristotle, Josephus, and Philo

ORIGINS OF THE CONCEPT OF THEOLOGY The concept of theology originates from philosophical discourse. This is a matter of historical coincidence, but it remains significant nonetheless. The term first appears in Plato meaning "legend of the gods," that is "myth" (Plato, *Resp.*, 379a). The noun θεολογία (*theologia*) in Plato denotes myths that call for critical evaluation and should only be used selectively for educational purposes. In Aristotle (*Metaph.*, 1026a.18–19; 1064b.1–3), while θεολογία can be called one of the three "theoretical philosophies" along with mathematics and physics, he primarily uses it to denote mythology.

Θεολογία also appears in Josephus and Philo. Josephus (*C. Ap.* 1.225) uses the expression "our theology" for the Jewish religion, while Philo (*Mos.* 2.115) calls Moses a "theologian" in an analogous manner. However, this terminology does not imply a reflective or synthesizing approach to religion. *Theology* instead appears almost as an alternate term for religion. The proximity of the use of the term to Greek philosophical use is noticeable.

---

1. For more detail, cf. Konrad Schmid, *Is There Theology in the Hebrew Bible?*, Critical Studies in the Hebrew Bible 4 (Winona Lake, IN: Eisenbrauns, 2015). See also the surveys provided by Walter Brueggemann, *Theology of the Old Testament: Testimony, Dispute, Advocacy* (Minneapolis: Fortress, 1997), 1–60; Paul R. House, *Theology of the Old Testament* (Downers Grove, IL: InterVarsity Press, 1998), 13–53.

2. *The Bible and the Early Church*

Neither the Greek Old Testament nor the New Testament uses the term θεολογία. Although absent in both Paul and John, their comprehensive intellectual efforts in both letter and narrative forms take on considerable significance for the later development of the concept of theology. It is noteworthy that John the Evangelist has been known as "the theologian" since Origen, an epithet that still endures for him in the Orthodox Church.

MARGINALIZATION OF THE CONCEPT OF THEOLOGY IN THE EARLY CHURCH Nevertheless, the concept of theology was not accorded central importance in the first centuries of the Christian church. It reached a preeminent status in the following periods, from Late Antiquity to the High Middle Ages. The adoption of the philosophical notion of God into Christian doctrine in the second century CE was especially important in this process.

Drawing a programmatic distinction from the traditional pagan use of the concept of theology, Eusebius of Caesarea held that the gods of myths and cults are not the focus of theology but rather only the one God whom the church recognizes as creator (*Hist. eccl.* 2.1.1). Therefore, writers of myths and mystical teachers do not qualify as "theologians," while the prophets, Paul, and John do.

3. *Scholasticism and the Emergence of Academic "Theology"*

In terms of the concept's reception, it was not so much the developments of Antiquity and Late Antiquity but rather of the Middle Ages that proved decisive for current notions of "theology." Observable contours of the modern conceptualization of "theology" first arise in the High Middle Ages. These dimensions especially concern the expansion of the concept of theology from the doctrine of God to the entirety of Christian doctrine.

THEOLOGY IN THE UNIVERSITY FRAMEWORK This extension of the concept is intrinsically linked to the contemporaneous reception of Aristotle, which helped to systematically expound Christian doctrine for the first time, treating it as an academic task. Especially conspicuous in this context are the schools of theology that emerged in the universities in the eleventh and twelfth centuries to deal with Christian doctrine. These bore the name *facultas theologica*. This development provided the foundation for the further predominance of the concept of theology in the history of Christianity. More than anything else, the result was the academic connotation of the concept, which would remain intact in the following period. Theology became a process involving reason and systematic reflection. The modern period would also add the methodological principle of criticism and doubt. It thereby pertains to a meta level of lived religion.

The character of theology as influenced by Scholasticism and the early universities prepared the foundation for the later historical development of the concept. Particularly in the English-speaking realm, the scholastic connotations of "theology" have largely persisted into the modern period; theology essentially consists of intellectualizing and systematizing. For this reason, biblical studies has occasionally and sometimes vehemently rejected "theology" as a subject of investigation from various perspectives and motivations. For example, "theology" does not do justice to the diversity of the witnesses of faith, it leads to reductionism, and it is an inappropriate subject for historical inquiry. However, it is critical to note that such understandings of "theology" generally present caricatures of what Scholasticism intended, with the result that such blanket criticisms should be qualified and understood accordingly.

§3 The Reformation's Reconstrual of the Concept of Theology

Christian Danz, *Einführung in die Theologie Martin Luthers* (Darmstadt: Wissenschaftliche Buchgesellschaft, 2013) ♦ Johannes Wallmann, *Der Theologiebegriff bei Johann Gerhard und Georg Calixt*, Beiträge zur historischen Theologie 30 (Tübingen: Mohr, 1961)

1. *The Existential Reinterpretation of the Concept of Theology in the Reformation*

THE CONNECTION OF THE NOTION OF THEOLOGY WITH RELATIONSHIP WITH GOD The roots of the Reformation movement were planted in an academic context, and, if for no other reason, the movement was quite familiar from the beginning with the scholastic conceptualization of theology. But the Reformation introduced an influential modification to the concept, without which the contemporary debates regarding its usage would be incomprehensible. This semantic shift involved a change from defining "theology" in terms of the doctrine of God to defining it in terms of the relationship of the person with God. "The proper subject of theology is man, sinful, guilty, and abandoned, and God the justifier and savior of sinful man."[2] Very pointed declarations conforming to this view appear against theology as a speculative system: "true theology is practical, therefore speculative theology belongs in hell with the devil."[3] In this respect it is noteworthy that Luther continued to hold firmly to the notion of theology despite his rejection of Aristotelian-influenced scholasticism. Luther's decision, followed almost without exception in Protestant theology, ultimately became the basis for later confusion on the distinction between theology and religion. Theology was no longer concerned with a speculative doctrine of God, it instead essentially concerned a matter of faith, namely the *relationship* with God in both its practical and existential dimensions, which Luther poignantly formulated "God and faith belong in one heap."[4] Thus the later applicability of its focus *also* moves in the direction of the notion of religion. The interchangeability of theology and religion emerged in the period of the Reformation, which did not have a problem with this overlap.

REFORMATIONAL REDEFINITION OF THEOLOGY The Reformation's new definition of theology arose in part through a new understanding of the Bible, which was read anew as a testimony of human experiences with God. It no longer sufficed simply to use the Bible to illustrate the pre-established correctness of doctrine. On the contrary, doctrine was now to be measured by the Bible, not least concerning how Christian teaching as a whole ought to be understood. In this sense, the Reformation can be seen as having developed in part out of attention to the distinction between Bible and doctrine. The gap between church practice and theology and the Reformation's own understanding of Scripture led to a reform movement aiming to reunite the Bible and the church, in line with reorienting the church toward the Bible. Judging from his body of work, had Luther taught in a modern school of theology he most likely would have belonged

---

2. Martin Luther, *Vorlesungen über Psalm 2, 45 und 51 1532* [Lectures on Psalm 2, 45, and 51, 1532], WA 40:2; 328:17.

3. Martin Luther, *Tischreden* [Table Talks], WA 172:16, no. 153.

4. Martin Luther, *Die Bekenntnisschriften der evangelisch-lutherischen Kirche* [The Confessions of the Evangelical Lutheran Church], 560:21–22: "Gott und Glaube gehören zuhauf."

to the department of Hebrew Bible. Yet the historical and content-related otherness of the Bible hardly represented a problem worthy of reflection in Luther's day. Although the Reformers' writings often demonstrate a sense of tension between biblical tradition and doctrine, the tension was not regarded as a foundational issue for theology. Rather, the ideal consisted of tying theology to biblical teaching, an aim whose chances of success few people doubted. Consciousness of a fundamental historical divide between the biblical and the contemporary periods was faint, so readers were able to imagine the biblical authors as speaking directly to them.

AFTEREFFECTS OF THE REFORMATION'S UNDERSTANDINGS OF THEOLOGY IN HEBREW BIBLE STUDIES In spite of all the historical conditions influencing understandings of theology in the Reformation, the articulation of theology as an interpretation of experiences with God has broadly permeated Hebrew Bible studies, as will demonstrated below. The present theology of the Hebrew Bible also participates in the effects of this fundamental decision. Is it then a Protestant theology of the Hebrew Bible? This is true in one sense. It also shares this fate with other subdisciplines of Hebrew Bible studies. Historically speaking, Protestant biblical scholarship bears the primary responsibility for forming and developing the disciplines and methods of Hebrew Bible studies since the eighteenth century. Therefore, while the present volume on the theology of the Hebrew Bible does not set a particularly Protestant accent in terms of its outline or content, it is Protestant in terms of the history of scholarship.

2. "Theology" in Protestant Orthodoxy

Protestant orthodoxy of the later sixteenth and seventeenth centuries returned to the systematizing forms of theology that were common prior to the Reformation. Melanchthon used the term "theology" with hesitation, preferring to speak of *doctrina christiana*. The term returned as a description of Christian teaching in the work of Bartholomäus Keckermann. In his work on the philosophy of science, *Systema S.S. Theologiae* (Hannover: Antonius, 1602) inspired by Jacopo Zabarella, Keckermann listed theology alongside other academic disciplines. Following Johann Gerhard's description of his *Loci theologici* (9 vols., Jena, 1610–1622), Keckermann understood theology as a comprehensive academic presentation of Christian doctrine.

DICTA PROBANTIA As a result, the convergence of Bible and doctrinal instruction became decisive in Protestant orthodoxy. The text was consulted in an eclectic fashion as a source of quotations to supply evidence for doctrinal positions. Of special importance was the identification of *dicta probantia* (prooftexts) to provide the biblical undergirding of doctrine. The best-known work of this kind was Sebastian Schmidt's *Collegium biblicum in quo dicta scripturae Veteris et Novi testamenti iuxta seriem locorum communium theologicorum disposita dilucide explicantur* (Strassburg: Staedeius, 1671; 2nd ed., 1676; 3rd ed., 1689), which separately listed Old and New Testament quotations of theological *loci* but avoided explicit evaluation of them. Bible and theology interacted with one another such that the former served as the implicit groundwork, while the latter was the systematic explication. However, the emergence of historical-critical biblical scholarship brought about the rapid dissolution of this relationship.

§4 From Biblical Theology to the Theology of the Old Testament

Hans Hübner and Bernd Jaspert, eds., *Biblische Theologie: Entwürfe der Gegenwart*, Biblisch-theologische Studien 38 (Neukirchen-Vluyn: Neukirchener Verlag, 1999) ◆ Reinhard G. Kratz, "Auslegen und Erklären: Über die theologische Bedeutung der Bibelkritik nach Johann Philipp Gabler," in *Johann Philipp Gabler (1753–1826) zum 250. Geburtstag*, ed. Karl-Wilhelm Niebuhr and Christfried Böttrich (Leipzig: Evangelishe Verlagsanstalt, 2003), 53–74 ◆ Hans-Joachim Kraus, *Die Biblische Theologie: Ihre Geschichte und Problematik* (Neukirchen-Vluyn: Neukirchener Verlag, 1970) ◆ Otto Merk, *Biblische Theologie des Neuen Testaments in ihrer Anfangszeit: Ihre methodischen Probleme bei Johann Philipp Gabler und Georg Lorenz Bauer und deren Nachwirkungen*, Marburger theologische Studien 9 (Marburg: Elwert, 1972) ◆ Walther Zimmerli, "Biblische Theologie I.," *TRE* 6:426–55

1. Biblical Theology as a Result of the Emancipation of Exegesis from Systematic Theology

THE EMERGENCE OF BIBLICAL THEOLOGY With the first steps toward historical-critical interpretation of the Bible in the seventeenth century, it quickly became clear that the systematic theology of the Reformation was not simply biblical. The Bible did not reason the same way the Reformers did. The biblical texts in fact said more, less, or even something different than systematics. The results were unavoidable: there was a slackening of the unity between text and systemization, between exegesis and dogmatics, that had been found in the premodern and continued into the Reformation period. The initial solution to this budding issue was the introduction of a mediating element between Bible and systematics.

BIBLICAL THEOLOGY AND SYSTEMATIC THEOLOGY Biblical theology emerged as an independent theological pursuit alongside systematic theology. It is noteworthy and important for reception history that this discipline includes the word "theology" as part of its title. Theology is understood in this context as an intellectual but unfinished endeavor that mediates rationally and systematically between existing settled entities.

JOHANN PHILIPP GABLER The beginning of the biblical theology movement is usually dated to Johann Philipp Gabler's inaugural lecture in Altdorf in 1787, *Oratio de justo discrimine theologiae biblicae et dogmaticae regundisque recte utriusque finibus.* However, Gabler's lecture was more a bundling of earlier efforts than a completely new starting point. The step toward a "biblical theology" independent from systematics was already announced in Johann Georg Hofmann's *Oratio de Theologiae biblicae praestantia* (Nürnberg: Bauer, 1770), in Jean Alphonse Turretini's *De Sacrae Scripturae interpretatione tractatus bipartitus* (Frankfurt a. d. O.: Straus, 1776), in the works of Anton Friedrich Büsching, both his *Dissertatio theologica inauguralis exhibens epitomen theologiae e solis sacris litteris concinnatae et ab omnibus rebus et verbis scholasticis purgatae* (Göttingen: Luzac, 1756) as well as his *Gedanken von der Beschaffenheit und dem Vorzug der biblisch-dogmatischen Theologie vor der alten und neuen scholastischen* (Lemgo: Meyer, 1758)—the latter of these brought him into conflict with the Göttingen school of theology—as well as in Johannes Cocceius and Georg Calixt. The fact that Gabler has gone down as the founder of "biblical theology" in the memoirs of historical theology is justified in terms of the programmatic nature of his lecture. Gabler in no way lamented the breakup of the Bible and systematics; he instead attempted to conceive of an appropriate determination (*discrimen*) of the process. He believed that one should distinguish between biblical and dogmatic theology. Biblical theology is a *historical* undertaking that reconstructs the theology of the biblical authors. Systematic theology, on the other hand, aims at the formulation of a *contemporary* theology. By necessity it must be separate from biblical theology, which arose from a different, bygone epoch. In order for systematics to remain connected to biblical theology, Gabler introduced a further differentiation within biblical theology, between "true" and "pure" biblical theology. "True biblical theology" remains within the *historical* framework of the biblical world and its thought paradigm. "Pure biblical theology" attempts to articulate universal, *timeless* perspectives behind this historically conditioned outlook of the Bible, thereby building a bridge to contemporary systematics. According to Gabler, one might view biblical theology and systematics in terms of a division of labor. However, it will soon become clear that Gabler's attempt did not really reconcile the Bible and systematics, but merely organized the differences into a multi-stepped model, reducing them only on the surface. Bible, true biblical theology, pure biblical theology, and systematics persisted next to one another, offering various degrees of systemization and applicability of the same message to the contemporary world.

Gotthilf Traugott Zachariä conceived of the relationship between biblical and systematic theology somewhat differently, namely in a polemical manner, in his *Biblische Theologie oder Untersuchung des biblischen Grundes der vornehmsten theologischen Lehren* (Tübingen: Schramm, 1780). Biblical criticism of systematics aims to "compare systematic and biblical ideas with one another and to investigate closely what of the accepted systematic ideas, which always have their sources in specific biblical expressions, are correct or incorrect."[5] In reality, however, Zachariä was in danger of replacing traditional dogmatism with the biblicism that also consumed him.

2. *The Rise of an Independent Theology of the Old Testament*

Gabler's edifice was not stable. Specifically, "pure biblical theology" was shown to be a Trojan horse that served the purpose of allowing for continued adherence to a trans-historical biblical truth, even if it was of necessity later converted into a particular temporal form by systematics. In terms of later reception history, what remains relevant is not Gabler's classification of biblical and systematic theology but rather his differentiations, which became even more pronounced. Not only did historical-critical biblical perspectives increasingly distance themselves from traditional dogmatics (which also resulted in several nineteenth-century biblical scholars such

---

5. Zachariä, *Biblische Theologie oder Untersuchung*, 8.

as Julius Wellhausen withdrawing from the schools of theology), but the unity of biblical theology was also shown to be of a provisional nature only. The Old and New Testaments are, as became increasingly clear, distinct from one another in terms of their theological message. They do not even fit together in terms of a progressive linear sequence, as is often intended through the conceptions of promise and fulfillment or of law and gospel.

GEORG LORENZ BAUER According to a growing consensus, from then on the theology of the Old Testament and the theology of the New Testament were to be portrayed separately. Georg Lorenz Bauer's *Theologie des A.T. oder Abriß der religiösen Begriffe der alten Hebräer: Von den ältesten Zeiten bis auf den Anfang der christlichen Epoche: Zum Gebrauch akademischer Vorlesungen* (Leipzig: Weygand, 1796) is usually seen as the first stand-alone representative of the new subdiscipline. Subsequent theological, or rather religious-historical, treatments of the Bible increasingly offered separate treatments of the testaments. Those treating the Old Testament include Carl Peter Wilhelm Gramberg, Bruno Bauer, Heinrich Andreas Christoph Hävernick, Ferdinand Hitzig, August Kayser, and August Dillmann.

Nonetheless, approaches taking the entire Bible into consideration—especially from a historical-developmental perspective—remained important. Especially noteworthy are Wilhelm Martin Leberecht de Wette's *Biblische Dogmatik Alten und Neuen Testaments: Oder kritische Darstellung der Religionslehre des Hebraismus, des Judenthums und des Urchristenthums* (Berlin: Realschulbuchhandlung, 1813; 3rd ed., 1831) and Wilhelm Vatke's *Die biblische Theologie wissenschaftlich dargestellt. I: Die Religion des A.T.* (Berlin: Bethge, 1835). Arising especially from the subtitle of de Wette's "dogmatics," they attempt to bridge the distance between and within the testaments by interpreting them in terms of historical development.

The sundering of the biblical theology of the whole Bible into separate theologies of the Old and of the New Testaments is an extremely significant event in the context of the overall history of the concept of theology. It results in the first conception of theology that contains a notion of *plurality*. The Bible does not have a single theology, but, when viewed from current perspectives, *at least* two theologies: one of the Old Testament and one of the New Testament. After establishing this distinction, no fundamental obstacles stood in the way of the further pluralization of theology that unfolded over the course of the twentieth and the beginning of the twenty-first centuries.

§5 The Romantic Devaluation of the Concept of Theology

Botho Ahlers, *Die Unterscheidung von Theologie und Religion: Ein Beitrag zur Vorgeschichte der praktischen Theologie im 18. Jahrhundert* (Gütersloh: Gütersloher Verlagshaus, 1980) ♦ Martin Laube, "Die Unterscheidung von Theologie und Religion: Überlegungen zu einer umstrittenen Grundfigur in der protestantischen Theologie des 20. Jahrhunderts," *ZTK* 112 (2015): 449–67 ♦ Axel Michaels, ed., *Klassiker der Religionswissenschaft: von Friedrich Schleiermacher bis Mircea Eliade* (Munich: Beck, 1997) ♦ Werner H. Schmidt, "'Theologie des Alten Testaments' vor und nach Gerhard von Rad," *VF* 17 (1972): 1–25 ♦ Udo Tworuschka, *Einführung in die Geschichte der Religionswissenschaft* (Darmstadt: Wissenschaftliche Buchgesellschaft, 2015)

1. The Differentiation between Religion and Theology

Friedrich Schleiermacher The late eighteenth and early nineteenth centuries were also pivotal for the issue of the adequacy of the application of the concept theology to Hebrew Bible texts. During this period arose the distinction between religion and theology that would become definitive for subsequent periods. At the same time discovery of religion as the "individual province of the mind" (Friedrich Schleiermacher) also took place. Religion is not simply a matter of the spirit, the intellect, or feeling, but a unique phenomenon. As a result, it cannot be evaluated sufficiently with the traditional tools of theology and philosophy. Religion is always more than what theology and philosophy are able to comprehend.

Johann Salomo Semler's Separation of Religion and Theology In the eighteenth century, the basic distinction between religion and theology began to gain prominence. This separation became especially accentuated within the movement of Neology (the reception of the Enlightenment in Lutheran theology)—specifically with Johann Salomo Semler. Theology came to be understood as reflection on religion. This development resulted in the fundamental classification of religion and theology, including the nature of the relationship between the two concepts in current discussion.

This distinction was strongly supported first by Johann Gottfried Herder and then by Friedrich Schleiermacher. Schleiermacher's formulation of the concept was especially influential for Hebrew Bible studies. De Wette explicitly referred to Schleiermacher's notion of religion and injected it into the exegetical disciplines. On the flip side, Hebrew Bible studies developed an increasingly negative view of theology. Religion is experience, feeling, sensibility, and sensitivity for the eternal that theology cannot explain and define, but rather corrupts.

BERNHARD DUHM Bernhard Duhm's position provides one of many possible examples. He views his primary task in his work on the Hebrew Bible as "examining the stage of religion prior to theology, or at least prior to being fully dominated by theology."[6] He points to this danger especially in the realm of prophecy. In his commentary on the book of Jeremiah, he writes of Jeremiah's opponents:

> In reality, those first theologians known from the history of biblical religion unwillingly brought a deep antagonism to light, that which exists eternally between inspiration and scholarliness, between the forward-looking and living impulse of the creative spirits and the aspirations of epigones and imitative laypersons toward the achievements of an earlier age that treats the words of a master as dead treasure, as an idol that cannot tolerate anything new or better. It is actually a tragedy of religion that the dead prophet kills the living one. The thought of the former prophets, such as Amos, Hosea, or Isaiah, is that which the Deuteronomistic theology is believed to have systematized, and for their sake that Jer[emiah] needed to become a martyr.[7]

One must unearth the living religion of the Hebrew Bible that lies beneath the theologically shaped and revised form of each prophet. In the end, this conviction was one of the most important motivations for the success of historical-critical biblical scholarship in the theological schools of the nineteenth century. Duhm, like many colleagues in Hebrew Bible studies, practiced historical criticism so intensively, with an almost unexplainable passion and intuitively accepted sense of necessity, because he was convinced that this was the only means to push through the (pejoratively viewed) theology of the biblical writings to get to true religion. The necessity of the task of biblical criticism was self-evident.

---

6. Bernhard Duhm, *Das Geheimnis in der Religion: Vortrag gehalten am 11. Februar 1896* (Leipzig: Mohr, 1896), 7.

7. Bernhard Duhm, *Das Buch Jeremia*, KHC 11 (Tübingen: Mohr, 1901), 90.

WILHELM VATKE Schleiermacher's inspiration was not the only source for the conceptualization of religion and the investigations of the history of religions in Hebrew Bible studies during the nineteenth century. It is helpful for understanding the history of scholarship to observe that the origins of the question of the history of religion was also strongly marked by Hegelianism, especially through the work of Wilhelm Vatke. Vatke's magnum opus, *Die biblische Theologie wissenschaftlich dargestellt: I, Die Religion des A.T.* (Berlin: Bethge, 1835), treats its subject, the history of religion, "both from historical-critical and dogmatic perspectives,"[8] and for this reason it can also bear the name "biblical theology," though this point of view is only presented in the first section. Vatke outlines the intention of that section as follows:

> Biblical theology presents the idea of religion in the form of the basic consciousness of the Hebrew people and the early Christian period, or, expressed differently, it portrays the religious and ethical views of the holy writings in their historical development and with their internal contexts.[9]

The concern for the religious history of ancient Israel—which on the basis of the source material available at the time could also be called biblical religious history—served as considerably more than a simple critical historiographic interest based on its historical scholarly context. The history of ancient Israelite religion was set in a larger universal historical context:

> All pre-Christian religions, including that of the Old Testament, are prerequisites, preparations, anticipations of the one true religion. They first appear in their true light when viewed from the standpoint of the final [one true religion].[10]

In keeping with this conceptual formulation, biblical theology was set within the context of a broader theological method of operation:

> One the one hand, biblical theology assumes those theological disciplines that investigated the text as their immediate subject, such as

8. Vatke, *Die biblische Theologie*, vi.
9. Vatke, *Die biblische Theologie*, 2.
10. Vatke, *Die biblische Theologie*, 18.

canonical studies, hermeneutics, historical criticism, and exegesis; and it brings together the results that are delivered by those [disciplines] from the strictly religious sphere. On the other hand, biblical theology also influences those disciplines in reverse to the degree that these borrow their principles from an overall view of the content in treating the religious content of the text.[11]

In Vatke's view, biblical theology is based on the normal analytical steps of historical criticism, but these steps are also dictated by their synthetic perspective. Remarkable when viewed from current scholarship is the recognition of the importance of the eighth century BCE as a break in the source material:

> The sources for the older stories of Old Testament religion flowed from the later saga and are therefore fragmentary and unreliable. From the period of the Judges and even more so from the Davidic period, the tradition takes on historical character. Yet it can be followed with complete reliability first from the eighth century on the basis of the prophetic writings that begin at this time.[12]

In addition to Vatke, representatives of the idealist historical approach to Old Testament theology include Daniel von Cölln, Bruno Bauer, Ferdinand Hitzig, and August Dillmann. Heinrich Ewald still interpreted the intellectual history of Israel as the process of its religious development that increasingly perfected itself. However, toward the end of the nineteenth century, the orientation propounded by Abraham Kuenen, Julius Wellhausen, Bernhard Stade, and Karl Budde prevailed, which—under the contemporary influences of positivism and evolutionary thought—dictated a critical and historically-oriented approach. Wellhausen was, of course, strongly influenced by Vatke and must also defend himself against the allegation of Hegelianism, but the differences between his scholarly work and those of the Hegelian influenced idealist-historical approach are quite clear. Wellhausen employed the historical standards of his time, though the progressive history of Israelite religion still played a decisive role:

11. Vatke, *Die biblische Theologie*, 8.
12. Vatke, *Die biblische Theologie*, 177–78.

Israelite religion first lifted itself out of paganism; this itself is the content of its history.[13]

Wellhausen interpreted the emergence of Judaism, to which the history of Israelite religion pointed, as the process of intellectual history concerning the detachment from paganism. The history of religion was thus a meaningful process that leads from baser to more developed forms of reflection.

2. The Emergence of Religious Studies

F. MAX MÜLLER Religious studies developed into an independent discipline in the late nineteenth century. This process is also significant for the conception of theology, which was still unproblematic in the discipline's early days. One of the pioneers of this new field was F. Max Müller, whose primary contribution in terms of content was introducing the English-speaking world to Sanskrit literature. He conceived and began the series Sacred Books of the East, which was published between 1879 and 1910 by Oxford University Press. Its fifty volumes offer the most important texts from Hinduism, Buddism, Taoism, Confusianism, Zoroastrianism, Jainism, and Islam translated into English (F. Max Müller himself undertook the volumes on the Upanishads, Vedic hymns, Mahâyâna texts, and various others). The series originally planned to include the Old and New Testaments. However, Müller was forced to distance himself from this proposal on account of resistance from church circles, which recognized, correctly, that a basic relativization would occur if the Bible were set within a larger assortment of holy texts from Asia. This collection constituted the basis for Müller to carry out the comparative study of religion, of which he was the founder.

He followed Schleiermacher closely in his delineation of the nature of religion. He conceived of religion as "that spiritual facility . . . which allows humans to engage the eternal under the most diverse names and various forms."[14] The following quotation shows clearly his view of religious stud-

---

13. Julius Wellhausen, *Israelitische und jüdische Geschichte*, 3rd ed. (Berlin: Reimer, 1897), 34.

14. F. Max Müller, *Einleitung in die vergleichende Religionswissenschaft: Vier Vorlesungen im Jahre MDCCCLXX an der Royal Institution in London gehalten, nebst zwei Essays "Über falsche Analogien" und "Über Philosophie der Mythologie"* (Strassburg: Trübner, 1876), 17.

ies as analogous to comparative linguistics and initially conceived in terms of historical philology.

> What would classically trained academics say to people who attempt to evaluate Homer's religion without ever learning Greek; what would theologians say if one wagers to speak about Moses and the prophets without any knowledge of Hebrew![15]

But Müller was not only interested in the concrete forms of religions' appearances. He also assigned evaluative and theoretical tasks to religious studies:

> Because of the two meanings that we saw inherent to the word "religion," religious studies divides into two parts. The first, which concerns itself with the historical appearances of religion, is called *comparative theology*; the second, which explains the conditions under which religion in its highest or basest forms is possible, is called *theoretical theology*.[16]

What is striking in this proposal of an inner distinction within the task of religious studies is Müller's use of the concept of theology for both subdisciplines (comparative and theoretical). This position assumes that reflection on the forms of religion's appearance could be called theology.
Differently than Vatke's work, for example, Christianity does not receive a preeminent role a priori:

> I must admit that those who view comparative study of religion as a means to push down Christianity and raise up the other religions are just as unwelcome as partners as those who find it necessary to degrade all other religions in order to elevate Christianity. Academics does not need partisanship.[17]

Nonetheless, Müller accords Christianity *de facto* an exceptional position among the religions in that it is the only one religion employed to provide the foundation for "comparative theology." Yet Christianity

15. Müller, *Einleitung*, 33.
16. Müller, *Einleitung*, 19.
17. Müller, *Einleitung*, 34.

does not constitute the consummate religion, the apex and culmination of all religious history. Following Johann Wolfgang von Goethe, Müller holds:

> The same [as with the languages] applies with the religions. Whoever knows [only] one, knows none.[18]

This position prepared an even-handed path for the study of the history of religion, yet it has encountered considerable opposition, as the incisive response by Adolf von Harnack on the significance of Christianity observes thirty years later in a reversal of Müller's position:

> Whoever does not know this religion, knows none, and whoever knows it along with its history, knows them all.[19]

In time, however, Müller's position prevailed over von Harnack's. Christianity is not the religion par excellence, but instead represents one historical embodiment among others. At least according to the direction developed in the phenomenology of religion, neither can the various concrete forms of religion be easily unraveled into individual comparable elements. Each form exists within its own universe of meaning with specific accentuations.

3. *The Virtual Disappearance of the Subdiscipline "Theology of the Old Testament"*

HERMANN SCHULTZ Within Christian theology during the nineteenth century, Hebrew Bible studies established an increasingly historical and descriptive approach with regard to the representations of processes and developments of the theology of the Hebrew Bible. This movement was vigorously supported by the development of ancient Near Eastern

---

18. Müller, *Einleitung*, 14.

19. Adolf von Harnack, "Die Aufgabe der theologischen Fakultäten und die allgemeine Religionsgeschichte: Rede zur Gedächtnisfeier des Stifters der Berliner Universität König Friedrich Wilhelm II. in der Aula derselben am 3. August 1901," in *Reden und Aufsätze* (Gießen: Ricker, 1905), 2:168. Cf. Carsten Colpe, "Bemerkungen zu Adolf von Harnacks Einschätzung der Disziplin 'Allgemeine Religionsgeschichte,'" *Neue Zeitschrift für Systematische Theologie und Religionsgeschichte* 6 (1964): 51–69.

studies as well as the rise of ethnography. The enthusiasm for religious-historical work did not take place without consequence for theology. In fact, the effects were decisive for Hebrew Bible studies. As a result, Hermann Schultz, for example, opted for a purely historical approach to the subject in his *Alttestamentlichen Theologie*, which was reprinted multiple times:

> The task of biblical theology is, then, a purely historical presentation whose sources are the biblical books. . . . Biblical theology should present in purely historical manner the faith perspectives and customary conceptions on offer in the times of the emergence of Israelite and Christian religion. . . . What biblical theology demonstrates to be the religious and ethical content from a particular time of its development should not at all for that reason be deemed the doctrine of Christian faith or practice.[20]

With comparable focus but considerably more radical, Bernhard Stade writes, "By biblical theology of the OT one understands the history of the religion under the old covenant."[21] Smend concludes, "It is therefore the task of OT biblical theology to expound the formation and the content of the religious belief of Judaism and its ideals, on which Jesus in his proclamation, on which the NT writers draw in their report on [Jesus's proclamation] and in interpreting his person, and which are therefore the historical preconditions to Christianity."[22]

Like Heinrich Schultz and Karl Marti, Ernst Kautzsch proceeded without introductory methodological reflections in his posthumously published *Biblische Theologie des Alten Testaments* (Tübingen: Mohr, 1911), which is laid out as a "history of Israelite religion."[23]

The comprehensive establishment of this approach is on display in the fact that the somewhat more conservative theologies of the Hebrew Bible appearing at the time also conceived of their task in this manner:

---

20. Hermann Schultz, *Alttestamentliche Theologie: Die Offenbarungsreligion auf ihrer vorchristlichen Entwicklungsstufe*, 5th ed. (Göttingen: Vandenhoeck & Ruprecht, 1896), 4.

21. Bernhard Stade, *Die Religion Israels und die Entstehung des Judentums*, vol. 1 of *Biblische Theologie des Alten Testaments*, Grundriss der theologischen Wissenschaften II/2 (Tübingen: Mohr, 1905), 1. Cf. also Rudolf Smend, *Lehrbuch der Alttestamentliche Religionsgeschichte*, 2nd ed. (Freiburg: Mohr, 1899), 1.

22. Smend, *Lehrbuch der alttestamentlichen Religionsgeschichte* (Freiburg: Mohr, 1893), 2.

23. Kautzsch, *Biblische Theologie des Alten Testaments*, 2.

The theology of the Old Testament, the first main part of biblical theology, is a historical-genetic presentation of the religion contained in the canonical writings of the Old Testament.[24]

However, a completely different conception of history forms the foundation of this historical description that was developed in the wake of the salvation-history theology of Johann Christian Konrad von Hofmann:

The theology of the Old Testament should follow the stages through which Old Testament revelation progressed on its way to the culmination of salvation in Christ. It should present the forms in which the communion between God and humans took shape under the old covenant . . . its task, stated in short, is the presentation of the entire economy of revelation.[25]

KARL MARTI The results of this conviction are palpably on display in the choice of titles of Rudolf Smend and Karl Marti's "theological" projects: *Textbook of Old Testament Religious History* and *History of Israelite Religion*. Characteristic of this approach is the action taken by Karl Marti in 1897 for the revision of August Kayser's *Theologie des Alten Testaments in ihrer geschichtlichen Entwicklung dargestellt* (Strassburg: Schmidt, 1886), in which Marti simply changed the title to *Geschichte der Israelitischen Religion* (3rd ed., Strassburg: Bull, 1897). This was not difficult because Marti determined the aim of both approaches to be without any difference as follows:

By *History of Israelite Religion*, as well as by *Theology of the Old Testament* is meant that discipline concerned with the presentation of the religious and ethical content of the Old Testament.[26]

As a result, theology of the Old Testament as a project and as a nominally identifiable discipline basically disappeared from the stage. This movement was analogous to New Testament studies, prominently represented by William Wrede. His *Über Aufgabe und Methode der sogenannten*

24. Gustav F. Oehler, *Theologie des Alten Testaments*, 3rd ed. (Stuttgart: Steinkopf, 1891), 7.
25. Oehler, *Theologie des Alten Testaments*, 8.
26. Karl Marti, introduction to *Geschichte der Israelitischen Religion*, by August Kayser, 3rd ed. (Strassburg: Bull, 1897), 1.

Neutestamentlichen Theologie (Göttingen: Vandenhoeck & Ruprecht, 1897)[27] was a decisive milestone in the history-of-religions approach to its subject:

> I must state from the outset that my comments presuppose the strictly historical character of New Testament theology.[28]

It was clear for Wrede that the New Testament could only be appropriately elucidated through the historical approach. As long as one accorded the theology of the New Testament "a direct link with dogmatics . . . [then] some things, such as, for example, serious contradictions within the New Testament, are not allowed to emerge."[29] Martin Dibelius characterized Wrede's program in the following way:

> In place of the "succession of doctrinal concepts," the presentation of the living development of early Christian *religion* appeared, and as a result one was not able to maintain the boundaries of the canon.[30]

HERMANN GUNKEL Hermann Gunkel formulated the radical change that took place around the turn of the century in Old and New Testament studies in a particularly clear manner:

> Without a doubt, the emergence of biblical theology as a specific discipline separated from systematics was a great advancement that can never be reversed. Now, however, after the almost 200 years that biblical theology has dominated, many voices in this generation are calling for the renewal of this discipline. It has become increasingly acknowledged that errors are preserved in both the word "theology" and in "biblical." First "theology": Ever since Schleiermacher one has distinguished with growing clarity between "religion" itself and the

27. Pages 7–80 are reprinted in *Probleme der Theologie des Neuen Testaments*, ed. G. Strecker, Wege der Forschung 367 (Darmstadt: Wissenschaftliche Buchgesellschaft, 1975), 81–154; trans. as "The Task and Methods of 'New Testament Theology,'" in *The Nature of New Testament Theology: The Contribution of William Wrede and Adolf Schlatter*, ed. and trans. Robert Morgan, SBT Second Series 25 (London: SCM, 1973), 68–116.

28. Wrede, "Task and Methods," 69.

29. Wrede, "Task and Methods," 69.

30. M. Dibelius, "Biblische Theologie und biblische Religionsgeschichte: II des NT," *RGG*, 2nd ed., 1:1091.

academic, i.e., the cognitive treatment, namely "theology." And especially for the O.T. it is clear that the living religion of the heart was quite prominent, while reflection on religion plays a comparatively minor role. Neither the nature of the Israelite people nor the period tended toward reflection. If one intends to treat the content of the O.T. appropriately, then the emphasis should be placed on *religion* . . . At the same time, the fence implied in the word *'biblical'* continues to fall. The maturing and blossoming religion from the soil of the Israelite nation is an extraordinarily diverse picture, in which all its forms and orientations, higher and baser, should be recognized . . .[31]

If one looks deeper and attempts to recognize the ultimate basis for the shortcomings of biblical theology, one notices that it is dominated by the early church doctrine of inspiration. As a result, it views the entire content of the Bible on the same plane and is able to organize systematically with uniform character the unity of thinking that it believes the Bible to possess. If this organization is now rejected, then this ultimately means that the spirit of historical scholarship has moved into this area of study. The appearance that our generation has experienced in the "history of Israelite religion" replacement of biblical theology is therefore explained by the spirit of historical scholarship beginning to replace the doctrine of inspiration.[32]

Gunkel postulates the necessity of replacing the consideration of biblical theology of the Old Testament with that of the history of Israelite religion on the basis of the disintegration of the foundational framework of theology. Historical thought rather than the doctrine of inspiration shaped theology during his time. While this final statement is correct, the immediately following period in the history of scholarship brought other developments than those that Gunkel expected with regard to biblical theology. They will be considered in a later section. However, because of its contemporary appearance, the next section will

31. H. Gunkel, "Biblische Theologie und biblische Religionsgeschichte: I des AT," *RGG*, 2nd ed., 1:1089-90.

32. Gunkel, "Biblische Theologie," 1089-90. Especially noteworthy in this context is Gunkel's statement in the foreword to his commentary on Genesis: "Whoever calls himself a theologian must study religion." *Genesis: Übersetzt und erklärt*, HKAT I/1 (Göttingen: Vandenhoeck & Ruprecht, 1901) n.p.; trans. as *Genesis: Translated and Interpreted by Hermann Gunkel*, trans. M. E. Biddle (Macon, Ga.: Mercer University Press, 1997).

treat the reception of the concept of "theology" in nineteenth-century Jewish scholarship.

§6 The Reception of the Concept of Theology in Judaism

Michael Fishbane, *Jewish Hermeneutical Theology* (Leiden: Brill, 2015) ♦ Shimon Gesundheit, "Gibt es eine jüdische Theologie der Hebräischen Bibel?," in *Theologie und Exegese des Alten Testaments / der Hebräischen Bibel: Zwischenbilanz und Zukunftsperspektiven,* ed. Bernd Janowski, SBS 200 (Stuttgart: Katholishes Bibelwerk, 2005), 73–86 ♦ Isaac Kalimi, ed., *Jewish Bible Theology: Perspectives and Case Studies* (Winona Lake, IN: Eisenbrauns, 2012) ♦ Jon Levenson, "Why Jews Are Not Interested in Biblical Theology," in *Judaic Perspectives on Ancient Israel,* ed. J. Neusner et al. (Philadelphia: Fortress, 1987), 281–307 ♦ Dalit Rom-Shiloni, "Hebrew Bible Theology: A Jewish Descriptive Approach," *JR* 96 (2016): 165–84 ♦ Benjamin Sommer, "Dialogical Biblical Theology: A Jewish Approach to Reading Scripture Theologically," in *Biblical Theology: Introduction and Conversation,* ed. Leo G. Perdue et al. (Nashville: Abingdon, 2009), 1–53 ♦ Benjamin Sommer, *Jewish Concepts of Scripture: A Comparative Introduction* (New York: New York University Press, 2012) ♦ Marvin A. Sweeney, *Tanak: A Theological and Critical Introduction to the Jewish Bible* (Minneapolis: Fortress, 2012)

The concept of "theology" has a comparatively short and controversial history in Judaism, essentially limited to the modern period. Though Josephus and Philo were acquainted with and used the term "theology" and its derivatives, they remained non-specified applications, essentially within the horizon of the profane Greek fields of meaning.

ACADEMIC STUDY OF JUDAISM The nineteenth-century "Jewish studies" movement, grounded and advanced by Leopold Zunz and others, was the first to take up the concept of theology in a programmatic fashion. In this context, the *Wissenschaftliche Zeitschrift für jüdische Theologie* was published beginning in 1835 by Abraham Geiger, and the Jewish Theological Seminary in Breslau was founded in 1854, which beginning in 1886 had a partner (and then from 1939 on a replacement) institution—the Jewish Theological Seminary of America in New York.

The aim to establish the written records, traditions, and history of Judaism as an object of academic investigation analogous to Christianity is clearly visible in the background of these efforts. These initiatives were quite formative. The concept of theology was also used in external descriptions of Jewish traditions in the latter nineteenth and twentieth centuries, though the relationship and differentiation between the concept of theology and the concept of religion often remained murky, similar to its use in Christianity. Ferdinand Wilhelm Weber, a Christian pastor, published a book about the Talmud entitled *Jüdische Theologie auf Grund des Talmud und verwandter Schriften* (Leipzig: Dörffling & Franke, 1897). Solomon Schechter treated *Major Concepts of the Talmud* (the subtitle) in his *Aspects of Rabbinic Theology* (New London: Black, 1909); Kaufmann Kohler published a *Jewish Theology Systematically and Historically Considered* (New York: Macmillan, 1918). A volume by Arthur Marmorstein appeared with the title *Studies in Jewish Theology* (Oxford: Oxford University Press, 1950), treating such subjects as "The Background of the Haggadah," "The Unity of God in Rabbinic Literature," and "The Holy Spirit in the Rabbinic Legend," among others. Samuel S. Cohon's *Jewish Theology: A Historical and Systematic Interpretation of Judaism and Its Foundations* (Assen: Van Gorcum, 1971) presents an understanding of theology that corresponds exactly in formal terms to that of Christianity, namely in connection with the organization of religion:

> Theology conceptualizes religious experience. It translates the life and faith of a religious community into ideas that are intelligible and communicable and give coherent answers to the spiritual questions which press upon the mind. The function of Jewish theology is to render the nature and goals of Judaism understandable and to show Judaism's relevance for our times. . . . Religion, supplying the data of theological investigation, naturally precedes theology, even as flowers precede botany, or as health precedes hygiene or medicine.[33]

Theology is understood here completely in keeping with its understanding in the Christian tradition—as the form of reflection on faith. Nonetheless, in the larger picture the use of the concept of theology in Judaism remained marginal. This can be explained by the nature of the content in postbiblical Jewish tradition. In the article "Theology," the *Encyclopedia Judaica* asserts:

> The Bible contains no systematic treatment of theological problems. . . . All this is largely due to the severely concrete, 'organic' nature of

33. Cohon, *Jewish Theology*, xv, 1.

ancient Hebraic thought which hardly bears any resemblances to the philosophical thinking that is the heritage of the Greeks and to which the Western world owes its theology. To a greater or lesser extent the same is true of rabbinic thought.[34]

PHILOSOPHY OF RELIGION INSTEAD OF THEOLOGY There is also a further aspect to consider. Like the authoritative Islamic tradition of the time, Medieval Jewish reflections on the Bible and the rabbinic tradition were expressed in religious-philosophical rather than in theological terms for determining the outline of the whole. Especially well-known examples of this approach are the works of Saadia Gaon and Moses Maimonides. Saadia Gaon's *'Emunot we-De'ot* [Beliefs and Opinions] is considered one of the first philosophically grounded and systematically formulated presentations of Jewish doctrine. The book first appeared in 933 CE in Arabic, entitled *Kitab al-Amanat wal-l'tikadat,* and it was first translated into Hebrew in the twelfth century. Also arising during this period was Maimonides's principal work, *Dalālat alḥā'irīn,* which became known by its Hebrew title as *Moreh Nevukim* [Teacher/Guide of the Perplexed]. It attempts to comprehend philosophically such topoi as God, creation, mysticism, ethics, and eschatology.

In keeping with these approaches, the concepts of both theology and philosophy were used in attempts to synthesize the Hebrew Bible. One noteworthy example is David Neumark's *The Philosophy of the Bible* (Cincinnati: Ark, 1918), which neither elucidates the meaning of the title nor explains how it is distinct from theology. He instead attempts to offer a "presentation of the history of thought in biblical Judaism."[35]

This type of inquiry appears to prosper in more recent times, though it has yet to produce a clear research profile.[36] A similar approach appears recently in Yoram Hazony, *The Philosophy of Hebrew Scripture: An Introduction*, which has, however, encountered intense criticism.

---

34. Louis Jacobs, "Theology," *EncJud,* 1st ed., 15:1104 (cf. the 2nd edition as well, *EncJud* 19:694–95).

35. Neumark, *Philosophy of the Bible*, iii.

36. Cf. Yoram Hazony, *The Philosophy of Hebrew Scripture: An Introduction* (Cambridge: Cambridge University Press, 2012); Seizo Sekine, *Philosophical Interpretations of the Old Testament,* BZAW 458 (Berlin: de Gruyter, 2014); Jaco Gericke, *The Hebrew Bible and Philosophy of Religion,* RBS 70 (Atlanta: SBL Press, 2012); Jaco Gericke, *What Is a God? Philosophical Perspectives on Divine Essence in the Hebrew Bible* (London: T&T Clark, 2017).

§7 The Devaluation of the Concept of Religion in Neo-orthodox Theology

Ulrich Körtner, *Theologie des Wortes Gottes: Positionen—Probleme—Perspektiven* (Göttingen: Vandenhoeck & Ruprecht, 2001) ◆ Jürgen Moltmann and James M. Robinson, eds., *The Beginnings of Dialectic Theology*, trans. Keith R. Crim and Louis De Grazia (Richmond, VA: John Knox, 1968)

Shortly after the virtual disappearance of theology as an independent concern from Christian Old Testament studies at the end of the nineteenth century, a countermovement set in, influenced by the experience of the First World War. Rudolf Kittel, Wilhelm Staerk, Carl Steuernagel, and Otto Eissfeldt called, each in his own way, for an independent theology of the Hebrew Bible distinct from the history-of-religions perspective.

NEO-ORTHODOX THEOLOGY AND THEOLOGY OF THE OLD TESTAMENT The renaissance of Old Testament theology in the 1930s, as will be shown below, cannot be understood without casting a glance at the marginally earlier emergence of neo-orthodox theology. This movement resisted the history-of-religions and social-scientific monopolization of the Bible, favoring the rise of theological investigations of the Bible.

1. Neo-orthodox Theology

KARL BARTH The resurgence of the theology of the Old Testament in the 1930s hinges on the fate of the concept of religion in neo-orthodox theology, which receives its severest formulation in Karl Barth's thesis that "religion is *unbelief*. It is a concern, indeed, we must say that it is the one great concern, of godless man."[37]

Religion stands in opposition to revelation for Barth. Religion as such is the work of humans and should therefore be minimized: "Religion is never true in itself and as such."[38] Attempting to place Christianity in connection with the concept of religion should only occur with great caution. "If the statement is to have any content," says Barth, "we can dare to state that the Christian religion is the true one only as we listen to divine revelation."[39]

---

37. Barth, *Church Dogmatics*, I/2 (Edinburgh: T&T Clark, 1956), 299–300.
38. Barth, *Church Dogmatics*, 325.
39. Barth, *Church Dogmatics*, 326.

With this harsh declaration against the notion of religion, Barth took a stand against the mainstream position of the nineteenth century. Accompanying the gradual success of neo-orthodox theology, whose influence shaped German-speaking Protestant theology after 1945, skepticism towards "religion" increased. On the flip side, the concept of theology, generally used in a pejorative manner in nineteenth-century biblical studies, bloomed again.

However, this development also led to a lack of clarity in the conceptual distinction between religion and theology, especially in Hebrew Bible studies. This is documented most clearly in Gerhard von Rad's *Old Testament Theology*, which discusses religious, literary, and theological aspects of the Hebrew Bible all under this one title. While not a product of the 1920s and 1930s, it still remains broadly within the tradition of neo-orthodox theology. It is difficult to explain the brittle use of the concept of religion in this work otherwise.

The stigmatization of the concept of religion and the emphasis on divine revelation in Jesus Christ within the framework of neo-orthodox theology also led to the programmatic conclusion by Emil Brunner and Rafael Gyllenberg that a theology of the Hebrew Bible is impossible.[40] Because the Hebrew Bible is neither familiar with nor documents this revelation, there can be no independent theology of the Hebrew Bible. While these opinions came from outside Hebrew Bible studies, such views were also heard from within.

In retrospect, there have been numerous voices that have critiqued, at times quite harshly, the influence exerted by neo-orthodox theology on biblical studies:

> [Neo-orthodox theology] did indeed address itself to the task of defining more closely the unique nature of Christianity and its God, a problem that had not been solved by religio-historical theology; at the same time, though, it did OT studies great harm through its renunciation of any religio-historical perspective, its disregard for an appropriate understanding of the uniqueness of Israelite religion, and its revival of allegorical and typological interpretation of the OT.[41]

---

40. Emil Brunner, *Offenbarung und Vernunft: Die Lehre von der christlichen Glaubenserkenntnis* (Zurich: Zwingli-Verlag, 1941), 287: "There is no 'theology of the Old Testament'"; and before him Rafael Gyllenberg, "Die Unmöglichkeit einer Theologie des Alten Testaments," in *In piam memoriam Alexander von Bulmerincq*, ed. Rudolf Abramowski, Abhandlungen der Herder-Gesellschaft und des Herder-Instituts zu Riga 6 (Riga: Plates, 1938), 64–68.

41. George Fohrer, *History of Israelite Religion*, trans. David E. Green (Nashville: Abingdon, 1972), 21–22.

It is likely that a particular personal resentment lay behind this declaration, and it is difficult to evaluate the history of the humanities and of academic developments in terms that are intersubjective and meaningful when using the categories of "damaging" and "useful." However, this estimation points to an important deficit that can be observed in Hebrew Bible studies during the middle of the twentieth century.

BIBLICAL THEOLOGY MOVEMENT Neo-orthodox theology, which originated in German-speaking scholarship, quickly developed into a globally significant movement, though with different accents and different spokespersons in various geographic regions. Neo-orthodox theology had considerable resonance in Great Britain and the United States in particular, leading both during and after the Second World War to the biblical theology movement. This movement attempted both to highlight the importance of the Bible for theology and to increase the biblical imprint of theology. In terms of the interpretation of the biblical text, Krister Stendahl's well-known article on "Biblical Theology" in the *Interpreter's Dictionary of the Bible* insisted that biblical exegesis consider not only "what [the Bible] meant," but also "what it means."[42]

Theological approaches to the Bible should, therefore, push beyond historical concerns in that they should consider the current significance of biblical texts. John J. Collins reformulates and adapts this position in the following manner:

> Biblical theology should not, however, be reduced to the "historical fact that such and such was thought and believed" but should clarify the meaning and truth-claims of what was thought and believed from a modern critical perspective.[43]

John W. Rogerson, who belongs to the broader circles of this tradition, authored a short theology of the Old Testament that is dedicated almost exclusively to the latter question ("what it means"):

> *A Theology of the Old Testament* is a work which, to paraphrase Bultmann, will use the resources of historical criticism in the service of

---

42. Krister Stendahl, "Biblical Theology, Contemporary," *IDB* 1:419.
43. John J. Collins, *Encounters with Biblical Theology* (Minneapolis: Fortress, 2005), 18.

the interpretation of Old Testament texts, on the assumption that they have something to say to the present.[44]

The "Biblical Theology Movement" argued for an independent discipline of biblical theology that investigates the present relevance and normativity of the historical witness of the Bible. Behind this conviction was the theological perspective that biblical studies is not only responsible for the historical description of the biblical texts, but also for the application of the biblical texts to the present context.

2. New "Theologies of the Old Testament"

OTTO EISSFELDT After the complete merger of theology of the Hebrew Bible and the history of Israelite religion and subsequent movement of neo-orthodox theology in the early twentieth century, the cry for an independent theological investigation of the Hebrew Bible grew louder. Otto Eissfeldt called most forcefully for the separation of religious-historical and theological approaches to the Hebrew Bible:

> The historical approach on the one hand and the theological on the other belong on two different planes. They correspond to two differently constituted functions of our spirit, to knowing and to believing."[45]

Eissfeldt considered the intermixing of the two perspectives "harmful,"[46] that is, "dangerous."[47] This opinion is conspicuous in that it comes from the primarily historically-oriented Eissfeldt, yet he clearly understood the theological dimension of the Hebrew Bible to be qualitatively separate from that of the historical. "Historical understanding of the Old Testament," Eissfeldt warns, "may never go beyond the relative and the imma-

---

44. John William Rogerson, *A Theology of the Old Testament: Cultural Memory, Communication, and Being Human* (London: SPCK, 2009), 12.

45. Otto Eissfeldt, "The History of Israelite-Jewish Religion and Old Testament Theology," in *Old Testament Theology: Flowering and Future*, ed. and trans. B. C. Ollenburger, Sources for Biblical and Theological Study 1 (Winona Lake, IN: Eisenbrauns, 2004), 16; trans. of "Israelitisch–jüdische Religionsgeschichte und alttestamentliche Theologie," *ZAW* 44 (1926): 1–12.

46. Eissfeldt, "History of Israelite-Jewish Religion," 109.

47. Eissfeldt, "History of Israelite-Jewish Religion," 111.

nent."[48] However, theology calls for just this further perspective, and as a result it must go beyond the historical. With a similar impulse, Eduard König lamented at the beginning of his *Theologie des Alten Testaments,* published in 1921:

> Works concerning "biblical theology of the Old Testament" that have appeared recently offer merely a history of Israelite religion. They do not contain a systematic presentation of the elements and ideas that have been proven vital for the salvation history of the Old Testament.[49]

WALTHER EICHRODT AND LUDWIG KÖHLER But the situation began to change in the following decades. In the 1930s two strongly systematic-oriented theologies of the Old Testament appeared, those of Walther Eichrodt and Ludwig Köhler.[50] Rather than concentrating on historical reconstruction, these works instead offer a synthesis of the theologically relevant ideas of the Hebrew Bible. Jörg Jeremias calls the departures of the 1930s the actual "hour of birth of the 'theology of the OT' as an independent discipline . . . because for the first time since J. Ph. Gabler, exegetes . . . interacted confidently and free of fear with regard to the foreignness [of the text] when interacting with the themes of systematic theology."[51] Both Eichrodt's and Köhler's works show an unmistakable proximity to the concerns of systematic theology. Their theologies could almost be described as systematic theologies of the Hebrew Bible, organized with similar structures to Christian systematic theologies. Yet their subject was not the Bible *and* the early church—or, as the case may be, the doctrinal development stemming from the Reformation—but was limited to the Hebrew Bible. One could term these projects, given their subject as the Old Testament rather than the Bible as a whole, something like "provisional" systematic theologies.

48. Eissfeldt, "History of Israelite-Jewish Religion," 109.

49. Eduard König, *Theologie des Alten Testaments* (Stuttgart: Belser, 1921), 3.

50. Walter Eichrodt, *Gott und Welt—Gott und Mensch*, parts 2–3 of *Theologie des Alten Testaments*, 5th ed. (Stuttgart: Klotz; Göttingen: Vandenhoeck & Ruprecht, 1964); trans. as *Theology of the Old Testament*, vol. 2, trans. J. A. Backer, OTL (London: SCM, 1967); Ludwig Köhler, *Theologie des Alten Testaments*, 4th ed., NTG (Tübingen: Mohr, 1966); first edition [1953] trans. as *Old Testament Theology*, trans. A. S. Todd (Philadelphia: Fortress; London: Lutterworth, 1957).

51. Jörg Jeremias, "Neuere Entwürfe zu einer 'Theologie des Alten Testaments,'" in *Theologie und Exegese des Alten Testaments / der Hebräischen Bibel: Zwischenbilanz und Zukunftsperspektiven*, ed. Bernd Janowski, SBS 200 (Stuttgart: Katholisches Bibelwerk, 2005), 129.

The approaches of Eichrodt's and Köhler's projects were occasionally marked by striking differences. While Köhler chose a more systematic outline that distinguished between theology, anthropology, and soteriology, Eichrodt allowed the theme of the covenant, a principle found in the Old Testament itself, to guide his organization. Nonetheless, a look at the subtitles of Eichrodt's three volumes alone shows that his structure was quite similar to Köhler's: "God and World," "God and the Nation," "God and Human."[52] On the flip side, Köhler actually allowed the formulation of his theology to be guided by the terminology and intellectual world of the Hebrew Bible, which was less the case with Eichrodt. It is clear, however, that both Köhler's and Eichrodt's theologies are descriptive rather than normative in orientation.[53]

It is striking, however, that Köhler, an author of one of the central works of the period, was actually a representative of liberal theology. While Eichrodt, following in the steps of his Erlangen teacher Otto Procksch, displayed considerable interest in theology both formed and bound by the confession of the church.

THEODOR VRIEZEN Belonging to the wider circle of this approach was *An Outline of Old Testament Theology* by Theodor Christiaan Vriezen.[54] "Revelation" appeared early in the progression of subheadings,[55] while "Theology" did not appear until considerably later.[56]

Old Testament theology is a form of scholarship differing from the history of Israel's religion in its object as well as in its method. In its object, *because its object is not the religion of Israel but the Old Testament*; in its method *because it is a study of the message of the Old Testament both in itself and in its relation to the New Testament*.[57]

52. The structure follows that of *Die Theologie des Alten Testaments* (Gütersloh: Gütersloher Verlagshaus, 1950) by Eichrodt's teacher, Otto Procksch, though Procksch's study appeared after Eichrodt's (1936–1939). Eichrodt likely became familiar with the content of Procksch's theology through his lectures.

53. Eichrodt professes in the introduction to the 5th edition of his *Theologie* to his "rejection of all temptations that would allow [Old Testament theology] to extend its reach to the realm of normative studies" (vi).

54. Theodor Christiaan Vriezen, *An Outline of Old Testament Theology*, trans. S. Neuijen (Oxford: Blackwell, 1958); first published as *Hoofdlijnen der Theologie van het Oude Testament* (Wageningen: H. Veenman & Zonen, 1949).

55. Vriezen, *An Outline of Old Testament Theology*, 12.

56. Vriezen, *An Outline of Old Testament Theology*, 118.

57. Vriezen, *An Outline of Old Testament Theology*, 121 (emphasis original).

Nonetheless, the approach taken by Eichrodt, Köhler, and Vriezen did not endure for the long term, despite the wide dissemination of Eichrodt's *Theologie*. Even though they attempted to link the systematizations of their theology closely to the Bible, this proved to be a Procrustean bed. The witness of the Hebrew Bible proved too diverse to be sufficiently categorized.

§8 Developments since the Mid-Twentieth Century

Walter Brueggemann, *Theology of the Old Testament: Testimony, Dispute, Advocacy* (Minneapolis: Fortress, 1997) ♦ Hans-Jürgen Hermisson, *Alttestamentliche Theologie und Religionsgeschichte Israels*, Forum Theologische Literaturzeitung 3 (Leipzig: Evangelische Verlagsanstalt, 2000) ♦ Jesper Høgenhaven, *Problems and Prospects of Old Testament Theology*, BibSem 6 (Sheffield: JSOT Press, 1987) ♦ Jörg Jeremias, *Studien zur Theologie des Alten Testaments*, ed. Friedhelm Hartenstein and Jutta Krispenz, FAT 99 (Tübingen: Mohr Siebeck, 2015) ♦ Othmar Keel, "Religionsgeschichte Israels oder Theologie des Alten Testaments?" in *Wieviel Systematik erlaubt die Schrift? Auf der Suche nach einer gesamtbiblischen Theologie*, ed. Frank-Lothar Hossfeld, QD 185 (Freiburg im Breisgau: Herder, 2001), 88–109 ♦ Othmar Keel and Christoph Uehlinger, *Gods, Goddesses, and Images of God in Ancient Israel*, trans. Thomas H. Trapp (Edinburgh: T&T Clark, 1998); trans. of *Göttinnen, Götter und Gottessymbole: Neue Erkenntnisse zur Religionsgeschichte Kanaans und Israels aufgrund bislang unerschlossener ikonographischer Quellen*, QD 134 (Freiburg im Breisgau: Herder, 1992) ♦ John Kessler, *Old Testament Theology: Divine Call and Human Response* (Waco, TX: Baylor University Press, 2013) ♦ Manfred Oeming and Andreas Schüle, eds., *Theologie in Israel und in den Nachbarkulturen: Beiträge des Symposiums "Das Alte Testament und die Kultur der Moderne" anlässlich des 100. Geburtstags Gerhard von Rads (1901–1971), Heidelberg, 18.–21. Oktober 2001*, Altes Testament und Moderne 9 (Münster: LIT, 2004) ♦ Gerhard von Rad, *Old Testament Theology*, trans. D. M. G. Stalker (Edinburgh: Oliver & Boyd, 1962/1965); trans. of *Theologie des Alten Testaments*, 2 vols. (Munich: Kaiser, 1957/1960) ♦ Henning Graf Reventlow, *Problems of Biblical Theology in the Twentieth Century*, trans. John Bowden (Philadelphia: Fortress, 1986); trans. of *Hauptprobleme der alttestamentlichen Theologie im 20. Jahrhundert*, EdF 173 (Darmstadt: Wissenschaftliche Buchgesellschaft, 1982) ♦ John Sandys-Wunsch, *What Have They Done to the Bible? A History of Modern Biblical Interpretation* (Collegeville, MN: Liturgical Press, 2005) ♦ Ben C. Ollenburger, *Old Testament Theology: Flowering and Future*, SBTS 1 (Winona Lake, IN:

Eisenbrauns, 2004) ◆ Josef Scharbert, "Die biblische Theologie auf der Suche nach ihrem Wesen und ihrer Methode," *MTZ* 40 (1989): 7–26 ◆ Werner H. Schmidt, "'Theologie des Alten Testaments' vor und nach Gerhard von Rad," *VF* 17 (1972): 1–25

1. *Gerhard von Rad's* Old Testament Theology

Gerhard von Rad wrote his epochal *Theologie des Alten Testaments* (1957/1960) in the context of postwar German-speaking scholarship, and he viewed the retelling of the Hebrew Bible as the only legitimate option.[58] This is a surprising choice when considered in light of, first, the works of his predecessors in the discipline, Eichrodt and Köhler, and second, the layout of the standard work of the neighboring discipline, Rudolf Bultmann's *Theology of the New Testament*, which formulates theology in terms of anthropology.

THEOLOGY OF THE OLD TESTAMENT AS RETELLING However, von Rad clearly did not allow the genre specifications either for a theology from his own discipline or for the neighboring one to influence him. Decisive instead were insights about the unique content of the Hebrew Bible that seemed to have been established at that time as especially characteristic of the Hebrew Bible. According to the information von Rad himself provides, the most important changes to be found in Hebrew Bible studies since Köhler and Eichrodt are those that came in the wake of Gunkel's form-critical scholarship. Here one "encounters quite ancient creedal formulas"—von Rad points to the results of his study on "The Form-Critical Problem of the Hexateuch" from 1938[59]—which prove that the theme of story belongs to the historical nucleus of the Hebrew Bible. On the other hand—and here von Rad paid deference to his colleague Martin Noth—he asserts:

> The history of tradition has taught us in a new way to see in the three gigantic works of the Hexateuch, the Deuteronomistic history, and the Chronicler's history, the most varied forms of the presentation of

58. Von Rad, *Old Testament Theology*, 1:121.

59. Gerhard von Rad, "The Form-Critical Problem of the Hexateuch," in *The Problem of the Hexateuch and Other Essays*, trans. E. W. Trueman Dicken (New York: McGraw-Hill, 1966), 1–78.

God's history with Israel in its different strata. It has also shown how Israel was at all times occupied with the task of understanding her history from the point of view of certain interventions by God, and how what God had rooted in the history presented itself in different ways in every age.[60]

Both changes led to an emphasis on the theme of story in the theology of the Hebrew Bible and to the structural decision to formulate such a theology in the mode of retelling. Von Rad thereby separates theology considerably from a program of the history of religion of ancient Israel:

The theological task proper to the Old Testament is not simply identical with this general religious one, and it is also much more restricted. The subject-matter which concerns the theologian is, of course, not the spiritual and religious world of Israel and the conditions of her soul in general, nor is it her world of faith, all of which can only be reconstructed by means of conclusions drawn from the documents: instead, [the theological task] is simply Israel's own explicit assertions about Yahweh. . . . [These] Old Testament writings confine themselves to representing Yahweh's relationship to Israel and the world in one aspect only, namely as a continuing divine activity in history. This implies that in principle Israel's faith is grounded in a theology of history.[61]

CRITICISM OF VON RAD It cannot be said that von Rad really stuck to his own narrow understanding of "theology of the Old Testament" in his composition. In reality he treated the texts of the Hebrew Bible in such a way that recognized various forms of theology in them. Von Rad speaks of the "theological world" of Jeremiah,[62] and the prophets "tread [a] new theological path."[63] According to his program, the "theology" that was the object of investigation was not really the "theological world" of Jeremiah, but rather "what Israel directly proclaimed about Yahweh." Von Rad constructed a differentiation that, as Friedrich Baumgärtel notes, correctly in my opinion, does not really exist:

60. Von Rad, *Old Testament Theology*, 1:v–vi.
61. Von Rad, *Old Testament Theology*, 1:105–6; cf. 1:111.
62. Von Rad, *Old Testament Theology*, 2:192.
63. Von Rad, *Old Testament Theology*, 2:187.

The problem that is treated in [the *Theology*] is according to v. R. the following: On one hand is the depiction formulated by historical-critical studies of the course of Israel's history and its intellectual-religious world and its world of belief—a task that can also be carried out by non-theologians. This aspect remains stuck in the history of religion. Against this rationally constructed historical world is the depiction of Israel's faith that has witnessed to the "continual divine action in history" (1:112 [ET: 1:106]), so that Israel's faith "is fundamentally based on a theology of history" (ibid.). In this depiction one does not encounter historical facts established by historical-critical scholarship, it instead concerns facts "which [are] drawn up from the faith of Israel" (ibid. [ET: 1:107]). In this divergence v. R. sees the current heavy burden of biblical studies: it deals with "completely different intellectual activities." One is [a] rational-historical method, the other is "confessional, personally involved in the events," Israel speaks only "with the passion of glory and regret about its history." Historical scholarship "cannot explain the phenomenon of this faith (1:113–14 [ET: 1:107–8]).[64]

Baumgärtel views this "divergence" between the historically reconstructable world of Israel's faith and Israel's confession of faith in God's activity in history as a pseudo problem.

To this can be said: there is nothing that diverges here, at least not for current critical biblical studies. The fact that the depiction constructed by Israel's confessional faith of history often does not correspond to the actual historical sequences is a result of critical scholarship. This scholarship labors not only to ascertain the actual historical progression, but certainly also with regard to the portrayal of the perspective that Israel itself had of its history (salvation-history). . . . This perspective is certainly also a part of history . . . and it should be investigated and depicted with the tools of historical criticism.[65]

64. Friedrich Baumgärtel, "Gerhard von Rad's 'Theologie des Alten Testaments,'" *TLZ* 86 (1961): 804.

65. Baumgärtel, "Gerhard von Rad's 'Theologie,'" 804. Cf. also p. 805: "Stated succinctly: the 'confessional portrayal of history' that comes from faith is a part of the religious history of Israel and as such can be investigated with the current historical-critical research methodology."

As a result of this quite hazy distinction between the world of faith and the confession of faith, von Rad's program headed de facto straight towards an identification of literary history (including the oral pre-history of the texts of the Hebrew Bible) with theology. Carl A. Keller describes the problem incisively: "Von Rad's book is basically not a theology, but rather an introduction."[66]

It is interesting to note that this judgment can actually be based on a declaration by von Rad himself in the preface to the first volume of his *Old Testament Theology* from 1957:

> The characteristic thing in today's situation, in my opinion, is the surprising convergence—indeed the mutual intersection—which has come about during the last twenty or thirty years between introductory studies and Biblical theology.[67]

One can in fact say that Gerhard von Rad's *Old Testament Theology* is many things, but it is not true to its genre. With regard to the concept of theology, he relates it closely and in programmatic fashion to Israel's direct confessions of the activity of God in history. He then extends it, without any methodological explanation, to the historically actualized forms of this confession. As a result, the doors stand open to use the concept of theology in a historically descriptive manner in order to describe the particular content of religious texts. Von Rad certainly saw this pluralization of theologies, but he only mentions it outside his *Old Testament Theology*:

> This reality of the restless actualization of historical facts of salvation with the result that each generation saw itself set to march toward a new fulfillment is in the foreground of the Old Testament in such a way that a "theology of the Old Testament" must accommodate it. This of course takes place first in the sense of the deconstruction of various earlier notions of the unity of the Old Testament to the extent that the Old Testament contains not only one, but a number of theologies that diverge greatly both in their structure and in the nature of their argumentation.[68]

---

66. C. A. Keller, "Review of G. von Rad, Theologie des Alten Testaments I," *TZ* 14 (1958): 308.

67. Von Rad, *Old Testament Theology*, 1:v.

68. Gerhard von Rad, "Offene Fragen im Umkreis einer Theologie des Alten Testa-

Von Rad's ambiguous distinction between history of faith—thirty years before or after him one would have spoken of the history of religion—and confession of faith, as well as the pluralization of theology, had wide-reaching consequences. His approach raised questions with regard to the legitimacy of the discipline of "theology of the Old Testament"— analogous to the developments at the close of the nineteenth century—as an independent investigation within Hebrew Bible studies.

2. Contemporary Discussions and Ambiguities

THEOLOGY OF THE HEBREW BIBLE IN THE SECOND HALF OF THE TWENTIETH CENTURY About a decade passed after the appearance of von Rad's theology before new conceptions appeared, for example from Georg Fohrer, Walther Zimmerli, Claus Westermann, Horst Dietrich Preuß, Otto Kaiser, and Rolf Rendtorff.[69] They exhibit a certain impulse to return to the recognition of more systematization or at least focusing—even if this is only of a partial nature. At the same time, however, they clearly attest to the desire to maintain the level of complexity found in von Rad's theology with regard to the plurivocality of the Hebrew Bible. Werner H. Schmidt opts for a rather peculiar approach in his *Alttestamentlicher Glaube in seiner Geschichte*, which attempts a mixed form between history of religion and theology.[70] From the eighth (1996) to eleventh editions (2011), it appears with the shorter title, *Alttestamentlicher Glaube*, which implicitly indicates a weighting in the direction of theology.

THEOLOGY OF THE HEBREW BIBLE OR THE HISTORY OF ISRAELITE RELIGION The investigation of the nature of the relationship between the

ments," in *Gesammelte Studien zum Alten Testament II*, TB 48 (Munich: Kaiser, 1973), 293–94. Cf. the reflections on this citation in Hermann Spieckermann, "Theologie II/1.1. Altes Testament," *TRE* 33: 268; J. C. Gertz, *Grundinformation Altes Testament: Eine Einführung in Literatur, Religion und Geschichte des Alten Testaments*, 3rd ed., Uni-Taschenbücher 2745 (Göttingen: Vandenhoeck & Ruprecht, 2009), 598 n. 17; trans. as *T&T Clark Handbook of the Old Testament: An Introduction to the Literature, Religion and History of the Old Testament* (London: T&T Clark, 2012), 781 n. 3.

69. Jörg Jeremias, "Neuere Entwürfe zu einer 'Theologie des Alten Testaments,'" in *Studien zur Theologie des Alten Testaments*, ed. Friedhelm Hartenstein and Jutta Krispenz, FAT 99 (Tübingen: Mohr Siebeck, 2005), 15–46.

70. Werner H. Schmidt, *Alttestamentlicher Glaube in seiner Geschichte,* 7th ed. (Neukirchen-Vluyn: Neukirchener Verlag, 1990; originally published 1975).

theology of the Hebrew Bible and Israelite history of religion was widely discussed in the early 1990s. Only in the wake of von Rad's *Old Testament Theology,* as Rainer Albertz argues in his *History of Israelite Religion in the Old Testament Period* from 1992, could "the history of religion" be a "more comprehensive Old Testament discipline" than "theology."[71] He names the following advantages, among others: a history of religion "corresponds better to the historical structure of large parts of the Old Testament," "takes seriously the insight that religious statements cannot be separated from the historical background from which they derive," does not fall under the compulsion "to bring down its varying and sometimes contradictory religious statements to the level of intellectual abstraction to one theoretical abstract level," and need not present "any claims . . . to absoluteness."[72]

Nonetheless, in many ways Albertz's own outline presents a mix of different approaches to the Hebrew Bible. While Albertz *also* offers a history of religion, he refers first and foremost to the Hebrew Bible, which provides both the themes and also the structure for his approach. This remains true even though he highlights the differentiations of private and official, local and family religion in his classification. How differently a history of Israelite religion appears when not based primarily on the biblical witnesses and themes is demonstrated in the contemporary volume by Othmar Keel and Christoph Uehlinger. For this reason Albertz's book is fundamentally just as much a literary history as it is a history of the theology of the Hebrew Bible.

Discussion since Albertz has shown that the replacement of theology by the history of Israelite religion is an inadequate model, but this in itself does not resolve the search for the nature of the concept of theology in Hebrew Bible studies.

THE STATE OF THE HUMANITIES The current questions and ambiguities surrounding theology in the Hebrew Bible and theology of the Old Testament cannot be understood without casting a glance at the state of the humanities in the German-speaking university environment as a whole. Theology was a leading branch of study for the humanities into the twen-

71. Rainer Albertz, *A History of Israelite Religion in the Old Testament Period,* 2 vols., trans. John Bowden, OTL (Louisville: Westminster John Knox, 1994), 1:16.

72. Albertz, *History of Israelite Religion,* 1:16–17. Albertz names additional church and ecumenical aspects that do not deal with the question of the content under discussion.

tieth century. The essential questions and methods, but also the defining research paradigms of the humanities were determined by theology. One need only recall the interdisciplinary importance of hermeneutics from Friedrich Schleiermacher to Wilhelm Dilthey to Hans-Georg Gadamer. At the same time, the humanities enjoyed a prominent position in the public's perception of the university.

Since the second half of the twentieth century, these leadership functions have diminished and in part even disappeared. Motivated especially by the rapid technological advancements of the 1950s and 1960s that fundamentally changed everyday life, the natural sciences have gained importance and simultaneously begun to exercise considerable influence over the humanities. A good index of the meaning of these changes is the discussion surrounding Charles Percy Snow's theory of the "two cultures" (1959) of the humanities and the natural sciences, which would exist to a large degree in unmediated fashion next to one another. Two decades later, Habermas speaks of a "colonialization of the living world" by the exact sciences. A further indicator appears in the rise of empirically oriented social sciences that increasingly separate themselves from the humanities in terms of their philosophical approach and organization.

These developments are at minimum indirectly relevant for Hebrew Bible studies. The theology and the hermeneutics of the Hebrew Bible are not central questions in current scholarship. The study of the Hebrew Bible is far more focused on clarifying religious history, literary history, and social history with regard to its object of study. All these investigations are, of course, interesting, and the study of them has provided vital expansion of the state of knowledge of the Hebrew Bible in recent years. Nonetheless, the process sometimes described as the "social scientification" and "cultural scientification" in the humanities has also served to distance Hebrew Bible studies from the questions of content that have traditionally belonged at its center, even if they have in the meantime reached levels of rhetorical excess.

The current question, in spite of all thematic ambiguities, regarding one or more "theologies" of the Hebrew Bible—a question that remains strongly anchored within the makeup of the discipline—keeps biblical studies focused on the content. Simultaneously, however, the need to maintain a degree of historical analysis when approaching "theological" questions has emerged. If this is the case, then there is no way to avoid the pluralization of the "theology" of the Hebrew Bible; it is a direct result of its historicization. Hand in hand with the recognition that extrabiblical texts (note as well the development of the history of this concept in the past two centuries) can contain "theologies" or be formed "theologically," is that the discussion of "theological" questions cannot be limited to the texts that later became canonical.

§9 Implicit Theologies in the Hebrew Bible and the Search for a Theology of the Hebrew Bible

Jan Assmann, *The Search for God in Ancient Egypt*, trans. David Lorton (Ithaca, NY: Cornell University Press, 2001) ◆ Angelika Berlejung, "Theologie in Babylon?—Theologien in Babylonien!," in *Theologie in Israel und in den Nachbarkulturen: Beiträge des Symposiums "Das Alte Testament und die Kultur der Moderne" anlässlich des 100. Geburtstags Gerhard von Rads (1901–1971), Heidelberg, 18.–21. Oktober 2001,* ed. Manfred Oeming et al., Altes Testament und Moderne 9 (Münster: LIT, 2004), 105–24 ◆ Esther Eidinow, Julia Kindt, and Robin Osborne, eds., *Theologies of Ancient Greek Religion* (Cambridge: Cambridge University Press, 2016) ◆ Georg Fischer, *Theologien des Alten Testaments*, NSKAT 31 (Stuttgart: Kohlhammer, 2012) ◆ Jörg Jeremias, "Neuere Entwürfe zu einer 'Theologie des Alten Testaments,'" in *Theologie und Exegese des Alten Testaments / der Hebräischen Bibel: Zwischenbilanz und Zukunftsperspektiven,* ed. Bernd Janowski; SBS 200 (Stuttgart: Katholisches Bibelwerk, 2005), 125–58 ◆ Matthew R. Schlimm, *This Strange and Sacred Scripture: Wrestling with the Old Testament and Its Oddities* (Grand Rapids: Baker Academic, 2015) ◆ Brent A. Strawn, *The Old Testament Is Dying: A Diagnosis and Recommended Treatment* (Grand Rapids: Baker Academic, 2017) ◆ Meir Weiss, *The Bible from Within: The Method of Total Interpretation* (Jerusalem: Magnus, 1984)

1. The Inadequacy of the Concept of Theology in Relation to the Hebrew Bible and the Impossibility of Avoiding It

The previous journey through the history of scholarship on the various aspects of meaning of the concept of theology has demonstrated that there is no "theology" along the lines of the understanding of the concept by the Scholastics. Or, stated differently, it is anachronistic to speak of theology in the Hebrew Bible. Even if the situation with regard to New Testament literature is not fundamentally different, the beginnings of a change in perspectives can at least be observed there: "In threefold manner the NT is familiar with statements that are acquainted with how the nature of God appears: 'God is spirit' (John 4:24); 'God is light' (1 John 1:5); 'God is love' (1 John 4:8). The OT is not acquainted with any such statements."[73] Without attributing any kind of evaluation to this observation, the New Testament literature appears to have developed new ways of speaking and new genres that separate it from the literature of the Hebrew Bible in terms of what later became classified as "theology."

WHILE THE CONCEPT OF THEOLOGY IS INADEQUATE, IT IS ALSO UNAVOIDABLE As ready at hand as it might seem to conclude from this observation that one should forego the use of theological terminology in application to the texts of the Hebrew Bible, such an alternative is also problematic. For while the Hebrew Bible *does not contain theology*, at the same time, *neither are its contents simply nontheological*. One can attempt to articulate this situation more precisely in various ways. Perhaps one of the most appropriate formulations comes from Christoph Levin, who spoke of "the way of the Old Testament to its theology."[74] While Rudolf Smend hesitated to use theological terminology for the Hebrew Bible in his epoch-making essay on "Theology in the Old Testament," he still found it appropriate to speak of the texts of the Hebrew Bible as having "at least a strong convergence with theology."[75]

Nobert Lohfink also demonstrates caution, summarizing the ambiguous results as follows: "The text type 'theological treatise' first emerged later and in a different cultural context. The Old Testament texts do *not* belong to it in terms of genre. 'Theology' appears in them only implicitly, indirectly, or reduced."[76] Nonetheless, this final sentence points to a perspective worthy of investigation.

IMPLICIT AND EXPLICIT THEOLOGY The distinction between *implicit* and *explicit* theology appears quite helpful for the Hebrew Bible, even if one

73. Köhler, *Theologie des Alten Testaments*, 4th ed., NTG (Tübingen: Mohr Siebeck, 1966), 2.

74. Christoph Levin, "Das Alte Testament auf dem Weg zu seiner Theologie," *ZTK* 105 (2008): 125–45.

75. Rudolf Smend, "Theologie im Alten Testament," in *Verifikationen: Festschrift für Gerhard Ebeling zum 70. Geburtstag*, ed. Eberhard Jüngel et al. (Tübingen: Mohr, 1982).

76. Norbert Lohfink, "Alttestamentliche Wissenschaft als Theologie? 44 Thesen," in *Wieviel Systematik erlaubt die Schrift? Auf der Suche nach einer gesamtbiblischen Theologie*, ed. F.-L. Hossfeld, QD 185 (Freiburg im Breisgau: Herder, 2001), 15.

might retort that the expression "implicit theology" is an oxymoron. But this would really only be the case for a very narrowly conceived conception of theology, one which could hardly be considered a majority view in contemporary discussion. The breadth of the concept of theology established in its reception history in fact allows for the paradoxical formulation that the Hebrew Bible *neither* contains theology *nor* contains *no* theology. In the context of its ancient Near Eastern environment, the Hebrew Bible is a unique corpus of tradition whose uniqueness is observable in its scribal exegetical character. The Hebrew Bible should, to a large degree, be viewed as the reflective interpretation of preexisting religious texts. It thereby fulfills—at least for the texts containing reflective interpretations—a basic requirement of theology, if "theology" is understood as the reflective examination and interpretation of religious phenomena.

RUDOLF BULTMANN The term *implicit theology* is not a neologism. It draws on a noble tradition, at least within the twentieth century. It appears as early as Bultmann in reference to the New Testament: "The science called New Testament theology has the task of setting forth the theology of the NT; i.e., of setting forth *the theological thoughts of the New Testament writings*, both those that are explicitly developed (such as Paul's teaching on the Law, for example) and those that are implicitly at work in narrative or exhortation, in polemic or consolation."[77] A formulation that illustrates this differentiation even better appears in the following context: "*Theological propositions . . .* can never be the *object* of faith; they can only be the *explication* of the understanding which is inherent in faith itself."[78] According to Bultmann, implicit theology with regard to the Bible designates the understanding inherent in its texts, which assumes a corresponding potential for reflection in them. This does not, however, allow for them to be seen as basically nontheological. Bultmann does not attempt to keep the concept of theology at a distance from the Bible simply because of a conscious decision to favor a solely intellectual understanding of theology. His perspective also bears an existentialist stamp, which can be traced back to the Reformation. Bultmann, therefore, declares in his *Theology,* "the presentation of New

77. Bultmann, *Theology of the New Testament,* 2 vols., trans. Kendrick Grobel, Scribner Studies in Contemporary Theology (New York: Scribner's Sons, 1951/55), 2:237 (emphasis original).

78. Bultmann, *Theology of the New Testament,* 2:237–38.

Testament theology offered in this book stands, on the one hand, within the tradition of the historical-critical and the history-of-religion schools and seeks, on the other hand, to avoid their mistake which consists of the tearing apart of the act of thinking from the act of living and hence as a failure to recognize the intent of theological utterances."[79] For this reason, Bultmann demands that biblical studies strive not only for "reconstruction," but also "interpretation."[80] It is important for him that "neither exists, of course, without the other, and they stand constantly in a reciprocal relation to each other."[81]

The terminology of "implicit theology," which Bultmann did not, however, use programmatically, failed to establish itself within traditional biblical studies terminology. It appears that the later usage of the concept does not refer specifically to Bultmann, but rather represents the independent categories of its users. For example, Jan Assmann uses the distinction between implicit and explicit theology with regard to extrabiblical, in his case Egyptian, texts.[82] He finds in *implicit theology* an opportune term for the Egyptian texts. Assmann does not envisage polar opposites with this distinction, but rather conceives of different degrees of theological explication. However, he views the simplest conceivable form of implicit theology as present in every religion; implicit and explicit theology relate to one another like language and grammar. However, this determination may be formulated too universally. In light of the actual facts, it is more advisable to employ the category of "implicit axioms" suggested by Dietrich Ritschl.

Assmann does not directly reference Bultmann's terminology. In reality, the prominent usage by Assmann, anchored in the title of the book itself, is more likely to have been inspired by von Rad, whose decision to present the theology of the Hebrew Bible in terms of a narrative in fact opened the way for the use of the concept in relation to other ancient texts.[83]

---

79. Bultmann, *Theology of the New Testament*, 2:250–51.

80. Bultmann, *Theology of the New Testament*, 2:251.

81. Bultmann, *Theology of the New Testament*, 2:251.

82. Jan Assmann, *Ägypten: Theologie und Frömmigkeit einer frühen Hochkultur*, 2nd ed. (Stuttgart: Kohlhammer, 1991), 21–23, 192–93; trans. as *The Search for God in Ancient Egypt* (Ithaca, NY: Cornell University Press, 2001).

83. In the English-speaking realm, the differentiation between "implicit" and "explicit" with regard to theology appears less prevalently. Instead it could be that the adjective "theological" and the noun "theology" are distinguished from one another in similar fash-

THE APPLICATION OF THE CONCEPT OF THEOLOGY TO TEXTS OF THE HE-BREW BIBLE The parameters resulting from the above reflections for the portrayal of a theology of the Hebrew Bible are as follows: Even if the terminology of theology is inadequate for texts of the Hebrew Bible, including those that demonstrate a clearly reflective character, this still provides little ground for keeping theology at a distance from them. The Hebrew Bible is acquainted with varying degrees of implicit and explicit pre-forms of theology. The passages of the Hebrew Bible that reflect on earlier biblical texts could, therefore, be called "theological," because their reflective character with regard to the fundamentally "religious" statements appears "theological." They relate to their object in the same intellectual manner as other kinds of scholarship do as well. The further determination of the reflective nature of these texts of the Hebrew Bible as "implicit" highlights the fact that the Hebrew Bible does not yet know explicit scholarship. These texts were written within a worldview that does not differentiate between experiences and their interpretations in a clear-cut way.

In keeping with the implicit nature of the theology of the texts of the Hebrew Bible, it would entail a certain narrowness to limit the reconstruction of the theological propositions of the Hebrew Bible to the experiences, perceptions, depictions, and conceptualizations of *God.* In the Hebrew Bible, considerations about humanity, nation, and world, all of which took place within the purview of God in ancient Israel and Judah, are also part of the theological propositions up for investigation. Finally, it is clear that the theology of the Hebrew Bible—considered in historical and critical terms—always incorporates a plurality of theologies. At the same time, these theologies do not stand side by side in a disconnected fashion. Thanks to the nature of the Hebrew Bible as scribal literature, these theologies are connected and interlinked with one another such that the Hebrew Bible appears as an observably multi-perspectival theological discussion. Therefore, the theology of the Hebrew Bible should not be broken up into the description of its various theologies, even though it comprises these as well.

---

ion. In his interaction with Hans Hübner concerning the question of theology in the Bible, James Barr proposes qualifying the Bible as "theological," while its texts themselves should not be spoken of as "theology." *The Concept of Biblical Theology* (Minneapolis: Fortress, 1999), 498.

2. Stereometric Theology as Implicit Theology

The implicit theological character of many texts of the Hebrew Bible requires the description of a further basic characteristic of the Hebrew Bible with regard to its theology. Implicit theologies can become more explicit over time through the development of a text's redactional history. However, the explication can also be functionally transferred to the audience's imagination, located in a new, unarticulated dimension *beyond* the text.

One example that combines both characteristics appears early in the Jeremiah tradition. An oracle of the prophet appears in Jer 6:1 that is clearly directed to Jeremiah's compatriots from Benjamin, calling them to flee from Jerusalem because of the approaching Babylonian military force.

> Flee for safety, Benjaminites, out of Jerusalem! And blow the trumpet in Tekoa, and raise a smoke signal on Beth-Kerem; for evil looks down from the north, and great destruction.

This text deals with political advice, but the ensuing evil does not receive further theological interpretation. Such a construal first appears in Jer 4:6–7:

> Raise a standard towards Zion, flee for safety, do not delay, for I am bringing evil from the north, and a great destruction. A lion has gone up from its thicket, a destroyer of nations has set out; he has gone out from his place to make your land a waste; your cities will be ruins without inhabitant.

Here as well a call to flee is issued, but the approaching evil is explicitly interpreted as brought about by God. There is no doubt that Jer 4:6–7 presupposes and interprets Jer 6:1, as demonstrated through the word-for-word adoption ("evil" and "great destruction"). While the evil is interpreted as brought about by God, Jer 4:7 simultaneously ascribes the Babylonian army its own activity ("The lion has gone up").

The approaching evil in Jer 4:6–7, therefore, contains both divinely directed and human directed components. The Babylonians actively set out, but their approach is ultimately attributed to divine control.

A combination of material from Jer 6:1 and Jer 4:6–7 then appears in Jer 1:13–14:

The word of Yhwh came to me a second time, saying, "What do you see?" And I said, "I see a boiling pot, tilted away from the north." Then Yhwh said to me: "Out of the north evil shall break out on all the inhabitants of the land."

This vision in the opening chapter of the book preemptively opens the discussion in Jer 4 and 6 of the approaching evil. However, it remains silent with regard to whether God himself is active in this or not. Yet the vision eradicates all doubt with regard to whether the evil descending on Judah is part of the plan of God himself. While God stands behind the evil according to Jer 1:13–14, the specific formulation chosen is so open that the theological distinctions found in Jer 4:6–7 and 6:1 are not overplayed.

One might call this evocation of different dimensions of meaning "stereometric reading."[84] Interpretations are not made explicit in the text. They instead emerge through the process of the audience's reception. This characteristic of the biblical texts is highly important for its theology. It shows that certain nuances of meaning appropriate to a text can only be presented by remaining silent about them. At the same time, however, the audience is pushed to perform particular synthesizing conclusions themselves during the process of reading, without unequivocally identifying the textual meaning.

This literary strategy appears clearly in what is called *parallelismus membrorum*, a widespread form within Biblical Hebrew poetry. Numerous declarations appear in wisdom literature on the so-called act-consequence nexus,[85] which are traditionally understood as support for a "doctrine of retribution" within the Hebrew Bible:

84. Cf. Benno Landsberger, "Die Eigenbegrifflichkeit der babylonischen Welt," in *Die Eigenbegrifflichkeit der babylonischen Welt: Leistung und Grenze babylonischer Wissenschaft*, ed. Benno Landsberger and Wolfram von Soden (Darmstadt: Wissenschaftliche Buchgesellschaft, 1965), 17. The notion of stereometry was adopted by Gerhard von Rad, *Wisdom in Israel*, trans. James D. Martin (Nashville: Abingdon, 1974); see also Andreas Wagner, "Der Parallelismus membrorum zwischen poetischer Form und Denkfigur," in *Parallelismus membrorum*, ed. Andreas Wagner, OBO 224 (Freiburg: Universitätsverlag; Göttingen: Vandenhoeck & Ruprecht, 2007), 11–13; Bernd Janowski, *Konfliktgespräche mit Gott: Eine Anthropologie der Psalmen*, 4th ed. (Neukirchen-Vluyn: Neukirchener Verlag, 2012), 13–21.

85. Cf. Bernd Janowski, "Die Tat kehrt zum Täter zurück: Offene Fragen im Umkreis des 'Tun-Ergehen-Zusammenhangs,'" in *Die rettende Gerechtigkeit*, Beiträge zur Theologie des Alten Testaments 2 (Neukirchen-Vluyn: Neukirchener Verlag, 1999), 167–91.

> A generous person will be enriched, and one who gives water will get water. (Prov 11:25)

However, consideration of the parallel structure of this statement shows that the connection between act and consequence is not only or primarily safeguarded by divine action. This proverb does not even mention God. While one might interpret the first colon "be enriched" as a divine passive, one could also think of social interactions that ensure this course of events. In any case, the second colon suggests by the use of the same root רוה (*rwh*) *hiphil* / *hophal*, "give to drink" / "be given drink," the conception of a reciprocal action within the community, which at the same time interprets the first colon. The theological dimension of the proverb is evoked by means of the parallelism, without explicitly being named.

The proverb that follows appears to have something similar in mind:

> The people curse those who hold back grain, but a blessing is on the head of those who sell it. (Prov 11:26)

The first colon primarily has the social realm in view, while the second colon implies a theological dimension. By means of the parallelism of the two cola, this theological dimension swings back to the first statement. The curse of the people takes on theological legitimacy.

Virtually in the sense of a climax—the proverbs become increasingly universal—Prov 11:27 is formulated in a foundational manner:

> Whoever diligently seeks good finds favor, but evil comes to the one who searches for it. (Prov 11:27)

God is not mentioned here either, but he is implied in the second colon, which again interprets the first.

Therefore, it appears characteristic of this type of poetic formation to suggest God's action in the background without explicitly mentioning it. One can conclude that this form of presentation rests on a theological judgment that was consciously chosen in order to account for the complexity and ambiguity involved in identifying God's action in the world.

C. Hebrew Bible and Old Testament

HEBREW BIBLE AND OLD TESTAMENT According to the conception of theology outlined above (Part B), a theology of the Old Testament must also—within the framework of its traditional formulation of the title—clarify the terminology of "Old Testament." First, "Old Testament" was not the original determination for the inventory of texts under discussion. Second, there is, strictly speaking, no such thing as *the* Old Testament—the texts included in the Old Testament vary among denominations, sometimes quite considerably. Furthermore, different language versions are viewed as authoritative. Therefore, it is more precise to speak in the plural of "Old Testaments."[1] The plural term admittedly comes across as artificial, and the different "Old Testaments" only come into view when considered from an ecumenical perspective. Every Christian denomination claims implicitly or explicitly to have *the* Old Testament.

The "Old Testament" denotes a Christian form of reception of the Hebrew Bible, the Tanakh (an acronym consisting of the beginning letters of Torah "Law," Nevi'im "Prophets," and Ketuvim "Writings"), which itself takes many forms. Christian Old Testaments can be limited to the inventory of writings in the Hebrew Bible, the Tanakh—though they arrange the writings in another order—or they can expand the inventory of writings, but they never reduce it. Furthermore, the "Old Testaments" are usually only encountered within a book in the context of the whole Christian Bible, which also contains a "New Testament."

---

1. Cf. the overview in Peter Brandt, *Endgestalten des Kanons: Das Arrangement der Schriften Israels in der jüdischen und christlichen Bibel*, BBB 131 (Berlin: Philo, 2001).

§10 The Pluriformity of the Tradition

Roger T. Beckwith, *The Old Testament Canon of the New Testament Church and Its Background in Early Judaism* (Grand Rapids: Eerdmans, 1985) ◆ Peter Brandt, *Endgestalten des Kanons: Das Arrangement der Schriften Israels in der jüdischen und christlichen Bibel,* BBB 131 (Berlin: Philo, 2001) ◆ Thomas Hieke, ed., *Formen des Kanons: Studien zu Ausprägungen des biblischen Kanons von der Antike bis zum 19. Jahrhundert,* SBS 229 (Stuttgart: Katholisches Bibelwerk, 2013) ◆ Jan Joosten, "The Origin of the Septuagint Canon," in *Die Septuaginta: Orte und Intentionen,* ed. Siegfried Kreuzer, WUNT 361 (Tübingen: Mohr Siebeck, 2016), 688–99 ◆ Sid Z. Leiman, *The Canonization of Hebrew Scripture: The Talmudic and Midrashic Evidence,* 2nd ed. (New Haven, CT: Connecticut Academy of Arts and Sciences, 1991) ◆ Folkert Siegert, *Zwischen Hebräischer Bibel und Altem Testament: Eine Einführung in die Septuaginta,* Münsteraner judaistische Studien 9 (Münster: LIT, 2001) ◆ Michael Tilly, *Einführung in die Septuaginta* (Darmstadt: Wissenschaftliche Buchgesellschaft, 2005

Neither *the* Old Testament nor *the* Hebrew Bible exists. Instead, the Jewish and Christian traditions are familiar with different arrangements of the biblical books. In addition, the Christian traditions—in the divergent canons of various religious communities and confessions—have different inventories of books.

ORDER OF THE BOOKS The standard order of the Hebrew Bible and the Old Testament in the most important forms of the tradition are as follows:

HEBREW BIBLE	SEPTUAGINT	VULGATE	PROTESTANT BIBLE
Torah	*Historical Books*	*Pentateuch*	*Historical Books*
Genesis	Genesis	Genesis	Genesis
Exodus	Exodus	Exodus	Exodus
Leviticus	Leviticus	Leviticus	Leviticus
Numbers	Numbers	Numbers	Numbers
Deuteronomy	Deuteronomy	Deuteronomy	Deuteronomy
Nevi'im		*Historical*	
Former Prophets		*Books*	
Joshua	Joshua	Joshua	Joshua
Judges	Judges	Judges	Judges
	Ruth	Ruth	Ruth
1–2 Samuel	1–2 Kingdoms	1–2 Kingdoms	1–2 Samuel

HEBREW BIBLE	SEPTUAGINT	VULGATE	PROTESTANT BIBLE
1–2 Kings	3–4 Kingdoms	3–4 Kingdoms	1–2 Kings
	1–2 Chronicles	1–2 Chronicles [+Prayer of Manasseh]	1–2 Chronicles
	[1 Ezra (= 3 Ezra in the Vulgate)]	1 Ezra (= Ezra)	Ezra
	2 Ezra (= Ezra+Neh)	2 Ezra (= Nehemiah) [3 Ezra] [4 Ezra]	Nehemiah
	Esther+Additions	Tobit	Esther
	Judith	Judith	
	Tobit	Esther+Additions	
	1 –2 Maccabees		
	[3–4 Maccabees]		
Latter Prophets	*Wisdom Books*	*Wisdom Books*	*Wisdom Books*
Isaiah		Job	Job
Jeremiah	Psalms	Psalms	Psalms
Ezekiel	[Odes of Solomom+Prayer of Manasseh]		
Hosea			
Joel			
Amos	Proverbs	Proverbs	Proverbs
Obadiah	Qoheleth	Qoheleth	Qoheleth
Jonah	Song of Songs	Song of Songs	Song of Songs
Micah	Job		
Nahum	Wisdom of Solomon	Wisdom of Solomon	
Habakkuk			
Zephaniah			
Haggai	Sirach	Sirach	
Zechariah	[Psalms of Solomon]		
Malachi			
Ketuvim	*Prophets*	*Prophets*	*Prophets*
Psalms	Hosea	Isaiah	Isaiah
Job	Amos	Jeremiah	Jeremiah

HEBREW BIBLE	SEPTUAGINT	VULGATE	PROTESTANT BIBLE
Proverbs	Micah	Lamentations	Lamentations
Ruth	Joel	Baruch	Ezekiel
Song of Songs	Obadiah	Ezekiel	Daniel
Qoheleth	Jonah	Daniel+Additions (incl. Susanna, Bel and the Dragon)	Hosea
Lamentations	Nahum	Hosea	
Esther	Habakkuk	Joel	Joel
Daniel	Zephaniah	Amos	Amos
Ezra–Nehemiah	Haggai	Obadiah	Obadiah
1–2 Chronicles	Zechariah	Jonah	Jonah
	Malachi	Micah	Micah
	Isaiah	Nahum	Nahum
	Jeremiah	Habakkuk	Habakkuk
	Baruch 1–5	Zephaniah	Zephaniah
	Lamentations	Haggai	Haggai
	Epistle of Jere- miah = Baruch 6	Zechariah	Zechariah
	Ezekiel	Malachi	Malachi
	Daniel+Additions 3:24–90 (= Prayer of Azariah; Song of the Three Young Men)	1–2 Maccabees	
	Susanna = Dan 13		
	Bel and the Dragon= Dan 14		

DIVERGENT ORDERS OF THE HEBREW BIBLE The Hebrew Bible—as the Holy Scripture of Judaism in the customary order—is made up of three parts, Torah, Nevi'im, and Ketuvim. The Torah consists of the books of Genesis, Exodus, Leviticus, Numbers, and Deuteronomy; the Nevi'im comprises Joshua, Judges, 1–2 Samuel, 1–2 Kings, Isaiah, Jeremiah, Eze-kiel, as well as the Book of the Twelve; lastly, the Ketuvim contains the books of Psalms, Job, Proverbs, Ruth, Song of Songs, Qoheleth, Lamenta-tions, Esther, Daniel, Ezra-Nehemiah, and 1–2 Chronicles. In the section of the Nevi'im, a further subdivision is common: Joshua through Kings are in sum the Former Prophets; Isaiah through Malachi are the Latter Prophets. Within the Ketuvim, Ruth, Song of Songs, Qoheleth, Lamentations, and Esther form what is called the "Megillot," that is the five "scrolls" read at specific festivals, a practice first attested in the sixth century CE. Ruth belongs to Shavu'ot (Feast of Weeks), the Song of Songs to Pesach, Qoheleth to Sukkot (Feast of Booths), Lamentations to the Ninth of Ab, and Esther to Purim.

The manuscript tradition of the Hebrew Bibles also attests to divergent orders of the books. However, the number of books and the three sections of the canon, Torah, Nevi'im, and Ketuvim, always remain constant. If one calculates the number of theoretically possible variations inherent in these conditions, one arrives at 120 variations for the five books of the Torah, 40,320 variations for the eight books of the Nevi'im (when counting the twelve Minor Prophets as a single book according to ancient custom), and around 40 million variations for the Ketuvim.

In any case, the tradition did not even come close to exhausting these possibilities. The Torah appears almost exclusively in the same order. There are at least nine variations attested for the Nevi'im, and these are all found in the Latter Prophets, as Genesis to Kings constitutes a chronologically ordered narrative constellation that presents a stable block of content. The order of the Ketuvim is relatively flexible, attesting to at least seventy different orders.[2]

The most important variations in the "Nevi'im" appear in the Babylonian Talmud (b. B. Bat. 14b–15a). Here the four books of the prophets are attested in the order Jeremiah, Ezekiel, Isaiah, Book of the Twelve. This is justified with a theological observation: Jeremiah is "entirely judgment," Ezekiel "half judgment, half consolation," and Isaiah "entirely consolation." However, even a cursory reading of these books reveals that this conclusion does not fit the content of the books. All three Major Prophets include both declarations of judgment *and* salvation and are, in this respect, "half judgment, half consolation." Why then does the Babylonian Talmud order the books in this way? The answer is very simple if one pays attention to the length of the four prophetic books: the book of Jeremiah comprises 21,835 words, the book of Ezekiel 18,730, the book of Isaiah 16,392, and the Book of the Twelve 14,355. The order in the Babylonian Talmud is, therefore, apparently motivated by the length of the books. The theological justification is a later rationalization of an order established on the basis of the length of each book.

---

2. Cf. the lists found in Beckwith, *Old Testament Canon*, 449–68.

The ordering of the Ketuvim sometimes attests to significant variation. Several examples must suffice at this point. The Aleppo Codex and Codex Leningradensis (Firkovich B19A), the two most important ancient manuscripts of the Hebrew Bible from 950 and 1008 CE respectively, place Chronicles at the very beginning of the Ketuvim. Apparently Chronicles, which provides an expansive narration of the establishment of worship at the Temple under David and Solomon, was understood as a "historical" introduction to the Psalms. The standard order now customarily places Chronicles at the very end of the Ketuvim, so as to close the Hebrew Bible with the important "exodus" declaration of 2 Chr 36:23b: "Whoever is among you of all his people, may the Lord his God be with him! Let him go up!"

A different tradition that is well attested in the manuscript evidence places Ruth before the Psalms. In this scenario, the genealogy of David that concludes the book of Ruth gives way to the Psalms, thereby offering an alternative "historical" contextualization of Psalms.

DIFFERENT ORDERS OF THE OLD TESTAMENT For the Christian Old Testament, it is best to differentiate between the various denominations. Common Protestant Bible editions offer the following structure: The first section gathers the "Historical Books": Genesis, Exodus, Leviticus, Numbers, Deuteronomy, Joshua, Judges, Ruth, 1–2 Samuel, 1–2 Kings, 1–2 Chronicles, Ezra, Nehemiah, Esther. The "Poetical Books" follow: Job, Psalms, Proverbs, Qoheleth, and Song of Songs. Last are the "Prophetic Books" of Isaiah, Jeremiah, Lamentations, Ezekiel, Daniel, Hosea, Joel, Amos, Obadiah, Jonah, Micah, Nahum, Habakkuk, Zephaniah, Haggai, Zechariah, and Malachi.

This Old Testament also presents a three-part structure, but it is of a different kind than the one in the Hebrew Bible. The first superscription of the "Historical Books" combines the Torah and the Former Prophets, and additionally comprises the narrative books of Ruth, Chronicles, Ezra, Nehemiah, and Esther. The second section ("Poetic Books") contains an important selection from the Ketuvim: Job, Psalms, Proverbs, Qoheleth, and Song of Songs. The third section ("Prophetic Books") comprises the Latter Prophets of the Hebrew Bible—that is, Isaiah, Jeremiah, Ezekiel, and the twelve Minor Prophets—but in addition includes Lamentations, whose Greek translation points to Jeremiah as its author (1:1). Also placed among the "Prophetic Books" is the book of Daniel, which was composed during the Maccabean period. For this reason it could no longer enter the already closed section of the Nevi'im in the Hebrew canon. In order to become part of the Hebrew Bible as a prophetic book, it had to be counted among the Ketuvim.

Roman Catholic editions of the Bible in the tradition of the Vulgate follow the same overarching structure, but they also have seven additional books. Tobit and Judith are placed after Nehemiah, the books of Maccabees follow Esther, the Wisdom of Solomon and Sirach follow Song of Songs, and Baruch follows Lamentations. Furthermore, Esther and Daniel contain several additional chapters (the so-called Additions to Esther and Daniel).

The larger extent of the Old Testament in the Roman Catholic Bible rests on the canonization of the Vulgate with its larger inventory of books by the Roman Catholic Church at the Council of Trent in 1545 as a ruling of the Counter-Reformation. This conciliar decision concerns the one and only decree regarding the canon. In other words, only the Roman Catholic Church has determined its inventory of books by means of an authoritative ruling. The broader extent of the Old Testament in the Vulgate itself goes back to the Septuagint, the oldest Greek translation of the Old Testament. It also gives rise to the different order of the Christian Bibles when compared to the Jewish Bible.

Following their humanistic recourse to the Hebrew Bible, the Protestant churches stipulated that only books of the Hebrew Bible should remain in the canon of the Old Testament. The Reformers declared the other books of the Septuagint and Vulgate Old Testament apocryphal or deuterocanonical books worthy of reading, but of a lower theological rank and value than the canonical writings.

In addition to the larger canon of the Old Testament of the Roman Catholic Church, there are the even more extensive canons in the eastern churches. Especially worthy of mention are the Ethiopic Christians, who include Enoch and the book of Jubilees as part of their Old Testament.

It is theologically noteworthy that the different Old Testaments of the various denominations do not serve the special theological interests or accentuations of the various churches. The books of Sirach and Tobit contribute just as little to the support of Roman Catholic doctrine as does the book of Jubilees to the Ethiopian church. The divergent canonical boundaries are instead based in different philological and historical developments and decisions.

§11 The Tanakh as the Hebrew Bible

Jan Assmann, "Five Stages on the Road to the Canon: Tradition and Written Culture in Ancient Israel and Early Judaism," in *Religion and Cultural Memory: Ten Studies*, trans. Rodney Livingstone (Stanford: Stanford University Press, 2006), 63–80 ◆ John Barton, "The Significance of a Fixed Canon," in *Hebrew Bible / Old Testament: The History of Its Interpretation*, vol. 1: *From the Beginnings to the Middle Ages (until 1300): Part 1, Antiquity*, ed. Magne Sæbø (Göttingen: Vandenhoeck & Ruprecht, 1996), 67–83 ◆ Michael Becker, "Grenzziehungen des Kanons im frühen Judentum und die Neuschrift der Bibel nach 4. Buch Esra," in *Qumran und der biblische Kanon*, ed. Michael Becker and Jörg Frey, Biblisch-theologische Studien 92 (Neukirchen-Vluyn: Neukirchener Verlag, 2009), 195–253 ◆ Roger T. Beckwith, *The Old Testament Canon of the New Testament Church and Its Background in Early Judaism* (Grand Rapids: Eerdmans, 1985) ◆ David M. Carr, "Canonization in the Context of Community: An Outline of the Formation of the Tanakh and the Christian Bible," in *A Gift of God in Due Season: Essays on Scripture and Community in Honor of James A. Sanders*, ed. Richard D. Weis and David M. Carr, JSOTSup 225 (Sheffield: Sheffield Academic Press, 1996) ◆ John J. Collins, "Before the Canon: Scriptures in Second Temple Judaism," in *Old Testament Interpretation: Past, Present, and Future: Essays in Honor of Gene M. Tucker*, ed. James L. Mays et al. (Nashville: Abingdon, 1995), 225–44 ◆ Frank Crüsemann, "Das 'portative Vaterland': Struktur und Genese des alttestamentlichen Kanons," in *Kanon und Zensur*, ed. Aleida Assmann and Jan Assmann, Archäologie der literarischen Kommunikation 2 (Munich: Fink, 1987), 63–79 ◆ Stephen G. Dempster, "Torah, Torah, Torah: The Emergence of the Tripartite Canon," in *Exploring the Origins of the Bible: Canon Formation in Historical, Literary, and Theological Perspective*, ed. Craig A. Evans and Emanuel Tov (Grand Rapids: Baker Academic, 2008), 87–127 ◆ Heinz-Josef Fabry, "Das 'Alte Testament,'" in *What Is Bible?*, ed. Karin Finsterbusch and Armin Lange, CBET 67 (Leuven: Peeters, 2012), 283–304 ◆ Tal Ilan, "The Term and Concept of Tanakh," in *What Is Bible?*, ed. Karin Finsterbusch and Armin Lange, CBET 67 (Leuven: Peeters, 2012), 219–34 ◆ Bernhard Lang, "'The 'Writings': A Hellenistic Literary Canon in the Hebrew Bible," in *Canonization and Decanonization: Papers Presented to the International Conference of the Leiden Institute for the Study of Religion (LISOR). Held at Leiden 9–10 January 1997*, ed. Arie van der Kooij and Karel van der Toorn, SHR 82 (Leiden: Brill, 1997), 41–65 ◆ Lee M. McDonald, *The Biblical Canon: Its Origin, Transmission, and Authority*, 3rd ed. (Peabody, MA: Hendrickson, 2007) ◆ Tobias Nicklas, "The Development of the Christian Bible," in *What Is Bible?*, ed. Karin Finsterbusch and Armin Lange, CBET 67 (Leuven: Peeters, 2012), 393–426 ✦ Nahum M. Sarna, "The Order of the Books," in *Studies in Jewish Bibliography, History, and Literature in Honor of I. Edward Kiev*, ed. Charles Berlin (New York: Ktav, 1971), 407–13 ✦ Nahum M. Sarna, *Ancient Libraries and the Ordering of the Biblical Books: A Lecture Presented at the Library of Congress, March 6, 1989*, The Center for the Book Viewpoint Series 25 (Washington, DC: Library of Congress, 1989) ✦ Konrad Schmid, "Der Kanon und der Kult: Das Aufkommen der Schriftreligion im antiken Israel und die sukzessive Sublimierung des Tempelkultes," in *Ex oriente Lux: Studien zur Theologie des Alten Testaments: Festschrift für Rüdiger Lux zum 65. Geburtstag,* ed. Angelika Berlejung and Raik Heckl, Arbeiten zur Bibel und ihrer Geschichte 39 (Leipzig: Evangelische Verlagsanstalt, 2012), 523–46 ✦ Konrad Schmid, "Die Entstehung des Alten Testaments als Kanon: Welche Schriften gehörten dazu?" *Welt und Umwelt der Bibel* 71 (2014): 18–21 ✦ Odil H. Steck, "Der Kanon des hebräischen Alten Testaments," in *Verbindliches Zeugnis I*, ed. Wolfhart Pannenberg and Theodor Schneider, DiKi 7 (Freiburg im Breisgau: Herder; Göttingen: Vandenhoeck & Ruprecht, 1992), 11–33 ✦ Julius Steinberg, *Die Ketuvim: Ihr Aufbau und ihre Botschaft*, BBB 152 (Hamburg: Philo, 2006) ✦ Julio C. Trebolle Barrera, "Origins of a Tripartite Old Testament Canon," in *The Canon Debate*, ed. Lee M. McDonald and James A. Sanders (Peabody, MA: Hendrickson, 2002), 128–45 ✦ Eugene C. Ulrich, "The Canonical Process, Textual Criticism, and Latter Stages in the Composition of the Bible," in *Sha'arei Talmon: Studies in the Bible, Qumran, and the Ancient Near East Presented to Shemaryahu Talmon*, ed. Michael Fishbane et al. (Winona Lake, IN: Eisenbrauns, 1992), 269–76 ✦ Eugene C. Ulrich, *The Dead Sea Scrolls and the Developmental Composition of the Hebrew Bible*, VTSup 169 (Leiden: Brill, 2015) ✦ Eugene C. Ulrich, "The Non-Attestation of a Tripartite Canon in 4QMMT," *CBQ* 65 (2003): 202–14 ✦ James VanderKam, *The Dead Sea Scrolls and the Bible* (Grand Rapids: Eerdmans, 2012)

THE BIBLE IN JUDAISM The Hebrew Bible consists, as shown above, of Torah, Prophets, and Writings. Before presenting its formation in a concise manner, it should be highlighted that the Bible receives a different status in Judaism than the Holy Scriptures of the Old and New Testaments in Christianity. It is true that ancient witnesses such as 4 Ezra and Flavius Josephus offer clues about the acceptance of a clearly delineated corpus of writings of twenty-four or, as the case may be, twenty-two books that count as normative. However, the three-part Jewish Bible never received the same normative and exclusive status that was accorded the Bible in

Christianity. The conception of canon with respect to the collection of the books of the Bible is first attested for the Christian Bible from the fourth century CE. In Judaism, it only became common in the wake of its expansion to classical texts by classicist David Ruhnken (1723–1798) in his *Historia Graecorum Oratorum* (Leiden: Luchtmans, 1768). The acronym "Tanakh" as an abbreviation for Torah ("Law"), Nevi'im ("Prophets"), and Ketuvim ("Writings") is first attested in the Middle Ages.

After 70 CE, rabbinic Judaism developed its own tradition in the talmudic literature. It quickly became more important for religious performance than the Bible, which was essentially read and interpreted in the light of this traditional literature. In addition, the Torah moved to the forefront through its liturgical use, as it was read in its entirety, though in various arrangements.

The Prophets received a voice in the "Haftarot" (the readings from the prophetic books), but in a limited manner, while the Writings (except for the so-called "Megillot," that is, the books of Ruth, Song of Songs, Qoheleth, Lamentations, and Esther, assigned for reading at the five festivals of Shavu'ot, Pesach, Sukkot, Ninth of Ab, and Purim) do not have a set liturgical location. Thus the Talmud and Midrash take on marked importance in comparison with the Bible, and within the Bible there is a clear focus on the Torah.

TERMINOLOGY The fact that Judaism did not formulate a clear and universal designation for its "Bible" might be connected to this specific significance for the Tanakh. Ancient texts often speak of the "Law and the Prophets," "Moses and the Prophets," sometimes even only of the "Law" (*pars pro toto* for the Tanakh), and of the "Scriptures," the "Holy Scriptures," "God's book," or "the divine word." And there are many more examples one might add.[3] The fact that the Bible received a stable name quite late in Jewish tradition is related to the relative importance granted the Talmud in comparison with those texts. The Talmud, surpassed only by the Torah, became the predominant object of study in Jewish scholarship. Bible and tradition—"written and oral Torah," which according to Jewish traditions were both received on Sinai—were not viewed hierarchically in terms of their normativity in Judaism, and each was appreciated in a selective manner.

How was the Hebrew Bible formed into a coherent literary entity so that today it is called a "canon"? For the discussion of the order of the

3. Cf. Beckwith, *Old Testament Canon*, 105–7.

biblical writings, one should first introduce a distinction concerning the technology of books, namely the difference between the scroll and the codex. The common form of the book was the scroll. For a scroll, the material on which one wrote, whether leather or papyrus, was rolled onto two rods. The text would then be rolled out and rolled up so that one column came into view and could be' read. For practical reasons, such scrolls usually contained a single biblical book. The great Isaiah scroll from Qumran alone is over eight meters long. Use of the so-called codex, an early form of the modern book, first emerged in the Christian era. It was bound at the back and its pages could be turned to the desired portion of the text.[4]

From these observations it is clear that the question of the order of the biblical books is difficult to determine when using scrolls. Individual books appear on separate entities. How can one speak of an order? The order of the books also appears quite arbitrary in the period when the form of the text was no longer the scroll. Two observations are important here: First, redactional texts that reach beyond individual books in the Hebrew Bible indicate that the order of books was subject to editing (see below, Part E). Second, the practices of ancient libraries show that collections of individual scrolls were also intended to have a specific sequence. Therefore, one can also reckon with certain arrangements of books in the pre-Christian era, even if the larger part of the formation of the traditions of the Jewish Bible and the Christian Old Testament took place at a time when the codex was the customary form of the book.

1. The Closing of the Hebrew Bible at the Turn of the Era

Historically speaking, the Hebrew Bible in the sense of a complete list of holy writings, set in terms of its textual inventory, constitutes a post-biblical phenomenon. Or, to formulate it the other way around, the writings contained in the Bible, are, strictly speaking, *pre-biblical* and only become *biblical* through the process of canonization. The biblical texts from Qumran show that the texts of the Hebrew Bible were not fixed down to the letter at the turn of the era. While the individual books were quite stable in terms of their content, there were still different versions of the

---

4. Cf. Martin Wallraff, *Kodex und Kanon: Das Buch im frühen Christentum*, Hans-Lietzmann-Vorlesungen 12 (Berlin: de Gruyter, 2013).

same biblical book that continued to contain small variations. Neither does the inventory of "biblical" books appear set. At least in Qumran, the book of Jubilees and the Enochic literature do not appear to have been less important than what later turned out to be included in the standard inventory of canonical books. However, the prominence of the book of Jubilees and the Enochic literature in Qumran is also due to the nature of their content: they present a solar calendar of 364 days a year that accords with the cultic convictions of the Qumran community.

FLAVIUS JOSEPHUS The notion of the Hebrew canon as a closed collection of writings becomes more recognizable in witnesses from the late first century CE, in Josephus and 4 Ezra 14. In his apologetic polemic *Contra Apionem*, the Jewish historian Josephus characterizes the traditions of the Hebrew Bible as follows:

> For we do not have 10,000s of books among us, disagreeing from and contradicting one another, but only twenty-two books, which contain the records of all the past times [of the history of Israel]; which are justly believed to be trustworthy; and of them five belong to Moses, which contain his laws and the traditions of the origin of mankind till his death. This interval of time was little short of three thousand years; but as to the time from the death of Moses till the reign of Artaxerxes, king of Persia, who reigned after Xerxes, the prophets, who were after Moses, wrote down what was done in their times in thirteen books. The remaining four books contain hymns to God, and precepts for the conduct of human life. Our history has been written since Artaxerxes till our time very particularly, but it has not been esteemed to have the same authority with the former by our forefathers, because an exact succession of prophets has been absent since that time. (1.8, author's translation)

Josephus reckons with a set number of twenty-two biblical books, which conforms to the number of letters in the Hebrew alphabet, therefore denoting completeness and perfection. The categorization of books in his list is not totally clear. The thirteen "prophetic" books likely contain Job, Joshua, Judges (including Ruth), Samuel, Kings, Isaiah, Jeremiah (including Lamentations), Ezekiel, the Twelve, Daniel, Chronicles, Ezra-Nehemiah, and Esther, while the "remaining four" likely mean Psalms, Proverbs, Qoheleth, and Song of Songs. However, these identifications are not completely certain.[5] Josephus also provides a theory of prophetic authorship, which links the composition of the biblical books to an uninterrupted succession of prophets from Moses to the time of Artaxerses, under whom Ezra and Nehemiah appear in the biblical witness.

4 EZRA The book of 4 Ezra, an apocalypse from the last decade of the first century CE, lays out a theory of canon in its final chapter. It describes the renewed composition of the biblical and other books after they were burned in the destruction of Jerusalem. Ezra dictates them through divine inspiration to his circle of scribes:

> And the Most High gave understanding to the five men [the scribes to whom Ezra dictated], and by turns they wrote what was dictated, in characters which they did not know. They sat forty days, and wrote during the daytime, and ate their bread at night. As for me, I spoke in the daytime and was not silent at night. So during the forty days ninety-four books were written. And when the forty days were ended, the Most High spoke to me, saying, "Make public the twenty-four books that you wrote first and let the worthy and the unworthy read them; but keep the seventy that were written last, in order to give them to the wise among your people. For in them is the spring of understanding, the fountain of wisdom, and the river of knowledge." (4 Ezra 14:42–47)

The first twenty-four books are the Hebrew Bible. They are accessible to all, while the seventy other books are meant to remain hidden and apparently concern the "Apocrypha," to which 4 Ezra itself belongs.[6] Here as well there is a set number of books (twenty-four), which deviates from that of Josephus, but likely because it rests on an older tradition rather than that it represents a theologically loaded symbol like the number twenty-two in Josephus. The deviation in the number probably does not point to a differ-

---

5. Steve Mason, "Josephus and His Twenty-Two Book Canon," in *The Canon Debate*, ed. Lee M. McDonald and James A. Sanders (Peabody, MA: Hendrickson, 2002), 110–27.

6. Cf. Christian Macholz, "Die Entstehung des hebräischen Bibelkanons nach 4 Esra 14," in *Die hebräische Bibel und ihre zweifache Nachgeschichte: Festschrift für Rolf Rendtorff zum 65. Geburtstag,* ed. Erhard Blum (Neukirchen-Vluyn: Neukirchener Verlag, 1990), 379–91; Michael Becker, "Grenzziehungen des Kanons im frühen Judentum und die Neuschrift der Bibel nach 4. Buch Esra," in *Qumran und der biblische Kanon,* ed. Michael Becker and Jörg Frey, Biblisch-theologische Studien 92 (Neukirchen–Vluyn: Neukirchener Verlag, 2009), 195–253.

ent inventory of books. More likely Josephus subsumed Lamentations into Jeremiah and Ruth into Judges in order to come to the Hebrew number of completion of twenty-two books. The motif of prophetic authorship also appears in 4 Ezra 14 in Ezra's dictation.

THE SYNOD OF JAMNIA AS AN ACADEMIC FALLACY   The scholarship of the late nineteenth and early twentieth centuries often brought the verifiable evidence of a canon from Josephus and the book of 4 Ezra together with the assumption of a synod in Jamnia, which supposedly decided upon this canon. In 1871 Heinrich Grätz interpreted statements from the Mishnah and Talmud as supporting such a synod. While Jamnia did in fact become a center of Jewish scholarship after 70 CE, there was neither a synod that took place there, nor was the canonical nature of the writings of the Hebrew Bible as a whole discussed, but only the status of Qoheleth and Song of Songs.[7]

THE PROLOGUE OF BEN SIRA   These comparatively fixed conceptions of a closed collection of Hebrew writings in the first century CE stand, however, in stark contrast to quite different conceptions from the Second Temple Period. At that time the books of the Hebrew Bible were unstable with regard to both their extent and order. The prologue to the Greek translation of the book of Sirach, written by the author's grandson (ca. 132 BCE), is of great importance in this regard:[8]

> Many great teachings have been given to us through the Law and the Prophets and the [other writings] that followed them, and for these we should praise Israel for instruction and wisdom. . . . So my grandfather Jesus, who had devoted himself especially to the reading of the Law and the Prophets and the other books of our ancestors, and had acquired considerable proficiency in them, was himself also led to write something pertaining to instruction and wisdom, so that by becoming

---

7. Cf. Günter Stemberger, "Jabne und der Kanon," *JBTh* 3 (1988): 163–74.

8. Cf. Armin Lange, "The Law, the Prophets, and the Other Books of the Fathers (Sir, Prologue): Canonical Lists in Ben Sira and Elsewhere?," in *Studies in the Book of Ben Sira: Papers of the Third International Conference on the Deuterocanonical Books, Shime'on Centre, Pápa, Hungary, 18-20 May 2006*, ed. Géza G. Xeravits and József Zsengellér, JSJSup 127 (Leiden: Brill, 2008), 55–80; Benjamin G. Wright, "Why a Prologue? Ben Sira's Grandson and His Greek Translation," in *Emanuel: Studies in Hebrew Bible, Septuagint and Dead Sea Scrolls in Honor of Emanuel Tov*, ed. Shalom Paul et al., VTSup 94 (Leiden: Brill, 2003), 633–44.

familiar also with his book, those who love learning might make even greater progress in living according to the law. . . . Not only this book, but even the Law itself, the Prophecies, and the rest of the books differ not a little when read in the original. When I came to Egypt in the thirty-eighth year of the reign of Euergetes [132 BCE] and stayed for some time, I found opportunity for no little instruction. It seemed highly necessary that I should myself devote some diligence and labor to the translation of this book. During that time I have applied my skill day and night to complete and publish the book for those living abroad who wished to gain learning and are disposed to live according to the law.

Two elements in particular should be highlighted from this text. First, the introduction clearly demonstrates that the Hebrew Bible essentially consisted of two parts for Jesus Ben Sira's grandson: the Law and the Prophets. In addition to these two parts were "other" (or "leftover") books, to which—as the example from his grandfather shows—could be added further: "So my grandfather Jesus . . . was himself also led to write something pertaining to instruction and wisdom." According to this prologue, the inventory of books contains closed textual material in the Law and the Prophets, while the remaining books represent an open and generic category that can be extended.

A second feature is also recognizable: the Law receives a marked authority, which is demonstrated by the repetitious and emphatic manner of speech that points out the lifestyle according to the Law.

MOSES AND THE PROPHETS The Sirach prologue, with its quite open terminology "in the Law and in the Prophets as well as in the others [Writings]," does not yet presuppose the latter three-part Hebrew Bible. This is confirmed by witnesses from Qumran and the New Testament. At the turn of the era, the Hebrew Scriptures apparently consisted of essentially two parts, as indicated by the common expression "Moses and the Prophets" or similar (e.g., 1QS 1.1–2, "As [God] commanded through Moses and all his servants, the prophets"; 1QS 8.15–16; CD 5.21–6.2; 4QDibHam (=4Q504) frag. 2, 3.11–13; Luke 16:16, "The Law and the Prophets were in effect until John"; Luke 16:29, 31, "If they do not listen to Moses and the Prophets"; Luke 24:27, "Then beginning with Moses and all the Prophets, he interpreted to them what all the Scriptures say about him"; Acts 26:22; Acts 28:23, "both from the law of Moses and from the Prophets"). In addition to Moses and the Prophets, individual documents also explicitly attest to the

Psalms, e.g., 4QMMT^d (=4Q397): "so that you gain insight into the book of Moses [and] into the book[s of the pro]phets and into Davi[d's psalms]"; or Luke 24:44: "Everything must be fulfilled that is written about me in the law of Moses and in the Prophets and in the Psalms." However, on the basis of the note in the Psalms scroll 11QPs^a 27.11 that interprets the Psalms as the "prophecy" of David, one can assume that the Psalms were not counted as an addition to the prophets, but were a highlighted part of them:

> And [David] spoke all this through prophecy, which was given to him by the Exalted One. (11QPs^a 27.11)

The canon of the Hebrew Bible at the turn of the era appears to have been conceived primarily as a two-part textual entity. The three-part structure that later became familiar is not yet recognizable. Instead the bipolar and unevenly weighted unity of the "Law and Prophets" was reckoned as Scripture.

2. The Formation of the Torah

PERSIAN IMPERIAL AUTHORIZATION It can be recognized from the Hebrew Bible itself that its historical and functional core is the Torah, the so-called five books of Moses. Chronicles and Ezra-Nehemiah in particular refer to the Torah (cf. esp. Neh 8:1–8), which arguably already has in view a rather fixed collection of the books from Genesis to Deuteronomy. The translation in around 250 BCE of the Torah into Greek, called the Septuagint, also shows that this body of text was, on the one hand, considered authoritative and, on the other hand, that it was considered complete by this time.

The Torah can therefore be considered the oldest as well as the most important part of the scriptures that later developed into the canon. Yet how did the formation of the Torah take place? The answer to this question remains disputed. It seems somewhat concrete that it took place in the Persian period. A number of scholars link its compilation to the so-called Persian imperial authorization of local laws, which seemed to have played an important role.[9] The Persian Empire did not have a central system of laws. Instead, the peoples within the empire could live according to their own laws, as long as these laws received Persian authorization. Was the Torah the corpus of laws

---

9. Cf. Konrad Schmid, "Persische Reichsautorisation und Tora," *TR* 71 (2006): 494–506.

produced by the Jewish community in the province of Yehud for the Persian administration, according to which they wanted to live? It is conceivable, and the portrayal in Ezra 7 may contain a memory of such a process.[10] It is unsurprising that the Torah itself provides no detailed information. The Torah has no interest in disclosing its historical origins as a normative text; it receives its authority from the depiction of its connection to the revelation at Sinai.

In any case, the combination of quite heterogeneous material in the Torah speaks in favor of its formation within the framework of Persian imperial authorization. The conflicting content between the Deuteronomistic and Priestly sections of text, which differ above all else in their covenantal and legal theologies (cf. below, §§33–34) is especially conspicuous. The Torah bears clear signs of a theological and legal compromise, so its emergence is more easily conceived with the assumption of external pressure than without it.

3. Torah and Nevi'im

NEVI'IM AS A PRE-MACCABEAN COLLECTION The formation of the Torah was accompanied by a corresponding application and exegesis of the Torah in the collected prophetic books of Joshua–Malachi. The closing of the Nevi'im section of the canon (Joshua–Malachi) around 200 BCE led to the development of a commentary literature of its own, available especially in the pesharim from Qumran.[11] The fact that the Nevi'im was constructed in the pre-Maccabean period is revealed especially in the book of Daniel's inclusion in the Ketuvim. Daniel is a prophetic book, but it apparently could no longer make it into the Nevi'im because its composition took place in the Maccabean period. The literary content of Joshua–2 Kings and Isaiah–Malachi is earlier than the formation of the Torah, and one should likely reckon with the fact that the cores of Joshua–2 Kings and Isaiah–Malachi were just as normative as the growing corpus of the Torah at that time. However, in accompaniment with the formation of the Torah, these prophetic texts apparently underwent theological redaction and received a new orientation.

10. Cf. Sebastian Grätz, *Das Edikt des Artaxerxes: Eine Untersuchung zum religions-politischen und historischen Umfeld von Esr 7,12–26* (Berlin: de Gruyter, 2004), who argues for a Hellenistic date for Ezra 7.

11. Cf., e.g., Christian Metzenthin, *Jesaja-Auslegung in Qumran*, ATANT 98 (Zurich: TVZ, 2009).

The most conspicuous manifestation of this development is, in the first place, the reference to the "Torah of Moses" in numerous places within the section from Joshua–2 Kings (e.g., Josh 8:31–32; 23:6; 1 Kgs 2:3; 2 Kgs 14:6; 18:6, [12]; 21:8; 22:8–13; 23:25), as well as in Mal 3:22 (Eng. 4:4) in the prophetic books (cf. Dan 9:11). Apparently the stable written Torah of Genesis–Deuteronomy is in view, which is now meant to function as the standard for the actions of the king and the people in history (or rather, it should have functioned in that way). Historically speaking, this is anachronistic. However, after the formation of the Torah, it was understood as the standard for history insofar as it further developed the earlier Deuteronomistic interpretative perspective in Joshua–2 Kings and in books like Amos or Jeremiah, which determined the entirety of the law or the will of Yhwh as the criterion for the experience of salvation and disaster in history.

LITERARY FRAME OF THE NEVI'IM The *inclusio* around the entire Nevi'im section of the canon (Joshua–Malachi) created through Josh 1:7, 9 and Mal 3:22–24 (Eng. 4:4–6) is especially important. It subordinates this part of the canon to the Torah, while presenting itself as the interpretation of the Torah to its audience:

JOSH 1:7–8, 13:

Only be strong and very courageous, being careful to act in accordance with all the law that my *servant Moses* commanded you; do not turn from it to the right hand or to the left, so that you may be successful wherever you go. This book of the *law* shall not depart out of your mouth; you shall meditate on it day and night, so that you may be careful to act in accordance with all that is written in it. For then you shall make your way prosperous, and then you shall be successful. . . . *Remember* the word that *Moses the servant of the Lord commanded* you, saying, "The Lord your God is providing you a place of rest, and will give you this land."

MAL 3:22 (ENG. 4:4):

Remember the teaching of my servant Moses, the statutes and ordinances that I commanded him at Horeb for all Israel.

The reference of the first chapter to the last chapter of the Nevi'im and, *vice versa*, the reference from the last chapter to the first demonstrate that the perspective of these interpretive passages views all the intervening textual material from Joshua–2 Kings, and also the future, within the framework of success or failure based on the observance of the Torah.

THE CANONICAL COMPLETION OF THE BOOK OF THE TWELVE PROPHETS In the course of the formation of the Nevi'im as a part of the canon attached to the Torah, it appears that the book of Malachi was separated from the Zechariah tradition, of which it may originally have been part. This made the Minor Prophets into twelve, the number of completion, and the three Major and twelve Minor Prophets come to function as something of an analogy to Abraham, Isaac, and Jacob and the twelve tribal ancestors of Israel, the sons of Jacob. As a result, the Prophets parallel the Torah. The fact that the book of Malachi first emerged as an independent book through a redactional process is suggested—in addition to the structural uniformity of Mal 1:1 with the system of superscriptions in Zech 9:1; 12:1 as well as the connections in context (e.g., the citation of Zech 1:3 in Mal 3:7)—by the fact that the name "Malachi" is not attested in either the biblical or epigraphic evidence. It instead appears to be an artificial name taken from Mal 3:1, meaning "my messenger," coined from the promise of Elijah's return at the end of the book (Mal 3:23-24 [Eng. 4:5-6]). This reminiscence of Elijah, who according to 2 Kgs 2:11-12 did not die, but instead was taken up into heaven, appears to reflect the fact that prophecy as an actual phenomenon had ended, and a prophet with unmediated experience of God will arise once again when Elijah comes. Until that time, Israel is referred to the literary canon of the Prophets.

4. Ketuvim

The formation of the Ketuvim, which took place in a comparatively flexible construction (the order of the Writings varies quite considerably in the various manuscripts),[12] presupposes the closure of both the Torah and Nevi'im, and its content interfaces with both corpora. The Psalms likely form the core of the Ketuvim. They were possibly considered part of the Nevi'im before the formation of the Ketuvim, but the notion of a three-

12. Cf. Beckwith, *Old Testament Canon*, 449-68.

part canon obviously prevailed over a two-part Holy Scripture in Judaism. There were several discussions in the Judaism of the first and second centuries CE on the topic of which writings in the Ketuvim "render the hands unclean" (that is, are of canonical quality) and which are not. Especially Qoheleth and Song of Songs appear to have been controversial. What finally led to the formation of the Ketuvim is disputed and likely cannot be clarified beyond doubt. There are different hypotheses on the emergence of the Ketuvim. The standard hypothesis states that the Ketuvim were the melting pot of further authoritative literature after the closure of the Nevi'im. A second hypothesis views the emergence of the Ketuvim as an instrument to safeguard the tradition in the Maccabean period.[13] While a third hypothesis assesses the Ketuvim as an anthology of exemplary Jewish literary genres, which was set up to resist the cultural influence of Hellenism.[14] These hypotheses are neither mutually exclusive nor incorrect, but the nature of the theological content of the Ketuvim should be stressed more strongly. This concern—despite all divergences in detail—appears in the relationship of these newly formed writings with the Law and the Prophets, in their mundane everyday application.

§12 Reception and Transformation into the Old Testament

Anneli Aejmelaeus, "Die Septuaginta als Kanon," in *Kanon in Konstruktion und Dekonstruktion*: *Kanonisierungsprozesse religiöser Texte von der Antike bis zur Gegenwart: Ein Handbuch,* ed. Eve-Marie Becker and Stefan Scholz (Berlin: de Gruyter, 2012), 315–27 ◆ Jürgen Becker, *Mündliche und schriftliche Autorität im frühen Christentum* (Tübingen: Mohr Siebeck, 2012) ◆ Ivan Z. Dimitrov et al., eds., *Das Alte Testament als christliche Bibel in orthodoxer und westlicher Sicht*: *Zweite europäische orthodox-westliche Exegetenkonferenz im Rilakloster vom 8.–15. September 2001*, WUNT 174 (Tübingen: Mohr Siebeck, 2004) ◆ Heinz-Josef Fabry, "The Biblical Canon and Beyond: Theological and Historical Context of the Codices of Alexandria," in *Text-Critical and*

---

13. Beckwith, *Old Testament Canon.*

14. Albert de Pury, "Zwischen Sophokles und Ijob: Die Schriften (Ketubim): Ein jüdischer Literatur-Kanon," *Welt und Umwelt der Bibel* 28 (2003): 24–27; Bernhard Lang, "'The 'Writings': A Hellenistic Literary Canon in the Hebrew Bible," in *Canonization and Decanonization: Papers Presented to the International Conference of the Leiden Institute for the Study of Religion (LISOR). Held at Leiden 9–10 January 1997*, ed. Arie van der Kooij and Karel van der Toorn, SHR 82 (Leiden: Brill, 1997), 41–65.

Hermeneutical Studies in the Septuagint, ed. Johann Cook and Hermann-Josef Stipp, VTSup 157 (Leiden: Brill, 2012), 21–34 ◆ Wolfgang Hage, *Das orientalische Christentum* (Stuttgart: Kohlhammer, 2007) ◆ Thomas Hieke, ed., *Formen des Kanons: Studien zu Ausprägungen des biblischen Kanons von der Antike bis zum 19. Jahrhundert,* SBS 228 (Stuttgart: Katholisches Bibelwerk, 2013) ◆ Hermann von Lips, *Der neutestamentliche Kanon: Seine Geschichte und Bedeutung, Zürcher Grundrisse zur Bibel* (Zurich: TVZ, 2004) ◆ Tobias Nicklas, "The Development of the Christian Bible," in *What Is Bible?,* ed. Karin Finsterbusch and Armin Lange, CBET 67 (Leuven: Peeters, 2012), 393–426 ◆ Eugen J. Pentiuc, *The Old Testament in Eastern Orthodox Tradition* (Oxford: Oxford University Press, 2014)

1. The "Scriptures" in the New Testament

THE LAW AND THE PROPHETS Earliest Christianity—that is, the first generations of Christians after Paul—were familiar neither with an Old Testament nor a New Testament. There was not even a stable collection of literature, let alone one identified with this terminology. Predecessors did exist, of course. The Torah had been a completed unit since the late Persian period (that is, the end of the fourth century BCE) and was perceived as a normative corpus. Similarly, the prophetic books—in the larger sense including Joshua to Malachi, perhaps also including the Psalms and Daniel—were viewed as its complement. They were considered to be interpretations of the Torah and accorded differing levels of normativity. As a result, texts of the New Testament generally refer to Israel's scriptures as the Law and the Prophets:

> The *law and the prophets* were in effect until John came; since then the good news of the kingdom of God is proclaimed, and everyone tries to enter it by force. (Luke 16:16)
> Abraham replied, "They have *Moses and the prophets*; they should listen to them." (Luke 16:29)
> He said to him, "If they do not listen to *Moses and the prophets*, neither will they be convinced even if someone rises from the dead." (Luke 16:31)
> Then beginning with *Moses and all the prophets*, he interpreted to them what all the scriptures say about him. (Luke 24:27)
> Then he said to them, "These are my words that I spoke to you

while I was still with you—that everything written about me in the *law of Moses, the prophets, and the psalms* must be fulfilled." (Luke 24:44)

To this day I have had help from God, and so I stand here, testifying to both small and great, saying nothing but what *the prophets and Moses* said would take place. (Acts 26:22)

After they had fixed a day to meet him, they came to him at his lodgings in great numbers. From morning until evening he explained the matter to them, testifying to the kingdom of God and trying to convince them about Jesus both from *the law of Moses and from the prophets*. (Acts 28:23)

The New Testament writings, which are nevertheless not the focus here, were in turn first collected into a fixed collection of books in the second and third centuries CE. Several texts, such as the Pauline letters, were already prominent among the first Christians, not as a part of the New Testament but as the occasional writings that constituted their original emergence. Around 100 CE the Gospels were then added and over time became established in liturgical use, eventually becoming an integral part of the New Testament canon along with the other writings of the New Testament.

From the perspective of the history of theology, it is extraordinarily important that during the formation of the biblical canon, the writings of the New Testament were neither joined to the Hebrew Bible—in something like a fourth part of the canon after Law, Prophets, and Writings—nor made superior to the Hebrew Bible as the normative interpretive authority for the Hebrew Bible.[15] Christianity instead came up with a double canon in which neither part is superior or inferior to the other. The balance of this relationship has gone through more and less stable phases throughout the history of Christianity, but the basic parameters of the forthright categorization have never been abolished.

Early Christianity was, sociologically speaking, originally a Jewish sect. The acceptance of the mission to the gentiles then initiated a break with Judaism, from which it became increasingly distanced. These developments also exercised a formative influence on Judaism, whose mission-

---

15. There are a small number of examples of the intermixture of Old and New Testament books in the canon lists and biblical manuscripts, such as the attribution of the Wisdom of Solomon to the New Testament in the Muratorian Canon and the mixture of Old and New Testament writings in several Vulgate manuscripts. Cf. Peter Brandt, *Endgestalten des Kanons: Das Arrangement der Schriften Israels in der jüdischen und christlichen Bibel*, BBB 131 (Berlin: Philo, 2001), 352 n. 1706.

ary activities gradually disappeared as it went on to formulate its identity as clearly distinct from the spreading Christianity. As a result, not only did Christianity emerge from Judaism, but in a certain sense Judaism also developed out of Christianity.[16]

2. Did the Septuagint Develop a Separate Canon?

It was only in the churches of the Reformation that the Hebrew Bible came to be identified as the Old Testament—in something of a hybrid form that adopted the number of books but not the order of the Hebrew Bible. Until that point in time, the books of the Old Testament were those of the Septuagint and Vulgate, that is, the Greek and Latin translations of the Hebrew Bible, as well as several additional books originally written in Greek. The Old Testament of the eastern churches was read primarily in Greek, while Latin was read in the West.

THE FORMATION OF THE SEPTUAGINT The Greek translation of the Hebrew Bible, the so-called Septuagint (Greek for "seventy"), began to emerge from the middle of the third century BCE onward in Alexandria. The Letter of Aristeas provides a legendary account of its origins: Ptolemy, the Egyptian king, commissioned seventy-two men from Jerusalem to translate the Torah in Greek for his library in Alexandria. The translation of the Torah led to the high regard for the Torah in the Hellenistic world. On the flip side, the translation was likely one of the decisive factors for the literary closure of the Hebrew Torah; a Torah that has already been translated can no longer be successfully extended. The translation of the Torah was followed by the translation of the other books of the Hebrew Bible into the second century CE. The books were generally translated by one, sometimes two, translators, so the translation techniques vary from extremely literal to relatively free. As a result, the Septuagint constitutes a conglomeration of a variety of individual translations, such that the theological nature of each book must be investigated.

CHRISTIAN OR JEWISH ORDER? The Christian Old Testament of the Septuagint and the Vulgate differs from the Hebrew Bible in terms of both

16. Cf. Peter Schäfer, *Die Geburt des Judentums aus dem Christentum* (Tübingen: Mohr Siebeck, 2010).

the extent and the order of its books. The Bibles of the Reformation relegated all books not belonging to the Hebrew Bible to the Apocrypha, but they still adopted the later standard order found in the Septuagint and the Vulgate (the older codices display a certain degree of variation; cf. below, §17), which group the historical books together at the beginning of the Old Testament, the poetic books in the middle, and the prophetic books at the end. It is debated whether or not this arrangement, with the prophetic books at the end of the Septuagint canon, goes back to the Hellenistic Jewish tradition in Alexandria. In that case, the librarians would have instituted a rather genre-oriented structure to the biblical books. Or perhaps this order arose in Christian circles. It is documented in the large Christian codices (which contain differences with respect to details; cf. below, Part E), while the prologue of Sirach, which originated in Alexandria, is oriented toward the Torah, Prophets, and Writings order.[17] Furthermore, placing the prophets in the final position appears most likely to serve Christian theological interests: then the Old Testament and the New Testament relate to one another as the prophecy of the Christ and the fulfillment of this prophecy in the emergence of Jesus of Nazareth.

3. The Old Testament in the Early Church

In the course of the second century CE, the New Testament began to take shape out of the writings of the New Testament that had apparently come to enjoy a special liturgical function. However, only Marcion[18] and certain streams of Gnosticism led to the dismissal of what had to that point been the Holy Scripture of the early Christians, the Old Testament. Early Christianity did not question whether or not one should accept the Hebrew Bible. The Hebrew Bible had always been taken for granted as the Holy Scripture of early Christianity. The disputes with the heresies of the second century—as they were later identified—led to the formation of a proper corpus of writings that safeguarded the identity of the early church. The New Testament that resulted was, therefore, neither understood nor conceived as a fourth section of the canon of the Hebrew Bible, nor was

17. It is possible that Sir 39:1 presupposes the progression Law—Wisdom—Prophets, but it is unclear whether this text is even considering the order of books.

18. Sebastian Moll, *The Arch-Heretic Marcion*, WUNT 250 (Tübingen: Mohr Siebeck, 2010).

it considered explicitly superior or inferior to the Old Testament. Instead, early Christianity established a double canon—a singularity in terms of the history of religion—which combined differing voices and embedded a fundamental reciprocal interpretive dynamic in the canon.

REACTION TO MARCION? Hans von Campenhausen's classic hypothesis that the formation of the New Testament canon should be understood as a reaction to Marcion remains disputed in current scholarship.[19] Marcion likely had some influence on the discussion. The development of a New Testament as a whole should be interpreted as a consequence of the further development of the divergent theologies in the New Testament as the second century progressed. At the same time, however, the New Testament canon did not fundamentally curtail these divergences. It instead largely integrated them, as the admission of four Gospels—rather than only one Gospel as in Marcion, the Didache, or Tatian—shows quite impressively.[20] As a result, the New Testament canon that was developed preserved the theological polyphony of early Christianity. The fact that early Christianity managed to maintain its collective identity in this process is due in large part to the continuation of the self-evident—and then deliberate after Marcion—acceptance of the Old Testament as Holy Scripture.

The term "Old Covenant" (παλαιὰ διαθήκη) is first attested in Melito of Sardis (cited in Eusebius, *Historia ecclesiastica* 4.26.14).[21] However, the differentiation between "Old" and "New Testament" was not yet entrenched in common parlance. Melito does offer a list for the Old Testament that largely agrees with b. B. Batra 14b–15a: Pentateuch, Joshua, Judges, Ruth, 4 books of Kings (= 1–2 Samuel, 1–2 Kings), 2 books of Chronicles, Psalms of David, Proverbs of Solomon or Wisdom, Qoheleth, Song of Songs, Job, Isaiah, Jeremiah, Book of the Twelve Prophets, Daniel, Ezekiel, and Ezra.[22]

19. Hans von Campenhausen, *Die Entstehung der christlichen Bibel*, BHT 39 (Tübingen: Mohr Siebeck, 1968, repr. 2003), 198–202, trans. as *The Formation of the Christian Bible*, trans. J. A. Baker (Philadelphia: Fortress, 1972), 170–75.

20. Cf. Gerd Theißen, *Die Religion der ersten Christen: Eine Theorie des Urchristentums* (Gütersloh: Gütersloher Verlagshaus, 2000), 356–84.

21. Rudolf Mosis, "Die Bücher des 'Alten Bundes' bei Melito von Sardes," in *Schätze der Schrift: Festgabe für Hans F. Fuhs zur Vollendung seines 65. Lebensjahres*, ed. Ansgar Moenikes, Paderborner theologische Studien 47 (Paderborn: Schöningh, 2007), 131–76.

22. Esther is conspicuously omitted from this list, which coincides with the evidence in Athanasius's Easter Letter from 367 CE. He offers a list of writings for the Old (and New) Tes-

In Clement of Alexandria (*Strom.* i.5; 5.85) and Origen (*Comm. Jo.* 10.28; *Princ.* 4.1.1) the terminology appears to have solidified and become increasingly established in the church. In Tertullian both *testamentum* as well as *instrumentum* still appear as translations for διαθήκη (*diathēkē*), but the concept of *Testament* prevailed. This makes it clear that both διαθήκη as well as *testamentum* carry out particular biblical-theological interpretations of the entire text. At the same time, the emergence of this concept is so late that it is just as clear that the formation of the Old and New Testaments did not take place under the guiding principle of "covenant" or "testament."

The Third Council of Carthage (397 CE) settled the liturgical use of Scripture. Its resolution envisions "that other than the canonical writings, nothing should be read in the church under the title of Holy Scripture. The canonical writings are: Genesis, Exodus, Leviticus, Numbers, Deuteronomy, Joshua, Judges, Ruth, four books of Kings [1–2 Samuel, 1–2 Kings], two books of Chronicles, Job, Davidic Psalter, five books of Solomon [Proverbs, Ecclesiates, Song of Songs, Wisdom of Solomon, Sirach], the book of the Twelve Prophets, Isaiah, Jeremiah [also including Lamentations, Baruch, the Epistle of Jeremiah], Daniel, Ezekiel, Tobit, Judith, Esther, Ezra–Nehemiah, 1–2 Maccabees."[23]

Jerome, the translator of the Vulgate, the authoritative translation of the Bible into Latin, displays a certain consciousness of the different status of the additional books in the Septuagint. He returns to the Hebrew for his translation of the Hebrew Bible, yet he still included these additional Greek writings into his work. In accordance with the so-called *prologus galeatus* ("helmeted preface"), which appears as an introduction to the books of Samuel and Kings, he classified Wisdom, Sirach, Judith, and Tobit as non-canonical (*non sunt canone*).

---

taments, and adds, "There are also other books in addition to these, that while not canonical, the fathers have determined that they should be read aloud to those who have been newly added and wish to be taught in the pious word: Wisdom of Solomon, the Wisdom of Sirach, Esther, Judith, Tobit; [for the New Testament] that called the Didache and the Shepherd."

23. Heinrich Denzinger and Peter Hünermann, *Enchiridion symbolorum definitionum et declarationum de rebus fidei et morum = Kompendium der Glaubensbekenntnisse und kirchlichen Lehrentscheidungen*, 40th ed. (Freiburg im Breisgau: Herder, 2004), 186: "ut praeter scripturas canonicas nihil in ecclesia legatur sub nomine divinarum scripturarum. Sunt autem canonicae scripturae: Genesis, Exodus, Leviticus, Numeri, Deuteronomium, Jesu Nave, Iudicum, Rut, Regnorum libri quattuor, Paralipomena libri duo, Iob, Psalterium Davidicum, Salomonis libri quinque, duodecimi libri Prophetarum, Esaias, Ieremias, Daniel, Ezechiel, Tobias, Iudit, Hester, Hesdrae libri duo, Maccabeorum libri duo."

The churches of the East vary strongly with regard to the inventory of writings in their Old Testaments. In terms of the Old Testament, the canon of the Ethiopic church is especially noteworthy; it has maintained writings such as the books of Enoch and Jubilees over the centuries until today, books that Judaism stopped passing on after 70 CE, such that the original Semitic versions only became accessible once more through the discovery of the writings from the Dead Sea.

The Reformation marks an important break in the history of the Old Testament in Christianity. Luther translated both parts of the Christian Bible from their original languages, in accordance with humanistic principles, so the Hebrew Bible was translated from Hebrew and Aramaic. This conforms to the inventory of texts in the Protestant Hebrew Bible. The order of the writings, however, follows the tradition of the Septuagint or rather the Vulgate. The writings of the Septuagint not found in the Tanakh, the "Apocrypha," appear in the German Lutherbibel (Luther Bible) of 1534 as a separate section between the Old and New Testaments under the superscription "Apocrypha: These are books that are not equal to the Holy Scripture and yet are useful and good to read," namely: Judith, Wisdom, Tobit, Sirach, Baruch along with the Epistle of Jeremiah, Maccabees, as well as parts of Esther and Daniel.

The German Zürcher Bibel (Zurich Bible) from 1531, which is therefore marginally older than the first Luther Bible, places the Apocrypha after the historical books from Genesis to Kings, Chronicles, Ezra-Nehemiah, and Esther. It includes 1 Esdras, 2 Esdras, Wisdom of Solomon, Sirach, Tobit, Baruch, Judith, Additions to Esther, 1–3 Maccabees, Susanna, and Bel and the Dragon. Following this first section (historical books) are Job, Psalms, Proverbs, Qoheleth, Song of Songs, Isaiah, Jeremiah, Ezekiel, and the twelve Minor Prophets. The integration of the Apocrypha continued into the seventeenth century, after which the Zurich Bible aligned itself with the Luther Bible to present the Apocrypha as an appendix to the Old Testament.

In reaction to the shorting of the Old Testament canon in the course of the Reformation's new translations of the Bible, the Roman Catholic Church at the Council of Trent in 1546 codified the inventory of texts of the Vulgate as the binding canon and declared the Vulgate the authoritative edition of Scripture (*session* IV on April 8, 1546):[24]

---

24. Denzinger and Hünermann, *Enchiridion*, 1501–6.

The 5 books of Moses, namely Genesis, Exodus, Leviticus, Numbers, Deuteronomy, Joshua, Judges, Ruth, 4 books of Kings, 2 books of Chronicles, the first book of Esdras and the second, which is called Nehemiah, Tobit, Judith, Esther, Job, David's book of Psalms with 150 Psalms. The Proverbs, Ecclesiastes, the Song of Songs, Wisdom, Sirach, Isaiah, Jeremiah with Baruch, Ezekiel, Daniel, the Twelve Minor Prophets, namely Hosea, Joel, Amos, Obadiah, Jonah, Micah, Nahum, Habakkuk, Zephaniah, Haggai, Zechariah, Malachi, 2 books of Maccabees, the first and second.[25]

4. Present Discussions about Nomenclature

The inventory of texts known in Christianity as the "Old Testament" can be characterized in fundamentally different ways. Within the Christian sphere, several alternative descriptions have taken hold because a certain unease with the terminology "Old Testament" has arisen in some contexts. Here and there the designation is taken as disparaging insofar as the Old Testament, under this name, is subordinated to the New Testament from the outset. Therefore, Christian circles also speak of the "Hebrew Bible," the "Jewish Bible," and the "First Testament." With regard to these designations, initially one can say that in principle they are neither appropriate nor inappropriate. Instead, they can and should vary according to the context of the use. On the flip side, however, they could also be right or wrong depending on the context. For example, when Old Testament is replaced by "Jewish Bible" and the New Testament by "Christian Bible" in Hubertus Halbfas's Bible with commentary,[26] this is inaccurate from two perspectives. What is presented by him as the Old Testament—or rather the selection he has made—is not the Jewish Bible: this would instead have been structured as Torah, Nevi'im, and Ketuvim. The New Testament is in no way the "Christian Bible" because the Christian Bible consists of the Old and New Testaments.

One can speak of "Hebrew Bible" when viewing what is called "Old Testament" in Christianity from a confessionally neutral or Jewish, but in any case non-Christian point of view. One should, however, be clear that

---

25. Denzinger and Hünermann, *Enchiridion*, 1502.

26. Hubertus Halbfas, *Die Bibel, erschlossen und kommentiert durch Hubertus Halbfas* (Düsseldorf: Patmos, 2001).

the Hebrew Bible also includes Aramaic portions (in Daniel and Ezra-Nehemiah), so the designation "Hebrew Bible" is particularly precise.

One can speak of "Old Testament" when looking at this inventory of texts as the first part of the Christian Bible. The designation "Jewish Bible" (or "Tanakh" or "Mikra") is recommended when addressing those texts as the Holy Scripture of Judaism.

Finally, the terminology "First Testament" has newly entered the discussion.[27] This concerns a neologism of the twentieth century that attempts to avoid the (apparently) discriminatory bias of the designation "Old Testament." Three considerations show that this designation is inadvisable. First, "Old Testament" only means "Out-of-Date Testament" for those thinking anachronistically. In antiquity, the old was better than the new. Secondly, a "Second" or "New" Testament would also supersede a "First" Testament, so the problem under discussion remains. And thirdly, it can be argued that the terminology of the "First Testament" is largely without tradition. While one can find a biblical reference point in the Letter to the Hebrews, which speaks of a "first covenant" (9:15), throughout the centuries of church history there is no attestation of the use of the terminology "First Testament."

§13 The Meaning and Relativity of the Canon for a Theology of the Hebrew Bible

Bernd Janowski, "Kanon und Sinnbildung: Perspektiven des Alten Testaments," in *Schriftprophetie: Festschrift für Jörg Jeremias zum 65. Geburtstag,* ed. Friedhelm Hartenstein et al. (Neukirchen-Vluyn: Neukirchener Verlag, 2004), 15–36 ♦ Stefan Krauter, "Brevard S. Childs' Programm einer Biblischen Theologie: Eine Untersuchung seiner systematisch-theologischen und methodologischen Fundamente," *ZTK* 96 (1999): 22–48 ♦ Christoph Landmesser, ed., *Normative Erinnerung: Der biblische Kanon zwischen Tradition und Konstruktion* (Leipzig: Evangelische Verlagsanstalt, 2014) ♦ Martin Ohst, "Aus

27. Cf. Erich Zenger, *Das erste Testament: Die jüdische Bibel und die Christen* (Düsseldorf: Patmos, 1998); Thomas Staubli, *Begleiter durch das Erste Testament,* 4th ed. (Düsseldorf: Patmos, 2010); John Goldingay, *Israel's Gospel,* vol. 1 of *Old Testament Theology* (Downers Grove, IL: InterVarsity Press, 2010), 15; James A. Sanders, "The 'First' or 'Old' Testament: What to Call the First Christian Testament," in *The Old Testament: Its Authority and Canonicity,* vol. 1 of *The Formation of the Biblical Canon,* ed. Lee M. McDonald (London: Bloomsbury, 2017), 36–38.

den Kanondebatten in der Evangelischen Theologie des 19. Jahrhunderts," in *Kanon in Konstruktion und Dekonstruktion: Kanonisierungsprozesse religiöser Texte von der Antike bis zur Gegenwart: Ein Handbuch*, ed. Eve-Marie Becker and Stefan Scholz (Berlin: de Gruyter, 2012), 39–70 ◆ Rolf Rendtorff, "The Importance of the Canon for a Theology," in *Canon and Theology: Overtures to an Old Testament Theology*, trans. Margaret Kohl, OBT (Minneapolis: Fortress, 1993)

The concentration on the Protestant and Catholic Old Testaments in their consolidated forms of transmission that came into play in the sixteenth century is important for the reception history and organization of the scholarly field. However, it should still be highlighted that the later canonical structure cannot be accorded the final say with regard to the limits of a historically oriented theology of the Hebrew Bible. This should receive special emphasis with respect to a theology of the Hebrew Bible understood to orient itself explicitly and decidedly as "canonical." Such canonically oriented theologies of the Hebrew Bible arose in part out of a certain weariness with regard to the uncertainties and divergences of historical-critical scholarship on the Old Testament. They attempt to find secure footing through the "canon."

THE POLYMORPHISM OF THE CANON In response, weighty historical reasons for the relativization of the canon can be invoked. They appear first and foremost in the variety of forms of the canon in different religious communities and churches, as well as in the differences in content within the canon. However, the decisive reason—at least in terms of a Protestant perspective— is theological: Christianity is not a religion of the book, and neither is the Bible a "paper pope," as Protestant dogmatics sometimes expresses the matter in polemical fashion. Every description of a formal, higher authority to the Bible—beyond everything that its content states and provides for consideration—must confront the charge of an authoritarian conception of the Bible.

The boundaries of the canon cannot serve fundamentally as absolute for a historically oriented approach to the theology of the Hebrew Bible. In the ancient Judaism of the second century BCE, other literature emerged alongside what later became canonical writings. These writings were also dedicated to the theological pursuit of treating and resolving difficulties in the preexisting tradition. They are highly important for the reconstruction of the historically complex thought world of the Bible, particularly because they are reckoned as part of the Bible in some canons.

Belonging to this group is, for example, the book of Jubilees, often called "little Genesis." It offers a retelling of Gen 1 to Exod 24, showing how Israel's ancestors could have followed the law, even though they did not have it. A narrative of an angel explaining the retelling to Moses on Sinai frames the story. The message of the book of Jubilees clearly lies in a Mosaic coloration of the primeval and ancestral narratives, so that they too can be gathered under the Torah theology that begins in Exodus with the onset of the Moses story. The book of Jubilees resolves this problem through "heavenly tablets" revealed to the ancestors of Genesis so that they can live in conformity to the law.

As a result, indications appear which show that this revelatory resolution of the "heavenly tablets" depends on a later interpretation. The earliest layer of the book of Jubilees might possibly have understood the ancestors' obedience to the law as intuitive adherence to the law—in the sense of a natural law—which gave rise to a re-interpretation of an explicit theology of law.

If this proposal is accepted, then even one of the fundamental questions driving the book of Jubilees—how could the law be valid even before its promulgation by Moses?—would have been treated in the course of another theological question that results from the first: how explicit could the law have been before Moses? However, even without the distinction between natural and revealed Law, the theological orientation of the book of Jubilees emerges.

The Enoch literature has primarily been preserved through its reception into the Old Testament of the Ethiopic church. Remains of the Aramaic text of the original have come to light since 1947 in Qumran. The Enoch manuscripts, which were yet to be combined into a book of Enoch at Qumran, give insight into a discrete apocalyptic thought world whose idiosyncrasies have even led to the postulation of a particularly "Enochic Judaism"[28] that led to the background for the composition of this literature. The book of Watchers (1 En 1–36) should be highlighted. It offers a wide-ranging elaboration of the biblical episode of the union between the sons of God and the daughters of humans from Gen 6:1–4, using this as a point of departure to describe the revelation of heavenly secrets to humanity.[29]

---

28. Cf. Gabriele Boccaccini, *Beyond the Essene Hypothesis: The Parting of the Ways between Qumran and Enochic Judaism* (Grand Rapids: Eerdmans, 1998).

29. Cf. Veronika Bachmann, *Die Welt im Ausnahmezustand: Eine Untersuchung zu Aussagegehalt und Theologie der Wächterbuches (1 Hen 1–36)*, BZAW 409 (Berlin: de Gruyter, 2009).

Not least because of the ascription to a pre-Mosaic bearer of revelation, Enoch, the literature became suspect and its reception stopped in rabbinic Judaism.

Also of value from the perspective of theological history are the prophetic commentaries, the so-called pesharim from Qumran. The pesharim follow the order of the text of a biblical book of prophecy and exegete its statements for their own time in the second century BCE. This prophetic hermeneutic also influences the literature of the New Testament; the Gospel of Matthew relates statements from the book of Isaiah without hesitation to the time of Jesus's appearance.

Finally, one can reference the so-called Temple Scroll (=11Q19–21), which also came to light as part of the discovery of the scrolls from the Dead Sea. Various markers indicate that it was not composed by the Qumran community itself, but is instead of pre-Qumran origins. As a result of its directives for the building of a temple that take the biblical prescriptions from the Priestly document (Exod 25–29 and 35–40) as well as the book of Ezekiel (Ezek 40–48) into account, it has been labeled the "Temple Scroll" in scholarship. The text has unfortunately not been completely preserved. It begins first with column 2, in which the adoption of Exod 34:1–16 interwoven with Deut 7:25–26 can be recognized, so the imagined narrative setting apparently concerns the revelation of the law prior to the conquest of the land. However, the Temple Scroll cannot be interpreted with certainty as presenting itself as an additional revelation from Sinai, because the Temple Scroll apparently views the promulgation of the law at Sinai and in the Transjordan (biblically speaking the location where Deuteronomy was delivered) as one, which it rearranges thematically and reformulates into the first-person speech of God. It is possible that the Temple Scroll also intends to be understood as superseding the Torah, but the extant text does not allow for a conclusive judgment.

It is clear in either case, however, that the Temple Scroll is a theological text both in terms of its interpretive method and in the literal sense. It attempts to produce a systematic order of the Torah and passes on its position as direct divine speech. However, the steep demands of the Temple Scroll apparently faded away in ancient Judaism—not one allusion to the Temple Scroll appears in the literature of the Qumran community that at least preserved the text, despite its close relationship in content to the highly esteemed book of Jubilees, with regard to the solar calendar, for example.

CENTER AND PERIPHERY From a historical perspective, instead of the strict differentiation between canonical and non-canonical texts, it is advisable to adopt the model of a center of recognized texts that is surrounded by different concentric circles of further writings that established themselves to successively lesser degrees in Judaism and Christianity. What belongs to the center and to the periphery depends on multiple factors determined more by historical coincidence than by the importance of the content of each text. The subsequent discussion focuses primarily on those texts, fields of texts, and themes that became especially prominent in the history of reception, though less known voices should also be given a hearing.

D. Methodological Reflections

The presentation thus far has adequately shown that no project of a theology of the Hebrew Bible is currently capable of reaching a consensus. Clarification is necessary not only with regard to the formulation of the problem reflecting the history of scholarship (see above, B) and the textual basis (see above, C), but also the basic methodological perspective. Namely, how is theology of the Hebrew Bible distinct from closely related questions about the Hebrew Bible? And, what is the authoritative basis for adjudicating between various points of view?

The following attempt to determine the relationships between positions does not intend to play right and wrong alternatives against one another. It will instead begin by demarcating various approaches and describing their specific character (even when such categorization will in turn remain disputed). The most controversial questions surrounding a theology of the Hebrew Bible—whether it be descriptive or normative; oriented toward history or the present; a Christian, a Jewish, or a Hebrew Bible endeavor—should for logical reasons not be decided axiomatically in one direction or another. They should instead be categorized and weighed in relation to one another. Theology of the Hebrew Bible can, for example, by all means be understood as a normative or a Christian endeavor, but such decisions bring into play basic convictions that assume developments from the history of scholarship, and these decisions should therefore be made with cognizance of the historical developments.

At the same time, the following considerations will not be limited merely to the categorization of the issues. They are more concerned with justifying the approach taken in this book. It would be foolish to deny that other possible approaches exist for a theology of the Hebrew Bible. Other approaches are also likely to be worthwhile. It is only a question of the particular end one has in mind. The goal of the approach proposed here is a theology of the Hebrew Bible that works, on the one hand, with

an explicit historical orientation and, on the other, is oriented toward a
clear division of tasks with other perspectives on theology. This approach
is bound to a particular theological and academic tradition, and, as such,
neither the method nor the result of this study produces truths of reason,
but rather—as with its object—historically contingent truths.

§14 Comparative Definitions

John Barton, "Should Old Testament Scholarship Be More Theological?,"
ExpTim 100 (1989): 443–48 ◆ Joachim Becker, *Grundzüge einer Hermeneu-
tik des Alten Testaments* (Frankfurt am Main: Lang, 1993) ◆ Achim Behrens,
*Das Alte Testament verstehen: Die Hermeneutik des ersten Teils der christlichen
Bibel*, Einführungen in das Alte Testament 1 (Göttingen: Ruprecht, 2013) ◆
Ingolf U. Dalferth, ed., *Eine Wissenschaft oder Viele? Die Einheit evangelischer
Theologie in der Sicht ihrer Disziplinen*, Forum Theologische Literaturzeitung
17 (Leipzig: Evangelische Verlagsanstalt, 2006) ◆ Christoph Dohmen and
Günter Stemberger, *Hermeneutik der Jüdischen Bibel und des Alten Testa-
ments*, Kohlhammer Studienbücher Theologie 1,2 (Stuttgart: Kohlhammer,
1996) ◆ Reinhard Feldmeier and Hermann Spieckermann, *God of the Living:
A Biblical Theology*, trans. Mark E. Biddle (Waco: Baylor, 2011) ◆ Jaco Ger-
icke, *The Hebrew Bible and Philosophy of Religion* (Atlanta: SBL Press, 2012)
◆ Elisabeth Gräb-Schmidt and Reiner Preul, eds., *Das Alte Testament in der
Theologie*, Marburger Jahrbuch Theologie 25, Marburger theologische Studien
119 (Leipzig: Evangelische Verlagsanstalt, 2013) ◆ Antonius H. J. Gunneweg,
Vom Verstehen des Alten Testaments: Eine Hermeneutik, 2nd ed., GAT 5 (Göttingen: Vandenhoeck & Ruprecht, 1988); 1st ed. trans. as *Understanding the
Old Testament*, OTL (London: SCM, 1978) ◆ Hans-Jürgen Hermisson, *Alttestamentliche Theologie und Religionsgeschichte Israels*, Forum Theologische Literaturzeitung 3 (Leipzig: Evangelische Verlagsanstalt, 2000) ◆ Hans Hübner
and Bernd Jaspert, eds., *Biblische Theologie: Entwürfe der Gegenwart*, Biblisch-
theologische Studien 38 (Neukirchen-Vluyn: Neukirchener Verlag, 1999) ◆
Bernd Janowski, ed., *Theologie und Exegese des Alten Testaments, der Hebräischen Bibel: Zwischenbilanz und Zukunftsperspektiven*, SBS 200 (Stuttgart:
Katholischer Bibelwerk, 2005) ◆ Bernd Janowski, "Vergegenwärtigung und
Wiederholung: Anmerkungen zu G. von Rads Konzept der 'Heilsgeschichte,'"
in *Heil und Geschichte: Die Geschichtsbezogenheit des Heils und das Problem der
Heilsgeschichte in der biblischen Tradition und in der theologischen Deutung*,
ed. Jörg Frey et al., WUNT 248 (Tübingen: Mohr Siebeck, 2009), 37–61 ◆

Manfred Oeming, *Biblische Hermeneutik: Eine Einführung*, 4th ed. (Darmstadt: Wissenschaftliche Buchgesellschaft, 2013) ♦ Konrad Schmid, "Sind die Historisch-Kritischen kritischer geworden? Überlegungen zu Stellung und Potential der Bibelwissenschaften," *Jahrbuch für Biblische Theologie* 25 (2011): 63–78 ♦ Konrad Schmid, "Dogmatik als konsequente Exegese? Überlegungen zur Anschlussfähigkeit der historisch-kritischen Bibelwissenschaft an die Systematische Theologie," *EvT* 77 (2017): 327–38 ♦ Hermann Spieckermann, "Das neue Bild der Religionsgeschichte Israels—eine Herausforderung der Theologie?," *ZTK* 105 (2008): 259–80 ♦ Hermann Spieckermann, "'YHWH Bless You and Keep You': The Relation of History of Israelite Religion and Old Testament Theology Reconsidered," *SJOT* 23 (2009): 165–82

NEIGHBORING AND RELATED QUESTIONS TO A THEOLOGY OF THE HEBREW BIBLE The discussion concerning the methodological approach and implementation of a theology of the Hebrew Bible can be simultaneously disencumbered and refined by shaping the question as neighboring, rather than covering the same ground as, comparable interpretive approaches to the Hebrew Bible. The divisions of the disciplines or subdisciplines of theology are not chiseled in stone. This is appropriate because scholarship must not adjust the objects of study according to the discipline, but rather the opposite; disciplines conform to the peculiarities of their object.

At the same time, it is reasonable to separate different questions from one another with a twofold aim: one is to formulate the issues of a discipline as coherently as possible, and the other is to ease the burden of each question as much as possible.

THEOLOGY AND CONTEMPORARY RELEVANCE A possible misunderstanding from Part A should be recalled, namely the idea that a theology of the Hebrew Bible is only actually "theological" if it provides a kerygmatic and contemporary message. And if this is not the case, it is either not a theology, or is only theological to a limited degree. The orientation from the history of scholarship in Part B has already demonstrated that the goal of a theology of the Hebrew Bible to provide immediate contemporary relevance represents a comparatively recent demand. It stems from the first three decades of the twentieth century and is connected with a related reorientation with regard to defining what is meant by "theology." From a certain historical distance, this view can now be evaluated in an unbiased manner as one of a number of options. As to how "theological" a theology of the Hebrew Bible is judged to be, this depends on various factors of reception that should not be privileged in a particular way. Especially in view of a theology of the Hebrew Bible, one must stipulate that "theological" cannot come at the expense of "Hebrew Bible" or "historical," if one attempts to avoid succumbing to a kind of pseudo-Docetism in theology. A "theology of the Hebrew Bible" is not by default "more theological" if it has a less "historical" orientation. Instead it runs the risk of missing the mark with regard to critical methodology.

1. The History of Israelite Religion

The similarity of the content of a history of Israelite religion to a theology of the Hebrew Bible[1] is evident merely in the many conceptions of a theology that contain a religious historical outline.[2] Nevertheless, the questions should be clearly distinguished from one another. Janowski distinguishes the different tasks of a history of Israelite religion from a theology of the Hebrew Bible as follows:

> The history of Israelite religion investigates the historical context of traditions of the Hebrew Bible and the religious, cultural, and historical circumstances behind them. Theology of the Hebrew Bible inquires about the traditions of the Hebrew Bible in their literary and redaction-historical context, as well as their theological shape.[3]

---

1. On the issue of a "historical theology of the Hebrew Bible," see below, §21.

2. Especially characteristic is the two-volume project by Ernst Sellin, *Alttestamentliche Theologie auf religionsgeschichtlicher Grundlage: Erster Teil: Israelitisch-jüdische Religionsgeschichte* (Leipzig: Quelle und Meyer, 1933); Ernst Sellin, *Alttestamentliche Theologie auf religionsgeschichtlicher Grundlage. Zweiter Teil: Theologie des Alten Testaments* (Leipzig: Quelle und Meyer, 1933). He describes his program as follows: "Israelite-Jewish religious history and theology of the O.T. together form an inseparable Christian theological discipline. The first describes the history, that is, the development and growth of the religion of the Israelite-Jewish people . . . The latter systematically describes the religious doctrine and faith that were gathered together in the scriptures of the Jewish community in the 5th to 2nd century BCE and declared holy, but only to the degree that Jesus Christ and his apostles recognized them to have formed the conditions and foundation of their gospel." *Israelitisch-jüdische Religionsgeschichte*, 1. Gerhard von Rad's "History of Jahwism and of the Sacral Institutions in Israel in Outline," which begins the first volume of his *Old Testament Theology* (pp. 3–102) without methodological comment, should also be mentioned here.

3. Janowski, *Theologie und Exegese*, 111. Cf. the illustrative compilation of thematic fields of investigation, pp. 111–12.

Acceptance of this characterization means that the theology of the Hebrew Bible initially has a narrower object of study than the history of Israelite religion. Rather than all the evidence related to the religion of ancient Israel, including the appropriate epigraphic and archaeological material, the focus is only the Old Testament or rather the Hebrew Bible (attested in its different scopes and forms). Overlap is found, on the one hand, wherever biblical literature (or parts of it) relate somewhat transparently to religious-historical circumstances (e.g., psalms used in the cult, prophetic oracles that trace back to oral pronouncements—in short, all material that classical form criticism could evaluate as having a concrete *Sitz im Leben*). On the other hand, the Hebrew Bible itself is a religious-historical product that can be investigated in accordance with religious-historical inquiry.

THE HISTORY OF ISRAELITE RELIGION OR THEOLOGY OF THE HEBREW BIBLE The alternative introduced into the discussion by Rainer Albertz and already addressed above in §8 concerning whether the theology of the Hebrew Bible or the history of Israelite religion is the appropriate synthetic discipline for Hebrew Bible studies has become an object of intense debate. At the same time, however, they are no longer pursued as mutually exclusive approaches.[4] Albertz's preference for the history of religion has not been followed in Hebrew Bible studies, likely in large part because his own "history of religion" does not exhibit a clear methodological separation, but rather combines elements of literary, social, religious, as well as theological-historical approaches to the Hebrew Bible in such a way that it amounts to more of a hybrid than a classic example of the genre of religious history.

THE MEANING OF EXOGENOUS INFLUENCES However, upheavals in the study of the history of religion in the past decades prove to be of great importance for the theology of the Hebrew Bible. For one, it has become clear that ancient Israel must be understood much more strongly in connection with its historical context than was accepted even in the middle of the twentieth century. Israel is part of the ancient Near East, both in terms of its cultural and its intellectual history. This does not mean that there were no indigenous and innovative internal developments in Israel, but rather that these must be understood in light of Israel's historical and geographic context. In a certain sense, with these convictions Hebrew Bible scholarship is returning to the viewpoints of the beginning of the twentieth century, which arose in light of

---

4. Cf. Albertz, *A History of Israelite Religion in the Old Testament Period*, 1:1–22.

the great discoveries in Mesopotamia and Egypt and led to the blossoming of the so-called "history of religions school."

BIBLE AND HISTORY On the other hand, and therefore connected, it has been demonstrated that the indisputable differences between Israel as documented in the Bible and its historical context must be understood in a much more complex manner than Gerhard von Rad's concordance model of Bible and history. It has become undeniable today that one must distinguish clearly between the biblical and the historical Israel. The Israel marked by monotheism, covenant, and law that we know from the Hebrew Bible only existed in history with these marks from the time of the Babylonian exile onward. The old paradigm under which von Rad still operated, that Israel was totally other than its surroundings from its beginnings, can no longer be maintained. The discontinuity between ancient Israel and its neighbors attested in the Hebrew Bible does not belong to the bedrock of the tradition. It is instead the result of complex and lengthy intellectual processes that have their historical roots in the crumbling of the old, self-evident certainties of the monarchic period concerning the state, identity, and religion.

INTERACTION BETWEEN TEXT AND HISTORY This means that a theology of the Hebrew Bible—if it intends to proceed historically—must take these intellectual processes into consideration. The theological substance of the texts of the Hebrew Bible cannot be deduced solely from the texts themselves, as if they depict a timeless revelatory witness. They must instead be elucidated with regard to their historical interactions, whether that be with other texts or with historical experiences.

2. *The Hermeneutics of the Hebrew Bible*

A theology of the Hebrew Bible will, at least logically, have a different shape than a hermeneutics of the Hebrew Bible, even if overlap again necessarily exists between the two lines of inquiry. This is especially true for "theologies of the Hebrew Bible" that make the contemporary relevance of texts of the Hebrew Bible central to their exposition.

THE RELEVANCE OF THEOLOGY AND HERMENEUTICS Theological and hermeneutic investigations share an interest in the organization of texts not simply in terms of the history of cultural studies, but also in discussing and unfolding their issues of content and thought. It should, however, be emphasized at the outset that the hermeneutical dimension must also have a fundamental interest in textual exegesis. One of the paramount advantages of biblical studies' institutional setting inside theological departments is that this context compels biblical studies to inquire not only about the historical and social contexts of historical texts, but also about their content and meaning.

PRODUCTION AND RECEPTION The fundamental difference between the tasks of a hermeneutics and a theology of the Hebrew Bible can be determined in the following way: If one understands hermeneutics, following Wilhem Dilthey, as "the art of understanding life expressions in fixed written form,"[5] then it becomes clear that hermeneutics is particularly oriented toward the receptive subject. A theology of the Hebrew Bible, on the other hand, is more strongly oriented toward the text, thus taking on a production-oriented accent.

THE ROLE OF THE HISTORY OF RECEPTION According to the hermeneutics of the Hebrew Bible, the perspective of the history of reception should be given its due. Because the current understanding of texts from the Hebrew Bible does not take place outside of the centuries of reception history, but rather through this history—and generally also where this history is denied. This perspective is especially important for Protestant exegesis,[6] which itself does not have a distinct tradition. If Protestant exegesis began with the framework of modern Lutheran theology that the application of historical criticism to the Bible generates the only sense of the text whose focal point is the doctrine of justification, then it has become clear over the 200 years of historical-critical scholarship that the historical sense of the texts of the Bible is far more divergent. The interpretation of the Bible in the sense of the doctrine of justification only remains historically and methodologically possible when taking Protestant tradition into account. Therefore, Protestant biblical hermeneutics also rely on a doctrine of tradition. This point of view plays an important role for a theology of the He-

5. Wilhelm Dilthey, "Die Entstehung der Hermeneutik," in *Materialien zur Ideologiegeschichte der deutschen Literaturwissenschaft*, 2 vols., ed. Gunter Reiß (Tübingen: Niemeyer, 1973), 1:55–68; originally published as "Kunstlehre des Verstehens schriftlich fixierter Lebensäußerungen" in 1900.

6. Cf. Friederike Nüssel, ed., *Schriftauslegung*, UTB 3991 (Tübingen: Mohr Siebeck, 2014).

brew Bible as well, but the present discussion will be limited to naming the necessity of consciously differentiating between the Bible and its effects as well as several smaller themes (see below, §§41–42).

HISTORICAL HERMENEUTICS Hermeneutics can also be practiced as a historically-oriented endeavor.[7] If this aspect is foregrounded, then a historical-hermeneutical approach to the theology of the Hebrew Bible remains, on the one hand, bound to the intrinsic meaning of the text and, on the other hand, simultaneously attempts to make this meaning comprehensible for modern subjects.

3. *The Ethics of the Hebrew Bible*

RITUAL LAW AND MORAL LAW Even if the investigation of an "ethics of the Hebrew Bible" does not belong among the most prominent fields of study in Hebrew Bible scholarship,[8] it remains helpful to call to mind the similarities and differences of a theology of the Hebrew Bible to this project. Within Christian theology since Thomas Aquinas (at the latest), a distinction has often been made between the ceremonial law and the moral law. While the ceremonial law would have been set aside through the gospel, the moral law, as natural law, remains in effect. To this extent, an ethics of the Hebrew Bible bears a broader theological importance in this traditional structure.

ETHICS OF THE HEBREW BIBLE AS A RECONSTRUCTION OF THE HISTOR-ICAL ORIGINS OF PROBLEMS AND VALUES Ever since the recognition of the historically conditioned and historically determined nature of biblical ethics—dealing with texts that were written over two thousand years ago with values that often remain imprisoned by their times, even if they sometimes point beyond this context—this approach has become impossible.

---

7. Cf. Friedhelm Hartenstein, "Autorität der Religionsgeschichte—Polyphonie der Religionsgeschichte?," in *Die bleibende Bedeutung des Alten Testaments: Studien zur Relevanz des ersten Kanonteils für Theologie und Kirche*, ed. Friedhelm Hartenstein et al., Biblisch-theologische Studien 165 (Neukirchen-Vluyn: Neukirchener Verlag, 2016), 131–61, esp. 157–58.

8. But see Eckart Otto, *Theologische Ethik des Alten Testaments*, Theologische Wissenschaft 3,2 (Stuttgart: Kohlhammer, 1994), as well as the instructive study by Uwe Becker, "Eine kleine alttestamentliche Ethik des 'Alltäglichen,'" *BTZ* 24 (2007): 227–40.

An unreflective and historically-unenlightened use of the Bible for current ethics would necessarily lead to fundamentalist and extremely conservative positions with regard to social politics because the Bible—in accordance with the conditions of its historical setting in antiquity—does not acknowledge the equality of genders, non-discrimination of foreigners, acceptance of homosexuality, etc. This does not exclude the Bible's ability to provide ethical impulses and stimuli with regard to particular issues, but it requires interpretation—and this includes an element of critical reflection. The Bible is of great importance to current ethical issues with regard to *understanding the historical origins of issues*; the biblical measures of value have played a role in deciding the range of questions that even appear ethically relevant.[9] As a result, the most recent German-language "ethics of the Old Testament" by Eckhart Otto took a historical-descriptive approach and outlines its task in the following manner:

> The task of the present theological ethics of the OT is, therefore, not an apologetic, moralistic resistance of the OT for people of today to resolve in order to confirm it as part of the Christian canon. Neither will it attempt to provide immediate guidelines for action. It will instead offer description for our historical understanding of the history of Old Testament guidelines, providing the criteria within the Old Testament to distinguish how they derive from Israel's belief in God, in order to show how the perspectives of the cultural-historical meaning of the Old Testament ethos open up as the basis for the spirit of modernity.[10]

One can lament the loss of biblical authority in such an approach to ethical questions, but, when viewed in the light of day, it also shields effectively against every dictum legitimated by the reception history in a past social order. The authoritativeness of the wording of the Bible is not a position of the Bible itself, but rather of its reception history. Especially with regard to legal and ethical questions, the Bible places the highest value on the necessity of interpretation and exegesis—this is seen especially well in the Pentateuch, which canonized not only the laws themselves, but also their interpretations. What is binding is, biblically speaking, the dynamic of interpretation, not the isolated position alone.

9. Cf. Johannes Fischer, "Die Bedeutung der Bibel für die Theologische Ethik," *ZEE* 55 (2011): 262–73.

10. Otto, *Theologische Ethik*, 11–12.

The possibilities and limitations of an ethical approach to the Hebrew Bible can be illustrated with, for example, Gen 1. One could conclude that this text calls for the prohibition of all consumption of meat today:

> God said, "See, I have given you every plant yielding seed that is upon the face of all the earth, and every tree with seed in its fruit; you shall have them for food." (Gen 1:29)

This would indeed render the biblical text directly relevant for the present. Furthermore, it cannot be disputed that vegetarianism is a valuable ethical option, at any rate superior to meat consumption. However, is this fair to Gen 1? Does this ethical position even need a biblical text as its support? One can initially note that Gen 1 is a narrative, rather than a normative text. Genesis 1 is not about required or prohibited behavior; it is instead a description of the original order of creation. It should also be emphasized that Gen 1 cannot be viewed in isolation according to either the present context or the recognized historical reconstructions, in which it is the head of a larger narrative complex, whose extension as far as Gen 9 is of great importance. Genesis 1 describes a counterworld whose rules no longer coincide with the world familiar to humanity. This familiar world first arose after the flood. With regard to human food, Gen 9 states:

> Every moving thing that lives shall be food for you; and just as I gave you the green plants, I give you everything. (Gen 9:3)

Therefore, Gen 1:29 does not provide a normative call to vegetarianism, but rather the counterpoint to Gen 9:3, which interprets human meat consumption as a diminution of an originally superior created order. One could draw the conclusion from this narrative constellation that there is a biblical justification for vegetarianism. However, this is more complicated than simply referring to the Bible verse of Gen 1:29.

The differentiation between theology and ethics is not foreign to the Hebrew Bible itself. Within the framework of a historically oriented and descriptive approach to the Hebrew Bible from a modern viewpoint, identifiable ethical issues can be integrated into the account that follows without subdisciplinary divisions as part of the genesis of the historical issue.

4. Biblical Theology

NEW TESTAMENT INTERPRETATION OF THE HEBREW BIBLE The view that the theology of the Hebrew Bible was to be understood as a biblical theology of the Old Testament—that is, that the theology of the Hebrew Bible should be treated from a New Testament perspective—was largely unquestioned until the nineteenth or even the twentieth century. This can be recognized in Christian scholarship quite clearly in Ernst Sellin's theology of the Old Testament, which completed his religious history and states on its first page:

> In the theology of the O.T. we are interested only in the large lines that reach their fulfillment in the gospel, the word of the eternal God in what over time became the Old Testament writings.[11]

The theology of the Old Testament viewed the Hebrew Bible largely retrospectively through the perspective of the New Testament—defined as unambiguous—and surveyed the Hebrew Bible's possible nature as preparation for the gospel.

Otto Procksch begins his *Theologie des Alten Testaments* yet more sharply with the sentence "All theology is Christology."[12] Different from Emil Brunner[13] or Rafael Gyllenberg,[14] however, it does not follow for Procksch that there could not be a theology of the Hebrew Bible. Rather, Procksch found a theology of the Hebrew Bible legitimate and necessary because it was formulated as a "proto-gospel"[15] and because it is only possible to understand Jesus's historical nature in light of the Hebrew Bible.[16]

COMPLEMENTARITY INSTEAD OF SUBORDINATION The goal of a biblical theology to place the two Testaments in relationship with one another is fundamentally important and correct from a Christian perspective. This

---

11. Ernst Sellin, *Theologie des Alten Testaments*, 2nd ed. (Leipzig: Quelle & Meyer, 1936), 1.

12. Otto Procksch, *Theologie des Alten Testaments* (Gütersloh: Bertelsmann, 1950), 1.

13. Emil Brunner, *Offenbarung und Vernunft: Die Lehre von der christlichen Glaubens-erkenntnis* (Zurich: Zwingli-Verlag, 1941), 287: "Es gibt keine 'Theologie des Alten Testaments.'"

14. Rafael Gyllenberg, "Die Unmöglichkeit einer Theologie des Alten Testaments," in *In piam memoriam Alexander von Bulmerincq*, ed. Rudolf Abramowski, Abhandlungen der Herder–Gesellschaft und des Herder-Instituts zu Riga 6 (Riga: Plates, 1938), 64–68.

15. Procksch, *Theologie des Alten Testaments*, 7.

16. Procksch, *Theologie des Alten Testaments*, 8.

raises the question of their theological relationship, which remains an ongoing task for Christian theology. However, solutions advocating the subordination of the Old Testament are backed neither by the Bible, the Old and New Testaments, nor Christian tradition. They are neither historically nor theologically acceptable. Therefore, a certain degree of restraint is appropriate with regard to the following formulation:

> A theology of the Hebrew Bible must provide an account of its *relationship to New Testament theology*. There can be no theological equality in this relationship. The differentiation of classic Protestant orthodox dogmatics between *norma normans* and *norma normata* retains its enduring claim. Namely, the Old Testament as a collection of texts is only part of the Christian Bible when read in relation to and from the perspective of the New Testament.[17]

This position should receive only limited consent. Classic Protestant orthodox dogmatics introduced the differentiation between *norma normans* and *norma normata* not with regard to the relationship between the Old and New Testaments, but rather with regard to the text and confession. The writings of the Old *and* New Testament *as a whole* are *norma normans*. The notion that the New Testament authorizes the Old Testament and that the Old must be authorized by the New is not in view. Instead, and this should be stated quite clearly: the Old Testament contains, with regard to its content, just as much "New Testament" as the New Testament does "Old Testament." Or, to use a different set of categories, it is not the case that the Old Testament contains merely "law" while the New Testament contains only "gospel." Both contain "law" and gospel," or both have "old" and "new."

NO DOWNWARD SLOPE FROM NEW TO OLD TESTAMENT There is in principle no canonical downward slope from the New to the Old Testament. It is instead the decision—or to be more precise, the theological dynamic—to respect the Christian tradition that created the double canon of the Old

17. Jörg Jeremias, "Alttestamentliche Wissenschaft im Kontext der Theologie," in *Eine Wissenschaft oder viele? Die Einheit evangelischer Theologie in der Sicht ihrer Disziplinen*, ed. Ingolf U. Dalferth, Forum Theologische Literaturzeitung 17 (Leipzig: Evangelische Verlagsanstalt, 2006), 19–20 (italics original). Cf., however, his considerations against this in Jörg Jeremias, *Theologie des Alten Testaments*, GAT 6 (Göttingen: Vandenhoeck & Ruprecht, 2015), 469–75.

and New Testaments rather than a tiered canon that would in principle subordinate the Old Testament to the New. Consideration of the basic differentiation between writing and the word of God should be maintained in any case in view of the canonicity of the canon from a Christian perspective. These two entities are not simply congruent; therefore, liturgical use of the writings is not limited to their being read. Instead a sermon takes a further step to interpretation. Not everything found in the Scripture is the word of God; however, it can at best become word of God in the proclamation.[18] On the other hand, not everything said in a sermon is word of God. Especially from a Protestant perspective, overly close identification of Scripture and word of God must be evaluated by theological reflection, because it tends to perceive the Scripture as law and not as gospel.

CHRISTIANITY WITHOUT THE OLD TESTAMENT? In the same way, calls for reforming the canon in the wake of, for example, Adolf von Harnack are likewise unhelpful:[19]

> To discard the OT in the second century was a mistake that the church at large correctly rejected; retaining it in the sixteenth century was a fate that the Reformation was not yet able to escape; but to still conserve the canonical document in Protestantism since the nineteenth century is the result of a religious and church paralysis. . . . To clear the table and to give the place of honor to the truth in confession and instruction is the feat that is required of Protestantism today—almost too late.[20]

18. In this respect, Otto Kaiser's description of the task of a theology of the Hebrew Bible remains underdetermined with regard to the differentiation between Scripture and the word of God: "Within the framework of a Protestant theology of the word of God, the theology of the OT must answer the fundamental question to what degree the OT is, contains, or witnesses to the word of God." Otto Kaiser, *Der Gott des Alten Testaments: Theologie des Alten Testaments*, part 1: *Grundlegung*, UTB 1747 (Göttingen: Vandenhoeck & Ruprecht, 1993), 21.

19. Cf. Notker Slenczka, *Vom Alten Testament und vom Neuen: Beiträge zur Neuvermessung ihres Verhältnisses* (Leipzig: Evangelische Verlagsanstalt, 2017), and debated by Friedhelm Hartenstein, "Zur Bedeutung des Alten Testaments für die evangelische Kirche: Eine Auseinandersetzung mit den Thesen von Notker Slenczka," *TLZ* 140 (2015): 739–51; Konrad Schmid, "Christentum ohne Altes Testament?," *Internationale Katholische Zeitschrift Communio* 45 (2016): 443–56.

20. Adolf von Harnack, *Marcion: Das Evangelium vom fremden Gott,* Texte und Untersuchungen zur Geschichte der altchristlichen Literatur 45 (Leipzig: Hinrichs, 1921), 217, 222. For current debate on this question, see Schmid, "Christentum ohne Altes Testament?"

The word of God cannot be defined or identified in a clear-cut textual manner, certainly not by excluding the Bible of early Christianity—the Hebrew Bible—from the Christian canon. The "canon within a canon" is not a textual excerpt of the canon, but rather a functional precept applied to the entire canon.[21]

More helpful for a Christian interpretation of the Hebrew Bible is the suggestion made by Jeremias in his *Theologie des Alten Testaments,* who speaks of "tendencies followed in the Old Testament that have channeled a path to the speech about God in the New Testament."[22] In the theological sense, "new" also appears in the "Old Testament," just as the reverse: the "New Testament" is not free of the "old."

5. Systematic Theology

If one follows, for example, James Barr, then the difference between the biblical theology of the Hebrew Bible and/or the New Testament and systematic theology is that systematics relies on further sources besides the Bible, such as philosophy, natural theology when appropriate, and church tradition in order to outline Christian belief in a systematic manner, while the measure and standard are found in the Bible.[23] Following this description, a theology of the Hebrew Bible must be treated simultaneously as both more and less than the subdisciplines of systematic theology that exhibit thematic affinities to the Hebrew Bible. The examples of the theologies of the Old Testament conceived as "preliminary systematics" by Ludwig Köhler[24] and Walther Eichrodt[25] demonstrate the proximity and distance of a theology of the Hebrew Bible to outlines of systematic theology. If one structures a theology of the Hebrew Bible into the main sections

21. Cf. Hans-Jürgen Hermisson, "Jesus Christus als externe Mitte des Alten Testaments: Ein unzeitgemäßes Votum zur Theologie des Alten Testaments," in *Jesus Christus als Mitte der Schrift: Studien zur Hermeneutik des Evangeliums: Festschrift für Otfried Hofius,* ed. Christof Landmesser et al., BZNW 86 (Berlin: de Gruyter, 1997), 199–233.

22. Jörg Jeremias, *Theologie des Alten Testaments,* GAT 6 (Göttingen: Vandenhoeck & Ruprecht, 2015), 479; cf. the similar perspective in Markus Witte, *Jesus Christus im Alten Testament: Eine biblisch-theologische Skizze,* Salzburger Exegetische Theologische Vorträge 4 (Münster: LIT, 2013).

23. Cf. James Barr, *The Concept of Biblical Theology* (Minneapolis: Fortress, 1999), 62–76.

24. Ludwig Köhler, *Theologie des Alten Testaments,* 4th ed., NTG (Tübingen: Mohr Siebeck, 1966).

25. Eichrodt, *Theologie des Alten Testaments.*

of God, humanity, and world (like Köhler) or rather God and people, God and world, God and human (like Eichrodt), then this structure is based on the traditional structures of Christian doctrine,[26] but then it is filled out with the content of the Hebrew Bible in something of a kaleidoscope fashion. A theology of the Hebrew Bible organized in this way meets the justified call for a certain systemization of the material, but in the end it remains a hybrid consisting of an overarching Christian form with fragmentary content from the Hebrew Bible.

DEGREE OF SYSTEMIZATION Moving a step further, systematic theologies have at least traditionally taken on the form of a doctrinal edifice. Even if the project of a theology of the Hebrew Bible views itself as legitimately confronted with the call for a certain systemization, then a theology of the Hebrew Bible can only reasonably be systematized to the degree that its object of study indicates.

SYSTEMATICS AS CONSEQUENT EXEGESIS? The degree to which the theology of the Bible, in this case the Hebrew Bible, and systematics move closer together or farther apart from one another depends, however, on the fundamental views taken by each. One model that compels them closer together is advocated by Eberhard Jüngel, who once described the task of systematic theology in an especially pointed manner as "consequent exegesis."[27] On the opposite side is James Barr, who sees a fundamental

---

26. However, cf. for example, Gunda Schneider-Flume, "Dogmatik erzählen: Ein Plädoyer für biblische Theologie," *Neue Zeitschrift für Systematische Theologie und Religionsphilosophie* 45 (2003): 137–48; Gunda Schneider-Flume, *Grundkurs Dogmatik: Nachdenken über Gottes Geschichte*, UTB 2564 (Göttingen: Vandenhoeck & Ruprecht, 2004), 27–28; Dietrich Korsch, *Dogmatik im Grundriß*, UTB 2155 (Tübingen: Mohr Siebeck, 2000).

27. Cf. Eberhard Jüngel, *Gottes Sein ist im Werden: Verantwortliche Rede vom Sein Gottes bei Karl Barth: Eine Paraphrase* (Tübingen: Mohr, 1965), 25 n. 43; Cf. Eberhard Jüngel, "Einführung in Leben und Werk Karl Barths," in *Barth-Studien*, ed. Eberhard Jüngel, Ökumenische Theologie 9 (Gütersloh: Mohn, 1982), 46 (characterization of Barth's dogmatics as "konsequente Exegese"); Eberhard Jüngel, "Glauben und Verstehen: Zum Theologiebegriff Rudolf Bultmanns," in *Wertlose Wahrheit: Zur Identität und Relevanz des christlichen Glaubens*, Theologische Erörterungen 3 (Munich: Kaiser, 1990), 16–77, esp. 22; Eberhard Jüngel, "Besinnung auf 50 Jahre theologische Existenz," *TLZ* 128 (2003): 471–84, esp. 476. On this cf. Ulrich Körtner, "Dogmatik als konsequente Exegese? Zur Relevanz der Exegese für die Systematische Theologie im Anschluß an Rudolf Bultmann," in *Exegese und Dogmatik: Beiträge zu einer gestörten Beziehung*, ed. Carsten Claußen and Markus Öhler, Biblisch-theologische Studien 107 (Neukirchen-Vluyn: Neukirchener Verlag, 2010), 73–102.

distance between biblical and systematic theology already in place simply through the different natures of their inquiries:

> Biblical theology [his terminology for a theology of the Old Testament] has the Bible as its horizon: its source material is the biblical text, its subject is the theology which lies behind or is implied by the Bible, and its scope is determined by the meanings as known and implied within the time and culture of the Bible. . . . Doctrinal theology, however much it works with the Bible and acknowledges the Bible as authoritative, is not primarily *about* the Bible: it is primarily about God and its horizon is God. . . . Even given the maximum authority of the Bible, the Bible is not the sole or even the sole controlling factor in its work.[28]

NECESSARY DIVERGENCE BETWEEN BIBLICAL AND SYSTEMATIC THE-OLOGY It is clear that there can be no conclusive determinations of the relationship between biblical and systematic theology. In spite of all the divergences, a certain amount of consensus ought to be conceivable such that the organization of the material within the framework of biblical theology would be more closely oriented to the text, while systematic theology would instead proceed more thematically. However, given the modern and historically informed conditions of understanding, it should be emphasized that the basic divergence between exegesis and dogmatics should not be overplayed, but rather represents an essential element of a critically conceived theology. Exegesis and dogmatics should not be harmonized, but ought instead to cultivate a mutual openness to differences within the framework of a multi-perspectival approach to theology. One of the merits of modern theology is that it has not only recognized the gulf between exegesis and dogmatics, but that it has also attempted to resist bridging it prematurely.[29]

28. Barr, *The Concept of Biblical Theology*, 74. Cf. also Friederike Nüssel, "Die Aufgabe der Dogmatik im Zusammenhang der Theologie," in *Eine Wissenschaft oder viele? Die Einheit evangelischer Theologie in der Sicht ihrer Disziplinen*, ed. Ingolf U. Dalferth, Forum Theologische Literaturzeitung 17 (Leipzig: Evangelische Verlagsanstalt, 2006), 77–98, esp. 96: "The view emerges from the development of systematic theological outlines in the nineteenth and twentieth centuries that the use of the textual witnesses as 'singular rule and standard according to which all instruction and instructors should be oriented and judged' [Bekenntnisschriften der Evangelisch-Lutherischen Kirche 767, 15–17], which can only be interpreted in the medium of the systematic reflection of its content that is relevant for faith."
29. Cf. in more detail Konrad Schmid, "Dogmatik als konsequente Exegese?"

§15 Fundamental Methodological Choices

John Barton and Michael Wolter, eds., *Die Einheit der Schrift und die Vielfalt des Kanons / The Unity of Scripture and the Diversity of the Canon*, BZNW 118 (Berlin: de Gruyter, 2003) ♦ Ernst Axel Knauf, "Hymnische Exegese: Der Psalter als Theologie des Alten Testaments," in *Data and Debates: Essays in the History and Culture of Israel and Its Neighbors in Antiquity = Daten und Debatten: Aufsätze zur Kulturgeschichte des antiken Israel und seiner Nachbarn*, AOAT 407 (Münster: Ugarit-Verlag, 2013), 475–97 ♦ Reinhard G. Kratz, *Historisches und biblisches Israel: Drei Überblicke zum Alten Testament* (Tübingen: Mohr Siebeck, 2013) ♦ Diethelm Michel, "Einheit in der Vielfalt des Alten Testaments," in *Studien zur Überlieferungsgeschichte alttestamentlicher Texte*, TB 93 (Gütersloh: Kaiser, 1997), 53–68 ♦ Manfred Oeming, "Viele Wege zu dem Einen: Die 'transzendente Mitte' einer Theologie des Alten Testaments im Spannungsfeld von Vielfalt und Einheit," in *Viele Wege zu dem Einen: Historische Bibelkritik—Die Vitalität der Glaubensüberlieferung in der Moderne,* ed. Stefan Beyerle et al., Biblisch-theologische Studien 121 (Neukirchen-Vluyn: Neukirchener Verlag, 2012), 83–108 ♦ Albert de Pury and Ernst Axel Knauf, "La théologie de l'Ancien Testament: kérygmatique ou descriptive?," *ETR* 70 (1995): 323–34 ♦ John W. Rogerson, "Die Bibel lesen wie jedes andere Buch? Auseinandersetzungen um die Autorität der Bibel vom 18. Jahrhundert an bis heute," in *Biblischer Text und theologische Theoriebildung,* ed. Stephen Chapman et al., Biblisch-theologische Studien 44 (Neukirchen-Vluyn: Neukirchener Verlag, 2001), 211–234 ♦ Werner H. Schmidt, "Pentateuch und Prophetie: Eine Skizze zu Verschiedenartigkeit und Einheit alttestamentlicher Theologie," in *Vielfalt und Einheit alttestamentlichen Glaubens,* vol. 1 of *Studien zu Hermeneutik und Methodik, Pentateuch und Prophetie* (Neukirchen-Vluyn: Neukirchener Verlag, 1995), 226–40 ♦ Ernst-Joachim Waschke, "Die Einheit der Theologie heute als Anfrage an das Alte Testament: Ein Plädoyer für die Vielfalt," in *Der Gesalbte: Studien zur alttestamentlichen Theologie,* ed. Ernst-Joachim Waschke, BZAW 306 (Berlin: de Gruyter, 2001), 267–77

The following considerations attempt to articulate in an explicit manner several foundational methodological decisions that are self-explanatory within the framework of modern historical-critical biblical exegesis. In this respect they are neither innovative nor revolutionary, but are instead the expression of the disciplined application of the approach and results of modern biblical scholarship to the field of theology, as Ernst Troeltsch classically formulated:

The historical method also took hold in theology, first in a fragmentary and timid manner with all sorts of reservations and limitations, then with increasing energy and comprehensiveness to the point that it had the same effects here as everywhere else, that is a principle change in the entire way of thinking and the whole stance toward the object.[30]

The following section formulates ten basic postulates: (1) Respect for the polyphony of the Hebrew Bible; (2) The renunciation of a sacred hermeneutic and the rejection of an autonomous "theological exegesis"; (3) The renunciation of a divorce between orthodoxy and heresy; (4) The differentiation between biblical and historical Israel; (5) The inclusion of concrete living contexts in the biblical texts; (6) The appreciation of processes of theologization of earlier traditions in the Hebrew Bible; (7) The appreciation of processes of reception and theologization in given extrabiblical traditions; (8) Consideration of later transformations; (9) Description and normativity; (10) Critique of the influences from the history of scholarship. These postulates possess neither an iconoclastic nor any anti-theological interest. On the contrary, they follow the conviction that theology cannot exist without critical reflection, that a theology of the Hebrew Bible can be reconstructed neither ideologically, in isolation, nor in a reductionist manner. Only in this fashion can biblical criticism offer an unfettered theological treatment of the Hebrew Bible that can claim to be both academic and theological.

1. *The Respect for the Polyphony of the Hebrew Bible*

The fact that a collection of texts in 39 books composed over a period of approximately a thousand years presents not one but numerous theological positions is only to be expected and is undeniably the case for the Hebrew Bible. The search for one message or a single theme for a theology of the Hebrew Bible is not an inquiry that arises in accordance with the object of study itself (cf. also below, §40).[31] This pursuit instead—when

---

30. Ernst Troeltsch, *Über historische und dogmatische Methode der Theologie* (Tübingen: Rheinischer Wissenschaftlicher Predigerverein, 1900); repr. in *Ernst Troeltsch Lesebuch: Ausgewählte Texte,* ed. Friedemann Voigt, Uni-Taschenbücher 2452 (Tübingen: Mohr Siebeck, 2003), 8.

31. Cf. the discussion in Matthias Büttner, *Das Alte Testament als erster Teil der christlichen Bibel: Zur Frage nach theologischer Auslegung und "Mitte" im Kontext der Theologie Karl Barths,* BevT 120 (Gütersloh: Kaiser, 2002), 123–258.

limiting the view to the modern context—stems from the German idealist (cultivated further in Romanticism) search for a unifying principle that must underlie such an eminent collection of texts like the Hebrew Bible or the Bible as a whole.

HISTORY OF RECEPTION INSTEAD OF HISTORICAL OR OBJECTIVE UNITY IN THE HEBREW BIBLE Such an inquiry will lead to many outcomes over which one can argue more or less profitably, but it will never find what it actually seeks because this singularity does not exist. The Hebrew Bible is at most a unity in terms of its history of reception, but not in historical or objective terms. Historically speaking, there are other texts from the time of the Hebrew Bible that did not become part of the Hebrew Bible, such as the Temple Scroll from Qumran or the Enoch literature. In terms of content, there is no idea or specific identity that would hold it together, for its identity has been produced by its history of reception, which was in turn defined by numerous deliberate and incidental factors and not by a unifying thematic principle. The historically contingent assembling of the Hebrew Bible does not exclude the possibility that some overarching concepts may have played a role as well—several will be presented below—but with regard to the whole, they are of secondary importance.

In light of the current form of the Hebrew Bible, one even has the impression that there was conscious guidance in the direction of broadness in its formation. Within the Pentateuch one might name, for example, the juxtaposition of the Deuteronomistic and Priestly perspectives, which stand in theological competition with one another.[32] In the Ketuvim one can point to the vastly different genres of the writings brought together in this part of the canon, apparently compiled more as a result of their diversity than their affinity.[33] A unity in "idealistic" or "romantic" terms would not reflect Hebrew Bible conceptions. The polyphony of the Hebrew Bible is instead one of its decisive marks, and it should be appreciated as such. One might even appreciate the historically established unity of the Hebrew Bible in a "rhetorical" manner, analogous to Philipp Melanchton's *Loci communes* (*Commonplaces*). It results from the categorization of different voices on different themes and establishes multiple perspectives on specific *topoi*.

32. See, e.g., Israel Knohl, *The Divine Symphony: The Bible's Many Voices* (Philadelphia: Jewish Publication Society of America, 2003).

33. Cf. Albert de Pury, "Zwischen Sophokles und Ijob: Die Schriften (Ketubim): Ein jüdischer Literatur-Kanon," *Welt und Umwelt der Bibel* 28 (2003): 24–27.

"THINKING IN COMMON" IN THE HEBREW BIBLE This points to a response to the early demand that arose in reaction to von Rad's theology of the Old Testament that a theology "to a large degree"—which was the case for von Rad—"must venture to think in common."[34] In reality, in the interest of a meaningful division of subdisciplines in Hebrew Bible studies, one must choose to keep "theology of the Hebrew Bible" from drawing too near to the introductory discipline, to the history of religion, or to the history of theology of the Hebrew Bible. On the other hand, the considerations that von Rad weighed when deciding to abandon a systematic presentation of a theology of the Hebrew Bible remain valid: if a theology of the Hebrew Bible remains more concerned with the Hebrew Bible than with its interpreters, then one cannot avoid the critical testing of aspirations for systemization, especially when they derive from later Christian doctrine.[35]

2. *The Renunciation of a Sacred Hermeneutic and the Rejection of an Autonomous "Theological Exegesis"*

READING THE BIBLE LIKE EVERY OTHER BOOK The notion that the Bible should be read in the same way as every other book is a relatively new achievement in its centuries-old interpretation,[36] and one universally established neither in Judaism nor Christianity, though it is of absolutely fundamental importance for modern western biblical scholarship and academic theology, where its validity is undisputed. This methodological maxim is necessary for biblical criticism, for only in this way is a scholarly responsible interpretation of the Bible possible, especially from a historical perspective. This precept is also important for theology in order that the conviction that theology does not allow double standards with regard to questions of truth may be carried out. Instead, both theology itself and its foundation—the Bible—are placed in the critical context of reason.

Gerhard Ebeling wrote: "So-called biblical criticism is only in apparent conflict with the authority of the Bible. Understood correctly, it

---

34. Walther Zimmerli, "Review of Gerhard von Rad, *Theologie des Alten Testaments*," *VT* 13 (1963): 105.

35. Cf. already Gerhard von Rad, *Old Testament Theology*, 1:120: "In particular, in tracing the different confessional material, we must beware of striving to reconstruct links between ideas, and systematic combinations, where Israel herself never saw or distinguished such things."

36. Cf. Rogerson, "Die Bibel lesen wie jedes andere Buch?"

is how the authority of the Bible is respected in the realm of exegesis."[37] This declaration turns the virulent skepticism of biblical criticism in many Bible-based and Evangelical circles on its head, proclaiming that one is not Bible-based by rejecting biblical criticism but rather by applying it correctly. Only in this manner is the Bible even given a chance to be understood in the modern world. Therefore, the Enlightenment principle of the renunciation of a sacred hermeneutic remains foundational for theology: "The interpretation of the Bible as the most important book takes place in principle the same way as the interpretation of every other book."[38]

RELEASE OF THE NATURAL SCIENCES This methodological conviction is of fundamental importance for the academic fate of theology because it brings with it the release of the natural and social sciences such that theology's place in the university remains justified and safeguarded.[39] No one must maintain the truth of certain statements against their better judgment—like the approximately 6,000 year age of the earth or creation in seven days—simply because they are in the Bible. The Bible should not be excluded from history, but should be understood in its context. And with regard to questions of a historical or natural scientific nature, the Bible is part of the scientific context of its own time, rather than of our time.[40] Therefore, it cannot be honored as a timeless stylite. It must instead be taken seriously as a denser, but historically influenced and historically conditioned conversation partner.[41]

THEOLOGICAL EXEGESIS AND DOCETISM Accordingly, caution is also advisable with regard to the call for a "theological exegesis." The expression "theological exegesis" could lead to thinking that, in addition to "historical-

37. Gerhard Ebeling, "Diskussionsthesen zur Einführung in das Studium der Theologie," in *Wort und Glaube* (Tübingen: Mohr, 1960), 1:451.

38. Ebeling, "Diskussionsthesen zur Einführung," 1:451.

39. Cf. Hans Schwarz, *400 Jahre Streit um die Wahrheit: Theologie und Naturwissenschaft* (Göttingen: Vandenhoeck & Ruprecht, 2012).

40. On this, cf. Konrad Schmid, "Von der Gegenwelt zur Lebenswelt: Evolutionäre Kosmologie und Theologie im Buch Genesis," in *Cosmologies et cosmogonies dans la littérature antique: Huit exposés suivis de discussions et d'un épilogue*, ed. Therese Fuhrer et al., Entretiens sur l'Antiquité classique 61 (Vandoeuvres: Fondation Hardt; Bonn: Habelt, 2015), 51–104.

41. Cf. the considerations by Michael Welker on the fourfold significance of the Scripture, "Sola Scriptura? Die Autorität der Bibel in pluralistischen Umgebungen und die interdisziplinäre Biblische Theologie," in *Reconsidering the Boundaries Between Theological Disciplines*, ed. Michael Welker and Friedrich Schweitzer (Münster: LIT, 2005), 15–29.

critical exegesis," there are certain special forms of exegesis that are less historical-critical, but in return more theological. Yet this position is not really feasible. A theological exegesis that is not accountable to history would reasonably come under the suspicion of Docetism, which would immediately forfeit its theological character. As a result, "theological" exegesis in the sense of exegesis that is compatible with the entirety of theology cannot be something fundamentally different than historical exegesis, if it wishes to remain scholarly.

No Double Standards In the end, the basic justification is itself theological in nature. From its beginnings, theology has chosen the path of philosophy and scholarship. While this path has been rocky and anything other than free of difficulties and interruptions,[42] it has ultimately been travelled consistently. Theology, according to this conviction, has not taken place within the framework of a special religious language. It has instead taken part in the discourse of scholarship and cannot accept double standards of truth. With all its positions, convictions, and theories, the Bible is an artifact of history, so historical access to it is not only permissible, but advisable if one attempts to understand the Bible without simultaneously turning it into an idol.

3. *The Renunciation of a Divorce between Orthodoxy and Heresy*

Within the framework of a historically and critically responsible theology of the Hebrew Bible, the concern will not be to differentiate between "orthodox" and "heterodox" positions in the Hebrew Bible. From the perspective of the history of reception, this is inadvisable simply because the Hebrew Bible *as a whole* was canonized, such that the singling out of "heterodox" or even "heretical" content would ignore the overarching canonicity of the Hebrew Bible. In light of that fact, "orthodoxy" and "heresy" can, in any case, only be defined after the fact. Stated in exaggerated terms, orthodoxy includes those potential heresies that were able to establish themselves.[43] Therefore, a historical approach to the Hebrew Bible must initially undertake descriptive evaluations. Schleiermacher formulated the task of biblical scholarship at his time as follows:

42. Cf. Hans Schwarz, *400 Jahre Streit um die Wahrheit*.
43. Cf. the classical argument of Walter Bauer, *Rechtgläubigkeit und Ketzerei im ältesten Christentum* (Tübingen: Mohr, 1934).

Criticism must undertake both investigations, whether or not there is something found in the canon that is non-canonical, and whether there is something canonical outside the canon that remains undetected.[44]

However, the consciousness of a difference between Christian doctrine and biblical theology was still emerging at the beginning of the nineteenth century. A current theological approach to the Hebrew Bible—at least from a Protestant point of view—denies the use of a preexisting understanding of the "canonical" to evaluate the actual canon. Instead, the reverse direction of questioning should be affirmed. What passes as "canonical" must first be established from the reading of the biblical canon. The fact that this "canonical" is diverse, requires interpretation, and is finally contingent on verification that is essentially of a reception-historical nature is understood from the historical perspective itself.

4. The Differentiation between Biblical and Historical Israel

It is self-evident in terms of the history of literature that one should differentiate, methodologically speaking, between the world of the narration and the world of the narrator for texts that are placed in a particular (real or fictive) historical setting. In the case of the Bible, however, it required many centuries for this self-evident fact to become established; in some fundamentalist circles it still has not taken place. There are cases in the Hebrew Bible in which one can assume that the world of the narrative and that of the narrator are the same or at least are not far from one another. In particular are certain prophecies that can be assigned to the historical prophetic figure. However, even in these cases one should reckon with a certain temporal distance between the oracle and the text that resulted, during which an extensive interpretive process could generally take place. For the vast majority of the rest of the traditions of the Hebrew Bible, a deep chasm opens up between the world of the narrative and that of the narrator. This is especially true for the traditions of origins in the books of Genesis–2 Kings, though even more so for 1–2 Chronicles, and also for the Psalms (in particular their ascription to David or other figures in the

---

44. Friedrich D. E. Schleiermacher, *Kurze Darstellung des theologischen Studiums zum Behufe einleitender Vorlesungen*, 2nd ed. (Berlin: Reimer, 1830), 52.

traditions of the Hebrew Bible), the books of Qoheleth and Song of Songs, as well as portions of Proverbs linked to Solomon.

WORLD OF THE NARRATIVE AND WORLD OF THE NARRATOR   It is indispensable for a historically enlightened interpretation of the text of the Hebrew Bible to account for the differing worlds of the narrative and its narrator, as well as the reciprocal relationship between the two. This difference will be applied and analyzed in both the subsequent outline of theological history as well as in the discussion of theological themes.

RUDOLF BULTMANN'S PROGRAM OF DEMYTHOLOGIZATION   But for what reason is a discussion of the narrator as well as the narration of theological importance? Would it not be sufficient for a theology of the Hebrew Bible simply to investigate its texts from a theological perspective? This points to a problem that Rudolf Bultmann encountered in the year 1941 that articulated the fundamental difficulties for understanding the biblical—in Bultmann's case New Testament—texts as modern readers (the problem also applies to the Hebrew Bible):

> We cannot use electric lights and radios and, in the event of illness, avail ourselves of modern medical and clinical means and at the same time believe in the spirit and wonder world of the New Testament. And if we suppose that we can do so ourselves, we must be clear that we can represent this as the attitude of Christian faith only by making the Christian proclamation unintelligible and impossible for our contemporaries.[45]

Bultmann immediately cites several practical examples in which mythological declarations confront the readers of the Bible:

> How can my guilt be atoned for by the death of someone guiltless (assuming one may even speak of such)? What primitive concepts of guilt and righteousness lie behind any such notion? And what primitive concepts of God? If what is said about Christ's atoning death is to be understood in terms of the idea of sacrifice, what kind of primitive

---

45. Rudolf Bultmann, "New Testament and Mythology: The Problem of Demythologizing the New Testament Proclamation," in *New Testament and Mythology and Other Basic Writings,* ed. and trans. by Schubert M. Ogden (Philadelphia: Fortress, 1984), 4–5.

mythology is it according to which a divine being who has become man atones with his blood for the sins of humanity?[46]

How can one still understand the Bible today, when it is marked by such primitive mythology? In response, Bultmann developed the program of demythologization. As Bultmann explicitly clarified, its intention is not to *delete* everything mythic in the biblical account—that would be the *elimination* of myth. To do so would be to throw the baby out with the bathwater. Myth must instead be interrogated with regard to its function; it must be *interpreted*.[47] How is that to be accomplished? According to Bultmann, what a myth attempts to communicate is ascertained through the reconstruction of the self-understanding of its narrator. The mythic worldview is temporary, but the anthropological self-conception that the myth expresses can be reconstructed and understood. Bultmann also speaks of the existential interpretation of the myth, which ascertains the existential understanding of the particular author.

But what understanding of existence? It is an understanding in which man finds himself in a world filled with riddles and mysteries and in which he experiences a destiny likewise enigmatic and mysterious. He is compelled to realize that he is not lord of his life, and he becomes aware that the world and human life have their ground and limit in a transcendent power (or powers) that lie beyond whatever he can calculate and control.[48]

This basic experience would be from mythology, which inherently speaks of "the unworldly as worldly, the gods as human,"[49] presented in such a way that it "naïvely objectifies the beyond as though it were something in this world."[50]

By contrast, demythologizing seeks to give full weight to myth's real intention to speak of man's authentic reality.[51]

---

46. Bultmann, "New Testament and Mythology," 7.
47. Bultmann, "New Testament and Mythology," 12.
48. Rudolf Bultmann, "On the Problem of Demythologizing," *The Journal of Religion* 42 (1962): 100.
49. Bultmann, "New Testament and Mythology," 10.
50. Bultmann, "Problem of Demythologizing," 100.
51. Bultmann, "Problem of Demythologizing," 100.

It is evident that by means of this hermeneutical program, historical biblical criticism arrives at immanent significance. To demythologize a myth, to interpret it existentially, one must first ascertain the existential understanding of the author by historical-critical means.

Biblical criticism leads from the biblical text to this existential understanding, but biblical criticism must be accordingly enlightened and aligned. Bultmann's demythologizing program has become outdated. It does not fit with the postmodern sensibilities of many readers of the Bible. Furthermore, myth is experiencing a revival in some places, which makes his program appear obsolete anyway. Some have accused Bultmann's insistence on existential interpretation of ahistoricism.[52] Whether or not these points of criticism are accurate, it remains the case that since Bultmann the hermeneutical problem of the Bible and the theological necessity of historical biblical criticism have rarely been stated with comparable poignancy.

5. The Inclusion of Concrete Living Contexts in the Biblical Texts

TEMPORAL CONTINGENCY OF THE TEXTS OF THE HEBREW BIBLE   In connection to the previous point, the authors and redactors of the biblical texts lived in particular historical, social, economic, and political contexts that influenced them both consciously and unconsciously. Many biblical texts receive their specific theological contour through these influences. While they can certainly be read and understood solely on the level of the text, investigation of the conditions surrounding their composition explains their accents, and such contemporary influences can then be critically evaluated.

Therefore, it is not at all self-evident that the texts of the Bible offer a unified conception of humans (humanity by default falls more into the different classes of king—free person—human; cf. below, §39). Political correctness should not be expected (the Bible originated from a world marked by patriarchy, and it only seldom breaks through this influence). Its worldview is not marked by the natural sciences, but rather by the shape of its society (the order of cosmology and mundane life are not considered separate from one another; cf. below, §31). The religious sphere in ancient

---

52. Cf. Michael Moxter, "Gegenwart, die sich nicht dehnt: Eine kritische Erinnerung an das Zeitverständnis R. Bultmanns," in *Religion und Gestaltung der Zeit*, ed. Dieter Georgi et al. (Kampen: Kok Pharos, 1994), 108–22.

Israel is (most often) marked by sacrifice and temple worship (cf. below, §35), and the possibility that there is no God is viewed as an absurd position afforded only to select fools (Pss 14:1; 53:1).[53] These are the contexts in which the texts of the Hebrew Bible were written, read, and heard. One cannot understand the Hebrew Bible without reconstructing and accounting for these contexts.

6. The Appreciation of Processes of Theologization of Earlier Traditions in the Hebrew Bible

In the past several decades, Hebrew Bible studies have changed profoundly. One of the most important changes concerns the recognition that many texts of the Hebrew Bible arise from inner-biblical interpretation. They were constructed for their particular contexts, without necessarily needing to have originated in an oral setting. They interact with other texts of the Hebrew Bible by differentiating from, confirming, or carrying them forward.

SCRIBAL TRADITIONAL LITERATURE As a result, it is possible to underline the "horizontal" and "vertical" interconnections of texts of the Hebrew Bible. This means that one can search for possible simultaneous literary interlocutors (horizontal references) of texts, as well as for analogous conceptions adopted in later literary positions (vertical references). Scholarship from the past several decades has taught that the books and texts of the Hebrew Bible should be appreciated not only as discrete points, but also in terms of their connections with biblical as well as ancient Near Eastern interlocutors.

The fact that the texts of the Hebrew Bible often engage with one another—whether with confirming, corrective, or conflicting intention—is well-known, though this interaction has by no means been treated exhaustively and will continue to occupy scholarship in the future. Inner-biblical references are recognized primarily through literary adoption and more or less verbatim citations. These are, however, quite rare in reality. One of the few explicit examples appears in Dan 9. The typical manner of an allusion that is not specifically introduced, but is identifiable for the scribal reader

---

53. Cf. Sonja Ammann, *Götter für die Toren: Die Verbindung von Götterpolemik und Weisheit im Alten Testament*, BZAW 466 (Berlin: de Gruyter, 2015).

through the choice of words and themes, presumably points to a narrow circle of scribes as the locus of the production and reception of the texts.

The argument for manifold interactions between the texts and writings of the Hebrew Bible can be sharpened further. Ever since the exegesis of the Hebrew Bible came to understand the once vilified "additions" in the biblical books often to be manifestations of inner-biblical exegesis and recognized that these "additions" can be quite extensive (to the point that in many cases they constitute the majority of a book) it became increasingly clear that the literary growth of the biblical books is not marginal, but rather marks the substance of the books themselves.

REDACTION AS INNER-BIBLICAL RECEPTION The redaction of the biblical books is not an objectively uncontrolled process of the proliferation of text. Rather, it generally consists of a productive process of inner-biblical *reception and interpretation* of preexisting textual material. Text and commentary are typically combined in the writings of the Hebrew Bible. Only after the closing of the canon does interpretation appear next to the text. Redaction history can, therefore, also be described as inner-biblical reception history, the reconstruction of which can reveal the inner-biblical theological discourse with their historical distinctions.

7. *The Appreciation of Processes of the Reception and Theologization of Given Extrabiblical Traditions*

Furthermore, fundamental connections in content and language between the biblical and ancient Near Eastern literature shows that investigations cannot be limited to the Hebrew Bible itself. "Horizontal" and "vertical" references by biblical texts do not stop at the post-biblical era canonical boundaries.

THE HEBREW BIBLE AS A PART OF THE ANCIENT NEAR EAST The realization that the Hebrew Bible should be understood as a subset of ancient Near Eastern literature rather than a foreign entity within it bars a simple model that views the Hebrew Bible as center that is separated from its peripheral environment, which was common in traditional scholarship of the nineteenth and twentieth centuries. The relationships are reversed when viewed historically; the great political and cultural centers lay in Mesopotamia and Egypt since the third millennium. Israel and Judah were small polities that first came on the political stage in the course of the first millennium and were linked through cultural exchange with the ancient Near Eastern empires from the beginning.

CULTURAL CONTACT IN THE ANCIENT WORLD The widely scattered finds show that there is no doubting the basic possibility of even vast geographic cultural contacts in the ancient Near East. The Babylonian Adapa myth is attested in Egyptian Amarna. North Syrian Ugarit was familiar with the Atrahasis Epic. The Gilgamesh Epic was read in northern Israelite Megiddo, according to fragmentary finds. An Aramaic version of the Iranian Bisitun inscription is attested on the Nile island of Elephantine. Cultural contact within the ancient Near East was so close that Israel's central position as well as its almost continuous political dependence on the respective empires located on the Euphrates and the Nile (within the so-called Fertile Crescent) from the eighth century BCE at the latest made it not only possible, but rather quite probable that the contemporary cultural and religious conceptions were known in Israel and were referenced, whether in agreement or disagreement.

Therefore, what is to a certain degree self-explanatory should be formally emphasized: the literature of the Hebrew Bible is not solely explained as a (positive or negative) historical reaction to ancient Near Eastern imperial ideologies. Every form of "parallelomania" is therefore ruled out.[54] However, several important literary and theological conceptions in the Hebrew Bible can only be adequately described in historical terms when one compares them with their ancient Near Eastern counterparts and accordingly recognizes the processes of theological reinterpretation taking place.

Several examples are worth pointing out. Especially clear is, for example, the basic outlook of Deuteronomy and its subsequent traditions, which clearly shows dependence on the theology of the Neo-Assyrian treaties, reformulating their demand for the vassal's unconditional loyalty to the Assyrian emperor with a Yahwistic orientation. A similar case appears in the anti-monarchic reception of the Neo-Assyrian legend of the birth of Sargon in Exod 2.

The exilic interpretations of the Pentateuchal legal traditions are directed against the Babylonian royal legal tradition, such that Yhwh reveals the law and Moses promulgates it. The well-developed depiction of the building of the Solomonic temple in 1 Kgs 6–8 can be considered in relation to either an Assyrian or Babylonian background. That kings are first

---

54. Cf. the critical comments by Samuel Sandmel, "Parallelomania," *JBL* 81 (1962): 1–13.

and foremost builders of temples is a prominent topos, primarily in Neo-Babylonian royal inscriptions.

The Priestly document is similarly linked to its context and affiliated texts, which adopt the Persian conception of world order and reproduce it from an Israelite point of view. Persian influences can also be accounted for in the conception of the succession of world empires in the book of Daniel.

Finally, the wisdom texts in Prov 1–9 and in Qoh can hardly be adequately understood without the Hellenistic background, showing a discussion with popular Greek philosophy.

As a result, the current scholarly situation offers the possibility and necessity for interpreting ancient Israelite literature in its ancient Near Eastern context—without the pseudo-theological obstacles from the time of the "Babel-Bibel" dispute.[55] The originality of the Bible does not lie in the lack of analogies to its materials, but rather in its interpretations and transformations of this material, which, however, can only be adequately grasped by looking beyond the Bible.

8. *Consideration of Later Transformations*

Recognizing the reality of the reception history and the history of the impact of the Hebrew Bible is also part of recognizing its historical nature. The Hebrew Bible has given rise to a two-thousand-year history of interpretation that is anything but irrelevant for present-day theological approaches to the Hebrew Bible.

Many historical interpretations of the Hebrew Bible in post-biblical Judaism and Christianity seem to be interesting today only as traditional positions from reception history. As a result of their textually distant character, one might even deny their nature as "interpretations." At the same time, however, their empirical parameters and culture-producing considerations should be taken seriously.

For the theology of the Hebrew Bible, on the other hand, the distance between the Hebrew Bible and its history of reception should be maintained; the foreign nature of the texts of the Hebrew Bible can hardly be overemphasized, because they are read in light of their effects rather than taking seriously the texts as literary creations in their own right.

---

55. Cf. Reinhard G. Lehmann, *Friedrich Delitzsch und der Babel-Bibel-Streit*, OBO 133 (Freiburg: Universitätsverlag; Göttingen: Vandenhoeck & Ruprecht, 1994).

9. Description and Normativity

The inquiry into the theology of the Hebrew Bible is often described as concerning not only the origins of the Hebrew Bible, but also its application (cf. also above, §1).[56] Sometimes this question is termed—apparently synonymously—as a "question of truth."[57] However, what conceptions are linked to the application of the texts of the Bible remains unclear.

APPLICATION OF BIBLICAL DECLARATIONS? Should this claim indicate that the texts of the Bible contain true and therefore valid declarations? This position is reasonable, if one has existential truths in mind, but much less so when one has physical, biological, or historical truths in view. The biblical creation account is not "true" in the sense of the natural sciences, and neither the Tower of Babel nor the Moses story is historically "true." And the existential truths that the biblical texts articulate are not primarily true because they are in the Bible, but rather because they establish certain resonances with human experience. Accordingly, they are not "valid" in a formal sense, but rather their validity is manifest after the fact.

ETHICAL NORMATIVITY FOR BIBLICAL TEXTS? Or is by normativity meant that biblical texts should provide norms for human behavior, such that their validity should be viewed from an ethical point of view? This holds true in certain communities of interpretation for texts like the Decalogue, but hardly for the slave or priestly laws of the Torah. Yet it should be stipulated here that—to remain with this example—the laws of the Decalogue are not valid *as such*, but rather this validity is granted them in virtue of their inherent plausibility. The normativity of the Decalogue in history and in the present, wherever it is maintained and advocated, is not really inherent in the text, but rather has to do with the nature of their reception. Normativity as such does not belong to the text, but is rather accorded to the text.

56. Bernd Janowski, "Theologie des Alten Testaments: Zwischenbilanz und Zukunftsperspektiven," in *Theologie und Exegese des Alten Testaments / der Hebräischen Bibel: Zwischenbilanz und Zukunftsperspektiven*, SBS 200 (Stuttgart: Katholisches Bibelwerk, 2005), 111–12.

57. Hermann Spieckermann, "Die Verbindlichkeit des Alten Testaments," in *Gottes Liebe zu Israel: Studien zur Theologie des Alten Testaments*, FAT 33 (Tübingen: Mohr Siebeck, 2004), 177.

RELIGIOUS NORMATIVITY Or should the Bible provide the norms for the religiosity and faith of its readers? It has played this role over many centuries in Judaism and Christianity; however, it was only one factor among many, albeit a central one. In light of its cultural power, the Bible has influenced the religions of Judaism and Christianity significantly, but can its texts count as normative for faith? However one answers this difficult question, hardly anyone would insist that the Bible provides the norms for faith *in every respect.* The Jewish and the Christian faiths would then have to be as multivocal with regard to their content as the Bible is itself, and they would not want to, attempt to, or be permitted to critique or reduce this multivocality. The *substance* of the Bible indeed determines lived faith in Judaism and in Christianity, but very often in a more unquestioned mode than a normative, objectively differentiated and specified demand. And wherever theological doctrine refers explicitly to the Bible, this takes place as a critical, selective, and reflective action, if this doctrine attempts to be theologically relevant.

NORMATIVITY OF THE BIBLE AS AN ENLIGHTENED POSTULATE This short description of the problematics shows that discourse on the validity of the Bible is highly complex and does not possess a clear outline. The call for a *normative* theology of the Hebrew Bible, or for a biblical theology generally, appears, when viewed in terms of the history of scholarship, to have less to do with the "internal demand"[58] of the text than with a residual concern of the Enlightenment's reception of the Bible. The Enlightenment granted the Bible validity to the degree that its normative standards were compatible with those of reason. The biblical worldview, the histories, and the historical presentation of the laws do not withstand the critique of reason, but the ethical commandments of the Bible are still acceptable. Accordingly, the Bible was primarily reduced to its ethics. In an interesting turn, this led to a process whereby the narrative content of the Bible, in order to prevent its loss, was interpreted normatively. Analogously, it became the practice to interpret texts of the Bible in the sense of a *moral imperative,* even when these texts belonged to *narrative genres*—such as, for example, the paradise narrative. It was read as a *warning* against eating from the Tree of Knowledge, that one *should* not desire to be like God, and that one *should* not squander paradise. However, all of this is a productive adaptation of the paradise narrative that itself only shares the commensu-

58. Spieckermann, "Verbindlichkeit," 173.

rate motifs with the actual text itself. The paradise narrative *narrates* that the humans ate from the Tree of Knowledge, that they *became* like God in recognizing good and evil, and that they *lost* paradise forever (cf. below, §31). These events are unchangeable and cannot be reversed. They are of such a fundamental nature that they have a primordial quality and were therefore explained at the very beginning of the Bible. As with many other texts of the Bible, especially in the Primeval History, the paradise narrative does not promote or forbid specific behavior; instead it intends to explain why certain circumstances of life are the way they are—why women experience birth pangs, why provisioning of food is an arduous task, or why snakes do not have legs. Finally, and connected to this, Gen 2–3 does not account for the disruption and destruction of the human world—though one might be hastily inclined to suggest such a present-day adaptation. It instead speaks of the loss of paradise, which is not the current human world, but rather a counterworldly projection.[59] According to Gen 2–3, the post-paradise order is in fact the world of human affairs, with birth pangs, work, and marriage. In this respect, the nature of the information coming from the paradise narrative does not lead one to expect results in the form of direct behavioral instructions. Rather, Gen 2–3 helps to understand reality in a differentiated way. Instructions for behavior can result only in an indirect manner. As a result, it is questionable whether one must conclude from the "membership of Hebrew Bible studies to the university department of theology"[60] the necessity of the introduction of normative questions. This is only necessary when following a particular understanding of theology.

HERMENEUTICS AND ETHICS   The extraction of ethical views from biblical texts is legitimate, but should take place in a methodologically controlled manner. At the same time, one should remain conscious that many texts of the Bible are more hermeneutically than ethically oriented. The Bible very rarely addresses the reader directly, and even in these cases one should note that the ancient audience experienced completely different life circumstances from the audiences of today. The Bible instead attempts to con-

59. Cf. Fritz Stolz, "Paradies und Gegenwelten," *Zeitschrift für Religionswissenschaft* 1 (1993): 5–24; Fritz Stolz, "Paradies," *TRE* 25 (Berlin: de Gruyter, 1995), 708–711.

60. Erhard Blum, "Notwendigkeit und Grenzen historischer Exegese: Plädoyer für eine alttestamentliche Exegetik," in *Theologie und Exegese des Alten Testaments / der Hebräischen Bibel: Zwischenbilanz und Zukunftsperspektiven*, ed. Bernd Janowski, SBS 200 (Stuttgart: Katholisches Bibelwerk, 2005), 38.

solidate particular life experiences, and its texts can be investigated for the worldview of their authors. This is a descriptive procedure, which is not for this reason less theologically valuable than normative considerations.

VALIDITY AS AN OVERARCHING CONCEPTION OF TEXT AND AUDI-
ENCE The above considerations do not question the legitimacy of normative approaches to the Bible. They instead try, first of all, to emphasize that the inquiry into the validity of biblical texts cannot take place solely within the text; it must rather be considered in relation to the corresponding interpretive community. Secondly, these considerations serve to highlight the theological capability of historical description.

10. *Critique of Influences from the History of Scholarship*

In keeping with the weight of its content and reception history, the Hebrew Bible is an extraordinarily thoroughly researched body of texts. The interpretation of its texts is dependent on various historical factors. Therefore, different imprints from the history of scholarship that influence the treatment of the Hebrew Bible can be identified. These influences should never be criticized as such, but they should be recognized and included in the thematic considerations. For example, the topic of creation was largely neglected in the wake of the order theologies of the postwar 1920s and 1930s, which is understandable but in reality unjustified. Furthermore, since the 1980s, intensive Jewish-Christian dialogue has cast the topic of law in a new light. One can also point to the processes of inner-biblical interpretation recognized in the past several decades, which has aroused understanding for the importance of so-called secondary passages in the Bible as well as for the theological history of the Second Temple period. Certain constellations of the history of scholarship require specific prioritization and approaches. It is advantageous for everyone to be informed of these.[61]

---

61. Cf. the comprehensive presentation in Magne Sæbø, ed., *Hebrew Bible / Old Testament: The History of Its Interpretation*, 3 vols. in 5 parts (Göttingen: Vandenhoeck & Ruprecht, 1996–2015).

E. Theologies of Extant Hebrew Bibles and Old Testaments

Following the formulation of the chosen approach to a theology of the Hebrew Bible, an initial inquiry should be made into the description of the identifiable theologies of the overall literary compositions of extant Hebrew Bibles and Old Testaments. What dimensions of meaning are accentuated by the various orders of the biblical canons in Judaism and Christianity?[1] It should be underscored that only the formation by the final editor will be discussed, whereas Part F will undertake steps back into the partial collections within Torah, Nevi'im, and Ketuvim.

---

1. Cf. Erich Zenger: "The project of 'theology of the Old Testament' is a typical product of Christian theology. It arose when critical exegesis increasingly shook the entrenched edifice of Christian doctrine. 'Theology of the Old Testament,' or rather 'biblical theology' was 'devised' in order to systematize and hold firm what one was able to and wanted to teach as the (revealed) truth of the Bible against the bewildering flood of the many individual observations and in light of the manifold challenges to incontrovertible truths by historical-critical exegesis." "Ist das Projekt 'Theologie der Hebräischen Bibel / des Alten Testaments' überhaupt bibelgemäß? Response auf den Vortrag von Shimon Gesundheit," in *Biblische Theologie*, ed. Paul Hanson et al., Altes Testament und Moderne 14 (Münster: LIT, 2005), 65–66. However, Zenger views the project as legitimate for two reasons: "1. While the Hebrew Bible is not a systematic textbook, neither is it an anthology and collection of aphorisms. Its final extant form arises from . . . a systemization recognizable in the text complexes themselves. . . . 2. If one assumes that the Bible is a literary work that, as such, can be interpreted with the methods of literary studies, then a systematic and summary interpretation of the whole at least of large recognizable literary complexes like, e.g., Torah, Prophets, Psalms is a legitimate *scholarly* task. Such an overarching interpretation cannot take the place of the interpreted texts, but it must hope to serve to understanding the texts themselves deeper and better." "Ist das Projekt," 67.

§16 Hebrew Bibles in Judaism and Their Theologies

Peter Brandt, *Endgestalten des Kanons: Das Arrangement der Schriften Israels in der jüdischen und christlichen Bibel*, BBB 131 (Berlin: Philo, 2001) ♦ Lester L. Grabbe, "The Law, the Prophets, and the Rest: The State of the Bible in Pre-Maccabean Times," *DSD* 13 (2006): 319–338 ♦ Timothy J. Stone, *The Compilational History of the Megilloth: Canon, Contoured Intertextuality and Meaning in the Writings*, FAT II/59 (Tübingen: Mohr Siebeck, 2013)

TORAH, NEVI'IM, AND KETUVIM   The Hebrew Bibles of Judaism follow the three-part structure of Torah, Nevi'im, and Ketuvim. However, the authoritative writings of Israel seem to still have essentially existed in two parts at the time of the New Testament (cf. above, §11). They were comprised of "Moses," that is the "Law," and the "Prophets" (cf. 1QS 1.1–2; Luke 16:16, 29, 31; 24:27; Acts 28:23). This organization is important for the hermeneutics of the whole document in itself. It is apparently understood as the preeminent Torah along with its historical application by the prophets.

In the framework of this two-part organization, the Prophets appears to have been a more extensive corpus than it is today. According to the statement in 11QPsᵃ 27.11, counted among them in a broader sense were also the Psalms, which were all attributed to David through נבואה (*nbw'h*), "prophecy" (cf. also 4 Macc 18:10–19). In any case, this division appears to represent the most widely spread structure of the Scriptures. One will, however, need to differentiate further according to sociological groups. Several attestations explicitly name the Psalms in addition to Moses and the Prophets (cf. 4QMMTᵈ [=4Q397]; Luke 24:44). However, these witnesses are rare and do not objectively conflict, because the "and" between the Prophets and the Psalms could have an emphatic rather than an additive sense.

Even the oft-cited prologue of Sirach from the last third of the second century BCE does not present a counter argument against the basic two-part division of the Scriptures around the turn of the era. The presence of a third part of the canon in the sense of the later Ketuvim is out of the question before 70 CE in light of further evidence from Qumran and the New Testament. The notion of a closed Bible is first attested in Josephus (*Contra Apionem* 1.8) und in 4 Ezra 14 (cf. above, §11).

OVERALL THEOLOGICAL PROFILE But what is the theological profile of the later three-part canon? Why did a third division of the Ketuvim ("Writings") emerge at all—apparently first after 70 CE and presumably at the exclusion of certain texts, like Psalms or Daniel for example, from what had earlier been more broadly conceived as the Prophets?

Psalms, Proverbs, Job, Qoheleth, etc., show—when read canonically—how the pious should act and what benefits such behavior can provide even in the face of all of life's adversities, as Job, for example, recognizes and articulates. As a whole, one could describe the new canonical logic of the progression from Law to Prophets to Writings as a "de-eschatologization" of the previous combination of Law and Prophets, the latter of which pointed to the application of the Torah in history. Rather than the historical journey of God with his people, now the individual and his well-being in everyday life stand in the forefront.

PSALM 1 AS THE OPENING OF THE KETUVIM The programmatic introduction of the Ketuvim presents this perspective. The Psalter, and therefore Psalm 1, begins the Ketuvim in the majority of the attested arrangements of the Hebrew Bible:[2]

> Happy is he who does not follow the advice of the wicked, or take
>   the path that sinners tread, or sit in the seat of scoffers;
> But his delight is in the instruction of Yhwh, and on his Torah he
>   meditates day and night.
> He is like a tree planted by streams of water.
> He yields his fruit in its season, and his leaves do not wither. In all
>   that he does, he prospers.
> The wicked are not so; they are like chaff that the wind drives away.
> Therefore the wicked will not stand in the judgment, nor sinners in
>   the congregation of the righteous;
> For Yhwh watches over the way of the righteous, but the way of the
>   wicked will perish. (Ps 1:1–6)

Psalm 1 stipulates that whoever is oriented towards Torah will succeed in life. It is surely not without deliberation that the Torah called to

2. Cf. Reinhard G. Kratz, "Die Tora Davids: Ps 1 und die doxologische Fünfteilung des Psalters," *ZTK* 93 (1996): 1–34; Bernd Janowski, "Freude an der Tora: Psalm 1 als Tor zum Psalter," *EvT* 67 (2007): 18–31.

mind here is the Torah of Yhwh (and not the Torah of Moses), recalling the parlance of the books of Chronicles, which in some arrangements of the Ketuvim appear before the Psalms. Psalm 1 subordinates itself, the Psalter, and—when read in terms of its reception—the whole Ketuvim to the Torah. The Torah is the entity towards which the pious orient themselves by means of the Ketuvim. In addition to this explicit reference on the surface level of the text, there are also implicit allusions in Ps 1 that allow for a specific interpretation of the canon's theology. Psalm 1 recalls, first of all, the previously discussed opening text from the Nevi'im, Josh 1:8, where God addresses Joshua after the death of Moses:

> This book of Torah should not depart from your lips, and you should meditate on it day and night so that you keep everything written in it. For then it will make your way prosperous and then you will be successful.

By means of this recollection, Ps 1 places its reader back into the position of Joshua immediately following the death of Moses. On the one hand, Ps 1 turns back the history of Israel's deliverance to the time before the conquest, which culminated in Israel's history of calamity in the exile. This means that everything is once again possible for the individual. On the other hand, Ps 1 renders every individual responsible. The task to obey Torah, to which well-being is linked, is given to *everyone*, not just the leaders like Joshua or the kings.

The fact that Ps 1 is tied to the beginning (Josh 1) and not the end of the canonical section of the Nevi'im indicates further that, from the perspective of Ps 1, the Ketuvim offer an independent, complementary, and non-prophetic interpretation of the Torah. The logic of the three-part canon of the Hebrew Bible is not constructed linearly in the sense that Torah, Nevi'im, and Ketuvim are connected to each other in a successive manner. Psalm 1 instead shows that the Ketuvim have an unmediated relationship to the Torah that virtually leaves out the Nevi'im. This direct orientation towards the Torah is indirectly supported by a second inner-biblical adoption in Ps 1. The image of the tree by the streams of water is apparently taken from Jer 17:7–8:

> Blessed is the man who trusts in Yhwh and whose hope is in Yhwh!
> He will be like a tree planted by the water, whose roots stretch out

toward the stream. It has nothing to fear when the heat comes; its leaves remain green. Even in the year of drought it is not anxious, it does not cease to bring fruit.

In the reception of Jer 17:8 in Ps 1, the Ketuvim fundamentally relativizes Jeremiah's prophecy of judgment. Whoever conducts himself in accord with Ps 1 does not even need to fear the kind of judgment that Jeremiah proclaimed and suffered through, for it will not take place (or, more precisely, according to Ps 1 it will not take place for those devoted to the Torah, but it will for the sinners).

The reception of Josh 1 and Jer 17 does not mean, however, that the overarching theology of judgment in the Nevi'im is invalidated *in every respect*. Psalm 1 instead maintains that the overarching theology of judgment will not have decisive effects at the level of the individual conduct of the devout.

VARIATIONS IN THE ARRANGEMENT As indicated earlier, the now standard order of the Tanakh was by no means authoritative from the beginning. The manuscript tradition of Jewish Bibles attests to numerous variant arrangements of the books. The three-part canon of Torah, Nevi'im, and Ketuvim and the number of books found within this division do, however, remain constant. Based on these two conditions, the number of possible mathematical variations comes to 120 variations for the five books of Torah, 40,320 variations for the eight books of the Nevi'im (if following the ancient practice of counting the twelve Minor Prophets as one book), and around forty million variations for the Ketuvim.

The tradition comes nowhere near exhausting the potential options. The Torah always appears in the same order. Nine variants are attested for the Nevi'im, and these all concern the Latter Prophets. Genesis to Kings presents a chronologically arranged combination, which orders the books by the logical sequence of their content. The order of the Ketuvim is relatively fluid; here at least seventy different arrangements are attested. The following examples are only of an illustrative nature.

The most important variants in the Nevi'im appear in the Babylonian Talmud (b. B. Bat. 14b–15a). It attests to the four prophetic books (Isaiah, Jeremiah, Ezekiel, Book of the Twelve Prophets) following the order Jeremiah, Ezekiel, Isaiah, and Book of the Twelve—arranging the books according to their lengths (see above, p. 65).

The arrangements of the Ketuvim also vary, sometimes quite dramatically. The Aleppo Codex and Codex Leningradensis, for example, view Chronicles as an introduction to the Ketuvim because it reports the installation of the temple cult under David and Solomon. It is therefore understood as the "historical" introduction to the Psalms (cf. in more detail above, §10).

JEWISH BIBLES IN GREEK In addition to the Hebrew Bibles, various Greek versions of Jewish Bibles existed in antiquity. The so-called Septuagint emerged—beginning with the translation of the Torah—as the Bible of the Greek-speaking Jewish community in Alexandria. After the adoption of the Septuagint by early Christianity, the need soon arose for new, separate translations for Judaism. This led to the translations of the Bible by Aquila, Symmachus, and Theodotion. Because of the unfortunate nature of transmission, however, it is hardly possible to garner information about the arrangement of the Greek Bibles of ancient Judaism. Whether the well-known configuration of the historical traditions in the Christian codices (cf. below, §17), in which the books of Chronicles–Ezra–Nehemiah follow immediately after 1–4 Kingdoms (1–2 Samuel, 1–2 Kings), goes back to a Jewish *Vorlage* can no longer be deduced. In any case, the rendering of the books of the Hebrew Bible into Greek that went on successively for over four hundred years shows, first of all, that the configuration of the books into a biblical corpus was a second-order procedure. Other variations in the arrangement were more than likely, despite the scarcity of available manuscripts.

§17 Old Testaments and Their Theologies

Anneli Aejmelaeus, "Die Septuaginta als Kanon," in *Kanon in Konstruktion und Dekonstruktion: Kanonisierungsprozesse religiöser Texte von der Antike bis zur Gegenwart: Ein Handbuch,* ed. Eve-Marie Becker and Stefan Scholz (Berlin: de Gruyter, 2012), 315–27 ♦ Heinz-Josef Fabry, "Der Beitrag der Septuaginta-Codizes zur Kanonfrage: Kanon-theologische Überlegungen zu Einheit und Vielfalt biblischer Theologie," in *Die Septuaginta—Entstehung, Sprache, Geschichte: 3. internationale Fachtagung veranstaltet von Septuaginta Deutsch (LXX.D), Wuppertal 22.–25. Juli 2010,* ed. Siegfried Kreuzer et al., WUNT 286 (Tübingen: Mohr Siebeck, 2012), 582–99 ♦ Lee M. McDonald, *The Old Testa-*

ment: Its Authority and Canonicity, vol. 1 of *The Formation of the Biblical Canon* (London: Bloomsbury, 2017) ◆ Matthias Millard, "Die alten Septuaginta-Codizes und ihre Bedeutung für die Geschichte des biblischen Kanons," in *Formen des Kanons: Studien zu Ausprägungen des biblischen Kanons von der Antike bis zum 19. Jahrhundert,* ed. Thomas Hieke, SBS 228 (Stuttgart: Katholisches Bibelwerk, 2013), 40–60 ◆ Tobias Nicklas, "The Development of the Christian Bible," in *What Is Bible?,* ed. Karin Finsterbusch and Armin Lange, CBET 67 (Leuven: Peeters, 2012), 393–426

THE OLD TESTAMENT IN GREEK Early Christianity primarily used the Greek Old Testament, which interpreted the Holy Scripture of Judaism into the *lingua franca* of the eastern Mediterranean region. This linguistic change arose initially due to practical reasons: it could be accessed much more easily by Christians who had not come from a Jewish background. However, it was also presumably connected with fundamental theological considerations. The Old Testament thus became accessible in the cosmopolitan language of the time. It could be communicated in that language, and now was also pointed directly at non-Jews.

VARIATIONS IN THE ARRANGEMENT Just as in the case of the Hebrew Bibles, but more pronounced due to the better condition of the literary sources for the early period, the manuscript evidence of the Greek Old Testaments demonstrates that the order within the manuscripts of Late Antiquity and the Early Middle Ages was not set. In the following, the examples of the arrangements of the books in the large uncial manuscripts of the Septuagint of the fourth and fifth centuries CE (Codex Vaticanus, Codex Sinaiticus, and Codex Alexandrinus) introduce the differing theologies of these three Old Testaments. These Old Testaments exist as part of whole Christian Bibles, so their theology should necessarily be placed within the horizon of the entirety of that Bible. While one could press forward with a complete investigation of all arrangements of the various confessions at this point, these three examples of the Septuagint will suffice.

THE GREAT UNCIAL MANUSCRIPTS The books of the Bible in Codex Sinaiticus, Codex Alexandrinus, and Codex Vaticanus are arranged as follows:

Codex Sinaiticus (א)	Codex Alexandrinus (A)	Codex Vaticanus (B)
Gen	Gen	Gen [from Gen 36]
. . .	Exod	Exod
	Lev	Lev
Num	Num	Num
. . .	Deut	Deut
	Josh	Josh
	Judg	Judg
	Ruth	Ruth
	1–4 Kgdms	1–4 Kgdms
1[–2] Chr	1–2 Chr	1–2 Chr
[1–]2 Esdras	Hos	1–2 Esdras
Esth	Amos	Pss
Tob	Mic	Prov
Jdt	Joel	Qoh
1+4 Macc	Obad	Cant
Isa	Jonah	Job
Jer	Nah	Wis
Lam	Hab	Sir
. . .	Zeph	Esth
	Hag	Jdt
	Zech	Tob
	Mal	Hos
	Isa	Amos
	Jer	Mic
	Bar	Joel
Joel	Lam	Obad
Obad	Ep Jer	Jonah
Jonah	Ezek	Nah
Nah	Dan	Hab
Hab	Esth	Zeph
Zeph	Tob	Hag
Hag	Jdt	Zech
Zech	1–2 Esdras	Mal
Mal	1–4 Macc	Isa
Prov	Pss	Jer
Qoh	Job	Bar

Codex Sinaiticus (ℵ)	Codex Alexandrinus (A)	Codex Vaticanus (B)
Cant	Prov	Lam
Wis	Qoh	Ep Jer
Sir	Cant	Ezek
Job	Wisd	Dan
	Sir	
	Pss Sol	
Matt	Matt	Matt
Mark	Mark	Mark
Luke	Luke	Luke
John	John	John
Rom	Acts	Acts
1–2 Cor	Jas	Jas
Gal	1–2 Pet	1–2 Pet
Eph	1–3 John	1–3 John
Phil	Jude	Jude
Col	Rom	Rom
1–2 Thess	1–2 Cor	1–2 Cor
Heb	Gal	Gal
1–2 Tim	Eph	Eph
Titus	Phil	Phil
Phlm	Col	Col
Acts	1–2 Thess	1–2 Thess
Jas	Heb	Heb . . .
1–2 Pet	1–2 Tim	
1–3 John	Titus	
Jude	Phlm	
Rev	Rev	
Barn	1–2 Clem	
Herm		

An initial comparison of the order of the Old Testament section shows clearly that the three codices agree on the order of the books from Gen–4 Kgdms (including Ruth) and 1–2 Chr. The historical books are placed together, which is expected due to the continuous narrative thread from Gen–4 Kgdms and the similar genres of the books. However, the three codices go different ways in their arrangements of the books that follow, though set or quasi-set group connections—similar to Gen–2 Chr—

can be recognized for the sequence Esth–Jdt–Tob / Esth–Tob–Jdt, the combination of Psalms and the "Solomonic writings," as well as the prophetic books.

Codex Sinaiticus In Codex Sinaiticus (א), Chronicles is followed (like in B) by the books of 1–2 Esdras (Ezra–Nehemiah), then Esther, Tobit, Judith, and 1+4 Maccabees to form a large historiographic corpus from creation to the Maccabees. The Prophets and the rest of the Writings follow, with Job in a conspicuous position at the end of the Old Testament.

Codex Alexandrinus In Codex Alexandrinus (A), 1 Esdras (Ezra) and 2 Esdras (Nehemiah) are separated from Chronicles. Here it is Gen–Kings + Chronicles and the books of the Prophets, and then the remaining writings with Pss Sol as the conclusion. The New Testament is completed by Revelation and the two letters of Clement.

Codex Vaticanus Codex Vaticanus (B) follows Chronicles and 1–2 Esdras (Ezra–Nehemiah) with Psalms, Proverbs, Qoheleth, Song of Songs, Job, Wisdom of Solomon, Sirach, Esther, Judith, and Tobit. It presents the Prophets (including the Jeremianic satellites Lamentations, Baruch, and the Epistle of Jeremiah, as well as the book of Daniel) in the concluding position, while the Minor Prophets (Hosea–Malachi) and the Major Prophets (Isaiah–Ezekiel), to which Daniel is also added, are interestingly inverted.

The New Testament in the Three Codices In the New Testament section, the three manuscripts agree in their placement of Matthew, Mark, Luke, and John in a fixed order at the beginning, and the letters follow the Gospels. Everything else, however, is quite open.

Codex Sinaiticus In Codex Sinaiticus (א) the four Gospels are not followed by Acts, as is familiar from the later standard arrangement, but first by the letters recognized canonically as Pauline (including Hebrews), after which Acts is presented. These are followed by James, 1–2 Peter, 1–3 John, Jude, and Revelation, as well as by the letter of Barnabas and—only extant in very fragmentary form—the Shepherd of Hermas.

Codex Alexandrinus The writings following the Gospels and Acts in Codex Alexandrinus (A) appear to have been arranged roughly according to a chronological conception, for which reason the catholic letters, which are traced back to the "older" figures of James, Peter, John, and Jude, appear before the "Pauline" letters. The New Testament is concluded by Revelation as well as the two letters of Clement (though 1 Clem. 57:7–63:4 as well as 2 Clem. 12:5 to the end are not extant).

CODEX VATICANUS To the degree extant, the New Testament in Codex Vaticanus (B) is structured like the one in Codex Alexandrinus. It cannot be determined whether further writings were added after Revelation.

BIBLICAL THEOLOGY OF THE CODICES How can these variations in arrangement be explained?

CODEX SINAITICUS The Old Testament of Codex Sinaiticus ends with the book of Job. This is hardly by chance, but likely serves to highlight the declaration of the theme of the "righteous sufferer," who—in accordance with the first additional concluding part of the book of Job in the Septuagint (Job 42:17a [LXX] instead of Job 42:17)—rises again, thereby accentuating a biblical-theological bridge between the two testaments.

> But it is written that [Job] will rise up again together with those that the Lord resurrects. (Job 42:17a)

Although this is not expressly stated, it is still clear that in this arrangement of biblical books, Job is seen as a prefiguration of Christ. The Old Testament culminates in the expected resurrection of the exemplary righteous sufferer, Job.

One can evaluate whether the specific arrangement of the New Testament in Codex Sinaiticus can be brought into connection with this emphasis on the "righteous sufferer." We have seen that Acts does not follow the Gospels in Codex Sinaiticus, where the Pauline letters instead come directly after the Gospels and only then the book of Acts. As a result, Acts is not the continuation of the Gospels, but rather a narrative counterpart to the Pauline letters and therefore primarily illustrates the resistance and suffering that Paul experienced as part of his mission. The fact that Codex Sinaiticus goes beyond the New Testament and also offers the letter of Barnabas and the Shepherd of Hermas, both of which present a strong paraenetic emphasis and doctrine of the two ways (one of the righteous and one of the wicked), would then be interpreted such that the biblical manuscript as a whole does not result in quietism, but rather motivates the righteous, in the face of all hostilities, to moral action.

CODEX ALEXANDRINUS According to its barely legible (and likely secondary) table of contents, Codex Alexandrinus concluded the latter books of the Old Testament with the Psalms of Solomon, which offers one of the most large-scale messianic promises known in all of Jewish literature.

Codex Alexandrinus's clear interest in declaring its biblical theology through the concluding Old Testament text is structurally comparable to Codex Sinaiticus. Alexandrinus also indicates a particular Christology, which, however, places a rather different emphasis from the one in Codex Sinaiticus. Rather than the theme of the "righteous sufferer," the theological goal of the Old Testament according to the arrangement in Codex Alexandrinus is the expectation of the "messiah," a son of David (v. 23), who—himself free from sin (v. 41)—wipes out the sin of the world (vv. 26–27), who is led by God (vv. 35, 38, 43), and whose power is especially found in his word (vv. 48–49; cf. v. 37). The Christological viewpoint of Codex Alexandrinus has something more of a traditional orientation; it emphasizes the classic "messiah" theme as a theological bridge between the two testaments. The letter to Marcellinus inserted before the Psalms also fits with this viewpoint because it explicitly opens the Psalter to messianic interpretation as well as the basic chronological order of the New Testament writings.

The New Testament of Codex Alexandrinus also includes the two letters of Clement. It is unlikely that this further inclusion into the New Testament can be connected with the messianic Christology evoked by the conclusion of the Old Testament with the Psalms of Solomon. The letter of 1 Clement in particular is a witness of an early claim to the primacy of the bishop of Rome. Therefore, read in the larger context of the messianic Christology of the codex, it leads to the legitimation of the *vicarious Christi* in Rome.

CODEX VATICANUS The Old Testament of the Codex Vaticanus (B) ends with the book of Daniel—a tradition followed by many other Septuagint manuscripts. As often presented, the concluding position of the book of Daniel within the Old Testament of Codex Vaticanus, especially in light of the expansive vision of the Son of Man in Dan 7, leads to the New Testament that follows.

Codex Vaticanus thereby emphasizes a *Son of Man* Christology. The Old Testament ends with the promise of the coming Son of Man, the New

Testament then reports of his arrival. As in the case of Codex Alexandrinus, here too the basic chronological arrangement of the New Testament connects well with the Old Testament as it is structured in Codex Vaticanus.

ARBITRARY OR PLANNED? These variations between the different codices could lead to the premature conclusion that the order of the books in the Old Testament is arbitrary. While the order is in fact undetermined, the variations do not indicate a basic arbitrariness. They instead point towards different theological intentions with regard to the forms of an overarching biblical theology.

F. Theologies of the Three Parts of the Canon and Their Collections

Having surveyed and described the theologies of overall biblical compositions, the following sections take a step backward to assess the formation of the biblical canon itself, as well as its component parts and their respective theological accentuations. The differentiation of Torah, Nevi'im, and Ketuvim offers a good starting point, though the earlier collections that make up these sections of canon will also be investigated in a more or less tentative manner. In the case of the Torah and the Nevi'im, one must also reckon with the fact that such earlier collections could have originally transgressed the boundaries of the later canonical division between the Torah and Nevi'im, becoming literarily divided during the formation of the Torah, such as the narrative connection between Deuteronomy and the book of Joshua.[1]

§18 Torah

Erhard Blum, *Studien zur Komposition des Pentateuch*, BZAW 189 (Berlin: de Gruyter, 1990) ◆ Erhard Blum, "Gibt es die Endgestalt des Pentateuch?," in *Congress Volume: Leuven 1989*, ed. John A. Emerton, VTSup 43 (Leiden: Brill, 1991), 46–57 ◆ Suzanne Boorer, *The Vision of the Priestly Narrative: Its Genre and Hermeneutics of Time*, AIL 27 (Atlanta: SBL Press, 2016) ◆ Stephen B. Chapman, *The Law and the Prophets: A Study in Old Testament Canon Forma-*

---

1. Cf. Christian Frevel, "Die Wiederkehr der Hexateuchperspektive: Eine Herausforderung für die These vom deuteronomistischen Geschichtswerk," in *Das deuteronomistische Geschichtswerk*, ed. Hermann-Josef Stipp, ÖBS 39 (Frankfurt am Main: Lang, 2011), 13–53; Thomas Römer, "From Deuteronomistic History to Nebiim and Torah," in *Making the Biblical Text: Textual Studies in the Hebrew and Greek Bible*, ed. Innocent Himbaza, OBO 275 (Fribourg: Academic Press; Göttingen: Vandenhoeck & Ruprecht, 2015), 1–18.

tion, FAT 27 (Tübingen: Mohr Siebeck, 2000) ◆ David J. A. Clines, *The Theme of the Pentateuch*, 2nd ed., JSOTSup 10 (Sheffield: Sheffield Academic, 1997) ◆ Frank Crüsemann, *The Torah: Theology and Social History of Old Testament Law*, trans. Allan W. Mahnke (Minneapolis: Fortress, 1996) ◆ Karin Finsterbusch, *Deuteronomium: Eine Einführung*, UTB 3626 (Göttingen: Vandenhoeck & Ruprecht, 2012) ◆ Jan C. Gertz, *Tradition und Redaktion in der Exoduserzählung: Untersuchungen zur Endredaktion des Pentateuch*, FRLANT 186 (Göttingen: Vandenhoeck & Ruprecht, 2000) ◆ Gary N. Knoppers and Bernard M. Levinson, eds., *The Pentateuch as Torah: New Models for Understanding Its Promulgation and Acceptance* (Winona Lake, IN: Eisenbrauns, 2007) ◆ Matthias Köckert, *Vätergott und Väterverheißungen: Eine Auseinandersetzung mit Albrecht Alt und seinen Erben*, FRLANT 142 (Göttingen: Vandenhoeck & Ruprecht, 1988) ◆ Christoph Levin, *Der Jahwist*, FRLANT 157 (Göttingen: Vandenhoeck & Ruprecht, 1993) ◆ Eckart Otto, *Das Deuteronomium im Pentateuch und Hexateuch: Studien zur Literaturgeschichte von Pentateuch und Hexateuch im Lichte des Deuteronomiumrahmens*, FAT 30 (Tübingen: Mohr Siebeck, 2000) ◆ Thomas Römer, "Zwischen Urkunden, Fragmenten und Ergänzungen: Zum Stand der Pentateuchforschung," *ZAW* 125 (2013): 2–24 ◆ Thomas Römer, "Der Pentateuch," in *Die Entstehung des Alten Testaments*, ed. Walter Dietrich et al., Theologische Wissenschaft 1,1 (Stuttgart: Kohlhammer, 2014), 52–166 ◆ Konrad Schmid, *Erzväter und Exodus: Untersuchungen zur doppelten Begründung der Ursprünge Israels innerhalb der Geschichtsbücher des Alten Testaments*, WMANT 81 (Neukirchen-Vluyn: Neukirchener Verlag, 1999) ◆ Konrad Schmid, "Der Pentateuch und seine Theologiegeschichte," *ZTK* 111 (2014): 239–71 ◆ Markus Witte, *Die biblische Urgeschichte: Redaktions- und theologiegeschichtliche Beobachtungen zu Genesis 1,1–11,26*, BZAW 265 (Berlin: de Gruyter, 1998) ◆ Markus Witte, "Methodological Reflections on a Theology of the Pentateuch," in *The Formation of the Pentateuch: Bridging the Academic Cultures of Europe, Israel, and North America*, ed. Jan C. Gertz et al., FAT 111 (Tübingen: Mohr Siebeck, 2016), 1109–20

1. The Theology of the Torah as an Overarching Complex

Of the three sections of the canon of the Hebrew Bible, the Torah has the clearest literary structure. Even though the narrative thread continues from the Torah into the book of Joshua as far as the end of the book of 2 Kings, the books of Genesis through Deuteronomy form a separate literary entity. The theology of the Torah can be ascertained from the redactional passages connected to the constitution of the Pentateuch—in canonical terms: as Torah. These passages have a horizon that extends clearly to the boundaries of the Pentateuch. One should not, however, speak of a "final redaction" of the Pentateuch in the singular, for the absence of a unified textual form of the Pentateuch shows that this did not take place. The term "final redactions" in the plural is also misleading because different final forms do not provide a unified profile with regard to content.

It should be emphasized, however, that the theology of the Torah is not exhausted by the statements and profiles of these redactional texts with the Torah as their horizon. Its theology includes countless further positions that will be addressed later in the discussion. At this point, however, the treatment concerns only the theology of the Torah on the level of its completed status—in other words, the theology of the Torah *as Torah.*

THE CONCLUSION OF THE TORAH In the final chapter of the Torah, Deut 34 (which was not, however, conceived as the conclusion of the Torah, but nonetheless contains elements that serve this purpose) one can identify three motifs whose content and literary nature can be brought together logically with the conclusion of the Torah.

The first is the sworn promise of the land to Abraham, Isaac, and Jacob in Deut 34:4, which traverses all the books of the Torah as a guiding theme but is missing afterwards, in Joshua–2 Kings. The second motif consists of the declaration in 34:10 that sets apart the Torah as the "arch-prophecy" of Moses in comparison with the subsequent "Former Prophets" in the books of Joshua through Kings. Finally, the third motif is the description of Moses's death while in perfect health at the age of 120 years in 34:7, which forms an *inclusio* with the relevant limit of the human lifespan in Gen 6:3. As a result, this motif literarily encircles the Torah. Deuteronomy 34:10 constitutes the connection of Genesis–Deuteronomy as Torah with a certain degree of distinction from Joshua–2 Kings. Deuteronomy 34:7 links Genesis–Deuteronomy to one another as Torah. These three motifs are treated individually below.

THE SWORN PROMISE OF THE LAND TO THE ANCESTORS The promise of the possession of the pledged land is a widely attested theme in the Pentateuch.[2]

---

2. Cf. for example Gen 12:7; 13:15, 17; 15:7, 18; 17:8; 24:7; 28:4, 13; 35:12; 48:4; 50:24;

However, the specific expression of the promise of the land to Abraham, Isaac, and Jacob—without אבות ('*bwt*) "fathers"—appears in comparably few places, limited to Gen 50:24; Exod 32:13; 33:1; Num 32:11; Deut 34:4. If one includes Lev 26:42, which is related in terms of its content, then this theological declaration is the only one that carries through all five books of the Pentateuch. Especially conspicuous in this context, it never again appears in the rest of the narrative books of the Enneateuch, from Joshua–2 Kings. The promise of the land to the ancestors is, therefore, an elevated theme that is exclusive to the Pentateuch.

Considered in terms of compositional history, this series of declarations appears to assume and combine both the Deuteronomistic and the Priestly traditions. The motif of the promise of the land seems fundamentally to have arisen from the Deuteronomistic portions of Deuteronomy, where it was originally directed to the exodus generation (see Deut 1:35; 6:18, 23; 7:13; 8:1; 10:11; 11:9, 21; 19:8; 26:3, 15; 28:11; 31:7, 20–21). Its transferal to the three patriarchs of Genesis (in Deut itself, cf. 1:8; 6:10; 9:5; 30:20) was motivated by the Priestly document, which sees the covenant with Abraham as the foundation for God's treatment of Israel. The meaning of the series of statements on the promise of the land to the ancestors within the Torah was then accentuated even more through the connection back from its last attestation in Deut 34:4 to the beginning of the Torah in Gen 12:7 and 13:15, where the theme of Israel itself begins. This establishes a large literary parenthesis surrounding the entire Torah. Deuteronomy 34:4 picks up on the promise of land from Gen 12:7:

DEUT 34:4:	GEN 12:7:
And Yhwh said to him, "This is the land of which I swore to Abraham, Isaac, and Jacob, saying, 'I will give it to your descendants.'"	Then Yhwh appeared to Abram, and said to him, "To your offspring I will give this land."

There is also a clear intertextual relationship between Deut 34:1–4 and Gen 13:10–15:

Exod 13:5, 11; 32:13; 33:1; Lev 18:3; 19:23; 20:24; 23:10; 25:2, 38; Num 11:12; 14:16, 23; 32:11; Deut 1:8, 35; 6:10, 18, 23; 7:13; 8:1; 10:11; 11:9, 21; 19:8; 26:3, 15; 28:11; 30:20; 31:7, 20–21; 34:4.

DEUT 34:1–4:	GEN 13:10–15:
And Moses went up from the plains of Moab to Mount Nebo, to the top of Pisgah, opposite Jericho, and Yhwh *showed him the whole land*: Gilead as far as Dan, all Naphtali, the land of Ephraim and Manasseh, and *all the land* of Judah as far as the Western Sea, the southland, and the *plain of the Jordan, the valley* of Jericho, the city of palms, *as far as Zoar*. And Yhwh said to him, "This is the land of which I swore to Abraham, to Isaac, and to Jacob, saying, '*I will give it to your descendants.*'"	Then Lot looked about him and *saw* that the whole *plain of the Jordan* was a well-watered land . . . *as far as Zoar*; . . . Yhwh said to Abram, after Lot had separated from him, "Raise your eyes now, and *look* from the place where you stand, northwards and southwards and eastwards and westwards; for *all the land that you see I will give* to you *and to your offspring forever.*"

In other words, Deut 34:1–4 takes up the network of promises from Gen 12–13 as a whole and emphasizes the fact that Israel continues to be entitled to the land promised to Abraham. In line with Gen 12:7, Deut 34:4 highlights the fact that the descendants are the recipients of the promise. Like Abraham, Moses can view the land, but Moses is not allowed to set foot in it.

This first motif of the promise of the land to Abraham, Isaac, and Jacob theologically accentuates the diaspora character of the Torah. This character emerges, in any case, from the fact that its narrative ends before the entrance into the promised land. The Torah is the foundational charter of an "exilic" Israel, a people whose history begins outside its land and whose moment of reading in large part also takes place outside this same land. The Torah thus contains an eminently "prophetic" note.

MOSES AS PROPHET WITHOUT EQUAL This characterization leads directly to the second motif in Deut 34 that serves a specific theological emphasis in the Torah. Deuteronomy 34:10 sets Moses apart from the prophets and depicts him as a prophet without equal, the heights of whom none of the later prophets can attain. This declaration is especially important because the notion of Moses's incomparability consciously assumes contradictions with the earlier text of Deuteronomy. Especially striking is the relationship with Deut 18:15. This text states:

A prophet like me will Yhwh raise up (יָקִים, *yqym*) for you from among your own people; you shall heed him.

The promise formulated with the *hiphil* impf. of קוּם (*qwm*) from Deut 18:15 is abrogated in Deut 34:10 (קוּם, *qwm, qal* pf.):

And no other prophet has arisen (קָם, *qm*) in Israel like Moses, whom Yhwh knew face to face.

Why does Deut 34:10 contradict Deut 18:15? The reason can be found in the succession of prophets in view in Deut 18:15 that begins with Moses, the arch-prophet, and all his successors, which is severed for the sake of Moses's incomparability. Deuteronomy 34:10 attempts to separate Moses from the subsequent prophets, and this separation between Moses and the prophets is most easily explained as the theological distinction of the Torah. Moses must be differentiated from the prophets if the Torah is to be qualitatively superior to the Prophets (that is, the prophetic books from Joshua to Malachi, the canonical section of the Prophets).

The statement that follows in vv. 10–12 also fits with such an intention:

And no prophet in Israel has arisen like Moses, whom Yhwh knew face to face, with regard to all the *signs and wonders* that Yhwh sent him to perform in the land of Egypt, against Pharaoh and all his servants and his entire land, and for all the *strong hand* and all the *terrifying horrors* [cf. Deut 4:34; 26:8; Jer 32:21] that Moses performed in the sight of all Israel.

Predicates associated with God are transferred in a rather conspicuous manner to Moses in this passage. Moses has performed "*signs and wonders*" with "*a strong hand*" and "*terrifying horrors*" are attributed to Moses in this case. Traditionally these are ascribed to God and to God alone.[3] Such is the case in Deut 4:34; 6:22; 26:8; Jer 32:21; and frequently elsewhere, but the most important reference here is Deut 29:1–2 (Eng. 29:2–3), which Deut 34:11 literally recalls.[4] In contrast to Deut 34:11,

---

3. Moses is also linked with "signs" and "wonders" in Exod 4:17, 21. In terms of composition history, Exod 4 should be placed after the Priestly document.

4. The expression "in the land of Egypt, against Pharaoh and all his servants and his entire land" appears only in these two places in the Hebrew Bible.

however, this text speaks of the great signs and wondrous deeds performed by *Yhwh*.

> And Moses summoned all Israel and said to them: "You have seen all that Yhwh did before your eyes in the land of Egypt, to Pharaoh and to all his servants and to all his land, the great trials that your eyes saw, those great signs and wonders.

In Deut 34:11, then—in contrast to Deut 29:1–2 (Eng. 29:2–3)—Moses is brought as close to God as possible, apparently in order to substantiate his nature as the "prophet without equal."

It is also said of Moses in Deut 34:10 that God communicated with him face to face (cf. Exod 33:11; Num 12:8; 14:14, in addition to Exod 24:10). This assumes a direct contradiction to a specific statement in an earlier pentateuchal tradition. Exodus 33:20 excludes this very thing; Moses is permitted to see Yhwh's back, but no one is allowed to see Yhwh's face. The opposite statement in Deut 34:10, that God communicates with Moses "face to face," fits with the overall profile of distancing of Moses from humanity and bringing him closer to God, so one might suspect the same intention as the declaration that follows in 34:11. The similarity of the content in Exod 33:11; Num 12:8; 14:14 presumably arises from the same hand as Deut 34:10 (or assumes it).[5]

One can make sense of this process of Moses's "deification" as an endeavor to provide the Torah with authoritative status. Moses is brought into close connection with God so that the Torah can command the appropriate authority.

MOSES'S DEATH AT THE AGE OF 120 YEARS   As the third motif, the remark in Deut 34:7 that Moses died at the age of 120 receives the surprising elaboration that he was in perfect health ("his sight was unimpaired and his vigor had not abated"). This information is especially remarkable because it establishes a contradiction to the previous context. It says in Deut 31:1–2:

---

5. It is also possible that the totally singular motif in the Hebrew Bible of Moses's burial by Yhwh himself (Deut 34:6), which was already "corrected" by the Samaritan Pentateuch (ויקברו [*wyqbrw*], "they buried," instead of ויקבר [*wyqbr*], "he buried"), is also driven by this perspective. Here, too, Moses moves into intimate proximity to God in an otherwise unmatched manner.

When Moses had finished speaking all these words to all Israel, he said to them: "I am now one hundred twenty years old. I am no longer able to go out or to go in."

While Moses is also 120 years old in this text, his health is anything but perfect. He is no longer able "to go out or to go in" (לצאת ולבוא, *lṣ't wlbw'*), probably "march out" and "return home"). In other words, he is no longer fit for military leadership. Why does Deut 34:7 emphasize Moses's sound health in contrast to the narrative flow?

The motif of "120 years" in Deut 34:7 refers back to Gen 6:3:

And Yhwh said, "My spirit shall not abide in mortals forever, for they are flesh; their lifespan shall be one hundred twenty years."

This functional reference can be interpreted in the following manner: Moses dies in Deut 34 for the sole reason that his lifespan had reached the limit set by Gen 6:3.

Deuteronomy 34:7 and Gen 6:3 together form the only literary *inclusio* that reaches all the way back from the conclusion of the Torah in Deut 34 not only to the beginning of the ancestral history in Gen 12–13, but also into the biblical Primeval History. This framing draws a specific theological outline around the Torah as an interpretive point of view. The statement in Deut 34:7 that Moses must die for the simple reason that the span of his lifetime has come to an end, and not from any kind of guilt, counters Num 20:12 (which likely belongs to the ongoing expansion of the Priestly document in the book of Numbers) on the one hand, and Deut 1:34–37; 3:25–27 on the other. Deuteronomy 34:7 offers a more neutral theological explanation for the interdiction against Moses crossing into the promised land. The Priestly influenced tradition in Num 20:12 assumes that Moses opposed a verbal miracle ("Speak to the rock . . ." [Num 20:8]) when he struck the rock and possibly reckoned that he could not make water appear, thereby being guilty of unbelief. The Deuteronomistic complex of tradition in Deut 1 and 3 includes Moses in the collective guilt of the people: "Even with me was Yhwh angry on your account (בגללכם, *bgllkm*)." Both explanations reckon with guilt on the part of Moses, whether individual, as in Priestly thought, or, conceived in Deuteronomistic terms, of a collective nature. In contrast, Deut 34:7 embraces neither of these two explanations, offering instead a thoroughly idiosyncratic interpretation. Moses is barred from entering the promised land because his 120 year lifespan concludes the day before the entrance. According to Deut 34:7, Moses's death in the Transjordan does not rest on his guilt, but rather on fate—the divinely ordained limitation of the human lifespan.

It is also indicative that this theological characteristic of Deut 34:7— that Moses's death has nothing to do with a transgression but with fate— agrees with the orientation of the content of Gen 6:3 within the context of Gen 6:1–4 itself.[6] The report here of the heavenly motivated assault by the sons of God on the daughters of humanity offers an independent explanation for the flood. The flood does not result from human guilt; it is instead traced back to a heavenly downfall. Responsibility is not seen as lying solely in human transgression, but events like the flood that can be interpreted as punishment can also be traced back to coincidences of destiny.

This is of primary importance for the later reception-historical equivalency between Torah and Law, which took place especially in the Greek tradition (νόμος, *nómos*). As a text complex with a considerable amount of legal material, the Torah neither exclusively nor largely takes a simple retributive approach. Nor is the divine theology of grace that the Priestly document inscribes in the Torah clearly dominant. The redaction that concluded and constituted the Torah formulates a third perspective—a wisdom perspective—one beyond punishment and grace as the divine regulator of world events. There are issues in the world that simply are the way they are because they were predetermined.

The three textual statements in Deut 34:4, 7, 10–12 are each in their own way connected with the constitution of the Pentateuch, and each adds its individual theological contour to it. The exclusive distribution of the theological statement of the promise of the land to the three patriarchs that appears once in each of the five books of Moses appears in Deut 34:4. Deuteronomy 34:10–12 sets the Torah apart from the subsequent Prophets (Joshua–Malachi). Finally, Deut 34:7 provides an allusion that spans the Pentateuch back to Gen 6:3.

In addition to this more narrowly conceived outline of the pentateuchal redaction, there are further noteworthy elements that characterize the theology of the Torah as a unity in a global sense.

6. Cf. Manfred Oeming, "Sünde als Verhängnis: Gen 6,1–4 im Rahmen der Urgeschichte des Jahwisten," *TTZ* 102 (1993): 34–50. See also Walter Bührer, "Göttersöhne und Menschentöchter: Gen 6,1–4 als innerbiblische Schriftauslegung," *ZAW* 123 (2011): 495–515.

LAW AND HISTORY There is, to begin with, the combination of historical and legal material in the Torah. In terms of the amount of material, they are about equal. But what does the narrative connection mean in the framework of the Torah? Through the narrative, laws receive a location within the history of the world. They are depicted as arising from the foundational history of Israel, which itself is contextualized within world history in Gen 1–11. The laws of the Torah are thereby interpreted as positive justice, given by God on Sinai and passed on by Moses to Israel in the Transjordan, while at the same time they possess a certain quality as natural laws, which coincides with the development of the world since creation.

INCLUSIVISM AND EXCLUSIVISM The combination of the two large narrative blocks in Genesis, on the one hand, and the exodus narrative (Exodus–Deuteronomy) on the other, should also receive mention, for together they provide the two focal points around which the ellipse of the Torah is arranged. Through this combination, the theologically exclusive, allochthonous, and aggressively oriented exodus narrative is provided with a prelude of the rather inclusive, autochthonous, and passively oriented Genesis. The exodus narrative presents an exclusive divine cult—Yhwh alone is the God of Israel. Genesis, on the other hand, conceives of God rather inclusively—different local or particular divinities with different names can be transparent for the one God. The exodus narrative depicts Israel as immigrating from outside its land; Genesis narrates a story of Israel's origins that is anchored in the land. Finally, the exodus narrative warns against making a covenant with the inhabitants of the land, while Genesis allows its protagonists to coexist peacefully with other groups of peoples in the Levant. The combination of Genesis and Exodus gives rise to a theologically ambivalent mold for the Torah, such that the two large blocks are placed in something of a dynamic balance with one another.

2. The Priestly Document

Among the partial collections found in the Torah is the so-called Priestly document, which likely once existed independently.[7] But as an entire com-

---

7. Cf. the discussion in Friedhelm Hartenstein and Konrad Schmid, eds., *Abschied von der Priesterschrift? Zum Stand der Pentateuchdebatte*, Veröffentlichungen der Wissenschaftlichen Gesellschaft für Theologie 40 (Leipzig: Evangelische Verlagsanstalt, 2015).

plex, it can only be reconstructed through literary and redactional analysis of the Pentateuch. Traditional pentateuchal scholarship identified the literary scope of the Priestly document from Gen 1 to Deut 34. As a result, the extent of the Torah was already prefigured in one of its sources, the Priestly document. Therefore, the Priestly document was already important for the theology of the Torah simply as a result of its literary congruence with the pentateuchal deliverance narrative. In current scholarship, however, the Priestly document is rarely seen as a source spanning the whole Pentateuch.[8]

CREATION AND SINAI It is much more likely that the original ending of the Priestly document is found in the Sinai pericope, even if exact scholarly determinations vary. In addition to exegetical difficulties that arise with regard to assigning portions of the text of Deut 34 to P, the Priestly document attributes considerable weight in its content to the promulgation of cultic law. The conspicuous literary *inclusio* between the creation and Sinai, which consists in the parallels between the creation of the world and the creation of the sanctuary, also points in this direction.

And God *saw* everything that he had made, *and look*, it was very good. (Gen 1:31a)	And Moses *saw* the whole work, *and look,* they had done it. (Exod 39:43a)
And on the seventh day God *completed* his *work,* which he had done. (Gen 2:2a)	*So was* all the work for the holy Tent of Meeting *completed*. (Exod 39:32a)
	And Moses *completed* the entire *work.* (Exod 40:33b)
And God *blessed* the seventh day. (Gen 2:3a)	And Moses *blessed* them. (Exod 39:43b)

According to the understanding of the most recent pentateuchal scholarship, the Priestly document does not constitute a *Vorlage* for the entire extent of the Pentateuch. It is, instead, of primary importance for another fundamental conceptual decision in the formation of the Pentateuch. As

---

8. However, cf. Christian Frevel, *Mit Blick auf das Land die Schöpfung erinnern: Zum Ende der Priestergrundschrift*, Herders Biblische Studien 23 (Freiburg im Breisgau: Herder, 2000).

the first conceptual combination of the ancestral and Moses-exodus tradi-tions, it made one of the most important conceptual and literary-historical syntheses of the Hebrew Bible.[9]

This innovative potential of the Priestly document may also have been the reason it first emerged as an independent source document, rather than as ongoing scribal expansion of the extant inventory of texts. Its particu-lar theological position could not be conveyed through the re-orientation of the content of traditional texts, which therefore brought about a fresh literary beginning.

COVENANTAL THEOLOGY The Priestly document's programmatic theo-logical texts appear in Gen 1; 9; 17; and Exod 6. The literary breadth of the Priestly document is especially on display in its description of the tab-ernacle in Exod 25–31 + 35–40. The theology of the Priestly document initially becomes accessible in its covenantal declarations, which enable an overview of its overall outline. Contrary to the view of Wellhausen, who still classified the Priestly document as a *liber quattuor foederum* (book of four covenants), thereby conferring upon it the siglum Q, the Priestly doc-ument speaks explicitly of the making of two covenants—one with Noah (Gen 9) and one with Abraham (Gen 17). These formulate the basic divine approach to the world and to the Abrahamic peoples—that is, Israel (Isaac/Jacob), but also the Arabs (Ishmael) and the Edomites (Esau). The Priestly document is accordingly structured in two large sections, which one can analogously call the "circle of the world" and the "circle of Abraham" re-spectively. In Gen 9 God places his slackened war bow in the clouds and guarantees creation a permanent existence. God thereby renounces all forms of comprehensive violence against his creation, having carried out once and for all the previously narrated flood against "all flesh":

Then God said to Noah: "The *end* (קֵץ, *qṣ*) of all flesh has come before me; for the earth is full of iniquity on account of them.[10] Therefore I will destroy them from the earth." (Gen 6:13)

9. Cf. the seminal discussion of Albert de Pury, "Pg as the Absolute Beginning," in *Les dernières rédactions du Pentateuque, de l'Hexateuque et de l'Ennéateuque*, ed. Thomas Römer and Konrad Schmid, BETL 203 (Leuven: Peeters, 2007), 99–128.

10. "All flesh" includes humans and animals; cf. Hermann-Josef Stipp, "'Alles Fleisch hatte seinen Wandel auf der Erde verdorben' (Gen 6,12): Die Mitverantwortung der Tierwelt an der Sintflut nach der Priesterschrift," in *Alttestamentliche Studien: Arbeiten zu Priesterschrift, Deu-teronomistischem Geschichtswerk und Prophetie*, BZAW 442 (Berlin: de Gruyter, 2013), 95–116.

The Priestly document did not devise this severe declaration of the "end" that "has come." It instead adopted it from the genre of judgment prophecy:

And he said, "What do you see, Amos?" I answered, "A basket of fruit (קָיִץ, *qyṣ*)." Then Yhwh said to me, "The *end* (קֵץ, *qṣ*) has come for my people Israel; I will no longer forgive them." (Amos 8:2)

You, son of man, speak: "Thus says the Lord Yhwh to the land of Israel: 'An *end* (קֵץ, *qṣ*) is coming! The *end* (קֵץ, *qṣ*) is coming upon the four corners of the land! Now the *end* (קֵץ, *qṣ*) comes upon you . . .'" (Ezek 7:2–3)

The Priestly document apparently adopts this message from judgment prophecy, enfolding it, however, into the Primeval History. Yes, there was a divine resolution to make an "end," but it lies in the past, not in the future. The Priestly document thereby takes a position contrary in substance to Deuteronomy and its announcement of curses (Deut 28).

Theologically analogous is the Priestly document's message for Israel. In the same way that the covenant with Noah guarantees a permanent existence for the world, the covenant with Abraham guarantees Israel's continuous proximity to God. In both cases, no conditions are issued.

It is part of the theological program of the Priestly document that the Sinai events do not qualify as a covenant, so that the sole covenant focus is on the covenant with Abraham. The Priestly document does not make the divine promises (increase, land, and divine proximity) conditional upon Israel's obedience to the law in the way envisaged by the Deuteronomistic form of the Sinai pericope. Instead, the Priestly document presents "covenant" as a one-sided promise by God. While individuals can surely fall out of this covenant (if, for example, they do not undergo circumcision), the collective entities of the Abrahamic nations as a whole cannot. This is displayed in detail in the characteristic adaptation of the so-called covenant formula in Gen 17:7: "for I will be God for you and for your descendants after you." The second half of the formula, at home in Deuteronomistic theology ("and you will be my people," or similar), is omitted, apparently on purpose. For whatever Abraham and his descendants do or do not do, it changes nothing with regard to the unconditionally promised closeness to God.

When further comparing the circle of the world with the circle of Abraham in the Priestly document, it is striking that the covenant with Noah follows the judgment of the world, while the covenant with Abraham precedes the national catastrophe of the judgment on Israel. The intention behind this composition is apparently that the change by God in the Primeval History that led to his covenant with Noah could now benefit the circle of Abraham from the outset in the promise of the covenant with Abraham.

CIRCLE OF THE WORLD, CIRCLE OF ABRAHAM, AND CIRCLE OF ISRAEL
The overall structure of the Priestly document is not two-part, though its covenantal theology could lead to this conjecture. It is instead structured in three parts, as indicated by its doctrine of God. In addition to the two circles—that of the world and that of Abraham—which relate to one another in concentric fashion, there is also a third, innermost circle, the circle of Israel. Although the Priestly document pursues an "ecumenical" theology that connects the Israelites, Arabs, and Edomites, it is clear that Israel alone is granted complete knowledge of God. Furthermore, only Israel, through the gift of the sacrificial cult, possesses a medium that makes a partial restitution of the "very good" creational order from Gen 1 possible.

The three circles correspond to three modes of divine revelation. God is held by the entire world to be "Elohim" (אלהים, 'lhym). The Priestly document in Gen 1 (to 9) uses the Hebrew term "god" in an undetermined manner, like a proper name. It identifies the category "god" with the only member of that category, thereby propagating an inclusive monotheism. In contrast, the deity presents himself to the patriarchs Abraham, Isaac, and Jacob as "El Shaddai" (אל שדי, 'l šdy) while his actual, cultically appropriate name is first unveiled to the generation of Moses as "Yhwh" (יהוה, yhwh [Exod 6:2–3]; cf. in detail below, §30).

PACIFISM On the whole, the Priestly document advocates a completely non-eschatological and pacifist (and in this sense also a political) position, which views the time of the Persian-period author as something akin to the divinely desired goal of history. The only God (אלהים, 'lhym, "Elohim," who can certainly be worshiped under different names, such as אל שדי, 'l šdy, "El Shaddai" in the Abrahamic ecumenical household, and as יהוה, yhwh, "Yhwh" in Israel) rules over the entire world he created, such that every nation lives together peacefully in perpetuity in their own place with their own language and their own cult. Only Egypt is viewed antagonistically in the Priestly document, which can be recognized in the plague cycle as well as in the notice in Exod 12:12. This likely reflects the historical composition of the Priestly document before the integration of Egypt into the Persian Empire under Cambyses in 525 BCE.[11] The Priestly document, with its pacifist and at least implicitly pro-Persian orientation, is virtually the absolute counter-conception of the Deuteronomistic strand of tradition, which itself viewed the Persian period as fundamentally lacking in terms of salvation. For according to the Deuteronomistic conception, as long as Israel was not united under its own king in its own land with national sovereignty, then God and his people could not have reached the goal of history. As a result, that time period remained a time of judgment, and reciprocally, this meant that Israel remained in a state of guilt, for Deuteronomism views judgment as punishment for guilt.

LITERARY STYLE The repetitive and enumerative style of the Priestly document criticized by nineteenth-century exegesis is closely connected to priestly interests: For the cult to be duly administered, even the smallest detail must be regulated. It must provide clarity such that the performance of each stipulation may follow that stipulation exactly. So, the numerous lists and "repetitions" in the Priestly document arise much more in connection with its theology than its "poor style."

3. The Non-Priestly Primeval History: Universalization and De-eschatologization

The non-Priestly Primeval History (Gen 1–11) constitutes a thematically independent section of the Torah. One of the most important breaks within the Torah appears between Gen 11 and 12. The story of Israel first begins in the Torah in Gen 12, while Gen 1–11 has a universal orientation and concerns humanity as a whole.

---

11. Cf. Konrad Schmid, "Taming Egypt: The Impact of Persian Imperial Ideology and Politics on the Biblical Exodus Account," in *Jewish Cultural Encounters in the Ancient Mediterranean and Near Eastern World*, ed. Mladen Popović, JSJSup 178 (Leiden: Brill, 2017), 13–29.

THE AUTONOMY OF THE PRIMEVAL HISTORY? It is debated whether the Primeval History (extending perhaps from Gen 2–8* or 2–11*) ever existed on its own,[12] or whether it instead emerged first as a literary elaboration on Gen 12–36* or Gen 12–50* and was placed at the beginning. Given its self-contained conceptual contour, in either case it can be described on its own in terms of its theology.

UNIVERSALIZATION AND DE-ESCHATOLOGIZATION The function of the historical theology of the non-Priestly Primeval History can be identified as the universalization and de-eschatologization of the subsequent Israel traditions. If one compares the entire text complex of Gen 12 to 2 Kgs 25, which continues to unfold in the prophetic books, then it is conspicuous that the so-called paradise narrative in Gen 2–3 anticipates its elementary structure and universalizes it. Just as Israel loses its land as a result of its disobedience to God's law, the first human couple is banished from the Garden of Eden as a result of disobeying God's command not to eat from the Tree of the Knowledge of Good and Evil. Therefore, the reigning Deuteronomistic judgment theology in Genesis–2 Kings becomes a special case of the human condition. All utopic sketches of the Hebrew Bible that reckon with a return to paradisiacal conditions (cf. e.g., Isa 11) are de-eschatologized. Genesis 2–3 (cf. esp. 3:24) instead boldly holds that there is no way out of the current human existence. Contrary to, for example, Deut 30; Jer 31; 32; or Ezek 36, which expect a "new heart" or a "new spirit" at least for the Israelites (cf. below, §39), humans will not fundamentally change—neither on their own nor with divine assistance. Humans will remain how they are: ambivalent. Therefore, human life will also remain ambivalent—at a distance from rather than close to God, but with a certain amount of personal responsibility and no longer like a child.

THE FLOOD PERICOPE The basic de-eschatologization of its "discussion partner" in the Hebrew Bible also appears in the non-Priestly frame of the flood pericope (Gen 6–9):

---

12. Cf. Jan C. Gertz, "The Formation of the Primeval History," in *The Book of Genesis: Composition, Reception, and Interpretation*, ed. Craig A. Evans et al., VTSup 152 (Leiden: Brill, 2012), 107–36.

GEN 6:5–8:

And Yhwh saw that human evil was great upon the earth, and that every impulse of the plan of their hearts was only evil <u>all days</u>, and Yhwh regretted that he had created humans upon earth, and it distressed him **in his heart.**
And Yhwh said, "I will destroy the humans that I have created from the earth, the humans as well as the livestock, also the creeping animals and the birds of the heavens, *for* (כִּי, *ky*) I regret that I have made them."
But Noah found grace from Yhwh.

GEN 8:20–22:

But Noah built Yhwh an altar. Then he took some of all clean animals and some of all clean birds and brought burnt offerings to the altar.
And Yhwh smelled the pleasant odor, and Yhwh said **in his heart:**
"I will never again curse the earth on account of the humans, *although* (כִּי, *ky*) the impulse of the human heart is evil from their youth.
And I will no longer strike what lives there, as I have done.
<u>All days</u> the earth will not cease to have seedtime and harvest, frost and heat, summer and winter, day and night."

The non-Priestly prologue and epilogue to the flood formulate an explanation in the Primeval History for the definitive renunciation of divine violence against creation after the flood. Humans remain "evil," but God has changed. Rather than divine regret and sorrow, God maintains the guarantee of life for humanity resulting from the assessment of human evil. Both take place—stated in daring anthropomorphic terms—"in the heart" of God (Gen 6:6; 8:21). The consequence is that the passage of time ("all days" 6:5; 8:22) will no longer be determined by the ongoing existence of human evil, but rather by the divine guarantee of life. It can be stated that the flood transformed God's logic, recognizable in the different uses of Hebrew כִּי (*ky*), which is used causally ("for") in 6:7, but adversatively ("although") in 8:21. As a result, the non-Priestly flood tradition contradicts the prophecies of judgment. God's nature is fundamentally not such that he allows himself to be provoked by human evil. This was originally the case (Gen 6:5–8), but God changed fundamentally into a God of grace (Gen 8:20–22) already at the beginning of world history.

THE TOWER OF BABEL NARRATIVE The non-Priestly Primeval History ends with the so-called narrative of the tower of Babel in Gen 11:1–9. It explains the reason for the multitude of languages among the nations in terms of God having thwarted humanity's building plans in Babel. The "tower" from Gen 11 has often been conceived of as a ziggurat, a Babylonian temple tower, but the Hebrew expression מגדל (*mgdl*) never identifies a sacred building. A more likely translation would be "citadel." Whether Gen 11 has in mind a specific architectural reality is debated and depends on how one dates the text, with proposals varying from the Neo-Assyrian period down into the Hellenistic period.

Gen 11 demonstrates a close relationship with Gen 2–4 (cf. Gen 11:6 and 3:22, as well as Gen 11:2 with Gen 4:16 "east"), but it does not appear to assume the Table of Nations in Gen 10, which takes for granted the linguistic diversity that Gen 11 attempts to explain. Gen 11 shares with Gen 2–4 the conviction that humans possess exceptional abilities and therefore require divine limitations. Gen 11 takes an anti-imperial point of view that analogously sets a pluralistic and piecemeal political organization of the world as corresponding to the divine will.

4. The Ancestral Narratives: The Promises

THE ANCESTRAL NARRATIVE AS AN INDEPENDENT FOUNDATION TRA-DITION FOR ISRAEL The so-called ancestral narratives, as recent penta-teuchal scholarship has recognized, once existed as an independent literary entity before they were expanded by the Primeval History and linked to the exodus narrative. The overarching salvation-historical conception of the Pentateuch, or rather the Hexateuch, was not present from the beginning, but instead emerged at the end of the formation of the tradition, so it cannot have formed the primary historical horizon of interpretation for the ancestral narrative.

This, therefore, means that the ancestral narrative was not originally a prelude; it was formerly an independent tradition of origins for Israel, which did not always lead to the exodus account, finding its sequel in that story. Behind the ancestral narrative, family and tribal traditions can be conjectured, but their oldest written versions already had a national orien-tation. The Jacob story provides reasons for the relationship with Edom, represented by Esau, the Abraham story those to Moab and Ammon (cf. below, §33).

While the independence of the ancestral narratives was also noted in traditional approaches, in these it rested on the influential reconstruction by Albrecht Alt of a religion of the god of the ancestors set in Israel's foggy nomadic prehistory.[13] However, the idiosyncrasy of the ancestral narratives has less to do with a past that reaches far back into prehistory than it concerns an independent literary history that continued into the expansion of the transmission of the independent tradition into the exilic period.

NARRATIVE CYCLES AND PROMISES The ancestral narrative goes back to the literary connection of the Abraham (Gen 13* + 18*), Isaac (Gen 26*), and Jacob traditions (Gen 25–35*). The Joseph story (Gen 37–50*) constitutes a further large building block with its own character. An overarching ancestral narrative reaching from Gen 12–50* likely emerged in the exilic period through the redactional connection of these preexisting circles of traditions as well as the Joseph story. They were brought together on the one hand by the genealogical concatenation of the protagonists Abraham, Isaac, Jacob, and Joseph as grandfather, father, son, and grandson, and on the other through the promises:

> Although the great narrative complexes covering the call of Abraham down to the death of Joseph consist in the coalescence of a great variety of traditional material, the whole has nevertheless a scaffolding supporting and connecting it, the so-called promise to the patriarchs. At least it can be said that this whole variegated mosaic of stories is given cohesion of subject-matter . . . by means of the constantly recurring divine promise.[14]

However, the promises vary in nature both with regard to their content as well as their compositional histories. They have two roots in the traditions: The first is in Gen 18 of the Abraham narrative, which is the only pre-Priestly ancestral narrative with an integrated promise—the promise of a son in v. 14b. The second is in the theme of blessing in the Jacob narratives.

COMPOSITIONALLY CENTRAL PROMISES Most important for the cohesion of the ancestral story are the promises in Gen 12:1–3; 13:14–17; 28:13–15; and 46:2–4. They contain the promise of descendants and land. Both are themes of great significance for Israel and Judah in the seventh to fifth cen-

---

13. Albrecht Alt, *Der Gott der Väter: Ein Beitrag zur Vorgeschichte der israelitischen Religion* (Stuttgart: Kohlhammer, 1929).

14. Gerhard von Rad, *Old Testament Theology*, 1:167.

turies BCE. The Assyrian and Babylonian deportations as well as economic problems led to substantial declines in population in a region no longer under its own kingship. The promises should be understood in light of this counterfactual historical moment.

TRANSFORMATION OF ROYAL IDEOLOGY A further important element of its theological outlook can be recognized especially in Gen 12:1–3:

GEN 12:1–3:	Ps 72:17:
And Yhwh said to Abram . . . "And I will make you into a great people, and I will *bless* you, and I will make your name great, and *it will be a blessing. . . . And in you* all tribes of the earth *will acquire blessing.*"	May [the king's] name endure forever, as long as the sun shines, may his name sprout. And in him may all nations *wish blessing*, and happily praise him.

By means of the motif of the "great name" and its mediation of blessing, Gen 12:1–3 adopts the fundamental elements of royal ideology as articulated in, for example, Ps 72:17, transferring them to the founding father of the nation, Abraham. These "democratizing" tendencies are hardly conceivable during the monarchic period. Instead, Gen 12:1–3 should be placed in the proximity of the analogous perspectives found in the tradition of Deutero-Isaiah, which at times addresses exilic Israel as "Abraham" or "Jacob," depicting them with royal qualities.

NOTES ON MIGRATION Of further interest are the connections between the system of promises comprised of Gen 12:1–3; 13:14–17; 28:13–15; and 46:2–4 and the migration notices (cf. Gen 26:2–3; 31:3, 13): "Go up out of your land" (12:1), "Do not be afraid to go down to Egypt" (46:3), etc. This demonstrates a definition of the people of God that is independent of a particular geographical location. Israel is Israel as a result of its relationship with God and not as a result of its residence in its land. On the flip side, these notices also burst the bounds of a locally or nationally defined understanding of God. God is with Israel, regardless of whether it resides in its land or in a foreign country. Neither is God bound to one or more sanctuaries; he can reveal himself to Israel wherever he desires.

INCLUSIVISM AND PACIFICISM The aggressive and exclusive orientation of the exodus tradition is absent from the ancestral story of Genesis. In terms of its political point of view, it is rather pacifistic.[15] The ancestors coexist with various ethnicities and groups in the land and agree to treaties with them, something that is strictly prohibited by the exodus tradition. In terms of its theological point of view, its inclusivism is conspicuous. The ancestors come into contact with a number of deities during their migrations and journeys, who reveal themselves under different names, and they erect places of worship to them in various places. Of course, it is clear to the audience of the ancestral story that one and the same God, Yhwh, is found behind these deities. This is less clear for the actors in the narratives, and their uncertainty doubtlessly has a historical background. Memories or oral traditions that originally dealt with numerous and different deities stand in the background of the ancestral narratives. On their journeys the ancestors discover what the development of the tradition yields—the different local deities are identified with the God of Israel. The ancestral narratives mirror an independent alternative conception of an assimilating and autochthonous emergence of Israel in its land in contrast to the exodus tradition, which locates Israel's origins in the foreign land of Egypt, and therefore propagates a vehement separation from all other national-religious identities.

5. The Moses-Exodus Narrative: From the Servitude of Slavery in Egypt to Service of God on Sinai

THE MOSES-EXODUS NARRATIVE AS AN INDEPENDENT TRADITION OF IS-RAEL'S ORIGINS The Moses-exodus narrative now functions as the continuation of Genesis in the current progression of the Pentateuch. Its natural conclusion, the presentation of the conquest of the land in the book of Joshua, also points beyond the Pentateuch. However, this narrative was initially—both in oral as well as written forms—a separate complex of tradition and remained this way until the late exilic or early postexilic period.[16] Its original independence arises from, on the one hand, its self-sufficient topic and theology, and on the other from the fact that the ancestral story

15. However, cf. Gen 14 and Gen 34, though both pieces do not belong to the narrative substance of the ancestral story. Genesis 14 attempts to provide the figure of Abraham with a fictive international coloring, while Gen 34 is a special narrative that assumes the topic of circumcision and develops it further in the narrative.

16. On this cf. Stephen Germany, *The Exodus-Conquest Narrative: The Composition of the Non-Priestly Narratives in Exodus-Joshua*, FAT 115 (Tübingen: Mohr Siebeck, 2017).

in Gen 12–50* in no way leads organically to the Moses-exodus narrative. Instead, the notion arises that in the ancestors and the exodus, two formerly independent complexes of tradition were secondarily connected with one another. Exodus 1:6–8 is especially conspicuous in this regard:

> And Joseph and all his brothers and that whole generation died. But the Israelites were fruitful, and it teemed with them; they multiplied and became overpowering, and the land became full of them. Then a new king arose over Egypt who knew nothing of Joseph.

Within these three verses, a reconciliation—readily recognizable as such—is forged between the previously narrated Joseph story and the following exodus story. First, all memory of Joseph's rise and his good deeds toward Egypt must be effaced so that the oppression motif can be introduced as plausible. Exodus 1:8 pays the price for this plausibility by having the new pharaoh forget Joseph, the second most powerful person in Egypt under his predecessor. This difficulty is explained by the attempt to connect the tradition of the ancestors and the exodus as succinctly as possible.

MOSES'S BIRTH NARRATIVE The Moses-exodus narrative was originally transmitted independently from the ancestral story. The literary Moses-exodus narrative opened with Exod 2:1–10, the birth narrative of Moses, through which several central and fundamental theological points of relevance for the entire Moses-exodus narrative can be elucidated.

The individual features of the birth narrative in Exod 2:1–10 reveal that it developed without awareness of the genocide topic in Exod 1. As the formulation of Exod 2:1 ("And a man from the house of Levi went and took the daughter of Levi") demonstrates in comparison with its closest biblical parallel of Hos 1:2 ("Go, take a whoring wife and [beget] whoring children"), it concerns the connection of parents who do not remain nameless by chance (the names Amram and Jochebed first arise in the later Priestly interpretation of Exod 6:20) but as a result of an illegitimate liaison. Exodus 2:1 speaks only of לקח (lqḥ), "take," not of לקח לאישה (lqḥ l'yšh), "to take as a wife" (cf. the contrast once again with Exod 6:20). Precisely this appears to be the reason for the abandonment, not the threat of genocide, which allows Pharaoh's daughter to identify the discovered boy unselfconsciously as a "Hebrew child" (Exod 2:6), seemingly unaware of her father's genocidal directive.

This interpretation also accords with the nature of the content in the closest ancient Near Eastern parallel to Exod 2, the Neo-Assyrian tradition of the Sargon Legend, referring to the great usurper Sargon I (2350–2294 BCE).

> I am Sargon the great king, king of Agade. My mother was a high priestess, I did not know my father. My father's brothers dwell in the uplands. My city is Azupiranu, which lies on Euphrates bank. My mother, the high priestess, conceived me, she bore me in secret. She placed me in a reed basket, she sealed my hatch with pitch. She left me to the river, whence I could not come up. The river carried me off, it brought me to Aqqi, the drawer of water. Aqqi, drawer of water, brought me up as he dipped his bucket. Aqqi, drawer of water, raised me as his adopted son. Aqqi, drawer of water, set (me) to his orchard work. During my orchard work, Ishtar loved me, Fifty-five years I ruled as king.[17]

Sargon tells that his mother was an *enitu* priestess, for whom marriage was forbidden. His father was unknown to him. In spite of his dubious parentage, however, he was chosen by the gods. This was demonstrated by his miraculous preservation in the basket, as well as by the fact that the goddess Ishtar chose him as her lover, meaning that she granted him kingship. The theological contours of Exod 2:1–10 correlate quite closely. The preservation and rescue of Moses when abandoned on the Nile shows that God was with him. If one assumes that Exod 2:1–10 was originally independent from Exod 1 and the motivation for Moses's abandonment did not arise from the planned genocide but from his illegitimate background, then Exod 2:1–10 also coincides with this feature of the Legend of Sargon.

In terms of theology, Exod 2:1–10 evokes God as an indirect guiding and preserving power. Within the narrative of Exod 2:1–10, no explicit theological explanation is offered for what happens; this is left to the audience alone.

CLIMAX OF THE THEOLOGICAL EXPLICATION IN THE SUBSEQUENT CONTEXT While God remains completely in the background in Exod 2:1–10, he moves progressively into the forefront in the further development of the narrative complex. In the further course of the Moses-exodus narrative,

17. "The Birth Legend of Sargon of Akkad," trans. Benjamin R. Foster (*COS* 1.133:461).

there is no room for doubt that it is God who frees Israel from Egypt. The point in the narrative at which this explicit theological perspective begins is dependent on one's view of the so-called call narrative of Moses in Exod 3–4. Should it be assessed, at least in part, as an integral element of the Moses-exodus narrative, or is Exod 3:1–4:18 as a whole a post-Priestly insertion?[18] If the former, then Exod 3 would anchor an explicit theological view comparatively early in the narrative. If the latter, then the theological explanation would have emerged step by step—especially through the plague cycle.[19] However, the miracle at the sea in Exod 14, which concludes the exodus event, concerns all Israel and not only the delivering figure of Moses. Exodus 14 and the so-called "great song of the Sea of Reeds" in Exod 15:1–18 mark the first turning point in the narrative as a whole with hymnal praise of God for his action.

ANTI-ASSYRIAN ORIENTATION The Neo-Assyrian background of the tradition of Exod 2:1–10 demonstrates in exemplary manner the critical, anti-Assyrian orientation of the Moses-exodus narrative. The non-royal figure of Moses takes the place of the Neo-Assyrian emperor as the object of divine election, and he liberates Israel from imperial corvée. This yields a remarkable perspective on the close proximity of the content of the Moses-exodus narrative to the perhaps somewhat older, but rather pro-Assyrian tradition of Judges (cf. below, §19). Moses too is one of Israel's deliverers, just as is the case for the "judges," but the Moses tradition competes in significant ways with Assyrian ideology. From this point of view, the Moses-exodus narrative can be understood as an anti-Assyrian consolidation of the pro-Assyrian tradition of Judges.

GOD AS SOVEREIGN POWER The Moses-exodus narrative emerges as the first clearly anti-imperial literary document in Israel. It instead acknowledges God alone as the absolute "imperial" power. The exodus story narrates the liberation of Israel from "servitude" to Egypt into "service" to God.[20] This foundational motif of the delineation of God as absolute sov-

---

18. Cf. the discussion in Thomas Römer, "Exodus 3–4 und die aktuelle Pentateuchdiskussion," in *The Interpretation of Exodus: Studies in Honour of Cornelis Houtman*, ed. Riemer Roukema et al., CBET 44 (Leuven: Peeters, 2006), 65–79.

19. Cf. Jan C. Gertz, *Tradition und Redaktion in der Exoduserzählung: Untersuchungen zur Endredaktion des Pentateuch*, FRLANT 189 (Göttingen: Vandenhoeck & Ruprecht, 2000).

20. Cf. Georges Auzou, *De la servitude au service: Etude du livre de l'Exode*, Connaissance de la Bible 3 (Paris: de l'Orante, 1961).

ereign, which is accompanied by his people's radical dependence on him, becomes a classic element in the history of theology. It is of central importance, especially for the formation of monotheism. The motif rests on borrowings from the Assyrian model, but it is applied with an anti-Assyrian twist (cf. below, §24 and §33). The Moses-exodus narrative transfers this anti-Assyrian orientation into the prototype conceived within an Egyptian setting. Egypt and its pharaoh—who purposefully remains unnamed—do not represent a concrete imperial power. They instead represent the institution of earthly empires as such.

COMPETING TRADITIONS OF ORIGINS The Moses-exodus narrative formulates an allochthonous foundation for Israel's existence. Israel is Israel from Egypt, and its roots have not always been in Palestine. This tradition, therefore, raises a certain amount of conflict with the ancestral narrative, which itself describes a tradition of origins for Israel. However, it sees these origins in the land itself. The Abraham and Jacob traditions are each, in and of themselves, considerably less "theologized" than the Moses-exodus narrative. Only once the Abraham and Jacob narratives have been combined through the promises is it essentially comparable with the Moses-exodus narrative. Only at this stage is a functional equivalence sufficiently discernable. Both the ancestral and the exodus narratives found the post-state existence of "Israel" as the people of God connected together after the fall of the northern kingdom in 722 BCE despite the absence of state structures. However, the ancestral narrative is more inclusive in orientation, while the Moses-exodus narrative is more exclusive. In terms of the history of its formation, the Moses-exodus narrative initially reacts to the still independent, somewhat older Jacob tradition in that it no longer determines Israel's identity in relation to the neighbors. Instead it determines Israel's identity—within the world of the narrative—in relation to the mythic, ungodly Egyptian Empire, or rather—in the world of the narrator—in relation to the Neo-Assyrian Empire.

6. Deuteronomy

A further, originally independent unit in the Torah is Deuteronomy. It was integrated both into the Pentateuch and also with the subsequent books of Joshua–2 Kings by means of its framing sections and its presentation as Mosaic discourse. However, its literary core initially existed on its own.

This core comprises the Deuteronomic legislation (Deut 12–26*), which was concluded by blessings and curses (Deut 28*). Its original introduction was possibly the Shema (Deut 6:4–9), with its emphasis on Yhwh's singularity ("Hear Israel, Yhwh our God is one Yhwh"), which provides the theological foundation for the singularity of the cult (Deut 12*).

REINTERPRETATION OF THE COVENANT CODE The Deuteronomic legislation is thoroughly dependent in literary terms on the Covenant Code (Exod 20–23*), which it reinterprets in light of cult centralization. This is also, though not exclusively, a consequence of its imperial interpretation of the concept of God. The God of Israel can only be worshiped at his "residence" in Jerusalem. At the same time, in light of this new interpretation, God himself becomes a legislator, which constitutes a new development in the world of the ancient Near East. The king is otherwise consistently viewed in this role.[21] Deuteronomy's specific character rests on the declaration of God as legislator, for it comprehensively substantiates all Deuteronomy's laws. This then has an impact on the Torah as a whole. The laws must manage to be followed simply by means of their own self-evident nature and authority. The justifications stand in a certain cognitive dissonance to the blessing and curse passages that conclude Deuteronomy, which themselves have something of a paraenetic function in the theology of judgment of Deuteronomy's larger context (within Genesis–2 Kings).

MOSES'S FAREWELL ADDRESS Deuteronomy was integrated into the literary progression of the Torah in the shape of Moses's farewell address (Deut 31:2; 32:48; 34:7). In it Moses conveys to the people of Israel the laws that they are to keep in the land they are entering. The narrative logic of the Torah thereby suggests that the material Moses passes on apparently accords with what he had received from God since Exod 20 on the mountain of God, but had not yet imparted to them. There are several small notes in the Sinai pericope beginning in Exod 20 that Moses had passed on some of it to Israel—for example, the "Covenant Code" (20:22–23:33; cf. Exod 24:7, proclaimed in 24:3), the Sabbath command (Exod 31:12–17, proclaimed in

21. In its present form, Deuteronomy is shaped as the law of Moses, yet texts like Deut 6:17 and 28:45 show that this rests on a secondary interpretation. Deuteronomy was originally conceived as the law of God; cf. Norbert Lohfink, "Das Deuteronomium: Jahwegesetz oder Mosegesetz?," *TP* 65 (1990): 38–391.

35:1–3), and the instructions for the construction of the Tent of Meeting (Exod 25–31; proclaimed in Exod 35:32, 34; Exod 35:4–19). However, missing from the larger narrative context of Exodus–Numbers is an unequivocal notice of execution that Moses actually followed through with what God continuously had instructed him to do: "Speak with the Israelites and say to them" (Lev 1:2; 4:2; 7:29; 11:2; 12:2; 15:2; [17:2, see on this verse below] 18:2; 19:2; 20:2; 21:1; 23:2, 10, 24, 34; 24:2; 25:2; 27:2; Num 5:2, 12; 6:2; 15:2, 18, 38; 19:2; 28:2; 34:2; 35:2; cf. Lev 22:2, 18; Num 6:23; 8:2). In the present context of the Torah, Deuteronomy appears to constitute the first significant proclamation of the law of God in the interpretation by Moses. This impression arises not only as a result of the order of the text; it is also supported by means of certain textual insertions.

THE DOUBLE TRANSMISSION OF THE DECALOGUE   First, the double transmission of the Decalogue from Sinai and in the promulgation of the law in the Transjordan can hardly be explained except as an attempt to maintain that the two legislative corpora are basically identical in substance, which is shown in their relevant summaries. The manner in which the double entrenchment of the Decalogue in the Pentateuch came about in diachronic terms is, as is well known, a hotly debated question. However, this changes nothing with regard to its function as identifying the promulgations of the laws of Sinai and of the Transjordan with one another.

Second, the current Mosaic fiction of the Deuteronomistic law can hardly be explained without seeing it in close connection with the law of the God of Sinai. A Mosaic law in and of itself is not a plausible construct within the context of ancient Near Eastern legal conceptions. The Mosaic fiction of Deuteronomy, which can hardly be original,[22] is instead first conceivable within the framework of Deuteronomy's characterization as an interpretation of the promulgation of the Sinai legislation.

Third, there are texts in Deuteronomy that expand on the idea that Deuteronomy contains the interpretation of the revelation of law from Sinai. Of note here is the superscription of Deut 1:5: "Beyond the Jordan in the land of Moab, Moses began to make clear/explicate (באר, *b'r*) this Torah." According to Deut 1:5, however, this means that Deuteronomy is to be understood as interpreted law—that is, an interpretation of the Sinai legislation (cf. also Deut 4:1–2, 5).

---

22. Cf. Lohfink, "Das Deuteronomium: Jahwegesetz oder Mosegesetz?"; Eckart Otto, "Deuteronomium," *RGG* 2:695.

Read in relation to Genesis–Numbers, Deuteronomy is therefore considered to be the Mosaic interpretation of the divine law of Sinai, whose same meaning is guaranteed by the two Decalogues. It is theologically noteworthy that the Torah does not solely contain God's legislation, but also its interpretation by Moses. Furthermore, the two—law and interpretation—are not separated from one another. The Torah is not presented as an unchangeable law of the Medes and Persians, but rather as a theological foundational text; its first interpretation can and needs to be done by Moses, and further exegesis is therefore justified canonically.

§19 Nevi'im

Ulrich Berges, *Jesaja: Der Prophet und das Buch,* Biblische Gestalten 22 (Leipzig: Evangelische Verlagsanstalt, 2010) ◆ Ulrich Berges and Willem Beuken, *Das Buch Jesaja: Eine Einführung,* Uni-Taschenbücher 4647 (Göttingen: Vandenhoeck & Ruprecht, 2016) ◆ Joseph Blenkinsopp, *A History of Prophecy in Israel,* 3rd ed. (Louisville: Westminster John Knox, 1999) ◆ Georg Fischer, *Jeremia: Der Stand der theologischen Diskussion* (Darmstadt: Wissenschaftliche Buchgesellschaft, 2007) ◆ Peter Höffken, *Jesaja: Der Stand der theologischen Diskussion* (Darmstadt: Wissenschaftliche Buchgesellschaft, 2004) ◆ Jörg Jeremias, *Hosea und Amos: Studien zu den Anfängen des Dodekapropheten,* FAT 13 (Tübingen: Mohr, 1996) ◆ Klaus Koch, *The Prophets,* 2 vols., trans. Margaret Kohl (London: SCM, 1982–83) ◆ Reinhard G. Kratz, *Die Propheten Israels,* Beck'sche Reihe 2326 (Munich: Beck, 2003) ◆ Karl-Friedrich Pohlmann, *Ezechiel: Der Stand der theologischen Diskussion* (Darmstadt: Wissenschaftliche Buchgesellschaft, 2008) ◆ Odil H. Steck, *Der Abschluß der Prophetie im Alten Testament: Ein Versuch zur Frage der Vorgeschichte des Kanons,* Bibilisch-theologische Studien 17 (Neukirchen-Vluyn: Neukirchener Verlag, 1991) ◆ Odil H. Steck, *The Prophetic Books and Their Theological Witness,* trans. James D. Nogalski (St. Louis: Chalice, 2000) ◆ Hermann-Josef Stipp, *Das deuteronomistische Geschichtswerk,* ÖBS 39 (Frankfurt am Main: Lang, 2011) ◆ Erich Zenger, ed., *"Wort Jhwhs, das geschah..."* *(Hos 1,1): Studien zum Zwölfprophetenbuch,* HBS 35 (Freiburg im Breisgau: Herder, 2002)

1. The Theology of the Nevi'im as an Overarching Complex

The Torah is followed by the text complex of the Nevi'im, combining the historical books of Joshua–2 Kings with the prophetic books of Isaiah–Malachi, which hardly seem to fit together at first glance. This combination is only comprehensible when viewed in light of the formation of the Torah (Genesis–Deuteronomy). On the one hand, the Torah presents Moses as the incomparable "prophet" (Deut 34:10) superior to all other prophets, while on the other it promises Israel a succession of prophets to follow Moses and instruct Israel (Deut 18:15–18). This chain of succession begins with Joshua and continues through figures like the judges, Samuel, and Ahijah of Shiloh, the deeds of whom the books of Judges, Samuel, and Kings report. The corpus of the prophetic books in the narrower sense from Isaiah to Malachi connects with these figures. From this perspective, the books from Joshua through Malachi do indeed form a unity as the Nevi'im ("Prophets") in contrast to the Torah ("Law").

INTERPRETERS OF THE TORAH Judging from the logic of the Hebrew canon, the prophets of the Hebrew Bible are just what people held them to be for centuries: preachers and interpreters of the Mosaic law. However, this is not historically accurate. The prophetic books were originally formed independently from the Torah—this was Julius Wellhausen's groundbreaking insight.[23] They only took on the role traditionally ascribed to them over time and were edited accordingly as the Torah ascended to its place as the most important body of tradition in the Hebrew Bible. Prior to being understood completely in the light of the Torah, the prophetic books were connected to the overarching complex of Genesis–2 Kings. They offered their own nuanced content and historical perspective on salvation, such that the theological low point ending the presentation of the history of salvation (Genesis–Joshua) and calamity (Judges–2 Kings) in Genesis–2 Kings might continue with the prospect of a new story of salvation.

23. Cf. Julius Wellhausen, *Prolegomena zur Geschichte Israels*, 3rd ed. (Berlin: Reimer, 1886), 417 and often; trans. as *Prolegomena to the History of Israel,* trans. John S. Black and Allan Menzies (Edinburgh: Black, 1885), 407. See also Konrad Schmid, "The Prophets after the Law or the Law after the Prophets? – Terminological, Biblical, and Historical Perspectives," in *The Formation of the Pentateuch: Bridging the Academic Cultures of Europe, Israel, and North America*, ed. Jan C. Gertz et al., FAT 111 (Tübingen: Mohr Siebeck, 2016), 841–50.

LITERARY *INCLUSIO* AROUND THE NEVI'IM The combination of the Former Prophets (Joshua–2 Kings) and Latter Prophets (Isaiah–Malachi) into the canonical section of the Nevi'im is reflected literarily by an *inclusio* between the first and the last chapters (Josh 1 and Mal 3 [Eng. 4]).

JOSH 1:7–8, 13

Only be very strong and steadfast to do scrupulously everything my *servant Moses* commanded. . . . You shall always speak from this book of *Torah* and meditate day and night, so that you will do scrupulously everything that is written in it, so that you will make your way prosperous and will be successful. . . . *Remember* what *Moses, the servant of Yhwh, commanded* you: Yhwh, your God, is providing you rest and giving you this land.

MAL 3:22 (ENG. 4:4)

Remember the Torah of Moses, my servant, to whom I *commanded* statutes and ordinances on Horeb for all Israel.

The content of this *inclusio* establishes the memory of the Mosaic Torah. The two-part concern to establish the Torah as the authoritative section of canon (cf. Deut 34:10–12) and to subordinate the Nevi'im to it is quite clear. Every prophet from Joshua to Malachi is a successor to Moses, towards whom they should orient themselves.

2. *The So-Called Former Prophets*

FORMER AND LATTER PROPHETS According to the structure of the canon, the books following the Torah—Joshua, Judges, Samuel, and Kings—belong together with the subsequent prophetic books and are themselves designated as "prophets." More specifically, they constitute the "Former Prophets" in contrast to the "Latter Prophets" comprised of Isaiah to Malachi. The fact that Joshua, Judges, Samuel, and Kings are counted among the prophets, and are not first and foremost integrated into the canon as the continuation of the Torah, arises primarily from the dominance of the Torah. The Torah is considered the pinnacle of prophecy by Moses, to which all later prophecy, from Joshua to Samuel and all further prophetic figures in the historical books including the complex from Isaiah and Malachi, are subordinate. At the same time, the separation between the Torah and the Former Prophets decouples the validity of the Torah from residence in the land.

In terms of the formational process, however, the combination of the books following the Torah as the "Former" and "Latter Prophets" represents an artificial and late step. The connection of the books of Joshua, Judges, Samuel, and Kings to the *Corpus propheticum* (prophetic corpus; that is, Isaiah to Malachi) concerns the latest texts in terms of literary history. The core of the book of Joshua probably arose as the conclusion of the Moses-exodus narrative. The book of Judges could have undergone a phase of independence before it was set within the complex of Joshua to Kings. Samuel to Kings also likely emerged as an independent work on the history of the kingdom from its beginnings to its end, which was then gradually linked with the preceding books.[24]

One can, in any case, assume that the connection of Joshua through Kings with the historical account in the Torah was dominant for long phases of the literary history of the Hebrew Bible, and the canonical separation belongs to the latest phases of the establishment of the Pentateuch as Torah.

DEUTERONOMISTIC HISTORY AND DEUTERONOMISTIC HISTORIES Scholarship often describes the books of Joshua to Kings, often including Deuteronomy, as the "Deuteronomistic History." The theological influence of Deuteronomy is certainly palpable in these books, though with varying intensity, which probably results from the extensiveness of the traditional material available in the "Deuteronomistically" influenced book contexts. For example, Judges and Kings are strongly marked with Deuteronomistic features, while this is less clearly the case for Joshua and Samuel.

However, in contrast to conventional scholarship, it should be noted that discussion of the "Deuteronomistic History" is only correct in the plural. There were different "Deuteronomistic Histor*ies*" within Genesis to Kings. The contours of a first "Deuteronomistic History" can be recognized in Samuel and Kings, the content of which (not yet in the language

---

24. Cf., e.g., Reinhard G. Kratz, *The Composition of the Narrative Books of the Old Testament*, trans. John Bowden (Edinburgh: T&T Clark, 2005); Thomas Römer, *The So-Called Deuteronomistic History: A Sociological, Historical and Literary Introduction* (London: T&T Clark, 2005).

of Deut 12) was governed by the idea of cult centralization in Jerusalem. A further "Deuteronomistic History" can be located in Exodus–Joshua combined with Samuel and Kings, which is governed by the first commandment and shaped theologically by the literary arc from Exod 32/1 Kgs 12, as well as the reciprocity of "exodus from Egypt" and "return to Egypt" in 2 Kgs 25:26. A third "Deuteronomistic"—now post-Priestly—"History" governs Genesis–Kings, which is already dominated by the concept of the "Torah of Moses" that should be observed in the history. It contains a great *inclusio* between Joseph in Egypt and King Jehoiachin at the table of the Babylonian king Evil Merodach, advocating a diaspora theology for Israel.[25]

THE BOOK OF JOSHUA The book of Joshua revolves around the acquisition of the land and is at the center of the goal toward which the Moses-exodus narrative flows. The coherence of the Moses-exodus narrative arises not only from the association of exodus and eisodus,[26] but also from the consistent Neo-Assyrian imaginative background. The conquest narratives are oriented in accordance with the standards of Neo-Assyrian campaign descriptions.[27] The older section of the book in Josh 1–12* should also be interpreted within the context of the Moses-exodus narrative. Especially theologically and compositionally important in the second part of the book (Josh 13–24), which contains material quite close to the Priestly document,[28] is the concluding chapter's report of the establishment of a theocracy in Israel. Joshua has the tribes of Israel commit themselves to Yhwh as their king in Shechem. As a result, Joshua 24 takes on an important hinge role between the Hexateuch (Genesis–Joshua) and the subsequent books of the Enneateuch (Judges–2 Kings), separating Israel's history of salvation from its history of destruction. Read in the light of Josh 24, the history of destruction presented in Judges–2 Kings is primarily characterized by violation against God's kingdom and the establishment of a separate earthly kingdom.

25. Cf. Michael J. Chan, "Joseph and Jehoiachin: On the Edge of Exodus," *ZAW* 125 (2013): 566–77.

26. Cf. Joachim Krause, *Exodus und Eisodus: Komposition und Theologie von Josua 1–5,* VTSup 161 (Leiden: Brill, 2014).

27. Cf., e.g., John Van Seters, "Joshua's Campaign of Canaan and Near Eastern Historiography," *SJOT* 4 (1990): 1–12.

28. Cf. Enzo Cortese, *Josua 13–21: Ein priesterschriftlicher Abschnitt im deuteronomistischen Geschichtswerk,* OBO 94 (Freiburg: Universitätsverlag; Göttingen: Vandenhoeck & Ruprecht, 1990).

THE BOOK OF JUDGES In its present form, the book of Judges is fashioned as an intermezzo between Israel's salvation history, which reaches from the promises to the ancestors through Israel's exodus from Egypt to the acquisition of the land, and the subsequent period of the monarchy.

The so-called judges—charismatic deliverers—arise during situations of distress and deliver Israel by their spiritual gifts. Yet Israel repeatedly falls away from God, such that the events form a cycle that the beginning of the book of Judges, taking an abstract view of history, describes as follows:

> And the Israelites did what was evil in the eyes of Yhwh. They served the Baals and abandoned Yhwh, the god of their ancestors, who had led them out of the land of Egypt. And they went after other gods. . . . And the anger of Yhwh burned against Israel, and he gave them into the hands of plunderers who robbed them. And he sold them into the hands of their enemies all around, and they could no longer stand against their enemies. . . . And Yhwh raised up judges, and they delivered them from the hand of those who robbed them. . . . And when Yhwh raised up judges for them, then Yhwh was with the judge and delivered them from the hand of their enemies as long as the judge lived, for Yhwh was moved to pity when they lamented over those who persecuted and oppressed them. But when the judge died, they again sinned, worse than their ancestors, and went after other gods, serving them and bowing down before them. . . . (Judg 2:11–19)

So the book of Judges leads to the portrayal of the monarchal period of Israel and Judah in the books of Samuel and Kings. They no longer tell of periodically recurring acts of divine deliverance, but rather about Israel and Judah's apostasy from God, which ends in the demise of each nation (2 Kgs 17 and 2 Kgs 25).

OLDER TRADITIONAL MATERIAL Yet the book of Judges was not drafted as the transition from the book of Joshua to the book of Samuel. Its literary core instead appears in Judg 3–9, which contain a collection of narratives about deliverers from the Assyrian period. The fact that, except for Othniel (Judg 3:7–11), all the judges—Ehud, Shamgar, Deborah, Barak, Gideon, and Abimelech—come from the region of the northern kingdom leads to the conclusion that Judg 3–9 preserves specifically northern Israelite traditions. These traditions propagate the possibility of a non-state existence for Israel without its own king. Especially the episode of the failed institutionalization by Abimelech in Shechem (Judg 9), which presupposes the historical destruction of Shechem in 722 BCE, warns against a separate kingdom in Israel. The incidences surrounding the establishment of a Shechemite kingdom in Judg 9 can be read as a summary of the worst atrocities of the northern kingdom. The story of Abimelech in Shechem concentrates two hundred years of Israelite kingship in one chapter. The specific profiles of Israel's enemies in Judg 3–9 also point to the Assyrian period: Moab first comes on the stage with King Mesha around 845 BCE as a state that was able to threaten Israel (Judg 3:12–14). The same is the case for the conflicts with the Midianites, which appear to reflect Israel's experiences with the Arabs beginning in the seventh century BCE. Therefore, the core of the book of Judges should probably be viewed as a post-monarchic programmatic writing that makes a statement in favor of a divinely led political approach through charismatic deliverers. It gives off the impression that this intra-Israelite leadership need not conflict with overarching political structures. The political program of Judg 3–9 is—understood within its historical location—thoroughly pro-Assyrian and therefore forms a political counterstatement to the Moses-exodus narrative.

THE BOOKS OF SAMUEL AND KINGS The books of Samuel report the establishment of the monarchy in Israel and Judah and should actually be called "the books of David" in light of their focus. They bear the title of Samuel, however, due to their location in the Former Prophets. Linked to Samuel are the books of Kings, depicting the further history of the kingdom and its demise. In terms of theology, a certain framework around the books of Samuel and Kings as a whole can be recognized in the stealing of the Ark in 1 Sam 4–6 and the destruction of the temple in 2 Kgs 25. The loss of the Ark offers a prelude to the centuries-later destruction of the central sanctuary.

CHARACTERIZATION AS HISTORY OF DISASTER In its present form, the books of Samuel and Kings are configured according to the perspective of Josh 24 and therefore depict the period of the monarchy as a period of disaster. The actual king should be Yhwh, but Israel chose differently and rejected Yhwh (cf. 1 Sam 8:6–12; 10:17–19). The tradition allows for the recognition, however, that behind this focus there is a pro-royal perspective that views the kingdom sympathetically (cf. 1 Sam 9:1–3).

AMBIVALENCE TOWARD THE MONARCHY The complex history of the formation of the books of Samuel and Kings (cf. below, §25) has led to a pronounced ambivalence in its presentation of the monarchy. On the one hand, the monarchy is placed under the fundamental verdict that it stands in competition with the kingdom of God. On the other hand, kings like David, Hezekiah, and Josiah are viewed unreservedly as positive figures that can serve as religious examples. The ambivalent view of the monarchy does not appear, however, only to be a product of the overlaying of a pro-royal layer with a redactional layer that is primarily critical of the king. The critical view too is anchored in older narrative material. The traditions of David's rise and succession in 1 Sam 16 to 1 Kgs 2 do not only chronicle David in a sugar-coated manner; they instead contain numerous incidents that allow the king to appear in a negative light—especially his affair with Bathsheba (2 Sam 11–12).

The Establishment and the Loss of the Kingdom   The largest block of the books of Samuel and Kings depicts the establishment and the loss of the institution of the monarchy in Israel and Judah. Within the context of the narrative books from Genesis to 2 Kings, only the two final books are aware of a monarchy in Israel and Judah. The monarchy is thereby introduced as a historically contingent entity, not as a fact of creation. As a result, according to Genesis–2 Kings, while the monarchy marks Israel and Judah's past significantly, it neither belongs to Israel's foundational period described in the Torah, nor is it necessary for the future. Though various prophetic texts develop the expectation of a restoration of the Davidic dynasty, these perspectives are in no way exclusive, nor do they remain unchallenged (cf. below, §37).

3. The Theology of the Four Books of the Prophets as an Overarching Complex

Four Prophetic Books   Judged in light of the standards of ancient book production, there are four prophetic books in the Hebrew Bible: the books of Isaiah, Jeremiah, Ezekiel, and the Twelve. The twelve so-called Minor Prophets are combined on one scroll, so they count as one book. In fact the books of the twelve Minor Prophets are also linked with one another through redactional insertions on their literary margins so that they are a unity not only in terms of the technology of writing, but also in literary terms.[29]

29. Cf. James D. Nogalski, *Literary Precursors to the Book of the Twelve*, BZAW 217 (Berlin: de Gruyter, 1993); James D. Nogalski, *Redactional Processes in the Book of the Twelve*, BZAW 218 (Berlin: de Gruyter, 1993); Elena Di Pede and Donatella Scaiola, eds., *The Book of the Twelve—One Book or Many? Metz Conference Proceedings, 5–7 November 2015*, FAT II/91 (Tübingen: Mohr Siebeck, 2016).

In the canonical sequence of the Hebrew Bible, it is striking that the four prophetic books are arranged in a specific order, wherein the books of Isaiah and the twelve Minor Prophets frame Jeremiah and Ezekiel.

Isa 1–39:			Hos, Joel, Amos, Jonah, Mic, Nah:
Assur			Assur
Isa 36–39:			
Assur/Babylon			
	Jer:	Ezek:	Hab, Zeph, Obad:
	Babylon	Babylon	Babylon
Isa 40–66:			Hag, Zech, Mal:
Babylon/Persia			Persia

The setting of the books of Jeremiah and Ezekiel pertain to a relatively limited section of Israelite history. They concern the time immediately before and after the catastrophe of Jerusalem and Judah in 587 BCE. The book of Isaiah and the Book of the Twelve, in contrast, provide information on a much broader section of the history of Israel. They begin in the Assyrian period and extend to the Persian period. The book of Isaiah even ends with a vision of the new creation of heaven and earth (Isa 65–66).

ALIGNMENT WITHIN HEBREW BIBLE PROPHECY This overarching organization of the four prophetic books of the Hebrew Bible shows that they were not perceived as individual books, but seen as a theological unity. At certain points the books are even aligned with one another through redaction.[30] This is most clearly recognized in cases of so-called double transmission, such as Isa 2:2–4 // Mic 4:1–3.[31] The Jeremiah and Ezekiel traditions are different from one another, which is also the case for the texts

---

30. On the book of Isaiah and the Book of the Twelve, see, e.g., Erich Bosshard-Nepustil, *Rezeptionen von Jesaja 1–39 im Zwölfprophetenbuch: Untersuchungen zur literarischen Verbindung von Prophetenbüchern in babylonischer und persischer Zeit*, OBO 154 (Freiburg: Universitätsverlag, 1997); Odil H. Steck, *Der Abschluß der Prophetie im Alten Testament*. For the books of Jeremiah and Ezekiel, see, e.g., Dieter Vieweger, *Die literarischen Beziehungen zwischen den Büchern Jeremia und Ezechiel*, BEATAJ 26 (Frankfurt am Main: Lang, 1993).

31. Cf. Irmtraud Fischer, "Schwerter oder Pflugscharen? Versuch einer kanonischen Lektüre von Jesaja 2, Joël 4 und Micha 4," *BL* 69 (1996): 208–16.

of the book of Isaiah and the Book of the Twelve, but in their redactional combination, they are interpreted as concordant in their substance despite different accents in terms of perspective. As a result, it is indirectly emphasized that prophecy rests on insight into the singular, indivisible will of God. Careful reading of the prophetic books allows for the reconstruction of this will, even though the individual books might diverge in certain details from one another.

4. *The Book of Isaiah*

ISAIAH AS "SPOKESMAN" The literary positioning of the book of Isaiah as the first book of the prophets (in the Hebrew tradition)[32] implies a leading role for this book. Isaiah is the "spokesman" for the prophets, who has an overview the entire passage of Yhwh's story with his people, which he writes down in his book. The fact that the book of Isaiah as a whole came to be understood as a comprehensive prophecy of history immediately after its literary completion is attested by the assertion in the book of Sirach, dated to around 180 BCE:[33]

> In bold spirit [Isaiah] looked into the future and comforted Zion's mourners. He declared what would take place at every time, and the hidden [he revealed] before it came. (Sir 48:27–28 [Eng. 48:24–25])

For the book of Sirach, Isaiah is a figure who speaks not only to his own time, but who, in accord with the present book of Isaiah extending from 1–66, foresaw the entire history of the world. The book of Isaiah owes its rise to the position of "spokesman" to the prominent position of the authority who lent his name to the book, Isaiah, as well as his historical location at the beginning of Israel's written prophecy.

An important consideration for the overarching theological structure of the book of Isaiah, which is what is of interest here, is that the Hezekiah-Isaiah narratives (Isa 36–39) separate the words of "Isaiah" in chaps. 1–35

---

32. The Greek and Latin tradition often places the Book of the Twelve before the book of Isaiah, for Hosea and Amos appear before Isaiah.

33. Cf. Johannes Marböck, "Jesaja in Sirach 48,15–25: Zum Prophetenverständnis in der späten Weisheit," in *Schriftauslegung in der Schrift: Festschrift für Odil Hannes Steck zu seinem 65. Geburtstag*, ed. Reinhard G. Kratz et al., BZAW 300 (Berlin: de Gruyter, 2000), 305–19.

from those in chaps. 40–66. Following primarily the announcement of judgment, but also conditional promises of salvation in chaps. 1–35, the narratives in chaps. 36–39 of the miraculous preservation of Jerusalem from Sennacherib in 701 BCE show the fundamental salvific intent of Yhwh, the god of Zion. They form the foundation for the further declarations of salvation by "Isaiah" offered in Isa 40–66, which are introduced there by a "second calling" (40:1–8), interpreted in terms of the progression of the book. The fact that the depiction of the events of 701 BCE in Isa 36–39 transition immediately to Isa 40, such that the Babylonian exile is skipped over in the presentation of the book, may be intentional on the level of the present composition. Isaiah declares the fundamental and steadfast salvific will of Yhwh for Zion, so the destruction of Jerusalem by the Babylonians only comes up through prospective and retrospective references.

INCLUSIOS SURROUNDING THE BOOK AS A WHOLE Isaiah 1 and 66 are strikingly related due to contact in content and vocabulary, such that one can interpret them as an *inclusio* surrounding the book as a whole.[34] This observation makes plain that the book of Isaiah as a whole (also in terms of literary production) is a redactional unity, and not merely a compilation of preexisting, unstructured florilegia. The observable change in content between Isa 1 and 66, which takes place within the transition from the prophecy of judgment against Israel in Isa 1 to the prophecy of salvation for the pious in Isa 65–66, shows that the book as a whole develops a reading progression, and it should be appreciated as such. The book of Isaiah surveys the history of the sinful people of God from the time of Assyrian hegemony, through the Persians, to the consummation of God's rule over his pious servants in the context of a new creation.

THEOLOGICAL THEMES IN THE BOOK OF ISAIAH At this point our concern is primarily with the theological form of the book of Isaiah and the further prophetic books as a whole. They deal with a multitude of theological themes, which will be discussed below in §§30–39.

---

34. Cf. "rebel" (1:2 [Israel]; 66:24 [Yhwh's enemies]); Zion as abandoned / Zion as surrounded by children (66:8, 10); false "new moon" and "Sabbath" (1:13–14) / Yhwh worshipped by the nations on "new moon" and "Sabbath" (66:23); false worship (1:11–13) / correct worship (66:20–21); pilgrimage of the nations (["sword"] 2:2–4; 66:12, 16); judgment by fire on Judah (1:31, cf. 1:7) / judgment by fire on the enemies of Yhwh (66:15–16, 24).

5. *The Book of Jeremiah*

THE HEBREW AND GREEK BOOKS OF JEREMIAH The first order of importance for the discussion of the theological nature of the present book of Jeremiah is the fact that the book has been transmitted in two different forms.[35] Unlike the Hebrew version, the Greek translation of the book of Jeremiah places the oracles against the nations (Jer 46–51) not at the end, but rather in the middle of the book.

Hebrew Version:

1–25	26–45	46–51	52
Oracles against Judah and Jerusalem	Narratives, including oracles of salvation (30–33)	Oracles against the nations	Historical context

Greek Version (with Hebrew numbering):

1–25	46–51	26–45	52
Oracles against Judah and Jerusalem	Oracles against the nations	Narratives, including oracles of salvation (30–33)	Historical context

In addition to this difference in order are divergences in the extent of the text. As a whole, the Hebrew is around 3,000 words longer than the Greek text, which works out to about one-seventh of the size of the book. The relatively faithful translation technique in the Septuagint of Jeremiah excludes the possibility that these differences arise exclusively or even primarily from the Greek translator. Rather, with a probability bordering on certainty, it should be accepted that the Greek book of Jeremiah goes back to a shorter Hebrew *Vorlage*. So the Greek translation of the Jeremiah tradition attests to the circulation of two versions of the book in the biblical period.[36]

35. Cf. Hermann-Josef Stipp, *Das masoretische und alexandrinische Sondergut des Jeremiabuches: Textgeschichtlicher Rang, Eigenarten, Triebkräfte*, OBO 136 (Freiburg: Universitätsverlag; Göttingen: Vandenhoeck & Ruprecht, 1994).

36. The discoveries from Qumran provide some confirmation. The fragments of Jeremiah from Qumran can be assigned to six scrolls, of which two (4QJer[b]; 4QJer[d]) are strikingly close to the LXX, showing that a Hebrew *Vorlage* of the Greek version of the book of Jeremiah did exist.

The theological contour of the likely more original—at least in terms of the order of the sections in the book[37]—Hebrew version of the book is primarily marked by the correlation between the sections of Jer 1–25 and 26–45, which place oracles and narratives in a relationship to one another. The redactional logic of this sequence can be interpreted such that the words of Jeremiah are the declaration and the narratives are their fulfillment. It is noteworthy that the oracles of salvation in Jer 30–33 appear within Jer 26–45. In judgment, the book of Jeremiah develops a view of salvation, which at first is declared to Jeremiah alone according to Jer 30:1–4, though it is left behind in written form for the audience of the book.

The Hebrew book of Jeremiah continues with a strong emphasis on the judgment of Babylon, which concludes the book, prior to the historically oriented chapter 52, which generally correlates with the texts of 2 Kgs 24:18–20 and 2 Kgs 25. This judgment against Babylon is the intermediate-term goal of God's act of judgment against his own people. Indeed the judgment against Jerusalem and Judah is quite analogously transferred to Babylon, as the correlation between Jer 6:22–24 and Jer 50:41–43 shows:

JER 6:22–24:	JER 50:41–43:
Thus says Yhwh:	
Behold, a nation is coming from the land of the north,	Behold, a people is coming from the north,
a great nation	a great nation
is stirring from the ends of the earth.	and many kings
They grasp bow and javelin	are stirring from the ends of the earth.
—it is cruel—	They grasp bow and javelin
And they are without mercy,	—it is cruel—
They roar thunderously like the sea and ride upon horses,	And they are without mercy,
equipped like a warrior against you,	They roar thunderously like the sea and ride upon horses,
Daughter *Zion*.	equipped like a warrior against you,
We heard the news—	Daughter *Babylon*.
Our hands slacken; fear has seized *us*,	*The king of Babylon* heard the news—
pains like an expectant mother.	*his* hands slacken; fear has seized *him*,
	pains like an expectant mother.

---

37. It is generally assumed that the shorter Greek text represents an older stage in the development of the text than the longer Hebrew version. This is probably correct in principle, but it is, at the same time, not always the case. There are also occasional plusses in the Greek text in comparison to the Hebrew version. Furthermore, it must also be determined, even if this does not concern very many passages in the Greek version (cf., e.g., Jer 27), if it should be seen as the result of abridgement.

The Greek book of Jeremiah, with its sequence of a "three-part eschatological schema," does not re-order all of the extant material in a disciplined manner according to this structure, but it demonstrates clearly that it understands the ensemble of the prophecies of Jeremiah in such a way that they combine into a great prophecy of history that envisages the three great stages of world history—judgment on the nation itself, judgment on foreign nations, and salvation for the nation. It is similar to Zephaniah and the book of Ezekiel, the general layout of Isa 1–39, as well as the Greek Book of the Twelve Prophets.

THE NARRATIVES ABOUT JEREMIAH A distinctive feature of the book of Jeremiah is the extensive narratives that concern Jeremiah himself and the events surrounding the demise of Jerusalem (Jer 26–29 and especially 36–45). Their extensive nature influences the book of Jeremiah in a particular manner. They are rarely explicitly theological, yet they make an impressive display of the diversity of interconnections between prophetic activity and its historical context. In Jer 36–45 Jeremiah on one hand appears defeatist because he is prosecuted and imprisoned for his message of judgment against Judah and Jerusalem. On the other hand, the narrative describes the last king of Judah, Zedekiah, as recognizing Jeremiah as a prophet and employing him for his purposes (Jer 37:3: "Please pray for us to Yhwh!"; 37:17: "Is there a word from Yhwh for us?"). Both Jeremiah's impact and lack thereof appear in the reflection of Judah's *Realpolitik* in the final years before the destruction. The tradition clearly shows that prophecy can be politically unwelcome and can hurt the prophets themselves. In response to Zedekiah's request to pray for Jerusalem, Jeremiah does receive a word from God that he should pass on to Zedekiah and that affirms the demise of the city once more (Jer 37:8), even though the Babylonians have temporarily withdrawn in the course of the appearance of the Egyptian army (Jer 37:7), which actually allows for the expectation that Jerusalem will be helped.

6. *The Book of Ezekiel*

THE BOOK OF EZEKIEL AS THE SELF-EVALUATIVE REPORT OF THE PROPHET The book of Ezekiel is the most rigorously organized book of the Hebrew Bible.[38] Except for the superscription in 1:3 and the no-

---

38. While fewer divergences are observed between the textual traditions of the book

tice in 24:24, it is consistently styled as a first person report, thereby constituting Ezekiel's autobiography in terms of its literary (not historical) perspective. It is recognizable that the prophet has become more important in contrast to his prophecy—a phenomenon that can be observed as parallel to the form of the Jeremiah narratives in the book of Jeremiah.

The book is arranged in four parts (though the final two can be taken together), which not only form thematic units but also call for understanding as a whole as a sequence. Following judgment against its own people (Ezek 1–24) and against foreign nations (Ezek 25–32), salvation for the nation follows (Ezek 33–39; 40–48). The book of Ezekiel therefore follows the "three-member eschatological schema" also found in the Greek book of Jeremiah.

1–24	25–32	33–39	40–48
Oracles of judgment against Judah and Jerusalem	Oracles of judgment against foreign nations	Promises for the people of Judah	Ezekiel's "draft constitution"

This order is not carried through in a mechanical fashion, so there are oracles of deliverance in 1–24 and oracles of judgment in 33–39. However, this does not speak against this structuring principle, but only demonstrates that, what was only likely to be the case, that this structure was laid over an entity that had grown literarily.

The sequence of the "three-member eschatological schema" is accompanied by the chronologically tiered motif of the prophet's muteness. The prophet remains mute (except for divine messages that he is supposed to deliver) for the period of judgment (beginning with the first deportation of Jerusalemites by the Babylonians in the year 597 BCE—this is the date of reference given in 1:2; 33:21; 40:1—until 586 BCE, the destruction of Jerusalem and the second deportation), so that he cannot appropriately advise the Jerusalemites (3:26; 24:27). Only after the ultimate fall of Jeru-

---

of Ezekiel and of the book of Jeremiah, the Greek translation of the Septuagint nevertheless shows several significant differences, especially the textual sequence in Papyrus 967 in the section of Ezek 36–39 (36 [without 23bβ–38]; 38–39; 37; 40–48), which is perhaps older than the Masoretic order.

salem is his muteness lifted (33:22). What becomes clear from this is that the book form of Ezekiel's prophecy is not suited to motivate the audience to repentance. It should instead provide the possibility for understanding the catastrophe after the fact.

Ezekiel 1–24 and Ezekiel 40–48 have a reciprocal relationship. Within Ezek 1–24, 11:23 reports the departure of the כבוד יהוה (*kbwd yhwh*),"the glory of Yhwh," that is the form of God's presence, from the temple. The corresponding reentry of "the glory of Yhwh" into the new temple is found within Ezek 40–48 in Ezek 43:1–5. The period of the exile is not only the time of the exile of the nation, but also the exile of God.[39]

The blueprint of the new temple in Ezek 40–48 is depicted as an antitype to the degenerate Solomonic Temple in Ezek 8–11. Its utopic dimension is highlighted through the fact that the details of the building only consist of two dimensions, the layout, and not the height. Therefore, Ezek 40–48 does not have a building in view, but it instead formulates a basic plan for a building.

BABYLONIAN FORMS OF THOUGHT A special characteristic of the book of Ezekiel, one that especially stands out in comparison with the book of Jeremiah, is its use of Babylonian ways of thinking.[40] The figures of speech used in the book of Ezekiel, especially those that mark the descriptions of the visions, clearly show their cognitive roots in the Babylonian sphere. For instance, Ezek 1 can be virtually decoded by means of concepts from Babylonian cosmology.[41] The imagery of the book of Jeremiah, on the other hand, is much more at home in the Levant. The juxtaposition of the Jeremiah and Ezekiel traditions with their different impressions shows the malleability of theology content according to the relevant cultural-

39. The same conception marks the frame of the basic layer of the book of Deutero-Isaiah in Isa 40:1–11 ad 52:7–10. The basis for the salvation announced by Deutero-Isaiah is the return of God from Babylonian exile, which must precede the return of the people, cf. Christina Ehring, *Die Rückkehr JHWHs: Traditions- und religionsgeschichtliche Untersuchungen zu Jesaja 40,1–11, Jesaja 52,7–10 und verwandten Texten*, WMANT 116 (Neukirchen-Vluyn: Neukirchener Verlag, 2007).

40. Cf. Othmar Keel, "Zeichensysteme der Nähe Gottes in der Büchern Jeremia und Ezechiel," in *Gottes Nähe im Alten Testament*, ed. Gönke Eberhardt and Kathrin Liess, SBS 202 (Stuttgart: Kohlhammer, 2004), 30–64.

41. Christoph Uehlinger and Susanne Müller Trufaut, "Ezekiel 1: Babylonian Cosmological Scholarship and Iconography: Attempts at Further Refinement," *TZ* 57 (2001): 140–71.

historical customs. Or, to state it more generally: prophecy does not exist on its own; it always employs historically and culturally contingent forms of expression.

7. The Book of the Twelve

THE UNITY OF THE BOOK OF THE TWELVE The fact that the so-called twelve "Minor Prophets" were counted as a single book in antiquity is attested from numerous pieces of evidence. First, the manuscript finds from Qumran and neighboring Wadi Murrabba'at attest that Hosea–Malachi always appear in a single scroll. Further, Sir 49:10 makes a summary reference to the "twelve prophets" around 180 BCE, which assumes that the "Minor Prophets" were perceived as a unity. Also the order of the books in the Septuagint within the prophets attests to the Book of the Twelve Prophets as a block placed before Isaiah, Jeremiah, and Ezekiel, such that the Book of the Twelve counts as an entity in itself. Finally, the information about the books of the Hebrew Bible in 4 Ezra 14 ("twenty-four") and in Josephus ("twenty-two") undoubtedly assume in their numbers that the Twelve are one book.

If it is the case that ancient Judaism treated the Book of the Twelve Prophets as one book, then the question arises as to whether a certain sequential meaning can be recognized in this composition as a whole. On this question one must differentiate between the Hebrew and Greek traditions because the Septuagint does not offer the Book of the Twelve Prophets before Isaiah, Jeremiah, and Ezekiel, but rather in a different internal order. It appears, however, that the Hebrew Book of the Twelve Prophets primarily attempts to order the partial books analogously to the chronological order of Isaiah, Jeremiah, and Ezekiel: Hosea, Joel, Amos, Obadiah, Jonah, and Micah stand for the eighth century; Nahum, Habakkuk, and Zephaniah for the seventh century, while Haggai, Zechariah, and Malachi are located in the sixth century. In terms of the chronological order, the Hebrew Book of the Twelve Prophets abides by the biblical superscriptions of the historical location of each prophet, which can in the best case actually point to the oldest texts of a book, though without guarantee. On the other hand, the Septuagint attempts—as in the case of the book of Jeremiah—to reproduce the "three-member eschatological schema." Following Hosea, Amos, Micah, and Joel, all of which contain judgment pronouncements against Israel, come Obadiah, Jonah, and

Nahum, with their declarations of judgment against nations like Edom and the Assyrians (especially Nineveh). The Greek Book of the Twelve Prophets is concluded by Habakkuk, Zephaniah, Haggai, Zechariah, and Malachi, which also develop perspectives on salvation for Israel.

MALACHI AS A REDACTIONAL SEVERING OF THE ZECHARIAH TRADITION The numerous literary and thematic connections of the book of Malachi with the preceding Zechariah tradition as well as the artificial name מלאכי (ml'ky), "my messenger," suggests the probability that the book of Malachi neither arose from a prophet by the same name, nor that it was originally an independent book.[42] It seems more likely that Malachi became a book of its own secondarily through its separation from the Zechariah tradition in order to reach the complete number of twelve Minor Prophets. This brought about the effect that Israel's prophets consist of three major and twelve minor figures to be seen as somehow analogous to Abraham, Isaac, and Jacob together with the twelve tribal ancestors of Israel.

§20 Ketuvim

Peter Brandt, *Endgestalten des Kanons: Das Arrangement der Schriften Israels in der jüdischen und christlichen Bibel*, BBB 131 (Berlin: Philo, 2001) ♦ Reinhard G. Kratz, "Die Tora Davids: Psalm 1 und die doxologische Fünfteilung des Psalters," *ZTK* 93 (1996): 1–34 ♦ Markus Saur, "Sapientia discursiva: Die alttestamentliche Weisheitsliteratur als theologischer Diskurs," *ZAW* 123 (2011): 236–49 ♦ Markus Saur, *Einführung in die alttestamentliche Weisheitsliteratur* (Darmstadt: Wissenschaftliche Buchgesellschaft, 2012) ♦ Markus Saur, ed., *Die theologische Bedeutung der alttestamentlichen Weisheitsliteratur,* Biblisch-theologische Studien 125 (Neukirchen-Vluyn: Neukirchener Verlag, 2012) ♦ Konrad Schmid, *Hiob als biblisches und antikes Buch: Historische und intellektuelle Kontexte seiner Theologie*, SBS 219 (Stuttgart: Katholisches Bibelwerk, 2010) ♦ Konrad Schmid, "Gott als Angeklagter, Anwalt und Richter: Zur Religionsgeschichte und Theologie juridischer Interpretationen Gottes im Hiobbuch," in *Die Anfechtung Gottes: Exegetische und systematisch-theologische Beiträge zur Theologie des*

---

42. Cf. Erich Bosshard and Reinhard G. Kratz, "Maleachi im Zwölfprophetenbuch," *BN* 52 (1990): 27–46.

Hiobbuches, ed. Leonie Ratschow and Hartmut von Sass, Arbeiten zur Bibel und ihrer Geschichte 54 (Leipzig: Evangelische Verlagsanstalt, 2016), 105–35 ◆ Johannes Schnocks, *Psalmen*, Uni-Taschenbücher 3473 (Paderborn: Schöningh, 2014) ◆ Julius Steinberg, *Die Ketuvim: Ihr Aufbau und ihre Botschaft*, BBB 152 (Hamburg: Philo, 2006) ◆ Georg Steins, *Die Chronik als kanonisches Abschlussphänomen: Studien zur Entstehung und Theologie von 1/2 Chronik*, BBB 93 (Weinheim: Beltz Athenäum, 1995) ◆ Georg Steins, "Torabindung und Kanonabschluss: Zur Entstehung und kanonischen Funktion der Chronikbücher," in *Die Tora als Kanon für Juden und Christen*, ed. Erich Zenger, HBS 10 (Freiburg im Breisgau: Herder, 1996), 213–56 ◆ Timothy J. Stone, *The Compilational History of the Megilloth: Canon, Contoured Intertextuality and Meaning in the Writings*, FAT II/59 (Tübingen: Mohr Siebeck, 2013) ◆ Erich Zenger, "Der Psalter im Horizont von Tora und Prophetie," in *The Biblical Canons*, ed. Jarie-Marie Auwers and Henk Jan de Jonge, BETL 163 (Leuven: Peeters, 2003), 111–34

1. The Theology of the Ketuvim as a Collection

Unlike the case of the Torah and the Nevi'im, no clear literary *inclusio* can be identified in the beginning and concluding texts of the Ketuvim. This hangs together with the fact that the sequence within the manuscript tradition of the Ketuvim varies strongly. The Ketuvim apparently never acquired a structure similar to the Nevi'im, much less the Torah. The books of the Ketuvim also reveal considerably fewer features of configuration that spread beyond individual books. These can be shown most easily for Chronicles and Ezra-Nehemiah, and in a limited manner for the writings attributed to Solomon as well (Proverbs, Qoheleth, and Song of Songs).

THE PSALMS AS THE OPENING OF THE KETUVIM However, there is a certain tendency to place the Psalms at the beginning of the Ketuvim. Psalms may even represent the historical nucleus of the third section of the canon (cf. Luke 24:44 and 4QMMT^c). The opening text of the Psalter is Ps 1, which refers back to the Torah and recommends the individual study of Torah as the *medium salutis* (cf. above, §16). One could also point to similar features in the wisdom literature within the framework of the Ketuvim, when read within the context of the canon as a whole. In any case, it is important that the canonical logic of the Ketuvim implements an anti-eschatological, post-cultic philosophy of life focused on mundane reality. While this theological perspective can be observed prior to 70 CE (Ps 1 itself, for example, certainly emerged before 70 CE and is assumed in Qumran), it only becomes dominant with the violent demolition of the temple establishment by the Romans, at which point the apocalyptic interpretation of Law and Prophets instead becomes entirely apocryphal.

2. Psalms

THE DIVISION OF THE PSALMS INTO FIVE PARTS THROUGH THE DOXOLO-GIES The final form of the Hebrew Psalter evinces a division into five parts, which forms an analogy to the Torah. The Torah of David is equivalent to the Torah of Moses.[43] This structure is established by the four doxologies in Ps 41:14 (Eng. 41:13); 72:18–19 (Eng. 72:19–20); 89:53 (Eng. 89:52); and 106:48. This "Torah shape" of the Psalter is also emphasized by the introductory Ps 1, as well as Ps 119. Given the strongly divergent orders of the Psalters still found in Qumran, as well as the theological proximity of the frame of the Psalter as a whole in Pss 1–2 and 146–150 with the contemporary, non-Essene wisdom texts (book of Mysteries [=1Q27; 4Q299–301]; 1Q/4QInstruction), this fivefold division can hardly be older than the second century BCE.

Analogous to the thematic emphases of the five books (shown in the graphic presentation below as I–V), but also corresponding to the content of the psalms connected with the doxologies of Pss 42, 72, 89, and 106, the present structure of the Psalter allows for the recognition of an impression of Israel inspired by Chronicles. It opens with the epoch of David (1–41) and Solomon (42–72), then continuing with the monarchy (73–89) and the exile (90–106), leading to the conclusion in a broad portrayal of the restoration (107–150).

43. Cf. Reinhard G. Kratz, "Die Tora Davids: Ps 1 und die doxologische Fünfteilung des Psalters," *ZTK* 93 (1996): 1–34.

David	Solomon	Monarchy	Exile	Restoration
I	II	III	IV	V
(Pss 1–41)	(Pss 42–72)	(Pss 73–89)	(Pss 90–106)	(Pss 107–150)
Ps 41:14 (Eng. 41:13)	Ps 72:18–19	Ps 89:53 (Eng. 89:52)	Ps 106:48	Pss 146:10; 147:20; 148:14; 149:9; 150:6
Praise be to Yhwh, *the God of Israel,*	Praise be to Yhwh, *the God of Israel,* who alone does great wonders! And praise be to his glorious name	Praise be to Yhwh	Praise be to Yhwh, *the God of Israel,*	
Forever and ever!	**forever**, all lands will be full of his glory!	**Forever!**	**from everlasting to everlasting!**	
Amen! Amen!	Amen! Amen!	Amen! Amen!	And let all people say: Amen! *Hallelujah!*	*Hallelujah!*

In terms of the direction of reading, this redactional structure in the Psalms generally develops an orientation toward the image of a peaceful world under the dominion of Yhwh, who fundamentally cares for it.[44]

The theocratic ordering of life spread through books IV and V makes the recognition of any national-political interests difficult to identify. Where views take on political perspectives, they concern social justice—protection for the foreigner, widow, and orphan. In terms of their theology of history as well as their political-theological orientation, therefore, the Psalms are quite close to the book of Chronicles.[45] Where David is

---

44. A clear exception appears in Ps 149; cf. Martin Leuenberger, "'. . . und ein zweischneidiges Schwert in ihrer Hand' (Ps 149,6): Beobachtungen zur theologiegeschichtlichen Verortung von Ps 149," in *The Composition of the Book of Psalms*, ed. Erich Zenger, BETL 238 (Leuven: Peeters, 2010), 635–42.

45. The theological imprint of the Greek Psalter differs substantially from the Hebrew. In addition to the differences in counting and extent, especially the eschatologization of spe-

named in books IV and V, he appears as an example for the godly, not as monarch.

OLDER PARTIAL COLLECTIONS IN THE PSALTER The book of Psalms shows that it is not a collection of individual psalms only, but also of collections of psalms, which may have once existed on their own. Conceivable as autonomous collections are the David (Pss 3–41; 51–64; 66–71), Korah (Pss 42–49; 84–85; 87–88), Asaph (Pss 50; 73–83), and pilgrimage psalms (Pss 120–134). The continuous use of אלהים (*'lhym*) for God in Pss 42–83 also suggests that this complex—the so-called "Elohistic Psalter"—likely once existed independently or was at least viewed and edited as an entity in itself. In terms of theology, however, these collections receive less of an accent than the fivefold division of the Psalter as a whole.

CULTIC AND POST-CULTIC MARKS OF THE PSALMS It remains a well-founded conjecture in scholarship that some psalms had a cultic function in the First or Second Temple. This is quite clearly apprehended in, for example, Ps 24, a so-called gate entrance liturgy, which is characterized by an antiphony and was obviously written for a cultic procession. In the present literary context of the Psalms, this cultic dimension has disappeared entirely and is replaced by the literary context of the Psalter. The Psalms as cultic songs have now become texts for meditation, which are transparent with regard to their original function but are now only used literarily. Many psalms likely never existed except as literature, so they should be understood as "post-cultic."[46] The secondary use of originally cultic texts in a literary "post-cultic" space, or rather the modeling of psalms from a cultic perspective, even though they were never used in the cult, is theologically noteworthy. The basic function of establishing nearness to God remains the same in both uses, though the present Psalter is now "only" an object of study.

---

cific psalms in the Greek version should be mentioned; cf. Joachim Schaper, *Eschatology in the Greek Psalter*, WUNT II/76 (Tübingen: Mohr Siebeck, 1995); Holger Gzella, *Lebenszeit und Ewigkeit: Studien zur Eschatologie und Anthropologie des Septuaginta-Psalters*, BBB 134 (Berlin: Philo, 2002).

46. Cf. Fritz Stolz, *Psalmen im nachkultischen Raum*, ThSt 129 (Zurich: TVZ, 1983).

3. The Wisdom Literature and the Megillot

The wisdom literature within the Ketuvim forms a comparatively amorphous complex,[47] which is demonstrated by the lack of clarity with regard to what counts as wisdom literature in the Hebrew Bible. One generally reckons with a nucleus consisting of the books of Job, Proverbs, and Qoheleth. Of these books, Proverbs and Qoheleth are connected to one another through their (at least partial) ascription to Solomon, which is of some relevance for the canon. However, the Hebrew Bible also ascribes the Song of Songs to Solomon. Job and Song of Songs thereby hinder the identification of wisdom literature too closely with the *Corpus Salomonicum.*

JOB The book of Job can be outlined comparatively clearly. It can first be separated into a frame (Job 1–2; 42:7–17) and dialogues (Job 3:1–42:6), whereupon the dialogue section can be further subdivided. It consists of Job's discussion with his three friends (Job 3–28), a monologue by Job (29–31), the speeches of a fourth friend, Elihu (32–37), two divine speeches (Job 38–41), as well as an answer by Job (42:1–6). This sequence is thoroughly significant, and the theological punch line of the book of Job emerges from the tense interplay between these three parts. The prologue (Job 1–2) expounds on Job's problem; however, it already offers the audience an answer to the question of why Job must suffer. He is the object of a heavenly test. The dialogues with the friends that follow go through the entire spectrum of possible explanations for Job's suffering. Perhaps, contrary to his wisdom and experience, Job did sin? Perhaps he must suffer because he is basically—like all humans—guilty? Perhaps he should also be instructed in a particular sense? Job rebels against all these attempts at explanation, and the audience of his book knows that Job is right. Job's suffering is neither grounded in the fact that he has offended God, nor that he, as human, cannot be righteous before God. Divine educational measures must also be eliminated as a reason. The reason for Job's suffering lies only in the heavenly test that God and the Satan conduct with him.

The progression from prologue to dialogues is apparently created so that the prologue preemptively criticizes the content of the friends' posi-

---

47. Wisdom writings within the Hebrew Bible also include particular psalms, as well as narratives like the Joseph story; wisdom passages also appear in the Prophets. Therefore, wisdom or wisdom-inspired literature only partially achieved an overarching literary grouping.

tions in the dialogues. However, the prologue is not only relevant for the speech cycles with the friends but also—even if it is not decisive—for the divine speeches in Job 38:1–40:2; 40:6–41:34. These speeches only indirectly answer the problem expounded in the prologue. The depiction of the ordered processes of the natural and animal worlds, as well as the example of the hippopotamus and crocodile extending from the *Chaoskampf* motif present a theology of the order of the world that, while it does not name Job's suffering, still places it in a larger interpretive framework. While Job does suffer, Job is not the world. Job's life does not function, but the world functions. While Job finds himself in chaos, the world as a whole is a divinely sustained cosmos. In any case, the order posited in the divine speeches receives a significant counterbalance in the prologue: Job's suffering does not fit into the world order, not even some kind of unseen or dynamic world order, but is instead the result of an exceptionally gruesome test. God makes no mention of the heavenly events of the prologue in his answer to Job.

This continues the same thematic line on another level that can be observed in the dialogues: the prologue not only criticizes the friends' theology, it also criticizes the divine revelation. Viewed in terms of the prologue of Job, God's nature is deducible neither from human nor divine speech. How then can one speak of God? A possible answer can be taken from the final divine declaration about Eliphaz and his friends in Job 42:7:

> My anger burns at you and your friends because you have not spoken rightly to me (כי לא דברתם אלי נכונה, *ky l' dbrtm 'ly nkwnh*) like my servant Job.

דבר אל (*dbr 'l*) in this verse should be understood succinctly as "speak to" and not as "speak of." The book of Job therefore issues a rejection of *disputare de Deo* (discussion of God), but at the same time it speaks of the transformational direction of address to God in the situation of suffering, namely of lament. The fact that Job laments in his distress, even turning to God with accusation, is explicitly justified by Job 42:7.

The theology of the book of Job develops through the equally artistic and suspenseful structure of the book. As a result of the fact that the book of Job does not directly formulate this theology, but instead allows it to emerge through the process of reading, its theology remains inconclusive and open, which is certainly appropriate for the problem treated in the book of Job.

PROVERBS The book of Proverbs is a complex entity made up of seven sub-books, of which three are ascribed to Solomon (1:1–9:18; 10:1–22:16; 25:1–29:27), two remain anonymous ("Words of the Wise": 22:17–24:22; 24:23–34), while the final two are attributed to foreign scholars ("Words of Agur" 30:1–33; "Words of Lemuel" 31:1–31). The sections ascribed to Solomon structure the book as a whole. After the introductory collection of ten instructive speeches in 1–9, each of the Solomon compositions (10:1–22:16; 25:1–29:27) is followed by two shorter series of proverbs that are anonymous or from non-Israelite sages. This is illustrated in the following chart:

1:1–9:18: "Proverbs of Solomon"

10:1–22:16: "Proverbs of Solomon"	25:1–29:27: "Proverbs of Solomon"
22:17–24:22: "Words of the Wise"	30:1–33: "Words of Agur"
24:23–34: "Words of the Wise"	31:1–31: "Words of Lemuel"

The significance of this compositional order might be found in the fundamental function of the fear of God for all attempts at wisdom that is highlighted in Prov 1–9:

The *fear of Yhwh* is the <u>beginning</u> of understanding, the fools despise wisdom and discipline. (Prov 1:7)

Wisdom's <u>beginning</u> is the *fear of Yhwh*, and the knowledge of the Holy is insight. (Prov 9:10)

It is clear in terms of compositional history that reference to God is unnecessary for the older sections, especially in Prov 10–22. However, the Yhwh proverbs cannot as a whole be classified as secondary. The earlier wisdom was in no way secular; it was in fact at least implicitly theological, which does not conceptually exclude the possibility of an explicit "theologizing" from the outset. Yhwh can certainly be designated as the originator and guarantor of the *Tun-Ergehen-Zusammenhang* (act-consequence connection). However, he is hardly ever seen as the immediate agent of retribution, which the *Tun-Ergehen-Zusammenhang* generally conceives as socially and historically mediated.[48] On the other hand, Solomon appears

---

48. Cf. Bernd Janowski, "Die Tat kehrt zum Täter zurück: Offene Fragen im Umkreis des 'Tun-Ergehen-Zusammenhangs,'" in *Die rettende Gerechtigkeit*, Beiträge zur Theolo-

in this overarching compositional structure of the book of Proverbs as the progenitor of all international wisdom. What the "wise" say is ultimately Solomon's legacy.

WAY OF LIFE AND INSIGHT INTO THE SOCIAL AND WORLD ORDER The topic dominating the book of Proverbs is the concrete way of life. The book of Proverbs collects various declarations about the successful and the unsuccessful life in poetic form. Typical is that the individual is not taken as an entity in itself and given guidance as such, but he is instead seen as part of a larger societal and cosmic whole. The successful life primarily arises from the appropriate approach to these contexts. Whatever the person does or does not do, they interact with the environment, which reciprocally defines their life, thought, and welfare. The book of Proverbs offers collected wisdom from experience on these interactions, which rests on the discovery of a certain regularity of human communal life, but also on the contingencies experienced within it.

DEALING WITH THE COMPLEXITY OF EXPERIENTIAL WISDOM The narrowing and banalization of experiential wisdom in light of the complexity of human life are avoided in the book of Proverbs through the balancing arrangement of individual proverbs that enables a system of reciprocal "checks and balances" between individual proverbs. An example appears in Prov 10:1–5:[49]

> . . . A wise son brings his father joy, but a stupid son is the sorrow of his mother.
> Wrongfully acquired treasures are useless, but righteousness delivers from death.
> Yhwh does not let the righteous hunger, but he pushes away the greed of the sinner.
> Whoever works with lazy hands[50] becomes poor, but diligent hands make rich.

---

gie des Alten Testaments 2 (Neukirchen-Vluyn: Neukirchener Verlag, 1999), 167–91. See also Klaus Koch, "Gibt es ein Vergeltungsdogma im Alten Testament," in *Spuren des hebräischen Denkens: Beiträge zur alttestamentlichen Theologie*, vol. 1 of *Gesammelte Aufsätze* (Neukirchen-Vluyn: Neukirchener Verlag, 1991), 65–103, esp. 65.

49. Cf. Thomas Krüger, "Komposition und Diskussion in Proverbia 10," *ZTK* 89 (1995): 413–33.

50. On the vocalization as *rēʾš ʿōśāh*, cf. *HALOT*, 2:1209.

> Whoever gathers in summer is an intelligent son, whoever sleeps at harvest is a disgraceful son.

Proverbs 10:1, 5 encompass a unit of proverbs that at first glance could each stand alone, but they are actually laid out as a deliberate composition. The thematic opposition between 10:1 "wise"–"stupid" becomes explicit in 10:5: "intelligent" is the one who harvests in summer; the one who does not do this behaves disgracefully. Linked to this explication is 10:2, which warns of the danger of only paying attention to economic efficiency, emphasizing the necessity of good behavior. Only legally gotten gain is of use. A problem is dealt with in 10:3 that could result from the position taken in 10:2. What happens when moral behavior leads to economic difficulties? At this point 10:3 brings in God as an argument. He will satisfy the pious. Finally, 10:4 makes clear that God's care in 10:4 does not render the self-initiative called for in 10:5 superfluous. Whoever does not work will remain poor. One can recognize the following: Prov 10:1–5 works out a complex position on the question of how wise action is concretely established, and it safeguards this position against possible side issues.

THEOLOGICAL RECEPTION OF WISDOM EXPERIENTIAL KNOWLEDGE Classical scholarship often differentiated between "earlier" and "later" wisdom. The "earlier wisdom," primarily represented by Prov 10–22, was based on the correspondence between human act and consequence, therefore still adhering to a just world order, while "later wisdom," such as that reflected in Job, Qoheleth, and Prov 1–9, was seen to have given up this connection and emphasized the inscrutability of the world order. This differentiation is correct in terms of identifying that there are clear differences in the wisdom literature with regard to the degree to which the social and natural mechanisms in the world can be recognized and described. This distinction is inaccurate, however, in categorizing the "earlier wisdom" as naïve and the "later wisdom" as reflective. Even the "earlier wisdom" is arguably quite critical in its declarations of a human view of the world that was always opaque.[51]

Within the framework of those texts traditionally categorized as "later wisdom," Prov 1–9 occupies a special role. The guiding principle of the emphasis on יִרְאַת יהוה (yr't yhwh), "fear of God" (cf. above on Prov 1:7; 9:10), highlights that knowledge cannot be obtained without godliness.

---

51. Cf. Thomas Krüger, *Kritische Weisheit* (Zurich: TVZ, 1997), v–viii.

Human effort alone is insufficient to attain insight into the world order that Prov 1–9 views as hidden. A person must first submit themselves spiritually to God and let themselves be led from this posture. This position is exceptional because the book of Qoheleth, treated below, follows a different viewpoint, which is more of a practical than a theoretical nature.

QOHELETH The book of Qoheleth is furnished with a double frame. The first frame consists of a prologue (Qoh 1:1–3) and epilogue (Qoh 12:8–14), which is set apart from the inner foreword (Qoh 1:4–11) and afterword (Qoh 11:1–12:7). The book bears the superscription as the "words of Qoheleth, the son of David, king in Jerusalem" (Qoh 1:1), so that Solomon is implicitly named as author, which introduces the form-critical imprint of the book as a collection of aphorisms. The design of the book recalls the form of address found in the so-called diatribes of popular Greek philosophy. The content of the book of Qoheleth is often postulated as bringing it into the proximity of ancient skepticism, as well as the life instruction from the Stoics and Epicureans. Doubtlessly there are points of contact that likely arose as a function of cultural contact, but the position of the book of Qoheleth is different on various points from the skepticism found within the scope of Greek philosophy. It is constitutive of skepticism that understanding itself is impossible, so one should refrain from judgment. Qoheleth underscores the narrow limits of human knowledge, but it does not conclude from these limits that one should refrain from judgment. Qoheleth instead designates the possibilities and limitations of human knowledge as the fundamental rationale for his practical philosophy. Humans may not be able to understand the world, but they can experience food, drink, and enjoyment as divine gifts that are available for human enjoyment.

> He [God] made everything so that it is beautiful in its time. He even placed the faraway time in the heart of humanity, simply so that humanity cannot grasp from beginning to end the work that God has made. I recognized that they can do nothing better than to enjoy and to do good in life. And when a person is able to eat and drink and enjoy good with all their labor, this too is a gift from God. (Qoh 3:11–13)

Here the book of Qoheleth evokes the basic approach to life on display in, for example, the Primeval History of the Torah. At the same time, it rejects all eschatological perspectives, especially those of the contemporary prophecy and emerging apocalypticism. There is "nothing new under the sun" (Qoh 1:9).

The well-known conclusion of the book of Qoheleth in 12:12–14 has sometimes been connected with the conclusion of the Ketuvim, but this cannot be substantiated by the concrete formulation.

> And beyond this—my son, be warned!—many books will be made without end, but much study tires the body. After hearing everything, the conclusion is: fear God and keep his commandments. This is the duty for everyone. For God will bring all deeds before judgment, on everything hidden, whether good or evil. (Qoh 12:12–14)

THE SO-CALLED MEGILLOT According to Jewish tradition, Qoheleth belongs to the so-called five Megillot ("feast scrolls"), which also include Ruth, Song of Songs, Lamentation, and Esther. These five writings are ascribed to the following five feasts: Song of Songs belongs to Passover, Ruth to the Feast of Weeks, Lamentation to the Ninth of Ab (the memorial on the destruction of the temple on the ninth of Ab), Qoheleth to the Festival of Booths, and Esther to Purim. The combination as Megillot and the assignment to the feasts are first attested in the Middle Ages. It is striking that all five Megillot display a certain distance from the explicit naming or direct discussion of God.

SONG OF SONGS Translated in some modern languages as the "highest song," which goes back to Luther, the Hebrew title is "Song of Songs" (שִׁיר הַשִּׁירִים, šyr hšyrym), which should be understood as a superlative. The book collects a series of originally profane love songs. The divine name Yhwh never appears throughout the entire book. Its inclusion into the Bible probably came about due to the ascription of Song of Songs to Solomon (1:1; cf. 1 Kgs 5:12 [Eng. 4:32]) and its—likely secondary[52]—allegorical interpretation as the love between God and Israel (and later in Christian contexts between God and the church). However, this reception itself requires explanation. It is rooted in the perception of love as a wonderful and inviolable gift to humanity that is experienced as surpassing the normal possibilities of the world.

---

52. Cf. the various contributions in Ludger Schwienhorst-Schönberger, ed., *Das Hohelied im Konflikt der Interpretationen*, ÖBS 47 (Frankfurt am Main: Lang, 2017).

RUTH The book of Ruth narrates the story of Ruth, a Moabitess, who comes to Bethlehem as the daughter-in-law of a Jewess. There she integrates into Judaism and finally becomes the ancestress of King David. Read canonically, the book of Ruth progresses to the concluding genealogy of David (Ruth 4:18–22) and points out that even King David can be connected to a Moabite ancestress. This relates the book of Ruth, similar to the content of the Joseph story, to a liberal position in the debate about mixed marriages in postexilic Judaism. The book of Ruth is marked literarily by a careful style of composition that is supported by guiding words (*Leitwörter*) and characterized by inner-biblical exegesis.

LAMENTATIONS Lamentations is a collection of five songs, of which the first four are arranged as acrostics—that is, their twenty-two verses or strophes (Lam 3 is comprised of sixty-six verses) follow the order of the Hebrew alphabet. The fifth song also contains twenty-two verses; however, they do not follow the alphabet. The Greek translation attributes authorship to Jeremiah (likely on the basis of the notice in 2 Chr 35:25). The songs reflect on the destruction of Jerusalem and develop a theology of guilt for the city that responds in particular to the prologue of the book of Deutero-Isaiah in Isa 40:1–2, pronouncing Jerusalem free from guilt. The city therefore becomes a figure that is to be taken as a character in its own right, not merely seen as the totality of its inhabitants.[53] The acrostic arrangement of the songs suggests closure and completion. The open arrangement of the fifth song might possibly suggest a dynamic for the book as a whole that leads beyond the lamentable state of Jerusalem. In any case, the concluding statement appears to have been consciously selected: "Bring us back, Yhwh, to you; we will return. Make our days new, as they once were. Or have you abandoned us completely, are you angry with us beyond all measure?" However, Lamentations has remained relevant with its air of mourning over the centuries because of Israel's ongoing exilic fortunes and has, as a result, continued to be transmitted.

ESTHER The book of Esther is a diaspora novella that tells of the endangerment and deliverance of the Jews in the Persian Empire. Its Hebrew version never mentions God;[54] however, it is clear that the guiding hand

---

53. Cf. Christl Maier, *Daughter Zion, Mother Zion: Gender, Space, and the Sacred in Ancient Israel* (Minneapolis: Fortress, 2008).

54. On the theological interpretations of the Greek version, cf. Kristin De Troyer and

of God should be recognized as indirectly behind the reported events. Mordechai speaks cryptically of God in Esth 4:14 when he expects help for the Jews ממקום אחר (*mmqwm 'ḥr*), "from another place." In addition, the Tetragrammaton Yhwh is located hidden in the first letters of Esther's four word statement, יבוא המלך והמן היום (*ybw' hmlk whmn hywm*), "Let the king and Haman come today," in Esth 5:4, which initiates the turning point in favor of the Jews. A theological dimension finally appears in 8:17, where an allusion is made that because of the events reported in the book of Esther, many pagans converted to Judaism.

Both in relation to the topic of diaspora and also the hidden work of God, the book of Esther is quite similar to the Joseph story. The conflict between the Jews and the Persians bears mythic features, which do not fit historically with the comparatively tolerant religious politics of the Persians but are more likely retrojections from the Hellenistic context. There is the confrontation between the Jewish protagonist, Mordechai, and his Persian counterpart, Haman, whose genealogy connects him with the legendary primordial conflict between Amalek and Israel (cf. Exod 17:8–16), which also occupied King Saul (cf. 1 Sam 15:3). Mordechai is introduced as "son of Jair, the son of Shimei, the son of Kish" (Esth 2:5), linking him with King Saul, who was the son of Kish (1 Sam 9:1–2). Haman's filiation as an "Agagite" (Esth 3:1), sounds like Agag, the king of the Amalekites (1 Sam 15:8). The distress of Judaism is therefore interpreted as the reiteration of the affliction of Israel by his archenemy Amalek, who failed as dramatically as the opponent of Judaism also will.[55]

4. Chronicles—Ezra—Nehemiah

The books of Chronicles are often viewed by scholarship in close connection to Ezra–Nehemiah as a connected "Chronistic History." Ezra–Nehemiah truly have been bound redactionally with 1–2 Chronicles through the hinge of 2 Chr 36:22–23 // Ezra 1:1–3 into a "Chronistic History." However, Ezra–Nehemiah are probably somewhat earlier in terms of their compo-

---

Gesine Schenke Robinson, *Die Septuaginta und die Endgestalt des Alten Testaments: Untersuchungen zur Entstehungsgeschichte alttestamentlicher Texte*, Uni-Taschenbücher 2599 (Göttingen: Vandenhoeck & Ruprecht, 2005), 26–48.

55. Cf. Hans Andreas Tanner, *Amalek: Der Feind Israels und der Feind Jahwes* (Zurich: TVZ, 2005).

sitional history than 1–2 Chronicles, even if these writings originate from a comparable theological milieu.

CHRONICLES AS "REWRITTEN BIBLE" The theological message of Chronicles can be determined through comparison with its *Vorlage* of Genesis–2 Kings. Immediately striking is the fact that Chronicles, as an independent work, is conceived as "rewritten Bible." Furthermore, its texts are not inserted into Genesis–2 Kings as an ongoing continuation (*Fortschreibung*). The conceptual differences were apparently too significant to allow for the possibility of revising Genesis–2 Kings. In addition, Chronicles arose at a historical point in time in which comprehensive additions were no longer possible, at least for the Torah portions. Historical placement of Chronicles varies between the late Persian to the Hasmonean periods, that is, between the fourth and second centuries BCE. One should likely reckon with a phased formation within the boundaries of this window in time.

THE PERIOD OF DAVID AND SOLOMON AS ISRAEL'S FORMATIVE EPOCHS The basic differences in content to Genesis–2 Kings are revealed in the basic outline of Chronicles. It summarizes the time before Saul in genealogy (1 Chr 1–9). Then, after the episode concerning Saul (1 Chr 10), it devotes its broadest and central area to the depiction of the kingdoms of David (1 Chr 11–29) and Solomon (2 Chr 1–9), who are depicted in idealizing form. Neither the ancestors nor the exodus, Sinai, the conquest, or any of the epochs of the classic salvation history of Israel, but rather the time of David and Solomon is the authoritative period of formation for Israel, while the "genealogical atrium" only functions as the summation of the pre-history. Chronicles therefore dates the essential foundational period of Israel much later than its *Vorlage*, placing it in the opening period of the monarchy. David and Solomon, as founders of the cult, are Israel's founders. They are portrayed in a certain way as analogous to the Persian kings Cyrus and Darius, though Cyrus is only prominent in 2 Chr 36:22–23 (העיר יהוה את רוח כורש [h'yr yhwh 't rwḥ kwrš], "Yhwh aroused the spirit of Cyrus"), and Darius is never mentioned in Chronicles. Just as David prepared for the construction of the First Temple, Cyrus does the same through the promulgation of the edict for the construction of the Second Temple. Just as the First Temple was built under Solomon, the Second Temple was built under Darius. This construction demonstrates the pro-Persian orientation of Chronicles. Cyrus and Darius are depicted as a second David and a second Solomon, being subtly brought near to the Davidic dynasty.

THE MARGINALITY OF MOSES AND THE EXODUS As a result, Chronicles presents a strongly autochthonous notion of the origins of Israel in which the period of the united monarchy follows closely on the period of the ancestors. While it does not completely silence the exodus and conquest, they move entirely into the background. Moses does not appear as the leader of the exodus, but rather as Israel's lawgiver. The exodus itself is mentioned only six times in the books of Chronicles (1 Chr 17:5, 21; 2 Chr 5:10; 6:5; 7:22; 20:10). The direct adoption of 1 Kgs 8:21 by 2 Chr 6:11 actually omits it. The covenant of Yhwh in 1 Kgs 8:21 is still made with the fathers, as he brought them out of the land of Egypt, while the parallel formulation of 2 Chr 6:11 merely describes it as made with the Israelites.

ALL-ISRAELITE PERSPECTIVE WITH JERUSALEM AS CENTER The highlighting of the period of David and Solomon carries with it the political perspective of a twelve-tribe ideal for Israel, presenting the inclusion of the north and south. It is striking that Chronicles completely omits the history of the cultically illegitimate northern kingdom; however, it is still clear that Israel in Chronicles is more than just Judah. It apparently sees Judah and Jerusalem as the center, but it campaigns for the annexation of the north, that is, the Samaritans to this center, in order to restore "Israel" as a cultic unity.

THEOLOGY OF INDIVIDUAL RESPONSIBILITY There is no historical accumulation of guilt in Chronicles. Instead, every generation is responsible to God themselves, and they will each—if they turn away from God—be punished. This theology of individual responsibility reflects a priestly background. The functioning of the cult of atonement assumes personal responsibility for guilt. The presentation in Chronicles is not thinking in moralistic terms, but instead brings the catastrophes of history into connection theologically with guilt. Times of prosperity, on the other hand, are begotten by just and godly behavior. This is quite clearly recognized in the presentation of Manasseh in Chronicles. Manasseh ruled for fifty-five years in Jerusalem (2 Kgs 21:1); therefore, he must—contrary to his depiction in 2 Kgs 21—have been a pious man.[56] In a similar manner, the exile is traced back to the guilt of the last king of Judah, Zedekiah, and his generation alone, which is accordingly portrayed in a negative light (2 Chr 36:11–14).

---

56. This notion appears in the deuterocanonical literature in the Prayer of Manasseh (*Oratio Manassae*) (cf. JSHRZ 4: 15–28).

DIFFERENCES FROM DEUTERONOMISM Primarily these conceptual differences from Deuteronomistic theology likely led to the formation of Chronicles as an independent work, rather than a layer of continuous writing in Genesis–2 Kings. Within the Hebrew Bible, this doubling of Genesis–2 Kings and 1–2 Chronicles and the idiosyncrasies of 1–2 Chronicles as an external new edition of Genesis–2 Kings remain the exception. From a hermeneutical perspective, it is quite significant. The mutual canonization of text and commentary anchors the interpretive dynamic itself within the Hebrew Bible.

RELATIONSHIP TO EZRA–NEHEMIAH Ezra–Nehemiah formed a single book in antiquity, which is indicated by the omission of the concluding masorah after Ezra. This book originates from the same circle of authorship as Chronicles, though it is probably somewhat earlier and only secondarily linked with Chronicles through the transportation of Ezra 1:1–3 into 2 Chr 36:22–23.

THEOLOGICAL INTERTWINING OF THE ACTIVITIES OF EZRA AND NEHEMIAH The complex of Ezra–Nehemiah reports on the restoration in Judah, interweaving in peculiar manner the activities of the priest Ezra and the commissioner for the reconstruction, Nehemiah. Immediately following the depiction of the return and temple construction in Ezra 1–6 is a section concerning Ezra's activities in Jerusalem (Ezra 7–10). Nehemiah 1–7 reports on the actions of Nehemiah; Neh 8–10 steers back to Ezra and his reading of the Law, and finally, further directives by Nehemiah appear in the reports in Neh 11–13. As a result, on the level of the composition, Ezra–Nehemiah appears to suggest consciously the simultaneity of Ezra's and Nehemiah's actions, though this was unlikely to have been the case in historical terms. Nehemiah can be located as a historical figure, while this is not completely clear for Ezra.[57] Regardless of what one decides, the reconstruction of the Jerusalem city walls initiated by Nehemiah is assumed to have already taken place by Ezra. So Nehemiah was active in Judah before Ezra. However, Ezra was placed earlier in the tradition because he should have priority as a priest.

PROPHECY IN EZRA–NEHEMIAH Prophecy plays a special role in Ezra–Nehemiah. In Ezra 1–6 the successful reconstruction of the temple requires

57. Cf. Thomas Willi, *Esra: Der Lehrer Israels*, Biblische Gestalten 26 (Leipzig: Evangelische Verlagsanstalt, 2012).

prophetic support, and the restoration is implicitly portrayed as the fulfillment of prophetic promises of salvation (cf., e.g., the reference from Ezra 7:27 to Isa 60:7, 9, 13). The theological consideration behind this depiction appears to lie in the conception of a positive counterpart to the Deuteronomistic theology of history in the Former Prophets (Joshua–2 Kings). If disobedience to the law and the rejection of the prophets lead to judgment, then Ezra–Nehemiah now show the opposite. That is, observance of the law and attention to the current prophets Haggai and Zechariah (cf. Ezra 5:1; 6:14) lead to prosperity for the community in Judah. In this way, both 1–2 Chronicles and also Ezra–Nehemiah as the broader "Chronistic History" can be understood as the comprehensive reception and reformulation of Genesis–2 Kings together with the subsequent *corpus propheticum* (Isaiah–Malachi). The foundational history of Israel and Judah no longer ends in catastrophe (2 Kgs 24–25), but in the restoration period of the Second Temple, in which the prophetic oracles of salvation begin to be fulfilled.

EZRA–NEHEMIAH BETWEEN DEUTERONOMISTIC AND CHRONISTIC THEOLOGY The book of Ezra–Nehemiah—in the form still independent from 1–2 Chronicles—is located on the threshold between the Deuteronomistic and Chronistic portrayals of history in terms of its theology of history. The linkage between law and well-being is marked by Deuteronomism, while the high opinion of Persian hegemony that provided the initiative for the construction of the temple according to Ezra 1–6 is close to Chronistic theology.

THE RELATIONSHIP TO THE TORAH Both 1–2 Chronicles and Ezra–Nehemiah are marked by a high view of the Torah, though both textual domains appear to present a flexible understanding of its contents. Moses is a marginal figure in 1–2 Chronicles and Ezra–Nehemiah; the Torah is generally called "the Torah of Yhwh" and not "the Torah of Moses." Chronicles remains completely silent about the revelation on Sinai, while it appears on the margin of the penitential prayer of Neh 9:13. However, both 1–2 Chronicles and Ezra–Nehemiah point to additional legal stipulations to those of the Torah. The priestly classes and priestly duties as well as the palace administration are regulated in 1 Chr 23–27. Additional social and cultic measures appear in Neh 11–13 after the commitment to the Torah is arranged in Neh 10.

G. The Principal Theological Guidelines in the Literary History of the Hebrew Bible

Having treated the theological contours of various biblical compositions overall, as well as their partial compositions, two further, larger sections follow. One (G) addresses the principal theological developmental lines of the literary history of the Hebrew Bible. The other (H) pursues individual theological themes in the complexities of their history and their history of scholarship.

§21 The Hebrew Bible on the Way to Its Theology

Jörg Jeremias, *Theologie des Alten Testaments*, GAT 6 (Göttingen: Vandenhoeck & Ruprecht, 2015) ♦ Othmar Keel, *Die Geschichte Jerusalems und die Entstehung des Monotheismus*, 2 vols., Orte und Landschaften der Bibel 4, 1 (Göttingen: Vandenhoeck & Ruprecht, 2007) ♦ Reinhard G. Kratz, *Historical and Biblical Israel: The History, Tradition, and Archives of Israel and Judah*, trans. Paul Kurtz (Oxford: Oxford University Press, 2015) ♦ Christoph Levin, "Das Alte Testament auf dem Weg zu seiner Theologie," *ZTK* 105 (2008): 125–45 ♦ Konrad Schmid, "Der Pentateuch und seine Theologiegeschichte," *ZTK* 111 (2014): 239–71 ♦ Konrad Schmid, *Is There Theology in the Hebrew Bible?*, trans. Peter Altmann, Critical Studies in the Hebrew Bible 4 (Winona Lake, IN: Eisenbrauns, 2015) ♦ Odil Hannes Steck, "Strömungen theologischer Tradition im Alten Israel," in *Wahrnehmungen Gottes im Alten Testament: Gesammelte Studien*, TB 70 (Munich: Kaiser, 1982), 291–317 ♦ Andrew Teeter, "The Hebrew Bible and/as Second Temple Literature: Methodological Reflections," *DSD* 20 (2013): 349–77

1. *Literary History and History of Theology*

The fact that the Hebrew Bible is a historical collection of books that grew over time means that its development can be described—insofar as its texts concern religious literary reflections—as theological history. In contemporary German scholarship on the Hebrew Bible, the expressions "history of literature" (*Literaturgeschichte*) and "history of theology" (*Theologiegeschichte*) are used quite promiscuously. The two investigatory questions overlap, but they should also be distinguished from one another.

The investigation of the literary history concerns the development of the literature of the Hebrew Bible as such, while the perspective of theological history concentrates on the theological positions in historical succession as they are formulated in this literature. To the degree that large spans of the literature of the Hebrew Bible are at least implicitly theological literature (which become explicit to different degrees), there is a certain overlap between literary and theological history, though the emphases of each are somewhat different. The distinction becomes especially clear wherever a discernible degree of explication of the theology is present in the literature of the Hebrew Bible.

RUDOLF BULTMANN'S UNDERSTANDING OF THEOLOGY At this point it is helpful to recall the first sentence of Rudolf Bultmann's *Theology of the New Testament:* "*The message of Jesus* is a presupposition for the theology of the New Testament rather than a part of that theology itself."[1] One can reconstruct an implicit theology from the proclamation of the historical Jesus, but Bultmann draws a hard line between the message of Jesus and the Christian kerygma about Jesus Christ as "the Crucified and Risen One."[2] New Testament theology in general no longer maintains such a clear separation. This is even less clear for the theology of the Hebrew Bible, but it does still exist. So, analogous to Bultmann, one could make a formulation to the effect that the hymnic tradition of the Psalms, the older legal tradition, the wisdom tradition, or the proclamation of the prophets are not the objects, but rather the prerequisites for the theology of the Hebrew Bible. While such a position would be overstated, it does have value. These bodies of texts are implicitly

---

1. Rudolf Bultmann, *Theology of the New Testament,* 2 vols., trans. Kendrick Grobel, Scribner Studies in Contemporary Theology (New York: Scribner's Sons, 1951/1955), 1:3 (italics original).

2. Bultmann, *Theology of the New Testament,* 1:3.

theological to a certain degree, such that they can certainly be differentiated from the explicitly theological re-interpretations that find their footing in them and substantially transform them. However, the fact remains that a clear line of separation cannot be drawn.

THEOLOGY AND THE HISTORY OF THEOLOGY Why should an outline of the history of theology even be found in a "theology of the Hebrew Bible"? Does this not threaten to drown the theology in the history of theology? As explained in Part A, a theology of the Hebrew Bible with today's state of knowledge should not overlook the historical complexities of theological positions. It must not only take into account these various positions as such, but also their developing dynamics and cross-linking networks. The observable character of considerable portions of the literature of the Hebrew Bible as traditional and interpretive is especially significant at this point. Therefore, it is appropriate to include such a sketch of the history of theology, albeit incomplete and preliminary, as part of a presentation of a theology of the Hebrew Bible.

2. Literary Continuation of Texts and New Literary Works in the Hebrew Bible

At this point a remarkable characteristic of the literary and theological development of the Hebrew Bible should be pointed out. As long as biblical literature was supplemented with commentary within the literature itself, by definition secondary literature (for theology as a form of reflection this is an important formal determination) could not develop. The commentary passages were affixed to the primary texts. As such, they are not textually differentiated from them, so they themselves also remain—at least when viewed formally—primary literature.

Within the framework of the literature of the Hebrew Bible, there are, however, several precursors to such external formations of written reflection. They can be recognized when preexisting textual material is not simply supplemented within the process of transmission, but when new operations of literary formation arise.

Such new operations can be observed in principle at many points within the formation of the tradition of the Hebrew Bible—whenever a new book (or rather more generally ספר [*spr*], "document") arises. However, several writings would have been expected to have been found as continuing supplements from the nature of their content. In any case, they appear to have arisen originally as independent literary works. Worthy of mention in this perspective are Deuteronomy, the Priestly document, the Deutero-Isaiah tradition, as well as Chronicles (though the literary independence of the Priestly document and the Deutero-Isaiah tradition rest on reconstructions). One could also add such texts as the books of Job or Qoheleth. With regard to their content, it becomes immediately clear where the decisive differences occur in relation to post-canonical theological commentary literature. Their form essentially remains similar to the preexisting literature—the texts remain "primary literature." However, their theological accents apparently require that they be set apart from the stream of tradition, such that they emerge as individual entities.

DEUTERONOMY With regard to Deuteronomy, it appears that this writing arose as an independent document, although the circumstances remain debated. At the same time, it is clear that Deuteronomy assumes and newly construes—especially under the perspective of cult centralization—the preexisting Covenant Code. The tradition of the Neo-Assyrian vassal treaties also lies in the background, which Deuteronomy adopts and applies in a new way to the relationship between God and nation. The relationship of the legal consequence between Deuteronomy and the Covenant Code can be seen in the application of the royal succession. Just as Assurbanipal succeeds Esarhaddon, Deuteronomy follows the Covenant Code.[3]

PRIESTLY DOCUMENT Historically speaking, a second new beginning within the pentateuchal tradition is found in the Priestly document. Within the formation of the tradition of the Pentateuch, it represents an anomaly. It probably did not arise as a supplement to preexisting textual material, but instead was authored as a literarily and conceptually independent entity. This still applies, even if one understands the alternation between source and redaction to be unsuitable, instead understanding the Priestly document as a literary entity that was initially conceived on its own, but then was immediately united with the non-Priestly Pentateuch.

However, why it was necessary that the Priestly document should be separated from the preexisting tradition in order to be conceived as an

---

3. Cf. Bernard M. Levinson and Jeffrey Stackert, "Between the Covenant Code and Esarhaddon's Succession Treaty: Deuteronomy 13 and the Composition of Deuteronomy," *JAJ* (2012): 123–40.

independent writing? Perhaps two issues were pivotal. The first is the requirement of cult centralization that the Priestly document adopts from Deuteronomy, which the preexisting tradition did not apply to the period before Moses. This is especially clear in non-Priestly Genesis, where the ancestral figures are brought into connection with sanctuaries outside of Jerusalem (Bethel, Shechem, Mamre, etc.) in active and legitimating ways. This does not appear to have been acceptable for the Priestly document.[4]

In addition, the Priestly document promotes its own understanding of covenant theology, which was not easily combined with the preexisting tradition. Avoiding the articulation of the promulgation of the law at Sinai as a covenant and moving forward the authoritative commitment by God into the times of Noah and Abraham also called for a new literary introduction.

DEUTERO-ISAIAH Within the scope of prophetic tradition, the tradition of Deutero-Isaiah is of special significance with regard to its conception as a literarily independent composition. The determination of the literary beginnings remains debated for the prophet whose tradition appears in Isa 40 and following, commonly referred to by the artificial name of "Deutero-Isaiah." However, it remains the case that it was composed with at least a certain amount of independence, suggested by the presence of a prologue (40:1–5) and an epilogue (52:7–10) that frame the conjectured kernal in Isa 40–48*. It was then integrated into the Isaiah tradition at a later point. In any case, the proclamations in Isa 40–52* do not link up to the text in Isa 1–39* as supplements. They instead form a separate, self-sufficient or semi self-sufficient writing.

The necessity of this action is once again recognized from the content. The traditional election traditions from monarchic Israel and Judah were annulled theologically by the demise of the northern and southern

---

4. The Priestly version of the narrative of Jacob in Bethel in Gen 35:9–15 presents something of an exception; cf. Albert de Pury, "Der priesterschriftliche Umgang mit der Jakobsgeschichte," in *Schriftauslegung in der Schrift: Festschrift für Odil Hannes Steck zu seinem 65. Geburtstag,* ed. Reinhard G. Kratz, BZAW 300 (Berlin: de Gruyter, 2000), 33–60. The pressure to pass on the tradition of the sanctuary in Bethel was apparently so strong that active contact had to take place in this prominent narrative of the Priestly document. Most striking in Gen 35:9–15 when compared to Gen 28:10–22 are the following elements: Gen 35:9 initially makes it clear that God allows himself to "be seen," that is, the divine appearance is not dependent on the special location of Bethel, which is only named in Gen 35:15, but rather on God's will to reveal himself. Concordant with this is Gen 35:13. After God speaks with Jacob, he leaves this place. So Bethel is not a sanctuary in the Priestly document, but rather a place of revelation. The description of Bethel as "House of God" and "Gate of Heaven" in Gen 28:16–17 is deliberately ignored.

kingdoms. The gift of the land as the objective goal of the exodus tradition and the establishment of the monarchy as the main concern of the David tradition were destroyed, so a new plan was necessary. Logically, this could no longer be attached to existing textual material as a supplement.

CHRONICLES A final example to be cited here—more would be possible—concerns Chronicles. Its date is controversial. Estimates fluctuate from the Persian to the Maccabean periods, though the redaction-historical differentiations can likely fill this entire spectrum (cf. above, §20). It is the first canonical representative of the genre "rewritten Bible," which is otherwise well attested in the literature of the second century BCE (the book of Jubilees should especially be noted). The reason for the need to formulate a new literary work in the case of Chronicles is also quite explicable. Its basic theological points of view could not be achieved within the framework of a revision or supplementation of Genesis–2 Kings. These concern, in particular, the theocratic orientation of the Jerusalem cultic community and the exclusive demarcation of Judah as the true Israel (though Chronicles attempts to maintain the all-Israelite focus in the sense of the twelve tribe ideal, insofar as the former northern tribes are invited to join Judah and the cult in Jerusalem). These could not be balanced out with the political orientation of the Deuteronomistic theology of the land in the *Vorlage* of the Former Prophets.

§22 The Destruction of the Northern Kingdom in 722 BCE

Angelika Berlejung, "Der gesegnete Mensch: Text und Kontext von Num 6,22–27 und den Silberamuletten von Ketef Hinnom," in *Mensch und König: Studien zur Anthropologie des Alten Testaments: Rüdiger Lux zum 60. Geburtstag*, ed. Angelika Berlejung and Raik Heckl, HBS 53 (Freiburg im Breisgau: Herder, 2008), 37–62 ♦ Angelika Berlejung, "Ein Programm fürs Leben: Theologisches Wort und anthropologischer Ort der Silberamulette von Ketef Hinnom," *ZAW* 120 (2008): 204–30 ♦ Erhard Blum, "The Jacob Tradition," in *The Book of Genesis: Composition, Reception, and Interpretation,* ed. Craig A. Evans et al., VTSup 152; FIOTL 6 (Leiden: Brill, 2012), 181–211 ♦ Walter Dietrich, *David: Der Herrscher mit der Harfe,* Biblische Gestalten 14 (Leipzig: Evangelische Verlagsanstalt, 2006) ♦ Israel Finkelstein, *The Forgotten Kingdom: Archaeology and History of Northern Israel* (Atlanta: SBL Press, 2013) ♦ Matthias Köckert, "YHWH in the Northern and Southern Kingdom," in *One God—One Cult—One Nation: Archaeological and Biblical Perspectives,* ed. Reinhard G. Kratz and Hermann Spieckermann, BZAW 405 (Berlin: de Gruyter, 2014), 357–94 ♦ Reinhard G. Kratz, *Historical and Biblical Israel: The History, Tradition, and Archives of Israel and Judah,* trans. Paul Kurtz (Oxford: Oxford University Press, 2015) ♦ Martin Leuenberger, *Segen und Segenstheologien im alten Israel: Untersuchungen zu ihren religions- und theologiegeschichtlichen Konstellationen und Transformationen,* ATANT 90 (Zurich: TVZ, 2008) ♦ Wolfgang Oswald, *Staatstheorie im Alten Israel: Der politische Diskurs im Pentateuch und in den Geschichtsbüchern des Alten Testaments* (Stuttgart: Kohlhammer, 2009) ♦ Albert de Pury, "The Jacob Story and the Beginning of the Formation of the Pentateuch," in *Die Patriarchen und die Priesterschrift: Gesammelte Studien zu seinem 70. Geburtstag = Les patriarches et le document sacerdotal: Recueil d'articles, à l'occasion de son 70e anniversaire,* ATANT 99 (Zurich: TVZ, 2010), 147–69 ♦ Konrad Schmid, "Anfänge politikförmiger Religion: Die Theologisierung politisch-imperialer Begriffe in der Religionsgeschichte des antiken Israel als Grundlage autoritärer und toleranter Strukturmomente monotheistischer Religionen," in *Religion—Wirtschaft–Politik: Forschungszugänge zu einem aktuellen transdisziplinären Feld,* ed. Antonius Liedhegener et al. (Zurich: Pano; Baden-Baden: Nomos, 2011), 161–77 ♦ Hermann Spieckermann, *Heilsgegenwart: Eine Theologie der Psalmen,* FRLANT 148 (Göttingen: Vandenhoeck & Ruprecht, 1989) ♦ Hermann Spieckermann, "Der Mythos Heilsgeschichte: Veränderte Perspektiven in der alttestamentlichen Theologie," in *Arbeit am Mythos: Leistung und Grenze des Mythos in Antike und Gegenwart,* ed. Annette Zgoll et al. (Tübingen: Mohr Siebeck, 2013), 145–66 ♦ Kristin Weingart, *Stämmevolk—Staatsvolk—Gottesvolk? Studien zur Verwendung des Israel-Namens im Alten Testament,* FAT II/68 (Tübingen: Mohr Siebeck, 2014)

Where does the theological history of the Hebrew Bible begin? It starts, gradually, with the emergence of what one can call *implicit theology* in the Hebrew Bible. Where are these beginnings to be found? There are two reasons that render a simple and unequivocal answer impossible. First, there is no consensus about the historical assessment of the writings of the Hebrew Bible, and this will remain the case given the state of empirical documentation. One is dependent on reconstructions that move between levels of probability. Second, it should not be expected that the rise of implicit theology would be a traceable literary process whose path could be observed or reconstructed from one sphere of literature into another. Rather, implicit theology should be recognizable in various strands of tradition, which does not, however, exclude that certain forms of implicit theology would be more likely to establish themselves than others.

PROPHETIC AND LEGAL TRADITIONS Nevertheless, it is reasonable to begin by highlighting two literary domains in particular that appear to have played a paradigmatic role in this process: the prophetic and the legal traditions. They developed under a certain amount of reciprocal influence from one another arising from the characteristic of prophetic literature—in part already from its beginning and in part redactionally—as normative divine word, which took on legal language and redactional forms very early. This did not remain without influence for the legal literature.

The reasons for the special importance of these bodies of literature are not difficult to articulate. First, concerning prophecy, the collection as well as the further transmission of prophetic oracles that arose from specific historical circumstances over a long period of time naturally demands the development of theological reflection, rules for adaptation, modernization of preexisting tradition, and the establishment of a historically complex whole. Within the sphere of the secondary passages in prophetic literature, the attempt to bring together the tradition and contemporary relevance in redactional formulations lies at the root of the formation of implicit theology in the Hebrew Bible.[5]

The same is the case for the legal literature in the Hebrew Bible, which was interpreted as divine law in ancient Israel from a rather early time (from the Neo-Assyrian period) and was analogously adapted and updated through the mode of literary supplementation to tailor it to changing historical relationships.[6] In view of the contemporary and parallel development of the prophetic tradition, the redactional techniques familiar to ancient Near Eastern legal traditions became available for use in the interpretive operations within prophetic literature.[7]

In terms of determining the time period when the first processes of theological reflection become observable, caution is recommended.[8] At

5. Cf. Hans-Jürgen Hermisson, "Zeitbezug des prophetischen Wortes," *KD* 27 (1981): 96–110; Odil H. Steck, *Gott in der Zeit entdecken: Die Prophetenbücher des Alten Testaments als Vorbild für Theologie und Kirche*, Biblisch-theologische Studien 42 (Neukirchen-Vluyn: Neukirchener Verlag, 2001).

6. Cf. Rainer Albertz, "Die Theologisierung des Rechts im Alten Israel," in *Geschichte und Theologie: Studien zur Exegese des Alten Testaments und zur Religionsgeschichte Israels*, BZAW 326 (Berlin: de Gruyter, 2003), 187–207.

7. Cf. Eckart Otto, "Techniken der Rechtssatzredaktion israelitischer Rechtsbücher in der Redaktion des Prophetenbuches Micha," *SJOT* 2 (1991): 119–50.

8. Under different scholarly persuppositions, Odil H. Steck places this starting point in the period of David and Solomon. "Strömungen theologischer Tradition im Alten Israel," in *Wahrnehmungen Gottes im Alten Testament: Gesammelte Studien*, TB 70 (Munich: Kaiser,

the same time, it can be said that the end of the eighth and especially the seventh century BCE, which was simultaneously the time after the destruction of the northern kingdom of Israel (722 BCE) and the period of the reception of Neo-Assyrian imperial ideology along with traditions from the northern kingdom in Judah, should be accorded special importance as the initial phase of the formation of theology in the Hebrew Bible. This does not mean that one should not reckon with texts from before the destruction of the northern kingdom that contain implicit theological reflections—one might think of particular narrative or proverbial compositions. However, the experience of the catastrophe of 722 BCE signified a qualitative break. In any case, it is difficult to weigh the importance of the beginnings of theologically reflective texts after 722 BCE in comparison with the reflective efforts around the time of the loss of the First Temple from 587 BCE onward. For while the experience of the destruction of the Jerusalem Temple had the *de facto* effect of leading to a considerable intellectualization and spiritualization of the religion of ancient Judah, at the same time it was in no way—when viewed in isolation—predestined to trigger processes of theological reflection. One would rather have expected the opposite,[9] but the course of the development of theological history that came about in the wake of the demise of the northern kingdom brought about the result that Judah's catastrophe led not to the abandonment, but rather to the intensification of theological thought.[10]

YHWH AS THE ROYAL DEITY IN THE NORTH AS WELL AS THE SOUTH It is very important that Yhwh was revered as the royal deity in both the northern and the southern kingdoms.[11] While several traditions from the northern kingdom as well as the name Israel itself allow one to suspect that

1982), 304. While Steck speaks of the "streams of theological tradition," he does not explain what he means by "theological." If one takes one's cue from Odil H. Steck, "Deuterojesaja als theologischer Denker," in *Wahrnehmungen Gottes im Alten Testament*, TB 70 (Munich: Kaiser, 1982), 204–20, then Steck uses the term "theological" almost indiscriminately in the sense of "religious."

9. Cf., for example, the "Plague Prayers of Muršili II," trans. Gary Beckman (*COS* 1.60:156–60).

10. Jörg Jeremias, *Theologie des Alten Testaments*, GAT 6 (Göttingen: Vandenhoeck & Ruprecht, 2015), 191–281, grants this circumstance appropriate weight in its second main section (of three), which bears the title "Die großen Neuentwürfe" (The great redesigns). This section treats Deuteronomy, Jeremiah and Ezekiel, Exod 32–34, the Deuteronomistic theology, the Priestly document, and Deutero-Isaiah.

11. Cf. Matthias Köckert, "YHWH in the Northern and Southern Kingdom," 357–94.

the process of Yahwehization took place in stages, both the onomastics of northern Israel[12] and the Mesha Stela, which attests to Yhwh as the God of Israel in the ninth century BCE, show that by the time of the Omrides at the latest, Yhwh was the central deity in the north.

The political demise of the north in 722 BCE marks an event that brings with it, on the one hand, the termination of kingdom and royal deity. However, on the other hand, it takes place in a historical-political context that was previously unknown for this royal deity in its normal function for Judah. The ideal foundation for the development of Judaism arose in this dialectic between a non-national and a national conception of God.

EXPERIENCES OF CATASTROPHES AS THE DRIVING FORCES FOR THEOLOGICAL REFLECTION It is clear in any case that the experiences of catastrophe—the demise of the northern kingdom as well as that of the southern kingdom—turned out to be the elemental driving forces for the formation of theological reflection. Therefore, it does not miss the mark to connect the Bible and its theological points of view with the concept of "resilience."[13] Biblical literature arose through tradition-oriented innovation, and it also attempted to conceive of God in conjunction with history when the conventional ways of thinking could no longer be maintained. Only as a result of this could biblical literature become the "Bible"; its efforts at reflection transgressed its own guidelines, such that its reflective endeavors survived, while its guidelines did not.

1. The Israelization of Judah

Although the Hebrew Bible is strongly oriented toward Judah and Jerusalem (books like Chronicles remain almost completely silent about the northern kingdom, and the whole canonical section of the Ketuvim is totally oriented toward Judah), it should still be maintained from a historical perspective that the balance was quite different in the early and middle periods of the monarchal period, in the tenth to eighth centuries BCE. The

12. Cf. Jeffrey H. Tigay, *You Shall Have No Other Gods: Israelite Religion in the Light of Hebrew Inscriptions*, HSS 31 (Atlanta: Scholars Press, 1986).

13. Cf. David M. Carr, *Holy Resilience: The Bible's Traumatic Origins* (New Haven: Yale University Press, 2014). See also Ruth Poser, *Das Ezechielbuch als Trauma-Literatur*, VTSup 154 (Leiden: Brill, 2012).

northern kingdom of Israel was—primarily because of its strategically and economically favorable location—the more important, powerful, and advanced of the two states.[14] Judah rose to a position of leadership only after the demise of the northern kingdom in 722 BCE, when Jerusalem became the center of literary activity, which arguably took place primarily in the temple though also in the palace.

ISRAEL AND "ISRAEL" Now the events of 722 BCE marked not only a political, but also an eminent theological break. After the demise of the northern kingdom of "Israel," the traditional and prestigious name of Israel apparently passed to the southern kingdom. While one can discuss whether the inclusive use of the term Israel—including both northern and southern kingdoms—had earlier roots (perhaps an "all Israel" political ideology was present under Jeroboam II, for example), the decisive re-coining of the view appears first to have taken place after 722 BCE.

In the book of Isaiah this transformation can be clearly observed at certain points, for example in Isa 1:3–4: "Israel recognized nothing; undiscerning is my people." In this parallelism, Isaiah clearly includes Judah and Jerusalem ("my people"), whom the Jerusalemite Isaiah primarily addresses. The so-called Song of the Vineyard of Isa 5 presents the notion of the progressive overview of Israel and Judah in an argumentative progression. According to 5:3, the Song of the Vineyard is directed to the "residents of Jerusalem and the men from Judah," but the explanatory verse in 5:7 then records, "The vineyard of Yhwh Almighty is the house of Israel, and the men from Judah are his favorite plant." In other words, Israel and Judah are not understood as complementary entities; Judah is a part of Israel, which in Isa 5:7 includes Israel *and* Judah.

This identification of Judah with Israel is of fundamental theological importance in the prophetic tradition of the book of Isaiah with regard to the impending judgment. The book of Isaiah goes to great lengths to show that the judgment announced by Amos on "Israel" concerning the demise of the northern kingdom remains unfinished. Perhaps the most important theological declaration and justification for the "judgment theology" unity of Israel and Judah appears in the so-called chorus refrain in Isa 5:25–30 + 9:8–21; 10:1–4, which refers to the tradition of Amos, the prophet to the northern kingdom, and therefore reflects on the topic of judgment on

---

14. Cf. Israel Finkelstein, *The Forgotten Kingdom: The Archaeology and History of Northern Israel* (Atlanta: SBL Press, 2014).

Israel and its meaning for Judah. The refrain, "For all this, his wrath has not turned away, and his hand remains outstretched" (cf. 9:12, 17, 21; 10:4; cf. 5:25), emphasizes the continuation of divine judgment against Israel. Within the refrain poem, the pronouncement of Isa 9:8 is, to begin with, meaningful in light of the connections to Amos:

> The Lord has sent (שלח, *šlḥ*) a word against Jacob, and it has fallen (נפל, *npl*) on Israel, and the whole nation should understand: Ephraim and those living in Samaria. One spoke with arrogance and with a presumptuous heart: Brick walls have fallen, but we will build with ashlar stones; sycamore tree (beams) were cut down, but we will replace them with cedar (wood).

Isaiah 9:8 takes an explicit look back at a prophetic oracle that had already gone forth (cf. the past tense forms, שלח [*šlḥ*], "has sent"; נפל [*npl*], "has fallen") against Israel (that is, the northern kingdom, as the addressees "Ephraim," "Samaria," and also "House of Jacob" demonstrate).

The addressee of the northern kingdom allows for hardly any other consideration than the Amos tradition. The allusion to the earthquake motif in Isa 9:8, central to Amos, as well as the following context in 9:13 also point to Amos:

> But the people did not turn back to the one who struck them, and they did not seek Yhwh Almighty.

The fact that the people did not "turn back" (לא שב, *lʾ šb*) to God adopts the refrain from Amos 4:6-12. The statement that the God of Israel "struck" (נכה, *nkh*, hi.) cites Amos 4:9. And the accusation that Israel did not "seek" (דרש, *drš*) God alludes to Amos 5:4-6, where the "House of Israel" is urged to "seek" (דרש, *drš*) God. The sense of these references to Amos is obvious: the judgment pronounced by Isaiah against Judah is not a new process; it touches on God's wrath against Israel, and it is still directed against his people.

Israel and Judah are therefore viewed as a unity in terms of the theology of judgment, though the compositional history need not presuppose Judah's demise in any way. It is instead more plausible that the conviction of the Isaiah tradition does not see the judgment of "Israel" as finished with the fall of Samaria. Therefore, it should be dated prior to 587 BCE, for the texts of Isaiah emphasize the rejection of the prophetic message in their hearing (cf. Isa 6:9–10) like no other prophetic book. This would make the most sense in a historical situation where Israel has perished as a political entity, but Judah still exists. This example illustrates the eminent importance of the history of theology in the time between the demise of the northern kingdom and the southern kingdom as an epoch of fundamental theological reorientations. The catastrophe of Jerusalem in 587 BCE and the Babylonian exile do not turn out to be the first elementary driving forces for the theology of the Hebrew Bible. Instead, the events of 587 BCE could only be theologically digested in a manner that did not lead to the demise of Yhwh religion, because the formation of tradition in the preceding century had already set the course in a decisive manner.

2. The Theologization of the Ancestral Narratives

THE PROMISE THEOLOGY IN GEN 12–50 The span of text from Gen 12–50 (cf. above, §18) contains many of the best known narratives of the Bible, but it is also one of the sections of the Bible that has the longest literary growth. Some of the narratives likely had oral precursors that reach back even into pre-Israelite times, so the timespan of the literary history of Gen 12–50 probably stretches over numerous centuries, maybe from the ninth to the fourth centuries BCE. During the course of the literary compositional history of Gen 12–50, different theological outlooks overlay one another in the textual complex. The most prominent of them in terms of theology are the promise texts, which link the different individual episodes and narrative cycles in Gen 12–50 to one another. The recognition that these promise texts do not belong to the original material of the tradition has become established in Hebrew Bible studies since the 1970s. Their theological interpretations and redactional networks are instead due to previously independent narratives and narrative cycles.[15] The promise theme does, however, have at least one point of contact within the range

---

15. Cf. the foundational study of Rolf Rendtorff, *The Problem of the Process of Transmission in the Pentateuch,* trans. John J. Scullion, JSOTSup 89 (Sheffield: JSOT, 1990); trans. of *Das überlieferungsgeschichtliche Problem des Pentateuch,* BZAW 147 (Berlin: de Gruyter, 1977); Erhard Blum, *Die Komposition der Vätergeschichte,* WMANT 57 (Neukirchen-Vluyn: Neukirchener Verlag, 1984); Matthias Kockert, *Vätergott und Väterverheißungen: Eine Auseinandersetzung mit Albrecht Alt und seinen Erben,* FRLANT 142 (Göttingen: Vandenhoeck & Ruprecht, 1988).

of the preexisting tradition, which is in Gen 18. The narrative of the visit by the three men to Abraham contains—in form-critical terms the promise in a divine visit narrative should be viewed as an integral element: deities that come as guests always bring a gift—the promise of a son, who will be born to the host within a year.[16] The gift in the case of Gen 18 is the promise of a son. The possibility cannot be excluded that this element belongs to the oral prehistory of the narrative and had been part of the formative tradition of the Abraham narratives that accompanied the ancestral history for an extended period of time.

LINKING THE NARRATIVE CYCLES The promise theme then took on enormous importance through its use within the process of establishing a wide-reaching ancestral narrative. The promises in Gen 12:1–3 and 28:13–15 play an especially fundamental role. Although their exact historical location is debated, they most likely at least presuppose the demise of the northern kingdom in 722 BCE (perhaps also after that of the southern kingdom in 578 BCE).[17] They recognizably presuppose a global diaspora that is viewed positively, which differs from what is seen in, for example, the prophetic tradition (cf., e.g., Jer 24:8–10). Israel is scattered throughout the world in order that the other nations can acquire blessing through it (cf. below, §36).

It is evident that the literary process of the combination of the individual narrative cycles of the ancestral history into the overarching complex of Gen 12–50 is quite important for the investigation of theologizing processes in the traditions of the Hebrew Bible. The redactional connections are created through explicit "theological" texts—that is, through proclamations by God himself. Therefore, it is unquestionable that this combination is connected with the development of theological meaning. What does it consist of?

DIVINE SPEECHES First, the most striking moment in the design of these tests are the divine speeches. The preexisting individual traditions and narrative cycles foster an image of God's interaction with humans that offers a much more restrained presentation of the meeting. This is perhaps most readily recognizable in Gen 28:10–22. Whether one views Gen 28:13aα

---

16. The individual narrative is adjusted to the Abraham-Lot cycle by means of the insertion of Gen 18:10b–15, which identifies the promised son with Isaac.

17. Cf. Matthias Köckert, "Verheißung I. Altes Testament," *TRE* 34:697–704.

("and Yhwh stood above/by him") as part of Jacob's original dream in Bethel or not, it changes little with regard to the fact that the recognition of the numinous nature of the place did not appear to be linked to the content of a divine verbal revelation in the original narrative of Gen 28:11–12*, 16–19*, which Jacob's surprised and substantially open reaction shows. Only upon the redactional integration of this narrative (or rather the Jacob cycle) into the larger complex of the ancestral history is an explicit divine speech (28:13–15) first inserted into the text.

RATIONALIZATION AND UNIVERSALIZATION One can describe this theological interpretation as rationalization and as universalization. In the promise texts, God appears not as a diffuse numinous entity, but rather as the giver of a revelation with a distinct message. He can appear wherever necessary, whether that be in Mesopotamian Haran or in Israelite Bethel. He is not bound to a particular sanctuary or a particular ethnic group.

Remarkable in this is that God provides a personal introduction in Gen 28:13: אני יהוה (*'ny yhwh*), "I am Yhwh." The promises in Gen 12:1, 7; 13:14 are not aware of this element. The reader of Gen 12–50 knows from the beginning that the revelatory God is "Yhwh," but the actors only recognize it bit by bit (cf. Gen 15:7; 28:13).

In terms of tradition history, this divine conception is characterized as integrative monotheism. Even when the "god of the ancestors" hypothesis of Albrecht Alt must be determined to have succumbed to critique in the meantime, it remains recognized that pre- and alternative Yahwistic conceptions of God can be seen behind the traditional materials of the ancestral history, which were apparently integrated into the conception of the one "Yhwh" in the course of the tradition.

INFLUENCE OF PROPHECY It is quite probable that the structural markers of the redactional synthesis of the ancestral history by means of the divine speeches was influenced by the prophetic literature of the Hebrew Bible that was taking shape at the same time. Scholarship has traditionally paid little attention to this question because the promises to the ancestors were viewed as considerably earlier than the beginnings of written prophecy. However, with the upheavals in pentateuchal scholarship, this perspective should be examined. In accordance with the knowledge of the production of literature in ancient Israel, one should not expect that the relationships can be recognized in every case by means of clearly identifiable citations. Such links would instead have been imparted through processes of memorization.

PROPHETIC COLORATION OF THE TRADITION The promise texts of Genesis add "prophetic coloring" to the preexisting tradition. They place the reported events inside the horizon of God's broader, future plans, which are disclosed to the actors in the narrative, and which still remain unfulfilled for the audience. These texts thereby construe God as a single entity whose power cannot simply be read in linear fashion from or defined by the political, economic, and demographic realities of the present, but instead transcends them.

As a result, the group of texts of the promises in Genesis are not exactly the model example in light of the investigation of implicit theology in the Hebrew Bible because they present clearly redactional supplements in literary terms, and in this "supplementation" they reflect on preexisting tradition, which they synthesize and reorient.[18] This also changes the concrete conception of how God reveals himself to humans, whether he is bound to particular cult sites, and how one can come into contact with him. The earlier traditions more or less reckon with dream revelations (Gen 28:11–19) and the visit by angels (Gen 18:1–10), as well as the local anchoring of the deity (Gen 28:16–17). Through the promise texts, God becomes a mental, but also a rationally dependable entity. He can speak to humans wherever they are, and his proclamations have a binding character for the future.

3. The Traditions Surrounding Saul, David, and Solomon

In the books of Samuel and into Kings, the presentations of the royal rule of the first kings, Saul (1 Sam 8–31), David (1 Sam 16–1 Kgs 2), and Solomon (1 Kgs 1–11), take up considerable space. The historical estimations of these presentations are debated, but it is assumed that they concern neither contemporary narratives nor thoroughly postexilic polemics

18. An empirical example of how a promise is subsequently inserted into an existing text is found in the Qumran text 4Q158 (frags. 1–2, 7–10), which augments the biblical text of Gen 32:29 ("and he blessed him there") with a promise ("and he said to him: May Yh[wh] make you fruitful [and multi]ply you [. . .] knowledge and insight, and may he deliver you from all violence and [. . .] till this day and until the eternal generations [. . .] And he went further on his way after he blessed him there.").

against the monarchy. This monarchal tradition is important theologically in two regards. First, in comparison with ancient Near Eastern traditions, it should be maintained that the Hebrew Bible does not view the monarchy as a given fact of creation. On the contrary, Gen 1 transfers the "image of God"—traditionally the prerogative of the kings—to all humanity. Not the king, but rather the kingly person is a reality of creation. While this transfer of royal ideology to the *species* of humanity is not the accomplishment of the tradition found in the books of Samuel (but rather of Gen 1), it remains a theological achievement of the biblical narratives about Saul, David, and Solomon that the topic of the monarchy in all its complexity is not treated at the beginning of world history, but rather within the framework of its historical development. A second moment is related: the explicit ambivalence with which the monarch is presented and evaluated. It is located in the, on the one hand, redaction-historically complex and tiered text in 1 Sam 8–12, in the well-known pro (1 Sam 9:1–3, 15–10:7) and anti-monarchic statements (e.g., 1 Sam 8:6–22; 10:17–19). On the other hand, however, it is also implicit in the tradition when individuals such as Saul, David, and Solomon are depicted both with their significance and dignity, but also in their transgressions and limits (cf. above, §19).

AMBIVALENCE OF THE MONARCHY The monarchy was not glorified in Israel and Judah, but remembered with ambivalence. The theological context of the presentation of the establishment of the monarchy is, therefore, its competition with the reign of God (cf., e.g., Josh 24; 1 Sam 8:6–22; 10:17–19). In the Hebrew Bible there is a diametrically opposed theological tension constructed between two poles that actually belong together in religious-historical terms. Every earthly kingdom in the ancient Near East had its counterpart in the heavenly realm. The earlier literature of the Hebrew Bible still shares this view; later literature, apparently from the context of the post-monarchic time, formulated the maxim that the election of an earthly king implied the rejection of the divine king. The tradition does not resolve this contradiction. One can spot the attempt at a certain theological synthesis in the expectations for a monarch in the prophetic books (cf. below, §37) as well as the idealized presentation of David in the books of Chronicles, which shape the tradition of the monarchy in such a way that it does not compete with the reign of God.

§23 The Preservation of Jerusalem in 701 BCE

Erasmus Gaß, *Im Strudel der assyrischen Krise (2. Könige 18–19): Ein Beispiel biblischer Geschichtsdeutung*, Biblisch-theologische Studien 166 (Neukirchen-Vluyn: Neukirchener Verlag, 2016) ◆ Lester L. Grabbe, ed., *"Like a Bird in a Cage": The Invasion of Sennacherib in 701 BCE*, JSOTSup 363; European Seminar in Historical Methodology 4 (London: Continuum, 2003) ◆ Friedhelm Hartenstein, *Das Archiv des verborgenen Gottes: Studien zur Unheilsprophetie Jesajas und zur Zionstheologie der Psalmen in assyrischer Zeit*, Biblisch-theologische Studien 74 (Neukirchen-Vluyn: Neukirchener Verlag, 2011) ◆ Corinna Körting, *Zion in den Psalmen*, FAT 48 (Tübingen: Mohr Siebeck, 2006) ◆ Nazek Khalid Matty, *Sennacherib's Campaign against Judah and Jerusalem in 701 B.C.: A Historical Reconstruction*, BZAW 487 (Berlin: de Gruyter, 2016) ◆ Reinhard Müller, *Ausgebliebene Einsicht: Jesajas "Verstockungsauftrag" (Jes 6,9–11) und die judäische Politik am Ende des 8. Jahrhunderts*, Biblisch-theologische Studien 124 (Neukirchen-Vluyn: Neukirchener Verlag, 2012)

The experience of the catastrophe by the Assyrian destruction of the northern kingdom in 722 BCE was not the only important mark on the theological history left by the Assyrians. Also significant was the experience of the preservation of Jerusalem in the face of the Assyrian pressure applied in the siege of 701 BCE by Sennacherib. This event appears both in the annals of Sennacherib[19] and in the book of Kings (2 Kgs 18:13–16). The Assyrian Emperor Sennacherib carried out the decisive attack against Lachish in Judah's south. The importance of this event can be measured by the representations of the victory in the Nineveh palace reliefs of Sennacherib, which fill a monumental room of 18.9 m x 2.5 m. King Hezekiah seems only to have been able to raise the Assyrian blockade of Jerusalem through the payment of heavy tribute and the loss of the Shephelah, connected with the fall of Lachish. However, this does not hinder the Hebrew Bible from seeing a powerful act of deliverance by Yhwh in the withdrawal of the Assyrians in 701 BCE. This is most clear in the Isaiah tradition, which leaves out the verses corresponding to 2 Kgs 18:14–16 in its parallel to 2 Kgs 18:13–16, thereby concealing Hezekiah's payment of tribute.

THE ISAIAH NARRATIVES IN THE BOOK OF ISAIAH The preeminent importance of the preservation of Jerusalem in 701 BCE has condensed primarily

19. "Sennacherib's Siege of Jerusalem," trans. Mordechai Cogan (*COS* 2.119B:302–3).

within the overall composition of the book of Isaiah. The narratives in Isa 36–39 were apparently understood as the legitimation for the proclamations of salvation in Isa 40–66. Because God had earlier delivered Jerusalem in 701 BCE, the announcements of salvation in Isa 40–66 are justified and trustworthy (cf. above, §19).

Interestingly, the Isaiah tradition does not itself make this argument explicit. It is only recognizable for the audience of the book, not for the direct addressees of its texts. One can recognize from this insight that the location of the theology from the perspective of the Hebrew Bible resides primarily in the receiving subject rather than on the surface of the text.

1. The Psalms of Zion

In the wake of the experience of the deliverance of Jerusalem from the Assyrian blockade in 701 BCE, the theological statement of the safety of Zion as a result of Yhwh's presence received a strong boost. This theological position formed the traditional orthodoxy of monarchal period Jerusalem, the location of Yhwh's temple. The presence of the God of Judah in the temple guaranteed the prosperity of the land as well as its political security. The Zion psalms of Pss 46* and 48* in their original form likely belong to the Assyrian period. For one, the texts of Isaiah seem to presuppose their tradition and the text of Jeremiah even their literary form. Furthermore, their theological content concerning the impregnability of Zion—at least as a newly emerging theological statement—loses its plausibility after 578 BCE. Their literary shape likely digests the events of 701 BCE. The motif of the nations raging against Zion could have been influenced by the Assyrian practice of incorporating foreign soldiers into the Assyrian army.[20]

A THEOLOGY OF SECURITY AND STRENGTH The theology of the psalms of Zion praises God for his strength and relies on it completely (cf. below,

---

20. Cf. Friedhelm Hartenstein, "'Wehe, ein Tosen vieler Völker . . .' (Jesaja 17,12): Beobachtungen zur Entstehung der Zionstradition vor dem Hintergrund des judäisch-assyrischen Kulturkontakts," in *Das Archiv des verborgenen Gottes: Studien zur Unheilsprophetie Jesajas und zur Zionstheologie der Psalmen in assyrischer Zeit*, Biblisch-theologische Studien 74 (Neukirchen-Vluyn: Neukirchener Verlag, 2011), 129–74.

§32). It is evident that the experiences to the contrary, which took place in the destruction of Jerusalem in 587 BCE, must have been disastrous for this position. They did not, however, perish completely, instead finding a modified reception in the theocratic sketches of the postexilic period (cf. below, §26).

2. The Command to Provoke Hardening in the Book of Isaiah

While the experience of deliverance in 701 BCE left its imprint on the basic organization of the completed book of Isaiah, at the same time it posed a powerful theological challenge in its immediate historical context for the Isaiah tradition. If God preserved Jerusalem, what then does this mean for Isaiah's pronouncements of judgment?

ISAIAH AS ANTI-PROPHET This problem is probably deposited in the so-called command to provoke hardening in Isa 6:9–10 more than anywhere else. In the process of his divine commission, Isaiah is informed that his message will neither be heard nor understood. This text has often been treated and discussed. The position of the so-called retrojections hypothesis in its various forms generally points in the right direction: the command to provoke hardening is formulated *after the fact* and views Isaiah's message and its lack of effect as one. The failure of the prophecy of Isaiah likely hangs together with the nature of political experience after 701 BCE. The command to provoke hardening likely mirrors the situation at that time. The motif of the people not hearing and not understanding reacts historically to the preservation of Jerusalem in the wake of its encirclement by Sennacherib in 701 BCE, which *de facto* reduced Jerusalem to a city-state. This could not, however, stretch the interpretation, even if desired, to a *complete* judgment of Judah and Jerusalem. Accordingly, the Isaiah tradition was reckoned as prophecy reaching to the events of 597 BCE and 587 BCE, for they had not or at least had not yet reached their fulfillment. At least for certain circles, the prophecy of Isaiah and the contemporary experience of the time of Manasseh must have diverged drastically, for this constituted a time of relative economic, architectonic, and even cultural and literary blossoming for Judah under Assyrian hegemony. Only through its general verification in the year 587 BCE did the Isaiah tradition first gain authority that extended beyond its original supporters.

§24 The Reinterpretation of Assyrian Imperial Ideology

Angelika Berlejung, "The Assyrians in the West: Assyrianization, Colonialism, Indifference, or Development Policy?," in *Congress Volume Helsinki 2010*, ed. Martti Nissinen, VTSup 148 (Leiden: Brill, 2012), 21–60 ♦ Israel Finkelstein and Thomas Römer, "Comments on the Historical Background of the Abraham Narrative: Between 'Realia' and 'Exegetica,'" *HBAI* 3 (2014): 3–23 ♦ Matthias Köckert, "Die Geschichte der Abrahamüberlieferung," in *Congress Volume: Leiden, 2004,* ed. André Lemaire, VTSup 109 (Leiden: Brill, 2006), 103–28 ♦ Eckart Otto, *Das Deuteronomium: Politische Theologie und Rechtsreform in Juda und Assyrien*, BZAW 284 (Berlin: de Gruyter, 1999) ♦ Eckart Otto, "Die Geburt des Mose: Die Mose-Figur als Gegenentwurf zur neuassyrischen Königsideologie im 7. Jh. v. Chr.," in *Die Tora: Studien zum Pentateuch: Gesammelte Aufsätze,* BZABR 9 (Wiesbaden: Harrassowitz, 2009), 9–45 ♦ Eckart Otto, "Assyria and Judean Identity: Beyond the Religionsgeschichtliche Schule," in *Literature as Politics, Politics as Literature: Essays in Honor of Peter Machinist,* ed. David Vanderhooft and Abraham Winitzer (Winona Lake, IN: Eisenbrauns, 2013), 339–47 ♦ Eckart Otto and Erich Zenger, eds., *"Mein Sohn bist du" (Ps 2,7): Studien zu den Königspsalmen,* SBS 192 (Stuttgart: Katholisches Bibelwerk, 2002) ♦ Wolfgang Oswald, "Auszug aus der Vasallität: Die Exodus-Erzählung (Ex 1–14*) und das antike Völkerrecht," *TZ* 67 (2011): 263–88

1. Deuteronomy and Reinterpretation in the Covenant Code

DEUTERONOMY AS THE CORE OF THE CANON The drafting of Deuteronomy represents a qualitatively new step in the scope of the theological history of the Hebrew Bible. It bears, for the first time, marks of a normative writing. As such, it can be viewed as the "core" of the canon of the Hebrew Bible.[21] A clearly recognizable theologization accompanies its design as an authoritative writing, which it owes in terms of its formation history to the assimilation of ancient Near Eastern tradition. Deuteronomy as a whole is shaped in the style of a Neo-Assyrian vassal treaty. However, it demands unconditional loyalty not to the Assyrian emperor, but rather to Yhwh. Its programmatic text, the Shema in Deut 6:4 ("Hear, O Israel, Yhwh, your

---

21. Cf. Frank Crüsemann, "Das 'portative Vaterland': Struktur und Genese des alttestamentlichen Kanons," in *Kanon und Zensur*, ed. Aleida Assmann and Jan Assmann, Archäologie der literarischen Kommunikation 2 (Munich: Fink, 1987), 63–79.

God, is one Yhwh") even uses the political vocabulary of the metaphor of love ("you shall love Yhwh, your God") found in its *Vorlagen*.

Viewed in terms of its tradition history, one can speak of Deuteronomy as a subversive reception of Neo-Assyrian vassal treaty theology (cf. above, §18). Even its characteristic program of cult centralization has a parallel in the Neo-Assyria realm in the bond between the deity Assur and the capital city of Assur and could at least have been motivated by this reality.

DEPICTING GOD AS EMPEROR   In this analogy God appears as outdoing the Assyrian emperor, thereby taking on an imperial dimension. Therefore, even if Deuteronomy does not yet push through to the theoretical monotheism that denies the existence of other deities, the imperial imprint of its conception of God represents an important step in the development toward monotheism. Deuteronomy presents an intolerant monolatry that is not yet monotheism.

In Deuteronomy, God rises to the position of an absolute sovereign. While this does not constitute an absolute innovation when gauged against the traditional declarations on God's kingdom in Israel, God's power is conceived here in closer competition with and surpassing all earthly political powers—especially foreign powers.

LAW AS DIVINE LAW   The formulation of divine law constitutes the most critical result of this concept.[22] God as sovereign is simultaneously conceived as lawgiver, so the law obtains a divine quality.

This represents a novelty within the framework of ancient Near Eastern law. Ancient Near Eastern law was understood as fundamentally concordant with the cosmic principles of *kittu* and *mēšaru*, which characterize the overarching concept of order, but ancient Near Eastern law is royal law. Deuteronomy introduces into the ancient Near East the idea of a divine promulgation of law. While the current form of Deuteronomy is conceived as the speech of Moses, verses like Deut 6:17 and Deut 28:45 show that Deuteronomy likely was originally conceived as divine law.[23]

---

22. Cf. Konrad Schmid, "Divine Legislation in the Pentateuch in Its Late Judean and Neo-Babylonian Context," in *The Fall of Jerusalem and the Rise of the Torah*, ed. Peter Dubovský et al., FAT 107 (Tübingen: Mohr Siebeck, 2016), 129–53.

23. Cf. Norbert Lohfink, "Das Deuteronomium: Jahwegesetz oder Mosegesetz?," *TP* 65 (1990): 387–91.

In its current form, the so-called Covenant Code (Exod 20–23) also appears as divine promulgation of law. However, one can clearly recognize that this impression first arose in accordance with a theological framing of the literary core, which now binds the impersonally formulated legal stipulations in third person to God. One can surmise in this case that the fundamental perspective of Deuteronomy, that the law is divine, had a retroactive literary effect on the Covenant Code. This step in the Covenant Code was even more vital because large stretches of Deuteronomy arose as interpretation of the Covenant Code, reformulated in light of cult centralization.

THE EMPHASIS OF FAMILY LAW AND THE FORMATION OF AN ETHIC OF BROTHERLY SOLIDARITY As classical scholarship already perceived and more recently underscored, the legal stipulations of Deuteronomy have a northern background.[24] One can reckon that traditions from the northern kingdom had a part in the scripturalization of Deuteronomy in the time of Josiah. One consequence of setting this anchor in the tradition history under the influence of the destruction of the northern kingdom is the expansion of the stipulations on family law and the accentuation on the shared solidarity ethic within Israel. No other legal collection in the Torah contains a similar number of stipulations concerning family law comparable to Deuteronomy (cf. Deut 21:15–21; 22:13–29; 24:1–4; 25:5–10; compare the one individual stipulation in the Covenant Code in Exod 22:16–17) or places similar emphasis on the social cohesion of the people of God. The fall of Samaria in 722 BCE and the influx of inhabitants of the former northern kingdom to the southern kingdom required a new consciousness for shared brotherly cohesion, which Deuteronomy attempts to cultivate and support. The new formation of a theological "brother" terminology, for example, demonstrates this in especially clear fashion. It comprises the "Hebrews," as displayed in the example deposited in Deut 15:12: כי־ימכר לך אחיך העברי או העבריה (*ky ymkr lk 'ḥyk h'bry 'w h'bryh*), "When your brother, a Hebrew man or woman, sells themselves to you . . ."

---

24. Cf. Gary N. Knoppers, "The Northern Context of the Law-Code in Deuteronomy," *HBAI* 4 (2015): 162–83.

2. *The Exodus Tradition*

THE KINSHIP BETWEEN THE EXODUS TRADITION AND DEUTERONOMY The narrative of Israel's departure from Egypt originally represented an independent entity whose tradition history may have reached back into the second millennium BCE. From a literary perspective, it also was initially conceived and circulated on its own. Like Deuteronomy, the origins of the exodus narrative also likely came from the northern kingdom, as its emphasis in the prophets originating from the northern kingdom, Amos and Hosea, shows. On the contrary, the exodus tradition plays no role in the early texts of Isaiah, which originate from Jerusalem. Furthermore, the tradition in 1 Kgs 12:28 links the two royal sanctuaries of the northern kingdom, Bethel and Dan, with the exodus tradition (הנה אלהיך ישׂראל אשׁר העלוך מארץ מצרים, *hnh 'lhyk yśr'l 'šr h'lwk m'rṣ mṣrym* "Behold, here are your gods, Israel, who led you out of the land of Egypt").

Judged in terms of its theological makeup, the earliest tangible written version of this narrative probably belongs to the Assyrian period. It shares Deuteronomy's anti-Assyria perspective, now providing this ideology with a narrative rationale.

One can perhaps read this in the introduction and presentation of the Moses figure in the exodus narrative. As already described, the closest parallel to Exod 2 appears in the Legend of Sargon, related to the great usurper Sargon I (2350–2294 BCE), which was transmitted in the Neo-Assyrian period. The tradition-historical background of the Legend of Sargon clearly demonstrates the critical, anti-Assyrian orientation of the Moses-exodus narrative, whose bias bears similarities to that of Deuteronomy. The non-royal figure of Moses takes the place of the Assyrian emperor as the object of divine election to free Israel from imperial corvée (cf. above, §18).

GOD AS ISRAEL'S ONLY LORD This perspective concurrently displays the fundamental theological argument that traverses the exodus narrative: Israel is liberated from "service" (עבד, *'bd*; עבדה, *'bdh*) to the Egyptians for "service" (עבד, *'bd*; עבדה, *'bdh*) to God, that is to worship. Israel recognizes no unconditional political loyalties to earthly imperial powers; Israel is bound only to its God.

The hymnic conclusion of the first stage of the exodus narrative in Exod 15 should be set within the framework of the orientation to the service of God alone. The great Song of the Sea in Exod 15 is—viewed in terms of the direction of reading of the Hebrew Bible—the first psalm outside the Psalter. As such, Exod 15 can be comprehended as a literary measure outside the Psalms that paradigmatically connects the Psalms to Israel's first decisive experience of deliverance.

§25 The Destruction of Judah in 587 BCE

Rainer Albertz and Bob Becking, eds., *Yahwism after the Exile: Perspectives on Israelite Religion in the Persian Era*, Studies in Theology and Religion 5 (Assen: Van Gorcum, 2003) ♦ Marc Z. Brettler, "Judaism in the Hebrew Bible? The Transition from Ancient Israelite Religion to Judaism," *CBQ* 61 (1999): 429–47 ♦ Christian Frevel and Katharina Pyschny, "A 'Religious Revolution' in Yehûd? The Material Culture of the Persian Period as a Test Case: Introduction," in *A "Religious Revolution" in Yehûd? The Material Culture of the Persian Period as a Test Case*, ed. Christian Frevel and Izaak Cornelius, OBO 267 (Fribourg: Academic Press; Göttingen: Vandenhoeck & Ruprecht, 2014), 1–22 ♦ Alexandra Grund, *Die Entstehung des Sabbats: Seine Bedeutung für Israels Zeitkonzept und Erinnerungskultur*, FAT 75 (Tübingen: Mohr Siebeck, 2011) ♦ Klaus Grünwaldt, *Exil und Identität: Beschneidung, Passa und Sabbat in der Priesterschrift*, BBB 85 (Frankfurt am Main: Hain, 1992) ♦ Johannes Hahn, ed., *Zerstörungen des Jerusalemer Tempels: Geschehen—Wahrnehmung—Bewältigung*, WUNT 147 (Tübingen: Mohr Siebeck, 2002) ♦ Friedhelm Hartenstein, "Der Sabbat als Zeichen und heilige Zeit: Zur Theologie des Ruhetages im Alten Testament," *Jahrbuch für biblische Theologie* 18 (2003): 103–31 ♦ Christoph Levin, "Die Entstehung des Judentums als Gegenstand der alttestamentlichen Wissenschaft," in *Congress Volume Munich 2013*, ed. Christl M. Maier, VTSup 163 (Leiden: Brill, 2014), 1–17 ♦ Martin Leuenberger, *"Ich bin Jhwh und keiner sonst": Der exklusive Monotheismus des Kyros-Orakels Jes 45,1–7 in seinem religions- und theologiegeschichtlichen Kontext*, SBS 224 (Stuttgart: Katholisches Bibelwerk, 2010) ♦ Marko Marttila, *Collective Reinterpretation in the Psalms: A Study of the Redaction History of the Psalter*, FAT II/13 (Tübingen: Mohr Siebeck, 2006) ♦ Marko Marttila, "The Deuteronomistic Heritage in the Psalms," *JSOT* 37 (2012): 67–91 ♦ Karl-Friedrich Pohlmann, *Die Ferne Gottes: Studien zum Jeremiabuch: Beiträge zu den "Konfessionen" im Jeremiabuch und ein Versuch zur Frage nach den Anfängen der Jeremiatradition*, BZAW 179 (Berlin: de Gruyter, 1989) ♦ Thomas Römer, "Beschneidung in der Hebräischen Bibel und ihre literarische Begründung in Genesis 17," in *Dem Körper eingeschrieben: Verkörperung zwischen Leiberleben und kulturellem Sinn*, ed. Matthias Jung et al. (Wiesbaden: Springer, 2016), 227–40 ◆ Andreas Ruwe, "Beschneidung als interkultureller Brauch und Friedenszeichen Israels: Religionsgeschichtliche Überlegungen zu Genesis 17, Genesis 34, Exodus 4 und Josua 5," *TZ* (2008): 309–42 ◆ Theo Sundermeier, *Was ist Religion? Religionswissenschaft im theologischen Kontext*, TB 96 (Gütersloh: Kaiser, 1999) ◆ Felipe Blanco Wißmann, *"Er tat das Rechte . . .": Beurteilungskriterien und Deuteronomismus in 1Kön 12–2Kön 25*, ATANT 93 (Zurich: TVZ, 2008)

1. Transformation Instead of Disappearance

THE DESTRUCTION OF JERUSALEM AS A WATERSHED The Babylonian conquest and destruction of Judah and Jerusalem marks the central date of Israel's history—"Israel" here in an inclusive sense—in the first millennium BCE. It concerns the most dramatic historical experience of ancient Israel and found its way into its religion, theology and literature in diverse, but always prominent ways. Turning first to the narrative traditions of the Hebrew Bible in Genesis–2 Kings, it is striking that—concordant with the mythical structure of ancient historical thought—the history prior to the central events is apparently viewed as more important than the history afterward. The books of Genesis–2 Kings report on the history of the world and Israel from creation to the destruction of the Jerusalem temple.

The year 587 BCE is, therefore, a date of superlative importance and it brought pivotal changes with itself. It could easily have been the case, in fact expected, that Judah and its culture, religion, and literature would perish in the wake of this military operation. Similar examples appear in various ways for the likes of Ammon, Moab, and Edom, even if their deities did not simply vanish with the cessation of their states, which one can reconstruct from the inscriptional evidence.[25]

THE EMERGENCE OF JUDAISM However, the situation in Judah developed in a decidedly different manner. The events of 587 BCE initiated a

25. Hani Hayajneh et al., "Die Götter von Ammon, Moab und Edom in einer frühnordarabischen Inschrift aus Südost-Jordanien," in *Neue Beiträge zur Semitistik: Fünftes Treffen der Arbeitsgemeinschaft Semitistik in der Deutschen Morgenländischen Gesellschaft vom 15.–17. Februar 2012 an der Universität Basel*, ed. Viktor Golinets et al., AOAT 425 (Münster: Ugarit-Verlag, 2015), 79–106; Manfred Weippert, *Historisches Textbuch zum Alten Testament*, GAT 10 (Göttingen: Vandenhoeck & Ruprecht, 2010), 513 n. 335.

transformation that one can term the "emergence of Judaism," even if this process cannot be pinned to a particular date. One might also locate the beginning of Judaism in the Persian period, as often determined above all in the nineteenth century, generally with a pejorative slant ("from the exile there returned, not a nation, but a religious sect"),[26] but also in the twentieth century in a neutral or even with positive and legitimizing force. Occasionally the break is also seen in the time of Alexander. The problem with determining such epochs is that they are placed on the historical phenomena from outside and can be determined differently based on the chosen perspective. For those attempting to limit the concept of Judaism only to the Judaism of rabbinical influence after 70 CE, the decisive difference will be the loss of the cult of the Second Temple and the resulting impact of the complete transformation into a book religion.

This is necessarily linked to the reduction of the inner plurality of Judaism, which one might even see as the most profound break. In English-speaking scholarship, one has appropriated the term "Judaisms" for the period before 70 CE. In any case, significant continuity exists between the "Judaism" of the Second Temple and rabbinic "Judaism," namely its post-state existence as well as the basic theological positions concerning monotheism, covenant, and law. Therefore, the recognized terminology of "antique or classical Judaism" is meaningful and justified, if one sufficiently provides for internal differentiations.

PRIMARY AND SECONDARY RELIGION With the transformation of the religion of ancient Israel and Judah to "Judaism," a "secondary" religion emerges for the first time.[27] "Secondary religions" means those religions whose nature and history cannot be explained by means of a certain religious linearity; instead specific information—generally in the form of "revelation"—takes center stage. The juxtaposition between "primary" and "secondary" religions coincides largely with the traditional differentiation of "nature religions" and "revelatory religions," but it attempts to avoid their discriminatory overtones.

---

26. Julius Wellhausen, *Prolegomena to the History of Israel*, 28; *Prolegomena zur Geschichte Israels*, 6th ed. (Berlin: Reimer, 1927), 28: "aus dem Exil kehrte nicht die Nation zurück, sondern eine religiöse Sekte."

27. Cf. Theo Sundermeier, *Was ist Religion?*; Andreas Wagner, ed., *Primäre und sekundäre Religion als Kategorie der Religionsgeschichte des Alten Testaments*, BZAW 364 (Berlin: de Gruyter, 2006).

REASONS FOR THE SURVIVAL OF JUDAH'S RELIGION But why did Judah's religion survive the catastrophe of 587 BCE? Various factors played a role. Without desiring or being able to claim comprehensiveness, one can name the following: Especially important was the situation already set in motion to some degree by the experience of the loss of their own monarchy, state, and sanctuary in the demise of the northern kingdom about 150 years earlier. One can surmise that an imposing number of refugees came to Jerusalem after 722 BCE and are responsible for the substantial expansion of the settlement area.[28] These refugees brought not only their possessions with them, but also their literature. The Israelization of Judahite tradition was likely accelerated by contact with this segment of the population, bringing about a theological "buffering" of the tradition in light of such central experiences of loss. This likely connects, second, to the development of the theological position of Deuteronomy, which should be dated to the late Assyrian—so still preexilic—period, which is important. The theological notion that Israel's relationship with God can be conceived in directly political terms—God (and not an earthly imperial power) is Israel's sovereign—would have immunized the religion of ancient Israel against political turmoil. Its existence does not depend on the survival of the monarchy and nation, but on God's will. Third and finally, one should mention the prophetic tradition, which in turn pays considerable attention to the notion of the extension of the judgment on Israel to judgment on Judah, which appears multiple times in the written prophetic tradition of the eighth century BCE. Of special importance is the Isaiah tradition. If it is correct that the command to provoke hardening formulates a literary reaction to the delay of arrival of judgment on Judah in the seventh century BCE, then the events of 597 and 587 BCE must have counted as the general historical verification of Isaiah's prophecy, whose views of judgment against Judah were now finally fulfilled. The tradition of Jeremiah also contributed in noteworthy fashion to the theological digestion of the catastrophe. In the destruction of Jerusalem and its temple in 587 BCE, something took place that, according to the traditional orthodoxy of the First Jerusalem Temple

28. Cf. the discussion between Nadav Na'aman, "Dismissing the Myth of a Flood of Israelite Refugees in the Late Eighth Century BCE," *ZAW* 126 (2014): 1–14; and Israel Finkelstein, "Migration of Israelites into Judah after 720 BCE: An Answer and an Update," *ZAW* 127 (2015): 188–206; and again Ernst Axel Knauf, "Was There a Refugee Crisis in the 8th/7th Centuries BCE?," in *Rethinking Israel: Studies in the History and Archaeology of Ancient Israel in Honor of Israel Finkelstein*, ed. Yuval Gadot et al. (Winona Lake, IN: Eisenbrauns, 2017), 159–72.

expressed in Ps 48, not only could not happen, but—even stronger—was totally unimaginable: Yhwh is the God imagined to be enthroned on Zion, whose divine presence there guarantees Jerusalem and Judah's protection and safety. The cultic recitation of the Psalms served as the ritual reassurance and safeguard of this conception. In the reality that it was confessed in the cult, it was implemented and held to be valid. The cultic tradition of Jerusalem was, to a certain degree, falsified as a conception by the historical experience of 587 BCE. However, certain passages in the book of Jeremiah link directly to this cultic tradition and transform it significantly. An especially clear example appears in Jer 6:22–26.

Ps 48:3–15*:

His holy mountain, towering beautifully, is the joy of the earth, Mount Zion high in the north is the city of a great king. God is in its palaces, as a fortress he has made himself known. For behold, kings assembled, they came near together. They looked and were astounded, fleeing away in panic.
Trembling took hold of them there, pangs like one in labor. . . . As we had heard, now we have seen in the city of the Almighty,
In the city of our God: God establishes it forever. . . . Walk around Zion, go around it, count its towers; marvel at its ramparts, go through its palaces, to tell it to a future generation. This is God, our God forever and ever; he will guide us.

Jer 6:22–26:

Thus says Yhwh: "Behold, a people coming from the land of the north, and a great nation will be awoken from the ends of the earth. Bow and javelin they take; it is hard and merciless. They sound like the sea when it roars, and ride on horses like a warrior armed against you, daughter Zion. We have heard the news—our hands fall slack; fear has gripped us, pangs like one in labor. Do not go out into the field and do not walk on the road! For the sword of the enemy is there—terror all around! Clothe yourself in sackcloth, daughter of my people, roll in the dust! Mourn as if for an only son, the bitterest mourning. For suddenly the destroyer will come upon us."

A range of motifs from Ps 48 reappear in Jer 6:22–26 but in succinct reversal. The kings attacking Zion are no longer stunned with fear and trembling. Instead the Jerusalemites themselves experience what was envisaged for the enemies. Furthermore, Jerusalem is no longer depicted as the unassailable cosmic mountain, but rather as a vulnerable, violated woman. The depiction of Jerusalem as a woman—likely as a reaction to Jerusalem's destruction—appears for the first time in the Hebrew Bible in Jeremiah and Lamentations.

That the approach of the Babylonians could be traced back to the action of God himself is a thought that only became possible over time. The earliest texts in the book of Jeremiah lament the onset of calamity, yet they do not interpret it as divine judgment (Jer 6:1). The tradition only takes a further step toward the recognition that the calamity brought upon Judah is from God himself (Jer 4:6–7) and was planned as such (Jer 1:13–14).

SABBATH AND CIRCUMCISION The loss of Judah's political continuity and the cult centered around the Jerusalem Temple brought about the need to develop new forms of religious belonging. During the period of the Babylonian exile, first and foremost the Sabbath and also circumcision gained importance in this regard. While the Sabbath is attested in the preexilic period (cf. Am 8:4–5; Hos 2:11; Isa 1:13; 2 Kgs 4:23), it always appears in these texts in parallel to "new moon." In combination with the observation that the related Akkadian term *šapattu* designates the full moon, one can assume that the "Sabbath" in Israel as well was not originally related to a work-free seventh day of the week, but instead meant the full moon feast, on which there were also certain restrictions, especially of an economic nature. The provision in Exod 23:12 that no work should be done on the seventh day does not require "Sabbath" terminology. From this one can conclude that there could have been rest from work on the seventh day in Israel already in the monarchic period, in the sense of a socially transformative analogy to the fallow land (there are no reports of actual observance of Exod 23:12), but one did not yet call this day "Sabbath." The Sabbath first developed into a foundational regulation in the Babylonian exile. The Decalogue of Deuteronomy in particular shows the fundamental importance of Sabbath. Its peculiar structure, which should instead probably be termed a "Pentalogue," given its five-parts (5:6–10; 5:11; 5:12–15; 5:16; 5:17–21), highlights the Sabbath command by means of its middle placement.[29] For the Decalogue, which first emerged in the exilic period at the earliest, cult centralization (cf. Deut 12) is no longer the chief commandment, but rather observation of the Sabbath, which self-evidently was also possible in the diaspora. In the Persian-period Holiness Code, the Sabbath appears in Lev 23:2–3, within the festival calendar, as the

---

29. Cf. Matthias Köckert, *Die Zehn Gebote* (Munich: Beck, 2007).

most important celebration before the Passover, the Feast of Unleavened Bread, and other feasts.

Circumcision was a common practice in the Levant and also in Egypt (cf., e.g., Jer 9:24–25); only the Philistines did not practice it. It could first function historically as a mark of differentiation for Israel in the context of the Babylonian exile because the Babylonians did not practice circumcision. In Gen 17, a Priestly text, circumcision is commanded for all male descendants. It is the sign of God's covenant with Abraham and his progeny; whoever does not practice it will be excluded from this covenant.[30]

JUDAISM AS A PRODUCT OF PERSIAN IMPERIAL POLITICS In addition to all the indigenous and especially religious factors that led to the formation of Judaism, it should also be underlined that Judaism as a semi-autonomous ethnicity in the province of Yehud can also be understood as a result of Persian imperial politics. This policy allowed the peoples united in the Persian Empire to identify themselves primarily in terms of their cultural and religious characteristics.[31]

2. Developments in Deuteronomism

THE GUILT OF THE KINGS Deuteronomy, with its primary demands for cultic unity and cultic purity, is quickly called on as the theological benchmark for the portrayal in the books of Kings. The evaluations of the kings evaluate every king of the northern kingdom negatively without exception because they did not refrain from the חטאת ירבעם (*ḥṭ't yrbʿm*), "sins of Jeroboam" (the exact formulation varies; 2 Kgs 17:22 states "sins" in the plural). The "sins of Jeroboam" refer to the establishment of two royal sanctuaries in Bethel and in Dan, which more likely go back to Jeroboam II than Jeroboam I.[32] However, several of the kings of the southern kingdom, Asa, Hezekiah, Josiah, and naturally David as well, are viewed entirely

30. Cf. Hermann-Josef Stipp, "'Meinen Bund hat er gebrochen' (Gen 17,14): Die Individualisierung des Bundesbruchs in der Priesterschrift," in *Alttestamentliche Studien: Arbeiten zu Priesterschrift, Deuteronomistischem Geschichtswerk und Prophetie*, BZAW 442 (Berlin: de Gruyter, 2013), 117–36.

31. Cf. Konrad Schmid, "Persische Reichsautorisation und Tora," *TRu* 71 (2006): 494–506.

32. Cf. Angelika Berlejung, "Twisting Traditions: Programmatic Absence-Theology for the Northern Kingdom in 1 Kgs 12:26–33* (the 'Sin of Jeroboam')," *JNSL* 35 (2009): 1–42, esp. 24; Juha Pakkala, "Jeroboam without Bulls," *ZAW* 120 (2008): 501–25.

positively. These judgments probably go back to Josiah and are pointed toward the depiction of his reform in 2 Kgs 22–23. The evaluation of the final four kings of Judah after Josiah—Jehoash, Jehoiakim, Jehoiachin, and Zedekiah—are thoroughly negative (כבל אשר־עשׂו אבתיו [*kkl 'šr 'św 'btyw*], "completely as his fathers had done" [23:32, 37]; cf. 24:9, 19:כבל אשר־עשׂה אביו [*kkl 'šr 'śh 'byw*], "completely as his father had done," or 24:19: כבל אשר־עשׂה יהויקים [*kkl 'šr 'śh yhwyqym*], "completely as Jehoiakim had done") and appear even to imply a collective judgment on all previous kings.[33] In these statements the books of Kings react to the destruction of the southern kingdom, which—in accord with ancient Near Eastern conceptions of order—are linked with the responsibility of the king. The king is considered the central figure of public life and was responsible for guaranteeing the prosperity of his land. The lack of prosperity allowed for the conclusion that he had failed.

THE GUILT OF THE PEOPLE However, the Deuteronomistic tradition did not stop with this consideration. After the loss of the monarchy, the conviction seemed to have emerged that the people too bore responsibility. This can be most easily recognized in the narrative of the golden calf in Exod 32, which apparently serves to anchor the "sin of Jeroboam," which was blamed on the kings of the northern kingdom in the books of Kings, in the foundational history and extend responsibility to the people as a whole. It was not Jeroboam—biblically speaking Jeroboam I, historically Jeroboam II—who made the golden calves; the original sin already took place in the departure from Egypt by the people themselves. The fact that Exod 32 is formed on the basis of 1 Kgs 12 can be read without difficulty from the adaptation of 1 Kgs 12:28b in Exod 32:4b. The choice of the plural formulation in Exod 32 ("Behold, these are your gods, Israel, who brought you up out of the land of Egypt") only makes sense in light of 1 Kgs 12, where, in contrast to Exod 32, the narrative actually concerns the fabrication of two calves.

33. However, it is debated whether 2 Kgs 23:32, 37 should be understood as collective judgment. Yet the only parallel formulation found to the expression in 2 Kgs 23:23, 37 of "completely as his fathers had done" in 2 Kgs 15:9 confirms the overarching horizon of 2 Kgs 23:32, 37, for Zechariah is viewed as the final representative of the Jehu dynasty in 2 Kgs 15:9. Likewise, 2 Kgs 23:32, 37 consider the Davidic dynasty as a whole. This also explains the divergent formula of the last two kings, Jehoiachin ("his father," 24:9) and Zedekiah ("Jehoiakim," 24:19), who are no longer reckoned as fully valid representatives of the Davidic dynasty after the accession of Nebuchadnezzar to world dominion.

EXOD 32:4:	1 KGS 12:28:
And [Aaron] took [the gold] from their hand, poured it into a clay form, and made from it a cast calf. Then they said: *"These are your gods, Israel, who brought you up out of the land of Egypt."*	The king took counsel and let two golden calves be made and said to the people: "You have gone on pilgrimage to Jerusalem long enough! *Behold, these are your gods, Israel, who brought you up out of the land of Egypt."*

The perspective of the guilt of the entire people, while already anchored in the book of Exodus, is also recorded in the books of Kings themselves, in 2 Kgs 17, the chapter offering a broad theological reflection on the destruction of the northern kingdom. The earlier statements in 2 Kgs 17:21–23 declare that Israel's guilt is rooted in the sin of Jeroboam, while the long, apparently secondary prelude in vv. 7–20 instead brings in the perspective that the people themselves are guilty. The reflections of the Hebrew Bible on the responsibility for the catastrophe of 587 BCE progress from royal to national responsibility.

THE TURN TO SALVATION Remarkably, the formation of the tradition also pushes forward to perspectives of overcoming the paradigm of guilt and punishment. The natural literary placement of such perspectives appears in the prophetic books appended to the historical books, but the books of Kings also offer an analogous outlook toward the future, appearing in the final (compositionally latest) verses of Solomon's so-called temple dedication prayer in 1 Kgs 8:46–53. In keeping with the literary fiction that these words belong to King Solomon, speaking in his time, the outlook on divine mercy and forgiveness for his people who will one day go into captivity is couched in the form of a supplication. Obviously, however, 1 Kgs 8:46–53 presuppose the Babylonian exile, and the expectations of the exiles are behind Solomon's words to benefit from what Solomon had prayed for them centuries before. However, 1 Kgs 8 formulates the condition as turning back to God: only then will God hear the supplication of his people.[34]

A similar conception appears in the latest chapter of Deuteronomy. Deuteronomy 4 contains a prophecy by Moses that looks ahead as far as

---

34. On 1 Kgs 8, cf. Michael Rohde, "Wo wohnt Gott? Alttestamentliche Konzeptionen der Gegenwart Jahwes am Beispiel des Tempelweihgebets 1 Könige 8," *BTZ* 26 (2009): 165–83.

the exile and the dispersion of Israel in the diaspora. Here, too, turning back to Yhwh is the precondition of future salvation, though this return is viewed as a future fact, just as is God's renewed attention (Deut 4:27–31).

3. Universalization and Individualization

The loss of temple, monarchy, and state brought on a series of innovations in terms of intellectual history. The most important include the universalization of the concept of God and, on the flip side, the individualization of anthropology.

THE EXPANSION OF THE CONCEPT OF GOD The universalization of the concept of God is primarily recognizable in the rise of monotheism, which appears in its clearest manifestations in the tradition of Deutero-Isaiah (Isa 40–55). Its starting point is that Israel will never again have kings of its own; instead the integration into the Persian Empire will be accepted as God's salvific will.

The proclamation of the Persian King Cyrus as "Yhwh's anointed" (45:1) is a novelty within ancient Near Eastern and also within ancient Israelite religious history. Ancient Near Eastern religions traditionally move within the framework of national religious conceptions, which deem everything foreign as belonging to the realm of chaos. When the Deutero-Isaiah tradition now views Cyrus as a legitimate ruler with God's favor, then a qualitatively new step is carried out. Yhwh, the God of Israel, is advanced as the sole ruler of the world, the one who appoints the Persian Emperor and who also deposes him if necessary.

THE THEOLOGY OF THE CYRUS CYLINDER Scholars have often pointed to the Cyrus Cylinder, a Persian document from the time of the fall of Babylon in 539 BCE, in relation to the Cyrus proclamations in Isa 40–48:

> Marduk . . . ordered him to march to his city Babylon. He set him on the road to Babylon and like a companion and friend, he went at his side. His vast army, whose number, like the water of the river, cannot be known, marched at his side fully armed. He made him enter his city Babylon without fighting or battle; he saved Babylon from hardship. He delivered Nabonidus, the king who did not revere him, into his hands . . . As for the citizens of Babylon . . . I [Cyrus] relieved their

weariness and freed them from their service (?). Marduk, the great lord, rejoiced over my [good] deeds.[35]

There is a structural similarity between the Deutero-Isaiah tradition and the Cyrus Cylinder in the choice of the Persian Cyrus by a foreign deity, here the Babylonian chief god Marduk.[36] Unlike Isa 40–48, the Cyrus Cylinder concerns a proclamation by Cyrus himself, who portrays himself as the legitimate ruler in Babylon in the view of the city's gods. In contrast, Isa 40–48 goes a step further. The designation of Cyrus as Yhwh's "anointed" is a third-person statement that sets the Persian Cyrus in the place of the dismantled Davidic dynasty. Analogously, it is probably first with Persian period declarations in the book of Jeremiah like Jer 25:9; 27:6; 43:10 that Nebuchadnezzar is designated God's "servant," which otherwise in the Hebrew Bible serves primarily as a title for David. Also comparable are the professions by foreign rulers of the God of Israel in Dan 1–6, which also bear similarities to this conception.

EXCLUSIVE AND INCLUSIVE MONOTHEISM The Deutero-Isaiah tradition advocates a strict monotheism that recognizes Yhwh alone as God, while all other deities worshiped by the nations are nothing: "I am Yhwh and there is no other" (Isa 45:6). One can describe this monotheism as exclusive—the class of deities is reduced to the single element of Yhwh. This contrasts with the inclusive monotheistic conceptions such as that of the Priestly document, which also reckons with only one God, but according to which this God could also be called upon and worshiped in different forms. The class of divinity in this case coincides with its only element, which can be named Yhwh, Ahuramazda, Zeus, etc.

The monotheism of Deutero-Isaiah marks an elementary upheaval in the history of Israelite religion. The exclusive faith in a single deity first appears here as an explicit configuration. It is an intensification of the formulation of the first commandment of the Decalogue, which forbids the worship of other deities, but still assumes their existence.

35. "Cyrus Cylinder," trans. Mordechai Cogan (*COS* 2.124:315).
36. Cf. Matthias Albani, "Religiöse Kommunikation zwischen Israel und Mesopotamien im 6. Jh. v. Chr. und der biblische Monotheismus: Abgrenzung und Entgrenzung der israelitischen Gottesvorstellung bei Deuterojesaja," in *Kommunikation über Grenzen: Kongressband des XIII. Europäischen Kongresses für Theologie. 21.–25. September 2008 in Wien*, ed. Friedrich Schweitzer, Veröffentlichungen der Wissenschaftlichen Gesellschaft für Theologie 33 (Gütersloh: Gütersloher Verlagshaus, 2009), 213–32.

Isa 45:6–7:	Deut 5:6–7:
I am Yhwh	*I am Yhwh,*
and there is no other,	your God, who brought you out of
who forms the light and creates the	the land of Egypt, out of the house of
darkness, who works salvation and	slavery; you shall have no other gods
creates calamity.	besides me.

Both texts begin with the self-presentation formulation at home in the ancient Near Eastern polytheism, אני יהוה (*'ny yhwh*), "I am Yhwh," by which a revelatory deity traditionally identifies himself. The first commandment then elaborates with "your God," that is Israel's God, "who brought you out of the land of Egypt, out of the house of slavery," which the universalizing conception in Deutero-Isaiah foregoes and moves immediately to the complementary negative proclamation, "and there is no other." This statement on the one hand strongly intensifies the Decalogue's stipulation, "you shall have no other gods besides me," while on the other hand it renders the self-presentation formula logically superfluous.

SALVATION AND CALAMITY With the declaration "who forms the light and who creates the darkness, who works (יצר, *yṣr*) salvation and creates (ברא, *br'*) calamity," Isa 45:6–7 then offers an analogue to the exodus statement of the first commandment. However, Isa 45:6–7 does not formulate a statement purely focused on salvation; it explicitly traces both salvation *and* calamity alike—a monotheistic logic—back to divine action. The monotheistic option in Deutero-Isaiah appears in direct connection to its conception of a sovereign. If the world ruler Cyrus should rule as the divinely legitimized king over Israel, then the reverse is clear, namely that God himself, of whom Cyrus is the earthly representative, rules the entire world. So one can maintain that the rise of monotheism rests on political foundations.

INDIVIDUALIZATION It need not be surprising that the loss of the state in 587 BCE led to an individualized anthropology. The opening chapter of the Priestly document (Gen 1) democratizes the royal ideology and applies it to every exemplar of the class homo sapiens (cf. in detail §39). Within the scope of the Psalter, every individual can locate themselves in the pious individual of the lament and thanksgiving songs (cf. below, §35).

238

JOB The biblical book of Job (cf. above, §20) presents an exceptional reflection on the catastrophe of 587 BCE. It was probably composed from a considerable historical distance of one or two hundred years from the events,[37] yet it allows the catastrophes encountered by the protagonist, Job, to point transparently to the events of 587 BCE. Among the hoards that steal his property and kill his servants are the "Chaldeans" (Job 1:17), that is the Neo-Babylonians. Although the scenery of the book of Job basically points to the time of the patriarchs and its location is outside the land of Judah in the land of Uz (Job 1:1), Job 1:17 superimposes this setting with the historical situation of Jerusalem in 587 BCE, allowing Job as an individual to experience what Judah as a whole encountered.

"EARLIER" AND "LATER" WISDOM One can take the book of Job as an example for what scholarship has characterized as the development of "later" wisdom. It documents the collapse of time-honored conceptions of order, from which the "earlier" wisdom, such as that observed in Prov 10–22, took its orientation and from which it presumed that a specific action would result in a corresponding result (cf. above, §20). This notion of order is no longer recognized by the book of Job, Qoheleth, or Prov 1–9. On the contrary, direction for life must function intellectually within a framework for which such concepts of order are concealed.

§26 The Theological Reception of Persian Imperial Ideology

Marc Z. Brettler, "Judaism in the Hebrew Bible? The Transition from Ancient Israelite Religion to Judaism," *CBQ* 61 (1999): 429–47 ♦ Friedhelm Hartenstein and Konrad Schmid, eds., *Abschied von der Priesterschrift? Zum Stand der Pentateuchdebatte*, Veröffentlichungen der Wissenschaftlichen Gesellschaft für Theologie 40 (Leipzig: Evangelische Verlagsanstalt, 2015) ♦ Gary N. Knoppers and Bernard M. Levinson, eds., *The Pentateuch as Torah: New Models for Understanding Its Promulgation and Acceptance* (Winona Lake, IN: Eisenbrauns, 2007) ♦ Reinhard G. Kratz, "Die Entstehung des Judentums," *ZTK*

---

37. Cf. the discussion in Jürgen van Oorschot, "Die Entstehung des Hiobbuches," in *Das Buch Hiob und seine Interpretationen: Beiträge zum Hiob-Symposiums auf dem Monte Verità vom 14.–19. August 2005*, ed. Thomas Krüger et al., ATANT 88 (Zurich: TVZ, 2007), 165–84; Konrad Schmid, "The Authors of the Book of Job and the Problem of Their Historical and Social Settings," in *Scribes, Sages and Seers: The Sage in the Mediterranean World*, ed. Leo Perdue, FRLANT 219 (Göttingen: Vandenhoeck & Ruprecht, 2008), 145–53.

95 (1998): 167–84 ♦ Christophe Nihan, *From Priestly Torah to Pentateuch: A Study in the Composition of the Book of Leviticus*, FAT II/25 (Tübingen: Mohr Siebeck, 2006) ♦ Otto Plöger, *Theokratie und Eschatologie*, 2nd ed., WMANT 2 (Neukirchen-Vluyn: Neukirchener Verlag, 1962) ♦ Albert de Pury, "P^g as the Absolute Beginning," in *Les dernières rédactions du Pentateuque, de l'Hexateuque et de l'Ennéateuque,* ed. Thomas Römer and Konrad Schmid, BETL 203 (Leuven: Peeters, 2007), 99–128 ♦ Peter Weimar, "Sinai und Schöpfung: Komposition und Theologie der Priesterschriftlichen Sinaigeschichte," in *Studien zur Priesterschrift*, FAT 56 (Tübingen: Mohr Siebeck, 2008), 269–317 ♦ Jakob Wöhrle, *Fremdlinge im eigenen Land: Zur Entstehung und Intention der priesterlichen Passagen der Vätergeschichte,* FRLANT 246 (Göttingen: Vandenhoeck & Ruprecht, 2012)

1. Theocracy and Eschatology

OTTO PLÖGER'S DUAL INTERPRETATION OF THE POSTEXILIC HISTORY OF THEOLOGY The theological history of the Persian period is imprinted by the antagonism that Plöger pithily characterized as the conflicts between "theocracy and eschatology." The blanket juxtaposition of "theocracy and eschatology" has often been criticized, but one should not misunderstand these concepts as complementary categories into which the literature of the Persian period should be distributed without remainder. It instead concerns two basic options to which individual texts or writings may draw closer or remain at varying distances.[38]

In the sense of the heuristic characterization of positions that certainly must be nuanced, the distinction between theocratic and eschatological positions without dichotomist points of view is still applicable. If the most important mode of reception of the traditions of the Assyrian and Babylonian Empires in ancient Israel was marked by rejection and subversion, the opposite can be observed with regard to the view of the Persian Empire and its dominion in the theocratic stream of postexilic literature. This circumstance is based on the fact that the Persians—unlike the previous empires—fostered a comparatively tolerant political approach to the peoples they subjugated, and they conceded considerable linguistic, cultic, legal, and cultural autonomy to them—more likely out

---

38. Cf. the discussion in Ernst Michael Dörrfuß, *Mose in den Chronikbüchern: Garant theokratischer Zukunftserwartung,* BZAW 219 (Berlin: de Gruyter, 1994), 92–115.

of sheer necessity, given the extent of its empire rather than out of (pre-) humanitarian convictions.

This Persian imperial ideology of a peaceful state made up of many nations maintaining the protection of the cultural and religious integrity of each, manifested in, for example, the Bisitun Inscription of Darius I,[39] which—as the discovery of its Aramaic version in Elephantine attests—also circulated as a school text, has primarily been adopted and appropriated in a positive manner by the priestly and cultically influenced conceptions of Persian period literature of the Hebrew Bible, such as the Priestly document and Chronicles.

THE EPOCH OF THE PERSIANS AS THE "END OF HISTORY" These writings presume that the salvific goal of Yhwh's history with Israel and the world has virtually been accomplished with Persian hegemony—stated pointedly, in the sense of a "realized eschatology."[40] This goal must be brought to completion in various places, but the turn to salvation had fundamentally taken place. This position is basically nothing more than the Jewish reception of the official Persian imperial ideology. In Chronicles one can read David and Solomon in their capacity as initiator and builder of the temple as the "primordial" models for Cyrus and Darius: one made the construction of the temple possible (Cyrus through his edict) and the other allowed it to be carried out (Darius).

Within the contemporary Priestly literature,[41] this Persian-period inspired image of an ordered world appears in the so-called Table of Nations in Gen 10, which describes the re-population of the world after the flood (Gen 6–9). It employs a refrain that describes the linguistic and culturally diverse order of the world according to languages, tribes, and peoples (Gen

39. Cf. Rüdiger Schmitt, "The Bisitun Inscriptions of Darius the Great," in *Corpus inscriptionum Iranicarum: Part I, Inscriptions of Ancient Iran*, vol. 1: *The Old Persian Inscriptions, Texts I* (London: Corpus Inscriptionum Iranicarum, 1991); and cf. Klaus Koch, "Weltordnung und Reichsidee im alten Iran," in *Reichsidee und Reichsorganisation im Perserreich*, ed. Peter Frei and Klaus Koch, OBO 55 (Freiburg: Universitätsverlag; Göttingen: Vandenhoeck & Ruprecht, 1984), 45–119.

40. To use the well-known terminology from Charles H. Dodd, *The Parables of the Kingdom* (London: Nisbet, 1936), 51, which he, however, applies to the proclamation of Jesus.

41. Cf. Konrad Schmid, "Distinguishing the World of the Exodus Narrative from the World of Its Narrators: The Question of the Priestly Exodus Account in Its Historical Setting," in *Israel's Exodus in Transdisciplinary Perspective: Text, Archaeology, Culture, and Geoscience*, ed. Thomas E. Levy et al. (Heidelberg: Springer, 2015), 331–46.

10:5, 20, 31, cf. below, §33). Within the framework of its Persian-period formation, the Priestly document is especially important for its contemporary history of theology.

UNIVERSALIZATION It initially appears that the Priestly document—at least in essential parts—is responsible for the Primeval History as the introduction of the Pentateuch. This is relevant for its theological imprint from two perspectives. First, the national religious traditions of Israel and Judah become contextualized as universal, and this takes place both in temporal as well as in spatial respects. This expansion logically connects to the attempt to set one's own particular tradition in relation to overarching perspectives, which is essentially a process driven by intellectual imperatives. In historical terms, however, it is understandable in light of the probable setting of its formation in the early Persian period. The universal contextualization of a particular tradition is still reasonable within the framework of an exilic location.

THE RECEPTION OF BABYLONIAN SCHOLARSHIP On the other hand, the presentation of the Primeval History within the Priestly document, and therefore in direct connection to it, is strongly marked by Babylonian scholarship.[42] The Priestly document quite obviously attempts to engage and interact with the level of knowledge at that time in its presentation of creation. The mediation of religious tradition with scholarly knowledge—even if this distinction remains foreign to Near Eastern antiquity—is an essential component of theological work.

THE PRIESTLY DOCUMENT AS THE BASIC LAYER OF THE PENTATEUCH In addition especially to the aspects conditioned by cultural contact with Babylon, there are also indigenous elements of the Priestly document that should be mentioned, in particular those related to the theological systemization of preexisting elements of tradition. First is its nature as the "basic layer"[43] of the Pentateuch. If its usual limits are correct, even only in their basic approach, and if recent scholarship is correct in its perception that the Priestly document constitutes the basic foundation of the Pentateuch

---

42. Cf. Jan C. Gertz, "Antibabylonische Polemik im priesterlichen Schöpfungs-bericht?," *ZTK* 106 (2009): 137–55.

43. Cf. the classic presentation by Theodor Nöldeke, "Die s.g. Grundschrift des Pentateuchs," in *Untersuchungen zur Kritik des Alten Testaments* (Kiel: Schwers, 1869), 1–144.

not only in literary, but also in conceptual terms, then the Priestly document must be considered the actual creator of a proto-Pentateuch.

Therefore, what appears here—in contrast to the context-dependent literary supplements in the prophetic literature or in the earlier parts of the Pentateuch—is a theological blueprint that allows for the recognition from the beginning of a new approach as a separate text in addition to previous traditions.

If it is correct that the ancestors and Moses-exodus narratives were first combined by P,[44] then one of the most important literary-historical syntheses of the Hebrew Bible goes back to it. Precisely this innovation in content could have been the reason why P did not emerge as a literary supplement to the existing inventory of texts, but instead first arose as a separate source text.

The theological conception of the Priestly document can be understood for large stretches as a new interpretation of Israel and Judah's religious traditions in light of the historical situation of its early Persian-period composition, which is marked, on the one hand, by the experience that the destruction and deportation apparently do not mark the end of Israel and Judah's history, and on the other by the view that the new Persian hegemony could possibly be understood as a divinely ordained form of Israel's political existence in the land and in the diaspora.

FOREIGN RULERS AS INSTRUMENTS AND DEVOTEES OF GOD Also belonging to the framework of this theocratic worldview are the conspicuous characterizations of foreign rulers as worshipers, even the elect of the biblical God. For example, the Babylonian Emperor Nebuchadnezzar, though having destroyed Jerusalem and God's temple, is titled in Jer 25:9; 27:6; 43:10 as God's עבד (*ʿbd*), "servant." The Persian Emperor Cyrus can be addressed in Isa 45:1 as משיחו (*mšḥw*), "his messiah" (cf. below, §33). Also to be mentioned here are the Daniel narratives in Dan 1–6*, which each end with a confession by the foreign ruler to Israel's God. These positions, viewed historically, first become conceivable in the Persian period, when the conception developed that God could also be served by foreign kings

---

44. Cf., e.g., Thomas Römer, ed., *Einleitung in das Alte Testament: Die Bücher der Hebräischen Bibel und die alttestamentlichen Schriften der katholischen, protestantischen und orthodoxen Kirchen* (Zurich: TVZ, 2013), 120–68; Thomas Römer, "Der Pentateuch," in *Die Entstehung des Alten Testaments*, ed. Walter Dietrich et al., Theologische Wissenschaft 1,1 (Stuttgart: Kohlhammer, 2014), 52–166.

in order to rule over the world. This "theocratic" conception presupposes the liberation of the religion of ancient Israel from an intellectual framework tied to a separate state and monarchy, as well as the universalizing extension, which first occurs in the Persian period.

THE ESCHATOLOGICAL COUNTER POSITION The eschatological position was primarily fostered during the Persian period in Deuteronomistic circles.[45] It primarily appears in the literary supplements to the prophetic books, but also in Deuteronomy and in the Former Prophets. Without their own land and their own monarchy, Israel remains under judgment according to the eschatological point of view. Included in a "chain of literary supplements" that promise the restoration of the Davidic monarchy within the framework of this theological current in multiple literary steps is, for example, Jer 23:1–6. It opens with an independent entity in 23:1–2 that is shaped form-critically as a prophetic judgment oracle and concludes with the formula of divine utterance. It contains an oracle of judgment against the kings of Judah ("shepherds"), who have become guilty for the scattering of their people:

> "Woe to the shepherds who have allowed the sheep of my pasture to go wild and scattered them!" The word of Yhwh. Therefore, thus says Yhwh, the God of Israel, concerning the shepherds who shepherd my people: "You have scattered my sheep and driven them away and have not cared for them. Behold, I will strike you with the evil of your deeds; oracle of Yhwh." (Jer 23:1–2)

In 23:3–4, a piece is then included that apparently arose from a different hand, for here it is not the kings who have driven their people away. Instead God himself is the actor behind this affair. So Jer 23:3–4 makes it abundantly clear that the deportation of Judah was no accident, but in the end is a part of God's plan for history, which therefore will also include the gathering of the diaspora:

> "And I alone will gather the remainder of my sheep from all the lands where I have driven them away, and I will lead them again to their pas-

---

45. On the problem surrounding the terminology in the context of the juxtaposition to theocracy, cf. Gunther Wanke, "Eschatologie: Ein Beispiel theologischer Sprachverwirrung," *KD* 16 (1970): 300–12.

ture, and they will bear fruit and increase. And I will place shepherds over them, and they will shepherd them, and they will no longer be afraid and no longer be frightened, and one will no longer need to care for them"—oracle of Yhwh. (Jer 23:3–4)

The subsequent verses in 23:5–6 are also separate from what came before and add the specification that the new shepherds that God will place over the people will be Davidides:

"Behold, days are coming," declares Yhwh, "when I will raise up for David a righteous offshoot. And he will reign as king and rule wisely and carry out justice and righteousness in the land. In his days, Judah will receive help, and Israel will dwell in safety. And this is the name that one will give him: Yhwh is our righteousness!" (Jer 23:5–6)

This chain of literary supplementation mirrors the literarily productive interaction in the book of Jeremiah with the basic declaration in 23:1–2, which over the course of time apparently required updating and further specification. The loss of the monarchy was compensated for by the increasingly concrete shape of a ruler for the time of salvation.

2. *Experiencing and Processing the Delay of the Parousia*

The theocratic positions possessed immediate concrete support in the Persian period: God's deliverance was realized in the experiences of the contemporary political situation. However, as time progressed, the nature of the experience changed. In spite of the construction of the temple, Judah and Jerusalem remained in a deplorable state, which was more easily interpreted as "the delay of the Parousia." Neither were the promises of the reinstallation of the Davidic dynasty found in, for example, Jer 23:3–6 fulfilled. With regard to the expectation of a Davidic ruler, a very late literary supplement, likely from the third century BCE (it is missing from the Greek version of the book of Jeremiah) in Jer 33:14–16 offers a surprising theological explanation. It combines Jer 23:5–6 with the promise of the return for the diaspora in Jer 29:10 in such a way that the diaspora must first return to the land before a Davidic ruler can be installed over Judah.[46]

---

46. Cf. in detail Konrad Schmid, "Die Verheißung eines kommenden Davididen und

THIRD ISAIAH AND THE DELAY OF SALVATION More than any other, the texts normally referred to as "Third Isaiah" in Isa 56–66, which belong to the later Persian period are marked by the problem of the "delay of the Parousia." The salvation promised in Deutero-Isaiah neither arrived to the degree nor in the proximate time presented by Isa 40–55. In the wake of the experience of this deficiency, Isa 56–66 investigates the causes and locates them in hindrances to salvation, in the wrong conduct of the people of God. Accordingly, Isa 56–66 offers admonitions and accusations. Contrary to the earlier hypothesis of a "Third Isaiah," Isa 56–66 does not rest on the previously oral proclamations of a separate prophet ("Third Isaiah"). These chapters should instead be viewed as the prophecy of scribal tradents, which never existed except as texts written for a book.[47]

An example of the scribal character as well as the new theological viewpoint of Isa 56–66 can be recognized in the adaptation of Isa 40:3 in Isa 57:14:

ISA 40:3:	ISA 57:14:
Hear, one calls out:	And he says:
"In the desert blaze	"Blaze, blaze,
the way of Yhwh;	level a street!
make in the steppe	Make way for my people,
a straight street	every obstruction out of the way!"
for our God!"	

In Isa 40:3 the call goes forth to level a processional street for Yhwh so that he can return to Zion/Jerusalem and into his sanctuary. Isaiah 57:14 adopts this call, but then interprets it in terms of ethics. The social and religious abuses of the people must be set aside so that salvation can break through.

The position of Isa 56–59 does not, however, prove to be a lasting resolution of the problems of the delay of salvation. The texts in Isa 63–66 transform Isa 56–59 into a form in which the hoped for arrival of the promised salvation is no longer dependent on ever expanding conditions. Instead, it

---

die Heimkehr der Diaspora: Die innerbiblische Aktualisierung von Jer 23,5f in Jer 33,14–26," in *Schriftgelehrte Traditionsliteratur: Fallstudien zur innerbiblischen Schriftauslegung im Alten Testament*, FAT 77 (Tübingen: Mohr Siebeck, 2011), 207–21.

47. Cf. Odil H. Steck, "Tritojesaja im Jesajabuch," in *Studien zu Tritojesaja*, BZAW 203 (Berlin: de Gruyter, 1991), 3–45.

will be limited to the "pious," who can also be devotees from the nations. As a result, the theological unity of the people of God is abandoned. The concluding texts of the book of Isaiah in chs. 65–66 only envisage salvation for the righteous; the sinners, on the other hand, will incur judgment (Isa 65:1–15; cf. Isa 57:20–21). In terms of the history of theology, this step marks a radical break. The surrender of the largely undisputed object of salvation in pre-Hellenistic times, "Israel," blazes the way to individualization, which is also something of a de-ethnicization of the Jewish religion. This trend would later become even more important, especially after the destruction of Jerusalem in 70 CE, and it had a significant influence upon Christianity in this respect.

§27 The Destruction of the Persian Empire in 333–331 BCE

Stefan Beyerle, *Die Gottesvorstellungen in der antik-jüdischen Apokalyptik,* JSJ-Sup 103 (Leiden: Brill, 2005) ♦ John J. Collins, "From Prophecy to Apocalypticism: The Expectation of the End," in *The Origins of Apocalypticism in Judaism and Christianity*, vol. 1 of *The Encyclopedia of Apocalypticism*, ed. John J. Collins (London: Continuum, 2000), 129–61 ♦ Florian Förg, *Die Ursprünge der alttestamentlichen Apokalyptik*, Arbeiten zur Bibel und ihrer Geschichte 45 (Leipzig: Evangelische Verlagsanstalt, 2013) ♦ Hans-Joachim Gehrke, *Geschichte des Hellenismus,* 3rd ed., Oldenbourg Grundriss der Geschichte 1a (Munich: Oldenbourg, 2003) ♦ Ernst Haag, *Das hellenistische Zeitalter: Israel und die Bibel im 4. bis 1. Jahrhundert v. Chr.,* Biblische Enzyklopädie 9 (Stuttgart: Kohlhammer, 2003) ♦ Othmar Keel and Urs Staub, *Hellenismus und Judentum: Vier Studien zu Daniel 7 und zur Religionsnot unter Antiochus IV.,* OBO 178 (Freiburg: Universitätsverlag; Göttingen: Vandenhoeck & Ruprecht, 2000) ♦ Christoph Markschies, *Hellenisierung des Christentums: Sinn und Unsinn einer historischen Deutungskategorie*, Forum Theologische Literaturzeitung 25 (Leipzig: Evangelische Verlagsanstalt, 2012) ♦ Konrad Schmid, "Das kosmische Weltgericht in den Prophetenbüchern und seine historischen Kontexte," in *Nächstenliebe und Gottesfurcht: Beiträge aus alttestamentlicher, semitistischer und altorientalistischer Wissenschaft für Hans-Peter Mathys zum 65. Geburtstag*, ed. Hanna Jenni and Markus Saur, AOAT 439 (Münster: Ugarit-Verlag, 2016), 409–34 ♦ Odil Hannes Steck, *Der Abschluß der Prophetie im Alten Testament*: *Ein Versuch zur Frage der Vorgeschichte des Kanons*, Biblisch-theologische Studien 17 (Neukirchen-Vluyn: Neukirchener Verlag, 1991) ♦ Michael Tilly, *Apokalyptik*, Uni-Taschenbücher 3651 (Tübingen: Francke, 2012)

1. The Experience of the Loss of Political Order and the Rise of Apocalypticism

THE ORIGINS OF THE APOCALYPTIC The hegemony of the Persians came to an abrupt end through the rise of Alexander the Great and his campaigns in the East. Contrary especially the classical impression of the Persians found primarily in Greek literature, in the view of the East, the Persians were in no way perceived as "barbarians." Instead, the *pax Persica*—at least in theocratic circles—was reckoned as the divinely ordained order, whose upheaval was interpreted as a catastrophe of cosmic proportions.

These interpretations are deposited in literary form primarily in the books of the prophets (cf. below, §32). These positions are important in terms of the history of theology insofar as they laid the intellectual foundation for the apocalyptic conceptions that emerged in their wake. The term "apocalyptic" is generally understood as a particular intellectual current along with the revelatory literature belonging with it that arose in the period between the third century BCE and the third century CE. However, it is a very complex historical entity. A certain amount of overlap within the texts usually considered apocalyptic appears in the motif of secret heavenly knowledge that appears to play a significant role. This partially justifies the collective designation of "apocalyptic" (esp. 1 Enoch, Daniel, 4 Ezra, 2 Baruch).

The importance of apocalypticism for the emergence of theology was negotiated above all in the 1960s around the provocative thesis of Ernst Käsemann that apocalypticism was the "mother of all Christian theology."[48] At that time Käsemann separated the un-apocalyptic Jesus from the apocalyptically marked theology of the New Testament in the Synoptics, Paul, and John. This debate only remains relevant today as history of scholarship. However, it led to the fact that one can today discuss apocalypticism as an intellectual current and literary phenomenon without a basic theological assessment—which was traditionally viewed as negative.

APOCALYPTICISM BASED IN THE PRIESTLY KNOWLEDGE OF THE LATE PERSIAN PERIOD Since the discoveries at Qumran it has become clear that the intellectual movement and corresponding literary expressions treated under the title "apocalyptic" must be older than the Maccabean book of Daniel, which one—on the basis of the Maccabean period ma-

---

48. Cf. Ernst Käsemann, "Die Anfänge christlicher Theologie," *ZTK* 57 (1960): 180.

terial in chapters 2 and 7–12—had commonly been viewed as the oldest apocalypse. The origins of apocalypticism were instead apparently to be found—irrespective of all historical nuances and definitional problems, which are closely interrelated to one another—in the domain of the Enoch literature attested in comparatively early manuscripts rather than in the Daniel literature. It belongs still in the third and not the second century BCE. This evidence is of considerable importance because it points to the significant role that priestly knowledge played in the astronomical portions of the Enoch literature for the development of apocalypticism.

ENDOGENOUS OR EXTERNAL FACTORS? Furthermore, it is also probable that the phenomenon of apocalypticism, which earlier was often viewed as an Iranian import, is much more strongly anchored in the intellectual history of ancient Judaism and more easily explained from within it than is commonly assumed. In particular, it is related to the destruction of the Persian Empire by Alexander the Great and the corresponding collapse of theocratically oriented—and commonly native to priestly circles—conceptions such as those of the Priestly document or later psalms. These could view the *pax Persica* as the divinely ordained end of history, so they may have significantly facilitated the formation of apocalyptic theology of judgment. The essential content of the (priestly) ideals of theocracy were basically maintained in the post-Persian era: God is ruler and guide of the world. However, the assertion of its earthly realization in the Persian period in the sense of a "realized eschatology" had to give way in light of the evidence and again became historically fluid. How God's dominion over the world would finally appear would now become the object of apocalyptic speculation about history.

TRANSFORMATIONS OF THEOCRATIC DESIGNS Just as the intellectual catastrophe of the collapse of the experience of the Persian-period order and the connected crisis of contemporary theocratic conceptions may have provided an initial ignition to the formation of apocalyptic conceptions, later experiences of the catastrophes of the desecration of the Jerusalem temple by Antiochus IV in 167 BCE and the temple's destruction in 70 CE by the Romans together with their destruction of the city of Jerusalem decisively marked its further development. Apocalypticism can be grasped as a theological reaction to the loss of the evidence for theocratic conceptions, for conflicting political events were motivated by these conceptions. This conjecture is supported even through the simple distribution of writings generally categorized as apocalyptic in the history of theology. They can largely be grouped around these two central dates and reflect, sometimes quite directly and—as much as possible within the historical fiction—explicitly on the related experiences. Reference should be made here especially to 1 En. 90:6–12; 93:9–10; 4 Ezra 10:21–23; 2 Bar. 7:1; 8:2; 10:5–19; Apoc. Ab. 27:3; cf. also Ps.-Philo 19:7.

EXPERIENCES OF GOD'S ABSENCE Apocalyptic conceptions arose in ancient Israel in the wake of historical encounters that appear to refute God's salvific presence in the world as traditionally postulated in theocratic circles. Where is God? Is he hidden from now on? Has he completely repudiated his people? Many apocalyptic texts answer these questions with a revelation presenting God's creational power that comprises all of history. This depiction can, however, take very different forms of manifestation—of weal and of woe—and must be differentiated historically.

TWO AGES The destruction of the temple in 70 CE depicts a limit experience of extreme proportions concerning the question of God's presence in the world. Therefore, one need not be surprised that this event demanded special efforts in order to cope theologically. Among the answers given in Jewish apocalypticism, one should mention 2 Baruch in addition to 4 Ezra. Of lesser importance are Apocalypse of Abraham and Pseudo-Philo. However, even 4 Ezra and 2 Baruch were unable to develop any influence in Judaism, which developed in the rabbinic direction after 70 CE. Their reception and transmission was preserved in Christianity.

Characteristic of these two writings is that their answers to the catastrophe of the destruction of the temple exhibit the first explicit attestations to the doctrine of two ages, which in some places becomes the constitutive feature for apocalypticism as a whole. It might originally have arisen from the experience of the destruction of the Second Temple.

Complementary to this negative discovery is that the doctrine of the two ages can be plausibly connected to the destruction of the Second Temple. Such an apparently ultimate elimination of the temple as the location of God's presence in the world pressed certain circles to the interpretation that the world as a whole could not continue in this form. Therefore, in the beginning God must have created not one, but two worlds (epochs)— the two ages. The first age is characterized not by the continual retreat of God himself from world history—as sometimes put forward as a blanket judgment for the apocalyptic view of history—but through a withdrawal of

God's salvific will from history. God of course remains the decisive power in history even in the catastrophe. His salvific presence is, in contrast, transferred to the second, coming age. As a result, the classic Priestly temple theology, which can be described concisely by the phrase "creation in the creation,"[49] transforms into a theology of the "creation after the creation." The coming age will bring God's creation to its fulfillment.

APOCALYPTIC THEOLOGY It is immediately recognizable that apocalyptic literature not only bears the marks of theological reflection, but it in fact owes its existence to such reflection. While it does not develop as a literary form of theological secondary literature, it instead links up to the prophetic tradition through its vision reports, depicting its positions as revelatory knowledge and not as the result of human reflection. However, this distinction is synonymous with that of the theory of an apocalyptic text and its actual formation. What the apocalypse presents as revelation is, of course, the theological position of its authors, which—as becomes identifiable through the historical investigation of such writings—arises through the theological integration of tradition and experience.

It is especially important to note the influence of the theocratic positions of the literature of the Hebrew Bible on apocalyptic theology. The basic orienting grid for the apocalyptic theology of history is the intellectual paradigm of universal history stimulated by a theocratic conceptualization. Apocalypticism can therefore be interpreted as a project of mediation between a fundamentally theological point of departure and apparently conflicting historical evidence. Its possible resolutions are so radical that they generally must call for new revelations. In form, apocalyptic literature is, therefore, more "revelatory" than "theological." However, its concern is genuinely theological.

2. Judaism and Hellenism

The most powerful intellectual movement in the post-Persian period is the rise of Hellenism. This term has been in use since Johann Gustav Droysen to designate the deep penetration of elements of Greek tradition into

---

49. Cf. Erhard Blum, *Studien zur Komposition des Pentateuch*, BZAW 189 (Berlin: de Gruyter, 1990), 289–332, esp. 311. The temple cult reactivates and restores features of the original creation.

the Mediterranean and Near Eastern culture in the wake of Alexander's campaigns. One should note, however, that the Greeks already played an important role in the Near East prior to Alexander. What was new under Alexander was the proliferation of their thought and culture as far as the Indus and its mix with indigenous traditions.

HELLENISM AS WORLD CULTURE It is unquestionable that the new world culture also exercised a powerful allure among the Jews, as one can deduce especially from the confrontations depicted in the book of 1 Maccabees. One can, however, receive the impression from the biblical and post-biblical Jewish literature of the Hellenistic period that resistance to Hellenism was a majority phenomenon. This point of view emerges primarily from the specific "orthodox" stamp of the related texts and writings that prevailed in the history of reception. However, viewed historically, it can be expected that Hellenism was broadly carried forward among the people and that the confrontations were in large part not exogenously but endogenously motivated. The interactive encounter of Judaism with Hellenism shows in an exemplary manner that religion is a cultural phenomenon and reacts sensitively (receptively or defensively) to various social and political constellations.

SEPTUAGINT Likely the most impressive example of the Hellenistic reception of the Hebrew Bible is the Septuagint.[50] The books of the Septuagint go back to different translators, and their translation techniques range from rather literal to quite free renderings. It is clear that traces of Hellenistic thinking appear in many places in the Septuagint.[51] For example, anthropomorphisms for the image of God are smoothed out, prophetic proclamations are actualized in contemporizing fashion, and

50. Cf. Siegfried Kreuzer, ed., *Einleitung in die Septuaginta* (Gütersloh: Gütersloher Verlagshaus, 2016).

51. Cf., e.g., Martin Rösel, "Towards a 'Theology of the Septuagint,'" in *Septuagint Research: Issues and Challenges in the Study of the Greek Jewish Scriptures*, ed. Wolfgang Kraus and R. Glenn Wooden, SBL Septuagint and Cognate Studies 53 (Atlanta: SBL Press, 2006), 239–52; Martin Rösel, "Der hebräische Mensch im griechischen Gewand: Anthropologische Akzentsetzungen in der Septuaginta," in *Der Mensch im alten Israel: Neue Forschungen zur alttestamentlichen Anthropologie*, ed. Bernd Janowski and Kathrin Liess, HBS 59 (Freiburg im Breisgau: Herder, 2009), 69–92; Michael Tilly, *Einführung in die Septuaginta* (Darmstadt: Wissenschaftliche Buchgesellschaft, 2005), 74–80. On older reception from the Greek realm in the Hebrew Bible, see Thomas Römer, "The Hebrew Bible and Greek Philosophy and Mythology: Some Case Studies," *Semitica* 57 (2015): 185–203.

Greek anthropology is conveyed in biblical terms. Especially impressive is the reconciliation of the creation portrayal with the Platonic dialogue *Timaios*. The terminology and the implicit conceptions in the Greek text of Gen 1 overtly strive for harmonization between biblical and Platonic cosmologies.[52] The world described by the Bible is, according to the understanding of the Septuagint, none other than that of Greek philosophy and scholarship.[53] The similarity to *Timaios* is apparent, for example, in Gen 1:2. The Septuagint renders the circumstances of the world before creation, which in Hebrew is described as the proverbial *thw wbwhw* (תהו ובוהו), that is, "life-antagonistic desert" (cf. Isa 34:11; Jer 4:23), as ἀόρατος καὶ ἀκατασκεύαστος ("unseen and unworked"), which appear analogously to allude to the distinction between the ideal world and the material world that is central in *Timaios*. The rendering of רקיע (*rqy'*), "firmament," in Gen 1:6 with στερέωμα ("structure") should probably likewise be explained in light of *Timaios*, for there the related adjective στερεός ("firm, solid") is used multiple times to refer to the celestial bodies (31b; 43c; and often).

WRITINGS OF HELLENISTIC JUDAISM FROM THE SECOND AND FIRST CENTURIES BCE Especially worthy of mention for Hellenistic Judaism are further writings like the book of Sirach, the book of Baruch, and the Wisdom of Solomon, which arose in the second and first centuries and try to mediate between Jewish tradition and the Hellenistic élan. This position appears especially marked in Sir 24:23 and Bar 4:1, where Torah and wisdom are identified with one another. The Jewish Torah is nothing other than wisdom in writing. Whoever grapples with Torah is occupied in concentrated form with the topic of Hellenistic philosophy. A certain claim to supremacy is implied: while the Torah is in substance equal with wisdom, it is superior because it originates from God, who rules over the entire world.

---

52. On this, cf. Martin Rösel, *Übersetzung als Vollendung der Auslegung: Studien zur Genesis-Septuaginta*, BZAW 223 (Berlin: de Gruyter, 1994), 31, 36, 60, 81–87.

53. Cf. the careful description in Martin Karrer, "Septuaginta und Philosophie," in *Juda und Jerusalem in der Seleukidenzeit: Herrschaft—Widerstand—Identität: Festschrift für Heinz-Josef Fabry*, ed. Ulrich Dahmen and Johannes Schnocks, BBB 159 (Göttingen: V&R Unipress, 2010), 191–212.

§28 Confrontations with the Maccabean Crisis (167–164 BCE) and the Question of the End of the Theological History of the Hebrew Bible

Ernst Haag, "Daniel 12 und die Auferstehung der Toten," in *The Book of Daniel: Composition and Reception*, ed. John J. Collins and Peter Flint, VTSup 83/1 (Leiden: Brill, 2001), 1:132–148 ◆ Othmar Keel and Urs Staub, *Hellenismus und Judentum: Vier Studien zu Daniel 7 und zur Religionsnot unter Antiochus IV*, OBO 178 (Freiburg: Universitätsverlag, 2000) ◆ Reinhard G. Kratz, *Translatio imperii: Untersuchungen zu den aramäischen Danielerzählungen und ihrem theologiegeschichtlichen Umfeld*, WMANT 63 (Neukirchen-Vluyn: Neukirchener Verlag, 1991) ◆ Reinhard G. Kratz, "The Visions of Daniel," in *The Book of Daniel: Composition and Reception*, ed. John J. Collins and Peter Flint, VTSup 83/1 (Leiden: Brill, 2001), 1:91–113 ◆ Martin Leuenberger, "Leben und Sterben für Gott? Religions- und theologiegeschichtliche Perspektiven aus dem alten Israel," in *Martyriumsvorstellungen in Antike und Mittelalter: Leben oder Sterben für Gott?*, ed. Sebastian Fuhrmann and Regina Grundmann, Ancient Judaism and Early Christianity 80 (Leiden: Brill, 2012), 5–19 ◆ Anathea Portier-Young, *Apocalypse Against Empire: Theologies of Resistance in Early Judaism* (Grand Rapids: Eerdmans, 2010) ◆ Gabriela Signori, *Dying for the Faith, Killing for the Faith: Old-Testament Faith-Warriors (1 and 2 Maccabees) in Historical Perspective*, Brill's Studies in Intellectual History 206 (Leiden: Brill, 2012)

1. The Maccabean Book of Daniel

The book of Daniel, whose literary core consists of the theocratic legends of chs. 1–6* from the Persian period resulting in the acclamation of the biblical God by the respective foreign ruler, received its earliest literary supplementation in the early Hellenistic period. However, its final and deepest revision took place in the Maccabean period. This revision is deposited primarily in the editing of the visions in Dan 2 and 7, as well as in the addition of chs. 8–9, 10–12. Daniel 8–12 is very familiar with the history of the period leading up to the death of Antiochus IV, whose death is wrongly predicted in Dan 11:45. Antiochus IV should have died between the sea and Zion, but he actually perished during the plundering of a temple in the east of the realm. Therefore, the date for the completion of the book of Daniel can be placed with high probability in the year 164 BCE.

DANIEL AS PROPHET The book of Daniel first became a prophetic book through its Maccabean expansion. It expected that the demise of the current and all foreign powers, and the turning point of Israel's salvation, was near—that the period of judgment enduring since the Babylonians would end. The visions make it clear that the confusing contemporary world events had long been preordained in heaven, and they could be recognized by the apocalyptic seer Daniel with the help of an interpretive angel. In Dan 8–12, the Maccabean religious plight is depicted in hues of the pronouncements of judgment of the book of Isaiah. What takes place in the Maccabean period is nothing other than a further fulfillment of the prophecy of Isaiah. However, there are other writings of the Hebrew Bible that also serve as sources of historical knowledge for the book of Daniel. This is the clearest for the great historical prophecy in Dan 9. Placed in an exilic setting, Daniel asks himself how long Jerusalem should still remain in ruins. He studies the texts concerning it in the writings where Jeremiah prophetically states seventy years (9:2). Yet Daniel reads more than just the book of Jeremiah. He formulates a penitential prayer in response and eventually receives an answer from the angel Gabriel. Not seventy years, but seventy weeks of years, that is, 490 years, are determined for Jerusalem's judgment. This does not simply concern an arbitrary extension from seventy to 490 years, but this prolongation is apparently derived exegetically from Lev 26:34–35 and 2 Chr 36:21, which indicate that the length of Israel's guilt should continue "until the land receives the compensation for its Sabbath years; for the entire time that it remains desolate, it rests until the expiration of seventy years" (2 Chr 36:21). The meaning of the biblical prophecy of the "seventy years" expounded by Gabriel, therefore, explains that the compensatory seventy years *are all* Sabbath years—not seventy regular years, in which only ten Sabbath years are compensated. As a result, Dan 9 arrives at the extension of the period of judgment to 490 years, which reach from the imagined historical setting directly until the present time of the Maccabean author. The chronology presented in Dan 9:24–27, which places the desolation of the Jerusalem Temple in the middle of the final week of years before the end of the 490 years of judgment, shows the degree to which the Maccabean book of Daniel reckons with an imminent expectation. It will only endure for another three-and-a-half years until the 490 years are up and salvation for Israel can arrive.

Apparently the Maccabean revolt was interpreted as the verification of this prophecy, which conferred a high amount of authority to the book of Daniel. However, it was too little to provide it with a permanent place in the Nevi'im—it is found in the Ketuvim.

2. *Martyr Theology in the Books of Maccabees*

The topic mentioned earlier in Dan 12 of martyrs has been discussed widely in the literature on the books of Maccabees, especially on the book of 2 Maccabees. The martyrs are of great importance both theologically and in the history of reception. They attest to the conception that one should take a stand for their faith for the first time in the religious history of the Levant.

The historical depiction of the Maccabean period is more loaded theologically than in 1 Maccabees. In 2 Maccabees, God intervenes actively in events either himself or through his messengers (3:2–34; 9:5; 14:3–35; 15:23–24, 34). His works are seen as dependent on Israel's actions. God helps the faithful, but he can also abandon his temple when Israel falls away from him (5:17).

A special text in the book is dedicated to the description of the martyrdom of the aged Eliezer and the mother with her seven sons in 2 Macc 6:12–7:42. They are cruelly tortured to death for their refusal to eat pork. Their martyrdom results, on the one hand, from Israel's sinfulness, which helps the Seleucids to desecrate the temple. On the other hand, their steadfastness in faith makes it so Judas Maccabee can proceed victoriously with God's assistance against Antiochus IV.

BELIEF IN RESURRECTION Their steadfastness till death is based on a belief in the resurrection, which makes such a martyrdom possible (cf. also 2 Macc 14:46). The conception of a resurrection from the dead is first encountered in late texts of the Hebrew Bible such as Dan 12:2–3[54] (cf. Ezek 37; Ps 88; Isa 25:8; 26:19), but it has a longer implicit prehistory, seen in a long process of God's "extension of authority" into the realm of the dead.[55]

54. Cf. Matthias Albani, "'Die Verständigen werden leuchten wie der Glanz der Himmelsfeste' (Dan 12,3): Die postmortale Hoffnungsperspektive der Weisheit in der frühen Apokalyptik," in *Ex oriente Lux: Studien zur Theologie des Alten Testaments: Festschrift für Rüdiger Lux zum 65. Geburtstag*, ed. Angelika Berlejung and Raik Heckl, Arbeiten zur Bibel und ihrer Geschichte 39 (Leipzig: Evangelische-Verlagsanstalt, 2012), 547–70.

55. Cf. Gönke Eberhardt, *JHWH und die Unterwelt: Spuren einer Kompetenzausweitung JHWHs im Alten Testament*, FAT II/23 (Tübingen: Mohr Siebeck, 2007); Johannes

INTERNAL CONFLICTS AND SETTING EXTERNAL BOUNDARIES One should probably assume, following the classic study by Elias Bickermann,[56] that the confrontation of the Maccabean period was not originally between the Jews and the Seleucids, but that it was instead rooted in differences between Jewish traditionalists and Jewish reformers. So it was essentially an endogenous conflict.

BIBLICAL AND HISTORICAL VIEWPOINTS It is interesting in theological terms, however, that the Maccabean conflict is overwhelmingly depicted in biblical tradition as Judaism's affliction from the outside. The internal conflict can only be inferred historically. The national religious point of view maintained the upper hand in the theological interpretation of history, and historical reconstructions have occasionally allowed themselves to be unduly influenced by this perspective.[57]

HISTORY OF RECEPTION The topic of the martyrs took on enormous importance in the Bar-Kochba revolt and in early Christianity. It is possible, especially in Christianity, that the formation of legends went far beyond historical reality, and martyrdom was depicted as considerably more widespread than was historically the case.[58]

3. The End of the Theological History of the Hebrew Bible

Where does the history of the theology of the Hebrew Bible end? This question can only be answered in a nuanced manner for the various available Hebrew Bibles and Old Testaments (cf. above, Part C). For the Hebrew Bible, it probably ends in the Maccabean period, even if Hasmonean dates have been proposed for individual psalms or Chronicles.[59] For the

---

Schnocks, *Rettung und Neuschöpfung: Studien zur alttestamentlichen Grundlegung einer gesamtbiblischen Theologie der Auferstehung*, BBB 158 (Göttingen: V&R Unipress, 2009).

56. Cf. Elias Bickermann, *Der Gott der Makkabäer: Untersuchungen über Sinn und Ursprung der makkabäischen Erhebung* (Berlin: Schocken, 1937). On Bickermann, cf. Albert Baumgarten, *Elias Bickerman as a Historian of the Jews: A Twentieth Century Tale*, TSAJ 131 (Tübingen: Mohr Siebeck, 2010).

57. Cf., e.g., Anathea Portier-Young, *Apocalypse against Empire*.

58. Cf. Candida Moss, *The Myth of Persecution: How Early Christians Invented a Story of Martyrdom* (New York: Harper Collins, 2013).

59. For Psalms, cf. Ernst Axel Knauf, "Psalm lx and Psalm cviii," in *Data and Debates:*

Old Testament with the standard scope of the Septuagint, the date is the first century CE, if one places the Wisdom of Solomon in this time.[60] For some of the eastern Old Testaments, the date is still later, depending on how one dates the book of Enoch, especially the so-called Similitudes (1 En. 37–71). These writings in part offer special theological material that does not appear elsewhere in the Hebrew Bible, especially, for example, the angelology of the book of Tobit (Tob 3:16–17; 12:6–15), the conception of the immortality of the souls of the righteous in the Wisdom of Solomon (Wis 3:1; cf. 4:10–11), and the well-developed theology of the son of man in the Similitudes. In view of their political-theological reception in the Hebrew Bible, the Greco-Roman period does, however, form a certain continuum. Wisdom of Solomon from the imperial period provides an especially critical view of the worship of images, directed against the Roman cult of the emperor (cf., e.g., Wis 14:16–20), yet this topic in itself is not new (cf., e.g., Ep Jer). Similar to the literature of the Maccabean period, the national-religious perspective in the Bible maintained the upper hand, even if one should reckon historically with the fact that the Romans were able to draw notable Jewish personalities or even entire groups to their side (cf., e.g., Flavius Josephus, *Jewish War*, 5.30).

Essays in the History and Culture of Israel and Its Neighbors in Antiquity = Daten und Debatten: Aufsätze zur Kulturgeschichte des antiken Israel und seiner Nachbarn, AOAT 407 (Münster: Ugarit-Verlag, 2013), 564; cf. also Manfred Oeming, *Das Buch der Psalmen: Psalm 1–41,* NSKAT 13/1 (Stuttgart: Katholisches Bibelwerk, 2000), 31–34. For Chronicles, cf. Georg Steins, *Die Chronik als kanonisches Abschlußphänomen: Studien zur Entstehung und Theologie von 1/2 Chronik,* BBB 93 (Weinheim: Beltz Athenäum, 1995); Israel Finkelstein, "Rehoboam's Fortified Cities (II Chr 11,5–12): A Hasmonean Reality?" *ZAW* 123 (2011): 92–107; Israel Finkelstein, "The Historical Reality behind the Genealogical Lists in 1 Chronicles," *JBL* 131 (2012): 65–83; Israel Finkelstein, "The Expansion of Judah in II Chronicles: Territorial Legitimation for the Hasmoneans?" *ZAW* 127 (2015): 669–95.

60. Cf., e.g., Helmut Engel, *Das Buch der Weisheit,* NSKAT 16 (Stuttgart: Katholisches Bibelwerk, 1998).

H. Themes in the Theology of the Hebrew Bible

THE PROBLEM OF SYSTEMIZATION Contrary to the tradition inaugurated by von Rad, a theology of the Hebrew Bible cannot refrain from a certain systematization of its topics. This is, it should be noted, not predominately called for by the Hebrew Bible itself (though this question is not completely foreign to it), but is primarily a question posed by theology. Just as with a presentation of Plato's philosophy, a theology of the Hebrew Bible requires both an analytical and a synthetic approach. However, "the choice and arrangement of the topics should not arise from conventional systematic-theological schemas, but from the material itself."[1] If one approaches the question of the thematic arrangement of the Hebrew Bible in this way, then—measured against the later reception in Judaism and Christianity (cf. below Part I)—either the foreignness or the familiarity of the themes is emphasized, or rather a whole spectrum between the two poles can be chosen. The following discussion opts for a middle road, which is justified by the fact that the later receptions and prioritizations can be interpreted not only as distortions, but each in their own way also as functional vanishing points that emanate from the Bible.

SELECTION AND ARRANGEMENT OF THE THEMES The subsequent selection and arrangement is one of many possibilities. It roughly follows the canonical sequence of Torah, Nevi'im, and Ketuvim, thus it follows the Hebrew Bible more than the Old Testament. It unavoidably lays a certain focus on the beginning of the Hebrew Bible (the Pentateuch), for on the one hand, the most important themes of the Bible are illuminated here,

---

1. Heikki Räisänen, "Die frühchristliche Gedankenwelt: Eine religionswissenschaftliche Alternative zur 'neutestamentlichen Theologie,'" in *Eine Bibel—zwei Testamente: Positionen biblischer Theologie*, ed. Christoph Dohmen and Thomas Söding, Uni-Taschenbücher 1893 (Paderborn: Schöningh, 1995), 260.

and on the other, the Pentateuch as the Torah also has historical primacy among the books of the Bible. Therefore, weighty themes that are actually attested more prominently in prophecy or in wisdom literature are already addressed comparatively early—namely where the Pentateuch already alludes to them—so that the order of the canon and the content overlap with one another.

HISTORY OF SCHOLARSHIP Added to the discussion of each theme is a section introducing the history of scholarship. It primarily serves the purpose of indicating the dramatic change in scholarship over the past thirty or forty years, which led to massive shifts in the perception and interpretation of each theme in recent Hebrew Bible scholarship. In keeping with the genre of textbooks, it cannot provide a detailed report on scholarship, but instead serves to highlight the dynamics and logic inherent to scholarly development and its importance for the understanding of current issues.

§29 Literary Genres and Forms of Theological Statements in the Hebrew Bible

Rainer Albertz, "Die Theologisierung des Rechts im Alten Israel," in *Geschichte und Theologie: Studien zur Exegese des Alten Testaments und zur Religionsgeschichte Israels*, BZAW 326 (Berlin: de Gruyter, 2003), 187–207 ◆ John J. Collins, "Changing Scriptures," in *Changing Scriptures: Rewriting and Interpretating Authoritative Traditions in the Second Temple Period*, ed. Hanne von Weissenberg et al., BZAW 419 (Berlin: de Gruyter, 2011), 23–45 ◆ Michael Fishbane, "Inner-Biblical Exegesis," in *Hebrew Bible / Old Testament: The History of Its Interpretation*, ed. Magne Sæbø (Göttingen: Vandenhoeck & Ruprecht, 1996), 1.1:33–38 ◆ Jan C. Gertz, "Schriftauslegung in alttestamentlicher Perspektive," in *Schriftauslegung*, ed. Friederike Nüssel, TdT 8 (Tübingen: Mohr Siebeck, 2014), 9–41 ◆ Jörg Jeremias, "Das Proprium der alttestamentlichen Prophetie," in *Hosea und Amos: Studien zu den Anfängen des Dodekapropheten*, FAT 13 (Tübingen: Mohr, 1996), 20–33 ◆ Melanie Köhlmoos, "Weisheit/Weisheitsliteratur II," *TRE* 35:486–97 ◆ Reinhard G. Kratz, "Innerbiblische Exegese und Redaktionsgeschichte im Lichte empirischer Evidenz," in *Das Alte Testament und die Kultur der Moderne: Beiträge des Symposiums "Das Alte Testament und die Kultur Moderne" anlasslich des 100. Geburtstags Gerhard von Rads 1901-1971: Heidelberg, 18-21. Oktober 2001*, ed. Manfred Oeming et al., Altes Testament und Moderne 8 (Münster: LIT, 2004), 37–69 ◆ Thomas Krüger, *Kritische Weisheit* (Zurich: Pano, 1997) ◆ Bernard M. Levinson, *Legal Re-*

vision and Religious Renewal in Ancient Israel (Cambridge: Cambridge University Press, 2008) ♦ Hindy Najman, "The Vitality of Scripture within and beyond the 'Canon,'" *JSJ* 43 (2012): 497–518 ♦ Eckart Otto, "Die biblische Rechtsgeschichte im Horizont des altorientalischen Rechts," in *Altorientalische und biblische Rechtsgeschichte: Gesammelte Studien,* BZABR 8 (Wiesbaden: Harrassowitz, 2008), 56–82 ♦ Markus Saur, *Einführung in die alttestamentliche Weisheitsliteratur* (Darmstadt: Wissenschaftliche Buchgesellschaft, 2012) ♦ Konrad Schmid, *Schriftgelehrte Traditionsliteratur: Fallstudien zur innerbiblischen Schriftauslegung im Alten Testament,* FAT 77 (Tübingen: Mohr Siebeck, 2011) ♦ Konrad Schmid, "Prognosen und Postgnosen in der biblischen Prophetie," *EvT* 74 (2014): 462–76 ♦ Hermann Spieckermann, "Der Mythos Heilsgeschichte: Veränderte Perspektiven in der alttestamentlichen Theologie," in *Arbeit am Mythos: Leistung und Grenze des Mythos in Antike und Gegenwart,* ed. Reinhard G. Kratz and Annette Zgoll (Tübingen: Mohr Siebeck, 2013), 145–66 ♦ Odil H. Steck, *Gott in der Zeit entdecken: Die Prophetenbücher des Alten Testaments als Vorbild für Theologie und Kirche,* Biblisch-theologische Studien 42 (Neukirchen-Vluyn: Neukirchener Verlag, 2001) ♦ Hermann Timm, "Das Alte Testament—ein Geschichtsbuch? Zu Gerhard von Rads Unionslektüren des Alten Testaments," *ZTK* 99 (2002): 147–61 ♦ Ernst-Joachim Waschke, "Mythos als Strukturelement und Denkkategorie biblischer Urgeschichte," in *Der Gesalbte: Studien zur alttestamentlichen Theologie,* BZAW 306 (Berlin: de Gruyter, 2001), 189–205

A theological approach to the Hebrew Bible is well advised to begin by clarifying what the Hebrew Bible itself understands literally with regard to "theology"—the speaking of God. Which forms have the texts and writings of the Hebrew Bible selected in order to speak of God, and what theological decisions are hidden behind such choices?[2] As is so often the case, the Hebrew Bible does not provide explicit reflection on these processes; instead its implicit logic must be deduced and interpreted.

WORD OF GOD AND WORD OF HUMANS A general principle on speaking about God in the Hebrew Bible should be stipulated: while the Hebrew Bible contains numerous passages of text marked by divine speech—this is the case for the historical books, the prophetic books, and also the Psalms

---

2. Jörg Jeremias treats this question in the first section of his *Theologie des Alten Testaments,* GAT 6 (Göttingen: Vandenhoeck & Ruprecht, 2015) under the rubric of "Denkformen" ("forms of thought"), which, however, also cover the first, preexilic section of the theological history of the Hebrew Bible.

as well as the wisdom literature; all of these are embedded as the words of God presented as declarations in interpretive contexts, which mark the divine speech as *mediated* divine speech—the Hebrew Bible does not attest to divine speech outside of human words.[3] Yes, it appears in the narrative of Moses's smashing of the two tablets "written with the finger of God," but only to reflect consciously on the fact that his writings do not possess a "divinely written" quality. According to the narrated world of the Hebrew Bible, there was only one time when there was a divine autograph, and that was long ago and only for a short time. This was the first edition of the Ten Commandments (Exod 32:16). However, this autograph was shattered by Moses shortly after he received them on Mount Sinai (Exod 32:19). Moses himself then wrote the second edition (Exod 34:27–28).

THE BOOK OF ESTHER NEVER NAMES GOD The book of Esther presents a singularity in that it never mentions God.[4] However, it still belongs to the biblical canon. It remains silent about God, but it is read as a writing that is perceived and understood as indirectly witnessing about God.

THE BEGINNING OF THE BIBLE IS NOT GOD'S SELF-REPORT Characteristic in this regard is the fact that the creation narrative of the Bible in Gen 1 from the very beginning consistently reports of God in the third person, and not in the first person, which would generally have been conceivable.[5] The Hebrew Bible is itself, then, also a self-testimony that it is not simply identical with God's word. It instead understands itself—where this even becomes a topic—as a witness, interpretation, and transmission thereof. Accordingly, various literary genres are used or developed in order to speak of "God," which will be presented in what follows. The list is not comprehensive, but representative.

STEREOMETRY One peculiarity already mentioned in §9 should be recalled here once again. A whole range of theological conceptions in the Hebrew

---

3. This first appears in the so-called Temple Scroll from Qumran; cf. Bernard M. Levinson, *A More Perfect Torah*, CSHB 1 (Winona Lake, IN: Eisenbrauns, 2015).

4. Cf. Harald Martin Wahl, "'Glaube ohne Gott?' Zur Rede vom Gott Israels im hebräischen Buch Esther," *BZ* 45 (2001): 37–54. On the theologically interpretative Greek version, cf. Kristin De Troyer, *Die Septuaginta und die Endgestalt des Alten Testaments*, Uni-Taschenbücher 2599 (Göttingen: Vandenhoeck & Ruprecht, 2005), 26–48.

5. Already highlighted by Johann Gottfried Eichhorn, *Einleitung in das Alte Testament* (Leipzig: Weidmann, 1803), 18.

Bible were not named explicitly in the first place, but rather rise stereo-metrically above the surface of the texts. Complex interrelated statements put forward a perspective of the meaning by means of the dynamic of reception they initiate for the audience that is not, however, condensed textually. This is an exceptionally remarkable manner by which to carry out theology, and it is also of great importance for addressing the question of how theology can be inspired by the Bible.

1. Narratives

In beginning to read the Hebrew Bible, initially the form of its texts as narrative holds sway. In the canon of the Hebrew Bible, this formal imprint carries through from Genesis to the end of 2 Kings, such that the Bible is introduced by a large and essentially continual (and therefore coherently readable) narrative from the creation of the world to the demise of Judah and Jerusalem that functions as Israel's founding story. In addition, the Hebrew Bible offers a second, structurally similar founding story in the books of Chronicles (together with Ezra–Nehemiah), which reaches from the first human (1 Chr 1) to the Edict of Cyrus (2 Chr 36), or rather to the restoration of Judah (Ezra–Nehemiah), which, however, stresses very different accents.

SOCIO-POLITICAL DIMENSION The thematic narrative orientation of Genesis–2 Kings has, in the first place, a socio-political nature. Just the fact that this large narrative ends with the loss of the monarchy, state, and temple grounds Israel's existence as an entity that in a political sense is "exilic." Genesis–2 Kings explains why Israel is not a people with its own land, ruler, and locally anchored cult. Why then is Israel nevertheless Israel? In order to answer this question, the actual theological substance of Genesis–2 Kings should be taken into account. The founding story offered in Genesis–2 Kings does not limit itself to a description of the development of specific political, social, or cultic regulations and institutions in the course of Israel's history, but it simultaneously if not predominantly narrates how God on the one hand in active, and on the other hand also in reactive manner became the God of Israel who, in a very complexly presented manner, is both the one responsible for Israel's *exilic* existence and also for Israel's exilic *existence*. The shared denominator of these declarations is the reciprocal relationship between God and Israel, which is the remaining central factor, together with Israel's genealogical cohesion, for its identity after the loss of the monarchy, state, and temple.

FUNCTIONAL MYTHIC STRUCTURE Why can narratives, especially in the prominent manner of Genesis–2 Kings, even come to be understood as forms of speaking about God? This question first took shape in the modern period. It never would have arisen in antiquity, primarily for two reasons. The first is that a theoretical approach to God was basically foreign to the ancient Near Eastern world; they speak of God in view of his actions and his experience. The second is that ancient literature generally uses mythical categories for fundamental questions, treating questions of existence as questions of origins, calling for narrative forms of presentation.[6]

Considering Genesis–2 Kings from this perspective, one recognizes that this narrative depiction treats and overlays with considerable complexity the questions of the universality and particularity of divine action, God's care and obligation, divine beneficence and human effort. It has been known for at least a quarter of a millennium that these overlapping phenomena are conditioned by the composition history, but only recent scholarship has developed perspectives that make these overlays comprehensible as inner-biblical interpretations.

Therefore, Genesis–2 Kings as a whole, for example, is readable as a comprehensive etiology for Israel in its diaspora existence, as an entity that maintains cohesion without monarchy, state, and temple—according to the information of Genesis–2 Kings, not in the least because of the history narrated there.

On a small scale, the narratives of the Primeval History in particular can be mentioned. The so-called paradise or Garden of Eden narrative in Gen 2–3 gives reasons for why humanity lives outside the divine garden.

6. If one maintains the classic, content-oriented definition proposed by Hugo Gressmann that myths are "stories of gods" that "take place outside of space and time" ("Mythen und Mythologie I.," *RGG*, 2nd ed., 3:618), then the Hebrew Bible contains no or almost no myths. However, it would be incorrect to deny that the Hebrew Bible has mythical qualities because its narratives are generally structured "mythically" from a functional point of view. That is, they treat questions of being as questions of origins. Cf. the classical definition of myth in Salust, *De diis et mundo*, 4.9, as a narrative that "never took place but always still is"; see also Hubert Irsigler, "Israels 'Urgeschichte'—ein Mythos? Zur Mythisierung von Geschichte und Historisierung des Mythischen im Alten Testament," in *Geschichte und Gott: XV. Europäischer Kongress für Theologie (14.–18. September 2014 in Berlin)*, ed. Michael Meyer-Blanck, Veröffentlichungen der Wissenschaftlichen Gesellschaft für Theologie 44 (Leipzig: Evangelische Verlagsanstalt, 2016), 233–66.

The flood tradition in Gen 6–9 separates humanity's existence from the condition of its good behavior. The narratives concerning Israel's ancestors account for the political relationships of Israel and Judah with their neighbors Edom, Ammon, and Moab. The exodus narrative offers an etiology explaining why Israel is God's people. The narratives concerning David justify in an ambivalent manner the political institution of the monarchy. The books of Kings then look back on the two monarchies in Israel and Judah from the perspective of their destruction.

2. Legal Stipulations

The Pentateuch offers extensive legal collections, especially in the range of Exodus–Deuteronomy. It may appear surprising for modern understanding that legal stipulations can be spoken by God. Then again, this is also conspicuous in the ancient Near East, where law is usually royal law. The specific presentation of the law of the Hebrew Bible as divine law represents a singularity among ancient Near Eastern legal corpora. The fundamental theological thought bound up with this peculiarity consists in the rational interpretation of Israel's relationship with God as a legally binding relationship: God relates to Israel in accordance with the legal order he has established.

DIVINE LAW The presentation of the law of the Hebrew Bible as divine law represents neither its literary nor theological bedrock; it instead rests largely on interpretation. The older legal traditions of ancient Israel, which can still be easily recognized primarily in Exod 20–23, do not yet appear in theologized form. Instead, they maintain the customary form of conditional statements.

Even this theologization of law,[7] which for its own sake, at least in parts, rests on the reception of prophetic tradition in the legal tradition of the Hebrew Bible, could have been one of the determining factors for why the legal stipulations became an integral part of the authoritative writings of ancient Israel. The legal tradition in its theological form is to some degree the institutional reception and anchoring of the prophetic social

7. Cf. in detail Konrad Schmid, "Divine Legislation in the Pentateuch in Its Late Judean and Neo-Babylonian Context," in *The Fall of Jerusalem and the Rise of the Torah*, ed. Peter Dubovský et al., FAT 107 (Tübingen: Mohr Siebeck, 2016), 129–53.

critique for Israel. The legal stipulations do not simply mirror the society's will for order, but also (following its presentation) God's will for this order, respectively (following the historical reconstruction) the theologically elucidated and mediated form of Israel's social configuration.

3. Prophecy

Prophecy is placed after the narrative books in the canon of the Hebrew Bible—which is primarily linked to the chronological order of the depicted scenery (Genesis–2 Kings covers the history of the world and Israel since the creation, while the prophetic books' locations in the Bible indicate placement, which is also appropriate for the literary core, beginning first in the eighth century BCE). But it is of exceptional importance for speech about God in the Hebrew Bible. For corresponding to their influence from the nature of ancient messages,[8] the authorial sense of the speech of God is most deeply anchored here.

PROPHECY IN THE ANCIENT NEAR EAST It should be underscored that prophecy was in no way a phenomenon limited to ancient Israel and Judah. Prophecy is something that occurred widely in the entire ancient Near East.[9] A particularity of biblical prophecy appears, however, in the fact that it was transmitted and actualized in multiple ages and as such received ongoing literary supplementation. The divine messages transmitted by the prophets could be related to various times and were seen as authoritative even beyond the lifetimes of the historical prophets themselves. Form-critical investigation has clearly demonstrated for the basic form of prophetic speech—the so-called prophetic judgment oracle—that what

8. Cf. the definition of prophecy formulated by Manfred Weippert: "A prophet is a man or a woman who 1. accesses the revelation of a deity or deities through a cognitive experience such as a vision, an auditory sound, a dream, etc.; and 2. is commissioned by the respective deity or deities to convey the revelation to a third party—the actual audience—in linguistic or meta-linguistic (symbolic actions) form." "Aspekte israelitischer Prophetie im Lichte verwandter Erscheinungen des Alten Orients," in *Ad bene et fideliter seminandum*: *Festschrift für K. Deller*, ed. Gerlinde Mauer and Ursula Magen, AOAT 220 (Neukirchen-Vluyn: Neukirchener Verlag, 1988), 289–90.

9. Cf. Jonathan Stökl, *Prophecy in the Ancient Near East: A Philological and Sociological Comparison*, CHANE 56 (Leiden: Brill, 2012); Stefan M. Maul, *Wahrsagekunst im Alten Orient: Zeichen des Himmels und der Erde* (Munich: Beck, 2013); Martti Nissinen, *Ancient Prophecy: Near Eastern, Biblical, and Greek Perspectives* (Oxford: Oxford University Press, 2018).

applies to other kinds of texts is especially true for the prophetic books: they are quite careful to distinguish between the word of the prophet and the word of God. The accusation is generally presented as the word of the prophet, the proclamation of the word of God.

THE PROPHETIC ORACLE OF JUDGMENT This can be illustrated by means of an example. Jer 22:13–19 presents an oracle against King Jehoiakim. In the indictment section (vv. 13–17), Jeremiah accuses him of wrongfully constructing magnificent buildings while neglecting justice and righteousness:

> Woe to him who does not build his house on righteousness and his upper rooms not on justice, who allows his neighbor to work without pay and does not give him his wage! He says, "I want to build a spacious house and airy upper rooms!" . . . But your eyes and your hearts are directed toward nothing more than your profit and to the shedding of innocent blood, and to oppression and blackmail.

The accusation of the prophet is followed by a harsh word of judgment that is expressly introduced as divine speech (v. 18) and announces to the king that he will forego a regular burial; instead his corpse will be thrown before the gate of Jerusalem (v. 19):

> Therefore, thus says Yhwh concerning Jehoiakim, the son of Josiah, the king of Judah: "One will not mourn over him, 'oh my brother!' And, 'oh sister!' One will not mourn over him, 'Oh, Lord!' and, 'Oh, his majesty!' As a donkey is buried will he be buried, dragged away and thrown far outside of the gates of Jerusalem.

This introduction of the proclamation of judgment as the word of God clarifies a duality. On the one hand, it becomes recognizable that the Hebrew Bible is not to be interpreted as a supernatural sword of Damocles that comes down from heaven here and there, but rather as an interaction of prophetic analysis and imagination and the received word of God, relating one to the other as cause and effect. On the other hand, an astonishing self-demotion is recognizable for the prophetic figure, who does not claim divine authority for himself from the outset in every case. Especially characteristic in this regard are texts like Jer 1:4–10 or Amos 7–9, which demonstrate the prophets' resistance to the imposition of the divine word upon them. These texts concern literary presentations, but their programmatic nature is clearly recognizable. The proclamations of Jeremiah or Amos do not spring from their own wills.

TRUE AND FALSE PROPHECY A further foundational feature of the prophecy of the Hebrew Bible can be described in Jer 22:13–19, which is the logic of their long-term transmission, which itself can be observed in cases of unfulfilled prophetic oracles. As chance would have it, for Jer 22:13–19 one can be almost certain that this prophecy was not fulfilled. This is revealed from 2 Kgs 24:6:

> And Jehoiakim lay with his ancestors, and Jehoiachin, his son, became king in his place.

The expression "lay with his ancestors" is the technical term in Kings for burial in the royal tomb, and there is no reason to doubt the historicity of 2 Kings at this point. The perspective of its own content is very critical with regard to the monarchy, and if Jehoiakim truly did come to the end that Jeremiah proclaimed for him, then 2 Kings would not have avoided a report of this event that accorded with the prophetic proclamation.

Apparently, however, it knows nothing of such an event. Jehoiakim was buried, one can therefore surmise, as per the custom in the tomb of the Judahite kings, and Jeremiah's proclamation was not fulfilled.

Yet this means, on the flip side, that it appears very likely that the proclamation that he will not be buried in Jer 22:18–19 is "real," that is, announced before the related event and also written down prior to it. There is no reason why the tradents of the book of Jeremiah should have put a demonstrably false proclamation into the mouth of the protagonist after whom their book is named *after the fact*.[10]

This raises the question of why the tradents would have preserved and passed on a false prophecy like Jer 22:18–19. The fact should first simply be established *that* this took place. This prophetic oracle received and maintained its place in the book of Jeremiah; it was not sorted out. The answer can probably be found in the fact that the tradents found the substance of the prophetic word—the charge against the king not to oppress

---

10. Flavius Josephus was unable to accept this. In his *Jewish Antiquities*, Jehoiakim's corpse is actually thrown from the gates of Jerusalem in accord with Jeremiah's word (10.6.3), which amounts to an *eventum ex vaticinio*.

his subordinates and instead to concern himself with justice and righteousness—more important than the arrival of the connected proclamation of judgment against the king. This consideration is quite significant for the assessment of prophecy in terms of the history of reception. The prophecies of the Hebrew Bible were quite openly more and different than mere guesswork about the future. The substance of certain prophetic oracles could even trump the accuracy of the foretelling, which this example shows with sufficient clarity.

The fact that exegesis is able to discern the authenticity or inauthenticity, primarily with false predictions, does not mean that the prophets only uttered false prophecies. It only means that one can be somewhat certain that one is dealing with pronouncements truly related to the future by verifiable false prophecies that did not come to pass. However, one cannot discern whether there were predictions that did actually come to pass. With these it is considerably more difficult to verify with sufficient certainty.

THE FULFILLMENT OF THE PROPHECY OF AMOS However, there are cases that one can show with some probability to have been true prophetic predictions that then actually were fulfilled. One example appears in the book of the prophet Amos. It begins in Amos 1:1:

> The words of Amos—he was among the sheep breeders from Tekoa—what he saw concerning Israel in the days of Uzziah, the king of Judah, and in the days of Jeroboam, the son of Joash, the king of Israel, two years before the earthquake.

This superscription was quite manifestly expanded over the course of the ongoing development of the book of Amos.[11] This emerges first and foremost from the fact that it contradicts itself, which leads to the conclusion that there was literary growth. The superscription of the book of Amos dates Amos's words, on the one hand, by specifying a duration ("in the days of Uzziah, the king of Judah, and in the days of Jeroboam, the son of Joash, the king of Israel"), and on the other hand with a punctiliar date ("two years before the earthquake"). The two do not fit together. If Amos's words really only belong in one particular year, then it would be expected

---

11. Cf. Jörg Jeremias, "Zwei Jahre vor dem Erdbeben," in *Hosea und Amos: Studien zu den Anfängen des Dodekapropheten*, FAT 13 (Tübingen: Mohr Siebeck, 1996), 183–97.

to identify this year with the royal chronology (e.g., in the fifteenth year of Uzziah, the king of Judah).

This is not the case. One can instead reckon that "two years before the earthquake" was the original date of a first edition of the words of Amos that related to this event.

For the earthquake motif appears prominently in the proclamation of the book of Amos:

See, I will make it *quake* under you like a cart *quakes*, one full of grain. (2:13)

I will strike the capital so that the thresholds *quake*! All your life ends with *quaking*. And those who remain from you, I will kill with the sword. None of them will escape, and none of them will save themselves! (9:1)[12]

The date of the oldest edition of the book of Amos, "two years before the earthquake," would make the most sense historically if one can assume that the early tradents of the prophecy of Amos understood this earthquake as an early verification of the proclamation of the prophet Amos. This conjecture only gains traction if this proclamation—of the earthquake motif—took place before this event. The earthquake itself is sufficiently secure in historical terms, both archaeologically and geologically, and also through its multiple attestations outside the book of Amos, in Zechariah (cf. Zech 14:5) and even still in Flavius Josephus (*Ant.* 9.10.4). It can be dated around 760 BCE.

One can also assume that the prophecy of Amos announced or at least contained the motif of an earthquake *before the fact* so that a corresponding event delivered the verification for this first prophetic book and then also played a central role in influencing subsequent prophets, who in part made reference to the prophecy of Amos and understood their own words

12. On the translation, cf. Jörg Jeremias, *Der Prophet Amos*, ATD 24/2 (Göttingen: Vandenhoeck & Ruprecht, 1995), 122. The date of Amos 9:1, however, is debated; cf. Jörg Jeremias, "Das unzugängliche Heiligtum: Zur letzten Vision des Amos (Am 9,1–4)," in *Konsequente Traditionsgeschichte: Festschrift für Klaus Baltzer zum 65. Geburtstag*, ed. Rüdiger Bartelmus et al., OBO 126 (Freiburg: Universitätsverlag; Göttingen: Vandenhoeck & Ruprecht, 1993), 155–67; Uwe Becker, "Der Prophet als Fürbitter: Zum literarhistorischen Ort der Amos-Visionen," *VT* 51 (2001): 141–65; Peter Riede, *Vom Erbarmen zum Gericht: Die Visionen des Amosbuches (Am 7–9*) und ihr literatur- und traditionsgeschichtlicher Zusammenhang*, WMANT 120 (Neukirchen-Vluyn: Neukirchener Verlag, 2008), 169–282.

as the extension of his prophecy (cf. esp. Isa 9:7). The beginnings of the prophecy of Isaiah refer to the prophecy of Amos from the outset and were interpreted as its continuation.

ALIGNMENT OF THE PROPHETIC BOOKS WITH ONE ANOTHER The interdependency of the prophetic books is recognizable from the fact that the prophetic books of the Hebrew Bible contain superscriptions—and, to be sure, to a certain extent comparable superscriptions, which is noteworthy. The superscriptions of the prophetic books generally consist of the name and the lineage of the relevant figure as well as information about a date for when this figure was active in the history of Israel. While not explicitly stated, this system of summarizing characterization of the subsequent oracles as the message of a specific prophet at a specific time clearly serves an overarching theology of history that shows that the word of Yhwh came at various times to various prophets and is accessible for study in the form documented in their books. It should be emphasized, however, that the books of the prophets apparently are neither shaped nor supplemented in such a way that they clearly and explicitly formulated the perceptible and reconstructable will of Yhwh *as such* behind the individual prophetic oracles. Rather, they understand themselves (and were also understood in their inner-biblical reception) in such a way that the prophetic material was always the object of necessary further exegesis and application, rather than simply offering this on its own.

PROPHETIC CRITIC ON PROPHECY The book of Jonah presents a peculiarity within the framework of the prophetic literature. It is not only idiosyncratic in form-critical terms in that as a whole it presents a prophetic narrative in which it also underlines God's freedom in contrast to its utilization of prophecy: Although prophets like Jonah are messengers of God, God is not, however, a slave to his expressed will. He can also change its sense—even if this does not please the prophet.[13]

4. Hymns, Laments, and Songs of Thanksgiving

Perhaps the most surprising genres for speaking about God in the framework of the literature of the Hebrew Bible come in the hymns, laments,

---

13. For more on Jonah, cf. Walter Bührer, "Der Gott Jonas und der Gott des Himmels: Untersuchungen zur Theologie des Jona-Buches," *BN* 167 (2015): 65–78.

and thanksgiving songs in the Psalter. Its Hebrew name is תהלים (*thlym*), which can be translated "praise songs." The Hebrew term תהלים (*thlym*) is morphologically a masculine plural, even though the singular תהלה (*thlh*) is feminine, so the regular plural form should be תהלות (*thlwt*). Apparently the ungrammatical form of the plural points out that these "praise songs" concern songs of a particular nature. The biblical Psalter contains genres other than praise songs, such as laments and songs of thanksgiving, but it is still indicative that the designation that became established in the Hebrew tradition and whose content came to the center—*pars pro toto*—was the praise of God.

PRAYERS AND SONGS AS A PART OF THE CANON   The sheer existence of the Psalter in the Bible is theologically and also literarily conspicuous. While most other biblical books claim to contain or witness to the words or deeds of God, the Psalms are explicitly formulated as human words, as songs and prayers directed toward God.[14] In the Psalms a literary genre entered the biblical canon that stands at a certain distance from the rest of the Bible. At the same time, they belong to the most beloved and most used texts of the Jewish and the Christian Bible, which can be recognized, for example, in the partial editions of the Christian Bible that contain just the New Testament and the Psalms. The Psalter became part of the canon of the Bible as a result of the conviction that one can speak of God in a legitimate and appropriate manner not only in revelatory writings, but also in the witness of songs and prayers that people have used in turning to God in various life circumstances.

VARIOUS EXPERIENTIAL BACKGROUNDS   It is paramount for the theological significance of the Psalms to see that they do not always arise from an analogous, but can also arise from a counterfactual background. The thanksgiving and praise songs of the Psalms in no way emerged solely from situations of thanksgiving and praise; nor were they only prayed, spoken, or read in such situations. These texts instead could have been written in and for times of distress, in which the thanksgiving rather then the lament appeared in the religious forefront for the one praying.

---

14. Isolated words of God also appear in the Psalms; cf. on them Klaus Koenen, *Gottesworte in den Psalmen: Eine formgeschichtliche Untersuchung*, Biblisch-theologische Studien 30 (Neukirchen-Vluyn: Neukirchener Verlag, 1996).

5. Wisdom Forms

As with the Psalms, it can be noted in the first place that the wisdom literature is not self-evidently worthy of consideration as a genre of theology of the Hebrew Bible. Of course, there are wisdom texts that speak extensively and explicitly of God, such as Prov 1–9, the book of Job, and also Qoheleth. However, the Hebrew Bible clearly understood traditional wisdom texts without an explicitly theological dimension as theologically relevant. This appears in the earlier proverbial wisdom, such as that attested in Prov 10–22, which gets along largely without mention of God, though this does not mean that it was simply "profane." Within the framework of ancient Near Eastern thought, this category makes no sense. The conception of order looming in the background of wisdom literature is—whether explicitly mentioning God or not—of a theological nature and can be seen as an implicit reason for the wisdom literature's placement in the Bible.

EXPERIENTIAL KNOWLEDGE The wisdom of Proverbs primarily condenses practical experiential life knowledge into compressed literary forms. This experiential knowledge often turns on the so-called act-consequence connection, which concerns human action and its consequences in sometimes complex ways. This connection can be brought into connection with God directly, indirectly, or not at all. In every case it is, however, the description and the concern of the social mechanism of human communal life that is viewed as theologically relevant within the framework of the biblical canon. The recognition or at least premonition of God does not appear separate from human experiential knowledge.

WISDOM SUBSTRUCTURE There is a further point as well. Many texts of the Hebrew Bible that do not belong to wisdom literature in a narrower sense still contain a wisdom substructure. One can interpret this substructure as a framework for theological reflection that confers an especially deep dimension to the texts. The wisdom imprint as such is explained by the fact that wisdom's traditional question about the order of the world provides appropriate intellectual access for the move into such a theological depth structure. Of course, this does not rest on conscious decisions by the biblical authors; it instead belongs to wisdom literature on the inventory of their foundational reflections.

MULTI-PERSPECTIVAL PERCEPTION OF THE WORLD A special feature of the wisdom interpretation of reality is the appreciation and recognition of a multi-perspectival perception of the world. An especially incisive example appears in Prov 26:4–5:

> Do not answer the fool according to his folly so that you do not
> become like him.
> Answer the fool according to his folly so that he will not consider
> himself wise.

The parataxis of two contradictory proverbs on how to answer a fool shows that wisdom thinking accounts for the ambivalence of reality in a foundational way. One cannot answer the fool correctly. Instead, his constitution is such that clear advice on relating to him cannot be given.[15]

6. Commentaries and Literary Continuations

While the genres of Hebrew Bible theology discussed up to this point took their orientation from form criticism and content, in conclusion one should be alerted to a formal characteristic that shaped the literature of the Hebrew Bible to a considerable extent. The Hebrew Bible is literature of ongoing supplementations (*Fortschreibungen*). Long stretches consist of text and commentary in one.

THE HEBREW BIBLE AS SCRIBAL TRADITIONS LITERATURE This fact is of fundamental theological importance, for it results from the consciousness that a text must change with the times if it hopes to preserve its meaning. It requires actualizing interpretation in order to speak into future times as well. This is the substantial reason why most biblical books have various literary layers that result primarily from the necessity of their scribal tradents not only to maintain the traditional texts themselves, but also their meaning, which was impossible without the work of literary supplementation. Therefore, the texts of the Hebrew Bible are characterized

---

15. Within the framework of the Greek translation the following disambiguation appears: before Prov 26:5 is an additional ἀλλά (*allà*), "instead," such that Prov 26:4 presents the rebuffing and Prov 26:5 the recommended answer. However, this is clearly the result of smoothing out the content.

as traditional literature that has incorporated its early commentaries into its own texts.

JEREMIAH 36   This circumstance is known within the Bible itself and is also explicitly discussed. A particularly clear example appears in the narrative of Jer 36, which reports on the production of a second scroll with the words of Jeremiah, after King Jehoiakim burned the first scroll:

> And Jeremiah took another scroll and gave it to Baruch, the son of Neriah, the scribe. And according to Jeremiah's dictation, he wrote down all the words of the writing that Jehoiakim, the king of Judah, had burned in the fire, *and many similar words were added to them* (נוֹסְפוּ, *nwsp*). (Jer 36:32)

The passive formulation נוֹסְפוּ (*nwsp*) does not exclude the possibility that these "similar words" originated from Jeremiah, but it also clearly opens up the horizon for the possibility of post-Jeremian literary supplementations. Therefore, one can read in the book of Jeremiah that these do not come from Jeremiah alone, but also to a large degree were added later.

Not only the book of Jeremiah, but the Bible as a whole looks back on a long history both of formation and reception in which the phases of the formation and reception history surprisingly—as scholarship in the last decade has clearly shown—overlap. This is the case to such a degree that it is almost possible that one can understand the formation history of the Bible as a part of its reception history. As soon as the first preliminary stages of a biblical text were present, they were then taken up, and in fact adopted in a literarily productive manner such that these first commentaries themselves became part of the biblical canon.

FIRST TRANSCRIPTION AS A PROCESS OF INTERPRETATION   Yet more radical is the reception-historical imprint in the formation history of biblical texts that are categorized as textual material going back to oral precursors. While scholars no longer view the preexistence and the extent of possible oral precursors of the Bible with the same importance as was the case in the nineteenth and the beginning of the twentieth centuries, there remain a considerable number of prophetic oracles, wisdom proverbs, psalms, and also narratives for which one reckons with oral stages. Even the procedure of the first transcription of such oral traditional material is a reception-historical process with a considerable amount of interpretation in which significant theological shaping can take place.

THE RECOGNITION AND EVALUATION OF THE DIACHRONIC DIFFERENTI-
ATION OF THE BIBLICAL TEXTS The appreciation of the Bible as interpre-
tive literature is unquestionably taken as a presupposition for historical criticism of the Bible. Without diachronic access to the Bible, it is hardly possible to differentiate between the text and commentary in it. It can also be seen that the books of Chronicles offer a new edition of the large narrative complex of Genesis–2 Kings—in English-speaking scholarship one terms this kind of literature "rewritten Bible."[16] Furthermore, Dan 9 interprets the book of Jeremiah, but this only renders visible the most miniscule fraction of the inner-biblical commentary activities, for these are written into the text in such a way that they are not initially differentiated and can only be recognized with difficulty.

While the recognition of this characteristic of the Bible is as old as his-
torical criticism of the Bible itself, it was originally understood especially in terms of theology as a necessity rather than a virtue. Where additions and commentaries were recognized, scholars attempted to purify the original text from them in order to present the text in its original beauty. This theological evaluative approach to the secondary sections has largely been overcome in present scholarly discussion. This change goes back to the beginnings of the redaction-historical investigation in the 1960s. It no longer exclusively sought the supposed original layers of biblical texts, but also the different accents and lines of assertions in the literary but still inner-
biblical post-history. The "supplementers" are not bumbling glossators, but scribal redactors who reinterpreted the traditions before them in light of their own experience in the mode of literarily productive supplementation. Biblical studies of the past decade has succeeded in demonstrating that these supplementations do not indicate a reduction of the quality of the underlying source text. They instead offer an interpretive and theological density that presents the conditions of the possibility for the Bible to impose itself as an authoritative text for its interpretive communities.

From this arises a fundamentally changed perception of the literary history of the Hebrew Bible in the Persian and Hellenistic epochs. No lon-

16. Cf. Antti Laato and Jacques van Ruiten, eds., *Rewritten Bible Reconsidered: Proceed-
ings of the Conference in Karkku, Finland, August 24–26, 2006*, Studies in Rewritten Bible 1 (Turku: Åbo Akademi University, 2008).

ger viewed merely as epigonal, they rise to the position of the authoritative periods of the formation of the Hebrew Bible. The dichotomic perception of the time of the Hebrew Bible in terms of Hebraic (before the exile) and Jewish (after the exile), which shaped the scholarship of the nineteenth and early twentieth century and is still occasionally reproduced today, is neither historically nor theologically justified. It has instead become clear that the Hebrew Bible is in large part a product of the intellectual efforts of postexilic Judaism. Even if considerable portions of text go back to the monarchic period, no book of the Hebrew Bible is found in anything other than its postexilic form. Ancient Hebrew literature can only be received through the interpretive appropriation of Judaism for later epochs; otherwise it would have fallen into oblivion.

§30 Perceptions and Impressions of God

Reinhard Feldmeier and Hermann Spieckermann, *God of the Living: A Biblical Theology,* trans. Mark E. Biddle (Waco: Baylor University Press, 2011) ♦ Friedhelm Hartenstein, "Die Theologie der Gefühle JHWHs: Zu den Anthropopathismen alttestamentlicher Gottesbilder," in *Theologie der Gefühle,* ed. Roderich Barth and Christopher Zarnow (Berlin: de Gruyter, 2015), 225–38 ♦ Friedhelm Hartenstein and Michael Moxter, *Hermeneutik des Bilderverbots: Exegetische und systematische Annäherungen,* Forum Theologische Literaturzeitung 26 (Leipzig: Evangelische Verlagsanstalt, 2016) ♦ Bernd Janowski, "JHWH und der Sonnengott: Aspekte der Solarisierung JHWHs in vorexilischer Zeit," in *Pluralismus und Identität,* ed. Joachim Mehlhausen (Gütersloh: Gütersloher Verlagshaus, 1995), 214–41 ♦ Othmar Keel, *Die Geschichte Jerusalems und die Entstehung des Monotheismus,* 2 vols., Orte und Landschaften der Bibel 4,1 (Göttingen: Vandenhoeck & Ruprecht, 2007) ♦ Klaus Koch, "Monotheismus und Angelologie," in *Ein Gott allein? Jahweverehrung und biblischer Monotheismus im Kontext der israelitischen und altorientalischen Religionsgeschichte,* ed. Walter Dietrich and Martin A. Klopfenstein, OBO 139 (Freiburg: Universitätsverlag; Göttingen: Vandenhoeck & Ruprecht, 1994), 565–81 ♦ Matthias Köckert, "Vom Kultbild Jahwes zum Bilderverbot: Oder: Vom Nutzen der Religionsgeschichte für die Theologie," *ZTK* 106 (2009): 371–406 ♦ Martin Leuenberger, *Gott in Bewegung,* FAT 76 (Tübingen: Mohr Siebeck, 2011) ♦ Jürgen van Oorschot, ed., "Anfänge und Ursprünge der Jahwe-Verehrung," *BTZ* 30 (2013) ♦ Jürgen van Oorschot and Markus Witte, eds., *The Origins of Yahwism,* BZAW 484 (Berlin: de Gruyter, 2017) ♦ Sven Petry, *Die*

Entgrenzung JHWHs: Monolatrie, Bilderverbot und Monotheismus im Deuter-onomium, in Deuterojesaja und im Ezechielbuch, FAT II/27 (Tübingen: Mohr Siebeck, 2007) ◆ Thomas Römer, *The Invention of God* (Cambridge: Cambridge University Press, 2015) ◆ Karel van der Toorn, ed., *The Image and the Book: Iconic Cults, Aniconism, and the Rise of Book Religion in Israel and the Ancient Near East*, CBET 21 (Leuven: Peeters, 1997) ◆ Christoph Uehlinger, "Vom Bilderkult zum Bilderverbot: Zeugnisse und Etappen eines Bruchs," *Welt und Umwelt der Bibel* 11 (1999): 44–53 ◆ Erich Zenger, "Der Monotheismus Israels: Entstehung—Profil—Relevanz," in *Ist der Glaube Feind der Freiheit? Die neue Debatte um den Monotheismus*, ed. Thomas Söding, QD 196 (Freiburg im Breisgau: Herder, 2003), 9–52

NO DOCTRINE OF GOD IN THE HEBREW BIBLE There is no question that a reconstruction and analysis of the Hebrew Bible's discussion of God belongs to the most important tasks of a theology of the Hebrew Bible. However, how can this be adequately achieved? It should initially be grasped that the Hebrew Bible reveals only the very limited beginnings of the development of a "doctrine of God." One can find such beginnings in certain hymnic predications or in, for example, the blessing formula (e.g., Exod 34:6–7),[17] but these are shaped by liturgical rather than didactic interests. On the contrary, God is spoken of primarily in view of his perceptions[18] and actions. Not who or what God is, but how he is recognized and described as an actor with regard to the world, his people, and individual humans is the focus of speech about God in the Hebrew Bible.[19]

---

17. Cf. Hermann Spieckermann, "'Barmherzig und gnädig ist der Herr . . . ,'" in *Gottes Liebe zu Israel: Studien zur Theologie des Alten Testaments,* FAT 33 (Tübingen: Mohr Siebeck, 2001), 3–19; Ruth Scoralick, *Gottes Güte und Gottes Zorn: Die Gottesprä-dikationen in Exodus 34,6f und ihre intertextuellen Beziehungen zum Zwölfprophetenbuch,* Herders Biblische Studien 33 (Freiburg im Breisgau: Herder, 2002); Matthias Franz, *Der barmherzige und gnädige Gott: Die Gnadenrede vom Sinai (Exodus 34,6–7) und ihre Parallelen im Alten Testament und seiner Umwelt,* BWANT 160 (Stuttgart: Kohlhammer, 2003).

18. The term comes borrowed from Odil H. Steck, *Wahrnehmungen Gottes im Alten Testament: Gesammelte Studien,* TB 70 (Munich: Kaiser, 1982).

19. This fundamental biblical perspective is also emphasized by the Reformation, with something of a Christological turn by Melanchthon: *"Hoc est Christum cognoscere beneficia eius cognoscere* [To know Christ is to know his benefits]." *Loci communes,* 1521, 65. It is also an indispensable element of current systematic-theological approaches to the doctrine of God.

GOD HAS A HISTORY Therefore, it is of significant importance that, on the one hand, God has a history—more precisely, the biblical presentations of God have a history—and on the other hand, the Hebrew Bible also preserves and correspondingly presents this history to a certain degree. Such texts as Deut 32:8–9 and Ps 82 still reveal memories of polytheistic convictions, even if these texts were not necessarily formed within a polytheistic referential system.[20] While the first commandment of the Decalogue demands exclusive worship of Yhwh, it does not deny the existence of other gods. This is instead presupposed, for otherwise the commandment would be unnecessary. Finally, the narrative style of the Primeval History in Gen 1–9 should be referenced, for it traces a "history of development" for God, which, as such, would hardly be conceivable without the memory of corresponding changes in the religious-historical conception of God that the Primeval History basically, in conceptual terms, also traces. Genesis 1–9 establishes the ultimate salvific will of God with regard to his creation that is not dependent on the behavior of humanity.

Therefore, the following discussion considers the religious-historical development of the idea of God in ancient Israel and Judah that underlies the explanations in the literature of the Hebrew Bible. The theological explanations of the Bible are to be evaluated in light of their proximity and distance to the religious-historical evidence.

IMAGES OF GOD AND THE PROHIBITION AGAINST IMAGES One peculiarity of the biblical notion of God is its lack of an image, as primarily expressed in the so-called prohibition of images in the Decalogue (Exod 20:4–5; Deut 5:8–9). The fact that God cannot be represented by a cultic image forms an exception within the religious history of antiquity that often provoked astonishment, admiration, as well as rejection from ancient cultures. When the Roman general Pompey conquered Judea in 63 BCE, his curiosity about the invisible God of Judaism drove him into the Holy of Holies, much to the dismay of the Jews. Does this mean that according to the Bible one cannot make an image of God? This conclusion is to be relativized in two respects. First, the prohibition of images in the Decalogue only concerns cultic images of the divine and does not have a

---

20. Cf. Konrad Schmid, "Gibt es 'Reste hebräischen Heidentums' im Alten Testament? Methodische Überlegungen anhand von Dtn 32,8f und Ps 82," in *Primäre und sekundäre Religion als Kategorie der Religionsgeschichte des Alten Testaments*, ed. Andreas Wagner, BZAW 364 (Berlin: de Gruyter, 2006), 105–20.

prohibition of art in mind at all. Indeed, the prohibition of images does not at all have figures of speech or thought of God in mind; the Hebrew Bible itself develops them comprehensively. Second, attention to the religious-historical evidence indicates that the lack of images in Judaism is the result of a religious-historical development. Rather than the cultivation of religious-historical bedrock, an ancient cult of images in Israel led to the lack of images. It is undisputable that there were images of God in ancient Israel and Judah in the monarchic period.[21] Numerous seal impressions and so-called pillar figurines attest to the goddess Asherah. Inscriptions from the ninth and eighth centuries BCE name her as consort to Yhwh. A terracotta figurine from the Judean highlands from the eighth century BCE may be interpreted as a depiction of Yhwh and his Asherah.[22] The tradition of the bull images in Bethel and Dan allows for the conclusion that Yhwh could also be conceived in the form of a bull (the identification of these steer images as "calves" [עֲגָלִים, 'glym] in 1 Kgs 12:28 [cf. Exod 32:4] rests on their pejorative rejection in the Bible). An Assyrian inscription of Sargon II presupposes that there were also cultic images in the sanctuary of Samaria: "I [Sargon II] counted as spoil 27,280 people, together with their chariots, and gods, in which they trusted."[23] For Judah, mention should first and foremost be made of the sanctuary in Arad, from whose holy of holies it can be recognized that Yhwh, possibly with his Asherah, was worshiped in the form of a maṣṣēbâ. The solarization of the conception of God, especially in Jerusalem (see below, §30.5) led to increased abstraction of the perception of God. A conception as completely unworldly, and therefore also not as an "image of anything that is above in heaven, below on the earth or in the water under the earth" (Exod 20:4), is first imaginable for the biblical God in and after the period of the Babylonian exile. Monotheism then asserted the strict separation between God and world (see below, §30.1), and the image prohibition followed logically. The ban on cult images presupposes, however, that what cannot be represented by an object can be described with language, to the degree that the literary universe of the Hebrew Bible with its manifold approximations of God is an appropriate expression of the prohibition on images.

21. Cf. Othmar Keel and Christoph Uehlinger, *Gods, Goddesses, and the Images of God in Ancient Israel* (Edinburgh: T&T Clark, 2008).

22. Cf. Christoph Uehlinger, "Ein Bild JHWHs und seiner Aschera? Nein! Vielleicht!," *Welt und Umwelt der Bibel* 11 (1999): 50–51.

23. "Nimrud Prisms D & E," trans. K. Lawson Younger, Jr. (*COS* 2.118D:295–96).

THE RELIGION OF THE HEBREW BIBLE IS NOT DEISM Viewed as a whole, the preoccupation with conceptions of God in the Hebrew Bible should, however, basically be relativized. It should be taken into consideration that the religion attested and construed in the Hebrew Bible is not to be characterized as deism. It is essentially conceived "from below" and thematizes human experiences of God, not God himself. As such, it is appropriate to treat what the Hebrew Bible offers in connection with God in this chapter, not everything, but to follow a broad and thematically complex approach (cf. the subsequent §§31–40).

1. Preliminary Remarks from the History of Scholarship

The assessment of the historical development of the conception of God in the Hebrew Bible has changed radically in the course of the past one hundred years. One can follow this change especially in the intensively contested monotheism debate of the past thirty years. To a certain degree, it can be described as a return to certain basic convictions of the history-of-religions school at the beginning of the twentieth century, which is also observable in other areas of the reconstruction of the religious-historical developments in ancient Israel.

ASSESSMENT OF MONOTHEISM Exemplary might be a comparison of the "Monotheism and Polytheism" articles in the second,[24] third,[25] and fourth[26] editions of *Religion in Geschichte und Gegenwart* [Religion Past and Present]. In 1930 Haller still states that "M[onotheism] as a defined formulated doctrine of the nature of a single God . . . [is attested] first from the exile"[27] and came about incrementally in Israel's intellectual history. The article by Baumgärtel from the year 1960 reads like a counter manifesto: "M[onotheism] in OT religion is a necessary result of its basic understandings of God, which protrudes like an erratic block from the surrounding religions."[28]

24. Max Haller, "Monotheismus und Polytheismus II. Im AT," *RGG*, 2nd ed. (Tübingen: Mohr, 1930), 4:192–94.

25. Friedrich Baumgärtel, "Monotheismus und Polytheismus II. Im AT," *RGG*, 3rd ed. (Tübingen: Mohr, 1960), 4:1113–15.

26. Hans-Peter Müller, "Monotheismus und Polytheismus II. Im AT," *RGG*, 4th ed. (Tübingen: Mohr Siebeck, 2002), 5:1459–62.

27. Haller, "Monotheismus," 192.

28. Baumgärtel, "Monotheismus," 1113.

Israel's religion and its monotheism cannot be explained in evolutionary terms, but on the "founding" by Moses.[29] Then in 2002, Müller determined once again, "A reflective M[onotheism] first comes as an answer to the crisis of the exile."[30] However, he specifies the previous religious history with the terminology of a "privileged reciprocal relationship."[31]

It is clear that the change in the presentation of the monotheism topic from the second to the third and then to the fourth edition of *Religion in Geschichte und Gegenwart* is linked not only, but also, with corresponding changes in the history of theology in the twentieth century. The *Religion in Geschichte und Gegenwart* of the first and second editions was solidly in the hands of the so-called history of religions school, and it was originally conceived as their voice. The history of religions school, coalescing around scholars like Johannes Weiß, Wilhelm Bousset, and Hermann Gunkel, explained Judaism and Christianity in terms of the verifiable external influences of other religions, which became accessible through the large archaeological finds and discoveries of the nineteenth century.

THE INFLUENCE OF NEO-ORTHODOX THEOLOGY Yet the debate changed significantly at the beginning of the 1920s, and the rising neo-orthodox theology around Karl Barth pushed the history of religions school increasingly off the theological beaten track. After the Second World War, neo-orthodox theology was able to establish itself as the authoritative position in German-speaking Protestant theology, and this significantly influenced the exegetical disciplines of Old and New Testament studies.

The earlier dominant explanatory paradigm of the religious-historical derivation of biblical assertions almost completely disappeared. The singularity of biblical faith instead moved to the forefront. Old Testament scholars rediscovered the central basic distinction of neo-orthodox theology between natural theology and revelatory theology in the religious history of the ancient Near East. Israel's neighboring religions worship gods that were extrapolated from the natural processes of growing and flourishing, while Israel believed in the one God revealed in history and was different from its neighbors from the very beginning.

This conception of the discontinuity and the line of explanation that it opened up for the Bible and theology was so successful that scholarship of

29. Baumgärtel, "Monotheismus," 1114.
30. Müller, "Monotheismus," 1461.
31. Müller, "Monotheismus," 1460.

the Hebrew Bible occasionally even helped itself to what Gerhard Ebeling innocently described as a "leading position."[32] The perspectives on many individual questions of the literature, theology, and religious history of the Hebrew Bible were quite divergent in this period of scholarship as well, but with regard to fundamental assumptions there was a surprising consensus. In particular, in pentateuchal scholarship the Documentary Hypothesis and its related religious-historical implications enjoyed an acceptance that led scholars of the Hebrew Bible to believe that they now had the essential coordinates of its historical reconstruction before their eyes.

NEWER DEVELOPMENTS The religious historical image derived from and supported by the Documentary Hypothesis has, however, virtually been falsified today through newer composition-critical conclusions of Hebrew Bible exegesis—namely in the wake of the inaccurately named so-called crises of pentateuchal scholarship—in connection with the massive primary sources from ancient Israel made available by archaeology in the last decade. Recent religious-historical scholarship reckons that historical monarchic Israel thought within the normal orientation coordinates of an ancient Near Eastern "national" religion, and the biblical image of Israel essentially arose from later receptions and interpretations, chiefly from the epochs of Persian-period and Hellenistic Judaism.

2. *Archaic Memories of God: A God of Mountain and Storm*

The clarification of the religious-historical origins of a deity is inevitably a difficult undertaking, for such beginnings are hardly documented by sources. And when specific texts address these origins, then they in no way display interest in historical illumination. On the contrary, they generally deal with retrojections that attempt to anchor the developed forms of a certain religion in the mythic period of their beginnings. Within the framework of a theology of the Hebrew Bible, however, it is not the religious-historical origins of Yhwh themselves that are addressed,[33] but only their memory or construction in the biblical texts.

---

32. Gerhard Ebeling, *Studium der Theologie: Eine enzyklopädische Orientierung*, Uni-Taschenbücher 446 (Tübingen: Mohr, 1972), 26–27.

33. The earliest epigraphic attestations for *Yhwh* appear, on the one hand, in Egyptian texts from the Late Bronze Age (Soleb, Amara West), in which it is, however, unclear

Yʜᴡʜ ᴀs Wᴇᴀᴛʜᴇʀ ᴀɴᴅ Mᴏᴜɴᴛᴀɪɴ Dᴇɪᴛʏ First, it is notable that texts like Judg 5; Deut 33; Ps 68; and Hab 3 (whose antiquity is, however, debated)[34] articulate the origins of Yhwh as a weather and mountain deity and bring Yhwh into connection with Edom and the Edomite mountains of Seʻir:

> Yhwh, as you set forth from Seʻir, as you strode forth from the fields of Edom, the earth quaked, also striking the heavens, even striking the clouds of water. The mountains staggered before Yhwh—the one from Sinai, before Yhwh, the God of Israel. (Judg 5:4–5)

> Yhwh came from Sinai and flashed forth before them from Seʻir. He shined from the mountains of Paran and came from Meribat-Kadesh. (Deut 33:2)

> God, as you went before your people, as you marched through the desert—Selah—the earth quaked, the heaven struck before God, the one from Sinai, before God, the God of Israel. (Ps 68:8–9 [Eng. 68:7–8])

> God comes from Teman, and the Holy One from Mount Paran. Selah . . . (Hab 3:3)

---

whether they designate a tribe, a region, or a settlement. As the unequivocal name of a deity, Yhwh is attested—remarkably in the long form typically found in the Bible as Yhwh rather than Yh or Yhw, as one could speculate on the basis of the Egyptian evidence and the onomastica—in the Mesha Stela, as well as in the inscriptions from Kuntillet ʻAjrud, both from the ninth century BCE. Kuntillet ʻAjrud also attests to the expression "Yhwh and his Asherah," which could indicate that at that time Yhwh had a consort, who was, however—as shown by the suffix of the personal pronoun—subordinate to him. The "Asherah" is also known from the Hebrew Bible (cf., e.g., Deut 16:21), but there it is exclusively from the distorted perspective of its rejection in the circles and followers of Deuteronomistic theology. The gendered differentiation of God was abandoned in the course of ancient Israel's religious history, which does not, however, preclude the use of both male as well as female metaphors for God's actions in the literature of the Hebrew Bible (cf. Isa 66:13).

34. Cf. Henrik Pfeiffer, *Jahwes Kommen von Süden: Jdc 5; Hab 3; Dtn 33 und Ps 68 in ihrem literatur- und theologiegeschichtlichen Umfeld*, FRLANT 211 (Göttingen: Vandenhoeck & Ruprecht, 2005). On the other side, cf. Martin Leuenberger, "Jhwhs Herkunft aus dem Süden: Archäologische Befunde—biblische Überlieferungen—historische Korrelation," *ZAW* 122 (2010): 1–19; Martin Leuenberger, "Noch einmal: Jhwh aus dem Süden: Methodische und religionsgeschichtliche Überlegungen in der jüngsten Debatte," in *Geschichte und Gott: XV. Europäischer Kongress für Theologie (14.–18. September 2014 in Berlin)*, ed. Michael Meyer Blanck, Veröffentlichungen der Wissenschaftlichen Gesellschaft für Theologie 44 (Leipzig: Evangelische Verlagsanstalt, 2016), 267–87.

Why does the Hebrew Bible provide information about these strange and non-Israelite origins for the biblical God? It is noteworthy from a theological perspective that the Hebrew Bible does not veil such versions of the religious-historical dimensions of God but mentions them instead. The fact that God can be grasped historically seems to be unquestionable for the Bible. The Bible provides insights into the historically complex process of how one is to think of God.

YHWH'S ORIGIN IN THE SOUTH With the establishment of God's origin from the south, from the Edomite hill country, these texts agree with most current religious-historical reconstructions. For Deut 33:2 ("Yhwh came from Sinai and flashed forth before them from Se'ir") one can assume that the parallelism of "Sinai" and "Se'ir" presents a harmonizing interpretation to reconcile the tradition of the Torah ("Sinai") with the religious-historical memories ("Se'ir"). This same motivation could motivate the glosses in Judg 5:5 and Ps 68:9 (Eng. 68:8) of "the one from Sinai," which emphasize the biblically primary but historically secondary connection of Yhwh with Sinai.

THE THEOPHANY FROM SINAI The Sinai pericope of Exod 19–24 and 32–34 truly is much more prominent in the Bible than the individual statements from Judg 5; Deut 33; Ps 68; and Hab 3. They describe God's central revelation on Mount Sinai, presented in more detail below, §38.

Even if the extensively developed Sinai tradition is arguably primarily of a literary nature, it is still indicative that the way in which God shows himself on Sinai is analogous in content to the accounts of theophanies found in Judg 5; Deut 33; Ps 58; and Hab 3, which also employ explicit or implicit mountain imagery (Deut 33:2; Hab 3:3). Their literary antiquity is not necessarily decisive; they could also have preserved earlier motifs in later literary garb. It should be maintained, however, that the question of how God reveals himself is determined by certain religious-historical limits. His revelation is not conceived completely anew; God remains true to his origins in the ways he appears.[35]

---

35. Cf. also Konrad Schmid, "Gibt es 'Reste hebräischen Heidentums' im Alten Testament? Methodische Überlegungen anhand von Dtn 32,8f und Ps 82," in *Primäre und sekundäre Religion als Kategorie der Religionsgeschichte des Alten Testaments*, ed. Andreas Wagner, BZAW 364 (Berlin: de Gruyter, 2006), 105–20.

3. The Name of God

The biblical God bears the name "Yahweh," or, consonantally, יהוה (*yhwh*) "Yhwh," which—as the Greek translation of the Hebrew Bible, the Septuagint, as well as the scrolls from Qumran suggest—was no longer vocalized from the third or second century BCE:[36] The Septuagint consistently translates the so-called Tetragrammaton with κύριος (*kyrios*), "the Lord," while several scrolls from Qumran write the Tetragrammaton either with paleo-Hebrew script or by means of four points set off from the otherwise used square script, thereby excluding it from the reading complex.

THE PRONUNCIATION OF THE TETRAGRAMMATON The consonantal nature of the divine name is reliably transmitted as "Yhwh." Its vocalization is supported by remarks from several early Christian writers (Clement of Alexandria, Epiphanius of Salamos, Theodoret of Cyprus, Origen of Alexandria, Phoetius of Constantinople), who attest to a written rendition as Ιαουε (*Iaoue*) or Ιαβε (*Iabe*),[37] which can also be deduced from the wordplay in Exod 3:14 and Hos 1:9. The short form "Yah," found many times in the Psalter, cannot have been more original than the long form, as occasionally assumed in the past, because the oldest inscriptional evidence of the divine name from the ninth century BCE (Mesha Stela, Kuntillet 'Ajrud) already attests to the long form "Yhwh." Therefore, "Yah" is a poetic version of "Yhwh" that arose from it and not the other way around.

THE MEANING OF THE NAME YHWH What does the divine name mean? Especially in light of the biblical statement in Exod 3:14—אהיה אשר אהיה (*'hyh 'šr 'hyh*), "I am who I am," or, more precisely, "I will be who I will be," a theological-historical discourse spanning centuries has unfolded concerning the meaning of the divine name, fueled not in the least by the Greek translation of Exod 3:14 as ἐγώ εἰμι ὁ ὤν (*egō eimi ho ōn*) "I am the existent one." However, on the one hand, the importance of a name should be relativized. Proper names often have an eloquent etymology, but this may not be important for the actual bearer (not every "Friedrich" or "Irene" must be peace-

---

36. Cf. Kristin de Troyer, "The Pronunciation of the Names of God: With Some Notes Regarding *nomina sacra*," in *Gott nennen: Gottes Namen und Gott als Name*, ed. Ingolf U. Dalferth and Philipp Stoellger, Religion in Philosophy and Theology 35 (Tübingen: Mohr Siebeck, 2008), 143–72.

37. Cf. the evidence in Römer, *Invention*, 44.

ful). On the other hand, one might ask with regard to Exod 3:14 whether the statement "I will be who I will be" is even an answer to a question about the meaning of the divine name. The immediate context indicates rather that "I will be who I will be" refers to and affirms the declaration כי אהיה עמך (*ky 'hyh 'mk*), "Surely I will be with you," in Exod 3:12. In terms of philological history, the etymology of the Yhwh name remains unsettled to this day. To some extent certain is only that it has nothing to do with the Hebrew verb הוה (*hyh*), "to be," as suggested by Exod 14. If the divine name has something at all to do with a verbal (and not a nominal) form,[38] then it instead likely arises from the south Semitic *hwh*, "fell, blow," which contains a further indication of the religious-historical origins of Yhwh as a storm god.[39]

WHY DO DEITIES NEED NAMES? In any case, the fact that the biblical God bears a name is of fundamental importance both in religious-historical and in theological terms. A deity needs a name when he would otherwise not be identifiable. Therefore, it is customary in polytheistic systems for gods to bear names and to introduce themselves in revelations, "I am so-and-so." This so-called "self-presentation formula" also appears in many places in the Hebrew Bible (cf., e.g., Gen 28:13, or massed together in the book of Ezekiel). The fact that the biblical God is called "Yhwh" demonstrates, for starters, that it arises from a religious-historical context that was also familiar with other deities. However, it is theologically noteworthy that the memory of the name of God continued to be preserved when the polytheistic context of the biblical God was negated. Certain very prominent texts of the Hebrew Bible—preeminently Gen 1—that are marked by monotheism use the designation "God" like a name and therefore make clear that the class conception "God" can be used for the only member of this class, namely "God." Yet "Yhwh" remains in use. Therefore, the theological formation of tradition preserved and did not suppress the polytheistic framework of the origins of the biblical God. As a result, the history of God is part of his biblical identity.

THE CONCEPTION OF GOD IN THE PRIESTLY DOCUMENT The theological conception of the Priestly document (cf. above, §18 and §26) is especially noteworthy in this regard because it links the various salvation-historical

---

38. Cf. Josef Tropper, "Der Gottesname *YAHWA," *VT* 51 (2001): 81–106.
39. Cf. Ernst Axel Knauf, "Yahwe," *VT* 34 (1984): 467–72, as well as the discussion in Römer, *Invention*, 37–50.

epochs of its Primeval History, which spans from creation to Sinai, with the use of various divine names. God reveals himself to the world as אלהים ('lhym) "Elohim," to the Abrahamic circle as אל שדי ('l šdy) "El Shaddai," and to Israel as יהוה (yhwh) "Yhwh." God's identity is not dependent on his name, which instead can vary according to divergent functional contexts. The Priestly document is familiar with and assimilates the knowledge of the fact that God bears one (or more) names and synthesizes this knowledge into a narrative that traces and justifies God's development from the God of creation to the God of Israel.

4. The Israelization of Yhwh and the Yahwehization of Israel

YHWH AND ISRAEL DID NOT BELONG TOGETHER FROM THE START The religious-historical relationships concerning the origins of Yhwh are unavoidably opaque, but it is sufficiently clear that Yhwh was not the God of Israel from the very beginning, and that, on the flip side, Israel was not bound with Yhwh from its beginning. On the one hand, the geographical roots of Yhwh worship lie outside Israel in the region of the southern Edomite hill country. On the other hand, Israel is constructed with the theophoric element *-el* and not *-yah* or *-yahu*.

In other words, the biblically central and frequently attested association of Yhwh and Israel—Yhwh the God of Israel and Israel the people of Yhwh[40]—developed over time. How this relationship came to be is dependent on, among other things, how one assesses Israel's ethnogenesis.[41] Recent scholarship has discharged the traditional models of the conquest, immigration, and infiltration hypotheses that determined the discussion of the twentieth century. It today sees that the process described from the biblical perspective as "the settlement of Israel" was a complex process of the formation of a people in Canaan of whom large parts were probably of endogenous origins, such that no clear rupture can be recognized between the civilizations of "Canaan" and "Israel." The so-called four-room house and the collared rim jar have proven themselves unsuitable to provide ex-

---

40. Rolf Rendtorff, *Die "Bundesformel": Eine exegetisch-theologische Untersuchung*, SBS 160 (Stuttgart: Katholisches Bibelwerk, 1995); Rudolf Smend, "Die Bundesformel," in *Die Mitte des Alten Testaments: Exegetische Aufsätze* (Tübingen: Mohr Siebeck, 2002), 1–29.

41. Cf. Volkmar Fritz, *Die Entstehung Israels im 12. und 11. Jahrhundert v. Chr.*, Biblische Enzyklopädie 2 (Stuttgart: Kohlhammer, 1996).

ternal archaeological indices of Israel's provenance.[42] Even if this does not exclude that certain populations like Asiatics in the Nile Delta joined Israel (it is even probable), the formation of Israel in its own land was primarily a process that can be explained along with the decline of the Late Bronze Age city culture and the accompanying dissolution of the division of labor between nomads and city-dwellers, leading to new forms of settlements in the land, especially in the middle Palestinian and Judahite hill country. Climatic factors also may have played a role.[43]

EARLY EVIDENCE FOR "ISRAEL" The first epigraphic attestations for Israel appear, in the first case, in the Merenptah Stela from 1219 BCE, which, however, attests to nothing more than an ethnic group of the designation "Israel" located in Canaan. The second case is in the Mesha Stela (ca. 850 BCE), which in addition to the mention of Israel, also witnesses to Yhwh as the national God of Israel, that is the northern kingdom under Omri. Also worthy of mention are the attestations for "Yhwh of Samaria" and "Yhwh of Teman" at Kuntillet 'Ajrud (ninth century BCE).[44]

The relationship between Yhwh and Israel must have been established between the twelfth and ninth centuries BCE, though one might especially consider the times of Saul and David—without necessitating the historical verification of the biblical associations of an empire.[45]

The epigraphic evidence of the theophoric elements in proper names in the period of the monarchy presents an uneven picture. The Samaria Ostraca from the eighth century BCE attest to about fifty personal names, of which eleven contain the theophoric element *-yah*, six that of *ba'al*,[46] though it is possible that they refer to the same deity that could be identified

42. Cf. Israel Finkelstein and Amihai Mazar, *The Quest for the Historical Israel: Debating Archaeology and the History of Early Israel*, ABS 17 (Atlanta: SBL Press, 2007), 77-78.

43. Cf. Fritz, *Die Entstehung Israels.*

44. Cf. Johannes Renz, "Der Beitrag der althebräischen Epigraphik zur Exegese des Alten Testaments und zur Profan- und Religionsgeschichte Palästinas: Leistung und Grenzen, aufgezeigt am Beispiel der Inschriften des (ausgehenden) 7. Jahrhunderts vor Christus," in *Steine—Bilder—Texte: Historische Evidenz außerbiblischer und biblischer Quellen,* ed. Christof Hardmeier, Arbeiten zur Bibel und ihrer Geschichte 5 (Leipzig: Evangelische Verlagsanstalt, 2001), 123-58.

45. Cf. Michael Huber, *Gab es ein davidisch-salomonisches Großreich? Forschungsgeschichte und neuere Argumentationen aus der Sicht der Archäologie,* Stuttgarter Biblische Beiträge (Stuttgart: Katholisches Bibelwerk, 2010).

46. Othmar Keel and Christoph Uehlinger, *Gods, Goddesses, and the Images of God in Ancient Israel,* trans. Thomas H. Trapp (Minneapolis: Fortress, 1998), 205.

as Yhwh or as Baʿal. In addition are other observable theophoric elements, such as Bes and Horus, but these do not appear in significant numbers. One must, therefore, avoid the false conclusion that the dominance of the theophoric names with the element -*yah* points to the rise of "Yahwistic monotheism." Instead, within the framework of a national religion, it can only be expected that in Israel, for example, most theophoric personal names will include the element -*yah*, for Yhwh is the God of Israel.

From a theological point of view, the resulting and ultimately arbitrary relationship of Israel and Yhwh as its God is of importance in view of the universal provisions that the Hebrew Bible deals with. If Yhwh was not always the God of Israel, then he can also be something more and other than the God of Israel—he is the God of the entire world and representatives from the nations can also join his worshipers.[47]

5. Solar Interpretations of God

RIGHTEOUSNESS AND JUSTICE AS THE FUNCTION OF THE SUN GOD IN THE ANCIENT NEAR EAST One of the most important and sustained developments of the conception of God in ancient Israel concerns its solarization. It depends first and foremost on the religious history of the city of Jerusalem. Canaanite Jerusalem was—as even the name *Uru-Šalim* "city of dusk" reveals (*Šaḥar* and *Šalim* designate the dawn and dusk)—connected cultically with the sun deity. The sun god was entrusted with the task in the ancient Near East of guaranteeing righteousness and justice, as for example the Hammurabi Stela demonstrates. Hammurabi receives a ring and staff from the sun god Shamash, which are generally interpreted as divine authorizations of the royal legislator.

As the biblical God, whose roots are as a storm god, becomes solarized over the course of Judaic religious history, he moves into the sphere of a God who creates and guarantees justice. One can illustrate this solarized depiction in, for example, Zeph 3:5:

Yhwh is righteous in [Jerusalem's] midst, he commits no injustice.
Every morning he creates justice, by every light without fail;
But the sinner knows no shame.

47. Cf. Volker Haarmann, *JHWH-Verehrer der Völker: Die Hinwendung von Nichtisraeliten zum Gott Israels in alttestamentlichen Überlieferungen*, ATANT 91 (Zurich: TVZ, 2008).

God's creation of justice is an activity linked with the morning, the rising sun, and the daylight. The sun symbolizes the divine will for justice.

The traditional connection between the solar traditions of Jerusalem and the theme of righteousness is reflected in the conception of Jerusalem as עיר הצדק (*'yr hṣdq*), "the city of righteousness," as it is presented in Isa 1:21–22, 26 or Ps 48:11–12 (Eng. 48:10–11). The process of the solarization of God in this intellectualized form succeeded in remaining influential and efficacious over the centuries—even in a religious context that had long been defined as monotheistic.

ASTRAL INFLUENCES OF NEO-ASSYRIAN RELIGION The Neo-Assyrian religion was strongly defined by the astral cult, so the tendencies toward religious acculturation in Judah, especially in the seventh century BCE, easily strengthened the solar elements of the Yhwh religion.

The solarization of God was simultaneously an expression and also a vehicle for the universalization of God. A God represented by the sun can have the entire earth in view. At the same time, God's solar connotations catalyzed his rule-governed character. God is a reliable entity in the same way that one can rely on the daily rising and setting of the sun.

These religious-historical backgrounds are only available by means of the corresponding statements about God in the Bible, but the solar imagery has proven itself theologically profitable and has become part of the implicit theology of the Hebrew Bible.

6. Imperial Influences

Belonging to the unavoidable insights of the study of religion in the nineteen century is the fact that a religion's conception of God is dependent on the particular political circumstances of its circle of devotees, even if the religion—this should be maintained contrary the study of religion in the nineteenth century—is not fully explained by its political circumstances. Small-scale, locally organized societies are generally familiar with a belief in ancestors and spirits, while the notion of "big gods" first develops in socially complex political entities.[48] In monarchies people envision God as king, and the idea of a God ruling over everything presupposes the intellectual influence of empires.

---

48. Ara Norenzayan, *Big Gods: How Religion Transformed Cooperation and Conflict* (Princeton: Princeton University Press, 2013).

ANCIENT NEAR EASTERN EMPIRES The ancient Near Eastern empires exercised different degrees of cultural-historical influence on Israel. In the first millennium BCE, hegemony over the Levant changed from the Assyrians (ninth–seventh centuries BCE), to the Babylonians (seventh–sixth centuries BCE), to the Persians (sixth–fourth centuries BCE), and to the Greeks (fourth–second centuries BCE). One can generally observe that the decline in military subjugation, which still represented a central element for safeguarding imperial power in the Assyrian Empire, was accompanied by a culturalization of power, which safeguarded the existence of the empire through alternative means. As a result, the Hebrew Bible basically views Persian foreign hegemony in a much more positive light than Assyrian hegemony, not in the least because the culturalization of Persian power was essentially oriented toward pluralization and local autonomy than was intended *mutatis mutandis* by Assyrian propaganda.

SUBSTANTIAL CULTURAL CONTACTS One should not doubt the basic possibility also for geographically far-reaching cultural contacts in the ancient Near East given the widely dispersed finds. According to the evidence, the Babylonian Adapa myth is attested in Egyptian Amarna, the Atrahasis Epic was known in north-Syrian Ugarit, and the Gilgamesh Epic was read in northern Israelite Megiddo. An Aramaic version of the Iranian Bisitun Inscription is attested on the Nile island Elephantine. The cultural contacts within the ancient Near East were so close that Israel's central position and almost continuous political dependence on the empires of the time on the Euphrates and on the Nile (within the so-called Fertile Crescent) from the ninth century BCE onward make it not only possible, but more than probable that the common fundamental cultural and religious conceptions were known in Israel and were received, whether in a circumscribing or affirming manner.

With the beginning of Assyrian hegemony in the ancient Near East, which reached its first high point in the middle of the eighth century BCE and held on until the end of the seventh century before succumbing to the Neo-Babylonians, Israel and Judah came into the sphere of influence of an imperial power that exercised extraordinarily strong political, military, and increasingly religious and cultural pressure as well. The Assyrians can be reckoned as one of the first powers to aspire in a determined fashion to political, economic, and military control over the then-known ancient world.

New insights place the first formation of a certain degree of statehood for Israel and Judah in this same time (the eighth century BCE) such that, according to this point of view, Israel and Judah were under Assyrian influence from the beginning. One could even go a step further: presumably cultural-historical influence from Assur triggered the development into statehood for Israel and Judah, such that these can be understood as "secondary states." However, it was military pressure from Assur that then led to the demise of the northern kingdom of Israel after several decades for this still new state in 722 BCE. Yet this catastrophe was of considerable intellectual historical importance. Reflection on this event had a strong effect in various spheres of the formation of tradition. It was in the formation and delimitation of its own cultural and religious identity juxtaposed to the declining Assyrian and traditionally very heavy propagandistic power at the close of the seventh century BCE that these traditions condensed into the contemporary litera-ture of the southern kingdom of Judah. Decidedly anti-Assyrian conceptions form in this time, which transpose the attestations of loyalty demanded by the Assyrians to their own relationship with God. The book of Deuteronomy should especially be mentioned in this regard, for it can be interpreted as a subversive reception of the Neo-Assyrian vassal treaty form (cf. above, §14).

The imperial interpretation of God carried out by the book of Deuter-onomy is theologically ambivalent. The intellectual configuration of God in the garb of an ancient Near Eastern emperor is, on the one hand, the elementary root of religious zeal in the later history of Judaism, Christian-ity, and Israel, which repeatedly induced the adherents of these religions to carry out deeds that do not always withstand critical evaluation in uncon-ditional dependence on their God. At the same time, this imperial sketch of God fundamentally relativizes all earthly power. The true ruler of the world is God himself; all other rulers are only indirect potentates.

7. *Mono-Yahwistic and Monotheistic Transformations*

As already noted, the fact that the biblical God bears a name, Yhwh, points to the fact that he arises from a polytheistic context. However, the situation is more complex. In the 1980s, inscriptions came to light from a caravanserai in the southern Negev, Kuntillet 'Ajrud, that can be dated to the ninth century BCE and mention "Yhwh of Samaria" and—somewhat less certain epigraphically—"Yhwh of Teman."[49] These

49. Cf. Ze'ev Meshel, *Kuntillet 'Ajrud: An Iron Age II Religious Site on the Judah-Sinai Border* (Jerusalem: Israel Exploration Society, 2012).

attestations show that Yhwh was known in different manifestations. In addition to the Yhwh of Jerusalem, who was able to assert himself over other expressions in the course of the Josianic Reform, there was obviously (at least) a Yhwh from Samaria and a Yhwh from Teman. One can speak in this case of "poly-Yahwism," but this "poly-Yahwism" is quite similar to the Yhwh-Asherah problem, which can be interpreted as a tendency toward differentiation. The manifestations are different from the divine origins.

The inscriptions present a picture of the religion of monarchic Israel that is only accessible in mediated fashion in the Bible. The fact that Yhwh had an Asherah at his side can only be detected from its negation. When Deut 16:21 forbids: לא־תטע לך אשרה כל־עץ אצל מזבח יהוה אלהיך (lʾ tṭʿ lk ʾšrh kl ʿṣ ʾṣl mzbḥ yhwh ʾlhyk), "You shall not plant for yourself any Asherah from any kind of wood next to the altar of Yhwh your God," the implication is that this idea was basically accessible. 2 Kgs 21:7 appears to show that Manasseh also put this idea into practice.

The "poly-Yahwism" of the inscriptions has its negative counterpart in the claim of the unity of Yhwh in the Shema (Deut 6:4). There it states, "Hear Israel, Yhwh, your God, is one Yhwh." The Shema ties all of Yhwh's manifestations to the one Yhwh of Jerusalem. Or perhaps formulated more poignantly, the true Yhwh manifests himself in Jerusalem. Contrary to "poly-Yahwism," the Shema propagates a "mono-Yahwism," which likewise only appears in the Bible as the end point of an extensive religious-historical development.

MONOTHEISM Explicit monotheistic conceptions first appear in the literature of the Hebrew Bible in the Priestly document and Deutero-Isaiah. Recent scholarship has placed significant emphasis on the importance of the Priestly document. Within the framework of the classic source model for the Pentateuch, the die had already been cast with regard to the worship of the one God by the Solomonic "Yahwist." The structure of the singularity of Yhwh was already sketched out there, so the epigones were only able to add further delimitations and clarifications, and nothing more. The actual theologian was the "Yahwist," and he was already a monotheist. However, if the Priestly document is considered the first literary layer of the Pentateuch to carry out the central theological efforts of the Pentateuch, then these should not be located before the early Persian period. And in fact one does find in the Priestly document theological arguments that indicate that neither the unity nor the singularity of God that it presents was readily familiar to its audience at that time. This is seen most clearly from the Priestly call of Moses in Exod 6:3:

> I am Yhwh. I appeared to Abraham, Isaac, and Jacob as El Shaddai, but by my name Yhwh I did not make myself known to them.

The Priestly document in Exod 6:3 formulates a staggered theory of revelation in order to show that the god of the ancestors and the god of the exodus are actually one and the same. Yhwh revealed himself to the ancestors as El Shaddai. The Priestly document summarizes the given tradition of the various deities of the ancestors together under this name, but El Shaddai is none other than Yhwh himself, as the audience of the Priestly document, by the way, secretly previewed in Gen 17:1, the only attestation of Yhwh in the Priestly document before Exod 6.

The efforts toward synthesis by the Priestly document are quite plainly on the surface of the text in the theory of revelation of Exod 6:3 with regard to its conception of God. They also appear elsewhere as a deep structure in the text. Here are two examples:

(1) Within the framework of the Priestly document, the description of the increase of the people in Exod 1:7 calls forth associations to central statements from preceding "P" texts. Exodus 1:7 states:

> But the Israelites were fruitful and multiplied; they increased and became exceedingly strong, so that the land (אֶרֶץ, *'rṣ*) became full of them.

The formulation of the increase of the Israelites adopts, in the first place, the creation mandate by God in Gen 1:28 to "be fruitful and multiply and fill the earth (אֶרֶץ, *'rṣ*) . . . ," which after the flood is issued word-for-word to Noah and his sons: "Be fruitful and multiply and fill the earth." (Gen 9:1)

The multiplying of the Israelites in Exod 1 therefore appears as a partial resolution of the creation mandate given to the first human couple and repeated after the flood to the family of Noah. The fact that the Israelites multiplied in Egypt is a divinely willed process. It is a creational event without it being stated anywhere explicitly. Only the unusual coupling of the heavy oppression of the Israelites with their simultaneous multiplication leaves a trace of this direction on the surface of the text:

> But the more [the Egyptians] oppressed the people, the more they grew and multiplied, so that they dreaded the Israelites. (Exod 1:12)

The fact that the Israelites increased further in spite of Egyptian oppression and did not decrease as the Egyptians both intended and justifiably expected took place because of the providence of the God of creation.

In addition to "fruitfulness" and "multiplying," Exod 1:7 also describes the Israelites—as English Bibles generally translate—as "increasing greatly." The use of the root שרץ (šrṣ), "swarm," by Exod 1:7 has a carefully considered meaning here. It only appears in relation to humans one other time in the Hebrew Bible, and this is in the context immediately following Gen 9:1, where God again speaks to Noah and his sons:

> Now you shall be fruitful and multiply, increase exceedingly (שרץ, šrṣ) upon the earth . . . ! (Gen 9:7)

When the situation of Noah's family after the flood is compared with the seventy-member clan of Jacob who moved to Egypt, it can easily be recognized that in both cases the narrative flow demands a rapid population increase. The whole earth must be populated by Noah's band (Gen 10), and the small clan of Jacob must become a great and strong people in just a few verses. Here, too, it is clear from the textual background that the multiplication of the Israelites is an event that is guided by God just as much as the repopulation of the world after the flood.

There is also a further aspect. The emergence of the Israelites as a people is not only a creational event, but also the fulfillment of a promise. Exodus 1:7 states that the Israelites have become "exceedingly" (במאד מאד, bm'd m'd) strong. This expression of growth seems to be an empty phrase, but closer observation shows its exact meaning. Previously it appears only in the great promise to Abraham in Gen 17, where God speaks to Abraham:

> I am El Shaddai. Walk before me and be perfect. I will establish a covenant between me and you, and I will multiply you exceedingly (במאד מאד, bm'd m'd). (Gen 17:1–2)

It is, therefore, the creator God of the Primeval History, who is also the God of the promise of the ancestral narrative, who is behind the increase of the Israelites in Egypt. Through the Israelites fulfillment takes place, on the one hand, of the creation mandate to the first humans, as well as of the promise given to Noah and his family and also to Abraham.

(2) In the Israelites' passage through the Sea, the Priestly depiction states in Exod 14:22:

> And the Israelites went into the Sea on the dry ground (יבשה, *ybšh*) and the water was a wall for them on their right and on their left.

The term יבשה (*ybšh*) appears in the Priestly document only once prior to Exod 14, namely at the very beginning in Gen 1:9:

> And God said: "Let the water under the heavens gather themselves in one place and the dry ground (יבשה, *ybšh*) will become visible." And it was so.

The fact that the same thing takes place in the miracle of the splitting of the sea as took place at creation, namely that the dry ground becomes visible, is evidently a careful presentation. This is demonstrated in the deep structure of the text, which shows that creational activity is behind the miracle of the Sea. Or, stated in terms of the conception of God, the God of creation and the delivering God of the exodus are one and the same.

One can already see in these explicit and implicit arguments that serve to connect the leading themes of pentateuchal tradition how the Priestly document undertakes enormous efforts to synthesize the extant traditions. The conception of God in the Priestly document can only partially be deduced through such observations of the compositional logic of the connection between the Primeval History, ancestral narrative, and exodus story. For they initially demonstrate God's unity but not God's singularity, though the latter is paramount for the Priestly document and also determinative for its overall theology.

THE LABEL "GOD" AS A MONOTHEISTIC PROGRAM The "monotheistic" argument of the Priestly document can be recognized primarily by its specific terminology of calling God אלהים (*'lhym*), "Elohim." Exodus 6:3 demonstrates that according to the Priestly document God appeared to the ancestors as El Shaddai, but the name Yhwh was first revealed in the time of Moses. On the level of the reader, God is notoriously introduced in yet another way, that is as Elohim. Its beginning in Gen 1:2–2:4a uses Elohim as a designation for God, which is extraordinarily prominent, appearing no less than thirty-three times as a subject, so the programmatic nature of this usage cannot be mistaken. The use of Elohim is especially conspicuous when juxtaposed to the use of the name of Yhwh in the non-Priestly material beginning in Gen 2:5. Elohim is a Hebrew noun with the meaning "god" or "gods." An undetermined Elohim without the definite article would then basically be translated as "a god" or "gods." This clearly is not the meaning of Elohim in the Priestly document, which is easily revealed from Gen 1. Elohim does not mean "a god," and certainly not "gods," which the singular predicates show, but rather "God," designating a so-called plural of majesty. Elohim in the Priestly document is therefore singular, and even though it does not have the definite article, it is used like a determined noun. This then means that the Priestly document uses Elohim with regard to its determined nature as a proper name, for only proper names are nouns that are determined enough in and of themselves to manage without the article, since they designate entities of which there is only one. The Priestly document therefore makes the class Elohim coincide with its only member, Elohim. The only thing that Elohim can, therefore, also be called is Elohim.

The point of the coincidence of the class and its only member can be described further when one juxtaposes the use of Elohim with the marginally earlier texts of Deutero-Isaiah. Isaiah 45:5 states, "I am Yhwh and no other; besides me there is no Elohim." In this case Elohim is clearly a designation for the class, and just like in the Priestly document there is only one member in Deutero-Isaiah, but it is called יהוה (*yhwh*), Yhwh, and not also Elohim. Class and sole member do coincide here, but they remain different. The resulting difference is minimal but of a rather fundamental nature. The Priestly document develops an *inclusive* theology—behind all divine manifestations, such as that of El Shaddai in the Abrahamic ecumenism, is quite simply God. Deutero-Isaiah, on the other hand, presents a strict *exclusive* theology: there is no other God besides Yhwh; all other gods are nothing.

One can, therefore, see that the Priestly document wrestles vehemently not only for the unity but also for the uniqueness of God, which is, however—as the use of the class term Elohim as a proper name clearly shows—structured inclusively.

CELESTIALIZATION AND TRANSCENDENCE OF THE CONCEPTION OF GOD The exilic period and the emerging monotheism brought with them fundamental changes to Israel and Judah's conception of God. It would be an underestimation if one were simply to interpret the process as the numerical reduction of the deities to one. First, there is a certain celestialization of the conception of God.[50] The presumably monarchic period texts from Jerusalem are largely silent about the "heavens" in connection to God's dwelling place (cf. esp. Isa 6:1–11). Clearly "the preexilic conception of Jerusalem as dwelling place [knew] no explicit localization of the divine throne in the cosmic realm of the heavens."[51] This explict location first arose in the course of the religious-historical transformations after the loss of the First Temple, which modified the close relationship between God and cultic place, though in various ways and with various accents. God's dwelling place was now located in heaven, which withdrew it from all political and military turmoil (cf. 1 Kgs 8:30, 38–39, 44–45; Ps 2:4, et al.).

The Priestly conception of God, however, goes one step further and removes any numinous quality from the heavens. The heavens are merely an edifice that separates the water above the inhabitable world from this world (Gen 1:9). God himself is not accorded a residence in the heavens. As the creator, God remains qualitatively and also topographically entirely separate. God is, therefore, fundamentally conceived as transcendent, even if he makes use of various modes of revelation in order to appear to humans.

GOD AS THE CREATOR OF WEAL AND WOE An immediate consequence of the conception of God as the only god consists in the fact that God is now seen as responsible for everything that takes place in the world. There can be no other power contrary to God that is responsible for suffering and calamity. All human experiences can be traced back to God. This conviction is formulated most clearly in Isa 45:6–7:[52]

I am Yhwh and no other, the one who forms the light and who creates the darkness, who performs salvation and creates calamity (עשׂה שׁלום

50. Cf. in more detail Konrad Schmid, "Himmelsgott, Weltgott und Schöpfer: 'Gott' und der 'Himmel' in der Literatur der Zeit des Zweiten Tempels," in *Der Himmel*, ed. Dorothea Sattler and Samuel Vollenweider, Jahrbuch für Theologie 20 (Neukirchen-Vluyn: Neukirchener Verlag, 2006), 111–48.

51. Friedhelm Hartenstein, *Die Unzugänglichkeit Gottes im Heiligtum: Jesaja 6 und der Wohnort JHWHs in der Jerusalemer Kulttradition*, WMANT 75 (Neukirchen-Vluyn: Neukirchener Verlag, 1997), 226; cf. further Friedhelm Hartenstein, "Wolkendunkel und Himmelsfeste: Zur Genese und Kosmologie der Vorstellung des himmlischen Heiligtums JHWHs," in *Das biblische Weltbild und seine altorientalischen Kontexte*, ed. Bernd Janowski and Beate Ego, FAT 32 (Tübingen: Mohr Siebeck, 2001), 126–79.

52. The intellectual prerequisite for such a statement was Israel's prophecy of judgment since the eighth century BCE; cf. the especially explicit statement in Amos 3:6: "Does calamity happen to a city (רעה בעיר, *r'h b'yr*) without Yhwh having acted?"

וּבוֹרֵא רָע, *'śh šlwm wbwr' r'*). I, Yhwh, am the one who accomplishes all this.

The terminology of the verbs chosen is especially striking: "performing salvation" is formulated with the normal Hebrew verb for making (עָשָׂה, *'śh*), while for the "creation of calamity" the specific verb used is the one used for the incomparable divine creation (בָּרָא, *br'*), which is also used multiple times in the biblical record of creation in Gen 1. These intend to emphasize that calamity too is the result of God's own and direct action. This thought has justifiably and repeatedly led to great problems in the history of interpretation. However, still greater problems would likely have resulted in the monotheistic religions if this thought had not been explicit. How could God be conceived as God if calamity was decoupled from him and could unfold uncontrollably? Tracing good and evil, salvation and calamity back to God himself thereby also transcends these categories themselves. If God creates salvation and calamity, then can they truly be characterized from every point of view as good or evil? Instead, texts like Isa 45:6–7 appear to reckon that good and evil are seen differently from God's perspective than they are from that of humans.[53] This argument shows that the transformation of the conception of God can also fundamentally change cornerstones of ethical orientation.

8. Angels and Mediating Beings

Both Judaism and Christianity are familiar with a complex angelology, the elaboration of which, however, took place in the post-biblical period.[54] The strict monotheism of the exilic period renounced the notion of angels and mythical creatures, but for the previous period it was normal to depict the earthly forms of divine appearances as angels (Gen 18:2; 28:11–12; 32:25). Also the period after the Babylonian exile was in no way characterized by the general dismissal of such beings. On the contrary, the fundamental

---

53. Cf. Heinz Günther Nesselrath and Florian Wilk, eds., *Gut und Böse in Mensch und Welt: Philosophische und religiöse Konzeptionen vom Alten Orient bis zum frühen Islam*, Orientalische Religionen in der Antike 10 (Tübingen: Mohr Siebeck, 2013).

54. Cf. Friedrich V. Reiterer et al., eds., *Angels: Concepts of Celestial Beings: Origins, Development and Reception*, DCLS 2007 (Berlin: de Gruyter, 2007).

theological distance established by monotheism between God and world, the creator and the creation, could not be maintained. The space between God and humanity was filled with numinous powers of various kinds. The arrangement of the basic monotheistic view brought about especially the traditional conception of a heavenly court in which all angels and mystical creatures are clearly subordinate to God.

ANGELS AS MESSENGERS The earliest witnesses to the depiction of angels in the Hebrew Bible are conceived completely in terms of the ancient Near Eastern institution of messengers. An angel is a divine messenger, who completely represents his sender. In Hebrew, the phrase מלאך יהוה (*ml'k yhwh*) is characteristic, and should be translated as "the messenger of Yhwh" rather than "a messenger of Yhwh." Because Yhwh is a proper name and therefore determined, the whole expression must be determined and translated as such. The messenger of Yhwh is met, for example, in Gen 22:11 and Exod 3:2, though in both texts the messenger of Yhwh alternates with Yhwh himself (cf. Gen 22:1; Exod 3:4, 7; and often). Both the determination as well as the alternation of terms make it clear that nothing differentiates the angel of God from God himself. The angel is the earthly form of the manifestation of God himself.

In addition to these terminologically set conceptions, the Hebrew Bible is also familiar with the occasional appearance of divine figures upon the earth that are never, or at least not at first, recognized as such in the course of the narrative. Worthy of mention are perhaps the three men who come to visit Abraham (Gen 18:2), the man who wrestles with Jacob at the Jabbok (Gen 32:24), the figure that appears to Joshua after the passage through the Jordan (Josh 5:13–15), and likely the man who points out to Joseph the way to his brothers in the open field (Gen 37:15–17). These figures are introduced quite unpretentiously as אִישׁ (*'yš*), "man." The fact that they concern messengers of God or God himself remains largely left to the imagination of the audience.

THE HEAVENLY COURT In connection with the angel thematic, mention should also be made of the members of the heavenly court that is presumed in Job 1:6; Isa 6:8; and 1 Kgs 22:19. Like an earthly king, God too rules over a court, in which various orders are divided among lower numinous beings. However, it would be a misinterpretation to understand this seemingly polytheistic conception solely under the aspect of the multiplicity of deities. It instead concerns ways of depicting the unity of the divine, but now interpreted as the distribution of diverse tasks and persons.[55] The Satan figure especially should be mentioned in this context. Primarily the book of Job leaves no doubt that the Satan is nothing other than a function within the sphere of God himself, who has no power besides or over God. God authorizes every single step that the Satan plans against Job; the calamity caused by Satan is calamity from God himself.[56]

In postexilic prophecy, the figure of an interpretive angel appears, who explains to the prophet what he has seen or heard (cf. Zech 1–6; Dan 9).[57] This conception is due to the increased theological awareness of divine messages. They initially had the character of a secret and could not immediately be understood by a prophet. They must instead be interpreted by a figure of divine descent. This complies with the prophetic hermeneutic,[58] which can be deduced from Qumran and also the New Testament. A pro-

55. Cf. for Egypt Jan Assmann, "Arbeit am Polytheismus: Die Idee der Einheit Gottes und die Entfaltung des theologischen Diskurses in Ägypten," in *Theologen und Theologien in verschiedenen Kulturkreisen*, ed. Heinrich von Stietencron (Düsseldorf: Patmos, 1986), 46–69; Jan Assmann, *Monotheismus und Kosmotheismus: Ägyptische Formen eines "Denkens des Einen" und ihre europäische Rezeptionsgeschichte*, Sitzungsberichte der Heidelberger Akademie der Wissenschaften, Philosophisch-Historische Klasse 12 (Heidelberg: Winter, 1993).

56. Cf. Hermann Spieckermann, "Die Satanisierung Gottes: Zur inneren Konkordanz von Novelle, Dialog und Gottesreden im Hiobbuch," in *"Wer ist wie du, HERR, unter den Göttern?" Studien zur Theologie und Religionsgeschichte Israels, Festschrift Otto Kaiser*, ed. Ingo Kottsieper (Göttingen: Vandenhoeck & Ruprecht, 1994), 431–44; Heinz-Josef Fabry, "'Satan'—Begriff und Wirklichkeit: Untersuchungen zur Dämonologie der alttestamentlichen Weisheitsliteratur," in *Die Dämonen: Die Dämonologie der israelitisch-jüdischen und frühchristlichen Literatur im Kontext ihrer Umwelt: Demons: The Demonology of Israelite-Jewish and Early Christian Literature in Context of Their Environment*, ed. Armin Lange et al. (Tübingen: Mohr Siebeck, 2003), 269–91; Martin Leuenberger, "Widersacher-Konstellationen in der Levante und im Alten Testament: Der Kampf des Wettergottes gegen die See(gottheit) und die Satansfigur in der perserzeitlichen Literatur," in *L'adversaire de Dieu / Der Widersacher Gottes. 6. Symposium Strasbourg, Tübingen, Uppsala. 27.–29. Juni 2013 in Tübingen*, ed. Matthias Morgenstern, WUNT 364 (Tübingen: Mohr Siebeck, 2016), 1–26, esp. 13–22; Susanne Rudnig-Zelt, "Der Teufel und der alttestamentliche Monotheismus," in *Das Böse, der Teufel und Dämonen / Evil, the Devil, and Demons*, ed. Jan Dochhorn et al., WUNT II/412 (Tübingen: Mohr Siebeck, 2016), 1–20.

57. Rüdiger Lux, "Der Deuteengel und der Prophet: Biblisch-hermeneutische Aspekte der Angelologie," in *Prophetie und Zweiter Tempel: Studien zu Haggai und Sacharja*, FAT 65 (Tübingen: Mohr Siebeck, 2009), 293–301.

58. Cf. Odil H. Steck, *The Prophetic Books and Their Theological Witness*, trans. James D. Nogalski (St. Louis: Chalice, 2000); Odil H. Steck, *Gott in der Zeit entdecken: Die Prophetenbücher des Alten Testaments als Vorbild für Theologie und Kirche*, Biblisch-theologische Studien 42 (Neukirchen-Vluyn: Neukirchener Verlag, 2001).

phetic message is dependent on an authoritative interpretation that is able to open up its full meaning. Only the Habakkuk Pesher (1QpHab 7.1–5) is able to explain that the biblical book of Habakkuk actually relates to the Teacher of Righteousness,[59] and only the Gospel of Matthew knows that the promise of the virgin birth relates to the birth of Jesus Christ (Matt 1:18–20).

WINGED ANGELS The notion of a winged angel appears for the first time in the Maccabean book of Daniel (e.g., Dan 9:21), a depiction which later became broadly established in the history of reception and iconography. It emphasizes the heavenly descent of the angel. At the same time, however, the moment of the surprising and secret appearance of the angel of God, known in earlier tests, retreats into the background.

DEVELOPED ANGELOLOGIES IN THE BOOKS OF TOBIT AND ENOCH Angels appear as independent actors that bear individual names (like Gabriel already in Dan 8:16) like Raphael in the book of Tobit or Semyaz, Arakeb, Rame'el, Tam'el, Ram'el, Dan'el, Ezeqel, Baraqyal, Asa'el, Armeaso, Batar'el, Anan'el, Zaqe'el, Sasomasp, We'el, Kestar'el, Tur'el, Yamayol, and Arazyal (1 En. 6:7) in addition to the archangels Michael, Uriel, Raphael, and Gabriel (1 En. 9:1) in the book of Watchers within the book of Enoch (1 En. 6–63). This represents the completion of a decisive step toward an autonomous angelology that no longer interprets the angel as direct forms of divine revelation, but instead, in various forms, as numinous actors in their own right.[60]

The book of Tobit plays with its main character's belief in angels and the actual appearance of angels. Tobit believes that his son Tobias is ac-

---

59. Cf. James C. Charlesworth, *The Pesharim and Qumran History: Chaos or Consensus?* (Grand Rapids: Eerdmans, 2002); Reinhard G. Kratz, "Die Pescharim von Qumran im Rahmen der Schriftauslegung des antiken Judentums," in *Heilige Texte: Religion und Rationalität, 1. Geisteswissenschaftliches Colloquium 10.–13. Dezember 2009 auf Schloss Genshagen,* ed. Andreas Kablitz and Christoph Markschies (Berlin: de Gruyter, 2013), 87–104.

60. Cf. Loren T. Stuckenbruck, "'Angels' and 'God': Exploring the Limits of Early Jewish Monotheism," in *Early Jewish and Christian Monotheism,* ed. Loren T. Stuckenbruck and Wendy E. Sproston North, JSNTSup 263 (London: T&T Clark, 2004), 45–70; Beate Ego, "Der Engel Rafael und die Witwe Judit: Aspekte vermittelter Gottespräsenz in den Apokryphen," in *Vermittelte Gegenwart: Konzeptionen der Gottespräsenz von der Zeit des Zweiten Tempels bis Anfang des 2. Jahrhunderts n. Chr.,* ed. Andrea Taschl-Erber and Irmtraud Fischer, WUNT 367 (Tübingen: Mohr Siebeck, 2016), 11–29.

companied by an angel on his trip to Media (Tob 5:17, 22), but he does not recognize that the angel Raphael is behind his companion Azariah, who reveals his identity first at the end of the narrative (Tob 12:15).

In the book of Watchers from the book of Enoch, the angels are primarily endowed with the function of the bringers of culture. They reveal to humans military technology, the art of cosmetics (1 En. 8:1), and the secrets of astrology (1 En. 8:3). Knowledge of civilization such as city building, music, and forging technology are achieved by humanity itself in Gen 4:17, 21–22. Genesis 4 and 1 En. 8 agree in their judgment of the ambivalence of this knowledge. In Gen 4, such knowledge is a characteristic of fallen humanity; in 1 En. 8 it is transmitted by fallen angels.

§31 From Counterworld to Everyday World: The Basic Precepts of Life

Bernd Janowski and Beate Ego, eds., *Das biblische Weltbild und seine altorientalischen Kontexte*, FAT 32 (Tübingen: Mohr Siebeck, 2001) ◆ Bernd Janowski, Friedrich Schweitzer, and Christoph Schwöbel, eds., *Schöpfungsglaube vor der Herausforderung des Kreationismus*, Theologie interdisziplinär 6 (Neukirchen-Vluyn: Neukirchener Verlag, 2010) ◆ Jörg Jeremias, "Schöpfung in Poesie und Prosa des Alten Testaments: Gen 1–3 im Vergleich mit anderen Schöpfungstexten des Alten Testaments," *Jahrbuch für Biblische Theologie* 5 (1990): 11–36 ◆ Othmar Keel and Silvia Schroer, *Schöpfung: Biblische Theologien im Kontext altorientalischer Religionen*, 2nd ed. (Freiburg: Universitätsverlag; Göttingen: Vandenhoeck & Ruprecht, 2008) ◆ Konrad Schmid, ed., *Schöpfung*, TdT 4 (Tübingen: Mohr Siebeck, 2012)

THEOLOGY OF CREATION Under the heading "From Counterworld to Everyday World" is concealed what is generally called the theology of creation in the Hebrew Bible. The reason for this choice of nomenclature in place of "Creation" is twofold. One is that the term creation is not found in the Hebrew Bibile—the Hebrew noun בריאה (*bry'h*) is first attested in the Qumran text CD 4.21 (cf. 12.15) and appears also in rabbinic literature.[61] The other is that both prominent creation narratives at the beginning of the Bible—those of Gen 1 and Gen 2–3—do not focus directly on the con-

---

61. The New Testament is familiar with and uses both the verb κτίζω (*ktízō*), "create," and unquestionably also the noun κτίσις (*ktísis*), "creation."

dition of the world as it was originally created by God (this condition is termed a "counterworld"), but on the condition toward which the further progression of the narrative develops ("everyday world").

Behind this narrative movement—from counterworld to everyday world—is a functionally mythical thought pattern. The foundational structures of the everyday world are explained genetically; that is, questions of being are treated as questions of origins. This is the most elementary characteristic of myth, which in this regard also describes the narrative world of the Hebrew Bible, even if it does not consist of "stories of gods that take place outside space and time," as Hugo Gressmann once poignantly defined the concept of myth.[62] The Hebrew Bible essentially concerns one God acting in space and time, thereby distancing itself in terms of its content from "myth." At the same time, however, it is functionally "mythic" in that it is familiar with the founding functions of these narratives and itself extensively uses them. This is especially the case in the Primeval History and in the creation narratives within it.

1. Preliminary Remarks from the History of Scholarship

DISCOVERIES OF THE NINETEENTH CENTURY Of primary importance for the topic of creation in the sphere of theology are the great archaeological discoveries in Mesopotamia in the nineteenth century. As soon as the Akkadian parallels to the biblical creation and flood narratives became known, the traditional and mythological nature of these traditions became clear. The assumption of the Bible's nonanalogous nature was empirically refuted, which many saw as curtailing its revelational quality. Now, from a distance of more than a century since these discoveries, scholars have learned, on the one hand, to view the relationship between Babel and Bible as more complex. The Bible was not written in complete isolation, nor is Pan-Babylonianism an adequate interpretive schema. On the other hand, scholars have also learned to value the reception-historical and tradition-historical aspects of the Bible from a theological perspective. The quality of the Bible does not lie in the unanalogous nature of its material, but in its specific interpretations. In order to work out this thesis, biblical studies in the twentieth century institutionalized the fundamental conviction that the Bible should be treated and interpreted in the same way as all other literature.

62. Cf. above, p. 264 n. 6.

MARGINALIZATION OF THE THEOLOGY OF CREATION Of still greater importance for the treatment of the topic of creation in theology was, however, the rise of neo-orthodox theology at the beginning of the 1920s. First, natural theology and the topic of creation fell into disrepute for internal theological reasons. Second, the topic of creation was severely marginalized as a result of the use of the concept of creational order in the sphere of the "German Christians" and the vehement combat against such positions within the context of the "Confessing Church" after the Second World War in theology. An example can be found in Gerhard von Rad's influential essay from 1936, "The Theological Problem of the Old Testament Doctrine of Creation,"[63] which prescribes the doctrine of creation a subservient role to salvation history within the theology of the Old Testament.

REDISCOVERY OF CREATION THEOLOGY It was first voices from the periphery from the last third of the twentieth century that recalled the theme of creation to mind.[64] In the wake of the ecological crises taking place since that juncture, the concept of creation has again become so popular in the public sphere of the church that its prior history appears—at least in public consciousness—largely to have been forgotten. However, difficulties have resulted not only in view of the unanswered problems of the past, but also with regard to the concept itself, which in eco-theological discussions is not clearly differentiated from the concept of nature. This became especially poignant within the context of the so-called conciliar process, which began in 1983 at the Vancouver general meeting of the World Council of Churches and was to work for justice, peace, and the preservation of creation. Specifically, the goal of the "preservation of creation" evoked criticism because nature and creation were not differentiated. From a theological perspective, humans cannot be the agents of the preservation of creation. More correctly, one must speak of the "preservation of nature in the knowledge of its character as creation." The internal theological ways of addressing the concept of theology also demonstrate a certain lack of clarity, which the following discussion will take into account.

63. Gerhard von Rad, "The Theological Problem of the Old Testament Doctrine of Creation," in *Creation in the Old Testament,* ed. Bernard W. Anderson, Issues in Religion and Theology 6 (Philadelphia: Fortress, 1984), 53–64.
64. Hans Heinrich Schmid, "Schöpfung, Gerechtigkeit und Heil," *ZTK* 70 (1973): 1–19; Hermann Spieckermann, "Schöpfung, Gerechtigkeit und Heil als Horizont alttestamentlicher Theologie," *ZTK* 100 (2003): 399–419.

THE TOPIC OF CREATION DOES NOT BELONG TO THE RELIGIOUS-HISTORICAL BEDROCK The fact that discussion of creation does not belong to the literary or religious-historical bedrock of the Hebrew Bible belongs to the accepted results of scholarship on the Hebrew Bible, which becomes clear from an initial, historically informed viewing of the main focus of the attestations. Neither the Primeval History, Deutero-Isaiah, nor the relevant psalms and wisdom texts reach—formulated conservatively with regard to their compositional history—far back into the preexilic period. This is also to be expected, for the creation thematic presupposes, first, an agrarian economy. Within pastoral nomadic societies, reflections on the world and natural order are of secondary importance. Second, Gen 1 in particular—which is in any case the most prominent configuration of the creation thematic that took place through continual interaction with Mesopotamian conceptions—presupposes the appropriate cultural contexts.

Reflections on the formation of the world and world order did not occur spontaneously in the ancient Near East. They were conducted at the height of the intellectual discourse of that time. In Israel, this was inconceivable without familiarity with the fundamental convictions of the contemporary leading cultures from Mesopotamia. The cultural exchange could, however, only become active in terms of reception history from the time when the scribal learning in Israel and Judah had itself reached an adequate stage of development.

Third and finally, one must take into account that the universalization of the religion of ancient Israel likely came about in the wake of the loss of the sovereign statehood leading to a pronounced accentuation on the presentation of God as the creator of the world. The development of this conception is connected to the imprint of biblical monotheism in this time (cf., e.g., Isa 45:5–7). In this respect, the concept of creation certainly did not first arise in the exile, but it underwent its most momentuous expansion at that time.

EARLIEST ATTESTATIONS The earliest extrabiblical attestation of a creational message in ancient Israel appears on a three-lined fragment of a storage jar from monarchic Jerusalem. The script points to the early seventh century BCE.[65] In the second line the name מכיהו (*mkyhw*), "Mikayahu," can still be read, while in the third the letters קנארץ (*qn'rṣ*) are

---

65. Cf. Nahman Avigad, "Excavations in the Jewish Quarter of the Old City of Jerusalem," *IEJ* 22 (1972): 193–200; cf. also *KAI* 256 A.III.18.

recognizable, which one can supplement to make אל] קנארץ] (['l] qn'rṣ), which either means "God, who created the earth," or perhaps, because of the missing article before קנה (qnh) as well as the missing ה (h) in the final position of קנה (qnh), intends the meaningful name of a deity Elqunirṣa, which still leads to the same conclusion.

Furthermore, the expression אל עליון קונה שמים וארץ ('l 'lywn qwnh šmym w'rṣ), "the highest God, who created heaven and earth" appears in Gen 14:19. However, the context as a whole, though very difficult to date, is an artificial product of the postexilic period.

The epigraphy can therefore confirm what was suggested from the internal considerations on the religious history of ancient Israel. The creation thematic was widely developed in the sphere of exilic and postexilic texts in the Hebrew Bible, but it is also familiar with isolated precursors.

CREATIO CONTINUA AND CREATIO PRIMA In any case, one should differentiate categorically between the age and the substance of the statements about creation in the Hebrew Bible. It seems worthwhile to introduce a distinction from Christian tradition at this point. While anachronistic in terms of terminology, it is meaningful in terms of the content. The conceptions of *creatio continua* and *creatio prima* can be differentiated from one another. The expression *creatio continua* denotes the ongoing preservation of the world by divine activity, while *creatio prima* indicates the first creation of the world by God. These conceptions do not act as equivalent in dogmatics or in their precursors in the Bible. The declarations about the creation of the world are instead understood as the culmination of the conception of divine preservation and control.

2. God as Creator and the World as Creation (Gen 1)

THE PRIESTLY REPORT OF CREATION Genesis 1:1–2:4a (in the following: Gen 1) is likely not only the most well-known text of the Bible, but of world literature altogether. However, the understanding of this text is often hindered by two basic misconceptions. First, Gen 1 is often interpreted as if it is an entity in itself. In reality, Gen 1 was never a stand-alone, independent text, but was always the opening piece of a larger literary complex—first of the so-called Priestly document and now of the Pentateuch. Therefore, the interpretation of Gen 1 should always pay attention to the network of connections with what follows. Second, the peculiar world order of Gen

1, in which animals and humans subsist as vegetarians and relate to one another without any conflict, is often understood as a moralistic appeal. In reality, Gen 1 appears to behold the deaths of animals and humans as one of the fundamental problems of the world. It should be noted, however, that Gen 1 is a narrative text. It contains no injunctions, only narrative. These two dangers will be considered and avoided in the following discussion.

Genesis 1 gives an account of how God created the world in seven days. However, the Greek-speaking tradition often speaks of a "six-day work." This is linked to a textual variant in Gen 2:2. The Hebrew text states: "And on the *seventh* day God completed the work that he had done." The Greek translation of the Septuagint instead offers: "On the *sixth* day God completed the work that he had done, and he rested on the seventh day from all the work that he had done." This version is smoother and more easily understood: God works for six days and rests on the seventh day. For just this reason it is probably secondary. The Septuagint dismissed the consideration that the rest belonged integrally to the work rather than being a resting from the work done, as the logic of the Hebrew text indicates. Regardless, it remains the case that the seventh day occupies something of a special position. Nothing is created on it, not even the Sabbath (the noun is not used; it is only the verb וישבת [*wyšbt*], "and he rested"). By his rest God primevally performs the later Sabbath.

THE CORRESPONDENCE OF DAYS AND WORKS In the first six days God creates eight works. The number of the works is easily recognized through formulaic presentation of the works—that is, in the operations of naming and the distribution of the approval formula ("and God saw that it was good"). They concern: (1) the separation of light from darkness, which lead to "day" and "night"; (2) the establishment of the firmament, which is then named "heaven"; (3) the collection of the waters under the firmament, which allows for the emergence of "land" and "sea"; (4) the creation of the plants; (5) the creation of the lights in the firmament, namely sun, moon, and stars; (6) the creation of the aquatic animals and the birds; (7) the creation of the land animals; and (8) the creation of humanity. This specific numeric discrepancy between the six days and the eight works has led many interpreters astray, such that they held the six-day schema as secondary in composition or tradition-critical terms, expecting a consistent author to distribute six works over six days. Such premature conjectures are easily falsified. The fact that Gen 1 relies on preexisting tradition is already likely from general cultural-historical considerations. However, the distribution of eight works over six days is not simply the result of an only partially successful reconciliation of assimilated traditional material. It is, rather, profoundly meaningful. Immediately striking—again simply in terms of numbers—is that the eight works are not distributed at random, but rather in a specific sequence over the six days:

Day 1:	1 work	Alternation of day and night
Day 2:	1 work	Heavenly firmament
Day 3:	2 works	Separation of land and sea
		Plants
Day 4:	1 work	Heavenly bodies
Day 5:	1 work	Aquatic animals and birds
Day 6:	2 works	Land animals
		Humans
Day 7:	Rest	

Genesis 1 thereby orders the works into a 1:1:2 rhythm that is played out twice. The fact that this is more than an aesthetic gimmick can be demonstrated by looking at the content. The formally denoted break between the third and fourth days is also of decisive importance in terms of content. It becomes immediately clear that the content of the second and the fifth as well as the third and the sixth days correspond to one another. The firmament, the "heaven" is established on the second day that separates the waters above and below so that a sphere of air is formed. These are the habitats for the aquatic animals and the birds that are created on the fifth day. On the third day, through the collection of the waters, dry land becomes visible that serves the land animals and humans as a habitat, who are created on the sixth day. This correspondence also provides the reason why the plants were already created on the third day. According to Gen 1, they are older than the stars that were first created a day later. The plants fundamentally belong to the creation of the dry ground, for without vegetation, the land offers no possibility for life.

In the same way that the second and the third days constitute the provision of the habitats related to the creatures that will reside in them that are created on the fifth and sixth days, the correspondence between the first and fourth days is also obvious. The structure of a day is created on the first day by the separation between light and dark, such that the progression of time is established. The structuring of time is the concern of the work of the fourth day, the creation of the heavenly bodies, which "are signs for feast times, for days and for years" (1:14).

THE WORLD OF GEN 1 Genesis 1 therefore describes the fundamental orders of time and life, as they emerge from the creation of the world. As the conclusion of the sixth day, Gen 1:31 finally stipulates, "And God saw everything that he had made, and behold, it was very good." "Good" here designates the nature of creation as supporting life. Described as "very good" means that it is completely geared for successful life.

One must now bear in mind, however, that Gen 1 does not result in the—at that time and today—*present* human and animal habitat. The world described in Gen 1 is similar to the present world in many ways, but it is not identical to it. The cosmology and biology of the creation do correspond to the experience of the world at that time, but not the fundamental order—namely that humans and animals subsist solely as vegetarians does not agree with the conventions of that time or of the present. In this regard, Gen 1 depicts an idealized world. At the same time, the following context is aware of the fact that this ideal state did not last for long.

THE CORRUPTION OF THE WORLD IN GEN 1 Five chapters later, Gen 6:11–13 states that the qualification of Gen 1:31 has become its complete opposite.

GEN 1:31:	GEN 6:11–13:
	But the earth became corrupt before God, and the earth became full of violence (חמס, ḥms).
And God saw everything that he had made, and behold,	And God saw the earth, and behold,
it was very good	it was corrupt for all flesh had currupted its ways on the earth. Then God spoke to Noah: the end of all flesh has come before me, for the earth is full of violence (חמס, ḥms) from them. So I will eradicate them from the earth.

The reason given for the compromising of the original creation is named in Gen 6:11-13 the corruption of the earth by "violence" (חמס, ḥms). The term חמס (ḥms) principally means "violence against life," especially the shedding of blood. With "all flesh," both humans and animals are in view, but not the fish, which biblically do not count as "flesh"—in verifiable manner—they are not punished by the flood. It should be maintained, however—against both a widespread and diminished interpretation of this section—that the guilt of the flood according to Gen 6:11-13 does not fall on humans alone, but with "all flesh," on both humans and animals.

The passage of Gen 9:1-6 reacts precisely to this problem of violence.

GEN 1:28-30	GEN 9:1-6
And God blessed them	And God blessed Noah and his sons
And spoke to them:	and spoke to them:
Be fruitful and multiply	Be fruitful and multiply
And fill the earth	And fill the earth!
And take possession of it and rule over the fish of the sea and the birds of the heavens, over the cattle and all animals that move on the earth!	Fear and terror of you will come upon all the animals of the earth, upon all birds of the heavens, upon everything that crawls on the earth, and upon all fish in the sea: they are given into your hands.
And God spoke: Behold, I give you all herbage that carries seeds on the whole earth, and all trees on which are seedbearing fruit: these shall be your food.	Everything that moves and lives shall be your food; like the green herbage, I give you everything. Only flesh that still has its soul—its blood—in it, you may not eat. Your own blood, however, I will require from all animals. I will require it and from humans each from one another, I will require the life of the human: whoever sheds human blood, their blood shall also be shed for the value of the human. For God made humans in his image.
But all animals of the earth and all birds of the heavens and everything that moves on the earth that has breath in it, I give grass and herbage as sustenance. And it was so.	

The divine speech offered in Gen 9:1-6 takes up the allocation of sustenance from Gen 1:28-30 and modifies it such that the consumption of meat is now permitted. Humans are permitted from now on to eat land animals, birds, and fish, in addition to food from plants. The diet of the animals is not explicitly regulated, but the shape of the texts indicates that the consumption of meat by animals is implicitly accepted. The death penalty only concerns cases when animals attack humans, or when humans turn against other humans, and it comes to the shedding of *human* blood.

THE DEATH PENALTY ACCORDING TO GEN 9 The formulation in Gen 9:6a does not allow for clear recognition of the subject that implements the death penalty: "Whoever sheds human blood, his blood shall also be shed by humans / at the value of the human." The answer to this question rests on the question of how בָּאָדָם (bāʾādām) is rendered. The Hebrew preposition בְּ (b-) can be understood as a *bet instrumentalis,* in which case the translation would be "by humans." It can also be interpreted as a *bet pretii,* in which case the translation "for the value of the human" is suggested. In favor of this later possibility is the structure of Gen 9:6a, in which the shed human blood from the first half of the statement (C) corresponds to the blood of the human in the second half of the statement (C'). The passive formulation "should be shed" would thus be understood as a divine passive. The implementation of the death penalty is reserved for God. It is also possible that the two meanings should not be separated.

Who sheds	blood	of the human:	the value of the human	shall his blood	be shed.
A	B	C	C'	B'	A'
יִשָּׁפֵךְ	דְּמוֹ	בָּאָדָם	הָאָדָם	דַּם	שֹׁפֵךְ
yiššāpēk	dāmô	bāʾādām	hāʾādām	dam	šopēk
A'	B'	C'	C	B	A

The permission of the consumption of meat as well as the introduction of the death penalty form the most important elements of the modifications of the creational order of Gen 1 in Gen 9. The world order experienced today is first established in Gen 9. Stated pointedly, the biblical creation narrative includes not only Gen 1, nor just Gen 1–3, but Gen 1–9.

The fact that Gen 1 is an opening text and is oriented toward and dependent on the progression in Gen 6 and Gen 9 can be verified by a small detail in Gen 1—the blessing motif. It appears in two places within Gen 1, in v. 22 and v. 28; Gen 2:3 speaks further of the blessing of the seventh day. In Gen 1:22 the blessing is directed according to the context to the aquatic animals created in Gen 1:21: "And God blessed them and said: 'Be fruitful and multiply and fill the water in the sea, the birds shall multiple on the earth.'" It is striking that the birds do not appear to be blessed. The divine speech reproduced in Gen 1:22 is directed in 2nd person only toward the aquatic animals, while the proclamation concerning the birds ("the birds shall multiply on the earth") breaks into 3rd person. Do the birds not receive a blessing? This may be likely, given that the second attestation of blessing within the framework of the sixth day, on which the land animals and humans are created, states a similar abnormality. Only the humans, whose creation Gen 1:26–27 has reported, are blessed in Gen 1:28: "And God blessed them, and God spoke to them: 'Be fruitful and multiply and fill the earth and take possession of it, and rule over the fish in the sea and the birds in the heavens and all animals that move on the earth!'" There is no mention in Gen 1 of a blessing for the land animals that were created immediately before. Were they not blessed as well?

Indeed, Gen 1 appears to develop the notion that of the living beings, only the aquatic animals and the humans receive a blessing (Plants are not living beings according to the Bible; according to Gen 1 they are features of the earth). Why?

The reason appears to lie in the structure of the world according to Gen 1. On the second and third days of creation, the habitats of the air, sea, and land with vegetation emerge, obviously in view of the living beings created on the fifth and sixth days—the birds, aquatic animals, land animals, and humans. It is evident that of these living beings, only the aquatic animals can have the habitat claimed by them all to themselves: the sea. While the birds alone have the air, for their sustenance and propagation—as the author of Gen 1 also knows, they rely on the habitat of the land. This means that birds, land animals, and humans must share the habitat of the land. According to the ordered thought of Gen 1, a difficulty results: If not every living being has a habitat for themselves, then it can lead to conflicts. Although Gen 1:31 maintains that the creation is "very good," it must be seen as endangered in light of this constellation. The absence of a blessing for the birds and land animals indicates that the author of Gen 1 was quite aware that the human receives its blessing only at a cost to the birds and land animals who must do without—for they share the same habitat. What exactly this costs the birds and land animals first becomes recognizable from Gen 9. They are given to the humans for consumption.

One now recognizes also from Gen 1 itself that the narrative casts a creational order for a utopian counter-world, which does, however, exhibit a certain fragility—and so it makes possible that development which in the end leads incrementally to the henceforth stable and experienced world. Its regulations are laid down in Gen 9. Genesis 1–9 narrates the evolution of the creation, its development into its present ambivalent form. In light of current debates, it is noteworthy that evolution appeared already to play an important role as a category of thought in ancient attempts to understand the world, at that time, however, in connection with the structures of mythic thinking.

THE DIFFERENTIATION BETWEEN CREATOR AND CREATION The opening statement of Gen 1:1 "In the beginning God created the heavens and the earth" is so well known that its basic theological point is often overlooked: the fundamental qualitative differentiation between creator and creation. The objective location of heaven and earth—certainly correctly interpreted as a merism that expresses the entirety of the world through the combination of heaven and earth—leaves no doubt that the heavens, otherwise belonging to the numinous sphere, are here degraded to a work of creation as the subsequent context elaborates: "And God said, let there be a firmament in the midst of the waters, let it separate water from water. And God made the firmament and separated the water under the firmament from the water above the firmament. And it was so. And God named the firmament heaven" (Gen 1:6–8). The heavens are nothing more, and also nothing less than a cosmological construction.

ANCIENT NEAR EASTERN *VORLAGEN* This demystification of the heavens is especially noteworthy in light of the Babylonian tradition digested in Gen 1. As already long recognized, the creation account of Gen 1 is closely related to the Babylonian epic Enuma Elish ("When on High"),[66] which, as a result of its points of contact, has been somewhat misleadingly described as an epic of the creation of the world. In actuality it concerns the rationale for the supremacy of the Babylonian god Marduk over the other gods, which is justified by his role in the creation event. This thought was likely taken up implicitly in Gen 1 and carried forward. God is the one and only authoritative God because he created the world. The cosmological conception of the world as an air bubble in the midst of water appears to be concretely inspired by Enuma Elish. In addition, the term used in Gen 1:2 for "primordial flood," תהום (*thwm*), recalls the name *Tiāmtu* in

66. "Epic of Creation," trans. Benjamin R. Foster (*COS* 1.111:391–402).

Enuma Elish, even if it remains uncertain whether *thwm* and *Tiāmtu* are immediately related in terms of etymology.[67]

Within the framework of Enuma Elish, it can be observed that the threefold layers of heaven then become the domicile of the deities after their creation—corresponding to their hierarchy. The difference from Gen 1 consists not only in that Gen 1—as a monotheistic text—is only familiar with one deity. Furthermore, the heavens in general are not considered the divine domicile. God instead appears to face the creation to some degree alocally.

THE DIFFERENTIATION BETWEEN THE CREATOR AND THE CREATION It becomes clear from this juxtaposition that, according to Gen 1, the creator and the creation are completely separate from one another. God has no worldly quality, and the world has no divine quality. In the later formation of tradition in Judaism and Christianity, this position basically became orthodox, though it is time and again discussed and also relativized. Gnostic and mystical conceptions find a "divine seed" or "spark" in the realm of humans that can be cultivated through techniques like meditation, contemplation, or enlightenment.

DEMYSTIFICATION OF THE WORLD The radical separation between God and world, between creator and creation brings with it almost inevitably the notion of a—anachronistically in the words of Max Weber—"demystification of the world," which is, however, already at work in the Babylonian tradition. This is most easily recognized in the weakening of the stars into mere "lamps." Evidently Gen 1 consciously avoids the Hebrew terms for "sun" (שמש, *šmš*) and "moon" (ירח, *yrḥ*). It instead only speaks of the

---

67. In Ps 104:6 the term תהום (*thwm*), "primordial flood," used in Gen 1:2 appears not as a given entity before creation but as a work created by God himself. It appears that Ps 104 is familiar with Gen 1 and composes the position formulated there more explicitly: the "primordial flood" too is part of God's creation. Psalm 104:10–13 speaks of the provision of water for the earth. Read sequentially, the impression arises that the spring water that supplies the humans and animals is nothing other than the "primordial flood." According to Ps 104:8, this water was displaced to the exact location from which the spring water arises. Cf. Thomas Krüger, "'Kosmo-theologie' zwischen Mythos und Erfahrung: Psalm 104 im Horizont altorientalischer und alttestamentlicher 'Schöpfungs'-Konzepte," *BN* 68 (1993): 49–74; differently Matthias Köckert, "Literargeschichtliche und religionsgeschichtliche Beobachtungen zu Ps 104," in *Schriftauslegung in der Schrift: Festschrift für Odil Hannes Steck zu seinem 65. Geburtstag*, ed. Reinhard Gregor Kratz et al., BZAW 300 (Berlin: de Gruyter, 2000), 259–79.

"greater" and the "lesser lamps" (מָעוֹר, *m'wr*), possibly to avoid associations with the corresponding deities, but more likely primarily from astronomical interests. Still more drastically, one could—extrapolating from the conception of light in Gen 1—also say "reflectors" instead of "lamps," for the heavenly bodies evidently do not have light of their own, but this light was created by God in Gen 1:3 and is only reflected by the stars.

CREATION THROUGH WORD The functional separation of creator and creation could also be responsible for the choice of the divine word as the means of creation in Gen 1. The fact that God creates through his word has become so well known in Middle Eastern and Western cultures as a result of the potency of the Bible that the peculiarity of this concept hardly attracts any attention. In actuality, however, it concerns a revolutionary concept that the Bible develops in its opening chapter (cf. its adoption in Ps 33:9 and Rom 4:16). For one, it therefore becomes clear that God is not a "demiurge," nor "foreman" of creation, who to some degree could have physical contact in the performance of his work. God as creator is instead so distinct from his creation that he completely stands opposite it. He can, however, by means of his word—in the sense of tangible contact—intervene in it with cataclysmic consequences. The heavens are created through his word, also air, water, and earth as habitats and the living beings that then reside in these habitats. While Gen 1 is not familiar with the concept of creation out of nothing (*creation ex nihilo*), which is first attested in 2 Macc 7:28, it is also clear, as it were, that the entire present world in Gen 1 results from the divine word. Without the divine word, the world would be a completely senseless and useless *tōhû-wa-bôhû*, as Gen 1:2 describes its state before the beginning of the divine speech.

Furthermore, the creation of creation by the word indicates that its structure is interpreted as textual. The creation is not a conglomeration of senseless elements; it instead arose step-by-step through linguistic decrees and is consequently readable as a "text"—even if its original form is no longer accessible in an unbroken manner (cf. also Prov 8:22–31).

3. Paradise Lost (Gen 2–3)

RECEPTIONAL OVERLAYS Since the beginnings of historical-critical biblical scholarship, it has been noted that a second creation narrative follows Gen 1 in Gen 2–3 that does not have an organic connection with the first but was only secondarily connected with it.[68] It also belongs among the most well-known and most often interpreted texts of the Bible, and it has given rise to a variegated history of reception. This reception history should be granted its appropriate worth, but at the same time it should be noted that it has covered over the original declaration of the biblical narrative. This can be clearly demonstrated; from Gen 2–3, the reception-historical memory has been primarily impacted by the elements of paradise, Adam, Eve, the apple, and the fall into sin. A look at the biblical texts establishes that of these elements, only Eve appears in the Hebrew narrative. The term παράδεισος (*paradeisos*), "paradise," arises from the rendering of the "Garden of Eden" in the Greek translation of the Hebrew Bible. The term itself is a Persian loanword. Adam is named for the first time in Gen 4:25. Genesis 2–3 mentions only "the human" (האדם, *h'dm*). This difference is undoubtedly clear in Hebrew by the use of the article ה (*h-*) before the noun אדם (*'dm*), which therefore cannot be a proper name, for proper names are not additionally marked as determined with an article. The forbidden fruit receives no botanical identification in the Bible. Its common designation as the apple is linked to the Latin history of reception of Gen 2–3, which makes a wordplay with the Latin homonym *malum* (evil/apple). And finally, the terms *sin* and *fall* never appear in Gen 2–3. The Bible first speaks of sin in the context of the narrative of Cain's fratricide of Abel (Gen 4:6–7). Therefore, in the interpretation of the story of the Garden of Eden, one must be careful not to mistake the content of its message with its reception.

THE MORTALITY OF THE HUMANS   The story of the Garden of Eden begins with God's planting of the Garden of Eden and the creation of the human that is placed in this garden. The description of the human as formed from עפר (*'pr*), "dust" (Gen 2:7) makes it sufficiently clear that the human is created mortal from the start. "Dust" is a common metaphor for perishability in the Hebrew Bible (cf., e.g., Qoh 3:20). This point is worth emphasizing

---

68. This occurs through the half-verse of Gen 2:4b (ביום עשות יהוה אלהים ארץ ושמים, "on the day / at the time when Yhwh God made the earth and the heavens"). The formulation ביום (*bywm*), "on the day/at the time" adopts the structure of days from Gen 1, which stands in competition to what is found in Gen 2–3 and generalizes it. What Gen 2–3 narrates takes place "at the time" of the creation of "heaven and earth," not on a specific day of the preceding depiction of creation in Gen 1. The fact that Gen 2–3 does not arise from the same hand as Gen 1 and cannot simply be understood as literary supplementation to it is revealed by the reverse order of the creation of the plants and humans. In Gen 1 the plants emerge on the third day and the humans on the sixth day. In Gen 2–3 the human is created before the plants.

because the interpretation is often presented that the human according to Gen 2–3 was originally immortal but then lost his immortality in the wake of the fall, as the early reception of Gen 2–3 in Sir 25:24, Wis 2:24, and Rom 5:12 attest.[69] The fact that this is incorrect for Gen 2–3 is further shown through the fact that the threat of punishment in Gen 2:17 consists of the conventional form of a legal statement, which imposes the death penalty (and not the penalty of mortality). The specific formulation in Gen 2:17, מות תמות (*mwt tmwt*), instead of מות יומת (*mwt ymwt*) is related to the consideration that God himself is in view as the enforcer of the death penalty (cf. Gen 20:6–7; Num 26:65; Judg 13:22; Ezek 3:18) and that in Gen 3:19b mortality does not appear as the sentences against the human and his wife, but rather as a justification for them.

Noteworthy from a theological perspective is the intensification of the reflection on human mortality in Gen 2–3. The original mortality of humanity remains a constant before and after the fall. The fact that the human must die does not result from guilt but is a part of God's original creation. What is problematic is not death itself, but rather the possibility of becoming immortal, which the Tree of Life offers.

THE TREES IN THE MIDDLE OF THE GARDEN In the middle of the garden are two trees, the Tree of Life and the Tree of the Knowledge of Good and Evil. The function of the Tree of Life is explained by Gen 3:22: whoever eats from it will live forever. But what is meant by the "knowledge of good and evil"? The occassionally presented sexual interpretation, which derives primarily from the language of "knowledge" and the scene of the fig leaves with its theme of nakedness and shame, must be eliminated to the greatest extent possible from the present text. Nowhere does this text speak simply of "knowledge"—terminology which does truly have sexual connotations in Hebrew. Instead it is always concerned with the knowledge of good and evil. A minimal, indirect justification for the sexual interpretation appears in the question concerning the fact that human propagation is not arranged for in any way prior to the fall. However, the further development of the narrative shows clearly that human propagation can in any case come as a result of "knowledge of good and evil"—to the degree that it is

---

69. Cf. in detail Konrad Schmid, "Loss of Immortality? Hermeneutical Aspects of Genesis 2–3 and Its Early Receptions," in *Beyond Eden: The Biblical Story of Paradise and Its Reception History*, ed. Konrad Schmid and Christoph Riedweg, FAT II/34 (Tübingen: Mohr Siebeck, 2008), 58–78.

actually "good" to have offspring—though it is not equivalent to having this knowledge. The divine proclamation in Gen 3:22 that states that the human has now become like God in that he knows about good and evil in no way refers to human sexuality, and the further attestations of "knowledge of good and evil" in the Hebrew Bible and its environment are also opposed to this (noteworthy are especially Deut 1:39–40; 1QSa 1,10–11; 2 Sam 19:35). This evidence instead shows that the knowledge of good and evil means the differentiation between life-supporting and life-demoting actions or entities. As Deut 1:39–40 and the evidence from the Qumran text 1QSa 1.10–11 show, knowledge of good and evil is especially the mark of adulthood, and indeed of every adult human life. Children do not yet have this knowledge, and as 2 Sam 19:35 suggests, aged people no longer have it. It should be emphasized that the knowledge of good and evil does not concern one avoidable ability, whatever that may be, but rather the indispensable human abilities on which every adult human relies every day.[70]

THE FORBIDDEN TREE With regard to the trees in the Garden, God only issues one instruction. The human is permitted to eat from all the trees except for the Tree of the Knowledge of Good and Evil. This means, conversely, that the enjoyment of the Tree of Life was still allowed at this time. The human was permitted to eat from the Tree of Life and could thereby obtain immortality. The narrative of the Garden, therefore, does not concern the loss of an original immortality, but rather the forfeited chance to acquire immortality.

However, at the encouragement of the serpent and the woman who had earlier been created from him, the human reaches for the Tree of Knowledge. The previous conversation between the serpent and the woman is of great importance for understanding the narrative as a whole. The woman answers the serpent's provocation, saying, "From the fruits of the trees of the garden we may eat, but of the fruit of the tree *that is in the middle of the Garden*, God said, 'Do not eat of it and *do not touch it*, so that you will not die'" (Gen 3:2–3). God's original prohibition from Gen 2:17 appears in the mouth of the woman in an intensified form; the fact that one may not *touch* the fruit was not previously mentioned. The intensification of the prohibition indicates first that the woman should be attributed special prudence. She in no way wants to transgress God's prohibition.

---

70. Cf. Gerhard von Rad: "No one would be able to live even for a single day without appreciable harm if he could not be guided by wide practical experience." *Wisdom in Israel* (Nashville: Abingdon, 1972), 6.

Second, the woman no longer specifically relates the prohibition to the Tree of the Knowledge of God and Evil, as was explicitly the case in Gen 2:17, but rather to the tree *in the middle of the Garden*. But according to Gen 2:9, *two* trees—the Tree of Life *and* the Tree of the Knowledge of Good and Evil—stand there. So according to the logic of the narrative, which one can deduce from the intensification of the prohibition, the woman included the Tree of Life in the prohibition, likely as a precaution. As a result, the humans did not eat from the Tree of Life, although it was fundamentally permissible till this point, nor will they eat from it in the future. The possibility that was present at the beginning, that the human would acquire eternal life and not the knowledge of good and evil, therefore, is shown merely as the appearance of a choice. The immortal life in paradise was not a real alternative to the so-called fall into sin. Out of pure caution, the first human pair would not have eaten from the Tree of Life. The experiment of humanity would have come to an end with the childlike pair, who therefore would also not have reproduced.

THE FALL Nevertheless, the humans ate from the Tree of Knowledge and acquired the ability to distinguish between "good and evil." With respect to terminology, the transgression of the prohibition is not brought into connection with the concept of sin; the Hebrew term for sin first appears in Gen 4:6–7 in relation to fratricide. So sin does not yet come into the world, from a biblical point of view, with the so-called "fall" into sin. The eating of the fruit provides the precondition—the ability to recognize good and evil, and therefore responsibility. The fratricide of Abel is the first actual "fall" into sin, which is recorded as such with the appropriate terminology.

Also noteworthy in Gen 3:1–6 is the narrative presentation of the woman's motivation to reach for the fruit. Not a single word in Gen 3:6 references the perspective brought up by the serpent one verse earlier, namely that the humans would become like God. The discussion solely concerns the woman's desire to "become wise" (השכיל, *hśkyl*)—a classic wisdom term. The frequent interpretation of hubris for Gen 2–3, therefore, has no support in the text. The eating from the Tree of Knowledge does not appear with the hubristic intent to elevate the human above God. The woman does not desire to take God's place; instead she desires wisdom.

AMBIVALENCE BEFORE AND AFTER THE FALL Seen in this manner, the narrative of the Garden concerns the original denial and then the successful acquisition of essential practical knowledge by humans. This acquisition resulted from the transgression of a command, but the theological scope of the narrative progression does not focus on God's desire to deprive humans of the faculty of insight, but on the fact that the faculty of insight itself is experienced as so ambivalent that the author of Gen 2–3 connects it with the necessity of distance from God.

HUMAN SIMILARITY WITH GOD REGARDING THE KNOWLEDGE OF GOOD AND EVIL There is no doubt at the end of the narrative—the human has acquired the knowledge of good and evil. This is stated in the divine speech in Gen 3:22 (formulated in the perfect): "Behold, the human *has become* like us, for he knows good and evil!"

This declaration has repeatedly puzzled interpreters. Older scholarship either retreated to the assumption that in 3:22 the plural "like us" had only equality with the angels in mind, but did not speak of human equality with God. Or, on the other hand, scholars attempted (following the reformers) to maintain an ironic understanding of the formulation of Gen 3:22.[71] And this only if one had not already dealt with the problem by pushing the verse to the margins by means of compositional criticism. However, these attempted solutions appear rather unconvincing and are fed primarily by the endeavor to avoid the unwieldiness of the content of the statement. The text itself is clear: The human had acquired a special knowledge, and he has become equal to God with regard to this knowledge. One should note that Gen 2–3 does not narrate a delusional human *desire* to be like God, but rather the human's *having become* like God, a status that the human in reality attained with regard to the knowledge of good and evil.

THE EXPULSION FROM THE GARDEN The very acquisition of practical life knowledge brings with it the mandatory expulsion of the human from the Garden. For if he were now also—as still permitted—to eat from the Tree of Life, then he would become completely like God: knowledgable *and* immortal. Therefore, the human is now excluded from God's presence and must serve out the period of his existence beyond Eden. The Garden in Gen 2–3 describes the origin, not the destiny of the human.

AMBIVALENCES Considering an overview of the Garden narrative after this discussion, it becomes immediately clear that it does not narrate the

---

71. Cf., e.g., Martin Luther: *est sarcasmus et acerbissima irrisio* [it is sarcasm and derisive ridicule]. *Genesisvorlesung von 1535–1545,* WA 42, 166, 13.

loss of a completely positive original condition in favor of a correspondingly negative present condition. Instead, it in fact leads from one ambivalent situation into another likewise ambivalent situation.

It is, therefore, also not by chance that the description of the life of the first humans in the Garden of Eden is completely omitted. The only statement on their condition appears in Gen 2:25: "and the two were naked, the human and his wife, and they were not ashamed before one another." This sentence merely serves to prepare for Gen 3:7, where the humans recognize their nakedness after the fall. The *supralapsarian human* was indeed near to God, but he did not have any knowledge of good and evil—what remains so serious is that he (as can be deduced from the woman's answer to the serpent's provocation) ate neither from the Tree of Life, nor discovered sexuality as the means to reproduction (Gen 2:25). The *infralapsarian human* must now live distant from God, but in return he is able to reproduce (Gen 4:1, 17, 25, etc.) and to achieve cultural feats like agriculture, crafts, music, art, etc. (Gen 4:17–24).

ETIOLOGY OF THE AMBIVALENCE OF HUMAN PLANNING AND ACTION The point of the Garden narrative is as follows: It attempts to explain why there is an indissoluble connection between the independent human directing of life, which is daily required *de facto* of every adult human, who must decide between good and evil, and a substantial distance from God. No road back to the original situation in the Garden opens up. First, one cannot simply forget the acquired knowledge. And second—as Gen 2–3 depicts—an angel with a flaming sword stands watch to make sure that the Garden remains sealed forever.

COMPARING GEN 2–3 AND GEN 1 Looking back from Gen 2–3 to Gen 1 renders it clear that these texts belong to completely different mentalities. While Gen 2–3 also bears a clear monotheistic imprint, God encounters the humans in the Garden of Eden in a much more immediate manner and is depicted in an almost shockingly anthropormorphic way. The confrontation with Babylonian learning is absent in Gen 2–3. In terms of cosmology, Gen 2–3 appears instead to be influenced by indigenous traditions that are not otherwise available. Genesis 2–3 focuses completely on the human condition, which is seen as much more problematic than in Gen 1. Human faculties of knowledge rest on a robbery and lead necessarily to a distance from God that is constitutive of human experience. In Gen 1, the humans are instead conferred the "image of God," so they are considered God's representatives on earth.

4. New Creation (Isa 65–66) and "Nothing New under the Sun" (Qoh 1)

THE PROPHETIC REVERSAL OF GEN 1–3 Contrary to the non-eschatological orientation of Gen 1–3, the theology of the third part of the book of Isaiah, which scholars have traditionally called Trito-Isaiah (Isa 56–66), develops the conception of a new creation. Contrary to the usual view of scholarship, Isa 56–66 does not concern an originally oral prophecy from the "Deutero-Isaiah" school. It is instead an entirely scribal interpretation of the prophetic texts from Isa 40–55. Divine action is already qualified in Isa 40–55 as creational action. However, the theology of Deutero-Isaiah—corresponding to the situation of its origin at the end of the so-called Babylonian exile with the expected return home for the people of Israel to its land—is completely determined by a "new exodus," which will far surpass the salvation-historical exodus from Egypt, as Isa 43:16–21 shows through its drastic formulations:

Isa 43:16–21:	Isa 65:17–18:
Thus says Yhwh, who makes a way in the sea and a path in the mighty waters, who brings forth wagons and horses, army and strength, they lie there together, never again will they rise, they are extinguished, put out like a wick.	For look, I am creating a new heaven and a new earth, and that which was earlier will no longer be remembered, and one will not consider it anymore.
"Think no more on what was before; And what was previously—do not be concerned with it. See, I am doing something new; it is already sprouting, do you not recognize it? Yes, I am making a way in the desert and rivers through the wasteland. The animals of the field will honor me, the jackels and the ostriches. For I am bringing water to the deserts, rivers to the wasteland in order to provide my people, my chosen ones with drink, the people that I formed for myself. They will tell of my glory."	Instead exult and rejoice without end over what I am creating! For look, I am creating Jerusalem as jubilation and her people as rejoicing.

For Isa 40–55, the "old" exodus from Egypt no longer contains any salvific quality (Isa 43:18: "Think no more on what was before!"). It obviously set in motion a history of calamity that culminated in the loss of the Israelites' own land. The relationship between Israel and its God could no longer support itself with this as its foundational experience. Isaiah 40–55 instead lays out that there will be a new exodus, now from Babylon, which will far surpass the old one. Initially Yhwh will himself set out from Babylon, and the people will then follow. A new relationship between God and the people will be established on this new exodus, so the old one can safely be forgotten. It is noteworthy that the new exodus is also familiar with a "water miracle," though no enemy will be destroyed like what took place in Exod 14. Instead Yhwh will provide water in the desert so that his people can drink.

NEW CREATION AS SUPERSEDING THE NEW EXODUS The idea that the new exodus from Babylon would be the new salvation experience on which Israel could depend did not, however, prove itself to be a sustainable theological supposition. A structurally very similar argument in Isa 56–66 now replaces not only the old exodus with a new exodus, but also the old *creation* with a new one (Isa 65:17: "that which was earlier will no longer be remembered!").

Within the realm of Isa 40–66, one can observe both the immediate composition and theological-historical steps prior to and also after Gen 1. Specifically, the earlier texts in Isa 40–55 interact more closely with Israel's traditions of election, such as the ancestor and exodus traditions, and the creation thematic only begins to establish itself as a continuous tenor. Furthermore, Isa 40–55 pushes strongly an exclusive conception of God, while Gen 1 thinks more inclusively. First in Isa 65–66, however, is the creation theology of Gen 1 reconditioned insofar as the expectation of a new creation is articulated. God will once again significantly re-shape his creation.[72] In addition, Isa 65–66 presents a theological position that abandons the idea of the unity of God's people. Also, repentance is no longer the means of salvation to overcoming hindrances to salvation such as cultic and social abuses, as it was in Isa 56–59. The differentiation between the

---

72. Odil Hannes Steck, "Der neue Himmel und die neue Erde: Beobachtungen zur Rezeption von Gen 1–3 in Jes 65,16b–25," in *Studies in the Book of Isaiah: Festschrift for Willem A. M. Beuken,* ed. Jacques van Ruiten and Marc Vervenne, BETL 132 (Leuven: Peeters, 1997), 349–65.

pious and sinners is alone relevant for the coming salvific turn. This new theological position is of such a fundamental nature that the juxtaposition of old and new exodus was no longer sufficient, for the exodus was a decidedly national conception.

THE OBJECTION IN THE BOOK OF QOHELETH However, the prophetic position of Isa 65–66 experienced hearty opposition in the wisdom literature. The book of Qoheleth issues a clear rejection of the wide-reaching hopes for a divine eschatological intervention in world history. In contrast to expectations for a new heaven and a new earth from the contemporary texts of the book of Isaiah, Qoheleth emphasizes that there is "nothing new."[73]

QOH 1:9–11:	ISA 65:17:
What was will again be, and what was done will be done again; there is nothing new under the sun. Perhaps one will say, "Look at this! It is something new!" It already existed long ago in earlier times that preceded us. There is no memory of the earlier, and also the later that will come. Of them there will also be no memory among those who will be last.	For look, I am creating a new heaven and a new earth; one will no longer think about the earlier things, and no one will still remember them.

Qoheleth is also rather reserved regarding a further fundamental conviction of Isa 56–66. In Qoheleth there is no theologically relevant separation between the sinners and the pious. There are certainly the wise and the foolish, righteous and unrighteous, but they do not have distinct fates in death (Qoh 3:19). In death all are alike; there is no compensation in the beyond, which one could have hoped from texts like Ps 49 and 73 (cf. Qoh 9:1).

Therefore, according to Qoheleth, humans are directed to the fundamental life provisions and life orders of creation. These are not optimal,

73. Cf. Thomas Krüger, "Dekonstruktion und Rekonstruktion prophetischer Eschatologie im Qohelet-Buch," in *"Jedes Ding hat seine Zeit . . .": Studien zur israelitischen und altorientalischen Weisheit: Festschrift für Diethelm Michel,* ed. Anja A. Diesel et al., BZAW 241 (Berlin: de Gruyter, 1996), 107–29.

but neither are they bad; they are instead ambivalent. As a result, Qoheleth agrees with the theological perspective of Gen 1–11,[74] and also with several statements in Psalms (cf. Ps 104).

IMMORTALITY OF THE SOUL Contrary to the rest of the Hebrew Bible, the Greek book of the Wisdom of Solomon from the first half of the first century CE in Alexandria presents the viewpoint of the immortality of the souls of the righteous (3:1) and of their rapture (4:10–11). This is the reward for the righteous if they are unable to attain remuneration in this life. The Wisdom of Solomon makes known to its audience that God did not create death (1:13–15), but that death came into the world through the jealousy of the devil (2:24), alluding to the figure of the serpent in the biblical story of the Garden (cf. Gen 3). This indicates that the Wisdom of Solomon stands a certain distance from the rest of the biblical writings.

NETWORK OF POSITIONS One can conclude, therefore, that the Hebrew Bible does not formulate a specific position on certain theological questions. It instead presents a network of positions that interact with one another textually, yet no one position is furnished with more or less authority. The Bible attests to a historically and functionally complex treatment of the theological questions that it addresses. This conclusion is only theologically problematic for a fundamentalist understanding of the Bible.

§32 Divine Intervention in History

Bertil Albrektson, *History and the Gods: An Essay on the Idea of Historical Events as Divine Manifestations in the Ancient Near East and in Israel,* Con-BOT 1 (Lund: Gleerup, 1967) ♦ Erhard Blum, "Ein Anfang der Geschichtsschreibung? Anmerkungen zur sog. Thronfolgegeschichte und zum Umgang mit Geschichte im alten Israel," in *Textgestalt und Komposition, Exegetische Beiträge zu Tora und Vordere Propheten,* FAT 69 (Tübingen: Mohr Siebeck, 2010), 281–318 ♦ Jan C. Gertz, "Die Stellung des kleinen geschichtlichen Credos in der Redaktionsgeschichte von Deuteronomium und Pentateuch," in *Liebe und Gebot: Studien zum Deuteronomium: Festschrift für Lothar Perlitt,*

---

74. Cf. Thomas Krüger, "Die Rezeption der Tora im Buch Kohelet," in *Das Buch Kohelet: Studien zur Struktur, Geschichte, Rezeption und Theologie,* ed. Ludger Schwienhorst-Schönberger, BZAW 254 (Berlin: de Gruyter, 1997), 173–93.

ed. Reinhard G. Kratz and Hermann Spieckermann, FRLANT 190 (Göttingen: Vandenhoeck & Ruprecht, 2000), 30–45 ◆ Bernd Janowski, "Vergegenwärtigung und Wiederholung: Anmerkungen zu Gerhard von Rads Konzept der 'Heilsgeschichte,'" in *Heil und Geschichte: Die Geschichtsbezogenheit des Heils und das Problem der Heilsgeschichte in der biblischen Tradition und in der theologischen Deutung*, ed. Jörg Frey et al., WUNT 248 (Tübingen: Mohr Siebeck, 2009), 37–61 ◆ Reinhard G. Kratz, "Geschichten und Geschichte in den nordwestsemitischen Inschriften," in *Was ist ein Text? Alttestamentliche, ägyptologische und altorientalische Perspektiven*, ed. Ludwig Morenz and Stefan Schorch, BZAW 362 (Berlin: de Gruyter, 2007), 284–309 ◆ Reinhard G. Kratz, *Historical and Biblical Israel: The History, Tradition, and Archives of Israel and Judah* (Oxford: Oxford University Press, 2015) ◆ Klaus Koch, "Gibt es ein Vergeltungsdogma im Alten Testament," in *Spuren des hebräischen Denkens: Beiträge zur alttestamentlichen Theologie: Gesammelte Aufsätze*, vol. 1 (Neukirchen-Vluyn: Neukirchener Verlag, 1991), 65–103 ◆ Klaus Koch, "Das aramäisch-hebräische Danielbuch: Konfrontation zwischen Weltmacht und monotheistischer Religionsgemeinschaft in universalgeschichtlicher Perspektive," in *Die Geschichte der Daniel-Auslegung in Judentum, Christentum und Islam: Studien zur Kommentierung des Danielbuches in Literatur und Kunst*, ed. Katharina Bracht and David du Toit, BZAW 371 (Berlin: de Gruyter, 2007), 3–27 ◆ Norbert Lohfink, "Die Priesterschrift und die Geschichte," in *Congress Volume Göttingen 1977*, ed. John A. Emerton, VTSup 29 (Leiden: Brill, 1978), 183–225 ◆ Thomas Römer, *The So-Called Deuteronomistic History: A Sociological, Historical And Literary Introduction* (London: T&T Clark, 2005) ◆ Thomas Römer, "Die Erfindung der Geschichte im antiken Juda und die Entstehung der Hebräischen Bibel," in *Geschichte und Gott: XV. Europäischer Kongress für Theologie (14.–18. September 2014 in Berlin)*, ed. Michael Meyer-Blanck, Veröffentlichungen der Wissenschaftlichen Gesellschaft für Theologie 44 (Leipzig: Evangelische Verlagsanstalt, 2016), 37–57 ◆ Michael Segal, *Dreams, Riddles, and Visions: Textual, Contextual, and Intertextual Approaches to the Book of Daniel*, BZAW 455 (Berlin: de Gruyter, 2016) ◆ Markus Witte, "Von den Anfängen der Geschichtswerke im Alten Testament: Eine forschungsgeschichtliche Diskussion neuerer Gesamtentwürfe," in *Die antike Historiographie und die Anfänge der christlichen Geschichtsschreibung*, ed. Eve-Marie Becker, BZNW 129 (Berlin: de Gruyter, 2005), 53–81

1. Preliminary Remarks from the History of Scholarship

THE HYPOTHESIS OF A SALVATION-HISTORICAL IMPRINT OF THE RELI-
GION OF ISRAEL The fact that the relationship of the literature of the Hebrew Bible to history itself has a history has not always been self-evident
in biblical studies. Even two generations ago, any question of the historical
development of the Hebrew Bible with regard to its relationship to history
would have been found rather implausible, for scholars were convinced
that the faith of the Hebrew Bible had been linked to history from the very
beginning. The God of Israel had revealed himself in historical events like
the exodus from Egypt, and in these very events he had proven himself to
be God. Therefore, Israel's faith had always pertained to history.

MARTIN NOTH As Martin Noth has stated, "One of the most fundamental
and frequently repeated statements of faith in the Old Testament is that
Yahweh, the God of Israel, is the one who 'led Israel out of Egypt.' . . . To
the act of God expressed in this confessional statement Israel traced its
existence and its special place among the nations."[75] Noth concisely articulates two points. First, Israel establishes its existence on God's saving act
in history. Second, Israel thereby takes a special position among the circle
of nations. The central theological concept in scholarship of the Hebrew
Bible at that time was called *salvation history*. The salvation-historical imprint of the religion of Israel was considered its unique feature within the
ancient Near East. Israel received God's salvation history from the promises to the ancestors, the exodus from Egypt, the wilderness wandering,
as far as the possession of the land as the content of its faith, while the
neighboring religions of the ancient Near East knew nothing of divine
action in history. Their gods rose and died cyclically with the seasons. In a
word, Israel found its God in history; the neighboring religions found their
gods in nature—such was the dominating distinction in the middle of the
1900s. One name within Hebrew Bible studies stands out with regard to
this conception: Gerhard von Rad. This is attested in exemplary fashion
in his epoch-making *Old Testament Theology*:

> The ancient east's view of the world bears to a greater or lesser degree
> the clear impress of cyclical thinking in terms of myth, that is to say, of

75. Martin Noth, *A History of Pentateuchal Traditions*, trans. Bernard W. Anderson
(Englewood Cliffs, NJ: Prentice Hall, 1972), 47.

a way of thinking which understood the cultic event on the basis of the rhythm of the fixed orders of nature. . . . This sacral understanding of the world is essentially non-historical; at least, it leaves absolutely no place for the very thing which Israel regarded as the constitutive element of her faith, the once-for-all quality of divine saving acts within her history.[76]

THE "SHORT HISTORICAL CREDO" Von Rad justified this sharp antithesis between "natural orders" and "historical faith" through what he called the credo texts in the Hebrew Bible, which have Israel's salvation history as their focus. For von Rad, at least the content of these was considered ancient.

Von Rad found the most important and also the most original imprint of this credo in Deut 26:5b–9:

A wandering Aramean was my father, and he went down to Egypt, and he sojourned there as a foreigner with few people, and there he became a great people, strong and numerous. And the Egyptians treated us poorly and oppressed us, and gave us heavy labor. And we cried to Yhwh, the God of our fathers, and Yhwh heard our voice and saw our suffering and our hardship and our oppression. And Yhwh led us out of Egypt with a strong hand and an outstretched arm and terrifying deeds and signs and wonders. And he brought us to this place and gave us this land, a land that flows with milk and honey.

This "short historical credo" describes in the briefest form the content of Israel's salvation-historical faith. In their own way—only much more elaboration—the authors of the older source texts of the Pentateuch, the Yahwist and the Elohist, repeated the same basic structure of this "short historical credo," thereby faithfully depicting the salvation-historical material of Israel's faith. The hexateuchal depiction of the history from the ancestors to the possession of the land is the most intrinsic material of Israel's faith, not in the least because it rested on relevant historical experiences—or so at least it was supposed.

CRITIQUE OF VON RAD However, it became clear in scholarship soon after von Rad that the antiquity of the short historical credo could not be maintained. The relinquishment of this thesis did not come as a surprise. The

76. Von Rad, *Old Testament Theology*, 2:110–11.

section of Deut 26:6–9 is markedly "Deuteronomistic," and one can even discover (post-)Priestly echoes (compare Deut 26:7 with Exod 2:23–25). In the meantime, linguistic and theological-historical evidence has been brought forth multiple times that the short historical credo is not a nucleus, but rather a later summary. As a result, however, one of the central supports for the classical depiction of Israel's religion as a historically conceived religion from the very beginning falls away.

Complementary to the late dating of the short historical credo is the widely accepted work in Hebrew Bible studies of the Swedish scholar Bertil Albrektson entitled *History of the Gods* from 1967, written as a refutation of the bipolar model of the differentiation of the historically shaped faith of Israel from the purely natural cults of its environment. This work received an especially warm reception in English-speaking scholarship. In his work Bertil Albrektson established that the self-manifestation of the gods in history was also common in the ancient Near East outside of Israel. Yet this thesis is comparatively trivial. Purely deist conceptions that separate God so radically from history, such that the two have nothing to do with one another, first arose with the Enlightenment, and the deities of the ancient Near East self-evidently have the ability to act within history. Otherwise one could not comprehend the entire complex of cult, sacrifice, and divination practices in the ancient Near East.

The triviality and also the success of Albrektson's thesis can basically be explained by the earlier almost uncontested triumph of the salvation-historical theory of Israel's faith from its beginnings, which provoked disagreement.

Moving beyond Albrektson, today one must say that the simple alternative between the historically active God of Israel and the non-historical deities of Israel's surroundings cannot simply be reproached with the counter argument that all deities in the Near East, including the god of Israel, are active in history.

CONCEPTIONS OF DIVINE ACTION IN HISTORY One must instead identify *how* divine action in history is conceived in the ancient texts. Of which modes of divine influence and permeation of history are ancient religions aware? Jan Assman proposes the differentiation of three conceptions of divine action in history:[77]

77. For the following, cf. Jan Assmann, *Das kulturelle Gedächtnis,* 7th ed. (Munich: Beck, 2013), 248–52.

DIVINE INTERVENTIONS The simplest and also most ancient conception is that of a single divine intervention in the historical reality, which is the functional presupposition of the entire ancient Near Eastern culture of divination. An example for this from the Hebrew Bible would be the miracle of fire on Mount Carmel in 1 Kgs 18, in which God sends lightning from heaven and sets Elijah's woodpile on fire, or such an event as the parting of the sea at the passage of the Israelites. Assmann calls these interventions "charismatic events." They are not to be understood as sacred intrusions into an otherwise profane history—the profane-sacred distinction would be anachronistic. Instead, time and history are themselves an unarticulated framework for the various powers—even divine interventions.

COVENANT-THEOLOGY INTERPRETED HISTORY A comparably advanced stage of the association between God and history is also found already where history is interpreted in light of a reciprocal relationship of obligation between the people or king and God. Times of weal or woe are correlated with human behavior that is measured by specific cultic requirements or divine laws, such that weal or woe follows them. Only at this stage does "history" even have a coherent, meaningful continuum in view. This kind of historical interpretation appears in ancient Mesopotamia in the Weidner Chronicle or in Egypt in the Demotic Chronicle. It appears most clearly in the Hebrew Bible in what are called the Deuteronomistic interpretive passages of the historical books, which correlate well-being or calamity in history with Israel's obedience. In this case Assmann speaks of "charismatic history."

DETERMINISTIC INTERPRETATIONS OF HISTORY A third step is the notion of a history that is completely directed and planned by God, which diverges from the other two. Apocalyptic interpretations of history such as the ten-week apocalypse of the book of Enoch can be mentioned as examples.

CONCEPTIONS OF HISTORY CAN OVERLAP These three identifiable stages of ideal types, of which alternatives and mixed forms also exist, will become clear in the following sections. They should not, however, be understood as conceptions that can be separated from one another into a linear sequence. The three steps supplement one another gradually, existing both interwovenly and next to one another.

Israel Is Not an Entity *Sui Generis* The scholarship of the twentieth century clearly demonstrated that, contrary to the notion of discontinuity in the wake of neo-orthodox theology, Israel was not completely independent from its environment, fostering a faith *sui generis*. The conception of divine action in history is not unique to ancient Israel. Conversely, Israel's faith was not simply marked by (salvation-)history from its very beginning. Instead, this imprint itself had a history that can be differentiated conceptually.

2. The Theology of the Jerusalem Cult

The theology of the Jerusalem cult was one strand of theological tradition that was fostered at the preexilic temple in Jerusalem and is condensed literarily into the Psalms more than anywhere else (cf. above, §23). It cannot be clearly classified by the typology sketched above. Instead, it forms, to some degree, the authoritative conceptual background in monarchic Jerusalem for various expressions of the conception of Yhwh's acts in history. The theology of the Jerusalem cult can be interpreted as a typical ancient Near Eastern theological conception. The theological conceptions of Judah's neighboring states—Ammon, Moab, Edom—can, *mutatis mutandis,* be conceived in the same way, even if this cannot be substantiated due to the lack of literary evidence. Yhwh is presented in the theology of the Jerusalem cult as the powerful king of the world, enthroned on Zion. He protects Jerusalem and its environs—the Judean highlands—and repels all chaotic threats, such as enemies as well as natural catastrophes.

> For Yhwh, the Highest, is awesome, a great king over all the earth. (Ps 47:2)

> The mountains melt like wax before Yhwh, before the lord of the entire earth. (Ps 97:5)

The sovereignty of Yhwh, the king of the world, is based in his majesty, which renders him exalted over all mythic and political challenges. It can by all means manifest itself in individual acts of history—especially those such as the preservation of Jerusalem from the siege by Sennacherib (701 BCE), which 2 Kgs 18–20 and the parallel passage in Isa 36–39 report. This event serves above all as the paradigm of divine deliverance for Israel in the late period. However, these are manifestations and not the foundation of God's identity as Israel's God. God's divine nature is based beyond history, which he dominates in punctiliar interventions.

THEOLOGIA GLORIAE Speaking anachronistically, the theology of the Jerusalem cult is a classic theology of glory, which describes God as a powerful protective force, sees him as unfailing, and especially as attached to the powerful and strong. Also in this aspect it is a classical counterpart to the other ancient Near Eastern religions that essentially think within this matrix. This form of thinking first dissolved in exilic and postexilic Judaism under the impact of the catastrophe of 587 BCE and the Babylonian exile, and God was then for the first time conceived as primarily attached to the poor (cf. below, §39).

THE THEOLOGY OF THE JERUSALEM CULT AS A "COLD" CONCEPTION Employing the well-known distinction from Claude Lévi-Strauss,[78] the theology of the Jerusalem cult is a "cold" conception. "Cold" in this context means that the theology of the Jersusalem cult is by nature not formulated in such a way that it could respond to historically contrary experiences and incorporate these into its framework. It instead attempts to resist and defensively immunizes itself against the conditions of historical experience. A "hot" conception instead reacts to historical experiences, adopting them and transforming itself by them constantly. One cannot say this about the theology of the Jerusalem cult. It is, therefore, not surprising that it did not outlive the demise of Judah and Jerusalem in 587 BCE.

3. God's Glory and the Glory of Assyria

THE HISTORICAL CONTEXT OF ISA 6–8 A special form of theologically construed interpretation of history appears in the so-called Isaiah Memoir in Isa 6–8. It refers to Judah's crisis that took place still prior to the Assyrian conquest of Damascus and Samaria in the eighth century BCE; however, as a literary document it likely emerged only in the seventh century BCE. The imagined political context allows for the identification of a coalition between Aram and Israel that attempts to force Judah into an anti-Assyrian alliance.

---

78. Cf. Claude Lévi Strauss, *Das wilde Denken*, 4th ed. (Frankfurt am Main: Suhrkamp, 1981), 270 = *The Savage Mind* (Chicago: University of Chicago Press, 1966).

One can still deduce from Isa 6–8 that the position of the prophet Isaiah initially foresaw deliverance for Judah from the harassment of the regional powers of Aram and Israel. However, this position changes in the written version, as especially Isa 6:1–13 and Isa 8:5–8 show, such that Judah itself is now also included in the impending judgment. Assyria will not only destroy Aram and Israel, but also Judah. One can assume with some probability that this expectation still belongs in the late eighth or early seventh century BCE, for the pronouncement of judgment against Judah—unlike that against Aram and Israel—was not immediately fulfilled, leading to the so-called commission to harden (hearts) in Isa 6:9–10, which indicates to the contemporary readers the apparent discrepancy between the prophetic message and experienced situation (cf. above, §23).

ASSYRIA AS GOD'S INSTRUMENT Within this conception, Isa 6–8 now develops a remarkable notion of God's acts of judgment against his own people by means of his instrument Assyria. The keywords "glory" (כבוד, *kbwd*) and "fullness" (מלא, *ml'*) in Isa 6:3 and 8:7 frame the complex of Isa 6–8, yet this is not simply an aesthetic literary measure. It instead establishes a theological, textually meaningful correspondence. The fullness of the world in Isa 6:3 is the glory of *God*. In Isa 8:7, Judah is instead affected by the glory of *the king of Assyria*. The term כבוד (*kbwd*), "glory," in this case serves as the Hebrew equivalent for the Akkadian *melammu*, "radiance." In Isa 8 this means "Taking the place of YHWH's 'glory' is the 'radiance' of Assyria, which God himself has made space for."[79] The biblical God is, therefore, willing and able to limit his own terrifying sphere of amazement so that Assyria's radiance can take its place.

This form of theological history in the Hebrew Bible is noteworthy for its employment of inter-religious ideas. It adopts the Neo-Assyrian conception of *melammu*, "radiance," and aligns the behavior of the biblical God in such a way that it relates in a complementary manner with the efficacy of the radiance of Assyria.[80] In this case Isaiah appears as a virtual

---

79. Friedhelm Hartenstein, *Das Archiv des verborgenen Gottes: Studien zur Unheilsprophetie Jesajas und zur Zionstheologie der Psalmen in assyrischer Zeit*, Biblisch-theologische Studien 74 (Neukirchen-Vluyn: Neukirchener Verlag, 2011), 11. German original: "An die Stelle der JHWH-'Herrlichkeit' tritt der 'Schreckensglanz' Assurs, dem Gott selbst Raum gibt."

80. As this example shows, not only depictions of deities were translatable between one another (cf. Mark S. Smith, *God in Translation: Deities in Cross-Cultural Discourse in the Biblical World*, FAT 57 [Tübingen: Mohr Siebeck, 2008]), but also theologies of history.

legitimator of Assyria's warlike actions against Aram, Israel, and Judah. The prophet thereby represents a mouthpiece against the dominant, orthodox theology of the Jerusalem cult.

4. The Deuteronomistic Theology of History

THE ORIGINS OF DEUTERONOMISM Toward the end of the monarchy, a weighty theological position arose in national religious circles in addition to the theology of the Jerusalem cult, arguably in opposition to the pressure of Assyrian culture and as a rejection of Assyrian treaty theology. This is the position of Deuteronomy (cf. above, §18 and §24). It likely had further tradition-historical roots in the northern kingdom and received significant impetuses from prophecy and wisdom.

DEUTERONOMY AND THE FURTHER DEVELOPMENT INTO DEUTERONOM-ISM After the catastrophe of Judah and Jerusalem in 587 BCE—which at the same time must have meant the declaration of the theological bankruptcy of the Jerusalem cult's theology of glory, which was not prepared for the fall of the city and temple of God but had conceptually excluded such a possibility in categorical terms—the theology of Deuteronomy and subsequently that of Deuteronomism gained the upper hand. It was able to formulate an answer to the historical experience of the national collapse. It is an answer that appears problematic from the perspective of today's theology, but at that time it seemed quite historically plausible. The collapse was divine punishment for human guilt. A very significant step took place here: with regard to the historical impress of Israel's religion, the comparably ahistorically formulated Jerusalem cult theology had abdicated. There was only one remaining viable intellectual conception capable of reacting to the historical experience of national catastrophe, so Deuteronomistic theology and Deuteronomism emerged.

At this point one of the most decisive choices in the theological history of ancient Israel can be observed. The decision was made to give up the conventional orthodox tradition and therefore to perish, instead choosing the "hot" option (Lévi-Strauss),[81] which takes seriously in theological terms the experience that strongly contravened the previous orthodoxy. It worked through that experience and then ventured initially heterodoxical

---

81. Cf. above, n. 78.

steps beyond the previous orthodoxy toward a new conception, which it was unclear in advance whether it would itself become orthodox. This decision is of the utmost importance for the history of theology and for theology itself, for it initiated an alliance in biblical tradition with every historical truth rather than with ideology.

Deuteronom(ist)ic Theology   Deuteronomic theology and Deuteronomism are essentially based on two basic presuppositions: First, there are two requirements for Israel with regard to its cult—cultic unity and cultic purity. Cultic unity means that Yhwh can only be worshiped cultically in Jerusalem. Cultic purity means that only Yhwh may be worshiped. Second, these requirements—or in the language of Deuteronomy, commandments—bring about blessing if they are kept, but curse if they are not. The corollary is also the case: the experience of blessing rests on obedience to the commandments; historical experience of curse is traced back to guilt.

With this classification, Deuteronomism offers the first thoroughly theologically-construed conception of history in Israel and presents the history of Israel from the exodus from Egypt to the exile in Exodus–2 Kings as a sustained history of guilt that therefore leads to catastrophe. Deuteronomism's interpretation of history is thoroughly marked by the close packaging of obedience to the commandments and the corresponding result. Israel's obligation to the commandments is the undertone that determines the history. It is worth noting that this theology of history is anchored in form-critical terms primarily in the speeches and prayers of the main characters in the historical books, found in the mouths of figures such as Joshua, Samuel, Solomon, etc. This makes the literary point clear that this theology of history rests on an interpretive process and is not inherent in the events themselves.

The Historical Reflection in 2 Kgs 17   An important exception to this is the long reflection on the demise of the northern kingdom in 2 Kgs 17:7–23, which undertakes an explicit theological interpretation of the catastrophe on the level of the narrator but is, however, tiered in terms of its content (and correspondingly also in terms of its composition). One perspective in 2 Kgs 17 places the guilt on the kings (vv. 21–23), the other, apparently added later, accuses the people (vv. 7–19).

Especially striking in light of 2 Kgs 17 is that a correspondingly long reflection on the demise of the southern kingdom is missing. While 2 Kgs 25 is not free of theological interpretation, the analogous passages do not compare with the massiveness of the interpretive effort put forth in 2 Kgs 17. This is noteworthy because Deuteronomism is fundamentally focused on Judah and Jerusalem, so such an interpretive perspective would also be expected in 2 Kgs 25. The absence of such an interpretation can perhaps be explained in a twofold manner. First, it may indicate in terms of the compositional history that there was a first edition of a Deuteronomistic history, perhaps only extending from *Sam–*Kings, already in the preexilic period, so the basic structure of this work did not reach to the demise of Judah and Jerusalem.[82] Second, one could, however, reckon that the book of Kings already pointed toward the prophetic literature that followed in the canon, and it as a whole provided this interpretation.[83]

DOXOLOGY OF JUDGMENT The Deuteronomistic complex of historical books is correctly described as a great confession of judgment,[84] which is a sweeping hymn to the just God of Israel. Yhwh is pronounced innocent of the historical catastrophe, for Israel was given obligations and responsibility but was guilty toward him—prominent, central, theological texts in Deuteronomy and in Deuteronomism do not allow for any doubt on this point. Worthy of mention here is, for example, the prelude to the famous Shema Israel ("Hear, O Israel") in Deut 6:1–3, which clearly shows the theme of the close connection between obedience and favorable well-being:

> And this is the commandment, the statutes and the ordinances, that Yhwh, your God, has commanded you, so that you will teach them, so that you will observe them in the land that you will cross into in order to possess it. Concerning how you will fear Yhwh, your God, for your whole life and keep all his statutes and commandments, which I give you—you, and your children, and your children's children—so that

---

82. This position was already presented by Wellhausen; cf. Konrad Schmid, "Hatte Wellhausen recht? Das Problem der literarhistorischen Anfänge des Deuteronomismus in den Königebüchern," in *Die deuteronomistischen Geschichtswerke: Redaktions- und religionsgeschichtliche Perspektiven zur Deuteronomismusdiskussion in Tora und Vorderen Propheten*, ed. Markus Witte et al., BZAW 365 (Berlin: de Gruyter, 2006), 23–47.

83. Cf. Ernst Axel Knauf, "Kings among the Prophets," in *Data and Debates: Essays in the History and Culture of Israel and Its Neighbors in Antiquity = Daten und Debatten: Aufsätze zur Kulturgeschichte des antiken Israel und seiner Nachbarn*, AOAT 407 (Münster: Ugarit-Verlag, 2013), 715–29.

84. Cf. von Rad, *Old Testament Theology*, 1:337.

your days will be long. So listen to them now, Israel, and be careful to do them, so that it will go well with you, and you will multiply greatly, as Yhwh, the God of your fathers, told you, in a land that flows with milk and honey.

One cannot say that this Deuteronomistic conception arose initially and solely after the fact, as a reaction to the catastrophe. This is hardly plausible historically. In order for a certain thought to be able to provide some orientation in the catastrophe, it must have already been conceived beforehand. Apparently a significant shuffling of the theologically dominant position took place in Israel with Deuteronomy and the beginnings of Deuteronomism at the end of the seventh century BCE, such that it could provide considerable succor throughout the historical experience of the catastrophe of Judah and Jerusalem. Israel was moved by Deuteronomism theologically to the place where it was also able to interpret contrary historical events in a religious manner. One might even entertain the possibility that Deuteronomists in the Babylonian exile were employed in the Babylonian palace. Their theology allowed the Babylonians to appear as God's legitimate instruments and relieved them of the allegation of willfully and arbitrarily destroying the Jerusalem temple.[85]

5. Prophetic Interpretations of History

PROPHETS AS "FORETELLERS" AND "FORTHTELLERS" The prophets of the Hebrew Bible have, according to the Bible, a very close relationship with history. In the biblical view, they are primarily reckoned as the foretellers of future events. This presentation of prophecy does not match the historical reconstructions of the prophets of the Hebrew Bible. On this a considerable difference can be illustrated with the double meaning of the Greek term προφήτης (*prophētēs*), which the Greek translation of the Hebrew Bible consistently uses to translate the Hebrew equivalent, נביא (*nby'*).[86] It is derived

---

85. Cf. Thomas Römer, *The So-Called Deuteronomistic History* (London: T&T Clark, 2005), 164.

86. The etymology of the Hebrew term נביא (*nby'*) is unclear. It has been suggested to derive it from the Akkadian verb *nabû(m)*, to which one ascribes the meaning "call," but this is both uncertain and motivated by a certain understanding of the biblical prophets (cf. Isa 6; Jer 1; Ezek 1–3) that is quite unreliable, and instead is likely based on the biblical construction of the prophetic figures.

from the verb προφήμι (*prophēmi*), which is made from the combination of the prefix προ- (*pro-*), "before," and the verb φήμι (*phēmi*), "say." The prefix προ- (*pro-*) denotes, in basic terms, the aspect "before" in either a temporal or spatial sense. The temporal interpretation would lead to the meaning "foretelling," while the spatial leads to the public "forth-telling."

Distinguishing these two aspects, they are, historically speaking, not *exclusively* but to a certain extent related to one another as *successive*. While it is true that the long-term biblical formation of tradition made them increasingly into tellers of the future, this characteristic of the prophets is primarily the creation of their books. They also proclaimed salvation and calamity for the near future, but they did not survey the entirety of world history, which is the case, for example, for the canonical Isaiah. According to the biblical image of the book of Isaiah extending from Isa 1–66, Isaiah prophesied about the subsequent centuries as far as the new creation of heaven and earth from his historical location in the eighth century BCE. The historical prophets offered social and cultic critique, carried out symbolic actions, intoned laments, and criticized the royal house. Their message is not dominated primarily by a view to the future, certainly not one still centuries removed. The difference between prophet and prophetic book is also mirrored in the different meaning of the topic of history.

THE EARLY ISAIAH TRADITION The so-called refrain poem in Isa 5:25–30 + 9:7–20; 10:1–4 refers to the tradition of Amos, the prophet of the northern kingdom and therefore the topic of the judgment on Israel, reflecting its meaning for Judah (cf. above, §22). The poem is marked by the refrain "For all this, his anger has not turned away, and his hand is still outstretched" (cf. 9:12, 17, 21; 10:4; cf. 5:25; see above, §22). It provides sufficient indications that the judgment was not finished with the destruction of the northern kingdom but would stretch further to include Judah. Isaiah 9:7, 12 are full of allusions to the Amos tradition, which shows that the judgment proclaimed by Isaiah against Judah was not a new operation. It rested on God's anger against Israel, which was still directed toward his people. The judgment against Judah was therefore an extension and continuation of the judgment proclaimed against the northern kingdom by Amos.

Prophetic interpretation of history in this case does not concern the future, but rather the past and the present. Of a similar nature is the section on the "prince of peace" in Isa 8:23b–9:7. In Christian tradition it is known as an Advent and Christmas text, understood as a messianic promise that speaks of the coming of a child who will bring eternal peace as a ruler. The original meaning of the text, however, is not a promise, as the past tense forms of the verbs show. The birth of this child was not expected; instead the text looks back in gratitude on the birth that already took place. Therefore, in this case prophecy is an elucidation of the present, not an announcement of the future.

The Construction of a Universal History Universal historical interpretations arise in prophecy in the period of the Babylonian exile. The experience of the change in imperial world domination from the Assyrians to the Babylonians and then to the Persians within a century appears to have brought about enormous attempts to interpret the way these processes fit in with the divine will that molds history. These efforts can be apprehended in such places as the book of Jeremiah or the Deutero-Isaiah tradition, where Nebuchadnezzar is designated as God's "servant" (Jer 25:9; 43:10) and Cyrus as "messiah" (Isa 45:1). The emperors from Babylon and Persia evidently took over the function of the Davidic dynasty as the divinely chosen and commissioned kings. In the book of Jeremiah, clear efforts can be discerned to replace the Davidic dynasty with Nebuchadnezzar's global dominion, which overlapped by several years in actual history (between the battle of Carchemish in 604 BCE and the demise of Jerusalem in 587 BCE). These passages attempt a theological harmonization by announcing the end of the Davidic dynasty (36:30) already in a narrative dated to the time of King Jehoiakim in 604 (Jer 36:1).[87] In subsequent texts, an awareness increasingly developed that prophetic declarations were not bound to particular times, even though the prophets themselves did not recognize the fulfillment of their announcements.

Prophetic Commentaries from Qumran Worthy of mention are especially the prophetic commentaries from Qumran, the so-called pesharim, which follow the textual sequence of a biblical book of prophecy and interpret its proclamations for their own day in the second century BCE. The commentary on the biblical book of Habakkuk is especially well preserved. In its seventh column it states:

87. Cf. in detail: Konrad Schmid, "Nebuchadnezzar, the End of the Davidic Rule, and the Exile in the Book of Jeremiah," in *The Prophets Speak of Forced Migration,* ed. Mark J. Boda et al., AIL 21 (Atlanta: SBL Press, 2015), 63–76.

And God spoke to Habakkuk, write what comes upon the last generation, but he did not make known to him the fulfillment of time. And when it says: *so that one running can read it* (Hab 2:2), then its meaning is about the Teacher of Righteousness, to whom God has made known the entirety of the mysteries of the words of his servants, the prophets. *For there is still a revelation set for its time, but it pushes to the end and does not lie* (Hab 2:3). Its meaning is that the last time drags on, and more than everything that the prophets have said because the mysteries of God are wonderful. (1QpHab 7,1–5, author's translation)

Two aspects are especially noteworthy in this interpretation. First, it is apparent that the Habakkuk commentary relates the prophecies of Habakkuk, who is located in the biblical tradition in the Neo-Babylonian period (that is ca. the sixth century BCE), to the time of the Qumran community in the second century BCE. This is explicit in the case of Hab 2:2, ". . . its meaning is about the Teacher of Righteousness," who was possibly the founder and leader of the Qumran community. He belongs to the middle of the second century BCE. The Habakkuk commentary claims that the prophecies of Habakkuk from the sixth century BCE in truth and deed refer to events that take place 500 years later. This connects to a second, even more important point. The Habakkuk commentary appears to assume that Habakkuk himself did not realize what he prophesied. This is based on the introductory statement from the column: "And God spoke to Habakkuk, write what comes upon the last generation, but he did not make known to him the fulfillment of time." The content of the prophecy that Habakkuk received from God concerns the end time. The Qumran community believed that it was already here, but Habakkuk apparently did not know *when* this end time would take place ("but [God] did not make known to him the fulfillment of time"). Instead, the Teacher of Righteousness was accorded this knowledge that had been withheld from the prophets themselves. For to him "God has made known the entirety of the mysteries of the words of his servants, the prophets."

UNDERSTANDING OF THE PROPHETS IN THE NEW TESTAMENT This understanding of the prophets also appears *mutatis mutandis* in the New Testament. The birth story of Jesus in the gospel of Matthew is written within this horizon, for the prophet Isaiah foresaw and proclaimed this birth and in particular its wondrous circumstances:

Now the birth of Jesus Christ took place as follows: Mary, his mother, was engaged to Joseph. Still before they had come together, she was found to be pregnant from the Holy Spirit. . . . This all took place so that what the Lord said through the prophet [Isaiah] would be fulfilled: *See, the virgin will become pregnant and will bear a son, and one will give him the name Emmanuel* [Isa 7:14]. (Matt 1:18–23)

At the same time, it becomes clear from this passage that the Gospel of Matthew does not assume that Isaiah himself had known that his prophecy was actually related to the specific figure of Jesus of Nazareth. Like Habakkuk in the Habakkuk commentary from Qumran, Isaiah is instead seen as a prophet who—to some degree unconsciously—spoke and pronounced truth but did not know about the exact temporal circumstances of his words' fulfillment. This latter case can be deduced first by Matthew the evangelist and his readers.

6. Sapiental Interpretations of History

The wisdom of the Hebrew Bible is usually ascribed a certain distance from the theme of history. Wisdom occupies itself with the structures and order of the world, not with history and its possible interpretations. This judgment is correct in tradition-historical terms. The so-called earlier wisdom appears truly to have placed weight on reflection on recognizable rules in nature and society. However, this does not exclude that wisdom treated the topic of the theology of history as well within the framework of its theological-historical development. Perhaps the clearest example is the long reminiscence on the exodus in Wis 11–19, a wisdom writing from the first century BCE that subjects the exodus narrative to a wisdom interpretation for over nine chapters.

THE THEOLOGY OF HISTORY OF THE JOSEPH STORY However, wisdom interpretations of history are also found in the core collection of the canon of the Hebrew Bible, such as in the Joseph story of Gen 37–50, whose close connection to wisdom has been repeatedly emphasized since Gerhard von Rad.[88] Especially important with respect to the interpretation of history is

---

88. Gerhard von Rad, "The Joseph Narrative and Ancient Wisdom," in *The Problem of the Hexateuch and Other Essays*, trans. E. W. Trueman Dicken (New York: McGraw-Hill, 1966), 292–300; Gerhard von Rad, "Die Josephsgeschichte," in *Gottes Wirken in Israel: Vorträge*

the closing sentence in Gen 50:20: "Even though you planned evil against me, God turned it to good in order to do what is now obvious: to keep a numerous people alive." The trials and tribulations surrounding Joseph and his brothers are now placed in a larger context.

One can call the famous quintessence of the Joseph story in Gen 50:20 a theology of history, but a theology of history always adheres to something known as heretical. In the Joseph story there are three features in particular worth highlighting. First, the declaration in Gen 50:20 does not say that God turned evil into good, but that God re-planned the evil planned by humans into good. The change evidently concerns the formulation, that is, the level of the planning, which indicates that "good" and "evil" as absolute categories of value for what takes place should be considered with caution.

Second, the interpretation that God re-planned evil into good appears in Joseph's mouth. This is critical. In Gen 50, the Joseph story steers clear of narrating directly the quintessence of the story to the reader. Instead it places the interpretation of the theology of history in the mouth of Joseph the protagonist, which makes it plain that the theology of history is a challenge of interpretation.

Finally, Joseph is not just any protagonist of the Joseph story; he is the victim of the evil plan of the brothers that he identifies. The theology of history formulated in Gen 50:20 is, therefore, not just any interpretive perspective. It is a very specific interpretive view. It takes place from below. The guiding hand in the events is recognized by the victim of the trials and tribulations of history. The theology of Gen 50:20, if placed in the mouth of the brothers or the narrator, would simply be a mockery. However, it is placed in Joseph's mouth, and this demonstrates the exceptional quality of the narrative and theology of the Joseph story, one which has rendered it an important text not only in the Bible, but also in world literature.

7. *The Removal of the Conditionality of God's Salvific Will in History according to the Priestly Document*

PRIESTLY DOCUMENT The so-called Priestly document presents one of the most important counter-reactions to the theology of history of Deuter-

---

zum Alten Testament (Neukirchen-Vluyn: Neukirchener Verlag, 1974), 22–41; with important theological-historical differentiations, Michael V. Fox, "Wisdom in the Joseph Story," *VT* 51 (2001): 26–41.

onomy and Deuteronomism. It was presumably composed as a direct and immediate counter-conception to Deuteronomism. It radically revokes Deuteronomism's theological-historical packaging of obedience and salvation, presenting the position that Yhwh unconditionally promises Israel his salvific presence, without which Israel would be able to distance itself from Yhwh. This position is especially conspicuous in the central theological text of the Priestly document, the Abrahamic covenant of Gen 17. The mere fact that the conclusion of a covenant with the ancestor Abraham represents the theological center of the Priestly document is an objection to the Deuteronomistic covenantal theology, which locates its salvation-history on Sinai. In that case Yhwh concluded a covenant with Israel on Sinai under the obligation of the law. The Priestly document moves Yhwh's covenant with Israel backward to the period of the ancestors, before there was a law.

THE COVENANT WITH ABRAHAM IN THE PRIESTLY DOCUMENT According to the Priestly understanding, this covenant, enacted before all laws, has prevailed over Israel's history since Abraham—regardless of what Israel does or does not do. Regardless of its action or inaction, Israel can in no way interfere with the survival of this covenant—the divine covenantal promise and Israel's behavior are completely decoupled. Rather than a two-sided relationship of obligations, Priestly covenantal theology advocates a one-sided relationship; the obligation lies only on God's side. At this point just two small features of Gen 17 shall be highlighted, both in v. 7:

> And I raise my covenant between me and you and your descendants, from generation to generation as an everlasting covenant, that I am God for you and your descendants.

It is striking in this verse that, on the one hand, the covenant concluded with Israel is an *everlasting* covenant—the determination of the covenant as everlasting from the start is completely inconceivable from a Deuteronomistic perspective, according to which it must first be shown how long this covenant will last. On the other hand, the special formulation of what is called the covenant formula ("I will be your God and you shall be my people") is striking in Gen 17. This formula is at home in the Deuteronomistic sphere, where it regularly exhibits two parts, stating, "I will be your God and you shall be my people." The second half is omitted in its Priestly reception, where the covenant formula only states, "I will be your God." The absence of the section "and you shall be my people" does not result from carelessness; it is a theological conception. Brought to a point, this omission can be interpreted as follows: It is irrelevant whether Israel wants to be God's people or not. God is Israel's God, whatever it does or does not do.

THE POSTEXILIC CONTEXT The Priestly document is a child of its times (cf. above, §18 and §26). It originates in the Persian period, the time of the two-hundred-year Persian hegemony over almost the entire known world of the time, which was marked by a noteworthy religious-political tolerance for the subjugated nations. From the perspective of the history of theology, the Priestly document clearly interpreted the time of its author as the theocratic end result of history. If Israel lived in its land and could duly perform its cult there, then history had reached its conclusion. Radical changes were no longer to be expected. The Priestly document does not foster any ambitions for a nation-state—the Persian hegemony does not pose a theological offence for it. All that counts is the guaranteed functioning of the Jerusalem cult under the exact observance of the appropriate laws—and this was granted under the Persians.

THE ANTAGONISM BETWEEN DEUTERONOMISM AND THE PRIESTLY DOCUMENT Precisely the Priestly understanding of the law illustrates clearly, once again in its own way, the contrast between the theocratic resolution of history in the Priestly document and the Deuteronomistic conception of law. While the laws in Deuteronomism serve—expressed as a catch-phrase—to *avoid* guilt, in the Priestly document they serve to *eliminate* guilt. They make possible the correct implementation of the cult of atonement established by God, which stabilizes in cultic terms the final resolution of history in righteousness. This overall orientation of the Priestly document again contrasts with Deuteronomism's pronouncedly cold conception. In terms of the theology of history, however, it is extraordinarily important to understand that the Priestly document did not simply replace Deuteronomism. Deuteronomism continued to exist next to the Priestly document. The postexilic history of theology proceeded not along one, but along multiple paths.

8. *The Judgment of the World*

THE COSMIC JUDGMENT OF THE WORLD While the idea that history is moving toward a comprehensive judgment of the world belongs in particular to the basic proclamations of the Christian understanding of the Bible, one must clarify that this conception took shape comparatively late in the Hebrew Bible. It was likely the experience of the collapse of the two-hundred-year world hegemony of the Persians (539–333 BCE) in the time of Alexander that perhaps the clearest literary sedimentation of declarations of world judgment found their way into the books of the Prophets (cf. above, §27). The conception of a comprehensive, cosmic judgment of the world developed by means of literary supplementation to existing judgment oracles (against the nations) can be observed in the books of Isaiah, Jeremiah, and in the Twelve Prophets.

THE CONSTRUCTION OF THE WORLD JUDGMENT IN ISA 34 The supplemental character is especially palpable in Isa 34:2–4:

> Draw near, you nations, and hear, and you peoples, give heed! Let the earth hear and all that fills it, the world, and everything that grows upon it. (34:1)

> For Yhwh is enraged against all nations and furious against its whole army; he has dedicated it to destruction, has given them over to slaughter. Their slain will then be cast out, and the smell of their corpses will rise, and the mountains will flow with their blood. And the whole army of heaven rot away, and like a scroll the heavens will be rolled together, and its whole army will wither like a leaf withers on the vine, and like foliage on the fig tree. (34:2–4)

> When my sword has drunk in heaven, look, it descends upon Edom, on the people that I have dedicated to destruction, to judgment; a sword of Yhwh, smeared with blood, gorged with fat, with the blood of lambs and goats, with the kidney fat of rams, for Yhwh has arranged a sacrifice in Bozra, a great sacrificial feast in the land of Edom. (34:5–6)

The preexisting original text of Isa 34:1, 5–6 speaks of a judgment by Yhwh in Edom to which the nations are called as witnesses. These same nations have a very different role in vv. 2–4. Here they are the ones judged.

Furthermore, in v. 5 the heavens still appear as a stable entity, while in vv. 2–4 they are rolled together "like a scroll." The present form of the text in Isa 34:1–6, therefore, speaks of a comprehensive judgment that involves the entire cosmos. It is noteworthy that the immediate context provides no other reason besides the rage and fury of God (34:2). The reader must deduce what this rage relates to from the preceding context (Isa 1–33). The supplemental character of Isa 34:1–6 supports the notion that the one adding vv. 2–4 did not consider the judgment of the world an isolated event. Instead, the judgment of the world is the culmination of all previous strokes of judgment that Israel and Judah had encountered since the Assyrian period.

WORLD JUDGMENT IN THE BOOK OF JEREMIAH It is also evident in the book of Jeremiah that the proclamations of world judgment are secondary expansions of preexisting texts. The notion of a judgment of כל בשר (*kl bśr*), "all flesh," in the final two verses of Jer 45:5–6 before the complex of oracles against the foreign nations in Jer 46–51 interprets the latter as a prophecy of world judgment. The same process is found in the supplement of the oracle of the cup in Jer 25, which also concerns a judgment of various nations, but by v. 27 is interpreted as "world judgment":

> And to them you shall say: Thus says Yhwh of Hosts, the God of Israel: Drink and become drunk and vomit! Fall and do not rise again before the sword that I am sending among you! But if they refuse to take the cup from your hand to drink, say to them: Thus says Yhwh of Hosts: You will drink! See, in the city called by my name, I am beginning to bring disaster, and will you remain unpunished? You will not remain unpunished, for I am calling forth the sword against all the inhabitants of the earth! Word of Yhwh of Hosts. And you, you will prophesy all these words and say to them: Yhwh will roar from the heights and from his holy habitation make his voice heard; he will roar mightily against the place of his pasture, a shout like those treading grapes he will intone over all the inhabitants of the earth. Unto the end of the earth will the clamor resound, for Yhwh has an indictment against the nations. He enters judgment will all flesh, the sinners—he has given them over to the sword! Word of Yhwh. (Jer 25:27–31)

PROCLAMATIONS OF JUDGMENT IN THE BOOK OF THE TWELVE Finally, there are also various insertions into the Book of the Twelve whose content can be linked to the corresponding texts in Isaiah and Jeremiah, such as Joel 3:12–16; Mic 7:12–13; and Zeph 3:8. The expectation of these proclamations is, like in the book of Isaiah, that the judgment of the world is not an additional, new attack by God against the world. These texts instead intend to show that the previous divine strokes of judgment are part of and precursors to a comprehensive divine judgment of the world.

It is evident that the content of this message runs counter especially to the theology of theocratic positions like the Priestly document, which formulates an eternal guarantee for the existence of humans and animals in the Noah covenant of Gen 9. And there are in fact passages among those texts on world judgment in the prophetic corpus, in particular in Isa 24–27, that clearly grapple with the Priestly theology. This can be grasped quite clearly in Isa 24:4–6. The end of the world is justified in this text by humanity's breaking of the eternal covenant. This covenant can hardly be any other than the covenant with Noah from Gen 9—the Hebrew Bible is not familiar with any other covenant with all humankind. The theme of bloodguilt that plays an important role within the context of Isa 24–27 also supports this conclusion. Therefore, Isaiah 24:4–6 argues against the theoretical possibilities of the Priestly document—the covenant of Noah can also be broken. As a result, the world order that the Priestly document viewed as final can also be overturned once more. Through a further allusion to Gen 6–9, Isa 26:20–21 assumes that Israel, like Noah, will be delivered from the coming judgment of the world.

9. Proto-Deterministic Ideology of History in the Book of Daniel

THE MACCABEAN BOOK OF DANIEL The book of Daniel is—in terms of reception history—of comparable importance for the theology of history as the first chapter of Genesis is for cosmology. Especially in its grand visions in Dan 2 and 7, it casts a universal view over the biblical period, which in later interpretation is widely adopted and re-interpreted.[89] At the same time, the book of Daniel can be located quite precisely. It was only finished in the course of the Maccabean revolts, around 164 BCE, and for this reason—despite its prophetically-shaped content—could not be admitted into the Nevi'im (Prophets) section of the canon, being placed instead among the Ketuvim

---

89. Cf. Katharina Bracht and David S. du Toit, eds., *Die Geschichte der Daniel-Auslegung in Judentum, Christentum und Islam: Studien zur Kommentierung des Danielbuches in Literatur und Kunst*, BZAW 371 (Berlin: de Gruyter, 2012).

(Writings). In its current form it belongs to apocalyptic literature—that is, to the literary condensation of an intellectual movement prominent between the third century BCE and the third century CE, which held that the divine course of history could be revealed in advance by visionary figures.

THE VISION OF DAN 2 According to Dan 2, God is the regulator of the world clock. Not only does he regulate the course of time, but he also fills its content in terms of politics. He deposes kings and installs kings—one should note this striking order. God determines history; he is not only the one who acts *in* time and *in* history, but he determines time itself. In the apocalyptic literature of the following period, this thought will be advanced substantially. God can even slow down or speed up time—speaking here of the apocopation or acceleration of the times. God's authority over time is conceived as so absolute that he not only can change the regular times and hours, he also has this change completely under his control.

COMPARISON WITH THE THEOCRATIC POSITIONS OF THE PERSIAN PERIOD If one compares the conception of Dan 2 with the theocratic positions of the Persian period, such as in the Priestly document, then there are two points that should be identified above all. After the two-hundred-year experience of the order of the Persian world hegemony, its collapse must have thrown into flux the theocratic notion of history reaching its conclusion in the Persian period. The experience fundamentally contradicted the theocratic theory of the end of history. The nature of experience changed completely from the Persian period with Alexander the Great and the subsequent Diadochean wars. The experience of a stable, divinely guided world empire under the administration of the Persian Emperor gave way to the confusion of the power-politics of the subsequent period. History had overtaken the end of history.

On the other hand, no theology of history in the subsequent period gave up on the theocratic conviction of God's absolute guidance of world politics and his power over history. The notion of a salvation history in a narrower sense, one in which history is thoroughly guided and kept working by God appears to have arisen from the breakdown of theocracy, for this conception of God's complete guidance of history continued to maintain the fundamental thought of theocracy. *God* determines who rules over the world—even if it is no longer simply the Persian Emperor in its dynastic unfolding to whom God has assigned world domination, but various kings that change in short intervals.

§33 Political Theology

Jan Assmann, *Herrschaft und Heil: Politische Theologie in Ägypten, Israel und Europa* (Darmstadt: Wissenschaftliche Buchgesellschaft, 2000) ◆ Angelika Berlejung, "The Assyrians in the West: Assyrianization, Colonialism, Indifference, or Development Policy?," in *Congress Volume Helsinki 2010*, ed. Martti Nissinen, VTSup 148 (Leiden: Brill, 2012), 21–60 ◆ Erhard Blum, *Die Komposition der Vätergeschichte*, WMANT 57 (Neukirchen-Vluyn: Neukirchener Verlag, 1984) ◆ Karin Finsterbusch, *Das Deuteronomium: Eine Einführung*, Uni-Taschenbücher 3626 (Göttingen: Vandenhoeck & Ruprecht, 2012) ◆ Christoph Koch, *Vertrag, Treueid und Bund: Studien zur Rezeption des altorientalischen Vertragsrechts im Deuteronomium und zur Ausbildung der Bundestheologie im Alten Testament*, BZAW 383 (Berlin: de Gruyter, 2008) ◆ Wolfgang Oswald, *Staatstheorie im Alten Israel: Der politische Diskurs im Pentateuch und in den Geschichtsbüchern des Alten Testaments* (Stuttgart: Kohlhammer, 2009) ◆ Eckart Otto, *Das Deuteronomium: Politische Theologie und Rechtsreform in Juda und Assyrien*, BZAW 284 (Berlin: de Gruyter, 1999) ◆ Adrian Schenker, "L'origine de l'idée d'une alliance entre Dieu et Israël dans l'Ancien Testament," in *Recht und Kult im Alten Testament: Achtzehn Studien*, OBO 172 (Freiburg: Universitätsverlag; Göttingen: Vandenhoeck & Ruprecht, 2000), 67–76 ◆ Konrad Schmid, "Anfänge politikförmiger Religion: Die Theologisierung politisch-imperialer Begriffe in der Religionsgeschichte des antiken Israel als Grundlage autoritärer und toleranter Strukturmomente monotheistischer Religionen," in *Religion—Wirtschaft—Politik: Forschungszugänge zu einem aktuellen transdisziplinären Feld*, ed. Antonius Liedhegener et al. (Baden-Baden: Nomos, 2011), 161–77

1. Preliminary Remarks from the History of Scholarship

POLITICALLY FORMED INTERPRETATION OF RELIGION The interaction between politics and religion left an immense imprint on the history of theology of the ancient Near East, and the adoption and further development of a politically inspired paradigm in the Hebrew Bible has also interpreted the relationship between God and Israel with prominent political terminology and conceptions, such that the relationship with God is conceived to a certain degree as politically formed.

IMPERIAL IDEOLOGIES AND THEIR RECEPTION Clear terminological correlations can be discovered between the intellectual configurations of ancient Israelite religion and the corresponding political ideologies of the respective hegemonic powers—the Assyrians, Babylonians, Persians, and Greeks. Therefore, the notion of a theologization of political terms is evident for this stage of the formation of biblical religion, which is of great importance for the history of reception.

RELIGION AS A POLITICALLY INFLUENCED CULTURAL ARTIFACT This recognition of the theologization of political terms is in no way revolutionary with respect to its main features. It arises from the fact that the conceptions of order and structures of the numinous sphere are conceived as having a certain correlation to the earthly realities. This is the *particula veri* (kernel of truth) in the critique of religion from Ludwig Feuerbach to Sigmund Freud, which, for that matter, also agrees with a basic element of Karl Barth's thinking, and for this reason should not have any whiff of theological illegitimacy. Religion is, as Barth expressed, "the work of humans."[90] Religions are historically evolving and culturally determined systems, and as such it cannot come as a surprise that they are significantly influenced by the contemporaneous political circumstances.

It does not take away any of the Bible's innovation and creativity if many of its thoughts and conceptions have been inspired from extrabiblical sources. Its originality lies not in the material itself, but rather in its adaptations and transformations.

2. Implicit Covenantal Theology

COVENANT AS TREATY At the center of the politically motivated religious language of the Hebrew Bible is the idea of a covenant between God and his people. The English translation of the Hebrew term בְּרִית (*bryt*) with "covenant" is, however, imprecise. "Treaty" would be more accurate and would also make the political background more clear. In any case, the covenantal terminology has claimed a fixed place in the history of interpretation of the Bible, and it has become a theological term in its own right.

The idea of a treaty between Israel and God is so elemental for the Hebrew Bible that the Bible anchors it at the very beginning of Israel's founding narrative in the context of the divine revelation on Sinai. Accordingly, it also moved to the center of focus for older presentations of the theology of

---

90. Karl Barth, *Church Dogmatics*, I/2, 325–61.

the Hebrew Bible. Walther Eichrodt's *Theologie des Alten Testaments* from 1933 took its orientation from the covenant idea. This biblical placement of the beginnings of covenant theology does not, however, correspond with history. Since the foundational work by Lothar Perlitt[91] from 1969 it has become clear that the covenant theology in the Hebrew Bible rests on a theological interpretation whose historical setting cannot have preceded the seventh century BCE, even if these beginnings of covenantal theology would be described differently today than was the case at Perlitt's time.

IMPLICIT COVENANTAL THEOLOGY At the same time, it should be maintained that at least the implicit notion of a covenant between God and nation is older than the well-known formulation nourished especially by the Neo-Assyrian treaty theology, which will be treated below. The fact that political entities in the ancient Near East, whether states or nations, could be attached to one or more deities belongs to the standard repertoire of ancient Near Eastern theology. Chemosh is the god of Moab, Qauṣ the god of Edom, and Yhwh the god of Israel—this was already known by the time of the Mesha Stela from the ninth century BCE—and Judah (cf. Judg 11:24). Indictments such as those in Hosea 4 or Amos 5 bemoaning Israel's apostasy from God are hardly comprehensible without the implicit conception of the association of God and Israel.

OATH TAKING AND VOWS A special form of association between God and people (whether it concerns a collective or an individual) appears in oaths and in vows. These are not characterized in the Hebrew Bible as ברית (*bryt*), "covenant," or "treaty," but their content implies the reciprocal obligations of those swearing or vowing on the one side and God on the other.[92] It is conceivable to find the root of the conception of a treaty between God and his people here.

THE TREATY THEOLOGY OF DEUTERONOMY The intellectual progress of the explicit formulation of this implicit determination of the relationship in the sense of a treaty should not be underestimated. Through the spec-

---

91. Lothar Perlitt, *Bundestheologie im Alten Testament*, WMANT 36 (Neukirchen-Vluyn: Neukirchener-Verlag, 1969).

92. Cf. Johannes Klein, *Beschworene Selbstverpflichtung: Eine Studie zum Schwur im Alten Testament und dessen Umwelt, mit einem Ausblick auf Mt 5,33–37*, ATANT 105 (Zurich: TVZ, 2015).

ification of the treaty theology, this relationship is placed on a textually identifiable basis, thereby setting Israel and Judah's relationship with God on a legal basis. This step was first taken in the Hebrew Bible in the first edition of Deuteronomy, which should probably be dated to the late pre-exilic period (cf. above, §18 and §24).[93]

3. The Formulation of Covenantal Theology in Deuteronomy

With the beginning of Neo-Assyrian hegemony in the Middle East, which reached its first high point in the middle of the eighth century and held on until the end of the seventh century BCE before it gave way to the Neo-Babylonians, Israel and Judah came under the sphere of influence of the imperial Assyrian power. It exercised exceptionally strong political and military power, which also took on an implicit religious and cultural dimension. The Assyrians can be reckoned among the first powers to strive resolutely for political, economic, and military control over what was then the known world.

Toward the end of their hegemony in the seventh century BCE, decidedly anti-Assyrian conceptions formed in Judah that transpose the political obligations demanded by the Assyrians to Judah's own relationship with God. This can be called a subversive reception of the Neo-Assyrian vassal treaty idea (cf. above, §18).

LOYALTY TO GOD INSTEAD OF TO THE ASSYRIANS The book of Deuteronomy demands unconditional loyalty, not to the Neo-Assyrian emperor but to the Judeans' own God. This can be recognized most clearly in the so-called Shema Israel ("Hear, O Israel") in Deut 6:4–5:

> Hear, O Israel: Yhwh, our God, is one Yhwh. And you shall love Yhwh, your God with your whole heart, your whole soul, and your whole strength.

LOVE OF GOD AS A POLITICAL TERM In particular the demand to love God carries political connotations in the world of the ancient Near East. "Love" is not an emotion, but rather a political term that designates loyal

93. Cf. Nathan MacDonald, "Issues in the Dating of Deuteronomy," *ZAW* 122 (2010): 431–35.

allegiance, for the injunction to "love" the Assyrian emperor also appears prominently in the Assyrian vassal treaties. Deuteronomy instead maintains that this form of love, of absolute loyalty, is reserved for God alone.

On the basis of these points of contact, two things become clear. One is the recognizable inspiration of the book of Deuteronomy by the theology of Neo-Assyria. The other, however, is the recognition that this influence simultaneously undergoes a fundamental re-interpretation: The treaty relationship is transferred from the Neo-Assyrian emperor to God himself. Loyalty is claimed for him, no longer for the king. Deities also play a role in the Assyrian treaties, but they are always guarantors, not partners in the treaty. In the book of Deuteronomy this is different. Ancient Israel reinterpreted the treaty relationship as a treaty between God and his people.

The subversive potential of this procedure is evident.[94] It engages in a profoundly critical way with the Assyrian Empire. Therefore, it is a short step to conjecture that it was historically possible only at a time when the Neo-Assyrian Empire was already in decline—i.e., shortly before the fall of the capital Nineveh in 612 BCE—and no longer possessed the military means to curb such dissident trends in the periphery of the empire.

IMPERIAL INTERPRETATION OF GOD   The imperial interpretation of God undertaken by the book of Deuteronomy is of preeminent importance. On the one hand it represents the drawing in of a transcendent horizon for the promulgation of the law, while at the same time it constitutes the most fundamental root of religious zeal in the later history of Judaism, Christianity, and Islam that has repeatedly beguiled adherents to these religions in unconditional dependence on their God to perform deeds for which they were no longer willing to maintain a critical and balanced view.

4. The Theology of Promise in the Ancestral Narratives and Its Problematization

POLITICAL DIMENSIONS OF THE FAMILY NARRATIVES IN GEN 12–50   Even if the ancestral narratives in Gen 12–50 take the form of family narratives and play out in a time in which there were not yet any states in the Levant,

94. This is debated, though not entirely convincingly, by Carly L. Crouch, *Israel and the Assyrians: Deuteronomy, the Succession Treaty of Esarhaddon, and the Nature of Subversion*, Ancient Near East Monographs (Atlanta: SBL Press, 2014).

they are still profoundly political literary entities. It is assumed that even their earliest literary precursors—the Jacob cycle as well as the Abraham-Lot cycle—were understood from the beginning as political entities represented by the relationship between the corresponding ancestral figures. Jacob is Israel; Esau is Edom; Abraham is the father of Isaac, who also stands for Israel (cf. Amos 7:9, 16); and Lot is the father of Moab and Ammon, who bear the names of the corresponding nations in the Transjordan.[95] For the ancestral narratives primarily in Gen 12–36, it is very probable that they had oral precursors, and it is possible that these earlier versions did not yet exhibit a political focus. However, the earliest written versions, which one can reckon with in the eighth century BCE, already place Israel and Judah in relation to the surrounding nations.[96]

No Royal Figures In light of this political imprint, however, it is striking that the ancestral narratives are not aware of any royal figures for Israel.[97] While figures like Abraham can be depicted with royal motifs (worthy of mention are, for example, the motif of the "great name" [ואגדלה שמך, w'gdlh šmk] and Abraham's mediation of blessing in Gen 12:1–3; cf. Ps 72:17), these motifs are accorded to him as the tribal ancestor. The lack of royal figures can probably be explained by the fact that the narrative cycle in Gen 12–50, at least in its written form, likely postdates 722 BCE—that is, it presupposes the demise of the northern kingdom. Because the kingdom has no fundamental or super-historical quality for the ancestral narratives, Gen 12–50 must have already formulated an identity for Israel that is essentially constituted as post-state.

The Promises as Redactional Connections It has been acknowledged since Rendtorff and Blum that the ancestor story is primarily linked together through the redactional promise texts. They are marked especially

95. Cf. already Julius Wellhausen, *Prolegomena to the History of Israel*, trans. J. Sutherland Black and Allen Menzies (Edinburgh: Black, 1885), 318: "The materials here [in the ancestral narratives] are not mythical but national . . ."

96. Cf. in detail Konrad Schmid, "Von Jakob zu Israel: Das antike Israel auf dem Weg zum Judentum im Spiegel der Fortschreibungsgeschichte der Jakobüberlieferungen der Genesis," in *Identität und Schrift: Fortschreibungsprozesse als Mittel religiöser Identitätsbildung*, ed. Marianne Grohmann, Biblisch-theologische Studien 169 (Neukirchen-Vluyn: Neukirchener Verlag, 2017), 33–67.

97. Other kings are presupposed and mentioned, e.g. Melchizedek of Salem (Gen 14:18) and other kings in Gen 14, Abimelech of Gerar (Gen 26:1) or Pharaoh in Gen 40-50.

by the themes of increase and land. There is disagreement about their historical placement, but it is clear that they should be dated after 722 BCE, probably even after 587 BCE, the destruction of the southern kingdom. Increase and land become explicit themes when they no longer represent self-evident realities.

The theme of promise itself, however, is earlier. Its tradition-historical origin appears in the narrative of the divine visitors in Gen 18 (cf. above, §18) and from there it dictated the pulse of the redaction-historical development of the ancestral narratives.

These promises can be read in a twofold fashion. On the one hand, they show that they can be read within the framework of Genesis alone, with an undetermined future. On the other hand, if read within the larger history of Genesis–2 Kings, then they already reach their fulfillment in the report of the growth into a nation at the beginning of the book of Exodus and the possession of the land narrated in the book of Joshua.

TWOFOLD FUNCTION OF THE PROMISES In any case, the fact that the promises themselves, except for the post-Priestly viewpoint in Gen 15:13–16, do not allow for the recognition that they will first be fulfilled after a long detour through the possession and subsequent loss of the land, indicates that the promises in Gen 12–50 originally constituted a literarily independent ancestral story whose substantial narrative looked back on the destruction of at least the northern kingdom, perhaps also even the southern kingdom. This ancestral story now promised a new existence for its post-national addressees. The political form of this new existence is remarkable in that its composition is not monarchic, but rather theocratic.

The great promise that Jacob receives in Gen 28:13–15, which corresponds in many ways to the analogous promise to Abraham in Gen 12:1–3, presupposes Israel and Judah's diaspora existence ("you will spread out to the west and east, to the north and south"), and that it simultaneously views this diaspora existence as theologically positive ("through you and your descendants all tribes of the earth will obtain blessing").

> . . . I am Yhwh, the God of your father Abraham[98] and the God of Isaac. The land on which you lie I will give to you and your descendants. And your descendants will be like the dust of the earth, and you will spread

---

98. Abraham appears here as Jacob's "father" אָב (*'b*), which can also be translated "grandfather," but perhaps the close relationship to Abraham is emphasized here.

out to the west and east, to the north and south, and through you and your descendants will all tribes of the earth acquire blessing. And look, I am with you and protect you wherever you go, and I will bring you back into this land. For I will not forsake you until I have done what I have said to you. (Gen 28:13–15)

As presented above, the scattering into the diaspora is explicitly interpreted as divine punishment in the books of Jeremiah and Ezekiel (cf., e.g., Jer 24:9–10). However, in Genesis another perspective seems to have taken hold. The diaspora existence serves Israel's role as the mediator of blessing (cf. below, §36).

In accordance with this, the promises to the ancestors also omit ideologies of political boundaries. While the promises are for Israel, they have a mediated effect on the nations who live among the Israelites and Judeans.

THE PROBLEMATIZATION OF THE PROMISE THEOLOGY IN GEN 22 The narrative of the sacrifice of Isaac in Gen 22 is one of the most unfathomable texts in the Hebrew Bible. It has called forth incomprehension, even revulsion in the history of exegesis. How can God want a father to sacrifice his son? The narrative becomes accessible through the observation that it does not speak of just any father and any son, but of Abraham, the bearer of the promise of many progeny, and of Isaac, the singular necessary link to the fulfillment of this promise. As the introduction of Gen 22:1 shows ("And it happened after these events . . ."), the narrative cannot be read as an entity in itself, but must be understood in connection with all the Abraham narratives related to it. The test of Abraham consists of whether he can also give back the promise that God has given him. Is it possible for him to trust God even when the promise of an abundant posterity is completely eclipsed? Genesis 22 is a Persian-period text that reflects the modest contemporary conditions in Yehud. Yehud is only sparsely populated. Jerusalem is a small provincial city. Is this what God has planned for his people? Does the fulfillment of the promises to the ancestors look like this? Genesis 22 answers these questions with the example of Abraham. Already for him it was no longer apparent that the promise would be fulfilled, but he trusted God. In the same way, the Judeans are called to adhere to Abraham's example in their deplorable historical situation.[99]

99. Cf. the extensive discussion in Timo Veijola, "Das Opfer des Abraham: Paradigma des Glaubens aus dem nachexilischen Zeitalter," in *Offenbarung und Anfechtung:*

5. The Political Theology of the Priestly Document

THE POSITIVE IMAGE OF THE PERSIANS   While the most important trajectory for the reception of Neo-Assyrian material in ancient Israel and Judah was marked by a basic rejection and subversion, as observed in Deuteronomy, the image of the Persian Empire and its hegemony over Israel meets the opposite result. The Persians are viewed in a strikingly positive light throughout the entire Hebrew Bible. Especially in contrast to the classical Greek tradition, which essentially characterizes the Persians as "barbarians," this is a noteworthy discovery.

PERSIAN IMPERIAL IDEOLOGY   It is surprising that there is not a single oracle against a foreign nation that is directed against the Persians. The reason for this lies in the fact that the Persians, unlike the previous empires, fostered a comparatively tolerant policy with regard to subjugated nations and granted them broad linguistic, cultic, legal, and cultural autonomy—likely more from sheer necessity given the size of the empire than from (pre-)humanitarian considerations. This policy was also well received in the Persian provinces of Samaria and Judah ("Yehud").

This Persian imperial ideology of a peaceful state of many nations, each preserving their cultural and religious character is expressed in, for example, the Bisitun inscription of Darius I.[100] The discovery of its Aramaic version in Elephantine attests to its circulation as a school text and points to its positive adoption in various conceptions of the Persian-period literature of the Hebrew Bible, such as the Priestly document and Chronicles.

These writings conclude that the salvific goal of Yhwh's history with Israel and the world was reached—stated pointedly, in the sense of a "realized eschatology"—with Persian hegemony. This goal still required completion at different points, but the salvific turn had basically been consummated. This position can be interpreted as the Jewish reception of official Persian imperial ideology. David and Solomon, in their capacities as initiator and builder of the temple, can be seen in Chronicles as precur-

---

Hermeneutisch-theologische Studien zum Alten Testament, ed. Walter Dietrich and Marko Marttila, Biblisch-theologische Studien 89 (Neukirchen-Vluyn: Neukirchener Verlag, 2007), 88–133; Konrad Schmid, "Die Rückgabe der Verheißungsgabe: Der 'heilsgeschichtliche' Sinn von Genesis 22 im Horizont innerbiblischer Exegese," in *Gott und Mensch im Dialog: Festschrift für Otto Kaiser*, ed. Markus Witte, BZAW 345 (Berlin: de Gruyter, 2004), 1:271–300.

100. Rykle Borger and Walther Hinz, "Die Behistun-Inschrift Darius' des Grossen," in *TUAT* 1/4, 419–50.

sors of Cyrus and Darius—Cyrus having made the building of the temple possible through his edict and Darius having allowed it to be carried out (cf. above, §20).

THE TABLE OF NATIONS IN GEN 10 Appearing within the contemporary Priestly literature (cf. §18) is the Persian-period inspired image of an ordered world in the so-called Table of Nations in Gen 10, which describes the repopulation of the world after the flood (Gen 6–9). It has a refrain that describes the linguistically and culturally diversified order of the world:

> . . . These are the sons of Japheth in their lands, with their languages, according to their tribes, in their nations. (Gen 10:5)

> . . . These are the sons of Ham according to their tribes, their languages, in their lands, according to their nations. (Gen 10:20)

> . . . These are the sons of Shem according to their tribes, their languages, in their lands, according to their nations. (Gen 10:31)

This worldview, strikingly pluralistic for ancient thinking, stands in stark contrast to the Assyrian imperial ideology, which presented a much stronger conception of unity.[101]

6. Renationalizing Tendencies in the Literature of the Maccabean Period

THE UPHEAVALS IN THE TIME OF ALEXANDER THE GREAT The literature of the Hebrew Bible did not stop with the integrative political vision of the Priestly document. It was finally the upheavals of the time of Alexander and the wards of the Diadochean kingdoms that robbed such universal political theologies of their credibility. In particular, the political positions that gained the upper hand in the Maccabean period and were later codified in biblical tradition were those that returned to the parameters of Deuteronomism. They argue that no salvation is possible under foreign rule without political sovereignty. This is the view of the Daniel tradition

---

101. Cf., e.g., Christoph Uehlinger, *Weltreich und eine Rede: Eine neue Deutung der sogenannten Turmbauerzählung (Gen 11,1–9)*, OBO 101 (Freiburg: Universitätsverlag; Göttingen: Vandenhoeck & Ruprecht, 1990).

of the Maccabean period (esp. in Dan 7–12) as well as in the books of Maccabees. Daniel 9 even maintains that the entire exilic and postexilic period up to the time of the author are marked by God's judgment on Israel, which has already continued for centuries, but now stands on the precipice of its eschatological sublimation.

THE ANTI-HELLENISM OF THE BIBLICAL TRADITION One can conclude with certainty that the book of Daniel and the books of Maccabees combat Hellenistic positions that were open to the new Seleucid cosmopolitan culture. They were both widely disseminated in the Judaism of the time, and they formulated their own theological justification. The books of Sirach and Baruch, as well as the writings of Philo of Alexandria, display diverse attempts to reconcile Jewish tradition and Hellenism. The literature focusing immediately on the Maccabean period had no space for the Hellenistic empires and combated them by every ideological means.

POLYPHONY OF THE POSITIONS A review of the theme of political theology in the Hebrew Bible shows that there is no biblical preference for one particular position. The Bible juxtaposes different perspectives—acceptance of the nations, rejection of the nations, theocracy, nationalism—and links them to specific historical points of view. It indicates that political theology cannot be formulated in absolute terms, but only in relation and reaction to particular historical events, in the light of which it will be judged.

§34 Law and Righteousness

Albrecht Alt, *Die Ursprünge des israelitischen Rechts* (Leipzig: Hirzel, 1934) ♦ Olivier Artus, *Les lois du Pentateuque: Points de repère pour une lecture exégétique et théologique*, LD 200 (Paris: Cerf, 2005) ♦ John J. Collins, *The Invention of Judaism: Torah and Jewish Identity from Deuteronomy to Paul* (Oakland, CA: University of California Press, 2017) ♦ Michael LeFebvre, *Collections, Codes, and Torah: The Re-characterization of Israel's Written Law*, LHBOTS 451 (London: T&T Clark, 2006) ♦ Bernard M. Levinson, *Legal Revision and Religious Renewal in Ancient Israel* (Cambridge: Cambridge University Press, 2012) ♦ Ulrich Manthe, ed., *Die Rechtskulturen der Antike: Vom Alten Orient bis zum Römischen Reich* (Munich: Beck, 2003) ♦ William S. Morrow, *An Introduction to Biblical Law* (Grand Rapids: Eerdmans, 2017) ♦ Eckart Otto, *Das Gesetz des*

Mose (Darmstadt: Wissenschaftliche Buchgesellschaft, 2007) ◆ Eckart Otto, *Altorientalische und biblische Rechtsgeschichte: Gesammelte Studien*, BZABR 8 (Wiesbaden: Harrassowitz, 2008) ◆ Raymond Westbrook and Bruce Wells, *Everyday Law in Biblical Israel: An Introduction* (Louisville: Westminster John Knox, 2009)

1. Preliminary Remarks from the History of Scholarship

THE LAW AS EXPRESSION OF POSTEXILIC "JUDAISM" It need not be surprising that the topic of law in the Hebrew Bible received little theological attention in traditional Protestant exegesis of the nineteenth and twentieth centuries. It was influenced by the poor overall estimation of law in theology, and the triumph of the Documentary Hypothesis added the dominant distinction between preexilic "Hebraism" and postexilic "Judaism." The most extensive passages of the law in the Priestly document (cf. above, §18 and §26) were classified as postexilic literature in a broad sense and seen as unimportant for this very reason. Wellhausen describes the conception of God from the law of the postexilic literature within the framework of the usual pejorative evaluation of Judaism in his time as follows:

The creator of heaven and the herd pupates in a small asylum, the living God abdicated the throne for the Law.[102]

The law suffocated the spirit, and therefore postexilic Judaism was seen merely as the executor of the living spirituality of preexilic Hebraism, which first revived with John the Baptist and Jesus of Nazareth. "Judaism" was the period lasting for five hundred years between "Hebraism" and the New Testament, which in terms of its content connected with the ingeniously identified period of "Hebraism."

APODICTIC AND CASUISTIC LAW The Decalogue constitutes an exception in the assessment of the ancient Israelite legal tradition, for it was attributed virtually transtemporal validity. Furthermore, the influential distinction by Albrecht Alt between apodictic and casuistic law reproduced the high estimation of the Decalogue as a genuine Israelite product in contrast to other,

---

102. Cf. Julius Wellhausen, *Skizzen und Vorarbeiten: Erstes Heft: Abriss der Geschichte Israels und Juda's; Lieder der Hudhailiten, arabisch und deutsch* (Berlin: Reimer, 1884), 97.

non-apodictically formulated legal materials, which were reckoned as being of Canaanite origins. Albrecht Alt's differentiation of Israel's own apodictic law from its very beginning, in contrast to the casuistic stipulations from the environment, has not, however, been maintained. His "apodictic law" gathers all too divergent legal traditions under one umbrella term, and this conception of law, it has been shown, is not limited to Israel.[103] It has also been shown that a strict differentiation between Israel and Canaan cannot be maintained. Accordingly, the different attributions of origins for apodictic and casuistic laws are no longer justifiable.

DISCOVERY OF THE THEME OF LAW In English-speaking scholarship, there was a long-standing interest in ancient Near Eastern and ancient Israelite legal history.[104] In the German realm, Hans Jochen Boecker first offered a monographic presentation of the legal thematic in the ancient Near East and in the Hebrew Bible in the 1980s,[105] and German-speaking scholarship's interest in the legal literature of the Bible is due in large part to the research of Eckart Otto.[106]

From a diachronic perspective, recent redaction-historical scholarship has shown that the earlier passages of the legal collections in the Hebrew Bible, all found in the Pentateuch, are still clearly rooted in the ancient Near Eastern legal tradition. In the so-called Covenant Code (Exod 20–23) there are compilations of legal statements that, like in their ancient Near Eastern counterparts, especially regulate special cases and like them have more of an orienting than a normative character within jurisprudence.

At the same time, however, it is clear that the legal collections of the Hebrew Bible *in their present, redactionally edited form* fundamentally diverge from ancient Near Eastern parallels, for they are composed as divine rather than royal law. God, not the king, is always the legal authority in the Hebrew Bible. The fact that this characteristic was not part of the legal historical beginnings of the Hebrew Bible but only emerged incremen-

103. Cf. Berend Meyer, *Das Apodiktische Recht*, BWANT 213 (Stuttgart: Kohlhammer, 2017).

104. Cf., for example, Raymond Westbrook, *Law from the Tigris to the Tiber*, ed. Bruce Wells and F. Rachel Magdalene, vol. 1: *The Shared Tradition*; vol. 2: *Cuneiform and Biblical Sources* (Winona Lake, IN: Eisenbrauns, 2009).

105. Hans Jochen Boecker, *Recht und Gesetz im Alten Testament und im Alten Orient*, 2nd ed. (Neukirchen-Vluyn: Neukirchener Verlag, 1984).

106. Cf., e.g., Eckart Otto, "Das Recht der Hebräischen Bibel im Kontext der antiken Rechtsgeschichte: Literaturbericht 1994–2004," *TR* 71 (2006): 389–421.

tally through correspondingly literarily productive redactions belongs to what has in the meantime become an undisputed matter in biblical studies. Therefore, it was not inherent to the substance of the text of the legal traditions from the very beginning, but it accrued incrementally through redaction.[107]

2. Codex or Law Book?

NORMATIVITY OR DESCRIPTIVITY In Western legal understandings it is self-evident that written law is normatively binding. However, historically speaking, particularly for ancient Near Eastern and biblical legal history, it must instead be maintained that the legal traditions originally had a more descriptive orientation. Rather than binding guidelines, they instead provided assistance for juridical questions. The king, not a text, was the final legislative authority in the monarchies of the ancient Near East. As a result, the ancient Near Eastern legal collections—Codex Hammurabi, Codex Eshnunna, Codex Lipit-Ishtar, Codex Ur-Nammu, etc.—have erroneously been described as *codices* in modern scholarship, because the term *codex* in itself ascribes the notion of normativity to its contents.

"LAW BOOKS" INSTEAD OF "CODICES" It would be more appropriate to call them law books. The large collections connected with the names Hammurabi, Eshnunna, and Lipit-Ishtar provide "a help, but no rules in finding justice."[108] The non-normative orientation of the ancient Near Eastern law books is especially supported by two observations. First, their legal stipulations do not cover anywhere near all possible legal cases that could arise in private or public life. The cases that are treated are often very special and complex and appear to have served as practice examples for legal learning. Second, the extant litigation records from the ancient Near East hardly if ever agree with the stipulations of the law books, nor are the latter cited.[109] The concrete search for justice, therefore, was not focused on the written law collections.

---

107. Cf. Rainer Albertz, "Die Theologisierung des Rechts im Alten Israel," in *Geschichte und Theologie: Studien zur Exegese des Alten Testaments und zur Religionsgeschichte Israels*, BZAW 326 (Berlin: de Gruyter, 2003), 187–207.

108. Jan Assmann, *Herrschaft und Heil* (Darmstadt: Wissenschaftliche Buchgesellschaft, 2000), 179.

109. Cf. "The Middle Assyrian Laws," trans. Martha Roth (*COS* 2.132:353–60).

System of Orientation from Traditional Knowledge Law in the ancient Near East was a system of orientation that arose from traditional knowledge and was applied with appropriate flexibility. There is no question that ancient Israel and Judah, as part of the ancient Near East, participated in this basic understanding of law.

3. The Legal Traditions of the Bible in Their Ancient Near Eastern Context

The Legal Corpora of the Torah The biblical legal texts appear in various places in the Torah. In the present version of the Torah, they are narratively integrated into the Moses biography from Exodus to Deuteronomy. Most stipulations are connected to Sinai, but the book of Deuteronomy is formulated as Moses's farewell address in the Transjordan before the entrance into the promised land. Three principal collections can be recognized: the so-called Covenant Code (Exod 20–23), which received its name from Exod 24:3; the Holiness Code (Lev 17–26), and the Deuteronomic laws (Deut 12–26). These collections in part comprise similar legal provisions that are related to one another as *Vorlage* and interpretation, making possible a relative dating of the three corpora. The Covenant Code appears to be the earliest collection. It was interpreted in Deuteronomy in line with the centralization of cult, and then the Deuteronomic laws are interpreted in the Holiness Code, balanced by the Priestly tradition. The two older collections, the Covenant Code and Deuteronomy, appear to have been originally literarily independent, while the Holiness Code presumably arose as a literary supplementation to a prespecified context. However, it is debated whether this context consisted of the still independent Priestly document or whether the Holiness Code presupposes the connection between the P and non-P materials in the Torah.

The Ancient Near Eastern Context In order to understand the peculiarity of even the earliest biblical legal texts, it is necessary to interpret them within their ancient Near Eastern context. The ancient Near East was familiar with an expansive written legal tradition ever since the end of the third millennium BCE. It is characterized by the fact that, on the one hand, it is formed as royal law, and on the other, as presented above, it is more descriptive than prescriptive.

THE KING AS THE LEGISLATIVE AUTHORITY The legislative authority in the ancient Near East is not the collection of written legal stipulations, but the king. The fact that there was no textually fixed law in pre-Hellenistic Egypt—except for a decree by Haremhab in the Eighteenth Dynasty—is, therefore, not an exception, but merely the logical illustration of this finding, of which the Greek and Roman conception of the king as *nomos empsychos* or *lex animata* provide an obvious expression.

THE CODEX ESHNUNNA The peculiarity of ancient Near Eastern law books is especially recognizable from the beginning of the so-called Codex Eshnunna, which emerged ca. 1770 BCE.[110] The first two paragraphs begin with a list of price equivalencies for goods:

(§1) 300 SILA of barley (can be purchased) for 1 shekel of silver. 3 SILA of fine oil—for 1 shekel of silver. 12 SILA of oil—for 1 shekel of silver. 15 SILA of lard—for 1 shekel of silver. 40 SILA of bitumen—for 1 shekel of silver. 360 shekels of wool—for 1 shekel of silver. 600 SILA of salt—for 1 shekel of silver. 300 SILA of potash—for 1 shekel of silver. 180 shekels of copper—for 1 shekel of silver. 120 shekels of wrought copper—for 1 shekel of silver.

(§2) 1 SILA of oil, extract(?)—30 SILA is its grain equivalent. 1 SILA of lard, extract(?)—25 SILA is its grain equivalent. 1 SILA of bitumen, extract(?)—8 SILA is its grain equivalent.

Up to this point one would characterize Codex Eshnunna as more of an economic than a legal text. In the following paragraphs, the text initially proceeds in a comparable manner, stipulating rent costs for means of transportation:

(§3) A wagon together with its oxen and its driver—100 SILA of grain is its hire; if (paid in) silver, 1/3 shekel (i.e., 60 barley corns) is its hire; he shall drive it for the entire day.

(§4) The hire of a boat is, per 300-sila capacity, 2 SILA; furthermore, [x] SILA is the hire of the boatman; he shall drive it for the entire day.

---

110. "The Laws of Eshnunna," trans. Martha Roth (*COS* 2.130:332–35).

Then in §5 the focus of the issue changes. Legal stipulations rather than economic price lists are offered, which take the classic "if . . . then" structure:

(§5) If the boatman is negligent and causes the boat to sink, he shall restore as much as he caused to sink.

(§6) If a man, under fraudulent circumstances, should seize a boat which does not belong to him, he shall weigh and deliver 10 shekels of silver.

One can see from this introductory passage that the genre of a legal book was not yet established. The Codex Eshnunna regulates prices, but also disputes that could arise from problems in economic life. Its following sections then progress further to common legal cases. Just like prices, which do not remain the same everywhere for all time, such is also the case for legal instructions. The Codex Eshnunna displays the legal traditions connection to reality roots in everyday life. The law was promulgated by the king; a divine component is, at most, suitable for directing the king to the cosmic order so that his promulgation of law accords with it.

THE CODEX HAMMURABI This is also the case for the famous Codex Hammurabi. The stela on which it is written has a graphic depiction of Hammurabi before the sun god Shamash, traditionally responsible for law and justice, on its upper part. Hammurabi receives a ring and staff presented by the sun god, presumably the insignia of his power as king. But he does not receive the text of the codex that can be read underneath on the stela (cf. above, §30.5). Therefore, Hammurabi's stela depicts the divine legitimation of the king rather than the divine parentage of his laws.

A COHERENT LEGAL CULTURE There can be no doubt that the legal books of the ancient Near East were not written in complete isolation from one another. They were instead part of a scribal legal culture. Their legal statements are often linguistically and thematically very closely related to one another, as shown by the stipulations concerning the goring ox, which appear both in Codex Eshnunna and also in Codex Hammurabi:

If an ox is a gorer and the ward authorities so notify its owner, but he fails to keep his ox in check and it gores a man [*awīlum*: i.e., a free man] and thus causes his death, the owner of the ox shall weigh and deliver 40 shekels of silver. If it gores a slave and thus causes his death, he shall weigh and deliver 15 shekels of silver.[111]

If an ox gores to death a man while it is passing through the streets, that case has no basis for a claim. If a man's ox is a known gorer, and the authorities of his city quarter notify him that it is a known gorer, but he does not blunt(?) its horns or control his ox, and that ox gores to death a member of the *awīlu*-class, he (the owner) shall give 30 shekels of silver. If it is a man's slave (who is fatally gored), he shall give 20 shekels of silver.[112]

It is immediately clear that these legal stipulations basically address the same case. At the same time, it is recognizable that the implementations and levels of detail clearly deviate from one another. One can deduce from this evidence that particular cases served as model cases, but in different legal traditions they could be implemented differently.

It is characteristic of law in the Hebrew Bible that it obviously takes part in ancient Near Eastern legal scholarship. This is illustrated most strikingly through the fact that the Torah is also familiar with the case of the goring ox.

If an ox gores a man or a woman so that they die, then the ox shall be stoned and its meat shall not be eaten. The owner of the ox, however, remains unpunished. If, however, an ox has gored for a longer time and his owner has been warned but still does not restrain it, and it kills a man or a woman, then the ox shall be stoned, and also its owner shall be killed. If a ransom is put upon him, then he shall pay the redemption for his life as much as is imposed upon him. If (the ox) gores a boy or a girl, then one shall treat it according to this stipulation. If the ox gores a male or a female slave, then he shall pay the owner 30 shekels of silver and the ox shall be stoned. (Exod 21:28–32)

This example shows that one must guard oneself from the assumption that law steadily becomes more humane over the course of legal history. Only the stipulation in the Torah envisages in the case of a goring ox that its delinquent owner can be killed, and only the Torah stipulates that the ox be stoned but that its meat not be eaten.

111. "The Laws of Eshnunna," trans. Martha Roth (*COS* 2.130:335).
112. "The Laws of Hammurabi," trans. Martha Roth (*COS* 2.131:350).

This legal stipulation is typical for the literary core of the Covenant Code. God neither appears explicitly nor implicitly in such stipulations. He is neither legislator nor judge. At the most he is guarantor and guardian of the legal order. The impression that arises from the present context that the entire law within the Pentateuch is divine law emerges in the Covenant Code primarily through the introduction in Exod 20:22–21:1, as well as through the insertion of further legal statements that explicitly mention God. The theologization of biblical law is, therefore, the result of a literary process rather than a characteristic inherent from the very beginning.

TALION IN THE ANCIENT NEAR EAST AND IN THE HEBREW BIBLE Among the legal statements of the Covenant Code are also the talionic stipulations (derived from the Latin *talis*, "same as"), which with the slogan "eye for an eye, tooth for a tooth" have participated significantly in the primarily Christian cultivated interpretation of the Hebrew Bible as a witness to the horrific doctrine of retribution.[113] Well-intentioned attempts have been made to defuse these stipulations so as to stem limitless blood vengeance by reading them as "only an eye for an eye" and "only a tooth for a tooth"—and not more, as far as the killing of the opponent for a small offense. It is not impossible that such a motivation lies behind the earliest oral precursors of such talionic stipulations. However, the logic in the Covenant Code is of another variety:

> If men fight with one another and injure a pregnant woman so that she delivers prematurely but no other harm follows, then the guilty party shall be punished with a fine that the woman's husband imposes upon him, and he shall pay it before the judges. However, if further harm follows, then you shall give life for life, eye for eye, tooth for tooth, hand for hand, foot for foot, burn for burn, wound for wound, stripe for stripe. When someone hits his male or female slave in the eye and destroys it, he shall set him free for his eye. If he knocks the tooth of his male or his female slave out, then he shall set him free for his tooth. (Exod 21:22–27)

It is striking in the first place that the talion stipulations are treated in the Covenant Code as a subset of a highly specialized legal situation: two

113. Cf. Eckart Otto, "Zur Geschichte des Talions im Alten Orient und Israel," in *Ernten, was man sät: Festschrift für Klaus Koch*, ed. Dwight R. Daniels (Neukirchen-Vluyn: Neukirchener Verlag, 1991), 101–30.

fighting men injure a woman in such a way that she suffers a premature delivery, and the resulting damages are to be settled through a fine. Only when further damages ensue do the talionic provisions come into play. But how exactly this is conceived remains unclear and, one must likely add for the legal context, deliberately open—to which damages do the talionic declarations apply? Are they the damages to the child or to the woman? And whose life or eye shall be "given" to whom? Important is, first, the observation that the Hebrew verb נתן (*ntn*), normally translated as "give," in the context of legal regulations in the Covenant Code means "pay." This meaning should also be adopted for Exod 21:22–27. The fact that the regulation of the penalty is not focused on the activation of further damages is also shown in the concluding provisions concerning the slaves. They should profit from the penalty, but the perpetrator shall not also be physically harmed.

This basic tendency can also be observed in the ancient Near Eastern models for the biblical talionic regulations. The talion regulation strikingly first appears in relation to bodily injuries in Codex Hammurabi; the earlier codices do not include it (only in the special case of murder, or rather homicide, which could not be legally differentiated from one another because ancient Near Eastern law is generally based on strict liability that does not take intent into consideration). They envision replacement payments (cf., e.g., Codex Ur-Nammu §§18–22).[114] Codex Hammurabi, on the contrary, introduces talion for the bodily injuries of free people (*awīlum*; cf. §§196, 197, 200). The meaning of this regulation is not to bring about more harm, but rather to obtain greater deterrence by means of the threatened penalty. Free people should not pursue their conflicts with violence. Whether talion actually was used as a legal principle in the ancient Near East is questionable. In any case, because of the basic status of the ancient Near Eastern legal collections, there was no compulsion to follow it.

DIVINE LAW AND ITS INTERPRETATION A significant consequence followed the theologized form of biblical law as divine law. Once the law was equipped with a divine quality, then it could no longer be changed without

---

114. Cf. Konrad Schmid, "The Monetization and Demonetization of the Human Body: The Case of Compensatory Payments for Bodily Injuries and Homicide in Ancient Near Eastern and Ancient Israelite Law Books," in *Money as God? The Monetization of the Market and Its Impact on Religion, Politics, Law, and Ethics*, ed. Michael Welker and Jürgen von Hagen (Cambridge: Cambridge University Press, 2014), 259–81.

hesitation. Only through inner-biblical interpretation was it possible to update such a law and put it in a new form, which was repeatedly necessary as time progressed and new problems arose. The interpretation of laws was a well-known process even before Deuteronomy—in the realm of the Covenant Code, but also in ancient Near Eastern legal literature—but the claim of divine origins for the law intensified these processes.

EXOD 21:2–7:	DEUT 15:12–18:
When you buy a Hebrew slave, he shall serve six years and in the seventh he shall go free without pay . . .	When your brother, a Hebrew man or woman, sells himself to you, then he should serve you six years, and in the seventh year you shall set him free. And when you set him free, you shall not send him out with empty hands . . .
But if the slave says: "I love my master, my wife, and my sons; I do not want to go free," then his master shall take him before God (האלהים, *h'lhym*). He shall take him to the doors or the doorpost, and there shall his master pierce his ear with an awl, and he will be his slave forever.	And if he says to you: "I do not want to go forth from you," then take the awl and thrust it through the ear into the doors, and he will be your slave forever. You shall also do this with your female slave. It should not be difficult for you when you must set him free. While he served you those six years that he was your slave, he only cost you half as much as a day laborer. And Yhwh, your God, will bless you in everything that you do.

The reformulation of the earlier slave laws from Exod 21:2–7 in Deut 15:12–18 shows a characteristic new interpretation. Slavery as such is viewed as self-evident in Exod 21 ("When you buy a slave"). In Deut 15, on the other hand, while it is accepted, it is viewed critically (cf. "sells himself to you," that is, "must sell himself to you"; "brother"). At the release in Deut 15 the slave is outfitted such that he can build up his own livelihood so that he will not immediately fall back into debt slavery. However, if the slave wants to serve in the house of his master, then this is sealed with a ritual that is obviously of a sacred nature in Exod 21 ("before God"), while in Deut 15 it appears in a profane form. Finally, the final passage in Deut 15 is especially striking. On the one hand, it formulates a motivational justification for the release of the slave, and on the other hand it promises divine blessing for keeping the commandment. The law in Deuteronomy apparently attempts to impose itself through this means, not through executive power.

A further interpretive step arguably takes place in the reception of the two stipulations in the framework of the Holiness Code in Lev 25:

> And if your brother beside you becomes impoverished and must sell himself, then you shall not lay the work of a slave on him.... For they are my slaves, whom I led up out of the land of Egypt. They shall not be sold as one sells a slave. You shall not rule over them with harshness (בפרך, *bprk*), but you shall fear your God. However, the male and female slaves that you may have, you shall buy from the nations around you. From them you may acquire male and female slaves. (Lev 25:39–44)

PARALLEL WITH THE EXODUS STORY Leviticus 25 forbids the ownership of slaves from Israel, for Lev 25:42 maintains that the Israelites are *God's* slaves, not slaves to one another. The formulation in Lev 25:43, 46, "rule with harshness (בפרך, *bprk*)," is adopted from Exod 1:13–14 (פרך, *prk*) and alludes to the oppression of Israel in Egypt. The Israelites are not permitted to rule over Israelites in the way that Egypt ruled over Israel. Only the possession of foreign slaves is permitted according to Lev 25.

THE PLURIVOCALITY OF THE LAW The legal provisions for slavery demonstrate quite clearly that the legislative materials of the Hebrew Bible were canonized together with their interpretive dynamic. This dynamic perception of law is of significant theological importance. A particular legal provision should always be interpreted in its inner biblical interpretive context.

LEV 10:16–20 AS LEGITIMATION OF THE CHANGEABILITY OF TORAH STIPULATIONS The fact that the Torah can also be changed in practice and should not be followed literally is justified by a short but remarkable passage from the book of Leviticus:

> But as Moses inquired about the goat for the sin offering, it had already been burned. And he became angry with Eleazar and Ithamar, the remaining sons of Aaron. And he said, "Why haven't you eaten the sin offering in the sanctuary?" ... And Aaron said to Moses, "See, today they have offered their sin offering and their burnt offering before Yhwh, and then such things happened to me. If I had eaten a sin

offering today, would Yhwh be pleased?" And Moses listened and it was good in his eyes. (Lev 10:16–20)

By means of a narrative, this text explains that the unauthorized behavior of Aaron's sons, which deviates from the stipulation of Moses, is nevertheless legitimate and can appear "good" in the eyes of Moses. As a result, the possibility for adaptations that do not affect the "Mosaic" character of the Torah is anchored in the Torah itself.[115] This small episode is rightly held to be the "founding legend of priestly exegesis."[116]

4. The Reception of the Prophetic Social Critique in the Legal Literature of the Hebrew Bible

SOCIAL RESPONSIBILITY AS AN ELEMENT OF THE LAW Even if the ancient Near Eastern conception of justice deviates significantly from the Roman influenced notion of *suum cuique* ("to each his own") and includes integral elements of grace and mercy for underprivileged persons, especially widows and orphans,[117] this emphasis receives special intensification in the legal literature of the Hebrew Bible, which is evidently linked with the adoption of prophetic claims and proclamations. "The Book of the Covenant takes up the shattering of everything that had been taken for granted, which the prophets of the late eighth and early seventh century lamented and subsequently declared to be God's judgment on a people that had become godless, in such a way as to derive a positive divine law from the lament and complaint of the prophets."[118]

In fact there are striking relationships between the prophetic tradition and the Covenant Code that can be interpreted accordingly. One might

115. Cf. Christian Frevel, "'Und Mose hörte (es), und es war gut in seinen Augen' (Lev 10,20): Zum Verhältnis von Literargeschichte, Theologiegeschichte und innerbiblischer Auslegung am Beispiel von Lev 10," in *Gottes Name(n): Zum Gedenken an Erich Zenger*, ed. Ilse Müllner et al., HBS 71 (Freiburg im Breisgau: Herder, 2012), 104–36.

116. Christophe Nihan, *From Priestly Torah to Pentateuch: A Study in the Composition of the Book of Leviticus*, FAT II/25 (Tübingen: Mohr Siebeck, 2007), 602.

117. The special emphasis on the royal responsibility to provide for widows and orphans may possibly be based in the husbands and fathers having died in battle or corvée for the king, whose task had been to carry out important military campaigns and monumental construction. It likely also concerns a compensatory diachronic measure.

118. Reinhard G. Kratz, *The Composition of the Narrative Books of the Old Testament*, trans. John Bowden (London: T&T Clark, 2005), 142.

compare a text such as Amos 2:6–8 with divine legal provisions in Exod 22:25–27 (retaining the second person):

Amos 2:6–8:	Exod 22:25–27:
Thus said Yhwh: "For three of Israel's transgressions or because of four I will not relent. Because they sell the innocent for money and the poor for a pair of sandals. They trample the head of the lowly into the dust and bend the path of the needy … They lie down on garments taken in pledge beside every altar and drink wine bought with fines in their house of God.	When you loan money to [one of] my people, the poor among you, do not treat him like a usurer; you shall not put any interest on it. If you take the coat of another as a pledge, then you shall return it to him before the sun sets, for it is his only blanket, the covering of his body. Otherwise on what shall he sleep? When he calls to me, then I will hear him, and I will be gracious.

The Covenant Code adopts the social criticism from the book of Amos and likely sees it legitimated through the attribution of this social criticism to the word of God in the book of Amos ("Thus said Yhwh"). It then adopts the stipulations in its legal collection as divine law.

PROPHETIC AUTHORIZATION OF THE LAW This process is highly noteworthy from a theological point of view. The plausibility of prophetic proclamation, based primarily on evidence of an ethical nature, is proclaimed in the Covenant Code as divine law—probably not least because these legal provisions could support themselves with prophetic authority. The idea of divine law is, however, not a genuine achievement of the Covenant Code. This was made possible by Deuteronomy, as will be explored next.

5. From Legal Regulations to Law: Deuteronomy

THE DEVELOPMENT OF NORMATIVE LAW A considerable step took place with the introduction and conception of divine law in the Hebrew Bible. The law in this form claims, in and of itself, to be binding and normative. The reasons for this can be historically identified. First, the transfer of normativity from king to textual corpus is rooted in the subversive reception of Neo-Assyrian treaty theology in Deuteronomy as described above, in which the authoritative sovereign of the Assyrian emperor is replaced by the God of Israel (cf. above, §18 and §24). Second is that it is heavily supported and expanded in the wake of the conquest and destruction of Samaria in 722 BCE by the Assyrians and of Jerusalem in 587 BCE by the Babylonians and—namely in the wake of these two events—through the oppositional reference to the expansive Babylonian legal tradition, which views the king as the final normative authority. The elimination of the monarchy in Israel meant the loss of the traditional ultimate legal authority. A replacement was found in the appointment of God to the function of the legislator, who, however—for comprehensible reasons—possessed no concrete executive abilities such that the adopted law cannot simply be implemented. Therefore, it is not surprising that biblical law, once having risen to divine law, now contains warnings and justifications for over 50% of the legal stipulations that emphatically call for the stipulations to be followed.[119]

For example, the stipulations on the release of slaves in the seventh year in Deut 15:12–18 even presents two motivations. The first is that the master of a slave shall remember that he himself was a slave in Egypt and was freed by God (Deut 15:15). The second points out that the slave has cost the master half of what he would have paid a day laborer in the six years (Deut 15:18). Without an external executive, legal consciousness itself must ensure that the law is enforced and that it is followed.

LAW AND INTERPRETATION OF THE LAW A further process accompanies the development of the divine law. Law classified as divine law cannot simply be changed or annulled, but only interpreted and construed. From the moment that the biblical law possesses this quality onward, there is hardly another way; the actualization of the law is self-evidently and necessarily to take place through inner-biblical exegesis. The expository actualization of biblical law can be clearly substantiated from various perspectives. Especially impressive is, on the one hand, the adoption of the Covenant Code (Exod 20–23) in Deuteronomy as well as, on the other hand, the adoption of Deuteronomy in the Holiness Code (Lev 17–26) and its adjustment with further legal texts.

THE AUTHORITY OF THE INTERPRETIVE PROCESS The final point mentioned is of decisive importance for the legal traditions conceived as divine

---

119. Cf. Tikva Frymer-Kensky, "Israel," in *A History of Ancient Law*, ed. Raymond Westbrook, vol. 2, HdO 72/2 (Leiden: Brill, 2003), 979.

law in the Bible. While it can be traced back to God as author and legislator, at the same time it is interpreted as temporary, in need of actualization, and open to actualization. Through the fact that text and commentary appear together in the biblical canon, the dynamic of interpretation is already inherent in the Bible itself and still has the potency, from its very beginning, to guard against every kind of fundamentalism that could be derived from the concept of divine law and—as is well attested in history—has been derived.

This special understanding is probably also the reason behind the great fluidity evident in the handling of the law in Judaism from Deuteronomy until the end of the Second Temple period. A fundamental observance of the Law first became significant for the identity of Judaism from the Maccabean period on, but the question of interpretation remained of central importance.[120]

6. Legal Interpretation in the Holiness Code

THE HOLINESS LAW AS LITERARY SUPPLEMENTATION TO THE PRIESTLY DOCUMENT The text complex of Lev 17–26 has been called the "Holiness Law" since August Klostermann[121] due to the repeated refrain "Be holy as I, Yhwh, your God, am holy." This corpus is not, however, an independent collection of laws. The Holiness Code either arose as literary supplementation to the Priestly document, or it may even have first sprung up after P had been integrated into the Pentateuch. In terms of content, Lev 17–26 is marked by the balancing of Deuteronomistic and Priestly legislation. This is especially tangible in the final blessing section of the Holiness Code in Lev 26. Leviticus 26:9, 11–13 adopts central promises from Priestly texts like Gen 17; Exod 6:2–8; and 29:45–46, making them dependent because they are now placed in the concluding blessing and curse section of the Holiness Code. This is introduced by "*If* you walk in my statutes and keep my commandments and follow them" (Lev 26:3). The promises will no longer be unconditionally fulfilled, but are instead made dependent on obedience to the law, which amounts to a certain "Deuteronomization" of Priestly theology.

---

120. Cf. John J. Collins, *The Invention of Judaism: Torah and Jewish Identity from Deuteronomy to Paul* (Oakland, CA: University of California Press, 2017).

121. August Klostermann, "Ezechiel und das Heiligkeitsgesetz," *Zeitschrift für die lutherische Theologie und Kirche* 38 (1877): 401-45.

GEN 17:6–7:

I will make you exceedingly fruitful;
and I will make nations of you, and
kings will descend from you. I will
establish my covenant between me
and you and your descendants from
generation to generation as an eternal
covenant, that I will be God to you
and your offspring.

LEV 26:3, 9–13:

If you follow my statutes and keep my
commandments and follow them, . . .
(9) then I will turn toward you and
make you fruitful and multiply you
and maintain my covenant with you.
. . . *I will place my dwelling among you*
and I will not abhor you. *I will* walk
among you and I will be your God,
**and you shall be my people. I am
Yhwh, your God, who led you out of
the land of Egypt,** so that you would
not be slaves there. And I broke the
bars of your yoke and made you walk
upright.

EXOD 6:4–7:

And I have established a covenant
with them. . . . I will free you from the
corvée labor of Egypt and deliver you
from your slavery with outstretched
arm and with mighty acts of judgment. I will take you as my people and
will be your God, and you shall know
that **I, Yhwh, am your God, who
frees you from the burden of the
corvée labor of Egypt.**

EXOD 29:45–46:

*And I will live in the midst of the
Israelites* and be their God, so that
they will know that **I, Yhwh, am their
God, who led them out of the land of
Egypt** *in order to live in their midst*, I,
Yhwh, their God.

Contrary to the theological program of the Priestly document, which
only uses the first half of the covenant formula, as the examples in Gen
17:7; Exod 6:7; 29:46 sufficiently attest, the now completely reproduced
covenant formula in Lev 26:11 points in the same direction: "I will be your

God, *and you shall be my people.*" The Holiness Code reformulates the one-sidedness of the Priestly theology in a Deuteronomistic sense. Now the promises of the Priestly document are no longer immediate divine grants; they are instead mediated by law theology.

RECEPTION OF THE DECALOGUE Especially striking as well is the role of the Decalogue in Lev 17–26. One receives the impression that the Decalogue and its theology represent a substratum of the content of the Holiness Code (cf. esp. Lev 19). The Holiness Code, therefore, attempts to showcase the suitability of its stipulations for daily life. Their self-presentation is that they are as fundamental as the commandments of the Decalogue.

§35 Temple Worship and Sacrifice

Ulrike Dahm, *Opferkult und Priestertum in Alt-Israel: Ein kultur- und religionswis-senschaftlicher Beitrag,* BZAW 327 (Berlin: de Gruyter, 2003) ◆ Christian Eber-hart, *Studien zur Bedeutung der Opfer im Alten Testament: Die Signifikanz von Blut- und Verbrennungsriten im kultischen Rahmen,* WMANT 94 (Neukirchen-Vluyn: Neukirchener Verlag, 2002) ◆ Friedhelm Hartenstein, "Zur symbolischen Bedeutung des Blutes im Alten Testament," in *Deutungen des Todes Jesu im Neuen Testament,* ed. Jörg Frey and Jens Schröter, WUNT 181 (Tübingen: Mohr Sie-beck, 2005), 119–37 ◆ Bernd Janowski, *Sühne als Heilsgeschehen: Traditions- und religionsgeschichtliche Studien zur priesterschriftlichen Sühnetheologie,* 2nd ed., WMANT 55 (Neukirchen-Vluyn: Neukirchener Verlag, 2000) ◆ Lee I. Levine, *The Ancient Synagogue: The First Thousand Years,* 2nd ed. (New Haven: Yale Uni-versity Press, 2005) ◆ Thomas Staubli, "Räuchern, libieren, spenden: Opfer im altisraelitischen Alltag," *BK* 64 (2009): 152–57 ◆ Guy G. Stroumsa, *The End of Sacrifice: Religious Transformations in Late Antiquity* (Chicago: University of Chi-cago Press, 2009) ◆ Ina Willi-Plein, "Ein Blick auf die neuere Forschung zu Opfer und Kult im Alten Testament," *VF* 56 (2011): 16–33 ◆ Ina Willi-Plein, "Opfer und Sühne," in *Die Welt der Hebräischen Bibel: Umfeld—Inhalte—Grundthemen,* ed. Walter Dietrich (Stuttgart: Kohlhammer, 2017), 271–84

1. Preliminary Remarks from the History of Scholarship

THE DEVALUATION OF THE CULT IN CHRISTIAN THEOLOGY Although Christian theology has traditionally had a very close relationship with the sacrificial thematic, given the New Testament's construal of the death of Jesus as a sacrifice,[122] it developed a remarkable distance, even devaluation of the sacrificial texts of the Hebrew Bible itself. As cultic instructions they were overtaken by Jesus's sacrificial death, and from this perspective, the sacrificial passages of the Hebrew Bible were sometimes outright discredited theologically. Paradigmatic is an interpretation such as that of Ludwig Köhler in his *Theologie des Alten Testaments* (1953), which treats the sacrificial cult under the title "Die Selbsterlösung des Menschen" ("The self-redemption of the person").[123] In Köhler's view the sacrifice is symbolic of Old Testament works-driven righteousness. Here the human attempts to make himself pleasing to God—unsuccessfully, of course.

THE DISCOVERY OF THE ATONEMENT THEOLOGY OF THE PRIESTLY DOCUMENT For the first time in the 1980s the discussion of the sacrificial texts began to change. It became clear that the sacrificial cult in the Torah should not be interpreted as a human effort, but that it was rather conceived as God's endowment, through which Israel was able to have healthy contact with God despite the ever accumulating guilt. While views in the 1980s, taking Lev 17:11b as their starting point, still had the blood rituals in the foreground of the atoning effect of the sacrifice, recent scholarship tends to interpret the pouring out of blood on the altar as the preparatory action to the actual sacrifice itself. The blood, which belongs to God anyway, is given back through the process of the sacrifice, while the sacrifice itself constitutes the burning of the offering and the rising of the ריח הניחוח (*ryḥ hnyḥwḥ*), "pleasing aroma."

THE DIVERSITY OF THE CULT Sacrifice is not the only thing that belongs to the cult. In fact, one must assume that there was less sacrificed in the First Temple than in the Second Temple. In addition to sacrifices, numerous other cultic experiences took place such as feasts, pilgrimages, reception of personal oracles, etc. The religion of ancient Israel and Judah in the preexilic period was primarily marked by such cultic celebrations, while texts and holy writings played a very subordinate role. Beginning with the destruction of the Jerusalem Temple in 587 BCE, fundamental processes

122. Cf. Jörg Frey and Jens Schröter, eds., *Deutungen des Todes Jesu im Neuen Testament*, 2nd ed., Uni-Taschenbücher 2953 (Tübingen: Mohr Siebeck, 2012).

123. Köhler, *Theologie des Alten Testaments*, 4th ed., NTG (Tübingen: Mohr Siebeck, 1966), 171–89.

of transformation start, marking the beginning of a scripturally-based Judaism. The basic religious-historical change during the sixth to fourth centuries has only been established in the last decade of scholarship, now that archaeology and epigraphy have successfully shown the fundamental difference between the biblical religion and the concretely lived religion in Israel and Judah.[124] Within the context of a theology of the Hebrew Bible rather than the religious-historical finds, this discussion will focus on the theological reflections and interpretations in the biblical texts.

2. Cultically Influenced Psalms

The book of Psalms is especially close to the temple cult. While current Psalms scholarship places much more emphasis on the literary character of the Psalter and also reckons with psalms that are of a redactional nature and never existed outside of the Psalter, current scholarship does not dispute that certain psalms arose within the cult and once had particular cultic functions.

THE TEMPLE AS THE LOCATION OF GOD'S PRESENCE Temples in the ancient Near East were not merely buildings that served sacred purposes; they were sanctuaries in which the divine and earthly spheres met. Therefore, they could not be built just anywhere. They were placed where the particular deity indicated, or the locations were discovered in some kind of miraculous way by the one establishing the cult (cf., e.g., Gen 28:11–19 for Bethel). For the Hebrew Bible, the temple in Jerusalem is the central sanctuary. While the Hebrew Bible is also aware of other sanctuaries in Shiloh, Bethel, Dan, and Samaria, according to its emphasis on cult centralization, these are unauthorized. The Jerusalem temples—the First Temple existing from Solomon to the destruction of Jerusalem in 587 BCE and the Second Temple from around 515 BCE till the destruction by the Romans in 70 CE—conformed to the known temple plans from the Levant with an inner court, main chamber, and Holy of Holies. It was, however—due to the strong solar tradition in Jerusalem—not aligned north to south, but rather east to west. The different rooms and courtyards of the temple signify a stepped holiness. All participants in the cult could

---

124. Cf. the overview in Othmar Keel and Christoph Uehlinger, *Gods, Goddesses, and the Images of God in Ancient Israel* (Edinburg: T&T Clark, 2008).

enter the inner court, the main chamber was reserved for the priests, and only the high priest was permitted to enter the Holy of Holies on Yom Kippur (Lev 16).

THE WILDERNESS SANCTUARY AS A PREFIGURATION OF THE JERUSALEM TEMPLE In addition to the historically verified buildings of the First and Second Temples in Jerusalem, the Bible is also familiar with the notion of a transportable tent sanctuary that receives an elaborate description in Exod 25–31 and 35–40. It concerns a mythic model for the Jerusalem temple that, according to Exod 25–31 and 35–40, was already designed and built in the Mosaic period. While tent sanctuaries are known in the ancient Near East, the tent designed in Exod 25–31 and 35–40 with its furniture and its wooden inner room (משכן [*mškn*], "residence") can only be of a fictive nature.[125] The splendid and sophisticated construction of the sanctuary rests on retrojections of the Jerusalem temple. The dimensions of the sanctuary from Exod 25–31 and 35–40 correspond to the later Solomonic Temple on a scale of 1:2. Exodus 25–31 and 35–40 belong to the Priestly document, which creates an indestructible literary temple with this model after the destruction of the temple. It is striking that in the current Pentateuch, the scandal of the Golden Calf is inserted in Exod 32–34 between the planning and construction of the tent. This demonstrates that the idea of the temple also exists independently from Israel's sin and punishment.

PSALM 24 AS A FORMERLY CULTIC TEXT Psalm 24:7–10 should be named within the Psalms that still show their roots in the cult:

> Raise up, you gates, your heads! Rise up, you ancient doors!
> That the king of glory may enter.
> Who is the king of glory?
> Yhwh, strong and mighty; Yhwh, the hero in battle.
> Raise up, you gates, your heads! Rise up, you ancient doors!
> That the king of glory may enter.
> Who is the king of glory?
> Yhwh of Hosts, he is the king of glory.

125. Cf. Hanna Liss, "The Imaginary Sanctuary: The Priestly Code as an Example of Fictional Literature in the Hebrew Bible," in *Judah and the Judeans in the Persian Period*, ed. Oded Lipschits and Manfred Oeming (Winona Lake, IN: Eisenbrauns, 2006), 663–89.

Psalm 24 clearly describes a procession—the entrance of God into his sanctuary—accompanied by a cultic antiphony. Psalm 24 was likely originally part of the official cult. However, this liturgy is now set in a literary context in Pss 15–24, within which it should be read. At least for the period after 587 BCE, if not already before, Ps 24 formulates the remembrance of a cultic event, which as such should be seen as theologically relevant—even if the original cultic context of this text no longer exists.[126]

PS 13 AS INDIVIDUAL LAMENT In addition to pieces like Ps 24, whose scenery points to the cultic sphere, one should also mention what are called the individual laments as cultic texts at home in the temple. A classic example is offered by Ps 13. The psalm can easily be structured in three parts: After the superscription, a lament appears in vv. 2–3 (Eng. vv. 1–2) followed by a request in vv. 4–5 (Eng. vv. 3–4). The psalm is concluded in v. 6 with a declaration of trust and a statement of praise:

> Ps 13:
> For the choirmaster. A psalm of David.
> How long, Yhwh! Will you forget me forever?   *Lament*
> How long will you hide your face from me?
> How long shall I bear worries in my soul?
> Sorrow in my heart day after day?
> How long shall my enemies be lifted up over me?
> Look at me, listen to me, Yhwh my God!   *Request*
> Give light to my eyes, so that I do not sleep the sleep
>   of death,
> So that my enemy not say, "I have overcome him,"
> My opponent not rejoice because I am shaken.
> But I have trusted in your goodness.   *Praise*
> May my heart rejoice concerning your help.
> I want to sing to Yhwh, for he has dealt bountifully with me.

The lament (vv. 1–3 [Eng. 2–3]) and request (vv. 4–5 [Eng. 3–4]) correspond closely thematically. They follow the theme God—I—enemy. Striking is that the theme "enemy," which is emphasized in the lament by means of its own "how long" sentence, is not accorded its own clause in

126. Cf. Thomas Podella, "Transformationen kultischer Darstellungen: Toraliturgien in Ps 15 und 24," *SJOT* 13 (1999): 95–130.

the request. The statement of the enemy is connected to the "I" declaration by means of "that not." This indicates that the psalm wants to show that the actual problem of the one praying is not—as one might superficially think—from the threat of the enemy, but from the experience of God's abandonment, based on its duration ("how long?"), which is especially threatening ("so that I not sleep the sleep of death"). Therefore, the theme of the enemy does not appear in the concluding v. 6, which is wholly focused on the relationship between the one praying and God.

THE PROBLEM OF THE REVERSAL IN TONE Psalm 13 is generally understood to have a linear temporal progression. The one praying first laments, then he requests, and finally he praises. Read in this way, the problem of the so-called reversal in tone arises, which also occurs in other individual songs of lament. This reversal is commonly explained by positing that a priestly oracle of salvation took place between the request and the praise (cf. Ps 22:22; Lam 3:57), promising divine support and help and allowing the petitioner, therefore, to progress from request to praise.[127]

PROLEPTIC TRUST This explanation, with unavoidable gaps, could be accurate or not; however, it does not really explain the theological function of Ps 13 in its context. Attention here should especially be paid to the perfective formulation of the trust motif in Ps 13:6 ([Eng. 5] בטחתי [*bṭḥty*], "I have trusted"). The situation of the one praying, should, therefore, not be understood such that he "trusts" in a somewhat counterfactual way that God will "do" good to him. Instead the psalm tells—taking the time structure into account—that first the one praying *had* trusted in the past—that is, before his hardship—and that God *had already* dealt bountifully with him. The psalm simultaneously calls for the one praying to also trust in God now, expecting good from him in the future, but the certainty of God's future salvific action lies in the retrospection of the one praying on God's acts of deliverance that have already taken place.[128]

127. Joachim Begrich, "Das priesterliche Heilsorakel," in *Gesammelte Studien zum Alten Testament,* TB 21 (Munich: Kaiser, 1964), 217-31. Cf. Federico G. Villanueva, *The Uncertainty of a Hearing: A Study of the Sudden Change of Mood in the Psalms of Lament*, VTSup 121 (Leiden: Brill, 2008).

128. Beat Weber, "Zum sogenannten 'Stimmungsumschwung' in Psalm 13," in *The Book of Psalms: Composition and Reception*, ed. Peter W. Flint und Patrick D. Miller, VTSup 99 (Leiden: Brill, 2005), 116-38; Felipe G. Villanueva, *The Uncertainty of a Hearing: A Study of the Sudden Change of Mood in the Psalms of Lament*, VTSup 121 (Leiden: Brill, 2008).

Therefore, Ps 13 provides a good example of how an originally cultically rooted text is stripped of its previous functional context and is now
placed as a theological text in the Psalter that can serve the scriptural meditation recommended as reading posture in Ps 1:2.

3. Sacrifice as a Constant in the History of Israelite Religion

SACRIFICE AS FOOD FOR THE GODS There is no doubt in the scholarship
of the history of religions that the sacrificial act belongs to the oldest cultic performances of humanity. How its function can be determined more
closely has primarily interested those crossing the boundaries between
the psychology of religion and early history and has called forth numerous
speculations.[129] Whether they are correct or not, they especially share the
perspective of offering structural mythic explanations for the significance
of sacrifice. From supposed primeval constellations, the attempt is made
to derive the ritual meaning of the sacrifice. Sacrificial acts are suitable
to anthropological and social depth dimensions. The original function of
sacrifice on the plane of religion itself may, however, have consisted of the
conception of sustenance for the deities. This can be clearly recognized in
a text such as the Gilgamesh Epic, which like the Bible (Gen 6–9) contains
a depiction of the flood that is, however, considerably earlier than Gen
6–9 and upon which the Bible drew literarily for its content. Like in Gen
8:21–22, the hero of the flood—Utnapishtim in the Gilgamesh Epic—offers
a sacrifice after the flood, but there it states:

> The gods smelled the scent, the gods smelled the sweet scent, the
> gods gathered like flies around the lord of the sacrifice. (Gilgamesh
> 11.159–61)

The gods pounce like flies on the first offering after the flood because
they had to undergo privation during the flood—there were no humans to
sacrifice to them. After the flood they could satisfy their hunger again on
the first sacrifice brought by the hero of the flood ("smell," cf. Gen 8:21:
"And Yhwh smelled the pleasant aroma . . .").

---

129. René Girard, *Violence and the Sacred* (London: Bloomsbury Academic, 2013);
Walter Burkert, *Homo Necans The Anthropology of Ancient Greek Sacrificial Ritual and Myth*
(Berkeley: University of California Press, 1987).

BIBLICAL SACRIFICIAL INTERPRETATIONS This original understanding of sacrifice attested in ancient Near Eastern texts primarily appears as a polemic distortion in the Hebrew Bible. Psalm 50:13 formulates it, for example, as a divine declaration: "Shall I eat the flesh of bulls and drink the blood of goats?" On the one hand, this adopts the traditional function of the sacrifice, but at the same time it turns it into its opposite. What God instead expects "as sacrifice" is "gratitude" (תודה, *twdh*; Ps 50:14). Psalm 50 should probably be interpreted historically as coming from a post-cultic context. From a theological perspective, it should be maintained that the psalm preserves the basic structure of the sacrifice as a medium to God, but this is now apprehended as spiritual rather than material.

In addition to this rejection of the cultic sacrifice, there are also numerous texts that not only approve of sacrifice but view it as essential for a relationship with God. This is especially the case for the Priestly sacrificial legislation (Lev 1–7), which views the sacrificial cult as Israel's prerogative within the world of the nations and signifies its special relationship with God. The Priestly sacrificial texts in this regard have a traditional orientation, for they primarily concentrate on the description of the ritual as such and hardly develop their own interpretive perspective. Especially noteworthy, however, is the use in them of the motif of the ריח הניחוח (*ryḥ hnyḥwḥ*), "pleasing aroma," that rises to God from the burning of the sacrificial offering and is received by him. On the one hand, this offers a clear memory of the original function of the sacrifice as sustenance for the gods, but on the other hand it appears in a theological shape that no longer views the smoke as serving to satiate the deity, instead signifying God's acceptance of the offering.

4. Sacrifice in Deuteronomy

Prior to the centralization of the sacrificial cult in Jerusalem, which the Bible links to Josiah's reform,[130] sacrifices were permitted to take place at open places, under trees, or in houses. Sacrifice was carried out by tribal or family heads or by local priests. Sacrificial affairs were festive events. The sacrificial legislation in Deuteronomy, which emphasizes the centralization aspect, still reflects this origin. Deuteronomy 12 names neither the

130. Cf. Michael Pietsch, *Die Kultreform Josias: Studien zur Religionsgeschichte Israels in der späten Königszeit*, FAT 86 (Tübingen: Mohr Siebeck, 2012).

meal, guilt, nor sin offerings, but underscores the social cohesion and the enjoyment associated with the sacrifice.[131] The sacrifice is traditionally linked with God's blessing: "An altar of earth you shall build for me and slaughter on it your burnt offering and your offerings of well-being, your sheep and your cattle. In every place where I will cause my name to be remembered, I will come to you and bless you" (Exod 20:24). In Deut 12:13–15 a theological interpretation has evidently already taken place. The blessing precedes the sacrifice; the bringer of the sacrifice offers what he has previously received from God.

COMMUNICATION WITH GOD AND COMMUNICATION WITH HUMANS From a theological perspective, it is noteworthy that the sacrificial texts of Deuteronomy stress the fact that the person's communication with God that takes place with the sacrifice cannot be viewed separately from the communication of humans with each other. The bringing of a sacrifice is not a process that concerns only the one bringing the sacrifice and the receiving deity; it includes the community of the one bringing the offering as well.

The centralization of the sacrificial cult—while the degree to which it was actually carried out or remained a theological program is difficult to say—implies, on the flip side, the profanation of everyday life. Slaughtering that does not take place within the framework of the prescribed pilgrimage feasts in Jerusalem (Deut 16) no longer had the same cultic character. This establishment of a profane sphere is of considerable importance in terms of the history of reception. It prefigures the living situation of the exile (according to other interpreters who date Deuteronomy to the exilic period, it portrays them), which moves far from the Jerusalem temple.

5. The Theology of the Cult and Sacrifice in the Priestly Document

The most prominent voice on cult and sacrifice in the Hebrew Bible is what is called the Priestly document (cf. §18 and §26). Likely originally an independent written source, presumably stretching literarily from creation to Sinai, it owes its name primarily to its cultic and priestly interests. It emerged at the time of the Second Temple in Jerusalem when Israel's sacrificial cult was in full bloom. To it is allocated almost all textual mate-

---

131. Cf. Peter Altmann, *Festive Meals in Ancient Israel: Deuteronomy's Identity Politics in Their Ancient Near Eastern Context*, BZAW 424 (Berlin: de Gruyter, 2011).

rial from Exod 25 until and including Lev 16 (with the exception of Exod 32–34), exhibiting a focus on the regulations of the sacrificial cult.

THE SACRIFICIAL TORAH IN THE BOOK OF LEVITICUS These texts, especially those of the book of Leviticus, claim an almost incomprehensible breadth for present-day understanding. From the perspective of the Hebrew Bible, however, Leviticus with its sacrificial stipulations is literally considered the center of the five books of the Torah. The division of the narrative material from Genesis to Deuteronomy into five books does not make sense in terms of the breaks in the course of the narrative (in particular, Exodus to Numbers forms a continuous context). Also the amount of material from Exodus to Numbers could easily be divided into two instead of three books. The present division likely took place in order to highlight the laws in Leviticus within the middle spot between Genesis and Exodus on the one side and Numbers and Deuteronomy on the other.

But what is the reason that the book of Leviticus with its sacrificial stipulations was held to be so significant from a biblical perspective that it could be accorded the concrete literary position in the middle of the Torah? Theologically, the establishment of the sacrificial cult with all its regulations basically constitutes the functional and theological counterweight to the Primeval History (Gen 1–11). If the Primeval History reports the proliferation of guilt—and not in the sense of moral misconduct that it would also be possible to avoid incrementally, but rather in the sense of guilt that necessarily marks human life in the creation of Gen 1 corrected by Gen 9, then the establishment of the sacrificial cult narrates a possibility initiated by God to redeem this guilt incrementally through atonement.

The nature of the sacrifice texts is such that they focus solely on the sequence of cultic performances and hardly formulate any perspectives on the purpose of sacrifice. The atonement terminology only appears occasionally, but sometimes prominently, such as in Lev 1:4:

And he shall lay his hand on the head of the burnt offering, so that it will be acceptable and effect atonement (כפר, *kpr*) for him.

The ritual of the laying on of the hand is sometimes understood as a transference of identity according to the presentation of a successor in Num 27:18 and Deut 34:9, such that the sacrificial animal would be identified with the bringer of the sacrifice and then in some sense die a substitutional death for the bringer of the sacrifice. This explanation is similar to the New Testament conception of Jesus's substitutionary death, but it can be maintained neither for the meaning of the laying on of the hand in Num 27:18; Deut 34:9, nor for the understanding of sacrifice in the Hebrew Bible. The transfer of identity is not present in either case.

BLOOD RITUALS There is also an important difference within the Priestly view in the book of Leviticus with regard to the blood rituals. In Lev 17:11 an explicit statement appears on the atoning function of blood:

> For the life-force (נפש, npš) of the flesh is in the blood, and I have given it to you for the altar in order to accomplish atonement (כפר, kpr), for it is the blood through which [its] lifeforce (נפש, npš) establishes atonement (כפר, kpr).

However, Lev 17:11 belongs to the literary context of the Holiness Code, which as such represents an expansion to the Priestly document. Within the Priestly texts themselves, this function of blood is not attested. Instead, three basic observations can be made. First, according to the sacrificial torah itself, blood does not appear to be sacrificed. It is poured out prior to the actual sacrifice by the bringer of the sacrifice (not by the priest) at the base of the altar. The understanding is, therefore, that the blood already belongs to God himself, so it cannot then be transferred to him. Second, the blood can take on a purification function within the view of the sanctuary and its inventory (Lev 4–5); it can be scattered within the context of a "small" (Lev 4:20, 25, 34) or "large" (Lev 4:5–7) blood ritual and thereby purify the sanctuary. The actual atoning function of the offering would be achieved through the burning of the offering and the rising of the aroma to God. Third, it should be observed that depending on the poverty of the offerer, instead of large or small cattle, also doves or even vegetable offerings could be brought (Lev 5:11). The blood is, according to this provision, not an indispensable part of a sacrifice.

In contrast, a shift in meaning takes place with Lev 17:11. The Holiness Code now truly attributes a central role to the blood. However, it is interesting that Lev 17:11 is framed completely as divine speech. God himself provides the blood for the altar—the idea of the sacrifice appears here in a completely theocentric form.

Thanks to the sacrificial cult established by God himself, a meaningful life is possible in a world that has stood under the mark of human guilt since its beginnings—this is the fundamental meaning of the sacrificial torah. Law here is not grasped as a collection of stipulations on how to avoid guilt, but rather how it is to be eliminated.

GOD AS THE SUBJECT OF ATONEMENT   The subject of the atonement is God, not the human. The sacrificial cult is precisely not the work of humans, but God's endowment, given for the redemption of guilt, which makes an auspicious life of righteousness possible. The rabbis, for example, maintained an entirely factual alignment with the book of Leviticus:

> Until the wilderness sanctuary was constructed, the world staggered; [but] from that moment on, the world was stabilized. (Pesiqta de Rab Kahana, 8–9)

> And you find also that in the entire time in which the service took place at the house of the sanctuary, blessing was on the earth. . . . Since the house of the sanctuary was destroyed, there is no more blessing on the earth. ('Abot de Rabbi Nathan, B 5 [9b])

CREATION IN THE CREATION   The wilderness sanctuary (the Tent of Meeting) that prefigures the temple in Jerusalem, as well as the temple itself, as the sites to which one brings the sacrifice, have a world-establishing function. Without sacrifice, the world "staggers," and there is "no blessing" on it. Why? Because a world with guilt that cannot be atoned through sacrifice is a world in which no meaningful, auspicious life is possible. One might even justifiably say that the establishment of the sacrificial cult in the Hebrew Bible can be characterized as a "creation in the creation."[132] Within the fallen first creation, the sacrificial cult forms a second creation that partially restores the integrity of the first creation. Perhaps the dietary laws should also be interpreted in this context, restricting the consumption of meat from Gen 9: only meat from pure animals may be consumed. This draws nearer to the original stipulation from Gen 1, which only allocated vegetarian food for the humans.

THE SACRIFICIAL CULT AS GOD'S ENDOWMENT   The sacrificial cult in the Priestly document is not human service for the divine world. Instead, it is the divine endowment to the world of humans that makes a righteous life

---

132. According to Erhard Blum, *Studien zur Komposition des Pentateuch*, BZAW 189 (Berlin: de Gruyter, 1990), 289–332, esp. 311.

possible for them. God is not thought of as the receiver according to the sacrificial texts of the Priestly document, but rather the donor. From this point of view, God does not demand food; instead he conveys life.

6. The Spiritualization of the Theology of Sacrifice and Individual Dietary Prescriptions

WISDOM INTERPRETATIONS Primarily in the wisdom literature and the wisdom influenced psalms,[133] but also in prophecy, the sacrificial theme is adopted in transformed shape. The basis of the prophetic and wisdom critique of sacrifice, or rather the spiritualization of sacrifice, is the conviction that sacrifices *ex opere operato* (in and of themselves) are worthless. Without the appropriate attitude on the part of the one sacrificing, the sacrifice cannot reach its goal—God. This is formulated in exemplary fashion in a text such as Prov 15:8:

> The sacrifice of the sinner is an abomination for Yhwh, but the prayer of the upright is his pleasure. (Prov 15:8; cf. 15:29)

This proverb is also shaped as a parallelism that contrasts the "sacrifice of the sinner" not with the "sacrifice," but with the "prayer" of the upright. This makes two things clear: more important than the distinction between sacrifice and prayer is the character of those that turn to God as "sinner" or "upright." And because the upright can reach God, prayer is enough for them to communicate with God. Proverbs 15:8 strikingly uses cultic language with רצונו (rṣnw), "his pleasure," which otherwise is connected with the acceptance of sacrifice. In the same way that God accepts sacrifice, he also accepts the prayer of the righteous. The text is silent about what happens with the sacrifice of the righteous. One can extrapolate that while this was authorized, prayer seems to take on a higher value. A general maxim in this direction is formulated in Prov 21:3:

133. Cf. Alexander Ernst, *Weisheitliche Kultkritik: Zu Theorie und Ethik des Sprüchebuchs und der Prophetie des 8. Jahrhunderts*, Biblisch-theologische Studien 23 (Neukirchen-Vluyn: Neukirchener Verlag, 1994); Christiane Radebach-Huonker, *Opferterminologie im Psalter*, FAT II/44 (Tübingen: Mohr Siebeck, 2010); cf. also the classic study of Hans-Jürgen Hermisson, *Sprache und Ritus im altisraelitischen Kult: Zur "Spiritualisierung" der Kultbegriffe in Alten Testament*, WMANT 19 (Neukirchen-Vluyn: Neukirchener Verlag, 1965).

To practice righteousness and justice is above sacrifice for Yhwh. (Prov 21:3)

However, here too sacrifice is not rejected, it is just not placed at the top of the hierarchy of what God finds desirable.

One should, therefore, beware of interpreting such statements as calls to replace the cult with ethics, an especially widespread explanation in the exegesis of the nineteenth century. The notion of ethics instead of cult is as foreign to the Hebrew Bible as it could possibly be. It is instead a matter of the right attitude in the cult and the right estimation of the cult.

JOB'S SACRIFICE Together with these texts one can place the striking mention of sacrifice in the prologue of the book of Job. According to Job 1:5, each time his children had a feast, he would present a burnt offering on the following morning. "Perhaps"—it explicitly states—they have sinned, and Job wants to insure against this "perhaps" by bringing a burnt offering before knowing whether this was actually the case and before the recognition of sin by his children. Even though the Hebrew Bible is familiar with sacrifice for atonement from indeliberate transgressions (cf. esp. Lev 5:1–13), Job's sacrificial prophylaxis remains a singularity in that it is, on the one hand, vicarious and, on the other hand, takes place before any recognition of guilt. This feature of the narrative is not in the first place a means to explain that other biblical figures were less pious than Job; it rests much more on the fact that such an insurance sacrifice in and of itself represents a theological impossibility. A burnt offering such as Job brings takes place after an atonement offering, conceived to eliminate guilt, and not as precautionary insurance against divine revenge for possible human wrongdoing. The fact that neither the narrator nor God criticizes Job's behavior integrates easily with the narrative character of the prologue, which does not shrink from presenting Job's piety in a virtually overstated manner that consists of legitimate (Job's uprightness) and also excessive elements (the preventative sacrifices).

These texts that distance themselves from the sacrificial cult—this is especially debated in the case of the book of Job—presuppose the destruction of the Jerusalem temple, even if this need not necessarily be the case for the wisdom critique of the cult.

DIETARY PRESCRIPTIONS With the loss of the temple cult, a new theme developed in biblical literature that itself evolved into a special marker of

Judaism but was also adopted in different ways by its daughter religions. The division of sustenance into permissible and impermissible foods, though the distinction of pure and impure animals is the focus here, is presented in Deut 14 and with somewhat more detail in Lev 11. One has often attempted to justify these distinctions with stringent zoological criteria. Although Deut 14 and Lev 11 themselves at least in part operate with the categories "ruminant" and "split hooves," the division in the end escapes a clear biological logic. Particularly Deut 14:7 and Lev 11:6, for example, are subject to the error that the hare is a ruminant. A basic factor appears to be that an animal must correspond completely with its type in order to be counted as pure. For example, the fish permitted for consumption must have scales and fins, in other words, they must be "fishy."

As archaeology shows, the dietary prohibitions were either unknown or, less probably, were not followed in the monarchic period. Remains of bones indicate that pigs were consumed in certain regions, and remains from fish bones also attest that the catfish prevalent in the upper Jordan region and in the Sea of Gennesaret, which has no scales, was regularly consumed. The emergence of the dietary prohibitions in Deut 14 and Lev 11 (a shared source possibly underlies them) is due probably to the end of the temple cult. Like the Sabbath and circumcision, they concern elements of the establishment of a temple-less religious community that connect to the traditional temple cult but transform it such that the new rituals can be implemented without a central sanctuary. Dietary prohibitions also appear in Mesopotamia and Egypt, but these are never formulated in a general fashion; they are instead limited spatially and temporally in each case in that they are, e.g., linked to specific feasts. Only the Bible has categorical statements—which are always in force—about what one may and may not eat.

PARTIAL RESTITUTION OF THE "VERY GOOD" CREATION The dietary restrictions connect with the thematic movement in the Priestly Primeval History that progresses from the complete abstention from consumption of meat for humans and animals in Gen 1 to the complete acceptance in Gen 9 by taking a mediating position. Not all, but only the "pure" animals may be consumed. This restores the "very good" (Gen 1:31) creation from Gen 1 at least in part.

The dietary prohibitions developed into the ultimate characteristic distinguishing Jews in the Maccabean period from their Hellenistic environment. Second Maccabees 6–7 reports of the first martyrs, who prefer death to eating the meat of swine (cf. above, §28).

7. *The Rise of the Synagogue and Word-Oriented Liturgy*

AGE OF THE SYNAGOGUE The rise of the synagogue is of significant importance for the question of the gradual replacement of the sacrificial cult by spoken liturgy. The beginnings of this institution lie, however, in darkness. The first epigraphic attestations appear in two Greek inscriptions from Egypt from the third century BCE (προσευχή, *proseuchē*).[134] These inscriptions need not indicate buildings erected specifically as houses of prayer. The more likely assumption is that they concern gathering locations in residences or communal rooms or even places in the open air. A Samaritan synagogue that was excavated on the Greek island of Delos likely goes back to the second or first century BCE. Within Israel, the synagogue of Gamla in northern Israel is reckoned to be the oldest such building (first century BCE).

FUNCTION OF THE SYNAGOGUE The function of the synagogue is that it was a place of religious gatherings. The Theodotos inscription from Jerusalem (*CIJ* 2:1404) mentions the reading of Torah and the teaching of the commandments as the purpose of the synagogue along with the lodging of guests.

While the synagogue is not mentioned in the Hebrew Bible, it is likely assumed. The scene depicted in Neh 8:5–8 of the reading of the Torah demonstrates considerable similarity to synagogue liturgy, so it can hardly be dated earlier than the third or second century BCE.

> And Ezra opened the book before the eyes of the entire people; for he stood higher than all the people. And as he opened it, the entire people arose. And Ezra praised Yhwh, the great God. And all the people answered with raised hands: Amen! Amen! And they bowed, and with their face to the earth, they threw themselves before Yhwh. . . . And they read aloud from the book, from the instruction of God, such that step by step it was explained, and they instructed them toward understanding, and one understood what was read aloud.

The first noteworthy detail from this depiction is the cultic veneration accorded to the Torah—the people bow before the Torah. Furthermore,

---

134. William Horbury and David Noy, *Jewish Inscriptions of Greco-Roman Egypt* (Cambridge: Cambridge University Press, 1992), 22, 117.

there is exegetical effort. The Torah was not simply read, but explained section by section. The Torah is understood here as a text requiring and amenable to interpretation, in other words a text with a deeper meaning that goes beyond the surface of the text.

THE END OF SACRIFICE The sacrificial cult in Jerusalem ended abruptly with the destruction of the Jerusalem temple in 70 CE.[135] In its wake, Judaism transformed completely into a religion of the book, so that one could maintain with the rabbis that "where one learns Torah, one does not need a temple."[136] However, this dictum is only partially correct. The Mishnah, for example, by no means abolishes the temple as an object of reflection. On the contrary, temple and sacrifice now become the object of highly detailed discussions, although they no longer presented cultic realities.

CULTIC FUNCTIONS OF SCRIPTURE At the same time, a cultic treatment of the Scripture itself became established. This is attested most convincingly by the manner in which one treats the Torah scrolls in rabbinic Judaism—they have been promoted to sacred objects. This process can already be observed schematically in Neh 8:5–8. The audience of the reading of Torah pay cultic respect to the Torah in that they first rise and then prostrate themselves.

This transformation was not a simple process. Just the fact that in the events surrounding 70 CE it was ensured until the last moment that the daily sacrifice could be brought shows that the loss of the temple cult must have presented a significant break. On the other hand, Israel was thoroughly prepared for existence without sacrifice. One can call to mind the wisdom critique of the cult and the synagogue worship. Even the cessation of the Qumran community showed that "prayer and complete change" (1QS 9.4–5) could replace the atoning function of sacrifice.

In a special way, it should also be mentioned that Judah had already lost its temple once, in 587 BCE through the Babylonians, and was therefore to some degree already experienced in post-cultic existence.

---

135. For the discussion on this break, cf. Daniel R. Schwartz and Zeev Weiss, eds., *Was 70 CE a Watershed in Jewish History? On Jews and Judaism before and after the Destruction of the Second Temple*, AJEC 78 (Leiden: Brill, 2012).

136. Cf. Stefan Schreiner, "Wo man Tora lernt, braucht man keinen Tempel: Einige Anmerkungen zum Problem der Tempelsubstitution im rabbinischen Judentum," in *Gemeinde ohne Tempel: Community Without Temple: Zur Substituierung und Transformation des Jerusalemer Tempels und seines Kults im Alten Testament, antiken Judentum und frühen Christentum*, ed. Beate Ego et al., WUNT 118 (Tübingen: Mohr Siebeck, 1999), 371–92.

However, it should continue to be maintained that the end of sacrifice in Judaism anticipated a general development of late antiquity by several centuries, ringing in a new epoch. Communication with God would no longer take place through gifts, but through immaterial media like prayer, meditation, or study. With the loss of the materiality of the medium of communication, a further transcendency of the relationship with God enters into the spiritual realm. However, cultic and transcendent understandings of God do not act in complementarity to one another. Cultic performances likewise possess elaborate, though often less explicit dimensions of transcendence than post-cultic forms of religion.

There is no text in the Hebrew Bible that addresses the events of 70 CE. Its latest passages are from the Maccabean, or perhaps the Hasmonean period. However, one can evaluate the prominent placement of Ps 1—at least in many of the arrangements (cf. above, §§10-11)—at the beginning of the Ketuvim as a striking expression of this new post-cultic understanding of the relationship with God. Rather than worship at the temple, continual Torah study (Ps 1:2) leads to God.

§36 People of a Nation, People of God, and the Individual

Daniel E. Fleming, *The Legacy of Israel in Judah's Bible: History, Politics, and the Reinscribing of Tradition* (Cambridge: Cambridge University Press, 2012) ◆ Judith Gärtner, "Das eine Gottesvolk aus Israel und den Völkern in Jes 66: Zur Bedeutung der Völkerwelt in der späten jesajanischen Tradition," in *Der eine Gott und die Geschichte der Völker: Studien zur Inklusion und Exklusion im biblischen Monotheismus*, ed. Luke Neubert and Michael Tilly, Biblisch-theologische Studien 123 (Neukirchen-Vluyn: Neukirchener Verlag, 2013), 1–29 ◆ Matthias Köckert, "'Land' als theologisches Thema im Alten Testament," in *Ex oriente Lux: Studien zur Theologie des Alten Testaments: Festschrift für Rüdiger Lux zum 65. Geburtstag*, ed. Angelika Berlejung and Raik Heckl, Arbeiten zur Bibel und ihrer Geschichte 39 (Leipzig: Evangelische Verlags-anstalt, 2012), 503–22 ◆ Reinhard G. Kratz, "Israel als Staat und als Volk," *ZTK* 97 (2000): 1–17 ◆ Nadav Na'aman, "Saul, Benjamin and the Emergence of 'Biblical Israel,'" *ZAW* 121 (2009): 211–24 ◆ Wolfgang Oswald, "Auszug aus der Vasallität: Die Exodus-Erzählung (Ex 1–14*) und das antike Völkerrecht," *TZ* 67 (2011): 263–88 ◆ Wolfgang Oswald, "Die Exodus-Gottesberg-Erzählung als Gründungsurkunde der judäischen Bürgergemeinde," in *Law and Narrative in the Bible and in Neighbouring Ancient Cultures*, ed. Klaus-Peter Adam et al.,

FAT II/54 (Tübingen: Mohr Siebeck, 2012), 35–51 ◆ Kristin Weingart, *Stämmevolk—Staatsvolk—Gottesvolk? Studien zur Verwendung des Israel-Namens im Alten Testament,* FAT II/68 (Tübingen: Mohr Siebeck, 2014)

1. Preliminary Remarks from the History of Scholarship

GOD AND HIS PEOPLE   Israel as God's people—this association is of such fundamental importance for the Bible that it is placed at the very beginning of the depiction of Israel's history. Even the first ancestor of Israel, Abraham, is brought at the very beginning from Mesopotamia by God and thereby marked as the object of divine election. Therefore, it must not be surprising that there are numerous theological outlines that reconstruct Israel's election according to the biblical presentation.[137]

A GROWING RELATIONSHIP   The theologically loaded conception of a chosen people of God is, however, strongly debated in current scholarship with regard to the conditions for its historical emergence. In any case it is clear that the theophoric element *-el* in *Israel* shows that the connection between Yhwh and Israel is one that came about over time, and not an original one. If Yhwh had been the God of Israel from the beginning, then one would expect a theophoric element containing Yhwh.[138]

The association of God and people was in particular a self-evident assumption within the framework of Albrecht Alt's hypothesis of a religion of the god of the ancestors. Individual groups represented by their clan ancestors could already have a privileged or even exclusive relationship to a particular deity in the nomadic prehistory. However, this hypothesis is no longer tenable.

POST-STATE BACKGROUNDS FOR EMERGENCE   The theological construction of a "people of God" was more likely due to the experience of the shattering of the political and religious givens that ceased with the destruction of the northern kingdom in 722 BCE. Such a conception did not develop

---

137. Cf., e.g., Paul Hanson, *The People Called: The Growth of Community in the Bible* (Louisville: Westminster John Knox, 2002).

138. The etymology of "Israel" is unclear. While Gen 32:29 and Hos 12:5 offer a folk etymology with a derivation from שרה *śrh,* "to fight," that alludes to Jacob's ("Israel's") wrestling at the Jabbok, this cannot be philologically confirmed.

out of nothing, for no intellectual separation of political, religious, and social contexts can be assumed for a particular population in the ancient Near East. In a certain sense, the inhabitants of the northern kingdom of Israel with their national deity Yhwh were already the people of Yhwh— but not in the highlighted and accentuated manner that first could have taken place after 722 BCE.

2. *Israel and Judah*

OLDEST REFERENCES TO ISRAEL Israel is first mentioned in the Merenptah Stela from the year 1209 BCE as a group of people in the Levant that Pharaoh Merenptah subjugated.[139] The monolithic inscription of Shalmaneser III from the year 853 BCE mentions the northern kingdom "Israel."[140] The marginally later Mesha Stela is also familiar with the northern kingdom as "Israel." Taking these data together, *Israel* in the Omride period appears to have designated a nation, though the name is evidently suitable to a certain ethnic component that has correspondingly been transformed and broadened.

JUDAH Judah is a name with less tradition. It likely first served as a geographic designation for the Judean hill country, but then became the name of the southern kingdom that remained in the shadow of the logistically better connected and economically stronger northern kingdom until the end of the eighth century BCE.

JUDAH BECOMES ISRAEL As presented above in Part G, the prestigious name Israel was transferred to Judah after the destruction of the northern kingdom in 722 BCE—not in an exclusive but prominent manner. Israel now designated three different entities: in historical retrospection the lost northern kingdom, the southern kingdom, and also the ideal unity of north and south as Israel. It cannot be determined conclusively whether this overarching linguistic use—from a pre-722 BCE standpoint—rests on tradition or innovation. This is dependent on composition-historical reconstructions.

---

139. "The (Israel) Stela of Merneptah," trans. James K. Hoffmeier (*COS* 2.6:40–41).
140. "Kurkh Monolith," trans. K. Lawson Younger, Jr. (*COS* 2.113A:261–64).

3. The Rise of the Question of Identity: Israel as the People of God

The fact that Israel is reckoned as the people associated with Yhwh is not distinctive within the context of ancient Near Eastern religiosity. Moab is equally the people of Chemosh, Ammon the people of Milcom, and Edom the people of Qauṣ (cf. Judg 11:24). However, it is different when Israel is perceived, on the one hand, exclusively as "the people of God"—namely, that Israel is constituted solely through its relationship with its God (and not, for example, with its land and its monarchy)—and on the other hand, when understood emphatically as the people of the one and only God.

ISRAEL AS GOD'S PEOPLE IN THE PENTATEUCH   This conception essentially influences the course of the narrative of the Pentateuch. This is especially the case in the books of Exodus through Deuteronomy; however, the ancestral stories of Genesis also integrate its pre-history. The Pentateuch narrates how the Israelites as the people oppressed in Egypt are liberated from compulsory labor and, through the exodus and Sinai, take refuge with God as their sole sovereign. The Pentateuch does not aim toward the establishment of a monarchy in Israel; its political imprint reveals a much more theocratic orientation. The description of the content of the present Pentateuch as "exilic" is completely correct. The promulgation of the law takes place outside the land. Moses never enters the promised land and is not a royal figure. And the people of Israel are an ethnic-religious rather than a geographic or culturally constituted entity. Through the emphasis on this characteristic of the people of Israel within the Pentateuch, it takes on a foundational quality.

HISTORICAL BACKGROUNDS   As much as the Pentateuch, likely primarily in the sphere of the Jacob tradition, contains very early texts, this overarching imprint indicates that the idea of a people of God had its decisive phases of formation in the periods after the destruction of the northern kingdom in 722 BCE and again after the fall of the southern kingdom in 587 BCE. The Pentateuch formulates the identity consciousness of an Israel that no longer self-evidently rediscovers itself in its land under the political organization of a monarchy.

PROPHETIC TRADITION   Something comparable can be extrapolated from the prophetic tradition. Especially the books of Hosea and Isaiah show

how Israel's identity around the time of the destruction of the northern kingdom did not rest on political matters of fact, but on its relationship with God.[141]

4. The Discovery of the "True Israel": The Babylonian Exiles

While the notion of a people of God marks large stretches of the literary history of the Hebrew Bible, it also underwent significant modifications.

ISRAEL VERSUS "TRUE ISRAEL" With the deportation of the upper class of Jerusalem in the year 597 BCE, the concept of a "true Israel" appeared for the first time, at least in substance, in the intellectual history of ancient Israel. Second Kings 24:14 reports of the proverbial "upper ten thousand" (upper crust)—King Jehoiachin and his entourage—being brought to Babylon, even if this number is arguably exaggerated from a historical point of view, as the competing information in Jer 52:28–30 suggests. This group apparently saw themselves as the Israel chosen by God, while those remaining back in the land and those that immigrated to Egypt were seen as cast out from it. This perspective can be recognized quite clearly in the vision of the basket of figs in Jer 24. It takes place after the events of 597 BCE (cf. 24:1, "This took place after Nebuchadnezzar, the king of Babylon led Jeconiah, the son of Jehoiakim, the king of Judah, and the princes of Judah and the artisans and the smiths from Jerusalem into exile and brought them to Babylon."). The prophet sees two baskets of figs, the one of very good figs, the other very bad. The very good figs stand for the exiles that had to go to Babylon with King Jehoiachin. For them it is the case that: "I will cast my eye favorably upon them, and I will bring them back to this land, and I will build them up and not tear them down, and I will plant them and not snatch them out. And I will give them a heart so that they will recognize me—that I am Yhwh. Then they will be my people, and I, I will be their God" (vv. 6–7). The covenant formula is narrowed to the exiles from 597 BCE; they and they alone are bound in a covenant with God. It is very different for the people of the land and the refugees in Egypt:

141. Cf., e.g., Reinhard G. Kratz, "Israel im Jesajabuch," in *Die unwiderstehliche Wahrheit: Festschrift für Arndt Meinhold*, ed. Rüdiger Lux et al., Arbeiten zur Bibel und ihrer Geschichte 23 (Leipzig: Evangelische Verlagsanstalt, 2006), 85–103.

And I will make them a calamity for all kingdoms of the earth, and into a horror, and into a mockery and into a proverbial scorn, and into a curse in every place to which I scatter them. And I will send upon them sword, hunger, and plague until they are destroyed from the ground that I gave to them and their forefathers. (vv. 9–10)

Jer 24 draws, therefore, a sharp boundary *within* the people of God, which from now on will fall into a chosen and a rejected part.

COORDINATION OF THE TRADITIONS OF JEREMIAH AND EZEKIEL Although Jer 24 provides perhaps the clearest text in the Hebrew Bible that formulates this boundary, the distinction is more at home in the book of Ezekiel (cf. Ezek 11; 33), which was written entirely from the perspective of the exiles of 597 BCE, to whom the prophet Ezekiel himself also appears to have belonged. The anchoring of this position in the book of Jeremiah shows that the traditions of Jeremiah and Ezekiel were theologically coordinated with one another, which, primarily in the book of Jeremiah, led to certain disruptions in the coherence of the content that the formation of the tradition evidently tolerated. The historical Jeremiah appears in no way to have imagined the total destruction of the people remaining in the land. His message instead stated that one could subject oneself to the Babylonians, which would be the only chance for survival (Jer 27–28).

5. Diaspora Theology

DIVERGENT JUDGMENTS OF THE WORLDWIDE DIASPORA The conception that the descendants of the exiles deported with King Jehoiachin in 597 BCE alone, this first group of deportees, were the true Israel, to whom God would exclusively turn in the future, simultaneously formulated the position that God would make the people remaining in the land "into a proverbial scorn, and into a curse in every place to which I scatter them" (Jer 24:9; see above). As a result, the scattering into the worldwide diaspora is explicitly interpreted as a result of divine judgment. The formation of tradition did not, however, stop with the position of Jer 24. In the previous chapter (in the Septuagint it is even placed at the end of Jer 23, immediately before Jer 24) there is a promise that God will turn toward the diaspora and integrate them into salvation:

"Therefore, look, the days are coming," says Yhwh, "that one will no longer say: 'As Yhwh lives, the one who brought the Israelites up out of the land of Egypt!' but: 'As Yhwh lives, the one who brought the descendants of the house of Israel up and has brought from the land of the north and from every land where he has scattered them!' Then they will live on their own land." (Jer 23:7–8)

It is clear that Jer 23:7–8 is familiar with the severe declaration in Jer 24:9 from the terminology of "scattering" (נדח, *ndḥ*, H) that is adopted from it. Jeremiah 23:7–8 does not even shy away from depicting the return of the diaspora as outdoing the exodus of the people of Israel from Egypt. This adopts a thought that had already appeared in the Deutero-Isaiah tradition (cf. Isa 43:16–21), which there still refers to the Babylonian exiles, and now is transferred to the worldwide diaspora. It is theologically noteworthy that Jer 23:7–8 newly relocates the mythic epoch of Israel's foundation to its own time, or, as the case may be, to the near future. The divine act that will constitute Israel will first take place in the very near future (following the formulation of the *futurum instans* [immediate future] הנה ימים באים [*hnh ymym b'ym*], "see, the days are coming").

DIASPORA THEOLOGY IN THE ANCESTRAL NARRATIVES A diaspora theology of its own shape appears in the promise to Jacob in Gen 28. God speaks with Jacob in his dream in Bethel:

I am Yhwh, the God of your father Abraham and the God of Isaac. The land on which you lie I will give to you and your descendants. And your descendants will be like the dust of the earth, and you will spread out to the west and east, to the north and south, and through you and your descendants will all tribes of the earth acquire blessing. (Gen 28:13–14)

Like most promises of Genesis, this text does not belong to the original Bethel narrative but arose through redactional expansion that along with Gen 12:1–3 guarantees the cohesion of the ancestral narrative in Gen 12–36. Its content apparently serves to declare that the worldwide scattering of Jacob's descendants does not rest on an oversight; it instead constitutes the divine plan that Israel become the blessing of all nations (cf. also Gen 12:2–3). Only through Israel's dispersion among the nations can the latter acquire this blessing.

The notion of Israel's mediation of blessing also appears in the Joseph story, where in Gen 39:2–6 Potiphar recognizes that God is "with" Joseph and supports Joseph further, so that God's blessing comes upon Potiphar's house. Genesis 39:4 expressly underlines that Potiphar identifies *Yhwh*'s work in Joseph—that is, an Egyptian recognizes the presence and the action of the God of the Hebrews, Yhwh, in Egypt. The appointment of Joseph over Potiphar's house then leads to God's blessing "on Joseph's behalf." Yhwh blesses the house of the Egyptian Potiphar, but only Joseph mediates it. This alludes to the motif of the mediation of blessing according to Gen 12:2.

THE DIASPORA THEOLOGY OF THE JOSEPH STORY Beyond Gen 39, the Joseph story as a whole is important for the diaspora theology in the Hebrew Bible. It justifies the unity of Israel as a nation of twelve tribes as a nation created by choice, disassociated from its geographic connection to Israel and Judah. The final chapter of the Joseph story narrates that after the death of their father, Jacob, Joseph and his brothers constitute the familial framework in a foreign land. Jacob's death is, therefore, transparent about the loss of Israel and Judah's statehood, which had unquestionably guaranteed the people's identity. The Joseph story by contrast emphasizes the necessity of a willful union.

In addition, the Joseph story presents the view that permanent life is both possible and theologically legitimate for Israelites in a foreign land. The Joseph story does not even see the marriage of pagan wives as problematic. Joseph marries Asenath, the daughter of an Egyptian priest.

Within the Hebrew Bible, the Joseph story can be considered an "anti-Deuteronomistic" historical work because of this theological perspective. It upholds what is reckoned as problematic from a "Deuteronomistic" perspective and even contrary to it: According to the Joseph story, Israel does not require its own king. Wise foreign rulers are, in its view, possible instruments of God within the context of a theocratically conceived ideal. Living in one's own land is not a theological necessity, and ethnic mixing is not sin.

6. *The Emergence of Judaism*

The most important reception-historical effect of the destruction of Jerusalem and the deportation of important parts of the population to Babylon is the emergence of Judaism.[142] The question of when Judaism began, however, is disputed and cannot be answered without ambiguity or imprecision. The extremes witnessed in published views specify Moses as the earliest beginning point of Judaism,[143] and the destruction of Jerusalem by the Romans in 70 BC as the latest.[144] Neither one nor the other of these positions can be sensibly maintained, but the two points mark the range within which Judaism gradually developed.[145] In English-speaking scholarship, the somewhat unattractive but factually justifiable expression *Judaisms* has developed.[146]

HISTORY OF THE TERM The term *Judaism* goes back to the Greek ἰουδαϊσμός (*ioudaismos*). The term ἰουδαϊσμός (*ioudaismos*) is first attested in the Hellenistic period and is shaped as a conception contrary to Hellenism. Especially meaningful are the attestations from the book of 2 Maccabees, such as 2 Macc 2:19–21:

> The history of Judas the Maccabean and his brothers . . . , who fought bravely for Judaism, so that in spite of their small number they seized [back] the whole land and pursued the barbarian armies.

Judaism is, therefore, an entity qualified especially by its rejection of the opposing position. The correlated social boundary is shown clearly in 2 Macc 8:1: "But Judas the Maccabean and his companions . . . took those in Judaism."

One is not an adherent to Judaism by means of lineage or domicile, but rather as the result of a conscious decision. The matter designated by the term *Judaism*—a distinct religion independent of state structures that is defined by specific creedal content and a specific genealogical coherence—is factually earlier and goes back to the beginnings of the Babylonian

---

142. Cf. Christoph Levin, "Die Entstehung des Judentums als Gegenstand der alttestamentlichen Wissenschaft," in *Congress Volume Munich 2013*, ed. Christl M. Maier, VTSup 163 (Leiden: Brill, 2014), 1–17.

143. According to the article "Judaism," in *Encyclopedia Judaica* (1972).

144. Martin Noth, *Geschichte Israels* (Göttingen: Vandenhoeck & Ruprecht, 1950), 386.

145. Cf. Marc Z. Brettler, "Judaism in the Hebrew Bible? The Transition from Ancient Israelite Religion to Judaism," *CBQ* 61 (1999): 429–47; Steve Mason, "Jews, Judaeans, Judaizing, Judaism: Problems of Categorization in Ancient History," *JSJ* 38 (2007): 457–512.

146. Cf., e.g., Diana V. Edelman, ed., *The Triumph of Elohim: From Yahwisms to Judaisms*, CBET 13 (Kampen: Pharos, 1995).

exile. Julius Wellhausen expressed this in the politically incorrect conceptual categories of his time as follows: "The Jewish church emerged as the Jewish state perished."[147]

The creedal content that gradually developed into the different forms of Judaism is based on central theological positions like monotheism, covenant, and law. The present form of the Hebrew Bible is clearly influenced by these themes, but at points its pre-Judaic origins are transparent.

7. Abrahamic "Ecumenism"

It necessarily attracts attention in the current portrayal of Genesis that the ancestor Abraham not only embodies the line that leads to Jacob and the twelve tribes of Israel—he is also reckoned as the ancestor of the Arabs and the Edomites. The Arabs are traced back to Ishmael, Abraham's first son with Hagar, and the Edomites are the descendants of Esau, Jacob's older brother and the son of Isaac. Do, then, the Arabs and Edomites form something of an "Abrahamic ecumenism" with Israel in Genesis?

HISTORY OF THE TERMINOLOGY The term *Abraham(it)ic ecumenism* has its origins in the 1990s. It goes back to the Tübingen Catholic theologians Karl-Josef Kuschel and Hans Küng.[148] It designates a project of conversation between the three monotheistic religions of Judaism, Christianity, and Islam, which all call on Abraham as a foundational figure and are bound with each other by the monotheistic belief in the creator God. This project is, however, problematic because of the extensive content and theological divergences between the Jewish, Christian, and Islamic images of Abraham, which make "Abraham" into anything but a simple cipher for understanding. In addition, the exclusivity of the perspective on the three classic revelatory religions has been criticized. Finally, it has not yet been decided whether the adoption of the terminology of *ecumenism* from the

147. Julius Wellhausen, *Israelitische und jüdische Geschichte* (Berlin: Reimer, 1894), 169 n. 1.

148. Karl-Josef Kuschel, *Abraham: Sign of Hope for Jews, Christians, and Muslims*, trans. John Bowden (New York: Continuum, 1995); cf. p. 13 n. 4 on the terminological distinction between "Abrahamic" and "Abrahamitic." Hans Küng, "Abrahamische Ökumene zwischen Juden, Christen und Muslimen: Theologische Grundlegung—praktische Konsequenzen," in *Stifterverband für die die Deutsche Wissenschaft. Jahresversammlung 1991 des Landeskurat* (Essen: Stifterverband für die Deutsche Wissenschaft, 1991).

intra-Christian dialogue into the sphere of inter-religious dialogue is truly helpful. In any case, the current discussion about a conversation between Judaism, Christianity, and Islam—with or without the help of the concept of an "Abrahamitic ecumenism"—is not the object of the discussion.

ABRAHAMIC THEOLOGY FROM GEN 17   The following is only concerned with describing the theological shape of the Abraham tradition in Genesis. Certain potential points will arise that could anachronistically be described as "ecumenical."[149] These are recognizable in Gen 17, the programmatic text of the Priestly document (cf. above, §18), especially in its opening verses (vv. 1–8). Here God explicitly promises his covenant with Abraham and his descendants. Among these are not only Isaac as the father of Jacob and grandfather of the twelve tribes of Israel, but also Ishmael, the ancestor of the Arabs, as well as Esau, who represents the Edomites. God's covenant, according to Gen 17—which includes increase, use of the land, and proximity to God—is therefore applied more broadly than just to Israel.

It is often pointed out that Gen 17:19–21 subsequently excludes Ishmael from the covenant, for this section only apportions him a blessing while the covenant remains reserved for the Israelite line of Abraham's descendants. However, vv. 19–21 do not primarily address *Ishmael's exclusion*, but rather *Isaac's inclusion* into the Abrahamic covenant. The fact that Ishmael is not immediately excluded from the just concluded covenant arises from Gen 17:7–8. Here it is explicitly emphasized that this covenant is concluded with Abraham and his descendants, to which Ishmael unquestionably belongs, as an "everlasting covenant." On the flip side, the explicit inclusion of Isaac in vv. 19, 21 is imperative in light of the fact that he was not yet born at the time of the scene of Gen 17. This is the reason why it must be specifically emphasized.

HISTORICAL BACKGROUNDS   From a historical perspective, this conception in Gen 17 can be explained from its contemporary context. The

149. Cf. Albert de Pury, "Abraham: The Priestly Writer's 'Ecumenical' Ancestor," in *Rethinking the Foundations: Historiography in the Ancient World and in the Bible: Festschrift for John Van Seters*, ed. Steven L. McKenzie et al., BZAW 294 (Berlin: de Gruyter, 2000), 163–81. Contrary to the position presented here is Matthias Köckert, "Gottes 'Bund' mit Abraham und die 'Erwählung' Israels in Genesis 17," in *Covenant and Election in Exilic and Post-exilic Judaism: Studies of the Sofja Kovalevskaja Research Group on Early Jewish Monotheism*, ed. Nathan MacDonald, vol. 5, FAT II/79 (Tübingen: Mohr Siebeck, 2015), 1–28.

Priestly document attempts to reconcile the political reality of Persian-period Yehud, as a modest province in "ecumenical" proximity to its neighbors, with the theologically required prerogatives of Israel. This compels it to fundamentally pacific political thought (cf. §33).

8. *The Separation between the Pious and the Sinners*

The fact that apocalyptic and New Testament literature unquestionably presuppose that there are pious and wicked in the world, who not only sometimes act piously or wickedly, but who can be identified as such, might belie the fact that this distinction first entered the Hebrew Bible quite late. While precursors can be identified, such as the position of Jer 24 (see above), the clear distinction between the pious and the wicked as classes of people can first be assumed for the Hellenistic period.

TRITO-ISAIAH Within the sphere of the latest passages of Trito-Isaiah, Isa 65–66 abandon the theological unity of the people of God. The concluding texts in Isa 65–66 only envisage salvation for the righteous; judgment will instead fall upon the wicked (Isa 65:1–15; cf. Isa 57:20–21). Therefore, the promise of a new heaven and a new earth in Isa 65:17–25, as its connection to the surrounding context shows, is only reckoned for the servants of Yhwh.

 The abandonment of the largely uncontested focus of salvation on "Israel" from the pre-Hellenistic era blazed the trail for the individualization of Jewish religion, which was further strengthened especially by the destruction of Jerusalem in 70 CE, and in this form also decisively influenced Christianity.

QOHELETH The determination of the fates of the pious and the wicked in Isa 65–66 did not remain unchallenged in the Hebrew Bible. The book of Qoheleth opposed it with considerable reserve. For Qoheleth as well there is a fundamental distinction between the wicked and the pious, the wise and the fool, the righteous and the unrighteous, but ultimately humans are not divided in their fate, namely in death. In death all are alike; there is no otherworldly compensation (cf. Qoh 9:1). Accordingly, the distinction between the wicked and the pious can be experienced in life, but theologically it presents a problem that Qoheleth neither can nor intends to resolve.

TORAH The Torah is not aware of this distinction, but the declarations of Deuteronomy that envisage favor for those obedient to the law and judgment for the disobedient were evidently understood in Qumran such that they relate not to the people of God as an entirety, but rather to each individual member. The prominent representation of Deuteronomy among the scrolls of Qumran, with remains of twenty-nine rolls, can hardly be explained otherwise. The Qumran community understood itself as the amalgamation of the pious in Israel, and they read especially those biblical texts that propagated and supported this distinction.[150]

§37 Monarchy, Theocracy, and Anticipation of a Ruler

Uwe Becker, "Der Messias in Jes 7–11: Zur 'Theopolitik' prophetischer Heilserwartungen," in *Ein Herz so weit wie der Sand am Ufer des Meeres: Festschrift für Georg Hentschel*, ed. Susanne Gillmayr-Bucher et al., Erfurter Theologische Studien 90 (Würzburg: Echter, 2006), 235–54 ♦ Martin Leuenberger, *"Ich bin Jhwh und keiner sonst" (Jes 45,5f): Der exklusive Monotheismus des Kyros-Orakels Jes 45,1-7 in seinem religions- und theologiegeschichtlichen Kontext*, SBS 224 (Stuttgart: Katholisches Bibelwerk, 2010) ♦ Stefan M. Maul, "Der assyrische König—Hüter der Weltordnung," in *Gerechtigkeit: Richten und Retten in der abendländischen Tradition und ihren altorientalischen Ursprüngen*, ed. Jan Assmann (Munich: Fink, 1998), 65–77 ♦ Matthew Novenson, *The Grammar of Messianism: An Ancient Jewish Political Idiom and Its Users* (Oxford: Oxford University Press, 2017) ♦ Wolfgang Oswald, *Staatstheorie im Alten Israel: Der politische Diskurs im Pentateuch und in den Geschichtsbüchern des Alten Testaments* (Stuttgart: Kohlhammer, 2009) ♦ Eckart Otto and Erich Zenger, eds., *"Mein Sohn bist du" (Ps 2,7): Studien zu den Königspsalmen*, SBS 192 (Stuttgart: Katholisches Bibelwerk, 2002) ♦ Markus Saur, *Die Königspsalmen: Studien zu ihrer Entstehung und Theologie*, BZAW 340 (Berlin: de Gruyter, 2004) ♦ Annette Schellenberg, *Der Mensch, das Bild Gottes? Zum Gedanken einer Sonderstellung des Menschen im Alten Testament und in weiteren altorientalischen Quellen*, ATANT 101 (Zurich: TVZ, 2011) ♦ Hans Heinrich Schmid, "Alttestamentliche Voraussetzungen neutestamentlicher Christologie," *Jahrbuch für Biblische Theologie* 6 (1991): 33–45 ♦ Konrad Schmid, ed., *Prophetische Heils- und Herrschererwartungen*, SBS 194 (Stuttgart: Katholisches Bibelwerk,

---

150. Cf. John J. Collins, *Beyond the Qumran Community: The Sectarian Movement of the Dead Sea Scrolls* (Grand Rapids: Eerdmans, 2009).

2005) • Horst Seebass, *Herrscherverheißungen im Alten Testament,* Biblisch-theologische Studien 19 (Neukirchen-Vluyn: Neukirchener Verlag, 1992) • Ernst-Joachim Waschke, *Der Gesalbte: Studien zur alttestamentlichen Theologie,* BZAW 306 (Berlin: de Gruyter, 2001)

1. Preliminary Remarks from the History of Scholarship

ANCIENT NEAR EASTERN CONTEXT The central importance of ancient Near Eastern royal ideology for the understanding of the Hebrew Bible (and also of the New Testament) only came to the attention of biblical scholarship once the related ancient Near Eastern texts and images became known and were actually received. This presupposes on one hand the great archaeological discoveries of the nineteenth century and, on the other hand, the abatement of the Babel-Bibel dispute that made possible a balanced understanding of the ancient Near Eastern parallels. Neither Pan-Babylonianism nor an insistence on the total isolation of the Bible represents viable religious-historical options. Not everything that was thought and written in Israel has a parallel in Mesopotamia, and not everything in the Bible is without analogy.

BIBLICAL ACCENTUATIONS From the biblical perspective, the institution of the kingdom is marginal and controversial. It first appears in the books of Samuel and becomes immediately marked by the stigma of competition with God's own kingdom (cf., e.g, 1 Sam 8:6).

However, the facts are presented differently in an ancient Near Eastern perspective. The kingdom is an object of creation, and the king is not simply an official but a qualitatively different entity from other people. There is no universal term for humanity that would also include the king. The class of humans instead disintegrates from the outset into three subsets: king, free person, and slave.

In ancient Near Eastern tradition, the king alone of these three is equipped with full insight and responsibility. First in Israel, during or after the Babylonian exile, is the *species* human as a whole equipped with these royal qualities in the Priestly creation report in Gen 1, so that the human assumes the status of "divine image"—a feature traditionally reserved for kings.

The connected processes of reception and transformation in view of the understanding of the human are objects of a historically operating anthropology (cf. §39).

2. *The Ancient Near Eastern Ideology of Kingship in the Hebrew Bible*

Royal ideology is a shared Near Eastern phenomenon in antiquity. It takes on different expressions, but the central convictions are comparable. The king is reckoned as God's son, though this declaration is to be understood as functional rather than biological. He receives the task of representing God on earth. He is to foster law and order. He creates cosmos and drives back chaos. He conquers the enemies. He is even responsible for the flourishing of nature, which supplies provisions for the population. These components appear most explicitly in the so-called royal psalms (Pss 2; 18; 20; 21; 45; 72; 89; 101; 110; 132), though they are also tangible as substrata in many other texts of the narrative, legal, and prophetic traditions.

The kings receive special emphasis in the judgments in the books of Kings, which characterize the kings of Israel and Judah positively, negatively, or with mixed reviews, in accordance with their cultic adherence (cf. §32). These judgments reflect the central importance of the king and his comprehensive responsibility. The political and economic wellbeing of the nation depends on him and his relationship with God. If he fails at his task, then he causes not only himself, but also the political community to suffer. In the further development of tradition in the exilic and postexilic period, this royal responsibility shifts to the people, but it is clear that these are derivative statements that still allow for the recognition of the original central place of the king.

3. *"Messianic" Prophecies*

The so-called messianic prophecies receive extraordinary attention in traditional Christian interpretation of the Hebrew Bible. These usually include Isa 7:14–16; 9:1–6; 11:1–10; Mic 5:1–5; and Zech 9:9–10, and in light of analogous receptions, Gen 49:10 and Num 24:17 have also been understood as "messianic." In addition, further texts, especially from the prophetic corpus, speak of a coming king of salvation, David or a Davidide, such as Jer 23:5–6; 33:14–26; Ezek 17:22–24; 34:23–24; 37:21–25; Amos 9:11–12; Hag 2:20–23; Zech 4:6–10; and 6:9–14.

The importance of the messianic prophecies in the prophetic books even led to the placement of the prophetic books at the end of Christian Old Testaments, so that the Old Testament as a whole pointed toward the end proposition of the pronouncement of the Messiah (cf §17).

From the perspective of the Hebrew Bible, however, the importance of the messiah thematic should be put in perspective. First, from the terminology itself it should be noted that while the Hebrew Bible is aware of and uses the expression *messiah*, it does not use it with regard to a future king of salvation. The designation משיח (*mšyḥ*), "messiah," that is "anointed," is reserved exclusively for contemporary rulers (Saul: 1 Sam 24:7, 11; 1 Sam 26:9, 11, 16, 23; 2 Sam 1:14, 16; David: 1 Sam 2:10, 35; 1 Sam 16:6; 2 Sam 19:22; 2 Sam 22:51 = Ps 18:51; 2 Sam 23:1; Ps 132:10, 17; Solomon: 2 Chr 6:42; as a general designation of the king: Hab 3:13; Ps 2:2; 20:7; 28:8; 89:39, 52: Lam 4:20; Cyrus: Isa 45:1) or the high priest (Lev 4:3, 5, 16; 6:15).

It should also be noted that the eschatological expectations of salvation in the Hebrew Bible focus neither exclusively nor centrally on a new Davidic ruler. The expectation of a coming ruler is one motif among others, and is often found in some connection with additional topoi. Eschatological expectations can appear in an ensemble with the conception of a judgment of the nations (e.g., Hag 2:20–23). They can be linked with the expectation of the return of the diaspora (e.g., Jer 33:14–16). They can be cast in the image of a utopia that also encompasses peace among animals (Isa 11:1–10) or in a fundamentally modified form, such as Zion moving into the function of the messiah (cf. §38).

In any case, it is the comprehensive potentiality of the royal metaphor that is able to bind together these divergent aspects of the human world. As a result, the expectation of a king of salvation is always connected to the establishment of a commensurate world order.

4. Cyrus and Nebuchadnezzar

The classification of foreign rulers like Nebuchadnezzar as the "servant" of God (עבד, *ʿbd*; Jer 25:9; 43:10) and Cyrus as "[God's] messiah" (משחו, *mšḥw*; Isa 45:1) is of great importance both theologically and reception-historically. From a historical perspective it is clear that these texts not only presuppose the emergence of the corresponding emperor, but also the end of the Davidic dynasty. The installation of foreign emperors into the honored, privileged relationship to the God of Israel as the true ruler of the entire world requires that the politics of Israel and Judah become completely dissociated from the conception of God.

From a literary-historical perspective, one would have to reckon that the theological explanation of the Persian King Cyrus precedes that of Nebuchadnezzar because it appears quite suggestive to the historical eye: Cyrus made the Jews' religious and cultural independence possible through Persian imperial politics, supported the reconstruction of the temple, and allowed the return to Judah.

The interpretation of Nebuchadnezzar as the "servant of God" in the book of Jeremiah likely presupposes the restoration and possibly also the interpretation of Cyrus as "the messiah" within the Deutero-Isaiah tradition.

In theological terms, the possibility of interpreting foreign rulers as kings installed by God depends on a comprehensively conceived monotheism. When God is understood as universal, then he also holds the events of world politics in his hand. Consequently, also figures like Nebuchadnezzar (though responsible for the destruction of the Jerusalem temple) or Cyrus may be chosen and led by God himself.

5. Theocracy

The notion that the earthly kingdom corresponds to a divine kingdom belongs to the unarticulated ideological presuppositions of an ancient Near Eastern monarchy like those in Israel and Judah. In terms of the history of religion, it is the reverse; the conception of a divine kingdom is a reflex of the corresponding form of political organization of the state system of that time. The divine world is structured analogously to the earthly world. In the end, traditional monarchies with an earthly governing figure are also theocratically oriented. God is the actual king; the earthly king is his representative on earth.

The demise of the kingdom after the destruction of Judah and Jerusalem in 587 BCE brought about the loss of the earthly component of this double kingdom. The prophetic tradition was partially able to cover over this loss through the elevation of divinely chosen foreign rulers like Nebuchadnezzar and Cyrus (see above). However, especially in the Psalms, a conception gained ground that propagated God's direct political rule. It is, however, striking that these perspectives of God's acts as ruler concentrate completely on his provision of the elementary necessities of life:

> Your kingdom is a kingdom for all times, and your dominion lasts from generation to generation. Yhwh supports all who fall and raises all who are bowed. All eyes wait for you, and you give them their food at the

right time. You open your hand and satisfy everything that lives with pleasure. (Ps 145:13–16)

God as royal ruler takes care of the nourishment of living things, humans and animals alike, upon the earth. The concrete political organization of human communal life moves to the background in this view. The form of earthly rule as such is not important, but rather God's attention to his creatures. Historically speaking, this conception mirrors the experience of the Persian period, which from a theocratically oriented perspective was experienced in Judah as extraordinarily wholesome due to the comparatively tolerant religious policies of the Persians, such that the satisfaction of the basic necessities of life could give space for the interpretation of God's action. It is noteworthy in terms of theology that seemingly self-evident things like one's own sustenance are explicitly traced back to God's good action for humanity. God's sphere of authority not only concerns areas of historical contingency like politics, military, or economy, but also comprises the elementary provision of human and animal life.

Theocratic conceptions in postexilic Judah can be conceived as both political and apolitical. They are political in the sense that God is designated as the only and the immediate king; they are apolitical in the sense that this conception is only linked with very elementary demands of daily human life, which are widely separated from concrete political expectations like the reestablishment of a separate state or kingdom.

§38 Zion and Sinai

Andreas Bedenbender, "Warum am Horeb? Zur Lokalisierung von Gottesoffenbarungen in der Hebräischen Bibel," *BK* 66 (2011): 219–23 ◆ George J. Brooke, "Moving Mountains: From Sinai to Jerusalem," in *The Significance of Sinai: Traditions about Divine Revelation in Judaism and Christianity*, ed. George J. Brooke et al., TBN 12 (Leiden: Brill, 2008), 73–89 ◆ Richard Clifford, *The Cosmic Mountain in Canaan and the Old Testament*, HSM 4 (Cambridge, MA: Harvard University Press, 1972) ◆ Friedhelm Hartenstein, "'Wehe, ein Tosen vieler Völker . . .' (Jesaja 17,12): Beobachtungen zur Entstehung der Zionstradition vor dem Hintergrund des judäisch-assyrischen Kulturkontakts," in *Das Archiv des verborgenen Gottes: Studien zur Unheilsprophetie Jesajas und zur Zionstheologie der Psalmen in assyrischer Zeit*, Biblisch-theologische Studien 74 (Neukirchen-Vluyn: Neukirchener Verlag, 2011), 127–74 ◆ Othmar Keel,

"Fern von Jerusalem: Frühe Jerusalemer Kulttraditionen und ihre Träger und Trägerinnen," in *Zion: Ort der Begegnung: Festschrift für Laurentius Klein zur Vollendung des 65. Lebensjahres,* ed. Ferdinand Hahn et al., BBB 90 (Frankfurt am Main: Hain, 1993), 439–502 ♦ Othmar Keel, *Die Geschichte Jerusalems und die Entstehung des Monotheismus,* 2 vols., Orte und Landschaften der Bibel 4,1 (Göttingen: Vandenhoeck & Ruprecht, 2007) ♦ Klaus Koch, "Ḥazzi-Ṣafôn-Kasion: Die Geschichte eines Berges und seiner Gottheiten," in *Religionsgeschichtliche Beziehungen zwischen Kleinasien, Nordsyrien und dem Alten Testament, Internationales Symposion Hamburg 17.–21. März 1990,* ed. Bernd Janowski et al., OBO 129 (Freiburg: Universitätsverlag; Göttingen: Vandenhoeck & Ruprecht, 1993) ♦ Matthias Köckert, "Wie kam das Gesetz an den Sinai?" in *Vergegenwärtigung des Alten Testaments: Beiträge zur biblischen Hermeneutik: Festschrift für Rudolf Smend,* ed. Christoph Bultmann (Göttingen: Vandenhoeck & Ruprecht, 2002), 13–27 ♦ Matthias Köckert and Erhard Blum, eds., *Gottes Volk am Sinai: Untersuchungen zu Ex 32–34 und Dtn 9–10* (Gütersloh: Gütersloher Verlagshaus, 2001) ♦ Corinna Körting, *Zion in den Psalmen,* FAT 48 (Tübingen: Mohr Siebeck, 2006) ♦ Martin Leuenberger, "Jhwhs Herkunft aus dem Süden: Archäologische Befunde—biblische Überlieferungen—historische Korrelationen," in *ZAW* 122 (2010): 1–19 ♦ Jon D. Levenson, *Sinai and Zion: An Entry into the Jewish Bible* (San Francisco: Harper & Row, 1987) ♦ Martin Metzger, "Zion: Gottes Berg, Gottes Wohnung, Gottes Stadt," in *Laetare Jerusalem: Festschrift zum 100 jährigen Ankommen der Benediktinermönche auf dem Jerusalemer Zionsberg,* ed. Nikodemus C. Schnabel, Jerusalemer Theologisches Forum 10 (Münster: Aschendorff, 2006), 41–63 ♦ Wolfgang Oswald, *Israel am Gottesberg: Eine Untersuchung zur Literargeschichte der vorderen Sinaiperikope Ex 19–24 und deren historischem Hintergrund,* OBO 159 (Freiburg: Universitätsverlag; Göttingen: Vandenhoeck & Ruprecht, 1998) ♦ Eckart Otto, *Das antike Jerusalem: Archäologie und Geschichte,* Beck'sche Reihe 2418 (Munich: Beck, 2008) ♦ Henrik Pfeiffer, *Jahwes Kommen von Süden: Jdc 5; Hab 3; Dtn 33 und Ps 68 in ihrem literatur- und theologiegeschichtlichen Umfeld,* FRLANT 211 (Göttingen: Vandenhoeck & Ruprecht, 2005) ♦ Johannes Renz, "'Jahwe ist der Gott der ganzen Erde': Der Beitrag der außerkanonischen althebräischen Texte zur Rekonstruktion der vorexilischen Religions- und Theologiegeschichte Palästinas," in *Israel zwischen den Mächten: Festschrift für Stefan Timm zum 65. Geburtstag,* ed. Friedhelm Hartenstein and Michael Pietsch, AOAT 364 (Münster: Ugarit-Verlag, 2009), 289–377 ♦ Konrad Schmid, "Der Sinai und die Priesterschrift," in *"Gerechtigkeit und Recht üben" (Gen 18,19): Studien zur altorientalischen und biblischen Rechtsgeschichte, zur Religionsgeschichte Israels und zur Religionssoziologie: Festschrift für Eckart*

Otto, ed. Reinhard Achenbach and Martin Arneth, BZABR 13 (Wiesbaden: Harrassowitz, 2009), 114–27 ◆ Konrad Schmid, "Zion bei Jesaja," in *Zion: Symbol des Lebens in Judentum und Christentum*, ed. Tanja Pilger and Markus Witte, Studien zu Kirche und Israel, NF 4 (Leipzig: Evangelische Verlagsanstalt, 2013), 9–23 ◆ Andrea Spans, *Die Stadtfrau Zion im Zentrum der Welt: Exegese und Theologie von Jes 60–62*, BBB 175 (Göttingen: V&R Unipress, 2015) ◆ Hermann Spieckermann, *Heilsgegenwart: Eine Theologie der Psalmen*, FRLANT 148 (Göttingen: Vandenhoeck & Ruprecht, 1989) ◆ Michael Tilly, *Jerusalem—Nabel der Welt: Überlieferung und Funktionen von Heiligtumstraditionen im antiken Judentum* (Stuttgart: Kohlhammer, 2002)

1. Preliminary Remarks from the History of Scholarship

HOLY MOUNTAINS In antiquity mountains were not perceived as merely geotectonic protrusions, instead they generally possessed a numinous quality. Especially outstanding or massive mountain peaks were considered the residences of deities. Weather and storm gods had their homes there.

ZION AND SINAI AS DIVINE MOUNTAINS The Hebrew Bible is familiar with two prominent divine mountains—Zion and Sinai. Within the context of Deuteronomic-Deuteronomistic tradition, Sinai is also called "Horeb." It is possible that the Sinai terminology associated with Edom, as texts like Judg 5:4 and Deut 33:2 show, was no longer acceptable after Edom's collaboration with Babylon in the destruction of Jerusalem in 587 BCE and that this motivated the rise of the name Horeb. This is, however, not provable. It is still clear that Sinai and Horeb mean the same mountain.

From a biblical perspective, Sinai initially appears to be an outstanding and predominant entity; on it Moses receives the revelation of God's laws for Israel (Exod 19 until Num 10). From a historical and a history of religions point of view, Zion is hardly inferior. The mountain of God in Jerusalem, as God's residence, and its fate in the years 701 BCE and 587 BCE are of decisive importance for the religion and literature of ancient Judah. Given the prominence of the two mountains, especially in light of their religious function as the place of God's revelation and residence, the scholarship of the Hebrew Bible has put forth surprisingly little effort into a systematic explanation of its literary, tradition, and religious-historical relationships, although such points of contact and connections are evident. The reasons for this are manifold. On the one hand, they lie in the fragmentation of scholarship on the Hebrew Bible, but on the other they reckoned with an age-old, pre-state Sinai tradition and a first monarchic Zion tradition, such that hardly any historical points of contact could be demonstrated.

With new developments in Hebrew Bible studies that have gripped almost all its subdisciplines in the past thirty years, this dissociative starting point is no longer present. On the contrary, Sinai and Zion traditions in the Hebrew Bible are no longer separated from one another a priori. They instead move together as possible objects of comparison on the scholarly horizon.

If it is the case that the religion of the monarchic period in ancient Judah, in particular in Jerusalem, was primarily marked by Zion theology, then the question virtually arises on its own as to how this tradition of a holy mountain that is considered the location of God's presence relates to the tradition of the divine mountain in the Pentateuch (esp. Exod 19–40). Do both traditions go back to an originally independent traditional core? When and how did the Sinai and Zion traditions influence one another?

INDEPENDENT SINAI TRADITION In the classical scholarship of the nineteenth century and also into the second half of the twentieth century there was an unquestioned consensus that the tradition of the divine revelation on Sinai must go back to a historical event interpretable as a theophany on the Sinai Peninsula (such as on *Ğebel Mūsā*) in the second millennium BCE, even if the Sinai tradition need not have necessarily been linked with the exodus tradition from the very beginning. In any case, the Sinai tradition was viewed as considerably earlier than the Zion tradition indigenous to Jerusalem, tangible especially in the book of Isaiah and in the Psalms.

With the upheavals in pentateuchal scholarship and also new assessments of the religious-historical developments of ancient Israel and Judah, such supposed certitudes are no longer givens. On the contrary, the literary-historical evaluations and religious-historical meanings of the pentateuchal Sinai traditions are highly contentious. The same is also the case for the poetic attestations of Sinai in Ps 68:8 and Judg 5:5, which were previously viewed as the bedrock of the biblical tradition but are no longer able to be considered certain (cf. above, §30).

Occasionally it has been attempted, following Wellhausen ("The true and ancient meaning of Sinai is completely independent of the legislation.

It was the seat of the Deity, the sacred mountain")[151] to rescue the antiquity of the Sinai tradition by separating Sinai from the law, but this position has been justifiably and resoundingly critiqued. The Sinai theophany is functionally dependent on a context. A mythic background should be reckoned for the Sinai tradition, but it is questionable whether this background can somehow be reconstructed through composition criticism.

One would have to assume that the Sinai tradition—and then also the Zion tradition—were not simply extant ahead of time as scripturally fixed entities, but that they developed step by step within the framework of the Hebrew Bible's transmission history. This provides an opening for the basic possibility but also necessity of comparing and correlating it in terms of literary, tradition, and religious history with the second prominent "divine mountain tradition," the Zion tradition.

The historical placement of the Zion tradition and its development primarily in the Psalms is, however, also contested. Yet because its literary location (but cf. Exod 15:13, 17) is not anchored in the contested pentateuchal origins—traditions and epigraphic witnesses can also be noted (Khirbet el Qom, Khirbet Beth Lei; see also the texts from Kuntillet 'Ajrud [cf. "Yhwh of Samaria"])—the literary-historical relationships can be made with comparably greater certainty. In particular, the events of 701 BCE likely played an important role in the shaping of the Zion tradition, and significant transformations appear in the wake of the fall of Jerusalem in 587 BCE—the mountain metaphor related to Zion is transformed in a tradition like Jeremiah into the metaphor of "daughter Zion."[152]

2. The Zion Theology in the Preexilic Period

TOPOGRAPHY OF JERUSALEM If one goes to Jerusalem today and asks for directions to Mount Zion, then one is pointed toward the southwest hill of the city, outside the city walls, where the Dormition Abbey is located. However, the name Mount Zion has been connected to this location only since the fourth century CE. Already the first archeological excavations in the nineteenth century showed that ancient Jerusalem could not have been located there. For the biblical period, Mount Zion is instead identified with the southeast hill of Jerusalem. The etymology of "Zion" is not completely

151. Julius Wellhausen, *Prolegomena to the History of Israel*, 343.
152. Cf. below, n. 156.

clear; the name may simply mean "mountain ridge," such as the one that goes along the southeast hill.

This is striking because, according to verses like 2 Sam 5:7, Zion appears to have been located originally in the somewhat lower City of David. Evidently, in particular with regard to the temple, the name "Zion" can also include the highest part of the ridge, the Temple Mount.

MOUNTAIN AND CITY "Zion" not only designates the mountain on which Jerusalem is located, but also the city of Jerusalem itself, in particular when it is perceived under the aspect of holiness. While the fact that the city of Jerusalem as a whole is designated as holy is commonplace in present-day perception, this should not be seen as religious-historical bedrock.[153] While the entire ancient Near East is familiar with the god of the city and the city of the god,[154] when it concerns God's presence in the city as a whole then such declarations are an indicator that the destruction of the Jerusalem temple already lies in the past. Traditionally the temple is the holy location in a city, and the city surrounds this location. Once Jerusalem as a whole is addressed as Zion, this means nothing less than that the whole city is qualitatively the temple, and this process is easiest to comprehend when there is no longer a temple.

PSALMS AND ISAIAH The Zion psalms as well as several texts from the book of Isaiah should be considered the most important texts for preexilic Zion theology, along with epigraphic declarations. One of the most important attestations appears in the inscription from Khirbet Beit Lei (ca. 700 BCE):

> YHWH is the god of the whole earth, The mountains of Judah belong to the God of Jerusalem. [155]

While one could also translate the first line "Yhwh is the god of the entire land," this is less likely in light of the otherwise recoverable univer-

---

153. Cf., from an archaeological perspective, Margreet Steiner, "The Notion of Jerusalem as a Holy City," in *Reflection and Refraction: Studies in Biblical Historiography in Honour of A. Graeme Auld*, ed. Robert Rezetko (Leiden: Brill, 2007), 447–59.

154. Cf. Hermann Spieckermann, "Stadtgott und Gottesstadt: Beobachtungen im Alten Orient und im Alten Testament," *Bib* 73 (1992): 1–31.

155. Cf. Johannes Renz and Wolfgang Röllig, *Handbuch der althebräischen Epigraphik: Teil 1: Text und Kommentar* (Darmstadt: Wissenschaftliche Buchgesellschaft, 1995), 242–51.

sal dimensions of monarchic period texts of the Hebrew Bible (Josh 3:11; Mic 4:13; Pss 97:5; 83:18; 47:2, 7; 2 Kgs 19:15). If one reads the inscription as suggested, then it would be clear that it combines a universal with a particular statement in a chiastic manner: Yhwh is the God of the entire earth (this means he rules over it), and therefore the mountains of Judah—where Khirbet Beit Lei is located—also belong to the God of Jerusalem. This is not in first order a statement of possession, but of protection: the mountains of Judah are under special protection by the God residing in Jerusalem, who rules over the world.

This perspective is in the background of many of the earliest texts of the book of Isaiah in chs. 1–12, though often changed into the form of judgment theology, as in the pronouncement of judgment in Isa 8:6–7:

> Because this people has refused the gently flowing waters of Shiloah ... therefore, see, may the Lord bring up the mightily flowing waters— the king of Assyria and all his glory—rising over them.

Because the Jerusalemites do not trust their God—depicted in this image as the necessary provider of water for Jerusalem—their God, who could sufficiently protect them, has therefore abandoned them to their enemy, the king of Assyria.

The background of Zion theology is especially tangible in Isa 7:1–9. The scene evoked here is that of the Syro-Ephraimite War in the eighth century BCE. In the course of the military pressure by imperial Assyria on the small states in the Levant, Aram and the northern kingdom of Israel attempted to compel Judah to join an anti-Assyrian coalition. In this situation, Isaiah reports to King Ahaz and issues a conditional salvation oracle to him. While Ahaz need not fear (v. 4), the promise of safety will only be fulfilled for Jerusalem if he remains calm and on guard, that is, if he trusts in the God of Jerusalem. Isaiah's implicit argument is that God himself will protect Jerusalem as long as Ahaz does not turn to the wrong political partner. This message is in no way an innovation in its historical context; it rests entirely on the traditional conviction of the deity's powerful presence in his city, making political alliances with further partners unnecessary and even appearing as a breach of trust.

3. Daughter Zion

In addition to the notion of Zion as a mountain and city, Zion also appears numerous times in the Hebrew Bible as a woman. How should this metaphor be construed?[156] It generally has a rather different accent in the contexts of the Hebrew Bible than the metaphor of the mountain. It reverses the protection metaphor, foregrounding Zion's defenselessness and need for protection (cf. Jer 6:26). This should probably be interpreted primarily as a reaction to the experience of the destruction of Zion by the Neo-Babylonians in 587 BCE, even though the conception of a city as a woman has a broad ancient Near Eastern pre-history and could therefore draw on certain models from the surroundings.

The symbol of the woman makes possible a further line of thinking. In keeping with the conceptual background of the ancient Near East, the conception of a city as feminine allows for the possibility of being connected through marriage to her city's god, so now the sins of Jerusalem in the Hebrew Bible can be depicted as adultery. What is meant is not the sinfulness of its residents, but rather the sins of the city itself, as addressed in texts such as Jer 4:14 or Lam 1. The city itself is perceived as a responsible entity that has distanced itself from God. Again like the ancient Near Eastern background, a failed policy of alliances is arguably in view. If a city or a state makes pacts with other powers, this is construed as adultery against the corresponding deity on the religious level.[157]

The proclamation of guilt upon Jerusalem as a city could belong to the oldest reflections of guilt in the wake of Jerusalem's catastrophe in 587 BCE, as shown especially by Lam 1 and the adoption of this motif in Isa 40:1–2. Then, in the sphere of Deuteronomistic theology, the king appears guilty. In a further step the guilt is broadened to include the people (Exod 32; 2 Kgs 17:21–23; cf. above, §32).

---

156. Cf. Marc Wischnowsky, *Tochter Zion: Aufnahme und Überwindung der Stadtklage in den Prophetenschriften des Alten Testaments*, WMANT 89 (Neukirchen-Vluyn: Neukirchener Verlag, 2001); Christl Maier, "Tochter Zion im Jeremiabuch: Eine literarische Personifikation mit altorientalischem Hintergrund," in *Prophetie in Israel: Beiträge des Symposiums "Das Alte Testament und die Kultur der Moderne" anlässlich des 100. Geburtstags Gerhard von Rads (1901-1971), Heidelberg, 18-21. Oktober 2001*, ed. Irmtraud Fischer et al., Altes Testament und Moderne 11 (Münster: LIT, 2003), 157–67; Christl Maier, *Daughter Zion, Mother Zion: Gender, Space, and the Sacred in Ancient Israel* (Minneapolis: Fortress, 2008).

157. Cf. Aloysius Fitzgerald, "The Mythological Background for the Presentation of Jerusalem as a Queen and False Worship as Adultery in the OT," *CBQ* 34 (1972): 403–16.

4. Sinai as the Mountain of Revelation

The prominence of Zion in Judah's religious history is matched by the prominence of Sinai in the Bible's literary history. Sinai is the most central and important location for divine revelation in the narrative cycle of the Pentateuch. From Exod 19 to Num 10, Israel halts at Sinai and Moses receives God's laws on the mountain. This expansive context is only interrupted as a narrative by the affair of the golden calf in Exod 32–34, which itself underscores the long duration of the revelation of the law on the mountain.

There can be no doubt from a biblical perspective—the most important mountain in the Hebrew Bible is Sinai. Yet even classical pentateuchal scholarship doubted the organic nature of the Sinai pericope within the exodus narrative:

> It appears as if the pilgrimage to Sinai had absolutely no place within the earliest saga. A form of it [i.e. the earliest saga] shimmers through that Israel went straight to Kadesh after the escape from Egypt and remained there for the forty years of their sojourn in the desert. The digression to a point so far [i.e. the Sinai] from the actual goal of the emigrants is quite unnatural.[158]

Outside the Torah, Sinai is first mentioned together with the exodus in the historical retrospective in Neh 9. This too nurtures the impression that the Sinai pericope is a large insertion into the present narrative context.

Some scholars have concluded that the Sinai pericope as a whole should be dated as post-Priestly. However, this can hardly be shown with certainty. It is possible that there was an old Sinai tradition that is remembered in texts like Judg 5:4–5; Deut 33:2; Hab 3:3; and Ps 68:8. Even if these cannot themselves claim to be of great antiquity, their Sinai references are somewhat in opposition to the mentions of Edom and Se'ir, evoking the impression of a later harmonization (cf. above, §30). Therefore, what is wrong in terms of the redaction-history of Exodus–Numbers is perhaps correct in terms of tradition history: namely, that Yhwh did reside on Mount Sinai and revealed himself from there—as God, but without concrete texts or laws. The Torah appears to have activated this tradition through its depiction of

---

158. Julius Wellhausen, *Israelitische und jüdische Geschichte,* 9th ed. (Berlin: Reimer, 1958), 12; cf. also Julius Wellhausen, *Prolegomena zur Geschichte Israels,* 357–58.

God's revelation on Sinai, which was then connected with the important and comprehensive promulgation of the law to Moses.[159]

The original edition of the Priestly document was probably unaware of this conception of "Mount Sinai"; the establishment of the cult and the construction of the tent in P instead took place in the "desert of Sinai."[160] In the present text, the Sinai pericope attaches the revelation of Exod 25–31, 35–40 to Mount Sinai only in Exod 24:15b–18, a post-Priestly introduction to Exod 25–31, 35–40.

Why, then, is the notion of Mount Sinai inscribed so prominently in the Torah? One cannot get around seeing this within the framework of a fundamental process of theological transformation that has transferred the previously central Zion motif to a mountain fundamentally removed from political and military turmoil and already vitally connected to the Yhwh tradition. Sinai went from being the old to being the new mountain of God, which became the symbol of mythic divine revelation that was already removed on basis of its location. When Elijah goes out for forty days and forty nights as far as the mountain of God according to 1 Kgs 19:8, the biblical narrative indicates that the divine mountain was seen as legendary and far away.

It is noteworthy that the Hebrew Bible also indicates a movement in the history of theology from Sinai back to Zion:

In the days to come, the mountain of Yhwh's house will be firmly established, the highest peak of the mountains, raised above the hills. And all nations will stream to it, and many peoples will go and say: "Come and let us go up to the mountain of Yhwh, to the house of the God of Jacob, so that he may teach us his ways, and we may walk in his paths." For Torah will go forth from Zion and the word of Yhwh from Jerusalem. (Isa 2:2–3)

The vision of the pilgrimage of the nations to Zion outfits Mount Zion with the function of Sinai, but universalizes it. The nations will receive Torah on Zion.

159. Cf. Matthias Köckert, "Wie kam das Gesetz an den Sinai?" in *Leben in Gottes Gegenwart: Studien zum Verständnis des Gesetzes im Alten Testament*, FAT 43 (Tübingen: Mohr Siebeck, 2004), 167–81.

160. Cf. Konrad Schmid, "Der Sinai und die Priesterschrift," in *"Gerechtigkeit und Recht zu üben" (Gen 18,19): Studien zur altorientalischen und biblischen Rechtsgeschichte, zur Religionsgeschichte Israels und zur Religionssoziologie*, ed. Reinhard Achenbach and Martin Arneth, BZABR 13 (Wiesbaden: Harrassowitz, 2009), 114–27.

5. Zion as Ruler and Eschatological Visions of Jerusalem

ZION AS MESSIANIC FIGURE Texts that describe Zion as ruler, like Isa 60 (cf. also Jer 33:16, where the messianic honorific "Yhwh is our righteousness" is related to Jerusalem), belong to the later conceptions of Zion in the Hebrew Bible. The personification of Zion as it is found in texts such as Jer 2–6 and Lam 1 is presupposed here and developed further. Isaiah 60 probably belongs to the historical context of the rebuilding of the temple as well as the return of the exiles, that is, in the early Persian period at the end of the sixth century BCE.[161] Here Zion is described as receiver of gifts that otherwise are known to have been delivered to the emperors of imperial powers in the ancient Near East. Poignant iconographic examples appear in the famous palace reliefs of Sennacherib from Nineveh, which depict the conquest of Lachish and afterwards present its inhabitants as the benefactors of tribute, or on the Black Obelisk, where Jehu brings tribute to Shalmaneser III. According to Isa 60, Zion itself moves into the function of the emperor. This is especially tangible through the adoption of Jer 27:8 in Isa 60:12. The proclamations related to the Babylonian emperor Nebuchadnezzar in the book of Jeremiah are now transferred to Zion. In Isa 60:12, Zion bears the characteristics of Nebuchadnezzar, in a certain sense replacing him in his role as ruler of the world.

JER 27:8	ISA 60:12
"But the nation and the kingdom that do not serve him, Nebuchadnezzar, the king of Babylon, and does not put its neck under the yoke of the king of Babylon, I will strike this nation with sword, hunger, and pestilence," says Yhwh, "until I have given it completely into his hand."	But the nation and the kingdom that do not serve you will perish and the nations will be destroyed!

However, Zion not only replaces the emperors, it also carries forward the Davidic dynasty in this capacity. This is especially recognizable in the light metaphor in Isa 60:1 ("Rise up, become light! For your light comes,

161. Cf. Odil H. Steck, *Studien zu Tritojesaja*, BZAW 203 (Berlin: de Gruyter, 2003), 14–19.

and the glory of Yhwh shines above you"), which adopts and digests Isa 9:1–6 (Eng. 9:1–7):

> The people going about in darkness have seen a great light, those living in the deepest darkness, a light has shined on them. . . . For a child is born to us, a son is given to us, and authority has come upon his shoulders. . . . The authority will grow continually, and peace shall be endless for the throne of David and his kingdom. (Isa 9:1, 5–6 [Eng. 9:1, 6–7])

The king of salvation described in Isa 9—contrary to customary interpretations and even many newer Bible translations—does not concern a coming king, but rather one who has come, as the perfective verb forms in 9:1–6 (Eng. 9:1–7) make clear. This figure no longer plays a role for Isa 60, for the functions and actions attributed to him are taken over by Zion. Zion no longer needs the shining light of a future king—instead she will be light herself.

A similar perspective is also found in the special proclamation that Zion will be the light for the nations (60:2–3). Here as well it concerns an adoption from a previous context, in this case the servant songs (cf. Isa 42:6 and 49:6), which are likely understood in the view of Isa 60 as messianic and therefore in need of reinterpretation. Messianic qualities belong to Zion alone in Isa 60.

This position in Isa 60, however, is understood appropriately only when Isa 60 is read within the context of the book of Isaiah as a whole. The messiah analogy of this text, which concentrates the functions of the ruler onto Zion, stands at the vanishing point of other, earlier positions that initially ascribed royal dignity to the Davidides (according to Isa 9 and 11). In the wake of the experience of the loss of the kingdom, this honor was then reckoned to have been transferred to the Persian King Cyrus. Finally, this entire process was considerably spiritualized and also renationalized so that now an entity like Zion was able to take on royal functions.[162]

162. Cf. in detail Konrad Schmid, "Herrschererwartungen und -aussagen im Jesajabuch: Überlegungen zu ihrer synchronen Logik und ihren diachronen Transformationen," in *The New Things: Eschatology in Old Testament Prophecy: Festschrift for Hendrik Leene*, ed. Ferenc Postma et al., Amsterdamse cahiers voor exegese van de Bijbel en zijn tradities, Supplement series 3 (Maastricht: Shaker, 2002), repr. in *Prophetische Heils- und Herrschererwartungen*, ed. Konrad Schmid, SBS 194 (Stuttgart: Katholisches Bibelwerk, 2005), 37–74.

Visions of Eschatological Jerusalem Elaborations of the expectation of an end times Jerusalem appear already in the Hebrew Bible itself, but then predominantly in the intertestamental literature and in the Apocalypse of John in the New Testament. The starting point for these expectations is taken from the temple blueprint in the book of Ezekiel (Ezek 40–48), which describes the layout of a new Jerusalem after the catastrophe. According to Isa 65:17–21, this newly created Jerusalem will be the place of eschatological joy for the righteous. From Qumran, various fragments (1Q32; 2Q24; 4Q554; 4Q555; 5Q15; and 11Q18) attest to a work that names "New Jerusalem" and also describes a new, end times Jerusalem. Then in Rev 21–22, the vision of a heavenly Jerusalem appears, which comes down and completely replaces the earthly one. These expectations no longer envision a future for the present Jerusalem and develop as compensation the conception of a heavenly replacement. However, they retain Jerusalem as the center of the world.[163]

§39 Interpretations of Humanity

Jan Assmann, "Zur Geschichte des Herzens im Alten Ägypten," in *Die Erfindung des inneren Menschen: Studien zur religiösen Anthropologie*, ed. Jan Assmann and Theo Sundermeier (Gütersloh: Gütersloher Verlagshaus, 1993), 81–112 ♦ Jan Assmann, "Konstellative Anthropologie: Zum Bild des Menschen im alten Ägypten," in *Der Mensch im alten Israel: Neue Forschungen zur alttestamentlichen Anthropologie*, ed. Bernd Janowski and Kathrin Liess (Freiburg im Breisgau: Herder, 2009), 95–120 ♦ Jan Assmann and Guy G. Stroumsa, eds., *Transformations of the Inner Self in Ancient Religions*, SHR 83 (Leiden: Brill, 1999) ♦ Walter Groß, "Die Gottebenbildlichkeit des Menschen nach Gen 1,26.27 in der Diskussion des letzten Jahrzehnts," in *Studien zur Priesterschrift und zu alttestamentlichen Gottesbildern*, SBAB 30 (Stuttgart: Katholisches Bibelwerk, 1999), 37–54 ♦ Bernd Janowski, "Die lebendige Statue Gottes: Zur Anthropologie der priesterlichen Urgeschichte," in *Gott und Mensch im Dialog: Festschrift für Otto Kaiser zum 80. Geburtstag*, vol. 1, ed. Markus Witte, BZAW 345/I (Berlin: de Gruyter, 2004), 183–214 ♦ Bernd Janowski, ed., *Der ganze Mensch: Zur Anthropologie der Antike und ihrer europäischen Nachgeschichte* (Berlin: Akademie Verlag Berlin, 2012) ♦ Bernd

---

163. Cf. Michael Tilly, *Jerusalem—Nabel der Welt: Überlieferung und Funktionen von Heiligtumstraditionen im antiken Judentum* (Stuttgart: Kohlhammer, 2002).

Janowski, "Anthropologie des Alten Testaments," *TLZ* 139 (2014): 535–54
♦ Bernd Janowski, "Der ganze Mensch: Zu den Koordinaten der alttestamentlichen Anthropologie," *ZTK* 113 (2016): 1–28 ♦ Thomas Krüger, "Das
menschliche Herz und die Weisung Gottes: Elemente einer Diskussion über
Möglichkeiten und Grenzen der Tora-Rezeption im Alten Testament," in *Das
menschliche Herz und die Weisung Gottes: Studien zur alttestamentlichen Anthropologie und Ethik*, ATANT 96 (Zurich: TVZ, 2009), 107–36 ♦ Christoph
Levin, "Das Amosbuch der Anawim," *ZTK* 94 (1997): 407–36 ♦ Carol A. New-
som, "Models of the Moral Self: Hebrew Bible and Second Temple Judaism,"
JBL 131 (2012): 5–25 ♦ Susan Niditch, *The Responsive Self: Personal Religion in
Biblical Literature of the Neo-Babylonian and Persian Periods* (New Haven:
Yale University Press, 2015) ♦ Jürgen van Oorschot, *Mensch: Anthropologie
und Theologie*, Uni-Taschenbücher 4763 (Tübingen: Mohr Siebeck, 2017) ♦
Jürgen van Oorschot and Andreas Wagner, eds., *Anthropologie(n) des Alten
Testaments*, Veröffentlichungen der Wissenschaftlichen Gesellschaft für Theol-
ogie 42 (Leipzig: Evangelische Verlagsanstalt, 2015) ♦ Johannes Unsok Ro, *Die
sogenannte "Armenfrömmigkeit" im nachexilischen Israel*, BZAW 322 (Berlin:
de Gruyter, 2002) ♦ Annette Schellenberg, *Der Mensch, das Bild Gottes? Zum
Gedanken einer Sonderstellung des Menschen im Alten Testament und in weiteren
altorientalischen Quellen*, ATANT 101 (Zurich: TVZ, 2011) ♦ Silvia Schroer,
"Grundlinien hebräischer Anthropologie," in *Die Welt der Hebräischen Bibel:
Umfeld—Inhalte—Grundthemen*, ed. Walter Dietrich (Stuttgart: Kohlhammer,
2017), 299–309 ♦ Andreas Schüle, "Die Würde des Bildes: Eine Re-Lektüre
der priesterlichen Urgeschichte," *EvT* 66 (2006): 440–54 ♦ Andreas Schüle,
"Anthropologie des Alten Testaments," *TR* 76 (2011): 399–414 ♦ Thomas
Staubli and Silvia Schroer, *Menschenbilder der Bibel* (Ostfildern, DE: Patmos,
2014) ♦ Andreas Wagner, ed., *Anthropologische Aufbrüche: Alttestamentliche
und interdisziplinäre Zugänge zur historischen Anthropologie*, FRLANT 232
(Göttingen: Vandenhoeck & Ruprecht, 2009) ♦ Manfred Weippert, "Tier und
Mensch in einer menschenarmen Welt: Zum sogenannten *dominium terrae* in
Genesis 1," in *Ebenbild Gottes: Herrscher über die Welt,* ed. Hans-Peter Mathys,
Biblisch-theologische Studien 33 (Neukirchen-Vluyn: Neukirchener Verlag,
1998), 35–55 ♦ Jakob Wöhrle, "Dominium terrae: Exegetische und religions-
geschichtliche Überlegungen zum Herrschaftsauftrag in Gen 1,26–28," *ZAW*
121 (2009): 171–88 ♦ Hans Walter Wolff, *Anthropologie des Alten Testaments*, ed.
Bernd Janowski, 8th ed. (Gütersloh: Gütersloher Verlagshaus, 2010)

The question of humanity has a privileged place in a theology of the Hebrew Bible and therefore consciously concludes the present thematic sec-

tion of §31–39, which generally follows the canon of the Hebrew Bible. In addition, the positioning of this section mirrors the fact that the reflection on humanity in the Hebrew Bible is especially anchored in the Psalms and in the wisdom literature.

A theology of the Hebrew Bible cannot be sufficiently biblically or theologically justified as developing exclusively as the doctrine of God, but it must also discuss humanity and its interpretation of self and other within the horizon of God. Theology and anthropology are not complementary questions with regard to the Hebrew Bible. They instead treat, in a certain sense, the same object with different emphases.[164]

1. Preliminary Remarks from the History of Scholarship

RUDOLF BULTMANN AND HANS WALTER WOLFF The status of an anthropology of the Hebrew Bible has become especially important in the wake of Rudolf Bultmann's works on the New Testament,[165] and its beginnings are linked especially with the name of Hans Walter Wolff.[166] In line with the philosophical-historical impression that the existentialism of Bultmann's time had on him, in particular as formulated by Martin Heidegger, Bultmann provided the perspective of defining and developing theology as anthropology. Already in 1925 Bultmann outlined this approach in his programmatic essay, "What Does It Mean to Speak of God?"

> If one understands speaking "of God" to mean speaking "about God," then such talk has no meaning at all. For in the moment when it takes place, then it has lost its object. For wherever the thought "God" is thought, it denotes God the Almighty, that is, the reality that deter-

164. Cf. the programmatic discussion by Shimon Gesundheit, "Gibt es eine jüdische Theologie der Hebräischen Bibel?," in *Theologie und Exegese des Alten Testaments / der Hebräischen Bibel: Zwischenbilanz und Zukunftsperspektiven*, ed. Bernd Janowski, SBS 200 (Stuttgart: Katholisches Bibelwerk, 2005), 73–86.

165. Cf. Konrad Hammann, *Rudolf Bultmann: Eine Biographie*, 3rd ed. (Tübingen: Mohr Siebeck, 2012), 397–408, esp. 404.

166. Cf. on him Jan C. Gertz and Manfred Oeming, eds., *Neu aufbrechen, den Menschen zu suchen und zu erkennen: Symposion anlässlich des 100. Geburtstages von Hans Walter Wolff*, Biblisch-theologische Studien 139 (Neukirchen-Vluyn: Neukirchener Verlag, 2013). For additional perspectives on Wolff, cf. Bernd Janowski, "Hans Walter Wolff und die alttestamentliche Anthropologie," in *Neu aufbrechen*, ed. Gertz and Oeming, 77–112, esp. 89–112.

mines everything. This thought is, however, not thought when I speak about God, that is, when I view God as an object of thought, toward which I can orient myself when I take a point of view from which I stand neutrally toward the question of God about God's reality and contrive considerations about his nature that I can reject or accept when they are illuminated. Whoever will be moved by reasons to believe in God's reality can be sure that he has not been captured by God's reality. And whoever reckons that he has said something about God with proofs of God disputes about a phantom. For every "speaking about" presupposes a point of view outside what is being spoken about. However, a point of view outside of God does not exist. Therefore, God cannot be spoken of in generalizing statements and general truths that are true without relationship to the concrete existential situation of the one speaking.[167]

To speak of God also means to speak of oneself. Theological statements are a function of human self-understanding. *Mutatis mutandis*, this program can also be applied to the biblical text. The self-understanding of the authors behind the biblical texts can be gathered through historical criticism, leading to the theological thinking of the biblical authors.

THEOLOGY AS ANTHROPOLOGY The question of anthropology, therefore, has a double function in a theology of the Hebrew Bible. On the one hand, in Bultmann's wake, theology as a whole can be developed as anthropology,[168] for theology—at least under Protestant influence—concerns the existential self-understanding of humans in their place before God (*coram Deo*) rather than abstract statements about God. On the other hand, however, anthropology can also be a partial topic of the theology of the Hebrew Bible, depicting and analyzing the theological statements about humanity in the Hebrew Bible.

167. Rudolf Bultmann, "Welchen Sinn hat es, von Gott zu reden?" in *Glauben und Verstehen*, vol. 1 (Tübingen: Mohr, 1958), 26; trans. as "What Does It Mean to Speak of God?" in *Faith and Understanding*, ed. Robert W. Funk, trans. Louise Pettibone Smith (London: SCM, 1969), 53–66 (author's translation).

168. Cf. the explicit statement in this direction by Shimon Gesundheit, "Gibt es eine jüdische Theologie der Hebräischen Bibel?," in *Theologie und Exegese des Alten Testaments / der Hebräischen Bibel: Zwischenbilanz und Zukunftsperspektiven*, ed. Bernd Janowski, SBS 200 (Stuttgart: Katholisches Bibelwerk, 2005), 73–86.

The investigation of historical anthropology in particular has found an entrance and fruitful application in recent scholarship of the Hebrew Bible. One might initially find the term *historical anthropology* contradictory because traditional anthropology concerns itself with the nature of humanity "in itself," which does not allow for any fundamental historical changes. However, the understanding of humanity as substantially socially, historically, and culturally conditioned has increasingly asserted itself so that historical anthropology has also found an established place. A historical anthropology of the Hebrew Bible concerns the diachronic reconstruction of various understandings of humanity in ancient cultures that significantly influenced the conceptions of anthropology of the Hebrew Bible.

FUNDAMENTAL ELEMENTS OF ANCIENT ANTHROPOLOGY There are two basic differences in particular between ancient and modern thinking about humanity that are of fundamental importance. The first is that the conception of humanity as a unified *species* is not of primary relevance. It is much more important to which social class a certain person belongs. Is one a king, a free person, or a slave? The second difference is causally dependent on the first: a person cannot be understood as a self-enclosed entity. His nature and also the functioning of his body are understood as depending on his social, political, and transcendental relations. Both differences will be discussed more below.

2. King—Freeman—Slave

As already laid out above in §37, the anthropological classification in the ancient Near East presupposes a strict social separation between king, free person, and slave. The reverse conception that these different classes together make up the genus *human* is only rudimentarily developed. This is shown, for example, in ancient Near Eastern mythology's general differentiation between the creation of the king and the creation of other people.[169] That is, the king is treated as an entity *sui generis*, set off fundamentally from the rest of humanity. Depending on social and political experience, however, the boundary between free and slave could occasionally be per-

---

169. Cf., e.g., John Van Seters, "The Creation of Man and the Creation of the King," *ZAW* 101 (1989): 333–42.

meated. Free persons could become slaves as a result of economic difficulty or war. On the other hand, it was also possible that slaves could benefit from liberation.

External and Internal Control   The special status of the king implies basic anthropological consequences for the understanding of his subjects. In ancient Egypt it can even be shown that the person in the Old Kingdom could be perceived as fully externally controlled—by the king and the state. The human heart as the organ of control plays no role in this period. When the term is used, it is related to the heart of the king.[170] A process only began with the demise of the Old Kingdom that increasingly discovered the concept of the person's internal control by his heart. This depends historically on the collapse of the Old Kingdom conception of the king, which led to the increased anthropological value of the individual.

The Heart as the Organ of Control   However, the newly discovered heart of the individual person corresponds in a fundamental manner with the powers and developments of the social sphere that determine it. As a listening and wise heart, it integrates itself—in the positive scenario—into the community and to its set of rules, leading the person to appropriate action. However, if the heart has no, or not enough receptivity to its environment, then the human falls into misery.

Israel and Judah   This constellation also influences the literature of the monarchic period in Israel and in Judah. Israel and Judah are part of the ancient Near East, and as such they participate in the surrounding intellectual world. As small states the differences between the various classes of humans are less strongly formed. However, the central figure of public life in Israel and Judah as well is the king. Yet every free person can and must place themselves within the order safeguarded by the king. While slaves are a separate class of people in the ancient Near East, in the legislation of ancient Israel they appear as potentially free people, for they should be released from their function as slaves in the seventh year (Exod 21:1–7; Deut 15:12–18). The Deuteronomic slave legislation even calls for the outfitting of the one released so that he would not immediately need to return to debt slavery.

The staggered end of the states of Israel (722 BCE) and Judah (587 BCE) had a pivotal effect on the importance of classes of humanity. The de-

170. Assmann, *Geschichte des Herzens*, 96.

struction of the monarchy meant the loss of the central orienting category of the king and the development of a new way to think about humans. The most efficacious conception was that of humans as "the image of God" (see below, Section 4), which accorded the human as such with a royal quality. However, the elevation of God to legislator (see above, §34) also newly designated a place for the human that was traditionally reserved for the king: humanity in general, and each and every person was now conceived as connected to God without intermediary.

3. Constellational Anthropology

The interconnectedness with the social, political, and transcendental spheres constitutive for the understanding of humanity in the Hebrew Bible can be described in terms of *konstellative Anthropologie* (constellational anthropology).[171] According to ancient thought, the person can only be fully appreciated within the context of relationships with his family, his friends, superiors and dependents, and also God.[172] A person is not primarily a separate individual; instead he is located in constant and changing constellations of relationships that influence and define him. The anthropology of the Hebrew Bible conceives of these relationships very closely with the human person. The human is a "bodily bound social being, that is, a being for which the bodily and social sphere is constitutive."[173]

BODILY ORGANS AND LIFE FUNCTIONS "Characteristic of this is the close connection between bodily organs and life function(s). Terms for bodily organs like the 'heart' can designate emotional and cognitive processes (Prov 23:15 and often), and conversely, social and psychic conflicts can affect certain bodily organs like the 'kidneys' (Ps 73:21–22 and often)."[174]

It is typical that this constellational anthropology is never literarily depicted on its own but is only articulated in connection with concrete narratives or proverbs. The naturalness with which it is presupposed indicates the enormous plausibility and obviousness that this concept could

171. See Jan Assmann, "Konstellative Anthropologie."
172. Assmann, "Konstellative Anthropologie," 101. Cf. also the references in Janowski, "Hans Walter Wolff und die alttestamentliche Anthropologie," 99 and n. 82.
173. Janowski, "Der ganze Mensch," 18.
174. Janowski, "Der ganze Mensch," 12.

lay claim to in the context of its emergence in antiquity. It is not actually unique to the Bible but characteristic for the premodern world as a whole. The human is not a self-contained entity in itself; he can instead only be defined in relationship to his lived environment. His sociality, his legal and political existence, and his religiosity define him in such a fundamental way that he cannot be viewed on his own.

Modern anthropology does not reject this approach as inappropriate. In the past decades, the classification of humans as an "ultra-social being" has placed the social and political dimensions of humanity in the foreground.[175] At the same time, the historical conditionality of the forms of human thinking and feeling have been highlighted and have led to a new branch of scholarship.[176] The similarity of biblical and modern anthropology is based in analogous observations whose distance is due primarily to the increasingly cultivated isolation of the individual within the context of modern thought, which has proven itself to be less appropriate.

4. Image of God

THE DISCOVERY OF THE *SPECIES* HUMAN Within the context of biblical anthropology, the *topos* of human being in the image of God in Gen 1:26–28 is extraordinarily well known, even though it only appears elsewhere in the Hebrew Bible in Gen 5:1 and Gen 9:6, so it is therefore limited to the Priestly literature. It is primarily its enormous history of reception within Christian atonement theology that has made it so prominent. It traditionally differentiated between the *imago Dei*, the natural image of God that cannot be lost, and the *similitudo Dei*, the further gift of grace that humanity lost through the fall into sin. *Imago* and *similitudo* are the Latin renderings in the Vulgate for בצלמנו כדמותנו (*bṣlmnw kdmwtnw*), "in our image, like our resemblance," in Gen 1:26. The Hebrew terms have almost the same meaning, as the selective adaptations of Gen 1:26 that have the same orientation in terms of content in Gen 5:1 (דמות, *dmwt*) and 9:6 (צלם, *ṣlm*) show.

Theologically groundbreaking in the fundamental anthropological statement of humanity as the image of God in Gen 1 is that—except for the

175. Cf. Michael Tomasello, *Warum wir kooperieren*, 2nd ed., Edition Unseld, 36 (Berlin: Suhrkamp, 2012).

176. Cf. Ute Frevert, *Vergängliche Gefühle* (Göttingen: Wallstein, 2013).

gender differences—it does not imply the formation of any further classes within the species of "human." Humans are not created as free or unfree, as nationals or foreigners, as kings or subjects, but "only" as man and woman.

THE RELIGIOUS-HISTORICAL BACKGROUND Namely, concerning the last-mentioned distinction, Gen 1 provides a revolutionary conception: in the world of the ancient Near East, only the king was originally reckoned as human in the full sense of the word. Rather than differentiating between the creation of the human and the creation of the king, Gen 1 draws them both together, which is recognizable in tradition-historical terms from the motif of the divine image. Elsewhere in the ancient Near East, only the king is considered "God's image," though "image" here would literally be translated as "statue" and intends the functionally fully valid presence of the one depicted. In the same way that a statue symbolized the divine presence—such as in the temple, the human according to Gen 1 is nothing less than the representative of God on earth—which was customarily intended for the king. Humanity's divine imageness consists in the assumption of God's royal function on earth. He is the trustee of creation, as the motif of *dominium terrae* makes directly explicit in the following context.

HISTORICAL CONTEXTS Viewed historically, the absence of an earthly royal figure can be explained by the post-monarchic formation of Gen 1. At the time of the composition of this text, there was no longer a monarchy in Israel and Judah, but this does nothing more than name a historical accident that in other texts of the Hebrew Bible could lead to the expression of the hope of the resurrection of the monarchy. The anthropology of Gen 1 instead appears consciously to discharge with the conception of the monarchy, or—said more precisely—to have "demoted" it: every human possesses royal quality.

Exegesis has always been exercised and continues to be exercised by the plural form נעשה (n'śh), "let us," of divine self-prompting in 1:26: נעשה אדם (n'śh 'dm), "let us make humanity." One must probably say that a resolution capable of consensus has yet to emerge. The interpretation of the Trinity by the church must be eliminated from a historical perspective from the outset. One has occasionally considered it a plural of majesty, but it is hardly attested in Hebrew; the only biblical attestation is Ezra 4:18 ("the writing that you sent to us"), which concerns the Persian king. Others have posited that here a heavenly court is being addressed, but this otherwise plays no role within the Priestly document to which Gen 1 is generally attributed. Finally, one has thought of a plural of deliberation, by which God makes the weighing of his decision-making clear, but this too does not fit with the conception of God in Gen 1. Perhaps the plural should be interpreted as the emphasis on the self-prompt, but its usage remains puzzling.

5. Distance from God and Capacity for Knowledge

THE THEME OF KNOWLEDGE IN THE GARDEN OF EDEN NARRATIVE It might be surprising to discuss the well-known narrative of the Garden of Eden (Gen 2–3) again at this juncture (cf. above, §31). It is, however, a foundational anthropological text of the Hebrew Bible and can be explained as a myth of adolescence of the human species. The Garden of Eden narrative reports how the first humans, as the other-directed "children" were created in the Garden of Eden, become "adults" who must master their lives with their own knowledge at a distance from God outside the Garden. The "knowledge of good and evil" that the humans attain is established by the parallel verses of Isa 7:15; 2 Sam 19:35 as the vital abilities of every adult human to lead their life with individual responsibility. According to Gen 3:22, the humans achieve and still retain this ability. However, it is the reason why they needed to be driven out of the Garden of Eden so that the tree of life remains withdrawn from them. If they would also have eaten from this tree, then the difference between human and God would completely disappear.

Therefore the narrative of the Garden of Eden offers a double etiology: why on the one hand humans have knowledge, and on the other hand why this knowledge repeatedly leads to experiences of distance from God. In the narrative this is symbolized by the expulsion of the human couple from paradise and the guarding of the Garden by the cherubim with their flaming swords.

6. Divine Care for the Poor

THEOLOGY OF LOWLINESS The postexilic anthropology of the Hebrew Bible places new accents on a topic that was not foreign but also in no way central to the monarchic period. God cares for the oppressed and the poor. The care for the poor belongs in the context of a comprehensively understood righteousness in preexilic literature.[177] Mercy for the underprivileged is part of socially-oriented justice. To care for the poor is, however, primarily an interpersonal task. In the postexilic period, the accent shifts in two ways. First, the poor become the primary object of God's attention, and it is even God himself who cares for them. This motif is encountered as prominent in particular in Deutero- and Trito-Isaiah.

> The needy and poor seek water and there is none there, their tongue parched with thirst; I, Yhwh, will answer them, the God of Israel, I will not abandon them. (Isa 41:17)

> Rejoice, you heavens, and be glad, you earth! The hills will break forth in jubilation, for Yhwh comforts his people, and he has compassion on his suffering ones. (Isa 49:13)

> The spirit of the lord Yhwh is upon me [i.e., Zion] because Yhwh has anointed me; to bring good news to the oppressed, he has sent me to heal the brokenhearted. (Isa 61:1)

God does not intend to be understood as the guarantor of present personal, social, political, or economic prosperity; he instead will be considered the one who attends to the oppressed.[178] These texts are conspicuously reserved in the formulation of concrete promises of salvation. The image of the exultant heavens, earth, and mountains in Isa 49:13 is noteworthy: it is not the oppressed who break out in exuberant rejoicing, but these cosmic entities; the oppressed instead received God's mercy.

The emphasis on God's attention to the poor is a clear expression of a newly emerging theology of the lowly, which turns the traditional character of the theological thinking of preexilic texts in the Hebrew Bible on its head. It presses forward the direction initiated by the Priestly document

177. Cf. Jan Assmann, Bernd Janowski, and Michael Welker, eds., *Gerechtigkeit: Richten und Retten in der abendländischen Tradition und ihren altorientalischen Ursprüngen* (Munich: Fink, 1998).

178. On the socio-economic backgrounds, cf. Johannes Bremer, *Wo Gott sich auf die Armen einlässt: Der sozio-ökonomische Hintergrund der achämenidischen Provinz Yəhūd und seine Implikationen für die Armentheologie des Psalters*, BBB 174 (Göttingen: V&R Unipress, 2016); see also Peter Altmann, *Economics in Persian-period Biblical Texts: Their Interactions with Economic Developments in the Persian Period and Earlier Biblical Traditions*, FAT 109 (Tübingen: Mohr Siebeck, 2016).

with its explanation of the royal quality of all humans in a theological bold manner. God not only pays attention to the king —as is known in the ancient Near East—as his son and representative (cf. in the Hebrew Bible texts such as Ps 2:7), but to all humans, and among them especially the lowly and oppressed. The fact that humanity is conceived as royal is also effective for the lowest of them all.

7. *The Problematization of the Human Ability to Act*

SEPARATION BETWEEN HUMAN WILL AND ACTION   One of the more recent recognitions in the scholarship of the Hebrew Bible is that the literature of the Second Temple period attests to the rise of anthropological conceptions that assume a separation between human will and human action. The human is not straightforwardly in the position to do what he plans. His will can be limited; he can be inhibited; he can be tarnished. The Pauline recognition from Rom 7:15 ("What I do, I do not understand; for not what I desire do I advance, but what I hate, this I do.") is only the endpoint of this development, which was initiated much earlier.

This anthropological problematization of human's ability to act is clearly detached from the earlier proverbial wisdom that assumed the correspondence of act and consequence and self-evidently reckoned that each human could control his own action. For this reason alone it is also possible and necessary for him to receive instruction and teaching.

THE ANTHROPOLOGY OF THE FLOOD PROLOGUE AND EPILOGUE   The skeptical anthropology of the postexilic period finds expression in particular in the non-Priestly flood prologue and epilogue, which, not least because of this skeptical image of humanity, cannot belong in the preexilic period.[179]

> And Yhwh saw that the evil of humanity was great upon the earth and that the whole inclination of the plans (וכל־יצר מחשבת, *wkl yṣr mḥšbt*) of his heart was always only evil. (Gen 6:5)

---

179. Cf. the decisive arguments in Jean-Louis Ska, "The Story of the Flood: A Priestly Writer and Some Later Editorial Fragments," in Jean-Louis Ska, *The Exegesis of the Pentateuch: Exegetical Studies and Basic Questions*, FAT 66 (Tübingen: Mohr Siebeck, 2009), 1–22. Also the allusion in Gen 6:7 to Gen 1 and the distinction between clean and unclean animals in Gen 8:20, whose content presupposes the Priestly sacrificial torah in Lev 1–7 speak in favor of a post-Priestly origin.

The prologue is thereby formulated even more strongly than the epilogue, which leaves out human childhood from the "evil inclination" and views this as beginning with its adolescence:

> For the inclination (יֵצֶר, *yṣr*) of the heart of humanity is evil from its adolescence onward. (Gen 8:21)

CORRECTIONS IN THE FINAL PASSAGES OF THE TORAH The Torah, however, according to its final passages, assumes that humanity is not completely at the mercy of this evil heart. The Law is not difficult for humanity to keep, as Deut 30:11–14 maintain: "but the word is close to you, in your mouth and in your heart so that you can keep it." A somewhat later supplementation that was inserted before Deut 30:11–14 envisages that the Israelites in exile will "consider in their hearts" (Deut 30:1) the word of God. In response God will "circumcise" (Deut 30:6) their hearts after their return to the land so that they will be able to observe the Law.

8. The Contractions of the New Human

THE NEW COVENANT AND THE NEW PERSON Persian-period texts, in particular in the prophetic tradition, developed visions of the transformation or the new creation of humanity (Jer 31:33–34; Ezek 36:26–27) that do not appear in the other sections of the canon. Within the context of the promise of a new covenant, Jer 31:33–34 promises that the Torah will be written in Israel's hearts so that reciprocal instruction will no longer be needed:

> "This is the new covenant that I will conclude with the house of Israel in those days," says Yhwh: "I will put my instruction inside them, and I will write it for them in their hearts. And I will be their God; they will be my people. Then no one will instruct his neighbor and no one his brother, saying, 'Know Yhwh!' Instead from the least to the greatest they will all know me, says Yhwh, for I will forgive their guilt and I will no longer consider their sins." (Jer 31:33–34)

In this vision Jer 31:33–34 sets itself against the basic conviction of the Shema (Deut 6:4–9) that the Law is in need of continual realization and circulation: "and you shall inculcate them [i.e., these words] into your children, and you shall speak of them when you sit in your house and when you go along the way, when you lie down and when you get up." The internalization of the Torah ultimately renders the written Torah and the reciprocal instruction superfluous. It need not be surprising that Jer 31:31–34 was not broadly received in Judaism (but cf. CD 14,19).

THE IMPLANTATION OF NEW CONTENT VERSUS THE TRANSPLANTING OF A NEW HEART In addition, there is a widespread notion that God will not only fill the human heart with new content but will replace the old heart with a new one:

> And I will give you a new heart, and inside you I will put a new spirit. And I will remove the heart of stone from your body and give you a new heart of flesh. And my spirit will I place inside you, and I will bring it about that you will live according to my statutes and keep my stipulations and perform them. (Ezek 36:26–27)

The implantation of new content into the human heart is not sufficient for the book of Ezekiel. Instead a new heart must first be transplanted that completely replaces the old one, and this new heart can be the location of God's spirit in the human.

DIFFERENCES BETWEEN THE NEVI'IM AND THE TORAH AND KETUVIM The human remains as he is for the Torah and the Ketuvim. Deuteronomy 30:6 alone indicates a future "circumcision" of the heart in the exile, but it avoids the terminology of "new." The prophetic declarations of a new creation of humanity found hardly any resonance in Jewish interpretation. They were hardly compatible with mainstream pharisaic-rabbinic piety. Christian theology also showed reserve in the reception of this idea. While faith makes every person "new," and God himself creates this newness, humans are not biologically changed. Their new creation is of a spiritual nature; it rests on a new self-understanding of the believing person.

The declarations from the prophecy of the Hebrew Bible generally concentrate on the human heart, into which the will of God is directly inscribed. The heart is renewed, or even completely replaced. It presupposes the conviction that the human as currently constituted is in itself incapable of conforming to God and his will. Only a fundamental anthropological change can provide a remedy.

CONTESTATIONS OF THE NEW HUMAN These perspectives did not, however, remain unchallenged within the Hebrew Bible. The wisdom literature, especially Qoheleth, insists that humanity is and remains what he is, and that he must live with his human condition. The Torah as well offers hardly any indication (but cf. Deut 30:6) that the human could undergo a fundamental anthropological change. Therefore, the formation of the tradition of the Hebrew Bible not only outlines the image of a new human, but it also includes the contestation of this very concept in its literature.

§40 Diversity and Unity in the Theology of the Hebrew Bible

John Barton and Michael Wolter, eds., *Die Einheit der Schrift und die Vielfalt des Kanons: The Unity of Scripture and the Diversity of the Canon*, BZNW 118 (Berlin: de Gruyter, 2003) ♦ Matthias Büttner, *Das Alte Testament als erster Teil der christlichen Bibel: Zur Frage nach theologischer Auslegung und "Mitte" im Kontext der Theologie Karl Barths*, BEvT 120 (Gütersloh: Kaiser, 2002) ♦ Jürgen Ebach, "Verbindliche Vielfalt: Über die 'Schrift' als Kanon," *Kirche und Israel* 20 (2005): 109–19 ♦ Heinz-Josef Fabry, "Der Beitrag der Septuaginta-Codizes zur Kanonfrage: Kanon-theologische Überlegungen zu Einheit und Vielfalt biblischer Theologie," in *Die Septuaginta: Entstehung, Sprache, Geschichte. 3. Internationale Fachtagung veranstaltet von Septuaginta Deutsch (LXX.D), Wuppertal 22.–25. Juli 2010*, ed. Siegfried Kreuzer and Marcus Sigismund, WUNT 286 (Tübingen: Mohr Siebeck, 2012), 582–99 ♦ Shimon Gesundheit, "Das Land Israels als Mitte einer jüdischen Theologie der Tora: Synchrone und diachrone Perspektiven," *ZAW* 123 (2011): 325–35 ♦ Ferdinand Hahn, "Vielfalt und Einheit des Neuen Testaments: Zum Problem einer neutestamentlichen Theologie," *BZ* 38 (1994): 161–73 ♦ Hans-Jürgen Hermisson, "Jesus Christus als externe Mitte des Alten Testaments: Ein unzeitgemäßes Votum zur Theologie des Alten Testaments," in *Jesus Christus als die Mitte der Schrift: Studien zur Hermeneutik des Evangeliums*, ed. Christof Landmesser et al., BZNW 86 (Berlin: de Gruyter, 1997), 199–233 ♦ Ernst Axel Knauf, "Die Mitte des Alten Testaments," in *Data and Debates: Essays in the History and Culture of Israel and Its Neighbors in Antiquity = Daten und Debatten: Aufsätze zur Kulturgeschichte des antiken Israel und seiner Nachbarn*, AOAT 407 (Münster: Ugarit-Verlag, 2013), 445–52 ♦ Thomas Krüger, "Einheit und Vielfalt des Göttlichen nach dem Alten Testament," *Marburger Jahrbuch Theologie* 10 (1998): 15–50 ♦ Manfred Oeming, "Viele Wege zu dem Einen: Die 'transzendente Mitte' eine Theologie des Alten Testaments im Spannungsfeld von Vielfalt und Einheit," in *Viele Wege zu dem Einen: Historische Bibelkritik—Die Vitalität der Glaubensüberlieferung in der Moderne,* ed. Stefan Beyerle et al., Biblisch-theologische Studien 121 (Neukirchen-Vluyn: Neukirchener Verlag, 2012), 83–108 ♦ Rolf Rendtorff, "Leviticus 16 als Mitte der Tora," *BibInt* 11 (2003): 252–58 ♦ Werner H. Schmidt, "Vielfalt und Einheit des alttestamentlichen Glaubens: Konstruktionsversuch an einem Pfeiler der Brücke 'Biblische Theologie,'" in *Psalmen und Weisheit, Theologische Anthropologie und Jeremia, Theologie des Alten Testaments,* vol. 2 of *Vielfalt und Einheit alttestamentlichen Glaubens* (Neukirchen-Vluyn: Neukirchener Verlag, 1995), 180–89 ♦ Werner H. Schmidt, "Die Frage nach einer 'Mitte' des Alten Testaments," *EvT* 68 (2008): 168–78 ♦ Hans-Christoph Schmitt, "Die Einheit der Schrift und die Mitte des Alten Testaments," in *Einfach von Gott reden: Ein theologischer Diskurs: Festschrift für Friedrich Mildenberger zum 65. Geburtstag,* ed. Jürgen Roloff and Hans G. Ulrich (Stuttgart: Kohlhammer, 1994), 49–66 ♦ Hermann Spieckermann, "From Biblical Exegesis to Reception History," *HBAI* 1 (2012): 327–50 ♦ Ernst-Joachim Waschke, "Die Einheit der Theologie heute als Anfrage an das Alte Testament: Ein Plädoyer für die Vielfalt," in *Alttestamentlicher Glaube und biblische Theologie: Festschrift für Horst Dietrich Preuß zum 65. Geburtstag,* ed. Jutta Hausmann and Hans-Jürgen Zobel (Stuttgart: Kohlhammer, 1992), 331–42

ASPECTS OF RECEPTION OR PRODUCTION? Within the context of a historically descriptive theology of the Hebrew Bible, the question of diversity and unity is posed in a calm fashion. The question is usually posed in relation to the *understanding* of the Hebrew Bible: How can one recognize a unity behind the different positions? What is the actual message of the Hebrew Bible? These questions concern the reception rather than the production of the Hebrew Bible. With regard to the texts and books of the Hebrew Bible itself, several observations can be invoked concerning the redactional combination of certain books and groups of books, leading sometimes even to a comprehensive structure of the entire Hebrew Bible or rather Old Testament (cf. Parts E and F). However, on the whole the Hebrew Bible does not have a historical or content-oriented unity. The Hebrew Bible neither comprises the entire literature of ancient Israel and Judah from the biblical period, nor can its writings be brought to a shared theological denominator. On the one hand it is held together over wide stretches by the specific nature of its literary formation—inner-biblical linkage. Yet on the other hand, it is still suitable as a reception-historical unity, or in light of the different canons (cf. Part C) more precisely as a plurality of reception-historical unities. The writings of the Hebrew Bible are reckoned in Judaism as well as in various Christian confessions in its (diversely accentuated and defined) entirety as "Hebrew Bible" or as "Old Testament."

However, before one considers this evidence further in view of the question of unity, a basic clarification of the problematic of the value of conceptions of diversity and unity is first necessary. Is unity more important or better than diversity?

1. Implicit Values

Linked to the religious-historical character of Judaism, Christianity, and Islam is the fact that over the course of their histories they have developed an awareness of the distinction between orthodoxy and heterodoxy. Jan Assmann has labeled this state of affairs the "Mosaic Distinction."[180] The formation of the tradition in the Hebrew Bible develops a foundational difference that is bound up with the distinction between "true" and "false" by the literary—not historical—figure of Moses. This foundational difference becomes symptomatic for Judaism and its daughter religions, especially Christianity and Islam. Does the "unity" of the Hebrew Bible establish its "orthodox" position?

ORTHODOXY VERSUS HETERODOXY From a descriptive-historical perspective can first be stated that the Hebrew Bible is objectively too plurivocal to allow one to settle on one position on various questions. Second, the identification of specific texts or declarations in the Hebrew Bible as orthodox or heterodox rests on particular reception-historical views. Ultimately the difference between orthodoxy and heterodoxy is only justifiable in terms of the history of reception. Formulated paradoxically, orthodoxy consists of those heterodoxies that were able to become established. One cannot escape the manifold political forces and contingencies guiding the history of reception by means of some supposed logic when investigating the possible unity of the Hebrew Bible. Third, one should bear in mind that the separation of "true" and "false" only makes sense within the context of a presupposed exclusivist orientation. The Hebrew Bible is familiar with numerous and divergent exclusivist positions, of course; however, it also

180. Jan Assmann, *The Price of Monotheism*, trans. Robert Savage (Stanford: Stanford University Press, 2010).

is aware of and attests to inclusive and pluralistic ones. The differentiation between "true" and "false," of "orthodox" and "heterodox" is relativized substantially within the framework of non-exclusivist approaches to the question of truth. Truth can appear in various shapes, in various linguistic forms. It can be captured differently from different presuppositions. It cannot be pinned down uniformly.

PRESERVATION OF A CERTAIN DIVERSITY AS THE GOAL OF THE FORMATION OF TRADITION Looking at the Hebrew Bible itself, the formation of tradition seems to have preserved and accentuated its diversity, though mediated by multiple textual allusions, much more clearly than its unity. But is this a loss?

It required the pluralization of the world of human life and its measures of value for the plurality of biblical positions to be interpreted as a virtue rather than a necessity in the end of the twentieth and beginning of the twenty-first century. In spite of all the sophisticated systems in modern societies that have been tasked with the establishment of the truth, pluralistic models have prevailed. This is no different in scholarship and art than it is in politics and finally also in religion, even when the various religions—each according to its degree of modernization—so far have developed different sensibilities. This option is also theologically justifiable. Whatever is stated about God religiously or theologically remains penultimate rather than ultimate. This is also the case for the Bible—it contains, therefore, witnesses of human experiences of God and not divinely revealed truths.

INNER-BIBLICAL REFERENCES AS AN ELEMENT OF ESTABLISHED UNITY With all respect to the diversity within the Hebrew Bible, noteworthy connections still remain that have brought about a historically differentiated unity in the course of the formation of the Hebrew Bible or, as the case may be, the Old Testament.

2. Historically Accumulated Connections

SUPPLEMENTING LITERATURE The textual character of the Hebrew Bible as discursive and agglutinative supplementary literature shapes large portions of the Hebrew Bible, though not exclusively. It involves the fact that its texts and books were linked to one another in numerous ways during the lengthy process of the Hebrew Bible's formation. The redaction-historical process harmonized the texts of the individual books as well as multi-book units with one another and created a relational structure with many accents so that it could be read and interpreted from divergent angles.

In this respect, an integrated interpretation of the Hebrew Bible or of certain multi-book sections is by no means a priori foreign to the Bible. On the contrary, it can be supported with appropriate literary observations for many text complexes, such as those presented in Part F.

In the end it is also this network of relationships that for the past fifty years has been responsible—at least in German-speaking exegesis—for the revival of redaction-historical scholarship on the Hebrew Bible. If one stands back from the traditional form-critical guidelines for the interpretation of texts of the Hebrew Bible, which essentially understand these texts as the textualization of originally oral and therefore independent units, then numerous verbal and content-related connections within the literature of the Hebrew Bible appear that can be most appropriately interpreted as literarily productive receptions of preexisting batches of texts.

EXAMPLES OF LITERARY HARMONIZATION Within the context of the redactional growth of the Hebrew Bible are blocks of text of different provenances that were incrementally bound together and harmonized with one another through the insertion of fitting passages of text, as was presented in Part C. For example, within the sphere of the ancestral narratives, the Abraham and the Jacob cycles were bound together by means of the parallel content of the promise texts (cf. Gen 12:1–3; 28:13–15). The ancestral narratives and the exodus narrative were linked to one another by means of two programmatic texts (Gen 15; Exod 3–4) that refer to one another. The Pentateuch was interpreted through the motif of the promise of the land to the three ancestors that traverses all its books and that from a particular perspective summarizes them thematically. The Former Prophets (Joshua–Kings) are bound together by a Deuteronomistic point of view. The Latter Prophets (Isaiah–Malachi) were harmonized with one another by a symmetrical structure and content-related alignments between the book of Isaiah and the Book of the Twelve, or, as the case may be, between the books of Jeremiah and Ezekiel. Within the Ketuvim, the evidence in the Psalter should receive special mention for its individual psalms placed in meaningful sequences through juxtaposition and concatenation (cf., e.g., Pss 3–14 or Pss 15–24). The Psalter as a whole is structured into a five-part unity through four doxologies that have been coordinated with one another.

Also important for the unity of the entire or at least substantial parts of the Hebrew Bible is the redactional parenthesis surrounding the Nevi'im (Josh 1:7–8, 13 / Mal 3:22 [Eng. 4:4]), which construes the Nevi'im as the interpretation and application of the Torah in history and pronounces all the prophets as Moses's successors. Psalm 1 as the opening text of the Ketuvim surveys almost the entire Hebrew Bible, and in this case alludes both to the Torah and the Nevi'im and now interprets the Ketuvim redactionally as pedagogical literature for the application of Torah and Nevi'im in daily life.

3. Unity as Canonically Differentiated and Limited Pluralism

There is, then, a redactionally accumulated unity of the Hebrew Bible and its sections, even if it is of different densities from one section of text to another. This unity is quite variable in itself and structured in divergent ways. Therefore, the formation of tradition did not have an interest in plurality in itself, but rather in a structured, functionally diverse, and interpretable plurality, which is only appropriate (cf. also §15 above on the anthropological character of the Hebrew Bible). Theological positions that were orthodox at a certain point in time necessarily degenerate into heterodoxy when they are not updated, accommodated, and further refined. The pressure toward inner-biblical interpretation is inherent within the canon in numerous ways and in the end has led to its diachronically differentiated unity.

In addition to all the plurality of the canon, the fact that it is closed should be emphasized as well. The canon did not grow in an unlimited manner, instead coming to a certain conclusion in the first century CE. While this closure did not mean the end of further interpretive activity on texts of the Hebrew Bible, such activity no longer took place within the text itself, but was now only outside the text and led to the development of a theological secondary literature of the Bible.

The closure of the canon of the Hebrew Bible took place rather accidentally (cf. above, §11). The loss of the Jerusalem temple in 70 CE and the rise of Christianity facilitated the concentration on the available traditions that were already comparably consolidated for the Torah and Nevi'im and would only still need an appropriate coincidence for the Ketuvim.

4. Is There a "Center" of the Hebrew Bible?

A RECEPTION-HISTORICAL QUESTION The identification of a theological center of the Hebrew Bible is a question for the history of reception that depends on certain theological decisions and declares either concrete texts or theologoumena inside or outside the Hebrew Bible as its "center," though this originally geographically connoted metaphor often remains unclear. The reception-historical nature of this question is most clear in the determinations from Christian perspectives that see this center as "external": Jesus Christ.[181]

DESCRIPTIVE EVIDENCE In the context of the approach chosen here, the sole question is whether the Hebrew Bible itself provides cause to inquire about certain accentuations or even a hierarchy of its positions. While this approach to the question is also reception-historical in nature, it remains within the historical framework of the inner biblical reception history of the writings of the Hebrew Bible. Here reference can be made to the evidence presented in Part C. Regardless of which Hebrew Bible (or Old Testament) one has in view, one will hardly find any indications of an especially highlighted "center." However, one will indeed find indicators of prominently highlighted books or sections of canon that appear either at the beginning or at the end of the sequence of books.

THE TORAH AS THE HIGHLIGHTED HEAD PIECE OF THE HEBREW BIBLE For the Hebrew Bible, there is no question that the Torah is not only the earliest, but also functionally the most important section of the canon by which the other books and sections of the canon are to be measured. The Hebrew Bible, therefore, does not have a "middle," but does have a prominent "head piece." With respect to the division of the Torah into books, the placement of the book of Leviticus in the middle does appear in fact to be due to an accentuation of this book. Looking only at the extent of the material, the books of Exodus to Numbers could also have been divided into two rather than three books.

---

181. Cf. Hans-Jürgen Hermisson, "Jesus Christus als externe Mitte des Alten Testaments: Ein unzeitgemäßes Votum zur Theologie des Alten Testaments," in *Jesus Christus als die Mitte der Schrift: Studien zur Hermeneutik des Evangeliums*, ed. Christof Landmesser et al., BZNW 86 (Berlin: de Gruyter, 1997), 199–233.

GRANTING OF HONOR TO THE PROPHETS IN THE OLD TESTAMENT The contrary is the case with the Old Testament in Christianity. Here too one cannot find—through literary indications—a "center." It is instead the final pieces that receive special significance. In the standard order, the Prophets are, first, in terms of the canon, understood receptionally as foretellers of Christ, presenting the quintessence of the Old Testament. The large uncial manuscripts of the Septuagint also allow for other books and their central themes to slop into this highlighted final location (cf. above, §17).

The inner-biblical references within the individual sections of the canon and the writings of the Hebrew Bible or Old Testament are often considered hierarchically from a formation-historical perspective. An interpreting text adapts the source text to be interpreted in a changed, corrected, or even accentuated manner. While it should be assumed that the earlier text was seen as authoritative for the later texts—from its own perspective—the editing hand retains the upper hand in the matter itself. However, there is hardly any passage in the Hebrew Bible or Old Testament that does not possess both interpreting and interpreted character. For this reason, the Hebrew Bible or Old Testament marked primarily by its character as "text" and "texts" does not have a "center."

I. The Question of a Jewish Theology of the Hebrew Bible or a Christian Theology of the Old Testament

In accordance with its historical and descriptive approach, the present theology of the Hebrew Bible is neither characterized as a Jewish nor a Christian, but essentially as a Hebrew Bible theology of the Hebrew Bible—or a Hebrew-biblical theology of the Hebrew Bible. If one places the beginning of "Judaism" in the Babylonian exile (cf. above, §36), then one can also speak of Jewish theology for the biblical texts from the Second Temple period. A Christian theology of the Old Testament is only historically possible from the time of early Christianity onward. Expressed differently, there is a Jewish redaction and supplementation of the Hebrew Bible, but no Christian redaction of the Old Testament (on the issue of individual Christian glosses in deuterocanonical writings like Baruch or Sirach, cf. below, §41). The Hebrew Bible has been edited and received in Judaism; the Old Testament has been received in Christianity.

A historically oriented approach makes possible a nuanced evaluation of the issue of a Jewish interpretation of the Hebrew Bible or a Christian interpretation of the Old Testament. Are such interpretations possible? Are they permissible? An initial answer to these questions is that Jewish and Christian interpretations of the Hebrew Bible or rather Old Testament are historical facts, and as such they belong to the theological-historical legacy of the Bible. The question of their legitimacy arises, in light of their existence, just as little or as much as with something like architectural structures that have integrated earlier buildings—like, for example, the cathedral of Syracuse on Sicily, which originated as a Greek temple, was then converted into a basilica, served as a mosque in the time of the Moors, and in the baroque period was furnished with a new façade. Are the secondary and tertiary elements of this building "illegitimate" in light of the fact that they rest on previous structures that they have integrated and transformed?

It belongs to the nature of important literary artifacts that they generated their receptions, which—if these receptions are themselves weighty—

not only reproduce the content of their precursors, but also add new accents and perspectives. In this respect Jewish and Christian interpretations of the Hebrew Bible or rather Old Testament are just as possible and permissible as musical, literary, and pictorial receptions, which does not exclude but rather includes that among these receptions are some that represent a theological or artistic dip in comparison with their originals.

§41 The Hebrew Bible and Judaism

Daniel Stökl Ben Ezra, *Qumran: Die Texte vom Toten Meer und das antike Judentum*, Uni-Taschenbücher 4681 (Tübingen: Mohr Siebeck, 2016) ♦ Martina Böhm, *Rezeption und Funktion der Vätererzählungen bei Philo von Alexandria: Zum Zusammenhang von Kontext, Hermeneutik und Exegese im frühen Judentum*, BZNW 128 (Berlin: de Gruyter, 2005) ♦ Devorah Dimant, "The Hebrew Bible in Jewish Context," in *What Is Bible?* ed. Karin Finsterbusch and Armin Lange, CBET 67 (Leuven: Peeters, 2012), 341–54 ♦ Shimon Gesundheit, "Gibt es eine jüdische Theologie der Hebräischen Bibel?" in *Theologie und Exegese des Alten Testaments / der Hebräischen Bibel: Zwischenbilanz und Zukunftsperspektiven*, ed. Bernd Janowski SBS 200 (Stuttgart: Katholisches Bibelwerk, 2005), 73–86 ♦ Matthias Henze, *A Companion to Biblical Interpretation in Early Judaism* (Grand Rapids: Eerdmans, 2012) ♦ Isaac Kalimi, ed., *Jewish Bible Theology: Perspectives and Case Studies* (Winona Lake, IN: Eisenbrauns, 2012) ♦ Michael Krupp, *Einführung in die Mischna* (Frankfurt am Main: Verlag der Weltreligionen, 2007) ♦ James Kugel, *The Bible as It Was* (Cambridge, MA: Harvard University Press, 1999) ♦ Gerhard Langer, *Midrasch*, Uni-Taschenbücher 4675 (Tübingen: Mohr Siebeck, 2016) ♦ Doron Mendels and Arye Edrei, *Zweierlei Diaspora: Zur Spaltung der antiken jüdischen Welt* (Göttingen: Vandenhoeck & Ruprecht, 2010) ♦ Daniel R. Schwartz, ed., *Was 70 CE a Watershed in Jewish History? On Jews and Judaism Before and After the Destruction of the Second Temple*, Ancient Judaism and Early Christianity 78 (Leiden: Brill, 2012) ♦ Folkert Siegert, *Einleitung in die hellenistisch-jüdische Literatur: Apokrypha, Pseudepigrapha und Fragmente verlorener Autorenwerke* (Berlin: de Gruyter, 2016) ♦ Benjamin Sommer, "Dialogical Biblical Theology: A Jewish Approach to Reading Scripture Theologically," in *Biblical Theology: Introducing the Conversation*, ed. Leo G. Perdue et al. (Nashville: Abingdon, 2009), 1–53 ♦ Benjamin Sommer, *Jewish Concepts of Scripture: A Comparative Introduction* (New York: New York University Press, 2012) ♦ Günter Stemberger, *Einleitung in Talmud und Midrasch*, 9th ed. (Munich: Beck, 2011); trans. as *Introduction to the Talmud and Midrash*, 2nd ed. (Edinburgh: T&T Clark, 1996) ◆ Marvin A. Sweeney, *Tanak: A Theological and Critical Introduction to the Jewish Bible* (Minneapolis: Fortress, 2012) ◆ Karin Hedner Zetterholm, *Jewish Interpretation of the Bible: Ancient and Contemporary* (Minneapolis: Fortress, 2012)

THE BIBLE IN JUDAISM Judaism has a complex relationship to the Hebrew Bible. Parts or at least precursors of the Hebrew Bible are earlier than Judaism—at least when one does not place Judaism's beginning before the Babylonian exile. In its reworked final form and also in broad sections of texts, the Hebrew Bible is a product of Babylonian, Persian, and Hellenistic Judaism. The latest texts of the Hebrew Bible belong to the Maccabean period—such as in the unanimous opinion of biblical scholarship the latest parts of the book of Daniel, possibly even in the Hasmonean period, which can be considered for individual psalms, perhaps even for several passages of Chronicles (cf. above, §28), but they only reach into the second and not the first century BCE. Therefore, the Hebrew Bible has a historical end, while the Judaism being formed from the Babylonian exile and in existence until today has experienced diverse changes and various expressions.

This discussion cannot trace the history of interpretation of the Hebrew Bible in the various strands of the Jewish formation of tradition.[1] However, the simple but oft neglected fact should be emphasized that the Hebrew Bible and its theologies should be differentiated from the later forms of reception, and that these should be appreciated as theological positions in their own right.

It is the nature of the traditional logic of religious literature that they like to depict themselves as conforming to Scripture in a supra-historical manner. Historically speaking, however, Scripture remains Scripture, and its interpretation remains its interpretation.

The substantial corpus of Jewish literature from the Second Temple period shows the enormous breadth of the adoption, continuation, and elaboration of biblical themes, which do not, however, continue to be transmitted in rabbinic Judaism. During the rabbinic period it is either lost or is initially only transmitted in translations in the broader scope of the Old Testament canons of the eastern churches, and it is only in part rediscovered in the original languages beginning in 1947 in the fragments from the caves at Qumran. Worthy of mention are, for example, the Enoch

---

1. Cf., for initial overviews, the articles in *Encyclopedia of Bible and Its Reception* (Berlin: de Gruyter, 2009–).

literature and the book of Jubilees, which survived in the Ethiopian canon of the Bible, while the so-called Temple Scroll, a harmonization between the temple texts in the Pentateuch and in the book of Ezekiel, was first rediscovered in Qumran Cave 11. One can only speculate as to why these writings did not become established in Judaism. It is probable, however, that both writings that claim for themselves a pre-Mosaic origin (such as the books of Enoch) and those that present excessive apocalyptic content were suspect to rabbinic Judaism and were eliminated from the process of transmission for those reasons.

THE TALMUD After the loss of the Temple in 70 CE, rabbinic literature began to develop. Its core consists of what is called the Mishnah, which ascribes itself to the oral Torah (תורה שבעל פה, *twrh šb'l ph*) that—in its self-perception—was communicated to Moses by God on Sinai in addition to the written Torah. It was supplemented by what is called the Gemara, which contains Aramaic commentaries and analyses of the Hebrew Mishnah. Together they form the Talmud, which was transmitted in a shorter Palestinian (or rather Jerusalem) and a longer Babylonian version.

Although the Talmud is closely related to the Bible, it can only indirectly be understood as biblical interpretation. For the most part, it is more an interpretation of the Bible of second or third order. The Gemara comments on the Mishnah, and the Mishnah itself does not refer directly to the Bible. It instead understands itself as Torah in its own right, as the textualization of the oral Torah from Sinai, which only reached its written form centuries after Moses in the Mishnah. The Mishnah primarily offers halakic material—that is, legal discussion on conduct—while in the Talmud as a whole, haggadic material—narratives with instructional content—predominates.

TALMUD AND BIBLE The Talmud became an essential object of theological study in Judaism in the first and second millennium CE. Learning in classical, especially then in Orthodox Judaism was Talmud learning, not biblical learning. The Torah, and its reading in particular, plays a prominent role in synagogue worship, in which various psalms or sections thereof are also used. On the Sabbath as well as on certain festival days, sections of the Prophets (the so-called *Haftarot*) are included, where "Prophets" means all the books of the canonical section *Nevi'im*. Furthermore, mention should be made of what is called the Megillot, which since the early Middle Ages have been assigned to specific feasts when they are each read:

Esther at Purim, Song of Songs at Passover, Ruth at Shavuot, Lamentations on the Ninth of Ab, as well as Qoheleth at Sukkot.

While a first beginning of philosophical interpretation of the Bible took place with Philo of Alexandria, who lived at the turn of the era and operated primarily by means of allegory, this thread was first picked up again in the High Middle Ages by figures such as Maimonides and his predecessors. This approach, however, belongs more to the context of Jewish philosophy of religion than to the formulation of a theology of the Hebrew Bible.

The Regulation of Orthopraxy A systematic theological formulation on the basis of the Bible did not take place in Judaism, due primarily to four factors. Because of the prevalence of the pharisaic-rabbinic strand of Judaism after 70 CE, classical Judaism developed a certain accent on orthopraxy rather than orthodoxy. Then, the character of the Hebrew Bible as interpreting literature as well as the continuation of interpretation of the sacred texts in the Talmud and Midrash led to the fact that these texts were appreciated more with regard to their plurality than if one had surveyed them for a potential received unity. Further, the confrontation with Greek (and Latin) philosophy was less intense than it was in Christianity, limiting itself primarily to the period before 70 CE. Finally, the two-part division of the biblical canon in Christianity more strongly provoked the question of the unity of the Hebrew Bible—whether one judges this now as appropriate or not—than was the case in Judaism.

§42 The Old Testament and Christianity

Albrecht Beutel, "Die Formierung neuzeitlicher Schriftauslegung und ihre Bedeutung für die Kirchengeschichte," in *Schriftauslegung*, ed. Friederike Nüssel, TdT 8 (Tübingen: Mohr Siebeck, 2014), 141–77 ◆ Volker Drecoll, "Exegese als Grundlage der Theologie in der Alten Kirche und im Mittelalter," in *Schriftauslegung*, ed. Friederike Nüssel, TdT 8 (Tübingen: Mohr Siebeck, 2014), 105–40 ◆ Gerhard Ebeling, *Kirchengeschichte als Geschichte der Auslegung der Heiligen Schrift* (Tübingen: Mohr, 1947) ◆ Elisabeth Gräb-Schmidt and Reiner Preul, eds., *Das Alte Testament in der Theologie*, Marburger Jahrbuch Theologie 25 (Leipzig: Evangelische Verlagsanstalt, 2013) ◆ Friedhelm Hartenstein, "Zur Bedeutung des Alten Testaments für die christliche Kirche: Eine Auseinandersetzung mit den Thesen von Notger Slenczka," *TLZ* 140 (2015): 738–51 ◆ Alan J. Hauser and

Duane F. Watson, eds., *A History of Biblical Interpretation*, 3 vols. (Grand Rapids: Eerdmans, 2003–2017) ♦ Henning Graf Reventlow, *From the Old Testament to Origen*, vol. 1 of *History of Biblical Interpretation*, trans. Leo G. Perdue (Leiden: Brill, 2010) ♦ Magne Sæbø, ed., *Hebrew Bible / Old Testament: The History of Its Interpretation*, 3 vols. (Göttingen: Vandenhoeck & Ruprecht, 1996–2015) ♦ Konrad Schmid, "Christentum ohne Altes Testament?" *IKaZ* 45 (2016): 443–56 ♦ Loren Stuckenbruck, "Henoch als Menschensohn in den Bilderreden von 1. Henoch und im breiteren traditionellen Kontext," in *Vermittelte Gegenwart: Konzeptionen der Gottespräsenz von der Zeit des Zweiten Tempels bis Anfang des 2. Jahrhunderts n. Chr.*, ed. Andrea Taschl-Erber and Irmtraud Fischer, WUNT 367 (Tübingen: Mohr Siebeck, 2016), 105–24 ♦ Markus Witte, *Jesus Christus im Alten Testament: Eine biblisch-theologische Skizze*, Salzburger Exegetische Theologische Vorträge 4 (Münster: LIT, 2013)

From a historical perspective, the correlation of the *Hebrew Bible* and Christianity is comparatively easy to evaluate: The Hebrew Bible as a whole is earlier than Christianity, and Christianity is later than the latest texts of the Hebrew Bible. Not a single book of the Hebrew Bible contains Christian glosses or editing. Their history of literary supplementation ends in the pre-Christian era, even if the—textually no longer productive—canon formation of the third division of the canon stretched into the first century CE. The Hebrew Bible first took on special meaning in the Reformation period when the Reformers—not least for humanistic reasons—restricted the Protestant Old Testament to the books of the canon of the Hebrew Bible, though the order of books remained bound to the traditional Christian Old Testament (cf. above, Part C).

CHRISTIAN GLOSSES IN THE HEBREW BIBLE? More difficult historically is the correlation between the *Old Testament* and Christianity. The various Old Testaments of different Christian confessions in part contain writings whose history of formation temporally overlaps with the formation of early Christianity and sometimes even reveals Christian glosses. A possible, though not undisputed example appears in Bar 3:38, which says concerning wisdom: μετὰ τοῦτο ἐπὶ τῆς γῆς ὤφθη καὶ ἐν τοῖς ἀνθρώποις συνανεστράφη, "Then she will be seen on earth and walk among humans."[2]

2. See Wolfgang Kraus, "Zur Frage der Ursprünglichkeit und Rezeption von Bar 3,38," in *Die Septuaginta: Orte und Intentionen*, ed. S. Kreuzer et al., WUNT 361 (Tübingen: Mohr Siebeck, 2016), 731–42. Kraus identifies Bar 3:38 as a Jewish gloss.

The Similitudes of the Ethiopian book of Enoch (1 En 37–71) should also be mentioned, which are perhaps entirely of Christian origin, even though they maintain the fiction of a pre-Christian, Hebrew Bible origin. Christian additions or interpretations are also discussed with regard to the Greek and Syriac books of Sirach.[3]

Neither can this section present the Christian history of interpretation of the Old Testament; it would have to cover almost the entire cultural history of Christianity.[4] Several basic indications of the meaning of the Old Testament in Christianity must suffice. It should first be highlighted that the Old Testament, not the New Testament, was the Bible of the first Christians. Easter in the year 30 or 31 CE was the hour of Christianity's birth. Christianity came into being with the death of Jesus on the cross and the belief in his resurrection. The historical Jesus was not a Christian; the historical Jesus was a Jew, and he was therefore familiar with and read only the Hebrew Bible, as Luke 4:16–17 describes:

> And Jesus came to Nazareth, where he had grown up, and he went, as was his custom, into the synagogue on the Sabbath and stood up to read aloud. And the book of the prophet Isaiah was handed to him.

The first writings of the later New Testament, the Pauline epistles, first originated twenty years after Jesus's death, and the completion of the New Testament required a further 100 years.[5]

WITNESS INSTEAD OF CODEX This fact that Jesus and the New Testament are not contemporaneous, do not even overlap historically, is of fundamental importance from a theological perspective. Christianity in

---

3. It is noteworthy that Christians sometimes composed writings that take the form of Jewish traditions. Worthy of mention are the Apocalypses of Daniel, Ezra, and Elijah, the Odes of Solomon, and the Ascension of Isaiah; cf. James R. Davila, "Did Christians Write Old Testament Pseudepigrapha That Appear to Be Jewish?," in *Rediscovering the Apocryphal Content. New Perspectives on Early Christian and Late Antique Apocryphal Texts and Traditions,* ed. Pierluigi Piovanelli and Tony Burke, WUNT 349 (Tübingen: Mohr Siebeck, 2015), 67–86.

4. Cf. Jörg Lauster, *Die Verzauberung der Welt: Eine Kulturgeschichte des Christentums* (Munich: Beck, 2016).

5. Cf. Hermann von Lips, *Der neutestamentliche Kanon: Seine Geschichte und Bedeutung* (Zurich: TVZ, 2004); Tobias Nicklas, "The Development of the Christian Bible," in *What Is Bible?* ed. Karin Finsterbusch and Armin Lange, CBET 67 (Leuven: Brill, 2012), 393–426.

almost all its various manifestations has maintained that its actual basis is not the New Testament but Jesus Christ. Said differently, ultimately normative in Christianity is not the aggregate of letters, but the figure of Jesus Christ, to whom the New Testament witnesses. The New Testament is first and foremost a witness oriented toward something outside itself, on which it reports. It is not a self-sufficient entity in terms of the theology of revelation. This basic structure of the New Testament has been adopted from the Hebrew Bible. Also the Hebrew Bible is first and foremost a witness: it witnesses to God's actions with his people Israel. Therefore, neither is the Old Testament simply codified revelation, but it attests to this revelation.

From a historical perspective, therefore, it is not the Old Testament that requires explanation as the sacred writing of Christianity, but rather the New Testament. It is noteworthy that the New Testament writings do not form a fourth division of the canon that could be added to the previous three divisions of the Hebrew Bible—Torah, Prophets, and Writings. They instead became the core of a separate collection of normative writings, the "New Testament." Actually, the fact that Christianity has an Old Testament does not require explanation, but rather the fact that it has a New Testament.[6]

THE SACRED TEXT OF EARLY CHRISTIANITY The sacred text of the early Christianity of the first three generations was the Hebrew Bible that one interpreted in light of Christ. In fact, the term "early Christianity" is even defined by the fact that this early Christianity did not yet have a New Testament, for one usually defines "early Christianity" as the first generations after Jesus until the completion of the final writings of the New Testament, which then, as they were written, had not yet become canonical. The early Christian writings arose in early Christianity, and they incrementally gained normativity. However, the sacred text of early Christianity was the Hebrew Bible.

THE DOUBLE CANON OF THE OLD AND NEW TESTAMENTS It was not a necessity in early Christianity that further scriptures had to be added in addition to the Hebrew Bible. Instead, the Pauline epistles and later the Gospels, as well as the further writings of the New Testament, were

---

6. Cf. Guy G. Stroumsa, *The Scriptural Universe of Ancient Christianity* (Cambridge, MA: Harvard University Press, 2016).

increasingly used in the first Christian communities and therefore could become a division of the canon in addition to the Old Testament. Christianity accomplished a religious-historical singularity in the second century CE—a double canon of sacred Scripture, whose parts were appreciated in dialogical relationship with one another. Christianity never decided to value one part of the canon more than the other. The double canon of Christianity, consisting of the Old and New Testament is not only remarkable because it represents a complete innovation in the history of Mediterranean religious history, but also because it was never appreciated in a hierarchical classification. The New Testament was placed next to, not above or below, the Old Testament. This decision of placing them next to each other likely suggested itself because the New Testament Scriptures were composed in Greek and not in Hebrew. In any case, it remains highly noteworthy that the Old Testament contains hardly any Christian redactions or glosses. In the Hebrew Scriptures of the Old Testament there is not a single verse that was added by a Christian hand (cf., however, above on Bar 3:38 and Sir 24:23–25). Apparently one was of the opinion that the Old Testament was readable and comprehensible in a Christian fashion just as it was transmitted.

Further books emerged in ancient Judaism and Christianity in addition to the writings of the New Testament, but they apparently did not become established in liturgical use and therefore remain "apocryphal."

It is indicative that the councils of the ancient church were extensively preoccupied with Christology and the doctrine of the Trinity, but not with the question of canon. This was first treated by the Council of Trent in the year 1545, in particular to guarantee that the larger Latin Old Testament would remain the sacred Scripture of the Catholic Church instead of the smaller Hebrew Old Testament to which the Reformers had wanted to limit it.[7]

While the question of which scriptures belong to the Bible remained unsettled even into the fourth century CE, in light of the confessional differences, it basically continues until the present. However, the fact that the core inventory of the biblical Scriptures was undisputed appears to have readily allowed for a certain degree of uncertainty about the margins of the scriptural canon. This renders it clear once again that the Christian

---

7. Cf. Guy Bedouelle, "Le canon de l'Ancien Testament dans la perspective du concile de Trente," in *Le canon de l'Ancien Testament*, ed. Jean-Daniel Kaestli and Otto Wermelinger (Geneva: Labor et Fides, 1984), 253–74.

Bible is not to be viewed as the exclusive and immediate codification of revelation. It is a witness, not a codex. Therefore, the Christian churches were able to live without a final fixed canon for centuries and instead made do with a canon of biblical Scriptures whose core inventory itself became established to a considerable degree as a function of its use in the church.[8]

8. Cf. the differentiated presentation in Christoph Markschies, *Christian Theology and Its Institutions in the Early Roman Empire: Prolegomena to a History of Early Christian Theology,* trans. Wayne Coppins (Waco: Baylor University Press, 2015), 295–300, in discussion with Adolf Martin Ritter, "Die Entstehung des neutestamentlichen Kanons: Selbstdurchsetzung oder autoritative Entscheidung?," in *Kanon und Zensur,* ed. Aleida Assmann and Jan Assmann, Beiträge zur Archäologie der literarischen Kommunikation II (Munich: Fink, 1987), 93–99.

Index of Authors

Index of Subjects

changeability of Torah stipulations, 372–73; combination of historical and legal material in the Torah, 150; Covenant Code, 166, 206, 223–25, 363, 365, 369–70, 373–74, 375; Deuteronomy and ancient Near Eastern legal conceptions, 122, 166–67, 206, 223–25, 336, 354–55, 365, 374–75; Deuteronomy and divine law, 167–68, 224–25, 370–72, 374–76; Deuteronomy's family law and ethic of brotherly solidarity, 225; Holiness Code, 365, 372, 376–78, 388; law as expression of postexilic "Judaism," 362; legal stipulations concerning goring ox, 368–69; legal stipulations in the Pentateuch, 265–66; preliminary remarks from the history of scholarship, 362–64; reception of the Decalogue, 378; reception of the prophetic social critique, 373–74; slave laws of the ancient Near East, 371–72, 375, 429–30; talionic stipulations, 369–70

Letter of Aristeas, 83

libraries of the ancient Near East, 13, 71

literature, Hebrew Bible as, 3, 10–14, 260–77; and ancient Near Eastern literature and culture, 121–23; commentaries and literary continuations, 274–77; dissemination of, 12–13; genres and forms of theological statements, 260–77; hymns, laments, and songs of thanksgiving, 271–72; and the Jerusalem temple library, 12–13; legal traditions/legal literature, 210–11, 265–66, 361–78; literary continuation of texts and new independent literary works, 205–8; narratives and functional mythic structure, 263–65; *parallelismus membrorum* form within Hebrew poetry, 59–60; prophecy, 210–11, 266–71; and scribal culture of ancient Israel, 10–14, 120–21, 274–75; thought world of, 8–9; wisdom literature, 190–98, 273–74; as witness to a literary religion, 14, 453; word of God/word of humans, 261–62

Maccabean period and crisis (167–164 BCE), 254–58, 349–50; and anti-Hellenism, 361; book of Daniel, 77, 248–49, 254–56, 349–50, 360–61; emergence of the term "Judaism," 403; Jewish identity and dietary prohibitions, 392; martyr theology in books of Maccabees, 256–57; political theology and renationalizing tendencies in literature of, 360–61; and question of end of the theological history of the Hebrew Bible, 254–58

Maimonides, Moses, 38, 450

Marcion, 84–85

Megillot (feast scrolls), 65, 70, 196–98; Esther, 197–98; Lamentations, 197; Qoheleth, 123, 195–96, 326–27, 406, 438; reading at certain feasts, 449–50; Ruth, 197; Song of Songs, 196

Merenptah Stela, 289, 397

Mesha Stela inscription, 11, 212, 289, 353, 397

messiah: Codex Alexandrinus and Christological expectation of the "messiah," 139; Cyrus as "God's messiah," 237, 341, 410–11, 423; the so-called messianic prophecies, 409–10; Zion as messianic figure, 422–23

Midrash, 70, 450

monarchy and royal ideology, 407–12; ambivalence toward (Samuel and Kings), 174–75, 218–19, 409; ancestral narratives and transformation of royal ideology, 160, 356; ancient Near Eastern kingship and royal ideology, 366, 408–9, 428–30, 432; Cyrus as "God's messiah," 237, 410–11, 423; destruction of Judah and the guilt of kings in Deuteronomistic tradition, 233–34; and eschatological expectations in the Hebrew Bible, 410; and the loss of the kingdoms Israel and Judah, 175, 337–38; Nebuchadnezzar as the "servant" of God, 237, 341, 410–11; preliminary remarks from the history of scholarship, 408; Psalmic perspectives on, 411–12; reinterpretation of Assyrian imperial ideology, 223–27; the so-called messianic

Index of Scripture